BUSINESS MANAGERS IN ANCIENT ROME

A Social and Economic Study of Institores, 200 B.C. - A.D. 250

BY

JEAN-JACQUES AUBERT

E.J. BRILL

LEIDEN · NEW YORK · KÖLN

1994

The publication of this work was aided by the Stanwood Cockey Lodge Foundation; the Fonds des publications de l'Université de Neuchâtel (Faculté de Theologie); the Fonds Paul Humbert du Séminaire des sciences de l'Antiquité classique de la Faculté des Lettres de l'Université de Neuchâtel; and the Swiss National Science Foundation.

The paper in this book meets the guidelines for permanence and durability of the Committee on Production Guidelines for Book Longevity of the Council on Library Resources.

Library of Congress Cataloging-in-Publication Data

Aubert, Jean-Jacques, 1958-
    Business managers in ancient Rome : a social and economic study of Institores, 200 B.C.-A.D. 250 / by Jean-Jacques Aubert.
        p.   cm. — (Columbia studies in the classical tradition, ISSN 0166-1302 ; v. 21)
    Includes bibliographical references (p.) and index.
    ISBN 9004100385 (cloth)
    1. Rome—Economic conditions.   2. Management—Rome.   3. Commercial agents—Rome.   4. Farm management—Rome.   5. Agency (Roman law)
    I. Title.   II. Series.
    HC39.A9   1994
    658'.00937—dc20   94-17201
                                                CIP

Die Deutsche Bibliothek - CIP-Einheitsaufnahme

Aubert, Jean-Jacques:
Business managers in ancient Rome : a social and economic study of institores 200 b.c. - a.d. 250 / by Jean-Jacques Aubert.
- Leiden ; New York; Köln : Brill, 1994
  (Columbia studies in the classical tradition ; vol. 21)
  ISBN 90-04-10038-5
NE: GT

ISSN 0166-1302
ISBN 90 04 10038 5

PRINTED IN THE NETHERLANDS

To Cheryl

and in memory of my grandparents

Gustave Aubert (1896-1988)
and Adeline Aubert (1905-1990)

CONTENTS

PREFACE

In his magisterial survey of Roman imperial economy and society, M. Rostovtzeff deplored the lack of an "adequate recent treatment by a specialist of the important subject of the development of ancient commercial law" (p. 625, n. 54). In the three decades that followed the second edition of the *Social and Economic History of the Roman Empire* (Oxford 1957), scores of legal historians have worked toward filling this lacuna and significant progress has been made on various aspects of the Roman law of obligations, in particular on the role of slaves in business activities. Among the most recent, far-reaching studies, one can cite the works of A. Claus, *Gewillkürte Stellvertretung im römischen Privatrecht* (Berlin 1973), A. Buti, *Studi sulla capacità patrimoniale dei servi* (Camerino 1976), A. di Porto, *Impresa collettiva e schiavo 'manager' in Roma antica (II sec. a.C. –II sec. d.C.)* (Milan 1984), A. Kirschenbaum, *Sons, Slaves and Freedmen in Roman Commerce* (Jerusalem/Washington, D.C. 1987), a slightly revised version of a 1969 Columbia University dissertation, and, most recently, T.J. Chiusi, "Landwirtschaftliche Tätigkeit und *actio institoria*," *ZRG* 108 (1991) 155-86. The last mentioned author made a breakthrough in explaining the connection between the legal system and the economic activity behind it.

Valuable though these studies are, they all fall short of fulfilling Rostovtzeff's wish to see a survey that would take account of "the vast amount of information which has been furnished by inscriptions and papyri as well as by some archaeological material (viz. the inscriptions on the so-called 'instrumentum domesticum,' which should be studied in connection with the 'instrumentum' itself)" (*ibid.*). Admittedly, the challenge put forth by Rostovtzeff was formidable and could not be accepted as such without completing first some thorough groundwork in each of the fields which would have to contribute to the type of synthesis that Rostovtzeff had in mind.

While jurists have been ploughing through the legal material, archaeologists and social and economic historians have been producing new material and interpretations of the Roman economy, taking the legal material into consideration, but without trying to reevaluate the legal system within which this economy functioned. J. Rougé showed the path in his thorough study of seaborne trade (*Recherches sur l'organisation du commerce maritime en Méditerranée sous l'Empire romain* [Paris 1966]), using mostly legal, epigraphical, and literary evidence. In an important article, ''Roman Terracotta Lamps: The Organization of an Industry,'' *JRS* 70 (1980) 126-45, W.V. Harris brought some specific archaeological material into the discussion. So did J.H. D'Arms in *Commerce and Social Standing in Ancient Rome* (Cambridge, MA 1981), where the author discusses the place of traders in Roman society, and the relationship between attitudes and behavior toward commerce in the Late Republic and Early Empire. More recently, D. Manacorda has been trying to use amphora stamps to support A. di Porto's conclusions (expressed in ''Impresa agricola ed attività collegate nell'economia della 'villa'. Alcune tendenze organizzative,'' *Sodalitas. Scritti in onore di A. Guarino VII* [Naples 1984] 3235-77) about the existence of integrated enterprises in the wine trade (''Schiavo 'manager' e anfore romane: A proposito dei rapporti tra archeologia e storia del diritto,'' *Opus* 4 [1985] 141-51, and ''Le anfore dell'Italia repubblicana: aspetti economici e sociali,'' *Amphores romaines et histoire économique* [Rome 1989] 443-67).

All the scholars mentioned above have recognized the importance of slaves and freedmen employed as agents in the production and distribution of goods, but none of them have tried to collect the ancient evidence about them. J.H. D'Arms, in particular, called for a special study on *institores* as business managers performing wide ranging transactions (*op. cit.* 143). The purpose of the present study is to sketch the social and economic history of an important chapter of the Roman law of obligations, the law governing indirect agency.

After surveying the references to *institores* in legal, literary, and epigraphical sources, I attempted to trace the activities of business managers in various areas of the Roman economy. As I came to realize the extent of the task ahead of me, I decided to restrict the geographical area to Italy and its most immediate vicinity, and to procede with case studies. One consequence of this choice was that I had to leave out—with some exceptions—the papyrological evidence, even though it might have provided valuable information on several points which I had to omit due to the lack of evidence from the area under investigation (for instance, the problem of accounting). The available material lead me to conclude that the core of the system of management featuring managers was developed in a rural setting, in connection with the villa economy, and therefore, I devoted a large place to the role of farm managers (*vilici* and *actores*).

From there I focused on some industrial activities carried out in both rural and urban conditions, namely the clay industry: this choice was of course influenced by the availability of stamped archaeological material. Finally, I examined the role of *vilici* and their likes as head of managerial units employing more or less numerous staffs (*familiae*) in various areas of private, public, and imperial administration.

Everyone has something to say about the Roman economy, and many have put it in print. It was therefore impossible to survey all the secondary literature on any of the subjects discussed in this study. I have tried to use mainly what has been published between 1970 and 1992, and even then I make no claim to comprehensiveness. In order to keep this study within reasonable length I refrained from reviewing the opinions previously expressed by others. My main concern was to collect and discuss the primary evidence (literary, legal, epigraphical, archaeological, and numismatic) that illustrates the activities of business managers in the Roman economy from the beginning of the second century B.C. until the middle of the third century A.D. Where the relevant ancient evidence was too inconclusive I tried, with due caution, to bring into the discussion later documents originating in the same area, as well as comparative material from Graeco-Roman Egypt, medieval Europe, antebellum America, and contemporary Switzerland.

Because of the circumstantial character of the evidence under examination, it is necessary to keep in mind that many of the conclusions drawn from this evidence reflect possibilities, plausibilities, and probabilities rather than certainties. Emphasizing this aspect of my study would have called for repetitive words of caution, which I kept to a minimum in order to spare the reader's patience.

This book is a revised and expanded version of my doctoral dissertation (*Business Managers in Ancient Rome, 200 B.C. –A.D. 250* [Columbia 1991]), which had been awarded a Special Prize from the University of Nice (*II Premio romanistico internazionale Gérart Boulvert*, Naples, 12 June 1993). I am grateful to my mentor, Prof. William V. Harris, for his continuous support since I started graduate school at Columbia University in 1984. The wide scope of his interests and his open-mindedness changed my way of thinking about ancient history and academe in general.

I also owe much to my other teachers at Columbia, Dean Roger

Bagnall, Profs. Richard Billows, Alan Cameron (all three as members of my doctoral committee), Lesley Ann Dean-Jones, Alfred Frazer, Peter Knox, William Metcalf, Daniel Selden, and the late Morton Smith and Nancy Waggoner for the training they gave me in ancient history and all kinds of ancillary disciplines.

Drs. Jesper Carlsen and Pasquale Rosafio read the whole book twice and generously shared with me the yet-unpublished results of their own research on the subject.

Profs. Ernst Badian, John Bodel, Dennis Kehoe, Elio Lo Cascio, James Rives (who was also on my doctoral committee), Margareta Steinby, and Susan Treggiari kindly read and criticized earlier drafts of this work.

I am indebted for information to Profs. Thomas Bisson, Emma Dench, Clayton Fant, George Frederic Franko, Regula Frei-Stolba, John Lenz, Myles McDonnell, Dirk Obbink, Giuseppe Pucci, Jonathan Roth, Glen Thompson, Andreas Wacke, Drs. Jairus Banaji, Peter Dorcey, Elizabeth Fentress, Seamus Ross, Katherine Welch, Messrs. Alexander Hahn, William Kraus, and Constantin Marinescu. I also owe many corrections to two anonymous referees (CSCT and SNSF).

My wife Cheryl not only tolerated my idiosyncratic pursuit, but also read the whole book with the eyes and mind of a lay person in ancient history, criticized my style, and corrected my English. She is, of course, responsible for all remaining shortcomings in form and content.

Deans Pierre Bühler and Denis Knoepfler, and Profs. André Schneider and Daniel Paunier were very helpful in securing funding for the publication of this book.

To all the people mentioned above I would like to express my gratefulness.

While I was writing this book I enjoyed the hospitality of the Classics Departments at Harvard and Stanford Universities (as an Exchange Scholar in 1989-1990), of the History Department at Columbia University (as a Visiting Scholar in 1991), of the American Numismatic Society, and of the Istituto Svizzero di Roma (as a Member in 1991-1992). While in Rome I was given access to the libraries of the Istituto di Diritto Romano (Università La Sapienza), the Ecole Française, the Deutsches Archäologisches Institut, the British School, and the American Academy. I also had the unique opportunity to participate in a year-long seminar on estate management at the Danish Academy.

Generous financial support from the Department of History at Columbia University (1984-1990), the Swiss Academy of Humanities (1988-1989), and the Swiss National Science Foundation (1989-1992) enabled me to devote the totality of my time to historical research and spared me the economic hardship experienced by most graduate and post-doctoral students.

Lausanne, 31 December 1992   J.-J. A.

ABBREVIATIONS

In matters of style, the names and works of ancient authors are abbreviated as in the *Oxford Classical Dictionary*[2] (Oxford 1970), and periodicals as in *L'année philologique*; sources of inscriptional material are expounded in F. Bérard *et al.*, *Guide de l'épigraphiste*[2] (Paris 1989), and references to occasional papyri are abbreviated as in J.F. Oates *et al.*, *Checklist of Editions of Greek Papyri and Ostraca*[4] (*BASP* Suppl. 7, Atlanta, GA 1992); Greek and Latin texts are quoted from the Loeb Classical Library, Oxford Classical Texts, Teubner or Budé editions, unless otherwise noted; translations are mine; the secondary literature is cited with full title and reference the first time it is used in each chapter and thereafter abbreviated by author's name, (periodical, issue number), and date of publication; the most important items are listed in the bibliography.

Other abbreviations of primary sources:

AE	*L'année épigraphique*
BMC	*British Museum Catalogue*
CIL	*Corpus Inscriptionum Latinarum*
CIG	*Corpus Inscriptionum Graecarum*
Cod. Iust.	*Codex Iustinianus*
Cod. Theod.	*Codex Theodosianus*
CVArr	*Corpus Vasorum Arretinorum*, ed. A. Oxé – H. Comfort
Dig.	*Digesta*
EJ	V. Ehrenberg – A.H.M. Jones, *Documents Illustrating the Reigns of Augustus and Tiberius*[2]
Eph. Ep.	*Ephemeris Epigraphica*
FIRA	*Fontes Iuris Romani Anteiustiniani*, ed. S. Riccobono *et al.*
IG	*Inscriptiones Graecae*
IGRR	*Inscriptiones Graecae ad Res Romanas Pertinentes*
ILLRP	*Inscriptiones Latinae Liberae Rei Publicae*
ILS	*Inscriptiones Latinae Selectae*
Inscr. It.	*Inscriptiones Italiae*
LSO	*Lateres Signati Ostienses*, ed. J. Suolahti, M. Steinby *et al.*

Not.Scav.	*Notizie degli scavi di antichità*
OGIS	*Orientis Graeci Inscriptiones Selectae*
PG	*Patrologia Graeca*
PIR	*Prosopographia Imperii Romani Saeculi I, II, III*
PL	*Patrologia Latina*
RIC	*Roman Imperial Coinage*
S	H. Bloch, "The Roman Brick-stamps Not Published in Volume XV,1 of the CIL," *HSPh* 56-57 (1947) 1-128
SEG	*Supplementum Epigraphicum Graecum*
SIG	*Sylloge Inscriptionum Graecarum*[3]
TLL	*Thesaurus Linguae Latinae*

Conventional signs

a) in legal texts:

[ ] interpolation
< > restoration

b) in papyri and inscriptions (Leiden system, cf. A.E. Gordon, *Illustrated Introduction to Latin Epigraphy* [Berkeley/Los Angeles/London 1983] 234-35):

[ ] restoration
( ) filled-out abbreviation
< . > omission
{ } unnecessary letter

Proper names

For the sake of consistency, I intentionally refer to all Roman jurists by their Latin names (Paulus, Ulpianus, Iulianus, etc.), while using English names to refer to celebrities, such as the emperors (Julius Caesar, Trajan, Hadrian, Diocletian, Julian, etc.).

CHAPTER ONE

BUSINESS AGENTS AND BUSINESS MANAGERS

A. Introduction

In 191 B.C., a Roman crowd could witness the following transaction: a soldier buys a female slave and makes a down payment to
her owner/pimp. Short of cash, he leaves the town without his new
acquisition, intending to pay the balance later. When he is able to
do so, he sends one of his slaves back to town with the money, with
a letter (*epistula*) expressing his intention, and with a token (*symbolum
obsignatum*) proving his connection with the buyer. In compliance
with his master's order, the slave looks for the seller or his representative (*atriensis*) in order to deliver the cash in exchange for the slave,
thus settling his master's debt and receiving ownership of the girl in
his master's name.[1]

The story is fictitious and forms the plot of Plautus's comedy *Pseudolus*, which follows a late-fourth-century-B.C. Greek model. However, a similar situation sounds plausible in a Roman context. The
transaction is interesting because both parties are represented by
agents who, as slaves, did not have any legal capacity of their own.
Harpax, the slave *armiger* (*stratioticus nuntius*)[2] who acts in the capacity of the buyer's agent, is capable of performing a valid legal transaction because he has received some precise instruction (*iussum*)
from his master, which the seller can verify on the basis of the letter
and token issued for this very purpose.[3] Besides, the audience is
told that Harpax holds a *peculium* which allows him to carry out
transactions on his own, for instance to buy his outfit.[4] Pseudolus,
his counterpart, pretends that he is a *procurator*, in spite of his slave

---

[1] Plaut., *Pseud. passim.*
[2] Plaut., *Pseud.* 603.
[3] Plaut., *Pseud.* 647-648.
[4] Plaut., *Pseud.* 1188-1189. On the *peculium* of slaves in Plautus's comedies, cf.
Merc. 89; 96; 524-525; *Capt.* 19-20; *Tri.* 727-728; J.-C. Dumont, *Servus. Rome et
l'esclavage sous la République* (Rome 1987) 368-71 and 404-05; and P.P. Spranger,
Historische Untersuchungen zu den Sklavenfiguren des Plautus und Terenz[2] (Wiesbaden/
Stuttgart 1984) 67-69.

status, and that he ranks higher than the *atriensis* with whom Harpax would like to deal.[5] According to Pseudolus, the role of a *procurator* is to take care of his master's property and accounts, and to receive and make payments in cash.[6] This may be a lie, since it is unlikely that the same person would be handling cash and keeping the accounts. Interestingly, Harpax refuses to give him the money, questioning both his identity and his legal capacity to accept payments while acknowledging that he would not have the same hesitation in dealing with the *atriensis*.[7]

Because the *atriensis* never shows up in the *Pseudolus*, we have to turn to another play by Plautus to understand what functions the *atriensis* held in the Roman household of the early second century B.C. In the *Asinaria*, the *atriensis* Saurea—who never appears on stage either—is supposed to receive payment from the agent of a merchant of Pella for some Arcadian asses he sold him earlier.[8] In a situation quite similar to that in the *Pseudolus*, the slave pretending to be Saurea tries to convince the merchant's agent of his identity, and for that purpose lists his daily activities: he has spent the last three days in the forum trying to place a loan with someone,[9] he had some oil shipped away, some wine sold to a vintner, some slaves hired out, and some tableware lent. In the management of his master's property, he is assisted by underlyings (*vicarii*) who belong to his *peculium* and have the same legal capacity as he has.[10] In Plautus's time, the *atriensis* gives orders to the staff of an urban household and acts as business manager on behalf of his master in his absence.[11] His role within the *familia urbana* is similar to that of the *vilicus* within the *familia rustica*. In a later period the managerial functions of the *atriensis* were taken over by other servants (*dispensatores*, *actores*, and *vilici*). *Atriensis* were thereafter mostly concerned with the supervision of the maintenance staff.[12]

[5] Plaut., *Pseud.* 608-610.
[6] Plaut., *Pseud.* 625-626: "Mihi hercle vero, qui res rationesque eri / Balionis curo, argentum accepto et quoi debet dato."
[7] Plaut., *Pseud.* 640-641.
[8] Plaut., *Asin.* 333-336.
[9] Plaut., *Asin.* 428-429.
[10] Plaut., *Asin.* 432-446.
[11] On *atrienses* in Plautus, cf. J.-C. Dumont (1987) 376-78; and P.P. Spranger (1984) 75-76.
[12] F. Fuchs, in E. de Ruggiero, *Diz.Epigr.* 1 (1985) 762-63, s.v. *atriensis*, who emphasizes the declining status of the *atriensis*; P. Habel, *PW* 2 (1896) cols. 2145-46.

It is clear that by the early second century B.C. slaves were capable of carrying out transactions on behalf of their master and of negotiating binding contracts,[13] but before the creation of the *actiones adiecticiae qualitatis* (cf. below), there was no guarantee for third contracting parties that agent or principal would honor the terms of the contract. Another difficulty lies in that slaves were not capable of transferring property through *mancipatio*. This was especially important for the management of agricultural estates, as land, cattle, and slave manpower, were—or should have been—fairly transient in order to permit landowners to adjust to economic fluctuations. But the problem of transfer of ownership of *res mancipi* does not seem to have prevented landowners from employing their slaves as agents even for this kind of transaction. In Plautus's *Persa*, Sagaristio is sent by his master from Athens to Eretria in order to purchase some oxen.[14] In the same play, a few slaves invent a stratagem whereby a free woman posing as a female slave would be sold to a pimp through *traditio*, following the mailed instruction of the alleged owner requesting that no *mancipatio* be performed.[15] Some later documentary evidence suggests that slaves could receive, but not transfer, property through *mancipatio*.[16]

If landowners wanted to transfer their property and were unable to do so in person, they could also rely on free middlemen who would negotiate a contract in their own name, acquire the *res mancipi* through a regular *mancipatio*, and transfer it in the same way to a third party. Although this procedure was cumbersome and could be

---

s.v. *atriensis*; and L.F. Smith – J.H. McLean – C.W. Keyes (eds.), *G.N. Olcott, Thesaurus Linguae Latinae Epigraphicae* 2 (New York 1935) 12, s.v. *atriensis*.

[13] Plaut., *Rud.* 1384-1386: "Quod servo meo / promisisti, meum esse oportet, ne tu, leno, postules / te hic fide lenonia uti: non potes."

[14] Plaut., *Pers.* 259-260.

[15] Plaut., *Rud.* 501-527, esp. 524-525: "ac suo periclo is emat qui eam mercabitur: / mancipio neque promittet neque quisquam dabit."

[16] *CIL* II 5406 = 5042 = *FIRA* III², no. 92, pp. 295-97 (*Formula Baetica*), a first/second century A.D. bronze inscription, probably from the colony of Hasta/Baetica, recording a general model of fiduciary agreement (*fiducia*) attached to the transfer of ownership of an estate and its slave manager. The landowner performed a *mancipatio nummo uno* to a slave representing the buyer. A. Oxé, "Zur älteren Nomenklatur der römischen Sklaven," *RhM* 59 (1904) 108-140, esp. 132 proposes, on the basis of the form of the slave's name, a date around Caesar's or Augustus's time. Cf. H. Ankum, "*Mancipatio* by Slaves in Classical Roman Law?" *Acta Juridica* (1976) 1-18, summarized in *RD* 56 (1978) 693-94, based on the evidence of Cic., *Att.* 12.50.2; Iulianus (57 *dig.*) *Dig.* 21.2.39.1; and Paulus, *Frg. Vat.* 51; and J. Andreau, *La vie financière dans le monde romain* (Rome 1987) 705-06.

risky for all parties involved, it is certain that free agents, friends, clients, or freedmen, were employed in Plautus's time. However, third contracting parties, such as Harpax in the *Pseudolus*, might be reluctant to make payment to a free agent, as they cannot be sure that the money will be subsequently transferred to the intended party.

The examples discussed above show agents carrying out isolated transactions. Such activities require an intensive involvement on the part of the principal, who gives instructions to his agent on a case by case basis. The agent is only an instrument in the hand of the principal, and his role is rather mechanical. He does not have to take any initiative, nor be creative. Faithful compliance is valued more than dynamism and entrepreneurial or managerial skills. This type of activity will not be examined in the present study.

By contrast, some economic activities were carried out on a permanent basis. In the *Captivi*, Hegion sends his delinquent slaves for punishment to his freedman Cordalus who is said to be in charge of some quarries (*lapidicina/latomia lapidaria*).[17] Cordalus might have been a self-employed entrepreneur owning or renting the quarries. He obviously employed slave labor. He might have started his activities before his manumission on the basis of the grant of a *peculium*. Even though a slave with *peculium* was legally dependent, his economic activities were practically kept separate from his master's.[18] For that reason, a slave with *peculium* was not acting as business manager on behalf of a principal, and this type of entrepreneur will not be discussed either in the present study.

It is possible, however, that the quarries were owned by Hegion, and that Cordalus was running the enterprise on Hegion's behalf. Hegion then would have been an entrepreneur (*dominus*) making major strategic decisions concerning the operation of the quarries. As a result of the appointment of Cordalus as business manager (*institor*), Hegion did not have to take part in the tactical day-to-day routine of their management. The enterprise and its profit remained his, and therefore he retained a right to supervise, and interfere with, Cordalus's management policy. He could go as far as firing

---

[17] Plaut., *Capt.* 735-736.

[18] In the parable of the talents (*Matth.* 25.14-30 and *Luke* 19.12-27), Jesus tells the story of three servants entrusted with a *peculium*, who were free to use the money the way they pleased, as long as their master was making a profit out of it.

him, or imposing on him a supervisor, a colleague, or an assistant, provided that there was no previous contractual agreement preventing him from doing so. As business manager, Cordalus was not an entrepreneur.[19] His functions consisted in rationally organizing the unit(s) of production, using the capital in an efficient way, controlling and supervising the workers employed in the enterprise, timing and coordinating their activities in order to achieve a definite purpose.[20] He might also have been expected to keep accurate written accounts.

The present study will focus on business managers (*institores*) and examine their social background and status, their role within the enterprise (*negotiatio*) as head of a managerial unit, and their relationship with the workers (*familia*), the entrepreneur (*dominus*), and outsiders, both suppliers and customers (third contracting parties).

B. DEFINITION AND SOURCES

1. *Institores in the legal sources*

Direct evidence about *institores* is scarce. Most of what we have consists of a collection of legal opinions dating from the late Republican period and early Empire. This juristic activity was prompted by the creation of a legal remedy called *actio institoria*, introduced in the late second century B.C. by the praetor in his Edict in order to supplement and correct the shortcomings of the Roman civil law. Consequently, it became possible for third contracting parties to sue the

---

[19] J. Andreau, "Originalité de l'historiographie finleyenne et remarques sur les classes sociales," *Opus* 1 (1982) 181-85, esp. 182, rightly points out that *institores* were not entrepreneurs, as opposed to slaves with *peculium*, but managers. For the distinction between entrepreneurship and management, cf. S. Pollard, "Industrial Management and the Beginnings of Industrialization in Europe," in S. Cavaciocchi (ed.), *L'impresa. Industria, commercio, banca (secc. XIII-XVIII)* (Florence 1991) 95-118, esp. 95-96.

[20] An adequate modern definition of management is provided by D.A. Wren, *The Evolution of Management Thought*[3] (New York 1987) 4: "For a broad working definition, let us view management as an activity which performs certain functions in order to obtain the effective acquisition, allocation, and utilization of human efforts and physical resources in order to accomplish some goal." Cf. also *ibid.* 10-11, where the author emphasizes the necessary combination of several elements (goal, personnel, tools, timing and coordinating), and 37, for the distinction between entrepreneur and manager, and between strategic and tactical decisions.

principal of the agent with whom they had done business.[21] The
purpose and modes of application of the *actio institoria* gave rise to
many problems of interpretation, which were discussed, as may be
expected, mostly in commentaries on the praetorian and provincial
Edicts. To judge from the legal sources, the economic, political, and
administrative changes that occurred in the third and fourth centuries A.D. do not seem to have made the *actio institoria* obsolete: as
we will see later on, the law governing indirect agency has been only
moderately affected by interpolations, at least in terms of substance
(*vs.* form), even though this point is still a matter of debate. The
compilers of the *Digest* collected whatever material they regarded as
relevant for this subject in one title (*Dig.* 14.3), which provides the
basis of our knowledge about *institores*.

Basic handbooks of Roman law, such as the *Institutes* of Gaius
(4.71) or Iustinianus (4.7.2), or the *Sentences* of Paulus (2.8), devote
a few lines to the *actio institoria*. It shows that this subject was deemed
important enough to be studied at an early stage in the education of
Roman lawyers during the Imperial period. It is true that these
writers are often idiosyncratic, derivative from one another, and
problematic, but I can think of no reason for dismissing beforehand
their account of this particular institution as mere antiquarianism.
One may postulate that the concerns of the jurists reflect the social
and economic importance of business managers in Ancient Rome,
but it will be necessary to look for confirmation of this fact in other
types of evidence. As Roman jurists were trained to extrapolate
from particular cases to general principles, it seems appropriate to
look through their writings for a definition of *institor*.

a. *occupations and transactions*

According to Paulus, an *institor* is an agent appointed to the head of
a shop or whatever place to conduct business.[22] Since "emere" and
"vendere", when used in legal texts, could refer to a wider range

---

[21] The text of the Edict has been reconstructed as follows on the basis of Gaius,
Inst. 4.71 and Ulpianus (28 *ad ed.*) *Dig.* 14.3.5: "Quod cum institore gestum erit
eius rei nomine, cui praepositus fuerit, in eum, qui eum praeposuerit, iudicium
dabo." Cf. *FIRA* I², no. 65, p. 355 and O. Lenel, *Das Edictum Perpetuum*³ (Leipzig
1927) 258-70. It is uncertain whether this edict was introduced by the urban or
peregrine praetor.

[22] Paulus (*sing. de var. lect.*) *Dig.* 14.3.18: "Institor est, qui tabernae locove ad
emendum vendendumve praeponitur quique sine loco ad eundem actum praeponitur."

of transactions than just purchase and sale, the passage does not say whether Paulus had anything specific in mind.[23] Consequently, *institores* could engage in various activities, such as hiring or renting commodities, facilities, or services, or acting as guarantors.[24] The ground for bringing a legal action against the principal was the transaction (*negotium*) performed by the agent on behalf of a principal against whom the remedy was given.[25] Paulus stresses that the place (*locus*) where business had to be conducted had no bearing on the issue: *institores* could be peddlers calling on the private homes of the upper class.[26] Paulus's opinion is shared by his contemporary, Ulpianus.[27] This unanimous insistence may reflect either an ongoing controversy regarding this matter, or some more or less recent change. At the time of its creation and for an indefinite period afterward, the *actio institoria* could have been granted only when the transaction had been performed by an agent in charge of a store, a workshop, or any permanent facility. This condition may have become less imperative at a later, perhaps fairly recent, stage. I will return to this point later on.[28]

Ulpianus, quoting late Republican or Augustan jurists (Servius Sulpicius and Labeo), presents a list of occupations in which *institores* usually engaged.[29] Superintendents of apartment buildings (*insularii*) and of other types of facilities (*aedificio praepositi*), food dealers (*frumento coemendo praepositi*), moneylenders and bankers (*pecuniis faenerandis praepositi (in mensa)*), farm managers (*agris colendis praepo-*

---

[23] According to P. Veyne, "Mythe et réalité de l'autarcie à Rome," *REA* 81 (1979) 261-80, "emere" and "venire" (= passive infinitive of "vendere") could refer to leases (263, n. 12) and to pledges (276, n. 50); cf. Labeo (5 *post. a Iav. epit.*) *Dig.* 18.1.80.2.

[24] Ulpianus (28 *ad ed.*) *Dig.* 14.3.5 *pr.* also says that *institores* were not restricted to certain types of transactions: "Cuicumque igitur negotio praepositus sit, institor recte appellabitur."

[25] Paulus (30 *ad ed.*) *Dig.* 14.3.4: "Nec mutat causam actionis locus vendendi emendive, cum utroque modo verum sit institorem emisse aut vendidisse."

[26] Paulus (30 *ad ed.*) *Dig.* 14.3.4: "cum interdum etiam ad homines honestos adferant merces et ibi vendant." For a different, sensible interpretation, cf. L. de Ligt, *Fairs and Markets in the Roman Empire* (Amsterdam 1993) 165, n. 35. Cf. also Ulpianus (28 *ad ed.*), perhaps following Labeo, *Dig.* 14.3.5.4: "Sed etiam eos institores dicendos placuit, quibus vestiarii vel lintearii dant vestem circumferendam et distrahendam, quos vulgo circitores appellamus."

[27] Ulpianus (28 *ad ed.*) *Dig.* 14.3.3: "Institor appellatus est ex eo, quod negotio gerendo instet: nec multum facit, tabernae sit praepositus an cuilibet alii negotationi."

[28] Cf. Chapters Two (*locus emendi vendendive*) and Three (*actor*).

[29] Ulpianus (28 *ad ed.*) *Dig.* 14.3.5.1-15.

siti), traders and (public) contractors (*mercaturis redempturis faciendis praepositi*), muleteers (*muliones*), launderers (*fullones*), tailors (*sarcinatores*), peddlers (*circitores*) employed by cloth dealers (*vestiarii, lintearii*), undertakers and morticians (*libitinarii, pollinctores*), stablekeepers (*stabularii*), bakers (*pistores*), shopkeepers of all kinds (*tabernarii*), etc. were performing services that forced them to enter into various types of contracts with their customers. The list is certainly not comprehensive, and the nature of the occupation does not determine the legal status of its holder: in juristic writings managers were labelled *institores* only insofar as they acted as someone else's agents. As we will see later on, this condition is ignored by literary writers.

Paulus and Ulpianus do not agree on every detail: they differ for instance on the case of farm managers. Ulpianus, following Labeo, considers that any farm manager is a kind of *institor* whose transaction makes his principal liable.[30] By contrast, Paulus explicitly says that no *actio institoria* would be available to those who negotiate a contract with a *vilicus*, because the *vilicus* was appointed for a different purpose.[31] The apparent contradiction between the two authors suggests that the liability of the principal was determined by the scope of the appointment (*praepositio*), which could vary from one

---

[30] Ulpianus (28 *ad ed.*) *Dig.* 14.3.5.2: "Labeo quoque scripsit, si quis pecuniis faenerandis, agris colendis, mercaturis redempturisque faciendis praeposuerit, in solidum eum teneri." A. di Porto, "Impresa agricola ed attività collegate nell'economia della villa. Alcune tendenze organizzative," *Sodalitas. Scritti in onore di A. Guarino* VII (Naples 1984) 3235-77, esp. 3247 ff. rightly considers the possibility that the three terms are complementary—and not exclusive—of each other. There is no doubt that farm managers were often involved in moneylending, trading, and contracting, but they were not the only ones to do so.

[31] Paulus (29 *ad ed.*) *Dig.* 14.3.16: "Si cum vilico alicuius contractum sit, non datur in dominum actio, quia vilicus propter fructus percipiendos, non propter quaestum praeponitur. Si tamen vilicum distrahendis quoque mercibus praepositum habuero, non erit iniquum exemplo institoriae actionem in me competere." The last part ("si tamen . . . competere") has been considered interpolated, especially because of the expression "exemplo institoriae actionem," cf. S. Solazzi, "L'età dell'*actio exercitoria*," *Riv. dir. navigaz.* 7 (1941) 185-212 (= *Scritti di diritto romano* IV [Naples 1963] 243-64, esp. 254-55). The substance of *Dig.* 14.3.16 is consistent with a text by the same author recorded in the *Sententiae* (2.8.2): "Si quis pecuniae fenerandae agroque colendo, condendis vendendisque frugibus praepositus est, ex eo nomine quod cum illo contractum est in solidum fundi dominus obligatur: nec interest, servus an liber sit." A possible restoration of the incriminated passage in *Dig.* 14.3.16, proposed by Solazzi (254), could read "[exemplo] institoria[e]<m> actionem in me [competere] <dari>." Cf. also A. di Porto, *Sodalitas* VII (1984) 3237-39 (esp. n. 12) and 3251 ff.

case to the other, even for the same type of business managers. Paulus's manager had been appointed "propter fructus percipiendos," and his master would incur full liability for all contracts negotiated in connection with this specific activity. However, any contract negotiated by the *vilicus* that fell outside the scope of the appointment would have no effect upon the principal, hence the importance of knowing the exact meaning and content of the *praepositio*.[32]

b. *praepositio*

By appointing an *institor* to the head of an enterprise, the principal was expressing his willingness (*voluntas*) to have his business run by an agent, and consequently to incur full liability for the legal transactions negotiated by him with third contracting parties, as long as these transactions pertained to the operation of the business.[33] The business managers' sphere of competence was strictly defined by the scope of their appointment (*praepositio*). Therefore, *praepositi* never enjoyed the same unlimited power of administration as *procuratores* or *servi cum peculio*. The appointment determined the extent and limits of the liability of the principal, but it had no bearing on the nature of the legal relationship between principal and agent. When the agent was a dependent—slave, descendant, or wife—of the principal, the relationship was non-contractual and was based on the power (*potestas* or *manus*) that the principal had over his dependent. When the agent was a free man, the relationship was defined by the rules pertaining to the contracts of mandate or hire (*locatio conductio*). If the agent was a slave and belonged to someone else (*ser-*

---

[32] A. Burdese, "*Actio ad exemplum institoriae* e categorie sociali," *BIDR* 74 (1971) 61-82, esp. 68-72, against the opinion of P. Angelini, "Osservazioni in tema di creazione dell'*actio ad exemplum institoriae*," *BIDR* 71 (1968) 230-248, esp. 245-48, who thinks that contracts negotiated by *vilici* did not give rise to an *actio (quasi-) institoria* before the Severan period; and T.J. Chiusi, "Landwirtschaftliche Tätigkeit und *actio institoria*," *ZRG* 108 (1991) 155-86, esp. 180-81.

[33] For *voluntas* as the basis of the principal's liability, cf. Gaius, *Inst.* 4.71: "Cum enim ea quoque res ex voluntate patris dominive contrahi videatur, aequissimum esse visum est in solidum actionem < in eum > dari." Cf. also Ulpianus (28 *ad ed.*) *Dig.* 14.1.1.22 and 14.3.7 *pr.* (where the will of the principal is expressed by subsequent ratification [*ratihabitio*]); G. Pugliese, "In tema di *actio exercitoria*," *Labeo* 3 (1957) 308-43, esp. 334; and S.E. Wunner, *Contractus. Sein Wortgebrauch und Willensgehalt im klassischen römischen Recht* (Cologne/Graz 1964) 105-33, esp. 114-25; against F. de Martino, *Diritto privato e società romana* (Rome 1982) [1941] 169 and [1958] 196-97.

vus alienus), the contract was negotiated between the principal and the slave's master. This question will be examined in Chapter Two.

We do not know whether any kind of formal or informal ceremony had to be performed at the time of the appointment. The event could have been comparable to a "house-warming" or to a "grand opening under new management." Since the purpose of the appointment was to inform every potential third contracting party of the liability of the principal for the transactions carried out by his agent in order to bolster the latter's credit, it is evident that the publicity surrounding the appointment was essential.[34]

The business manager's assignment was spelled out in a bill or charter called *lex praepositionis*. Thanks to Ulpianus, we have a sample of the level of specificity encountered in such a charter in the context of the operation of a ship:

> The appointment (of a shipmaster by a shipper) provides third contracting parties with a set charter. Thus, if someone has appointed an agent as shipmaster for the sole purpose of transporting people and goods at a fixed price, and not for the purpose of leasing the ship (perhaps because he had taken care of this himself), the shipper will not be liable if the shipmaster has leased the ship out. Conversely, if the appointment pertains to leasing only, and not to collecting fares and freight, the same opinion applies. Again, if the appointment pertains to transporting passengers, and not to loading the ship with goods, or vice versa, the shipper will not be liable for any obligation derived from the transgression of the terms of the charter by the shipmaster. But if the appointment pertains to leasing the ship for the transport of certain types of goods, such as vegetables or hempen rope, and if the shipmaster has leased the ship out for the transport of marble or some other material, the shipper will not be liable. For there is a difference between freighters and passenger ships. And I know that most shippers forbid shipmasters to take passengers on board, and, in the same way as trade is limited to a certain region inland or on the sea, there are ships transporting passengers from Cassiope or Dyrrachium to Brundisium which are not fit to carry freight, or again river boats which would not be fit for sea travel.[35]

---

[34] F. Serrao, *Enciclopedia del diritto* 21 (Milan 1971) 827-34, s.v. *institor*, esp. 829-30, stresses the necessity to publicize the scope and purpose of the appointment of an *institor*, in contrast with the appointment of a *procurator*, which requires no publicity.

[35] Ulpianus (28 *ad ed.*) *Dig.* 14.1.1.12: "Igitur praepositio certam legem dat contrahentibus. Quare si eum praeposuit navi ad hoc solum, ut vecturas exigat, non ut locet (quod forte ipse locaverat), non tenebitur exercitor, si magister locaverit: vel si ad locandum tantum, non ad exigendum, idem erit dicendum: aut si

Among the Greek papyri from Roman Egypt there is a category of documents that can be described as written agreements (or ὁμολο-γίαι), whereby a principal gives his authorization (σύστασις) to an agent to carry out certain transactions on his behalf, on a general basis or on a single occasion, with or without restriction pertaining to the nature of the transactions. A copy of the document (ἀντί-γραφον) was filed with the *agoranomoi* and deposited into one section of the city archive called the μνημονεῖον.[36] The purpose of such documents was (1) to define the scope of the agency in the event of a dispute arising between principal and agent; and (2) to advertise the agency to potential third contracting parties.[37]

If such a charter was missing, the principal's liability was established by long-time practices.[38] Consequently, if a principal wanted the scope of the appointment to differ from what was generally accepted in the context of a given trade, he had to make it known in

---

ad hoc, ut vectoribus locet, non ut mercibus navem praestet, vel contra, modum egressus non obligabit exercitorem: sed et si ut certis mercibus eam locet, praepositus est, puta legumini, cannabae, ille marmoribus vel alia materia locavit, dicendum erit non teneri. Quaedam enim naves onerariae, quaedam (ut ipsi dicunt) ἐπιβατηγοί sunt: et plerosque mandare scio, ne vectores recipiant, et sic, ut certa regione et certo mari negotietur, ut ecce sunt naves, quae Brundisium a Cassiopa vel a Dyrrachio vectores traiciunt ad onera inhabiles, item quaedam fluvii capaces ad mare non sufficientes." *Vecturas exigere* implies a series of transactions with several contractors, while *locatio* refers to a contract negotiated with a third party for the transport of goods supplied by this party, cf. J. Rougé, *Recherches sur l'organisation du commerce maritime en Méditerranée sous l'Empire romain* (Paris 1966) 390.

[36] A similar practice may have existed in Italy, as Frontinus reports (*Aq.* 96.1) that public contractors (*redemptores*) had to register "in tabulas publicas" the names of the slaves (*opifices*) they employed in the maintenance of water conduits.

[37] G. Hamza, "Einige Fragen der Zulässigkeit der direkten Stellvertretung in den Papyri," *AUB (iur.)* 19 (1977) 57-67, citing *P.Oxy.* II 261 (A.D. 55); *P.Oxy.* I 94 (A.D. 83); *P.Oxy.* III 501 (with *PSI* IX 1035, A.D. 179); and *BGU* I 300 (with *P.Mert.* I 18, A.D. 161). In *P.Oxy.* I 94, the principal (M. Antonius Ptolemaios) appoints an agent (Dionysios) to sell two slaves, and is said to συνεστακέναι αὐτὸν ... τοῖς προσελευσομένοις τῶι ἀγορασμῶι. The document is a contract in which Dionysios promises to pay the proceeds of the sale to the principal, but at the same time the document establishes the latter's ownership of the slaves for potential buyers.

[38] S.E. Wunner (1964) 117 ("typische Auslegung"), following G. Pugliese, *Labeo* 3 (1957) 315, against F. de Martino (1982) [1958] 173-75. Cf. also M. Just, "Ansätze zur Anscheinsvollmacht im römischen Recht. D. 14, 3, 19, 3; 14, 5, 8: ein Beispiel spätklassischer Rechtspraxis," in W. Barfuss (ed.), *Festschrift für K.H. Neumayer zum 65. Geburtstag* (Baden-Baden 1985) 355-87, esp. 384-87 demonstrates that in two cases an imperial decision contradicts the jurists' opinion by extending the principal's liablility to cases involving transactions falling outside the scope of the appointment, because long-time practice had almost made them tacitly part of the *lex praepositionis*. For customary rules in *locatio conductio*, cf. P.A. Brunt, *JRS* 70 (1980) 88, n. 37.

an unambiguous manner, through *iussum* or *proscriptio*. This could
be done, for instance, by posting a sign in a visible place, written
with clear letters in the language spoken in the area, i.e. in Latin or
in Greek, in order to avoid misunderstandings.[39] Other languages
were probably not excluded, but the possibility of having business
transactions enforceable in Roman law conducted in non-Romanized or non-Hellenized environments seems fairly remote. Still, it is
remarkable that Ulpianus addresses the problem of using non-classical languages in making trusts (*fideicommissa*).[40] It is possible that
the requirement of writing a document specifying the limits of the
appointment (*condicio praepositionis*) became a common practice when
businessmen began rely to increasingly on employees whom they
had to establish in distant places—for instance as guards (*custodes*) of
warehouses—but whom they did not want to entrust with the conduct of legal transactions.[41]

So far as I know, no actual *lex praepositionis*, no *iussum*, and no *proscriptio* have been preserved. The reason for this is, needless to say,
that they were probably written on perishable material. Cato may
be referring to the use of such documents when he recommends that

---

[39] Ulpianus (28 *ad ed.*) *Dig.* 14.3.11.2-3: "De quo palam proscriptum fuerit, ne
cum eo contrahatur, is praepositi loco non habetur: non enim permittendum erit
cum institore contrahere, sed si quis nolit contrahi, prohibeat: ceterum qui praeposuit tenebitur ipsa praepositione. Proscribere palam sic accipimus claris litteris,
unde de plano recte legi possit, ante tabernam scilicet vel ante eum locum in quo
negotiatio exercetur, non in loco remoto, sed in evidenti. Litteris utrum Graecis
an Latinis? Puto secundum loci condicionem, ne quis causari possit ignorantiam
litterarum. Certe si quis dicat ignorasse se litteras vel non observasse quod propositum erat, cum multi legerent cumque palam esset propositum, non audietur."
[40] Ulpianus (2 *fideicom.*) *Dig.* 32.1.11 *pr.*: "Fideicommissa quocumque sermone
relinqui possunt, non solum Latina vel Graeca, sed etiam Punica vel Gallicana vel
alterius cuiuscumque gentis." Cf. W.V. Harris, *Ancient Literacy* (Cambridge, MA
1989) 179-80, and n. 21.
[41] Paulus (4 *ad Plaut.*) *Dig.* 15.1.47 *pr.*: "Quotiens in taberna ita scriptum fuisset 'cum Ianuario servo meo geri negotium veto,' hoc solum consecutum esse dominum constat, ne institoria teneatur, non etiam de peculio." Cf. also Ulpianus (28
ad ed.) *Dig.* 14.3.11.6: "Sed si in totum prohibuit cum eo contrahi, praepositi loco
non habetur, cum magis hic custodis sit loco quam institoris: ergo nec vendere mercem hic poterit nec modicum quid ex taberna." On the non-exchangeable functions of guards (*custodes*) and managers (*vilici*), cf. Cato, *Agr.* 144-145 and M.E.
Sergeenko, "*Villicus*," in I. Bieżuńska-Małowist (ed.), *Schiavitù e produzione nella
Roma repubblicana* (Rome 1986) 191-207 (= *VDI* 4 [1956] 46-54), esp. 201-02. The
title of the employee is not sufficient in itself to allow us to determine whether or
not he was entitled to get involved in legal transactions. For instance, an *insularius*
could be a mere guard (Pomponius [5 *ad Sab.*] *Dig.* 7.8.16.1) or an appointed
superintendent (Ulpianus [28 *ad ed.*], quoting Servius, *Dig.* 14.3.5.1).

landowners leave written instructions with their *vilici*. As these instructions concern the performance of business transactions (purchases and sales, or hires and leases), it is possible that they were intended for outsiders as well.[42] As Cato's description suggests, the charter of appointment probably consisted of a collection of standardized instructions related to the occupation of the manager.

Ulpianus points out that an agent whose appointment had been nullified by *proscriptio* was barred from negotiating contracts with third contracting parties on behalf of his principal. Any transaction that the agent chose to perform in spite of the *proscriptio* was valid if the agent had a juristic capacity, i.e. if he was free or a slave with a *peculium*. The principal did not incur any liability in the first case, and only a limited liability (to the extent of the *peculium*) in the second case.[43] Similarly, if someone had lent the agent some money in defiance of the principal's prohibition and sued the latter on the basis of the manager's conduct, the principal had an *exceptio* to counter the *actio institoria* introduced by the third contracting party, unless the latter could demonstrate that the principal had personally benefited from his agent's transaction.[44]

Any uncertainty about the scope and existence of a valid appointment owed to negligence on the part of the principal or fraud on the part of the agent would result in making the former liable.[45] The case of Titianus Primus's slave, recorded and argued by Paulus against the prefect of the corn supply and the emperor, shows that the distinction between a widely conceived appointment and a general authorization—not available for slaves unless they had a *peculium*—was not always precisely drawn. The slave had been appointed with the purpose of lending money on security. On his own initiative, he was also dealing in the capacity of middleman between barley sellers and purchasers, and was shown to have been involved in renting storage facilities. At one point, after agreeing to pay the price of a certain quantity of barley, he took to flight and his principal was sued on the basis of the manager's conduct (*nomine institoris*). Titianus Primus claimed that the transaction fell outside the

---

[42] Cato, *Agr.* 2.6: "Siquid desit in annum, uti paretur; quae supersint, ut veneant: quae opus sint locato, locentur: quae opera fieri velit et quae locari velit, uti imperet et ea scripta relinquat." Cf. Chapters Two and Three.

[43] Cf. Chapter Two.

[44] Paulus (30 *ad ed.*), citing Proculus, *Dig.* 14.3.17.4.

[45] Ulpianus (28 *ad ed.*) *Dig.* 14.3.11.4-5.

scope of the slave's appointment and that, consequently, he should incur no liability. Paulus sided with the principal, and tried to suggest that the transaction of the slave was tantamount to acting as guarantor (*fideiussor*), but both the prefect and the emperor argued that the scope of the appointment should be regarded as general and that the third contracting party was entitled to an *actio institoria* against Titianus Primus. Their decision indicates that the principal was expected to ensure that his agent was not overstepping the limits of the original appointment. Had the principal paid attention to the activity of his agent, he would have known that the slave had been involved in the storage business on a regular basis.[46] This case shows that under normal circumstances the *actio institoria* was denied when the transaction fell outside the scope of the appointment.[47]

Circumspection was required on the part of a third contracting party entering into a business transaction with the agent, so that the transaction did not fall outside the scope of the appointment. For instance, a moneylender had to make sure that the money borrowed by the *institor* would likely be used in fulfillment of the task entrusted to him. There was no need, however, for the third contracting party to go through too much trouble to ensure that the money was actually used in the purported way, as Africanus points out in the case of a shipmaster.[48]

The Roman jurists were more concerned with establishing under which circumstances the *actio institoria* would be given to a third contracting party than with the historical profile of business agents. It is important to note, however, that in most cases cited by the jurists the manager is a person-in-power (*alieni iuris*), i.e. a slave or a son. Freedmen are occasionally mentioned: in a famous passage, Gaius refers to those who do business overseas and in distant areas through

---

[46] Paulus (1 *decret.*) *Dig.* 14.5.8: "Sed quia videbatur in omnibus eum suo nomine substituisse, sententiam conservavit imperator." Cf. A. Claus, *Gewillkürte Stellvertretung im römischen Privatrecht* (Berlin 1973) 280-81.

[47] Gaius, *Inst.* 4.71; Papinianus (3 *resp.*) *Dig.* 14.3.19.3; Ulpianus (28 *ad ed.*) *Dig.* 14.3.5.11; 14.3.13 *pr.*; and 14.1.1.7; Paulus (29 *ad ed.*) *Dig.* 14.3.16. Cf. M. Just, *Festschrift für K.H. Neumayer zum 65. Geburtstag* (Baden-Baden 1985) 382-84.

[48] Africanus (8 *quaest.*) *Dig.* 14.1.7.2: "Eadem fere dicenda ait et si de institoria actione quaeratur: nam tunc quoque creditorem scire debere necessariam esse mercis comparationem, cui emendae servus sit praepositus, et sufficere, si in hoc crediderit, non etiam illud exigendum, ut ipse curam suscipiat: an in hanc rem pecunia eroganda est."

their slaves and freedmen.[49] The appointment of the agent could occur prior to, or after, his manumission. Scaevola mentions a freedman who had been appointed to the head of a bank (*mensa nummularia*) and records elsewhere that some agents had started as slaves and continued their activities in the same position after their manumission.[50] Papinianus, who refers to a similar case, specifies that the relationship between agent and principal is not altered by the change of status.[51] Papinianus's opinion probably reflects a change whereby the *actio institoria* was probably extended to agents who did not belong to the family of the principal. I will argue later on that at the time of the creation of the *actiones institoria* and *exercitoria* the liability of the principal was recognized only when his agent was his dependent,[52] which could account for the relative unimportance of freedmen in *Dig.* 14.3.[53]

The term *institor* designates a person with reference to his/her legal situation, not to his/her profession. It represents one type, among others, of indirect agent. An *institor* can perform free of charge, or can be hired by the principal. These two features make it more difficult to tell apart *institores* from other business contractors, such as *mancipes*, *conductores*, *redemptores*, etc. *Institores* were engaged in land

---

[49] Gaius (1 *rer. cottid. sive aureor.*) *Dig.* 40.9.10: "Saepe enim de facultatibus suis amplius, quam in his est, sperant homines. Quod frequenter accidit his, qui transmarinas negotiationes et aliis regionibus, quam in quibus ipsi morantur, per servos atque libertos exercent: quod saepe, adtritis istis negotiationibus longo tempore, id ignorant et manumittendo sine fraudis consilio indulgent servis suis libertatem."

[50] Scaevola (5 *dig.*) *Dig.* 14.3.20: "Lucius Titius mensae nummulariae quam exercebat habuit libertum praepositum: is Gaio Seio cavit in haec verba: 'Octavius Terminalis rem agens Octavii Felicis Domitio Felici salutem...'" and *idem* (11 *dig.*) *Dig.* 26.7.58 *pr.*: "Qui negotiationem per Pamphilum et Diphilum prius servos postea libertos exercebat...."

[51] Papinianus (11 *quaest.*) *Dig.* 26.7.37.1: "Secundum quam sententiam servus institor dominicae mercis vel praepositus debitis exigendis si liber factus in eodem actu perseveret, quamvis tempore servitutis obligari non potuerit, praeteriti temporis nomine actione negotiorum gestorum non inutiliter convenietur, earum scilicet rerum, quae conexam rationem cum his, quae postea gesta sunt, habuerunt ..." and *idem* (3 *resp.*) *Dig.* 14.3.19.1: "Si dominus, qui servum institorem apud mensam pecuniis accipiendis habuit, post libertatem quoque datam idem per libertum negotium exercuit, varietate status non mutabitur periculi causa."

[52] As suggested by the title of the Edict (reconstructed by Lenel): *Quod cum magistro navis, institore eove, qui in aliena potestate erit, negotium gestum erit.*

[53] K. Visky, "L'affranchi comme *institor*," *BIDR* 83 (1980) 207-20; *contra*, A. di Porto, *Impresa collettiva e schiavo 'manager' in Roma antica (II sec. a.C. –II sec. d.C.)* (Milan 1984) 387-89. This point will be discussed at greater length later on, but cf. also Chapter Three, about freed *vilici*.

based activities as opposed to seaborne trade for which the equivalent of the *instritor* is the *magister navis* (''shipmaster''), whose principal is called *exercitor* (''shipper''). The legal remedy given to the third contracting party against the principal is called *actio exercitoria* (*Dig.* 14.1).[54] Both the *exercitor* and the *magister navis* could be found in the position of *institores*, because both were likely to conduct transactions not necessarily related to the management of a ship.[55]

2. *Institores in the literary sources*

If we consider now the picture provided by the literary sources, it is striking to note at first that ancient writers had little to say about businessmen in general, and even less about *institores*. The following survey is based on the references collected in the *Thesaurus Linguae Latinae*, which amount to about 60 occurrences.[56] This collection, which may not be comprehensive as far as Imperial sources are concerned, includes quotations excerpted from both pagan and Christian authors. As a whole, one can divide this material into two categories. On one hand, *institor* designates a merchant, a retailer, or a peddler. It is sometimes synonymous with *negotiator, mercator,* and the

---

[54] The text of the Edict has been reconstructed as follows on the basis of Gaius, *Inst.* 4.71 and Ulpianus (28 *ad ed.*) *Dig.* 14.1.1: ''Quod cum magistro navis gestum erit eius rei nomine, cui ibi praepositus fuerit, in eum, qui eam navem exercuerit, iudicium dabo. Si is, qui navem exercuerit, in patris dominive (alterius?) potestate erit eiusque voluntate navem exercuerit, quod cum magistro eius gestum erit, in eum, in cuius potestate is erit qui navem exercuerit, iudicium dabo.'' Cf. *FIRA* I[2], no. 65, p. 355 and O. Lenel, *Das Edictum Perpetuum*[3] (Leipzig 1927) 257-58. It is uncertain whether this edict was introduced by the urban or peregrine praetor.

[55] Ulpianus (28 *ad ed.*) *Dig.* 14.1.1.3: ''Magistri autem imponuntur locandis navibus vel ad merces vel vectoribus conducendis armamentisve emendis: sed etiamsi mercibus emendis vel vendendis fuerit praepositus, etiam hoc nomine obligat exercitorem;'' and *Dig.* 14.1.1.19: ''Si is, qui navem exercuerit, in aliena potestate erit eiusque voluntate navem exercuerit, quod cum magistro eius gestum erit, in eum, in cuius potestate is erit qui navem exercuerit, iudicium datur.'' In spite of its awkward wording, this second text is considered genuine by G. Pugliese, *Labeo* 3 (1957) 321-23 (whom I follow), against F. De Martino (1982) [1941] 160-64 and [1958] 187-90 and 198; and G. Longo, ''*Actio exercitoria, actio institoria, actio quasi institoria,*'' *Studi G. Scherillo* II (Milan 1972) 581-626, esp. 597. The chain of command on a merchant vessel is discussed by J. Rougé, ''La justice à bord du navire,'' *Studi E. Volterra* III (Milan 1971) 173-81; and *idem*, ''Prêt et société maritime dans le monde romain,'' *MAAR* 36 (1980) 291-303, esp. 297-98; cf. also F. Ghionda, ''Sul *magister navis*,'' *Riv. dir. navigaz.* 1 (1935) 327-55.

[56] *TLL* 7.1 (1964) cols. 1985-86, s.v. *institor*; and P. Fabricius, *Der gewaltfreie Institor im klassischen römischen Recht* (Würzburg 1926) 26-30, esp. 27, n. 11.

likes, although it ordinarily refers to a lower social stratum. On the other hand, the word seems to have acquired a derogatory meaning and has a flavor of greed, luxury, and debauchery. We will see that literary writers used the word in a different acceptation from legal writers.

a. *institores and seaborne trade*

In the literary sources, *institores* are presented as engaged in seaborne as well as land based trade. Horace associates *institores* with sailors (*nautae*) and with a shipmaster (*magister navis*).[57] This might be a coincidence, but it is not an isolated instance. Manilius mentions an "institor aequoreae...mercis" who trades on the seashore and exploits marine resources, such as pearls.[58] In later antiquity, Jerome translates ναῦς ἐμπορευομένη as "navis institoris,"[59] the *institor* being either the shipper or the shipmaster, as Salonius, a fifth-century bishop of Vienna, explains to his interlocutor Veranus:

> A merchant is called *institor*, because he always toils in order to acquire merchandise and to increase his profit. His ship loaded with various commodities available in greater quantities in his homeland, the *institor* sails across the sea to sell his cargo in foreign places before returning home with goods of a higher value.[60]

Sidonius Apollinaris, a contemporary of Salonius, alludes to the "plenas mercibus...carinas" that an *institor* trades in peace-time.[61] In conclusion, it seems that the term *institor*, at least in non-technical literature, applies to all persons engaged in commercial activities, regardless of the place—urban or rural areas, or overseas countries—where the operations are conducted.

The literary sources rarely provide any relevant information about the social background and the economic activities of *institores*, but they shed some light on the prejudicial attitudes of the upper

---

[57] Hor., *Epod.* 17.20; *Carm.* 3.6.29-32.
[58] Manilius 5.406-408: "tali sorte suas artes per litora tractat, / aut emit externos pretio mutatque labores / institor aequoreae varia sub imagine mercis."
[59] Vulgate, *Prov.* 31.14.
[60] Salonius, *In Proverbia Salomonis* 31.14 (= *PL* 53.990 B): "Institor dicitur negotiator, propterea quod semper instat ut acquirat et multiplicet merces et lucra sua. Navis ergo institoris onusta diversis mercimoniis, quae in sua patria magis abundant, per mare pergit ad loca peregrina, ut illic venditis quae attulit, cariora domum reportet."
[61] Sid. Apoll., *Carm.* 23.260.

classes of Roman society toward *institores*. These attitudes were
sometimes translated into official policies, whereby the political
authorities took repressive measures against this class of businessmen.

b. *prejudices against institores*
The widespread contempt for a broad range of economic activities
forms the basis of the derogatory connotation attached to the word
meaning small-scale traders.[62] This emphasis seems to go back to
the earliest dramatic reference to *institores*. Recording the events that
took place in 217 B.C., Livy tells the story—probably fictitious but
nonetheless plausible for this period—of a demagogic magistrate, C.
Terentius Varro, who supported a bill to which the nobility was
opposed. To add some discredit to the circumstances that motivated
Varro's political stand, Livy (or rather his source, Fabius Pictor)
emphasizes the social background of the incriminated magistrate
whose origin was not merely low, but even sordid: his father was a
butcher who performed the menial task of selling meat.[63] It is interesting to note that the term *institor* applies to the father, although
there is no evidence that he was the agent of the store's owner. His
disgrace would have been of lesser significance if he had been the
owner of a shop managed by slaves, which may have been the case,
but our source did not volunteer that information. After practicing
the same trade for a while as the assistant or agent of his father, the
future consul of 216 succeeded in working his way up and escaping
from this low position. By telling us that not only his ambition, but
also the money he inherited from his father were instrumental in
permitting him to rise on the social ladder, Livy suggests that the
occupation of butcher was very profitable: Varro's father may have
been a wealthy businessman. Still, Varro's past involvement in
petty trade, by which he was irrevocably branded, was viewed as the
cause of his questionable political attitude.

One can argue that Livy may be guilty of using an anachronistic

---

[62] Cic., *Off.* 1.42.151: "Mercatura . . . si tenuis est, sordida putanda est." Cf.
J.H. D'Arms, *Commerce and Social Standing in Ancient Rome* (Cambridge, MA 1981)
1-19, esp. 4-6.

[63] Livy 22.25.18-19: "Patrem lanium fuisse ferunt, ipsum institorem mercis,
filioque hoc ipso in servilia eius artis ministeria usum;" and 22.26. C. Terentius
Varro had been quaestor, twice aedile, and praetor (217 B.C.), and sided with
those who opposed the dictator Q. Fabius Maximus's policy before the battle of
Cannae. This position won him the consulship soon after (in 216).

terminology in writing about *institores* in a third-century context. The word is not used by Plautus or Terence, nor by any author before Cicero (in 44 B.C.). However, it is remarkable that (a) the term used in reference to Terentius Varro is not a unique case in Livy's work, as he uses it again in another passage to refer to a distinct, contemporary event; and (b) other Augustan or Imperial authors consider the word *institor* appropriate for describing a situation occurring in the mid-Republican period.

In the narrative concerning the settlement that took place after the crushing of the revolt of Capua (211 B.C.), Livy reports that the proconsul Fulvius Flaccus allowed only a large group of resident aliens, freedmen, *institores*, and craftsmen to stay permanently in the town, while all people commanding some degree of social prestige or respect, i.e. the nobility and the landowning middle class, were either put to death or sold as slaves.[64] It is established that economic considerations prevented the town from being completely destroyed and its whole population deported: the reason for the Roman government's leniency was due to the Campanian cultivators' probable reliance on the town for necessary tools, artifacts, and a market for the sale of their surpluses.[65]

According to Valerius Maximus, P. Cornelius Scipio Aemilianus banned civilian camp followers from military quarters in order to strengthen the discipline among his soldiers during the siege of Numantia in 134/3. The targeted crowd was composed of sutlers (*lixae*) and prostitutes (*scorta*), as well as *institores*, whom Valerius Maximus calls an "ugly and shameful scum." Appian records the same event, and we have good reason to think that the story is authentic because it probably goes back to Polybius, who is thought to have been present at Numantia as a personal friend of Scipio.[66]

---

[64] Livy 26.16.8: "multitudo incolarum libertinorumque et institorum opificumque." P. Jal (ed. Budé, vol. 16 [1991] 117) suggests that only non-citizens were allowed to stay in the town.

[65] J.-P. Morel, "La manufacture, moyen d'enrichissement dans l'Italie romaine," in Ph. Leveau (ed.), *L'origine des richesses dépensées dans la ville antique* (Aix-en-Provence 1985) 87-111, esp. 102.

[66] Val. Max. 2.7.1: "P. Cornelius Scipio ... edixit ut omnia ex his, quae voluptatis causa comparata erant, auferrentur ac summoverentur: nam constat tum maximum inde institorum et lixarum numerum cum duo milibus scortorum abisse. Hac turpi atque erubescenda sentina vacuefactus exercitus noster ...." Appian, *Hisp.* 14.85: Ἐλθὼν δέ, ἐμπόρους τε πάντας ἐξήλαυνε, καὶ ἑταίρας καὶ μάντεις καὶ θύτας, οἷς, διὰ τὰς δυσπραξίας οἱ στρατιῶται περιδεεῖς γεγονότες, ἐχρῶντο συνεχῶς. There is no evidence that Appian was using Valerius Maximus as his

As the Roman army relied mostly on private enterprise for its logistical support, it is likely that major campaigns provided business opportunities for dynamic tradesmen. An episode of the Gallic War illustrates that relationship between businessmen and the military. In his account of the year 52 B.C., Caesar reports the death of one Gaius Fufius Cita, a member of the equestrian order and a respectable merchant (*negotiator*) to whom he had entrusted the logistical supply of the Roman army.[67] In Caesar's own words, Cita was the equivalent of a *praepositus*, but his social status protected him from the suspicion of being an *institor*. Feeding and equipping an army of several thousand men required a rather sophisticated organization, so it is likely that Cita had access to an existing infrastructure (suppliers, storage spaces, relay stations, lines of communications, etc.) and was content with supervising the work of others, either his own servants and employees or some subcontractors, whose social status was similar to that of the *institores* in the Numantine War. The relationship between Caesar and Cita was possibly based on some kind of friendship or personal connection: Cita was then acting on the basis of a mandate or of a contract of work,[68] and could be considered the archetype of the *procuratores* or *conductores/redemptores* of the Imperial period. The Numantine episode in 134 B.C. and Caesar's personal experience should be considered as early signs of the existing and growing interaction between the army and private businessmen. Producers and distributors were always attracted by the huge military markets, and went through great trouble to maintain their control over them, especially when the army had settled in more permanent quarters—for instance on the Rhine *limes* in the first century A.D. We will see further on how the

---

source, but it is possible that he had access to Polybius's Numantine monograph directly or through Diodorus Siculus. Valerius Maximus also goes back to Polybius, probably through Livy (*Per.* 57).

[67] Caes., *BGal.* 7.3.1: "Carnutes...concurrunt civesque Romanos, qui negotiandi causa ibi constiterant, in his Gaium Fufium Citam, honestum equitem Romanum, qui rei frumentariae iussu Caesaris praeerat, interficiunt bonaque eorum diripiunt." Cita was killed by the Carnutes at Cenabum. Cf. A. Labisch, *Frumentum commeatusque. Die Nahrungsmittelversorgung der Heere Caesars* (Meisenheim am Glan 1975) 115-20.

[68] A. Steinwenter, *PW* 10 (1919) cols. 1306-08, s.v. *iussum*, stresses the variety of meanings of the word *iussum*, which stands for an unilateral order, an invitation, or an authorization to do something.

institorian arrangement may have facilitated the suppliers' task.[69]

In the moralistic writings of the early Empire, *institores* were despised for their greed, which they allegedly tried to satisfy through speculation and petty trade. Profit-making was the *raison d'être* of any *institor*, and this fact is supported by Paulus's statement that the principal of a *vilicus* would not be liable to an *actio institoria*, unless the latter had been appointed for the very purpose of doing business ("propter quaestum").[70] A Christian writer like Salonius is eager to stress that the very term *institor*—according to a fanciful etymology—is revealing of avarice.[71] Not all profits were censured, only those derived from banausic activities and those which brought about distress to others. *Institores* were notorious for taking advantage of weak, corrupted youths whom they supplied with superfluous luxury goods,[72] for which they were keen at creating a demand. As a result of the establishment of commercial networks that could rely on adequate transportation, processing facilities, storage spaces, and retail outlets, the commerce of exotic commodities—such as ice—became profitable and fashionable. Prices fluctuated according to seasonal variations.[73] The better skilled the *institor*, the more successful in anticipating rises and drops in prices and making the necessary adjustments. Pliny the Elder says that cloth dealers used to watch the sky on the night of November 10 and, on the basis of the position of certain stars, could determine whether the winter would be cold or wet, setting the prices of coats and cloaks accordingly.[74] Juvenal acknowledges the readiness of *institores* to accept

---

[69] Cf. Chapter Four, about the establishment of branch workshops to facilitate the distribution of pottery in the provinces.

[70] Paulus (9 *ad ed.*) *Dig.* 14.3.16: "Si cum vilico alicuius contractum sit, non datur in dominum actio, quia vilicus propter fructus percipiendos, non propter quaestum praeponitur." But cf. above, and Chapter Three.

[71] Salonius, *In Proverbia Salomonis* 31.14 (= PL 53.990 B): "propterea quod semper instat ut acquirat et multiplicet merces et lucra sua." Cf. above.

[72] Sen., *Ben.* 6.38.3: "Institores delicatarum mercium iuventus corrupta locupletat."

[73] Sen., *QNat.* 4b.13.8-9: "Itaque ne unum quidem eius est pretium, sed habet institores aqua et annonam, pro pudor! variam.... Quid illi [= Lacedaemonii] fecissent, si vidissent reponendae nivis officinas et tot iumenta portandae aquae deservientia, cuius colorem saporemque paleis quibus custodiunt inquinant."

[74] Plin., *HN* 18.225: "Hoc ipso Vergiliarum occasu fieri putant aliqui a.d. III Idus Novembris, ut diximus, servantque id sidus etiam vestis institores, et est in caelo notatu facillimum. Ergo ex occasu eius de hieme augurantur quibus est cura insidiandi, negotiatores avaritia. Nubilo occasu pluviosam hiemem denuntiat, statimque augent lacernarum pretia; sereno asperam, et reliquarum vestium accendunt."

wage adjustments and his scholiast comments on "institor hibernae
tegetis niveique cadurci" ("trader of winter blankets") by saying
that he is a "merchant who depends on the weather to sell his
product."[75] No credit is given for such flexibility and, in the mind
of upper-class Roman writers, a shrewd businessman is not considered worthy of the same respectability as an astute and knowledge-
able cultivator.

In addition to, or rather in consequence of, the discredit attached
to their economic pursuits, *institores* as petty traders were viewed as
a group sharing in some social stigma. Male *institores* were thought
to have been endowed with qualitatively and quantitatively superior
sexual power channeled into illicit or immoral activities. This attitude is widespread among racially biased people towards religious
or ethnic groups they scorn but, at the same time, fear, e.g., Jews
and Gypsies in Western Europe, and blacks in America.[76] Such
biases are not aimed exclusively at racial groups. The basis for the
stereotype is obvious: as peddlers, *institores* knocked at the door of
private houses in the daytime, when the men of the family were busy
outside. Then they had plenty of opportunities to chat with secluded
women and to seduce them with gifts. Ultimately they became so ar-
rogant as to not even mind the presence of a husband:

> An indecent *institor* will come to your craving mistress and will
> display his treasures in spite of your sitting there.[77]

Legitimate lovers and husbands were at a loss, not knowing how to
handle such a tricky situation while protecting their honor:

> If you let in old women, seers, charlatans, dealers in gems and silk gar-
> ments, your honor is at risk; but if you do not, you become suspect
> of being unfair.[78]

---

[75] Juv. 7.219-221: "Cede, Palaemon, / et patere inde aliquid decrescere, non
aliter quam / institor hibernae tegetis niveique cadurci;" and ΣJuv. 7.221: "negotiator, qui pro qualitate temporis mercem suam distrahit."

[76] The same remark applies to seventeenth-century English merchants, cf. N.
McKendrick, "The Typology and Organisation of Enterprise," in S. Cavaciocchi
(ed.), *L'impresa. Industria, commercio, banca (secc. XIII-XVIII)* (Florence 1991) 77-94,
esp. 82: "Such merchants were mocked because they were feared. They were feared
because they were seen as predatory, ambitious and aggressive, a threat to the established social order."

[77] Ov. *Ars Am.* 1.421-422: "Institor ad dominam veniet discinctus emacem
expediet merces teque sedente suas."

[78] Sen., *frg.* 52 (Haase) = Jerome, *Adversus Iovinianum* 1.47 (= *PL* 23.190):

It was not so much the incessant sexual activity of *institores* that was targeted as their promiscuity, want of discrimination, and lack of discretion. *Institores* had the reputation of switching partners and taking advantage of women's temporary boredom:

> She loves others, but she is tired of me: a peddler, alas!, enjoys the nights that she denies me.[79]

Institores saw nothing wrong with engaging in sexual intercourse with such outcasts as the witch Canidia "often loved by sailors and traders"[80] and could not refrain from interfering with the life of married couples:

> Her husband sees her get up to comply with the request of a business-man or of the shipmaster of the ship Hispana, who is ready to pay a high price for her dishonor.[81]

For Roman moralists there was only one step from adultery to prostitution. *Institores* were described in turn as prostitutes, pimps, or johns. P. Atilius Philiscus, a character embodying early Roman modesty, had been forced as a youth into prostitution by his master, but later killed his own daughter whom he had found guilty of debauchery. Valerius Maximus marvels at this "vendor of sex" turned "such a harsh avenger of chastity."[82] Arnobius indiscriminately labels as *institores* perfumers, muleteers, butchers, whores, etc.[83] It is unclear whether Pseudo-Quintilian's "merchants of shame" peddle their own virtue or someone else's, but the sexual allusion is unmistakable.[84] Seneca wishes that the prostituted *phi-*

"Anus et aruspices et hariolos et institores gemmarum sericarumque vestium si intromiseris, periculum pudicitiae est: si prohibueris, suspicionis iniuria."

[79] Ov., *Rem. Am.* 305-306: "Diligit ipsa alios, a me fastidit amari: Institor, heu, noctes, quas mihi non dat, habet."

[80] Hor., *Epod.* 17.20: "amata nautis multum et institoribus."

[81] Hor., *Carm.* 3.6.29-32: "sed iussa coram non sine conscio / surgit marito, seu vocat institor / seu navis Hispanae magister, / dedecorum pretiosus emptor."

[82] Val. Max. 6.1.6: "Quam sanctam igitur in civitate nostra pudicitiam fuisse existimare debemus, in qua etiam institores libidinis tam severos eius vindices evasisse animadvertimus?"

[83] Arn., *Adv. Nat.* 2.38: "Quid picarios salinatores bolonas unguentarios aurifices aucupes vannorum sirpiarumque vitores? Quid fullones lanarios phrygiones cocos panchristarios muliones lenones lanios meretrices? Quid institorum alia genera, quid professorum et artium, quibus enumerandis omnis aetas angusta est, rationibus conferunt et constitutionibus mundi, . . ."

[84] Ps.-Quintilian, *Decl. min.* 260.13: "Nihil obesse rei publicae videretur si vitiorum institores hos eosdem sumptus divisissent." Cf. M. Winterbottom's commentary (1984) p. 340.

losophia would barter her pimp for a priest.[85] As sexual intercourse
with prostitutes did not incur any social disapproval, Horace's
"buyer of dishonor", whose attempt at seducing a Roman matron
is understandably decried, was unlikely to be the chief target of
moralists if he chose his partner in lower circles; consequently, no
emphasis on this aspect of the sexual activity of *institores* is noticeable
in the sources.

Opportunist and libertine, yet playing a vital economic role, the
typical *institor* was viewed by the nobility as a necessary disease to
be contained within strict limits. This was mainly achieved by social
segregation, the upper classes pretending to abstain from potentially
very profitable activities which became the preserve of the lower
classes. Claim to respectability was inconsistent with petty trade,
which explains why slaves and freeborn have-nots are more likely to
be found in the shoes of *institores* than successful and socially ambitious freedmen. Respectable business agents of course were plenty,
but they can be expected to distance themselves from pettiness by
adopting an upper-class attitude or status. This is exactly what the
freedman M. Aurelius Zosimus did, with the generous cooperation
of his patron, M. Aurelius Cotta Maximus Messalinus, the consul
of A.D. 20. On his tombstone (dedicated by his wife), Zosimus
reports that, apart from being the attendant (*accensus*) of his patron,
he was regularly entrusted with the management of his affairs, for
which activity he was given on many occasions the financial means
to obtain the equestrian census in addition to career and financial
benefits for his children. Any specific title (*procurator, actor, dispensator, institor,* etc.) or job description are carefully and consciously
omitted in the dedication.[86]

---

[85] Sen., *Ep.* 52.15: "si modo non institorem, sed antistitem nancta est."

[86] *CIL* XIV 2298 (= *ILS* 1949, found on the Via Appia in the territory of
Alba): "M. Aurelius Cottae / Maximi l. Zosimus, / accensus patroni. / Libertinus
eram, fateor; / sed facta legetur / patrono Cotta nobilis umbra mea. / Qui mihi
saepe libens census donavit / equestris, qui iussit natos / tollere, quos aleret / quique
suas commisit opes / mihi semper, et idem dotavit / natas ut pater ipse meas, / Cot-
tanumque meum produxit / honore tribuni, quem fortis / castris Caesaris emeruit.
/ Quid non Cotta dedit? qui nunc / et carmina tristis haec dedit / in tumulo conspi-
cienda meo./ Aurelia Saturnia Zosimi." Cf. J.H. D'Arms, *CSSAR* (1981) 103-04,
with other examples of freedmen working for, or at least in possible connection
with, their patron.

c. *imperial policy against institores*

There were times, however, when the nobility felt that the barriers between them and the others were no longer visible enough and required some drastic intervention on the part of the political power. We know of a few occasions when a magistrate of the Roman state or the emperor tried to control the position or activities of *institores* as a social and economic group. According to Pliny the Elder, C. Sulpicius Galba, a favorite of the emperor Tiberius who became consul in A.D. 22, complained in the senate that *institores* were successfully escaping the fine to which innkeepers were subjected (*popinarum poenae*) by claiming exemption on the basis of their alleged equestrian status. This event took place in A.D. 23 and was elicited by the enforcement of a measure probably introduced by Galba himself in the previous year,[87] whereby profits derived from activities associated with bistros and hotels, e.g., sales of hot meals and drinks, gambling, prostitution, etc. were subject to some kind of inhibiting tax.[88] Pliny unambiguously states that a double standard was applied in the enforcement of the rule and that social prestige entailed legal privileges. What annoyed Galba was not so much the legally questionable application of double standard as the claim laid by a category of economic agents to determine their own social status without referring to the elite. This kind of initiative is known to have been particularly odious to the ruling class.[89] The debate that followed Galba's intervention resulted in a major purge of the equestrian order, the access to which was restricted to those who could boast a free origin. The wording of the decree reveals that *institores* were commonly viewed by the upper classes as slaves, freed-

---

[87] Pliny, *HN* 33.32: "...cum C. Sulpicius Galba, iuvenalem famam apud principem popinarum poenis aucupatus, questus esset in senatu, volgo institores eius culpae defendi anulis." R.J. Talbert, *The Senate of Imperial Rome* (Princeton 1984) 239 and 440, nos. 27-28; T. Kleberg, *Hôtels, restaurants et cabarets dans l'Antiquité romaine* (Uppsala 1957) 80 thinks that Galba acted in the capacity of aedile.

[88] For similar measures, cf. Suetonius, *Tib.* 34.1; *Claud.* 38.2 (about an incident that occurred probably during the reign of Tiberius or Caligula); *Nero* 16.2; Dio Cass. 60.6.7 (A.D. 41); 65.10.3 (A.D. 70); on first-century imperial regulation of eating-houses, cf. G. Hermansen, "The Roman Inns and the Law. The Inns of Ostia," in J.A.S. Evans (ed.), *Polis and Imperium. Studies in Honour of E.T. Salmon* (Toronto 1974) 167-81. The *popinarum poenae* are interpreted diversely by Kleberg, who understands them as fines collected by aediles when innkeepers transgressed the stiff imperial laws prohibiting the sale of certain commodities, and Talbert, for whom they were penalties for keeping eating-houses (cf. preceding note).

[89] This fact is best illustrated by the *Gnomon of the Idios Logos* (*FIRA* I², no. 99 =

men, or descendants of these within three generations.[90] The his-
toricity—though not the dating—of the anecdote recorded by Pliny
is warranted by the find at Larinum of a senatorial decree passed in
A.D. 19 that deals with the same issue.[91]

Further official intervention against *institores* is reported by
Martial, who alludes to the pervasiveness of shopkeepers in Rome.
In response to this state of affairs, the emperor Domitian reportedly
took steps to keep them off the sidewalk in order to improve the
fluidity of the traffic within the city.[92] Even though from a practical
point of view the official reason was sensible, the measure effectively
interfered with the occupation of shopkeepers and peddlers and
could be viewed by the lower classes as a deliberate show of power
toward a group whose economic dynamism was considered too
aggressive.

These two instances of intervention by public authorities against
institores recorded in the literary sources are supplemented by two
other instances recorded in epigraphical and legal sources. First,
Diocletian's Price Edict was promulgated in A.D. 301 with the expressed purpose of preventing greedy *institores* from doing further
damage to the economy through manipulation of prices of commodities and services. By targeting this specific group, the emperors
thought that they would be able to curb the monetary instability and
to impose a new economic order.[93] Second, an imperial decree

---

BGU V 1210, A.D. 150-61) and by the edict of A.D. 215 calling for the expulsion
from Alexandria of Egyptians who had assumed the insignia of another class
(*P. Giss.* 40). Trimalchio is portrayed as wearing a gilded ring as well as a small gold
ring (status symbol of an active *sevir*), which reveals his mannerism (Petron., *Sat.*
32.3).

[90] Pliny, *HN* 33.32: "Hac de causa constitutum, ne cui ius esset nisi qui ingenuus ipse, ingenuo patre, avo paterno HS $\overline{CCCC}$ census fuisset et lege Iulia
theatrali in quattuordecim ordinibus sedisset." On the whole question, cf. J.P.
Bodel, *Freedmen in the Satyricon of Petronius* (Diss. Univ. of Michigan 1984) Appendix
3: "The Jus Anuli Aurei in the Julio-Claudian Period"; M. Reinhold, "Usurpation of Status and Status Symbols in the Roman Empire," *Historia* 20 (1971)
275-302, esp. 285-86; and F. Kolb, "Zur Statussymbolik im antiken Rom," *Chiron*
7 (1977) 239-59.

[91] *AE* 1978, no. 145; and B. Levick, "The Senatus Consultum from Larinum,"
JRS 73 (1983) 97-115.

[92] Mart. 7.61: "Abstulerat totam temerarius institor urbem." Cf. also Mart.
1.41; R. MacMullen, *Roman Social Relations* (New Haven/London 1974) 64 and
169, nn. 19-20; and H. Wagner, "Zur wirtschaftlichen und rechtlichen Bedeutung
der Tabernen," *Studi A. Biscardi* III (Milan 1982) 391-422, esp. 396.

[93] Text and commentary by M. Giacchero, *Edictum Diocletiani et collegarum de*

issued by Theodosius II and Valentinian III in A.D. 436 barred *institores* and their like from holding public offices, as magistrates, military officers and civil servants in the provinces, not to say in both capitals:

> We also command that all people involved in various trading activities, bankers, vendors of gems, silverware, and garments, warehousemen, and all kinds of *institores* and workers be removed from public positions in provincial government so that the magistracy and the bureaucracy will be sheltered from infection of this kind.[94]

These independently recorded events leave no doubt that official notice of *institores* as a group was taken only to express the aristocratic attitude toward trade and commerce, which can be traced a long way back to the Republican period and is most explicitly represented in Cato's preface of his *De Agri Cultura* or by Cicero in a famous, often-discussed passage of his *De Officiis*.[95] Admittedly, the bias

---

pretiis rerum venalium (Genova 1974) and S. Lauffer, *Diokletians Preisedikt* (Berlin 1971). Cf. next section on epigraphical sources.

[94] *Cod. Iust.* 12.57.12.3: "Sed etiam cunctos, qui diversarum rerum negotationibus detinentur, trapezitas scilicet vel gemmarum argentique vestiumve venditores, apothecarios etiam ceterosque institores aliarum mercium quibuscumque ergasteriis adhaerentes iubemus a provincialibus officiis removeri, ut omnis honor atque militia contagione huiusmodi segregetur." Similar measures affected the Jews in the East, cf. in particular P. Johnson, *A History of the Jews* (New York 1988) 165; A.H.M. Jones, *The Later Roman Empire* (Norman, OK 1964) 948 and 1392, nn. 25-26, with reference to *Cod. Theod.* 16.8.16 (404) and 24 (418) for the Western empire; and *Nov. Theod.* 3.2.5-6 = *Cod. Iust.* 1.9.18 (438 or 439), for the Eastern empire, with the addition of the position of *pater civitatis* to the list of barred offices. Exclusion from the army was enacted in an edict of the emperors Gratian, Valentinian and Theodosius, addressed to provincial taxpayers (*Cod. Theod.* 7.13.8, A.D. 380): "Inter optimas lectissimorum militum turmas neminem e numero servorum dandum esse decernimus neve ex caupona ductum vel ex famosarum ministeriis tabernarum aut ex cocorum aut pistorum numero vel etiam eo, quam obsequii deformitas militia secernit, nec tracta de ergastulis nomina." Prof. S. Treggiari pointed out to me that these extreme social prejudices are not present in earlier municipal laws, and this is consistent with Callistratus's opinion that specifies ([6 *cognit.*] *Dig.* 50.2.12) that small traders ("qui utensilia negotiantur et vendunt"), who are exposed to physical punishment at the hands of the aediles, are not *infames* and can aspire to a municipal career if more honorable candidates are lacking; cf. F. Jacques, *Le privilège de liberté. Politique impériale et autonomie municipale dans les cités de l'Occident romain (161-244)* (Rome 1984) 330; and 533.

[95] Cato, *Agr.* Pref. 1: "Est interdum praestare mercaturis rem quaerere, nisi tam periculosum sit, et item fenerari, si item honestum sit;" and 3: "Mercatorem autem strenuum studiosumque rei quaerendae existimo, verum, ut supra dixi, periculosum et calamitosum." Cic., *Off.* 1.42.150-151: "Primum improbantur ii quaestus qui in odia hominum incurrunt, ut portitorum, ut feneratorum . . . Sordidi etiam putandi qui mercantur a mercatoribus quod statim vendant . . . Mer-

against *institores* must have varied in times and places according to
the fervor with which the traditional attitude toward trade and commerce was fostered and perpetuated. Discrepancies between attitudes and behavior must also be expected at the individual level, as
is clear from the writings and biography of Cato the Elder, who
reportedly engaged in seaborne trade and moneylending through
his freedmen while condemning loudly both occupations.[96]

d. *use and meaning of the word institor*
The word *institor*, which first occurs in a text by Cicero written in
44 B.C.,[97] was part of the vocabulary of classical (Livy, Horace,
Ovid, Propertius, Manilius, Valerius Maximus, Scribonius Largus,
Seneca, Pliny the Elder, Quintilian, Juvenal, Martial, Irenaeus)
and post-classical writers (Arnobius, Nonius Marcellus, Donatus,
Claudian, Prudentius, Jerome and his disciple Philippus [= Ps.-
Jerome], Sidonius Apollinaris, Salonius, Gregory the Great). The
sheer length of this list bears witness to the popularity of the word
which survived in Medieval Latin, but seems by then to have lost its
derogatory connotation. One of the latest instances where *institor* has
an unequivocally negative meaning occurs in the imperial constitution of Theodosius II and Valentinian III (436) quoted above.[98]

The manuscript tradition of Christian texts in which the word *institor* is used shows that some problem of understanding arose at
some point. Gregory the Great, who was Pope from 590 to 604,
points out that "in all Latin books we find the word *institutor* [=
teacher], while in Greek works the word for *negotiator* [= merchant]

---

catura autem, si tenuis est, sordida putanda est.'' S. Treggiari, "Urban Labour
in Rome: *Mercennarii* and *Tabernarii*,'' in P. Garnsey (ed.), *Non-slave Labour in the
Greco-Roman World* (Cambridge 1980) 48-64; and J.H. D'Arms, *CSSAR* (1981) 4-5
and *passim*.

[96] Plut., *Cat. Mai.* 21.5-7: Ἁπτόμενος δὲ συντονώτερον πορισμοῦ, τὴν μὲν γεωρ-
γίαν μᾶλλον ἡγεῖτο διαγωγὴν ἢ πρόσοδον, εἰς δ' ἀσφαλῆ πράγματα καὶ βέβαια
κατατιθέμενος τὰς ἀφορμὰς ἐκτᾶτο λίμνας,... (6) Ἐχρήσατο δὲ καὶ τῷ διαβε-
βλημένῳ μάλιστα τῶν δανεισμῶν ἐπὶ ναυτικοῖς τὸν τρόπον τοῦτον. Ἐκέλευε τοὺς
δανειζομένους ἐπὶ κοινωνίᾳ πολλοὺς παρακαλεῖν· γενομένων δὲ πεντήκοντα καὶ
πλοίων τοσούτων αὐτὸς εἶχε μίαν μερίδα διὰ Κουιντίωνος ἀπελευθέρου τοῖς δανειζο-
μένοις συμπραγματευομένου καὶ συμπλέοντος· (7) Ἦν [δ'] οὖν οὐκ εἰς ἅπαν ὁ κίνδυ-
νος, ἀλλ' εἰς μέρος μικρὸν ἐπὶ κέρδεσι μεγάλοις.

[97] Cic., *Phil.* 2.38.97: "Quid ego de commentariis infinitis, quid de innumer-
abilibus chirographis loquar? Quorum etiam institores sunt, qui ea tamquam gladiatorium libellos palam venditent.''

[98] I will discuss the etymology of the word in the section about the creation of
the *actio institoria* in its relationship with the *actio exercitoria*, cf. Chapter Two.

is used" and he attributes this change to the writers' ignorance.[99] One can argue (a) that the word became obsolete in the fourth or fifth century A.D. and, its meaning being unclear, was replaced by a more familiar word (*institutor* means "educator"); or (b) that some copyists felt uncomfortable using this word because of the continuing perception of its derogatory flavor, which was uncalled for in the present context, and indulged in a small alteration of the word; or (c) that the variant was the result of a scribal mistake: the copy of Diocletian's Price Edict found at Plataea (cf. below) reads *institutorum* instead of *institorum*.

It is worth stressing that in no place in the literary sources it is specified that *institores* were agents, dependent managers, middlemen, or foremen. This can be explained by the fact that literary writers were mostly members of the elite and therefore unlikely to draw attention to the principals who benefited from the activities of *institores* in spite of the general attitude of the upper classes condemning trade and business. However, self-restraint on the part of our sources cannot provide more than a partial explanation, as there are quite a few instances where upper class writers unreluctantly mention agents involved in transactions on behalf of the elite. For instance, Plutarch reports, without condonation, the avaricious attitude of Cato the Elder who took shares in business ventures through his freedman Quintio[100] or provided some of his slaves with a *peculium* for the purpose of slave-breeding.[101] In addition, principals could belong to the lower-middle class,[102] and moralists would have had no reason to spare them. The unanimous agreement of the literary sources on using the word *instantor* without reference to agency must reflect a semantic choice on their part and emphasizes the so-

---

[99] Gregorius Magnus, *Moralia in Job* 18.35 (*PL* 76.68): "In cunctis Latinis codicibus institutores positos reperimus, in Graecis vero negotiatores invenimus. Ex qua re colligi valet quod in hoc loco pro institoribus institutores scriptores quique ignorando posuerunt. Institores enim negotiatores dicimus, pro eo quod exercendo operi insistunt."

[100] Plut., *Cat. Mai.* 21.6-7; cf. above.

[101] Plut., *Cat. Mai.* 21.7-8: Ἐδίδου δὲ καὶ τῶν οἰκετῶν τοῖς βουλομένοις ἀργύριον· οἱ δ' ἐωνοῦντο παῖδας, εἶτα τούτους ἀσκήσαντες καὶ διδάξαντες ἀναλώμασι τοῦ Κάτωνος μετ' ἐνιαυτὸν ἀπεδίδοντο. (8) Πολλοὺς δὲ καὶ κατεῖχεν ὁ Κάτων, ὅσην ὁ πλείστην διδοὺς ἐωνεῖτο τιμὴν ὑπολογιζόμενος.

[102] Sex. Avidius Eutychus in *CIL* XI 1621 (= *ILS* 7607, Florence/*Regio* VII) was probably a freedman; Mocianus in *CIL* III 13523 (Tüffer/Noricum) has no identifiable connection with any known character, but the *cognomen* Mucianus is common.

cial and economic position of petty traders rather than their legal relationship towards a principal. The literary usage suggests that *institores* could be self-employed businessmen.

3. *Institores in the inscriptions*

A possible consequence of the contemptuous attitude of the nobility toward people engaged in petty trade is the rare occurrence of the term *institor* in Latin inscriptions. Most of those who wanted to record their own, or other people's, memory on tombstones probably did so either using the label of specialized craftsmen or tradesmen,[103] or without any mention of occupation. It is therefore difficult for modern historians to differentiate self-employed workers from business agents. When a slave occupied in some business activity is mentioned in connection with his master, it is possible, but not certain that the slave was employed as business agent by his master. A slave could also be employed by someone else as a *mercennarius*, or carry out a *de facto* independent activity on the basis of the grant of a *peculium*.

From Italy, there are only three inscriptions recording *institores*. One, found in Florence, is the tombstone of a certain Adiectus, the slave of Sextus Avidius Eutychus (himself perhaps a freedman), who was engaged in the perfume industry (*seplasiarius negotians*).[104] The second inscription, from Rome, records another perfumer (*unguentarius*), Faustus Po. . ., perhaps related to the *gens* Popilia which was known for its commercial interests in perfumes.[105] The third inscription has been found on the site of a Roman villa near Chieti and was dedicated by one Q. Avidius Bassus to the *institor* Dionysius, who was working as a cobbler (*sutor*) and shoemaker (*caligarius*) for a certain Cn. Mamilius Primus. The nature of the relationship between Dionysius and Q. Avidius Bassus is uncertain.[106] The connection with a Roman villa might be purely accidental, since one cannot assume that Dionysius was buried where he worked. If the discovery site of this inscription is significant, it could mean that

---

[103] S. Treggiari, in P. Garnsey (ed.) (1980) 48-64, esp. the list on pp.61-64.
[104] *CIL* XI 1621 (= *ILS* 7607).
[105] *CIL* VI 10007 (= *ILS* 7608).
[106] *CIL* IX 3027 (= *ILS* 7546, Teate Marrucinorum). The last word of the inscription is abbreviated and could be read *p(osuit)* or, less likely, *p(atronus)*.

the *institor* was attached to the villa in the capacity of manager of one of the activities carried out there.

The rest of the empire has yielded only two additional examples so far. One is a monument dedicated by a certain Tattus for himself and his dependent Tatton. The stone was found in the Roman baths in the vicinity of Tüffer (Noricum), which may indicate that the *institor* was the bathkeeper (*balneator*).[107] The most interesting example comes from the province of Macedonia: Vitalis, son and slave brought up in the house (*verna*) of C. La(e?)vius Faustus, died at age 16 while in charge of a shop, the so-called "Taberna Apriana."[108] The inscription records the credit that Vitalis had acquired with the local population ("a populo acceptus")[109] and apologizes for the occasional swindling of his customers in order to increase his principal's profit.

The only securely datable epigraphical evidence is provided by the imperial constitution promulgated by Diocletian and his colleagues as an introduction to the Edict on Maximum Prices (A.D. 301). To justify the drastic measure of setting a price ceiling on a list of commodities and services, the authors of the enactment blamed the greed of *institores* for the sharp rise in prices that affected the Roman economy and prevented its recovery. They objected to several foul practices: rich people were speculating on the price of grain after a bad harvest, and were employing business managers in market-places who pursued their own profit by charging murderous rates of interest.[110] Unfortunately, the text is corrupt and the Greek version is no longer extant.

---

[107] *CIL* III 13523; cf. Chapter Five.

[108] *CIL* III 14206, no. 21 (= *ILS* 7479, Karrakavak/Macedonia).

[109] H. Wagner, "Zur wirtschaftlichen und rechtlichen Bedeutung der Tabernen," *Studi Biscardi* III (Milan 1982) 391-422, esp. 398, n. 47 suggests that the expression "a populo acceptus" refers to a "publizistischen Superfiziarverhältnis" according to which the *Taberna Apriana*, located on public ground (*loco publico*), would have been rented out to Vitalis or his principal/owner/father on the basis of a state contract. Cf. Ulpianus (44 *ad Sab.*) *Dig.* 18.1.32 and below, Chapter Two.

[110] *ILS* 642, Praef. 12 = I 23-26 (Lauffer): "Et quibus senper (*sic*) studium est in questum trahere etiam beneficia divina, ac publicae felicitatis afluentiam (*sic*) stringere rursusque anni sterili[tate de seminum] iactibus adque institorum officiis nundinari; qui singuli maximis divitiis diffluentes, quae etiam populos adfatim explere potuissent, consectentur peculia et laceratrices centensimas (*sic*) persequantur: eorum avaritiae modum statui, provinciales nostri, communis humanitatis ratio persuadet."

C. Greek terminology

As Latin literary and epigraphical sources refer to *institores* as petty tradesmen or business managers, one can expect their Greek counterparts to have occasionally dealt with this category of people and to have used a Greek term to designate them. In order to be able to exploit Greek sources, it is necessary to determine how they would refer to business managers.

1. *Bilingual sources*

Our only bilingual source is the Bible, with the Greek Septuagint and Jerome's translation. The Vulgate includes six passages where the word *institor* is used. The corresponding passages in the Septuagint do not offer a homogeneous translation. In *Job* 28.8, "filii institorum" stands for υἱοὶ ἀλαζόνων, an ἀλαζών being a vagrant, a charlatan, or a braggart.[111] In *Isaiah* 23.8, *Ezekiel* 27.13, 17, and 20, "institores" translates ἔμποροι, and in *Prov.* 31.14, "navis institoris" translates ναῦς ἐμπορευομένη. Other works by Church Fathers bearing on these passages or others include the word *institor*, and often a tentative explanation is provided. On the other hand, there is no example of the use of the word *institor* in the Latin version of the New Testament. Yet, Jerome, commenting on *Matth.* 13.45-46 or 21.12-13, uses "institores" to translate ἔμποροι or πωλοῦντες. The Gospel according to Matthew provides one interesting case (24.45-47): a well-deserving slave in charge of a household (ὃν κατέστησεν ὁ κύριος ἐπὶ τῆς οἰκετείας αὐτοῦ) is promoted to higher functions (ἐπὶ πᾶσιν τοῖς ὑπάρχουσιν αὐτοῦ καταστήσει αὐτόν). The verb καθιστάναι of the Greek version is translated by the verb *constituere* in the Vulgate ("quem constituit dominus suus super familiam suam"), which is a synonym of the verb *praeponere*. The Lukan parallel (12.42-46) uses the word οἰκονόμος.

In the *Basilica*, a Greek adaptation of Justinianic codification made during the reign of Leo the Wise (886-911),[112] the Anonymous translates *institor/praepositus* as προεστὼς τοῦ ἐργαστηρίου, ἐμπορίας χάριν προστάς, or προβληθεὶς ἐπὶ τῷ πωλεῖν ἢ ἀγοράζειν.

---

[111] Elsewhere Jerome translates "filii arrogantium" (*PL* 29.97 B).

[112] W. Kunkel, *An Introduction to Roman Legal and Constitutional History*[2] (Oxford 1973, based on the sixth German edition) 179-81 and 226-27.

The *vilicus* of *Dig.* 14.3.16 is a διοικητής, while φροντιστής and ἐπίτροπος translate respectively *procurator* and *tutor*. The principal is referred to as προστήσας, δεσπότης, or προβαλλόμενος.[113] The scholiasts (Kyrillos, Stephanos) use the Latin terminology (ἰνστιτού-τωρ), but call the *vilicus* οἰκονόμος.[114]

Another source providing information about the Greek equivalents of the word *institor* is found in the *Corpus Glossariorum Latinorum* (vol. 6, p. 588), which offers as equivalents for *institor* the words ἐργαστηριάρχης ("head of a workshop"), ἐνθηκάριος ("broker"), and ἐργοδιώκτης ("taskmaster"). These words were rarely used in ancient texts. Worth mentioning, however, is a late second-century-A.D. inscription from Ephesus—but found in Magnesia-on-the-Meander—which records the measures taken by a proconsul and the city council after a strike by a group of bakers and their ἐργαστηριάρ-χαι: one of them, named Hermias, was in charge of a bakery appended to the temple of the goddess Gamilo and might have been a slave.[115] In this particular context, however, the word ἐργασ-τηριάρχης could mean "foreman" or "lessee" as well as "business agent."[116]

In Chapter Three of this study, I will discuss particular types of *institores*, i.e. the managers of agricultural estates, *vilici* or *actores*. Both categories are commemorated in bilingual inscriptions, which provide reliable evidence for Greek equivalents. In Italy, the Danubian provinces, Greece, Asia Minor, Syria, and Egypt, *vilici* are attested as οἰκονόμοι[117] and *actores* as πραγματευταί.[118] Two

---

113 *BT* 18.1.1-20 (ed. Scheltema, pp. 869-74).

114 *BS* 18.1.1-20 (ed. Scheltema, pp. 1063-73).

115 *SEG* IV 512, lines 15-16: τῆς δὲ ἀπονοίας τῶν ἐργαστηριαρχῶν [μέγι-] | στον δεῖγμα χθὲς Ἑρμείας ὁ πρὸς τῇ ΓΑΜΙΛΩ ΜΕΤ´[άλλων τὴν ἐργασί]αν τὴ[ν ἀρτο-κοπικὴν ἔχων παρέσχε]. Cf. W.H. Buckler, "Labour Disputes in the Province of Asia," in W.H. Buckler – W.M. Calder (eds.), *Anatolian Studies Presented to Sir William M. Ramsay* (Manchester 1923) 27-50, esp. 30-33.

116 Pollux, *Onom.* 7.183 (ed. Bette 1967) has a short section on the terminology used in Classical Greece: τοὺς δὲ ἐφεστηκότας τῇ τῶν ἔργων ἐπιμελείᾳ οἱ μὲν Ἀττικοὶ ἐπιστάτας ἔργων λέγουσιν, Ἐπίχαρμος (frg. 212 Kaibel) δὲ καὶ ἐργεπιστάτας.

117 For instance, *IGRR* I 464 (= *CIG* 5875, Venusia/*Regio* II); the only bilingual inscriptions that I know of refer to *vilici*/οἰκονόμοι in charge of collecting taxes (*CIL* III 447 = *ILS* 1862, Miletus, *portorium*; and *CIL* III 555 = 7287 = *ILS* 1867, Athens, *vicesima libertatis*). Athenion, the Cilician slave who played a leading role in the second slave revolt in 104 B.C. was undoubtedly a private *vilicus* in the territory of Segesta and Lilybaeum. Diodorus Siculus describes him as αὐτὸς οἰκονόμος ὢν δυοῖν ἀδελφῶν μεγαλοπλούτων (36.5.1). For the Greek East in the Ptolemaic and early Roman period, cf. P. Landvogt, *Epigraphische Untersuchungen über den* οἰκο-

inscriptions from Venusia (*Regio* II) could suggest that in fact the distinction between *vilicus*/οἰκονόμος and *actor*/πραγματευτής was not always respected. One Sagaris, who was the slave of one of the Bruttii Praesentes (a consular family well represented in second-century-A.D. inscriptions), dedicated two altars, one to Sol Mithra as οἰκονόμος[119] and the other to Mercurius Invictus as *actor*[120] on behalf of his master's good health. It is likely, however, that the same Sagaris dedicated both altars at two different moments of his career, being promoted from the position of (*vilicus*/) οἰκονόμος to that of *actor* (/πραγματευτής) in the meantime. That some time had elapsed between the two dedications would account for the switch from Greek to Latin as a result of Sagaris's further Romanization.

2. *Business managers in the papyri*

The Greek papyri from Roman Egypt have transmitted abundant and detailed information about agents in charge of running the property and business of wealthy Roman citizens. In contrast with the rest of the empire, we have for that province a set of collections of private correspondence exchanged between agents and their principals or third parties. Belonging to the period following the Roman conquest, for instance, are the archive of L. Bellienus Gemellus (first and second centuries),[121] the archive of Sarapion (first and

νόμος (Strasbourg 1908); L. Robert, *Hellenica* X (Paris 1955) 83, n. 3. The term οἰκονόμος, however, may also refer to the position of *dispensator*, as suggested by two bilingual documents, *CIL* III 333 (= *ILS* 1539 = *IGRR* III 25, Cios, Bithynia) and *SB* VI 9248 (Syene, Egypt, second half of second century A.D.), cf. A. Swiderek, "Les Καίσαρος οἰκονόμοι de l'Egypte romaine," *CE* 45 (1970) 157-60; and D.J. Crawford, "Imperial Estates," in M.I. Finley (ed.), *Studies in Roman Property* (Cambridge 1976) 35-70, esp. 51 and 178, n. 75.

[118] *IGRR* I 190; 349; and 359 (all three from Rome, probably from the second or third century A.D.); *AE* 1930, no. 67, who was the freedman of the consul of A.D. 238 (Rome); *AE* 1981, no. 401, commemorating the death of a Syrian agent who died at Tridentum (*Regio* X) probably on a business trip in the fifth century A.D. Cf. L. Robert, *Etudes anatoliennes* I (Paris 1937) 240-43; 263 and n. 1; and 309-11.

[119] *IGRR* I 464 (= *CIG* 5875); cf. Chapter Three.

[120] *CIL* IX 425 (= *ILS* 3197); cf. Chapter Three.

[121] *P.Fay. passim*; cf. W.L. Westermann, "An Egyptian Farmer," *University of Wisconsin Studies in Language and Literature* (Madison 1919) 170-90; N. Hohlwein, "Le vétéran Lucius Bellienus Gemellus, gentleman-farmer au Fayoum," *Et. Pap.* 8 (1957) 69-91; and I. Bieżuńska-Małowist, *L'esclavage dans l'Egypte gréco-romaine* II (Wroclaw 1977) 73, n. 1; 78, nn. 14-16; and 101-03.

second centuries),[122] the archive of Heroninus (third century),[123] the archive of Papnouthis and Dorotheus (fourth century),[124] and the archive of the Flavii Apiones (fifth-seventh centuries).[125] A systematic study of the role of private φροντισταί, προνοηταί, προεστῶτες, προστάται, ἐπιμεληταί, ἐπιστάται, ἐπίτροποι, πραγματευταί, οἰκονόμοι, ὑπόβλητοι, οἰκέται, ἴδιοι, and παιδάρια in the papyri would undoubtedly yield interesting results leading to a more thorough understanding of the economic importance and relative social status of various types of business agents in the Roman world.[126] A superficial survey of the papyrological evidence shows that the reality is not so clear-cut as modern historians would hope and warns against any attempt at establishing universal, standardized patterns in which institutions of private law would have to fit.

D. Conclusion

The term *institor* is generic and designates any person engaged in trade and commerce, mostly, but not exclusively, land based (as opposed to seaborne), and conducted on a small scale (as opposed to the activity of *negotiatores*). The derogatory connotation of the term—perhaps a semantic development of the late Republican period—did not hinder its use by the jurists who may have coined the expression *actio institoria* earlier.[127] It may account for the rare occurrence of avowed *institores* in the epigraphical sources. How-

---

[122] *P.Sarap.*; cf. J. Schwartz, *Les Archives de Sarapion et de ses fils: une exploitation agricole aux environs d'Hermoupolis Magna (de 90 à 133 p.C.)* (Cairo 1961).

[123] D.W. Rathbone, *Economic Rationalism and Rural Society in Third-Century A.D. Egypt* (Cambridge 1991), esp. 44-87.

[124] *P.Oxy.* XLVIII 3384-3429, A.D. 331-371 (or even later).

[125] The archive is composed of ca. 160 documents written between 460 and ca. 620; cf. for instance, among the documents recently published, *P.Oxy.* LVIII *passim*; *P.Oxy.* LI 3641; *P.Wash.Univ.* 26; *SB* XVI 12484; *P.Select.* 18. The phrase διὰ Μηνᾶ οἰκέτου τοῦ ἐπερωτῶντος καὶ προσπορίζοντος or the variant παρόντος Μηνᾶ οἰκέτου is standard in a series of contracts belonging to this particular archive, but does not appear elsewhere in the papyri. Cf. E.R. Hardy, *The Large Estates of Byzantine Egypt* (New York 1931); J. Gascou, "Les grands domaines, la cité et l'Etat en Egypte byzantine (recherches d'histoire agraire, fiscale et administrative)" *T&MByz* 9 (1985) 1-90; and J. Banaji, *Rural Communities in the Late Empire* (Diss. Oxford 1992), with a complete list of documents discussed in an appendix.

[126] D.P. Kehoe, *Management and Investment on Estates in Roman Egypt During the Early Empire* (Bonn 1992).

[127] Cf. Chapter Two.

ever, the scarcity of direct evidence does not imply that business managers were exceptional. The social and economic structure of the ancient world was characterized by the fact that those who owned the means of production (land, industrial and commercial facilities, ships, and all their equipment) and who had control over labor forces (slaves and clients) were reluctant to be actively involved in the process of production and distribution. This induces me to postulate the widespread activity of business managers at the head of units of production and networks of distribution, doing business on behalf of wealthy landowners, factory owners, and traders.[128] The restraint that agents affected in recording their links to their patrons, on their tombstones in particular, calls for an explanation that may lie in the degree of practical independence that these business managers were likely to achieve in the course of their career. If they had successfully escaped the initial bond by the time they appear in the inscriptions as dedicators or deceased, we may expect that their modest start would be carefully played down.

It is often impossible to establish who was carrying out an independent activity and who was not. The Latin terminology designating particular jobs makes no distinction between the owner of a business, his appointed or hired manager, if there was any, and the workers.[129] In most cases our sources are hopelessly elliptic. Freedmen are particularly likely to elude any attempt at categorization either as independent businessmen or as managers.[130] For instance, the freedman C. Baebius P[?] calls himself "idem danista" in an inscription from Rome.[131] Was he lending money on his own, or was he a partner or a subordinate of his patrons who are said to practice the same trade? The *Digest* refers to cases where freedmen were acting as competitors of their patrons.[132] It is well known that

---

[128] W.V. Harris, "Roman Terracotta Lamps: The Organization of an Industry," *JRS* 70 (1980) 126-45, esp. 140-41; and J.H. D'Arms, *CSSAR* (1981) 143.

[129] S. Treggiari, *Roman Freedmen during the Late Republic* (Oxford 1969) 99: "We are often in doubt whether a *balneator* is the owner of baths or an attendant, whether a *fullo* is the owner of a fullery or a malodorous labourer."

[130] P. Garnsey, "Independent Freedmen and the Economy of Roman Italy under the Principate," *Klio* 63 (1981) 359-71, esp. 365.

[131] *AE* 1984, no. 161: "C(aius) Baebius C(aiorum) l(ibertus) P[...] / idem danista. Hoc [...] commodum est [...] / factum ex testamento ar[bitratu ...] / Pamphili."

[132] J.H. D'Arms, *CSSAR* (1981) 143, n. 108, with reference to Ulpianus (1 *opin.*) *Dig.* 37.14.2; Scaevola (4 *resp.*) *Dig.* 37.14.18 and (2 *resp.*) *Dig.* 38.1.45;

the Cossutii were involved in the marble trade all over the Roman Empire during the Republican period. Were the freedmen connected with them working independently or under some kind of general direction? Who made the decisions about prices and investment, organized the transport of raw material or (semi-) finished products from the quarries to workshops and construction sites, opened and closed quarries, and appointed their managers?[133] A. Umbricius Scaurus was a famous producer of fish sauce in Pompeii in the first century of the Empire. How usual was it for him to set up agents at the head of shops to oversee the production and the distribution of his fashionable product?[134] Or conversely, how common was it for a wealthy and prosperous entrepreneur to play an active part in operating an estate, a workshop, a store, a ship, etc.?

The list of questions concerning the role of business managers in the Roman economy could be extended *ad nauseam*, but most of these questions are unlikely to find a satisfactory answer because of the lack of evidence. Consequently, it would be unrealistic to want to trace them in every corner of their economic and social life. In this study, I will focus on business managers as contracting parties within the scope of their appointment. The contracts negotiated by a business manager made his principal liable to an action on the manager's conduct (*actio institoria*) brought by third contracting parties. The legal basis of this liability, the historical circumstances in

---

Papinianus (13 *resp.*) *Dig.* 37.15.11; cf. also P. Garnsey, *Klio* 63 (1981) 366, with a counterexample, recorded and supported by Alfenus Varus (7 *dig*) *Dig.* 38.1.26 *pr.*, of a physician who does not allow his freedmen to practice the same trade in order to have more customers for himself; and W. Waldstein, *Operae libertorum. Untersuchungen zur Dienstpflicht freigelassener Sklaven* (Wiesbaden/Stuttgart 1986) 300-20.

[133] E. Rawson, "Architecture and Sculpture: the Activities of the Cossutii," *PBSR* 43 (1975) 36-47; M. Torelli, "Industria estrattiva, lavoro artigianale, interessi economici: qualche appunto," *MAAR* 36 (1980) 313-23; and J. Ward-Perkins, "The Marble Trade and its Organization: Evidence from Nicomedia," *MAAR* 36 (1980) 325-38. Some relevant questions about quarries, in particular the possible role of *magistri* supervising the quality of the production in the quarries, are discussed by J.C. Fant, "Seven Unedited Quarry Inscriptions from Docimium (Ischchisar, Turkey)," *ZPE* 54 (1984) 171-82; *idem* (ed.), *Ancient Marble Quarrying and Trade* (Oxford 1988); *idem*, *Cavum antrum Phrygiae: The Organization and Operations of the Roman Imperial Marble Quarries in Phrygia* (Oxford 1989). Other intertwining networks of various trading and commercial interests are discussed by J.H. D'Arms, *CSSAR* (1981) 28 (late-Republican Avianii from Puteoli) and *passim*.

[134] R.I. Curtis, "Product Identification and Advertising on Roman Commercial Amphorae," *AncSoc* 15-17 (1984-86) 209-28; cf. Chapter Four.

which praetorian remedies sanctioning this liability were introduced, and the nature of the legal relationship between principal and
agent will be discussed in Chapter Two.

Business managers did not form a homogeneous group. The environment in which they operated and the specific features of their
respective trades were likely to require very different types of skills;
farmers, potters, innkeepers, moneylenders, and undertakers may
have little in common, except that, in their capacity of business
managers, they were required to be trustworthy and resourceful,
and to display managerial skills. Ulpianus's commentary on the
praetorian Edict, based on the writings of earlier (Republican and
Augustan) jurists, contains a list of occupations which reflects what
classical jurists considered a likely context in which the Roman praetor would be asked to grant an *actio institoria*.[135] From the study of
the most important and best-documented economic activity in antiquity, namely agriculture, I will establish a model showing what
types of contractual transactions managers of agricultural estates
(*vilici* and *actores*) were expected to perform with outsiders within the
scope of their appointment (Chapter Three). The management of
agricultural estates is described in some detail in literary and legal
sources, but our understanding of the various systems of management has greatly benefited from the study of inscriptions and archaeological remains of Roman villas.

It has become clear, however, that the farmstead also harbored
other types of activities, for instance the productions of clay artifacts
such as building material and containers for agricultural products.
These products are identifiable by their "trademark" (cast potter-
mark), their typology, their size and color, and their petrochemical
composition. These features are common to other artifacts, the production of which was not limited to a rural setting. As W.V. Harris
has shown in the case of the lamp industry, this type of material
is likely to contribute much to our understanding of the organization of industry and commerce and will be the subject of Chapter
Four.[136]

Finally, a survey of the epigraphical material has shown that the
vilicus system developed in the context of the management of agricultural estates was adopted in other areas of private and public

---

[135] Ulpianus (28 *ad ed.*) *Dig.* 14.3.5.1-15; cf. above.
[136] W.V. Harris, *JRS* 70 (1980) 126-45.

(municipal and imperial) administration. The study of the collection of a specific type of tax, the custom dues (*portorium*), demonstrates that this system of management, which features a manager (*vilicus, actor, praepositus*, etc.) appointed to the head of a managerial unit (*statio, officina*, etc.) and overseeing a skilled staff (*familia*), was widely used during the Principate and was a factor of stability and efficiency. This will be the subject of Chapter Five.

Finally, a cautionary remark. One should be aware that the complementarity of the material used in this study is not always evident. The description of ancient private institutions is based on:

(a) random allusions made by classical authors belonging to a narrow stratum of Roman society and pertaining to widely-scattered geographical and chronological contexts;

(b) legal commentaries tainted with rhetorical and idiosyncratic devices, quoting opinions, sometimes three centuries old, out of their historical and narrative context;

(c) mostly undated, often stray, Greek and Latin inscriptions, the representativeness of which depends on the extent of archaeological work carried out in the area and the quality of its publication and cataloguing in the major corpora;[137]

(d) archaeological material known only through catalogues and reports of varying qualities.

This type of historical reconstruction may amount to comparing apples with oranges, but the absence of a more adequately integrated material compels modern historians to capitalize on this unique situation by studying each type of material separately and for itself, drawing the pieces together, comparing them, and filling the gaps with the help of comparative evidence. One should also keep in mind that it is hazardous to generalize from a material reflecting the views of a very small bracket of Roman society, and that any attempt at establishing a chronological development is vitiated by the fact that the result would inevitably be based on arguments from silence, which would at best provide weak *termini ante* or *post quos*. The impressionistic picture obtained through this approach will provide nothing more than a starting point for further research to disagree with.

---

[137] Cf. the important methodological remarks in S.R. Joshel, *Work, Identity, and Legal Status at Rome. A Study of the Occupational Inscriptions* (Norman, OK/London 1992), esp. ch. 1.

CHAPTER TWO

INDIRECT AGENCY IN ROMAN LAW

A. Introduction

In the social and economic context of the mid-Republican period, it is likely that many people engaging in economic activities were not always able or willing to be personally, or even physically, involved in the transactions that the pursuit of their interests required them to perform. Admittedly, contracts between absent parties were valid, as long as they were not formal (i.e. made through stipulation). The agreement of the parties to any transaction could be exchanged orally or in a written form through messengers (*nuntii*),[1] but this procedure was subject to unpractical delays and left room for misunderstandings. In the absence of reliable means of immediate, long-distance communication, the reliance upon agents capable of negotiating valid contracts on behalf and in the name of their principals was an obvious and most effective way to overcome such difficulties. However, the concept of direct agency, whereby one enters into a legal transaction, the consequences of which will bind or benefit a third party to the exclusion of the agent, was never accepted in Roman private law.[2] It seems that the Romans had devised such a sophisticated and adequate way of circumventing all difficulties arising from the lack of direct agency that the necessity

---

[1] Gai., *Inst.* 3.136 (= *Dig.* 47.7.2.2); Paulus (3 *ad ed.*), following Labeo, *Dig.* 2.14.2 *pr.*; Ulpianus (27 *ad ed.*) *Dig.* 13.5.14.3; Paulus (29 *ad ed.*) *Dig.* 13.5.15; Paulus (32 *ad ed.*) *Dig.* 17.1.1.1. Cf. R. Monier, *Manuel élémentaire de droit romain* II[4] (Paris 1948) 79; and M. Kaser, *Das römische Privatrecht* I[2] (Munich 1971) 526.

[2] The concept of direct agency was recognized in Roman public and corporate law, cf. *Dig.* 3.4; F. Schulz, *Principles of Roman Law* (Oxford 1936) 30, n. 2; *idem*, *Classical Roman Law* (Oxford 1951) 100, n. 173; A. Watson, *Contract of Mandate in Roman Law* (Oxford 1961) 2-3; M. Kaser, "Zum Wesen der römischen Stellvertretung," *Romanitas* 9 (1970) 333-55, who remarks (335) that direct agency, whereby one person acts and another sees the effect, smacks of magic; *idem*, "Stellvertretung und 'notwendige Entgeltlichkeit'," *ZRG* 91 (1974) 146-204, esp. 172 ff.; J. Plescia, "The Development of the Juristic Personality in Roman Law," *Studi Sanfilippo* I (Milan 1982) 487-524; and *idem*, "The Development of Agency in Roman Law," *Labeo* 30 (1984) 171-90. However, M. Kaser (*RP* I[2] [1971] 302-10, esp. 307, n. 33) points out that the (judicial) *actor municipum* is an indirect agent.

of renouncing deep-rooted, traditional rules of behavior regarding the performance of juristic acts was never regarded as compelling.[3]

The ban of direct agency in Roman civil law rests upon the twofold principle that (a) the parties to a contract must have an interest in that contract; and (b) a contract can have no legal effect upon anybody but the parties to the contract (privity of contract).[4] This principle can be illustrated with several situations. By the beginning of the first century B.C., Q. Mucius Scaevola remarks that "no one can legally bind someone else through compact, arrangement, or covenant."[5] Thus, an extraneous agent negotiating a contract with a third contracting party could not bind his principal. Conversely, an extraneous agent could not negotiate a contract with a third contracting party, the effect of which would benefit his principal only, because stipulations and promises on behalf of third parties were considered void.[6] By the late first century A.D., if an extraneous agent gave some money—his own or his principal's—to a third contracting party as a loan (*mutuum*) or as an unjustified payment (*indebitum solutum*) in the name of his principal, the latter had a claim (*condictio*) over this money.[7] But an extraneous agent could

---

[3] W.M. Gordon, "Agency and Roman Law," *Studi Sanfilippo* III (Milan 1983) 341-49.

[4] B. Nicholas, *An Introduction to Roman Law* (Oxford 1962) 199.

[5] Q. Mucius Scaevola (*sing.* ὅρων) *Dig.* 50.17.73.4: "Nec paciscendo nec legem dicendo nec stipulando quisquam alteri cavere potest." Cf. M. Kaser, *RP* I² (1971) 263 and 527. The beginning of the passage has been considered interpolated; cf. R. Monier, *Manuel* II⁴ (1948) 85, n. 3, following G. Cornil, "Explication historique de la règle *alteri stipulari nemo potest*," *Studi Riccobono* IV (Palermo 1936) 241-58, esp. 250-51. A. Claus, *Gewillkürte Stellvertretung im römischen Privatrecht* (Berlin 1973) 84-97; and 107-09 thinks that Q. Mucius's rule either put an end to a more liberal situation, or prevented the evolution toward one, which triggered a reaction on the part of the praetor with the creation of the *actiones adiecticiae qualitatis* (cf. below).

[6] Gai., *Inst.* 3.103: "Praeterea inutilis est stipulatio, si ei dari stipulemur, cuius iuri subiecti non sumus." Ulpianus (49 *ad Sab.*) *Dig.* 45.1.38.17: "Alteri stipulari nemo potest, praeterquam si servus domino, filius patri stipuletur: inventae sunt enim huiusmodi obligationes ad hoc, ut unusquisque sibi adquirat quod sua interest: ceterum ut alii detur, nihil interest mea" (with the possible interpolation of "huiusmodi obligationes"). *Cod. Iust.* 8.38.3 *pr.* (A.D. 290): "Ut inter absentes verborum obligatio contrahi non potest, ita alteri, cuius iuri subiectus non est, aliquid dari vel restitui, nisi sua intersit, nemo stipulari potest." *Inst. Iust.* 3.19.19. Cf. G. Cornil, *Studi Riccobono* IV (Palermo 1936) 241-58. About the nullity of promises and stipulations on behalf of third parties and the connection with the lack of direct agency, cf. R. Monier, *Manuel* II⁴ (1948) 96-100 and 257-58; and M. Kaser, *RP* I² (1971) 263 and 491.

[7] Ulpianus (26 *ad ed.*), citing Iulianus and Aristo, *Dig.* 12.1.9.8: "Si nummos

not request from his principal's debtor that he fulfill his obligation towards the principal without the latter's authorization,[8] the idea being that it was not necessarily in the best interest of the principal/creditor to lose his claim through settlement. On the other hand, by the middle of the second century A.D., it had become possible for an extraneous agent to discharge his principal's obligation toward his creditor even without his knowledge and against his will, for instance by paying his debts,[9] the rule being that an extraneous agent could always better, but not worsen, the economic condition of his principal.[10]

In accordance with an old principle recorded by Gaius, the Romans could not acquire ownership or possession through an extraneous agent.[11] Exceptions to this rule appeared as early as the Republican period, as Servius Sulpicius Rufus writes that purchases made by freedmen mandated by their patron belonged automatically and immediately to the latter.[12] At the end of the first century A.D.,

---

meos tuo nomine dedero velut tuos absente te et ignorante, Aristo scribit adquiri tibi condictionem: Iulianus quoque de hoc interrogatus libro decimo scribit veram esse Aristonis sententiam nec dubitari, quin, si meam pecuniam tuo nomine voluntate tua dedero, tibi adquiritur obligatio, cum cottidie credituri pecuniam mutuam ab alio poscamus, ut nostro nomine creditor numeret futuro debitori nostro.'' Cf. M. Kaser, *ZRG* 91 (1974) 177-79.

[8] Gaius (3 *de verb. oblig.*) *Dig.* 3.5.38 (39): "quod autem alicui debetur, alius sine voluntate eius non potest iure exigere.''

[9] Gaius (3 *de verb. oblig.*) *Dig.* 3.5.38 (39): "Solvendo quisque pro alio licet invito et ignorante liberat eum: quod autem alicui debetur, alius sine voluntate eius non potest iure exigere;'' and *idem* (5 *ad ed. prov.*) *Dig.* 46.3.53: "Solvere pro ignorante et invito cuique licet,...'' Cf. R. Monier, *Manuel* II[4] (1948) 219; and M. Kaser, *RP* I[2] (1971) 636-37.

[10] Gaius (3 *de verb. oblig.*) *Dig.* 3.5.38 (39): "Naturalis enim simul et civilis ratio suasit alienam condicionem meliorem quidem etiam ignorantis et inviti nos facere posse, deteriorem non posse;'' and *idem* (5 *ad ed. prov.*) *Dig.* 46.3.53: "...cum sit iure civili constitutum licere etiam ignorantis invitique meliorem condicionem facere.''

[11] Gai., *Inst.* 2.95: "per extraneam personam nobis adquiri non posse.'' Cf. also Paulus (3 *quaest.*) *Dig.* 45.1.126.2; and *idem, Sent.* 5.2.2. About the restrictions concerning the acquisition of ownership or possession through extraneous agents, cf. Gai., *Inst.* 2.86-96 (= *Dig.* 41.1.10) and 3.163-167; *Dig.* 41.1 and 2, *passim; Cod. Iust.* 4.27; *Inst. Iust.* 2.9 and 3.28; R. Monier, *Manuel* I[6] (1947) 391-92 and 413; and M. Kaser, *RP* I[2] (1971) 262-64; 392-93; 491; and 653.

[12] Paulus (54 *ad ed.*) *Dig.* 34.2.4: "Cum quidam libertum suum in Asiam misisset ad purpuras emendas et testamento uxori suae lanam purpuream legasset, pertinere ad eam, si quam purpuram vivo eo libertus emisset, Servius respondit.'' Cf. M. Kaser, *RP* I[2] (1971) 263, n. 31; and *idem, ZRG* 91 (1974) 192-93, n. 165. This seems to be confirmed by a first-century-A.D. document (*Tab. Herculan.* 87); cf. V. Arangio-Ruiz–G. Pugliese Carratelli, *PP* 10 (1955) 470-77, esp. 476-77; and P.

Neratius Priscus also reports that acquisition of possession and ownership through *procuratores* or guardians was valid.[13] A century later, the reform was completed and all extraneous agents could acquire possession for their principal, even though the latter was unaware of it.[14] By the same time, *procuratores* and mandataries could also receive valid payments from the debtors of their principals.[15] Considering how reluctant the Romans were to allow principals to benefit directly and exclusively from contracts negotiated by extraneous agents, it goes without saying that extraneous agents could not validly transfer their principals' property without their explicit and specific authorization, and only through informal conveyance.[16]

The situation was different when the agent was a dependent of the principal (master/*paterfamilias*). Dependents include (a) wives *in manu*; (b) sons and daughters *in potestate*, and their descendants, unless they had been emancipated; (c) all those who belonged to the category "in mancipio", such as *filiifamilias* transferred into the power of another person;[17] and (d) male and female slaves,[18] either

Cosentini, "La dote di Paolina," *Studi E. Volterra* III (Milan 1973) 715-33, esp. 716-17 (text) and 728-33.

[13] Neratius (6 *reg.*) *Dig.* 41.1.13 *pr.*-1: "Si procurator rem mihi emerit ex mandato meo eique sit tradita meo nomine, dominium mihi...adquiritur etiam ignoranti. (1) Et tutor pupilli pupillae similiter ut procurator;" and *idem* (7 *membran.*) *Dig.* 41.3.41: "...quamvis per procuratorem possessionem apisci nos iam fere conveniat,..." Cf. M. Kaser, *RP* I² (1971) 393; and *idem, ZRG* 91 (1974) 193-96.

[14] *Cod. Iust.* 7.32.1 (A.D. 196): "Per liberam personam ignoranti quoque adquiri possessionem et, postquam scientia intervenerit, usucapionis condicionem inchoari posse tam ratione utilitatis quam iuris pridem receptum est." Modestinus (14 *ad Q. Mucium*) *Dig.* 41.1.53: "Ea quae civiliter adquiruntur per eos, qui in potestate nostra sunt, adquirimus, veluti stipulationem: quod naturaliter adquiritur, sicuti est possessio, per quemlibet volentibus nobis possidere adquirimus." In the middle of the second century, there was still a lack of agreement on that issue, cf. Gai., *Inst.* 2.95; M. Kaser, *RP* I² (1971) 392-93; and J. Plescia, *Labeo* 30 (1984) 175. According to M. Kaser (*Romanitas* 9 [1970] 340), the concept of agency is more acceptable in the context of acquisition of possession than in the context of acquisition of ownership because possession is a fact, not a legal claim.

[15] Ulpianus (30 *ad Sab.*) *Dig.* 46.3.12 *pr.* Cf. R. Monier, *Manuel* II⁴ (1948) 219; and M. Kaser, *RP* I² (1971) 637.

[16] Gaius (2 *rer. cott. sive aureor.*) *Dig.* 41.1.9.4 (= *Inst. Iust.* 2.1.42); *Cod. Iust.* 2.12(13).16 (293); A. Burdese, *Autorizzazione ad alienare in diritto romano* (Turin 1950); M. Kaser, *Romanitas* 9 (1970) 341-42; *idem, RP* I² (1971) 267, esp. n. 59; and *idem, ZRG* 91 (1974) 198-202.

[17] Gai., *Inst.* 1.116-123. Cf. M. Kaser, *RP* I² (1971) 57-58; 69-70; and 302; and L. Amirante, "Sulla schiavitù nella Roma antica," *Labeo* 27 (1981) 26-33.

[18] Ulpianus (29 *ad ed.*) *Dig.* 14.1.1.21: "In potestate autem accipiemus utriusque sexus vel filios vel filias vel servos vel servas."

owned or held in legitimate possession and in usufruct.[19] Dependents were normally deprived of property rights,[20] and, except for sons, of juristic personality.[21] Consequently, dependents could not obligate themselves toward their master/*paterfamilias*,[22] nor toward any other person, but they could acquire property through formal conveyance (*mancipatio*), will, and through informal procedures (*occupatio, possessio, traditio*) for the sole benefit of their *paterfamilias*.[23] Thus, it appears that the lack of the concept of direct agency in Roman civil law was partly compensated by two prominent features of Roman society, the institution of slavery and the existence of a tightly-knit family, within which only the *paterfamilias* enjoyed a complete juristic personality and unrestricted property rights. Acquisitions through a slave or a family member on behalf of the *pater-*

---

[19] Gai., *Inst.* 2.91-95. Cf. M. Kaser, *RP* I² (1971) 262-63.

[20] Gai., *Inst.* 2.86-87: "Ipse enim, qui in potestate nostra est, nihil suum habere potest."

[21] Gai., *Inst.* 3.104: "Praeterea inutilis est stipulatio, si ab eo stipuler qui iuri meo subiectus est, item si is a me stipuletur. Servus quidem et qui in mancipio est et filia familias et quae in manu est non solum ipsi, cuius iuri subiecti subiectaeve sunt, obligari non possunt, sed ne alii quidem ulli." It is interesting to note that the *filiusfamilias* is omitted from the list, cf. F. de Zulueta, *The Institutes of Gaius* (Oxford 1946-53) *ad loc.*; M. Kaser, *RP* I² (1971) 287; 343; and 481; and J. Plescia, *Labeo* 30 (1984) 173, n. 5, with reference to Gaius (1 *ad ed. prov.*) *Dig.* 50.17.107: "Cum servo nulla actio est." Slaves lacked a legal capacity in civil law, but not in natural law, cf. Ulpianus (43 *ad Sab.*) *Dig.* 50.17.32; and Paulus (11 *ad ed.*) *Dig.* 4.5.3.1. In his discussion of "the development of juristic personality in Roman law," J. Plescia, *Studi Sanfilippo* I (1982) 487-524, points out (496-97) that the system developed over three periods (statutory – edictal/jurisprudential – statutory) "from a law of property where the dependent is *dead at law* to a law of obligation where the dependent becomes a party to a contractual relation."

[22] Gai., *Inst.* 3.104, with the exception of natural obligations; cf. Ulpianus (7 *disp.*) *Dig.* 44.7.14; and Tryphoninus (7 *disp.*) *Dig.* 12.6.64. Cf. also Pomponius (15 *ad Sab.*) *Dig.* 44.7.7: "Actiones adversus patrem filio praestari non possunt, dum in potestate eius est filius;" Paulus (15 *quaest.*) *Dig.* 46.1.56.1; and M. Kaser, *RP* I² (1971) 343, esp. n. 20; and 481, n. 24.

[23] Gai., *Inst.* 1.52: "Quodcumque per servum adquiritur, id domino adquiritur;" and 3.163: "Admonendi sumus adquiri nobis non solum per nosmet ipsos, sed etiam per eas personas quae in nostra potestate manu mancipiove sunt." Cf. also Gai., *Inst.* 2. 86-96 and 3.167; and *idem* (11 *ad ed. prov.*) *Dig.* 41.1.32: "Etiam invitis nobis per servos adquiritur paene ex omnibus causis." Ulpianus (2 *ad leg. Iul. et Pap.*) *Dig.* 29.2.79; Paulus (32 *ad Sab.*) *Dig.* 41.3.31.2; and J. Plescia, *Labeo* 30 (1984) 172, who remarks that everything dependents acquired "devolved by force of the law of *accessio* (based on *patria potestas* or *dominium*), and not of agency, to the *paterfamilias*;" and 173, n. 6. About the problems raised by the acquisition of possession through dependents, cf. H.-P. Benöhr, *Der Besitzerwerb durch Gewaltabhängige im klassischen römischen Recht* (Berlin 1972) and A. Kirschenbaum, *Slaves, Sons, and Freedmen in Roman Commerce* (Jerusalem/Washington 1987) 18-24.

familias were so easy and so common that there was no need to depart from the ancient rule. Only the disappearance or drastic weakening of these institutions would have created a legal vacuum calling for a change of attitude toward legal representation. These phenomena simply never happened—at least to such an extent that they would have provoked such a shift—in classical Roman times. And, as W.M. Gordon rightly puts it,

> Roman law gradually reached a position where the advantage of going further was more theoretical than practical and Roman law reached this situation in a way which gave practical results which were in certain respects preferable to those which would follow from the adoption of direct agency.[24]

On the other hand, in order to protect the *paterfamilias* against the consequences of unwanted initiatives on the part of his dependents, Roman law stipulated that the contracts negotiated by a dependent could have no negative—binding—effect upon the *paterfamilias*. Dependents could better, but not worsen, the situation of their *paterfamilias*.[25] This means that dependents, like extraneous agents, could not validly transfer property without the consent (*voluntas*) of their master/*paterfamilias*, expressed before or after the transaction by *iussum*, *permissio*, or *ratihabitio*.[26] This rule was designed to prevent unscrupulous or incompetent dependents from damaging the economic interests of their master/*paterfamilias*, but at the same time it deprived the latter from benefiting from more complex deals—in which both parties give and take—that a trustworthy agent could be required, and should be able, to negotiate. This loophole in the legal system was recognized at an early stage and corrected through the intervention of the praetor who granted to third contracting parties a set of five legal remedies (called by modern scholars *actiones adiecticiae qualitatis*) available under special conditions. The modern name of these remedies stems from the fact that the liability of the principal

---

[24] W.M. Gordon, *Studi Sanfilippo* III (1983) 343.

[25] Gaius (8 *ad ed. prov.*) *Dig.* 50.17.133: "Melior condicio nostra per servos fieri potest, deterior fieri non potest." Cf. also Papinianus (8 *quaest.*) *Dig.* 46.3.94.3.

[26] Iulianus (57 *dig.*) *Dig.* 21.2.39.1; Ulpianus (17 *ad ed.*) *Dig.* 6.1.41.1; Paulus (29 *ad ed.*) *Dig.* 13.7.20 *pr.*; *Cod. Iust.* 2.12(13).16 (293); M. Kaser, *RP* I² (1971) 267, n. 59; J. Plescia, *Labeo* 30 (1984) 173-74; and A. Kirschenbaum (1987) 27-29. Slaves could never transfer property through *mancipatio* or *in iure cessio*, cf. H. Ankum, "*Mancipatio* by Slaves in Classical Roman Law?" *Acta Iuridica* (1976) 1-18; and above, Chapter One.

was additional to that of the agent.[27] In the formula, the name of
agent appeared in the *intentio* ("si paret...") and the name of the
principal in the *condemnatio*.[28]

Before examining the history of the *actiones adiecticiae qualitatis*—
i.e. how early, under which circumstances, and in which chronological order the praetor included in his Edict the promise of a grant of
legal remedies through which third contracting parties would get
redress from principals made liable for the transactions performed
by their agents—it is necessary to describe how these legal remedies
were used in the classical period (second/third century A.D.), as
shown by Gaius in his *Institutes* (written ca. A.D. 161), by Pseudo-
Paulus in the *Sententiae* (late third century), and by several classical
jurists, from Servius Sulpicius Rufus (I B.C.) to Hermogenianus
(late III), whose works were excerpted in Iustinianus's *Digest*.

The purpose of this chapter is to show how the law was adjusted
to accommodate the needs of the business community. The large
quantity of primary sources makes a thorough discussion of the textual basis unfeasible. Consequently, text criticism is limited to the
bare minimum. Besides, it is one of the main contentions of this
book that apparent oddities and inconsistencies of the law should be
examined and explained in reference to the social and economic context in which it developed instead of being dismissed as the result of
post-classical interpolations.

B. RELATIONSHIP BETWEEN THIRD CONTRACTING PARTY AND
    PRINCIPAL/AGENT (*ACTIONES ADIECTICIAE QUALITATIS*)

In spite of the lack of direct agency in Roman civil law, people employed not only their dependents, but also free mandataries and
hired employees, to perform business transactions on an occasional

---

[27] The name is derived from a passage by Paulus (29 *ad ed.*) in the context of the
actio exercitoria, *Dig.* 14.1.5.1: "Hoc enim edicto non transfertur actio, sed adi-
citur." For a case of double liability in a situation featuring a *colonus* (acting *iussu
domini*) and his landowner, cf. Iulianus, quoted by Ulpianus (71 *ad ed.*) *Dig.*
43.24.13.7. M. Kaser, *RP* I[2] (1971) 609 rightly points out that the *actio tributoria*,
which is usually discussed in connection with the *actiones quod iussu, institoria, exercitoria, de peculio aut de in rem verso*, does not belong to the same category, and therefore it will not be examined below.
[28] A similar type of legal remedy seems to have been introduced ca. 118 B.C.
by the praetor P. Rutilius Rufus (*actio Rutiliana*), cf. Gai., *Inst.* 4.35; M. Kaser, *Das
römische Zivilprozessrecht* (Munich 1966) 262-64; and J. Plescia, *Studi Sanfilippo* I
(1982) 513-14, n. 85.

or permanent basis. Cicero, for instance, often alludes to extraneous agents (*liberti*, *procuratores*) working side-by-side with dependents (*familia*) for wealthy businessmen, such as A. Trebonius, L. Lamia, and L. Bruttius, known to have had important commercial interests in the provinces.[29] Business was carried out according to a triangular pattern, involving a principal, his agent (and/or subagent), and a third contracting party. The nature of the legal relationship between principal and agent will be examined later on. In this section, I will focus upon the position of third contracting parties towards principal and agent.

When an agent had negotiated a contract with a third contracting party, both parties to the contract were entitled to, and obligated by, the terms of the contract. When the parties could not agree on a particular point or when one of the parties unilaterally withdrew from the agreement (breach of contract), a settlement had to be reached through litigation in court. In the formulary procedure (probably introduced by the third quarter of the second century B.C.), the plaintiff had first to obtain the appropriate legal remedy (*actio*) from a magistrate, on the basis of which an arbitrator (*iudex*) had to make a decision by condemning or acquitting the defendant. The type of remedy was determined by the nature of the contract from which the obligation arose: for instance, litigation about a contract of sale was conducted through an *actio empti* or *venditi*.

In the time of Plautus and Cato, i.e. before the introduction of the praetorian remedies known as *actiones adiecticiae qualitatis* and described below, the legal position of the parties was defined by Roman civil law (*ius civile*). Let us envisage at first the case where the third contracting party was the plaintiff and tried to obtain the fulfillment of the obligation through threat of a lawsuit, or redress in the form of a monetary compensation through litigation. If the agent was a slave, a wife- or daughter-in-power, or a person *in mancipio*, he/she could not act as a defendant,[30] nor make his/her master/*paterfamilias* liable for any contractual obligation resulting from his/her transactions. Consequently, the third contracting party had no one to sue and was left with no legal means to get redress from the other party,

---

[29] Cic., *Fam.* 1.3 (56 B.C): ''. . . magna negotia et ampla et expedita;'' 12.29 (43 B.C); 13.38 (46 B.C); A. Bürge, *ZRG* 105 (1988) 861; and A. Kirschenbaum (1987) 122-99.

[30] M. Kaser, *RZ* (1966) 149, n. 14.

agent or principal, with whom he had negotiated a contract. If the agent was a son-in-power (*filiusfamilias*), he could act as a defendant,[31] but once condemned, he was not exposed to the execution of the judgement (*missio in bona* and *venditio bonorum*),[32] because dependents were incapable of ownership. Until the time of Augustus, who granted limited property rights (*peculium castrense*) to sons-in-power enrolled in the army, the third contracting party was left with an unenforceable remedy. In both cases, it was irrelevant whether the principal was the agent's master/*paterfamilias* or an outsider. If the agent was a free man, the third contracting party had to sue him directly and ignore his status of agent. If the defendant, once condemned, refused to comply with the arbitrator's decision, the plaintiff could proceed with the execution on the property of the defendant. Practically, however, the guarantees offered by agents of low social and economic statuses—who, as agents, needed to have no assets of their own—might have been out of proportion with the type of transactions they were performing on behalf of wealthier, more powerful principals. Thus, the proceeds of the execution on the agent's property were likely to be much lower than the amount of the debt. Consequently, the plaintiff was left with insufficient compensation. Because of the rigidity of the legal system, lower-class agents were likely to be seen as less reliable business partners than independent businessmen, who were usually endowed with some assets of their own.

Conversely, the third contracting party could be in the position of defendant. If the agent was a dependent—the principal's or someone else's—the legal remedy arising from the contract he had negotiated automatically belonged to his master/*paterfamilias*.[33] The latter had to act as plaintiff if he was also the agent's principal, but was expected, though not bound, to transfer the remedy to the principal if the dependent agent was employed by an outsider. By contrast,

---

[31] Gaius (3 *ad ed. prov.*) *Dig.* 44.7.39: "Filius familias ex omnibus causis tamquam pater familias obligatur et ob id agi cum eo tamquam cum patre familias potest." Cf. also Ulpianus (41 *ad Sab.*) *Dig.* 5.1.57; and M. Kaser, *RZ* (1966) 149, n. 12 and *RP* I² (1971) 343, n. 17.

[32] M. Kaser, *RZ* (1966) 149, n. 13; and 301-12.

[33] There were exceptions to the rule that *filiifamilias* were incapable of acting as plaintiffs in litigation, cf. Ulpianus (17 *ad ed.*), following Iulianus and Marcellus, *Dig.* 16.3.19; *idem* (43 *ad ed.*), following Iulianus, *Dig.* 5.1.18.1; *idem* (57 *ad ed.*) *Dig.* 47.10.17.10; *idem* (71 *ad ed.*), quoting Labeo, *Dig.* 43.24.13.1 (itp.); Paulus (9 *ad Sab.*), following Iulianus, *Dig.* 44.7.9; and M. Kaser, *RZ* (1966) 148-49.

free extraneous agents could act as plaintiffs, and the remedy arising from the contract belonged to them only, to the exclusion of the principal, who, from a legal point of view, had no influence upon the outcome of the judicial process and the execution of the judgement. When the principal's social status or economic power was significantly higher than the extraneous agent's, it would have been advantageous for the plaintiffs (both principal and agent) to benefit from the principal's economic and social clout.

To sum up, a few drawbacks were attached to indirect agency in Roman civil law at the time of the development of the formulary procedure. Principals could not sue third contracting parties on account of the contracts negotiated by their extraneous agents. Principals could of course sue their free extraneous agents or the masters/ *patresfamilias* of their dependent extraneous agents on the basis of the contractual relationship established between them (*mandatum*, *locatio conductio*, *negotium gestum*), but it is only in the middle of the second century A.D. that they became entitled to an *actio utilis* to sue directly third contracting parties on account of the contracts negotiated by their extraneous agents.[34] It is likely that this development occurred first in the context of the *actio exercitoria*, since Ulpianus reports that the prefects in charge of the food supply and the provincial governors granted shippers a remedy derived from the contracts negotiated by their agents and enforceable through extraordinary procedure.[35]

A more significant problem consisted in that third contracting parties could not sue the principals on account of the contracts negotiated by agents, either dependent or extraneous. In order to correct this situation, the praetor decided to provide third contracting parties with a set of legal remedies by which the claims derived from the contracts could be effectively enforced against both agent

---

[34] Ulpianus (36 *ad ed.*), citing Iulianus, *Dig.* 26.7.9 *pr.*; Ulpianus (28 *ad ed.*), quoting Marcellus, *Dig.* 14.3.1; Gaius (9 *ad ed. prov.*) *Dig.* 14.3.2; Ulpianus (32 *ad ed.*), quoting Papinianus (3 *resp.*), *Dig.* 19.1.13.25; Ulpianus (28 *ad ed.*) *Dig.* 14.1.1.18; Paulus (48 *ad ed.*) *Dig.* 46.5.5; A. Watson (1961) 80-81; M. Kaser, *RP* I² (1971) 263, nn. 28-30; 266-67, n. 51; 588, n. 13; and 605-06, n. 2.

[35] This legal privilege was meant as an incentive for shippers, whose role in the food supply of Rome and of the army was essential. Other fiscal privileges, such as immunity from local compulsory services, were introduced for the same purpose; cf. Scaevola (1 and 3 *reg.*) *Dig.* 50.4.5 and 50.5.3; and Callistratus (1 *de cogn.*) *Dig.* 50.6.6.3-6; cf. R. Duncan-Jones, *Structure and Scale in the Roman Economy* (Cambridge 1990) 162, n. 23.

and principal.[36] The principal's interests required that this type of remedy be available only when it was well established that he had commissioned (implying *voluntas* expressed through *iussum* or *praepositio*), or given his consent (implying *patientia* and *scientia*) to, the agent's activity. Short of that, the principal could only be held liable to the extent of his enrichment if it could be established that he had benefited from his agent's transaction, since enrichment to the detriment of others was considered unfair.[37]

1. *Actio quod iussu*

According to the terms of the praetorian Edict, principals (masters/ *patresfamilias*) who had authorized third contracting parties to do business with their dependents were liable for the whole debt arising from the agent's transaction.[38] The underlying principle was that whoever made a contract with a dependent in accordance with the principal's will was viewed as making a contract with the principal himself.[39] Paulus examines the case of a son-in-power who killed his slave after promising *iussu patris* to convey him to a third party. Pomponius states that the liability of the father was not in doubt, because he became an accessorial debtor by ordering the transaction.[40]

---

[36] The fullest, recent general treatment of the question is by E. Valiño, "Las *actiones adiecticiae qualitatis* y sus relaciones basicas en derecho romano," *AHDE* 37 (1967) 339-436; and *AHDE* 38 (1968) 377-480. Cf. also M. Kaser, *RP* I² (1971) 605-09; A. Claus, *Gewillkürte Stellvertretung im römischen Privatrecht* (Berlin 1973), with the review-discussion by M. Kaser, *ZRG* 91 (1974) 146-204; A. Kirschenbaum, *Slaves, Sons, and Freedmen in Roman Commerce* (Jerusalem/Washington 1987); and the forthcoming article by A. Wacke, "Die adjektizischen Klagen im Überblick. I. Von der Reeder- und der Betriebsleiterklage zur direkten Stellvertretung," *ZRG* 111 (1994), which the author kindly showed me before publication.

[37] Pomponius (9 *ex var. lect.*) *Dig.* 50.17.206: "Iure naturae aequum est neminem cum alterius detrimento et iniuria fieri locupletiorem." The substance of the text is classical, cf. M. Kaser, *RP* I² (1971) 221, n. 2; and 594, n. 5.

[38] The main sources are Gai., *Inst.* 4.70; *Dig.* 15.4; *Cod. Iust.* 4.26; *Cod. Theod.* 2.31.1; *Inst. Iust.* 4.7. Cf. also G. and M. Sautel, "Note sur l'action *quod iussu* et ses destinées post-classiques," *Mélanges H. Lévy-Bruhl* (Paris 1959) 257-67.

[39] Gai., *Inst.* 4.70; and Ulpianus (29 *ad ed.*) *Dig.* 15.4.1 *pr.*

[40] Paulus (17 *ad Plaut.*) *Dig.* 45.1.91.5: "An filius familias, qui iussu patris promisit, occidendo servum producat patris obligationem, videndum est. Pomponius producere putat, scilicet quasi accessionem intellegens eum qui iubeat." The end ("scilicet ...") is probably interpolated. Cf. R. Knütel, "Die Haftung für Hilfspersonen im römischen Recht," *ZRG* 100 (1983) 340-443, esp. 373, n. 139.

The principal's authorization, which was meant either for a specific transaction or on a general basis, could be given by will, by letter, orally, or through a messenger.[41] In contrast to a *praepositio*, a *iussum* could be directed at a single transaction.[42] It is not entirely clear whether the authorization was aimed at the third contracting party rather than at the agent, but it seems likely that a certain amount of publicity was required for the rule to have any meaning.[43]

The authorization could be expressed in various legal forms, from a simple *subscriptio* on a document drafted by the agent (*chirographum*) to the ratification of the agent's transaction (*ratihabitio*) by the principal, or to a contract of mandate.[44] Since the agent could not make a contract of mandate with his master/*paterfamilias*, it seems that this text bolsters the suggestion made above that the principal's authorization was addressed to the third contracting party. A *iussum* differed from a mandate in that the former was neither contractual nor consensual.[45] *Iussum* and mandate were similar in that they had to be fulfilled precisely. Paulus says that if a master had instructed ("*praeceperit*") his slave to proceed with a sale under certain conditions (e.g., imposing a certain price) the sale was void if these conditions were not respected—making the position of the master worse

---

[41] Ulpianus (29 *ad ed.*) *Dig.* 15.4.1.1: "Iussum autem accipiendum est, sive testato quis sive per epistulam sive verbis aut per nuntium, sive specialiter in uno contractu iusserit sive generaliter: et ideo et si sic contestatus sit: 'Quod voles cum Sticho servo meo negotium gere periculo meo' videtur ad omnia iussisse."

[42] On the similarity of the two concepts, cf. G. Hamza, "Fragen der gewillkürten Stellvertretung im römischen Recht," *AUB (iur.)* 25 (1983) 89-107, esp. 95.

[43] A. Steinwenter, *PW* 10 (1919) 1306-08, s.v. *iussum*, esp. 1307 concludes that the *iussum* was addressed to third contracting parties; cf. also G. and M. Sautel, *Mél. Lévy-Bruhl* (1959) 258-60. M. Kaser, *RP* I² (Munich 1971) 265 says that it originated in an order addressed to the agent, but later on the author states that the *iussum* had to be announced in an informal way to the third contracting party (*ibid.* 608). The wording of *Dig.* 15.4.3 (Ulpianus, 2 *resp.*) unambiguously indicates that the *iussum* was addressed to third contracting parties.

[44] Ulpianus (29 *ad ed.*) *Dig.* 15.4.1.3, 4, and 6.

[45] A. Watson (1961) 137 and 140-41, citing S. Solazzi, *L'estinzione dell'obbligazione nel diritto romano²* (Naples 1935) 74, remarks that "the *iussum* of a creditor to the debtor (Paulus [2 *man.*] *Dig.* 46.3.108) is a unilateral declaration, not a mandate, and one cannot talk of a mandate where there is no shadow of a contract." Further, Watson shows (151) that the passage has been interpolated and deals with *delegatio*. Cf. also *ibid.* 180 (about Paulus [67 *ad ed.*] *Dig.* 43.24.6), where the submandatary entrusted by the mandatary with the completion of the initial contract between mandator and mandatary is not bound toward the mandator ("Si ego tibi mandavero opus novum facere, tu alii, non potest videri meo iussu factum").

—and the master was entitled to claim the sold thing through a *vindicatio*.[46]

A special case concerns the liability of a city official (magistrate or *curator*?) or public servant on account of the contracts made with his authorization by a public slave.[47] Although magistrates and commissioners (*curatores*) were direct agents of the state or a municipality, they carried out their administrative duties through public slaves, whose transactions made them personally liable. As M. Rostovzeff suggests, it is probable that this was the result of a second-century development, whereby a transition was effected "from the principle of collective responsibility to that of individual liability."[48]

The *actio quod iussu*, like the *actiones de peculio* and *de in rem verso*, was available only when the agent was a dependent of the principal, i.e. a non-contractual agent.[49] In this sense, these three remedies were more restricted than the *actiones institoria* and *exercitoria*, which were available—at least in the classical period—to third contracting parties contracting with extraneous agents. On the other hand, the *actio quod iussu* was similar to the *actiones institoriae* and *exercitoriae* in that the liability of the principal was unlimited (*in solidum*).

2. *Actio institoria*

The *actio institoria*[50] was based on the idea that principals who bene-

---

[46] Paulus (32 *ad ed.*) *Dig.* 17.1.5.4: "Servo quoque dominus si praeceperit certa summa rem vendere, ille minoris vendiderit, similiter vindicare eam dominus potest nec ulla exceptione summoveri." *Contra*, Paulus, *Sent.* 2.15.3: "Certo pretio rem iussus distrahere si minoris vendiderit, mandati iudicio pretii summa poterit integrari; venditionem enim dissolvi non placuit." A. Watson (1961) 191-92 rightly says that this passage is "a complete aberration from classical and Justinianic law."

[47] Ulpianus (10 *ad ed.*), citing Pomponius, *Dig.* 15.4.4: "Si iussu eius, qui administrationi rerum civitatis praepositus est, cum servo civitatis negotium contractum sit, Pomponius scribit quod iussu cum eo agi posse."

[48] M. Rostovtzeff, *The Social and Economic History of the Roman Empire*[2] (Oxford 1957) 391. This aspect of agency will be discussed in Chapter Five on the basis of some evidence concerning the application of the *vilicus* system to various public services.

[49] Ulpianus (29 *ad ed.*) *Dig.* 15.1.1.1-2: "Est autem triplex hoc edictum: aut enim de peculio aut de in rem verso aut quod iussu hinc oritur actio. Verba autem edicti talia sunt: 'Quod cum eo, qui in alterius potestate esset, negotium gestum erit'." The extension of the remedies to cases involving independent agents was enacted by a law of A.D. 422 (*Cod. Iust.* 4.26.13), approved by Iustinianus; cf. M. Kaser, *RP* II[2] (1975) 103-07.

[50] The main sources are Gai., *Inst.* 4.71, with *P.Oxy.* XVII 2103; *Dig.* 14.3;

fited from the transactions of their dependent business managers should also incur liabilities arising from them.[51] According to the terms of the praetorian Edict, the principal who had appointed an agent (*institor*) to run his business expected him to negotiate contracts with customers, suppliers, and contractors, in a specifically designated place (estate, workshop, store, or any other facility) or elsewhere,[52] and accepted full liability for the transactions performed by his agent on the basis, and within the scope, of his appointment (*praepositio*).[53] Consequently, third contracting parties were given a legal remedy against either the agent or the principal. In the latter case, the formula of the remedy was drafted so that the *intentio* contained the name of the agent and the *condemnatio* the name of the principal (cf. above).

The appointment was usually performed by the principal, either a man or a woman.[54] Wards who appointed an agent with the authorization of their guardians were liable in full. Otherwise, their liability was limited to the extent of their enrichment derived from

Paulus, *Sent.* 2.8; *Cod. Iust.* 4.25: *Inst. Iust.* 4.7. The *actio institoria* is not mentioned in the *Codex Theodosianus*, which led G. and M. Sautel, *Mél. Lévy-Bruhl* (1959) 264 to suggest that it became obsolete after Diocletian. This is unlikely, since the sixth-century Compilers discussed it in great detail. What happened between Diocletian and Iustinianus is admittedly unclear. The bibliography on the *actio institoria* is enormous and can be traced back through F. Serrao, *Enciclopedia del diritto* 21 (1971) 827-34, s.v. *institor*. Cf. also the more recent discussions by M. Just, "Ansätze zur Anscheinsvollmacht im römischen Recht. D. 14, 3, 19, 3; 14, 5, 8: ein Beispiel spätklassischer Rechtspraxis," *Festschrift für K.H. Neumayer zum 65. Geburtstag* (Baden-Baden 1985) 355-87; A. Kirschenbaum (1987); N. Benke, "Zu Papinians *actio ad exemplum institoriae actionis*," *ZRG* 105 (1988) 592-633; and T.J. Chiusi, "Landwirtschaftliche Tätigkeit und *actio institoria*," *ZRG* 108 (1991) 155-86. A—somewhat hypercritical—review of the texts has been presented by G. Longo, "*Actio exercitoria, actio institoria, actio quasi-institoria*," *Studi G. Scherillo* II (Milan 1972) 581-626, esp. 603 ff.

[51] Ulpianus (28 *ad ed.*) *Dig.* 14.3.1: "Aequum praetori visum est, sicut commoda sentimus ex actu institorum, ita etiam obligari nos ex contractibus ipsorum et conveniri."

[52] Paulus (*sing. de var. lect.*) *Dig.* 14.3.18: "Institor est, qui tabernae locove ad emendum vendendumve praeponitur quique sine loco ad eundem actum praeponitur."

[53] Ulpianus (28 *ad ed.*) *Dig.* 14.3.5.11-15. For the definition of *praepositio*, cf. Chapter One.

[54] Ulpianus (28 *ad ed.*) *Dig.* 14.3.7.1: "Item quisquis praeposuit: nam et si mulier praeposuit, competet institoria exemplo exercitoriae actionis." The reference to the *actio exercitoria* can be explained by the fact that it is discussed first in Ulpianus's writing *Ad edictum* (*Dig.* 14.1.1.16), following the order in which they were listed and described in Iulianus's Perpetual Edict, cf. below.

the agent's activity.[55] *Institores* could also be appointed by several
principals united in joint ownership or partnership. Iulianus, cited
by Ulpianus, wonders whether the joint owners of a slave agent
should each be held liable (a) in proportion to their share in the
slave; or (b) in proportion to their share in the business; or (c) in full.
He decides in favor of the full liability of each principal, by analogy
with the *actio exercitoria* and with the *actio de peculio*. The owner who
had been sued by a third contracting party on the contract of a *servus
communis* could in turn sue his fellow principals on the contract of
partnership or for division of common property.[56]

It seems that general agents (*procuratores*), curators, and guardians
were also entitled to appoint a business manager on behalf of the
principal.[57] As we will see in Chapter Five, this aspect is most important in public administration, and the passage should not be rejected as interpolated. Ulpianus thinks that such an appointment,
once ratified by the principal, would result in making only the latter
liable, but Paulus considers that the *procurator* should bear a joint liability with the principal.[58] As the (joint) liability of the principal
arose from the appointment of an *institor* by the *procurator*, it seems
that the classical jurists were flirting with the concept of direct agency.[59] When a wealthy principal had wide-ranging business interests, it is unlikely that he had time to appoint all his agents himself.
Trimalchio's surprise while hearing that he owned some property
near or in Pompeii—or formerly belonging to one Pompeius—implies that the *vilicus* who managed the property was unknown to

---

[55] Ulpianus (28 *ad ed.*) *Dig.* 14.3.9 and 11 *pr.*; and Gaius (9 *ad ed. prov.*) *Dig.* 14.3.10.

[56] Ulpianus (28 *ad ed.*), citing Iulianus, *Dig.* 14.3.13.2. On this question, cf. A. di Porto, *Impresa collettiva e schiavo 'manager' in Roma antica (II sec. a.C. –II sec. d.C.)* (Milan 1984) 63-167.

[57] Ulpianus (28 *ad ed.*) *Dig.* 14.3.5.18: "Sed et si procurator meus, tutor, cura-tor institorem praeposuerit, dicendum erit veluti a me praeposito dandam institori-am actionem."

[58] Paulus (30 *ad ed.*) *Dig.* 14.3.6: "Sed et in ipsum procuratorem, si omnium re-rum procurator est, dari debebit institoria." The passage is probably interpolated ("si . . . est"), but the substance remains unchanged.

[59] A. Claus (1973) 273-74. However, one should keep in mind that the exten-sion by Papinianus of the *actio institoria* (*utilis*) to cases involving transactions per-formed by a *procurator* made *procuratores* and *institores* very much alike (cf. Papinianus [3 *resp.*] *Dig.* 14.3.19 *pr.*) and the three-level structure *dominus-procurator-institor* be-came equivalent to the structure principal-agent-subagent discussed by Ulpianus (28 *ad ed.*) *Dig.* 14.1.1.5 (cf. below).

him.[60] The story was meant as a joke about Trimalchio's pretentious attitude toward the daily management of his huge properties, but it indicates that it was probably common for low-level managers to be appointed by a general agent (*procurator*).

An agent could also appoint a subagent, provided that the (sub-) appointment was not in contradiction with the terms of the *praepositio* and that the principal knew of it, and consented to it. Iulianus accepts the principle of the full liability of the principal, provided that he was aware of, and did not object to, the appointment of the subagent. Ulpianus goes even further, and accepts the full liability of the principal when the (sub-)appointment has been made without his knowledge and in spite of his opposition. Ulpianus admits that Iulianus's and his interpretations are more acceptable in the concept of the operation of a ship, as Roman classical law was favorable to the shipping industry because of its role in the food supply of the city of Rome. The situation of the principal whose dependent had appointed an *institor* was slightly different. In this case, the principal's liability was full if the dependent was following his instruction (*voluntas*), and limited to the amount of the dependent's *peculium* if the dependent was acting on his own initiative. An action for distribution of the *peculium* was reserved when the principal was aware of his dependent's activity.[61]

---

[60] Petron., *Sat.* 53.5.

[61] Ulpianus (28 *ad ed.*) *Dig.* 14.1.1.5: "Magistrum autem accipimus non solum, quem exercitor praeposuit, sed et eum, quem magister. . . . Et facilius hoc in magistro quam institore admittendum propter utilitatem" (the last sentence refers only to Ulpianus's opinion that, in the context of the operation of a ship, not only the principal's *voluntas*, but also his *scientia* and *patientia*, and even his *ignorantia* concerning the (sub-)appointment provide a sufficient basis for his full liability) and 14.1.1.19-20: "At institorum non idem usus est: ea propter in tributum dumtaxat vocantur, qui contraxerunt cum eo, qui in merce peculiari sciente domino negotiatur;" (here again the difference between *actio institoria* and *actio exercitoria* consists in a more subtle distinction between levels of liability in the context of the operation of a land based business). Cf. below. Both passages have been considered non-classical by modern scholars, cf. S. Solazzi, *Scritti di diritto romano* IV (Naples 1963) 243-64, esp. 246-49; cf. also F. de Martino (1982) [1941] 155-57 and [1958] 175-80; and F. Serrao, *Enciclopedia del diritto* 21 (1971) 829, n. 7; against G. Pugliese, "In tema di *actio exercitoria*," *Labeo* 3 (1957) 308-43, esp. 312-16; S.E. Wunner, *Contractus. Sein Wortgebrauch und Willensgehalt im klassischen römischen Recht* (Cologne/Graz 1964) 125-31; and P. Garnsey, "Independent Freedmen and the Economy of Roman Italy under the Principate," *Klio* 63 (1981) 359-71, esp. 365. Even though the texts as they stand contain some spurious elements, I see no reason to reject their substance and therefore choose to side with Pugliese and Garnsey; cf. my paper on workshop managers. There is no doubt, in my opinion, that the question

A business manager could be either slave or free, *sui iuris* or *alieni iuris*, male or female, adult or minor, or even a ward.[62] Interestingly, Gaius reports that it was quite common to employ boys and girls as business managers.[63] A change in status on the part of the *institor*, through manumission or emancipation, had no necessary effect on the position and liability of the principal toward third contracting parties.[64] The nature of the legal relationship, either (quasi-) contractual or non-contractual, between principal and agent was irrelevant. So was the legal relationship between third contracting party and agent. Thus, the *institor* could be the slave of the third contracting party (for instance, a *vicarius* rented out by a *dispensator* or any slave with *peculium*), without impairing the validity of contracts concluded between them.[65] However, the classical jurists were aware of the irregular character of a transaction between a *dominus* and his own slave, and considered granting the master an *actio utilis* against the principal.[66] When the *institor* was a *servus alienus*, the third contracting party had the option to sue either the principal or the master.[67] Of course, the second option was not available if the third

of the appointment of subagents provoked some intense legal dispute in the second century A.D. Cf. also A. Kirschenbaum (1987) 101-03.

[62] Ulpianus (28 *ad ed.*) *Dig.* 14.3.7.1: "Parvi autem refert, quis sit institor, masculus an femina, liber an servus proprius vel alienus. . . . Nam et si mulier praeposuit. . . et si mulier sit praeposita, tenebitur etiam ipsa. Sed et si filia familias sit vel ancilla praeposita, competit institoria actio." Cf. A. Burdese, "*Actio ad exemplum institoriae* e categorie sociali," *BIDR* 74 (1971) 61-82 (= *Studi G. Donatuti* I [Milan 1973] 191-210); *contra*, P. Angelini, "Osservazioni in tema di creazione dell' *actio ad exemplum institoriae,*" *BIDR* 71 (1968) 230-48.

[63] Gaius (9 *ad ed. prov.*) *Dig.* 14.3.8: "Nam et plerique pueros puellasque tabernis praeponunt."

[64] Papinianus (3 *resp.*) *Dig.* 14.3.19.1: "Si dominus, qui servum institorem apud mensam pecuniis accipiendis habuit, post libertatem quoque datam idem per libertum negotium exercuit, varietate status non mutabitur periculi causa;" *idem* (11 *quaest.*) *Dig.* 26.7.37.1: "Secundum quam sententiam servus institor dominicae mercis vel praepositus debitis exigendis si liber factus in eodem actu perseveret, quamvis tempore servitutis obligari non potuerit, praeteriti temporis nomine actione negotiorum gestorum non inutiliter convenietur;" and Scaevola (11 *dig.*) *Dig.* 26.7.58 *pr.*: "Qui negotiationem per Pamphilum et Diphilum prius servos, postea libertos exercebat, . . ."

[65] Ulpianus (28 *ad ed.*) *Dig.* 14.3.11.8; and Iulianus (11 *dig.*) *Dig.* 14.3.12.

[66] O. Lenel, *Das Edictum Perpetuum*[3] (Leipzig 1927) 261 rejected by P. Fabricius, *Der gewaltfreie Institor im klassischen römischen Recht* (Würzburg 1926) 20-22. G. Longo, *Studi Scherillo* II (1972) 617 and 622, n. 74 considers that the *actio institoria utilis* is a creation of the Compilers and that it was referred to as *actio institoria ficticia* by classical jurists.

[67] Paulus (30 *ad ed.*) *Dig.* 14.3.17.1: "Si servum Titii institorem habueris, vel

contracting party was the master of the *instititor*. The remedy was given in consideration of the fact that it was usually possible to identify the status and standing of the business manager in charge of a shop, but this was admittedly more difficult in the case of a shipmaster.[68]

A principal could appoint several *institores* to the head of a single shop. Papinianus mentions the case of the owner of a *taberna purpuraria* who bequeathed it to his son with all the managers and dyestuff in the stores at the time of his death.[69] Scaevola, speaking of the staff and equipment of a wine cellar, refers to its managers in the plural,[70] and Ulpianus, citing Sabinus's *Ad Vitellium*, lists *vilici* and *monitores* as managers of an agricultural estate.[71] There is no doubt that this situation existed already in the early history of the *actio institoria*, since the Republican jurist Servius Sulpicius Rufus writes that the staff of an inn is composed of several managers and one female cook.[72] The principal could indicate in the *lex praepositionis* whether third contracting parties had to negotiate their contracts with all managers together, or whether they could validly deal with one of them.[73]

When a transaction carried out by an *institor* gave rise to litigation, the principal had to defend where the transaction was performed. Labeo mentions the case of a provincial businessman who had set up his *institor* in Rome to sell his merchandise, and says that any suit

---

tecum ex hoc edicto vel cum Titio ex inferioribus edictis agere potero. Sed si tu cum eo contrahi vetuisti, cum Titio dumtaxat agi poterit." *Inferiora edicta* refers to the *actio quod iussu, actio de in rem verso, actio de peculio*, and *actio tributoria*.

[68] Ulpianus (28 *ad ed.*) *Dig.* 14.1.1 *pr.*: "Aequum fuit eum, qui magistrum navi imposuit, teneri, ut tenetur, qui institorem tabernae vel negotio praeposuit, cum sit maior necessitas contrahendi cum magistro quam cum institore. Quippe res patitur, ut de condicione quis institoris dispiciat et sic contrahat: in navis magistro non ita, nam interdum locus tempus non patitur plenius deliberandi consilium."

[69] Papinianus (7 *resp.*) *Dig.* 32.91.2.: "Pater filio tabernam purpurariam cum servis institoribus et purpuris, quae in diem mortis eius ibi fuerunt, legavit."

[70] Scaevola (22 *dig.*) *Dig.* 33.7.7: "...item horreum vinarium cum vino et vasis et instrumento et institoribus, quos secum habere consueverat."

[71] Ulpianus (20 *ad Sab.*) *Dig.* 33.7.8 *pr.*: "In instrumento fundi ea esse, quae fructus quaerendi ... gratia parata sunt ... veluti homines qui agrum colunt, et qui eos exercent praepositive sunt is, quorum in numero sunt vilici et monitores...."

[72] Pomponius (6 *ad Sab.*), citing Servius, *Dig.* 33.7.15 *pr.*: "...et in cauponio institores et focariam...."

[73] Ulpianus (28 *ad ed.*) *Dig.* 14.3.11.5: "item si plures habuit institores vel cum omnibus simul contrahi voluit vel cum uno solo." Cf. *Dig.* 14.1.1.13, below.

will have to be brought in Rome.[74] A recently published document
from the Agro Murecine in Pompeii shows that the procedure was
sometimes more complicated. A businessman, C. Iulius Prudens,
whose slaves Hyginus and Hermes had taken out a loan in Puteoli
in A.D. 55, was sued by the moneylender C. Sulpicius Cinnamus.
The case was first brought before a local magistrate, one of the *duumviri* of the colony, who proceeded with an *interrogatio in iure* and ordered (by *denuntiatio*) the defendant/principal to produce (*exhibitio*)
his slaves before of an arbitrator (*iudex*) in Rome to verify the legal
relationship (*potestas*) between principal and agents. The point was
probably to verify the existence and scope of the *praepositio* in order
to establish the extent of the principal's liability.[75]

The legal consequences of the appointment outlived both principal and agent. Contracts negotiated by an *institor* after his principal's death were valid, and third contracting parties could sue the
principal's heir.[76] The remedy was perpetual and could be either
enforced against the principal's heir or transmitted to the third contracting party's heir.[77]

3. *Actio exercitoria*

According to the terms of the praetorian Edict, the principal/shipper
(*exercitor*) who had appointed an agent/shipmaster (*magister navis*) to
be in charge of a ship was fully liable for the transactions performed
by his agent.[78] The ship could be of any size and operate on the sea,

---

[74] Ulpianus (60 *ad ed.*), citing Labeo, *Dig.* 5.1.19.3: "Apud Labeonem quaeritur, si homo provincialis servum institorem vendendarum mercium gratia Romae
habeat: quod cum eo servo contractum est, ita habendum atque si cum domino
contractum sit: quare ibi se debebit defendere." Cf. M. Kaser, *RZ* (1966) 183; and
A. Kirschenbaum (1987) 111-12.

[75] *AE* 1973, no. 146 (Agro Murecine) = *Tab.Pomp.* 25 (cf. F. Sbordone, *RAAN*
46 [1971] 177-78); cf. M. Lemosse, "La procédure contre l'esclave débiteur, une
nouvelle révélation romanistique," *RD* 62 (1984) 225-29; L. Bove, *Documenti processuali delle Tabulae Pompeianae di Murecine* (Naples 1979) 85-93; and J. Andreau, *La
vie financière dans le monde romain* (Rome 1987) 706-07. On litigation involving
Italians, cf. M. Kaser, *RZ* (1966) 126-30; 138-42; and 183-84.

[76] Ulpianus (28 *ad ed.*) *Dig.* 14.3.5.17; and Paulus (30 *ad ed.*), citing Pomponius, *Dig.* 14.3.17.3.

[77] Ulpianus (28 *ad ed.*) *Dig.* 14.3.15: "Novissime sciendum est has actiones
perpetuo dari et in heredem et heredibus."

[78] The main sources are Gai., *Inst.* 4.71, with *P.Oxy.* XVII 2103; *Dig.* 14.1;
Cod. Iust. 4.25: *Inst. Iust.* 4.7. Cf. F. de Martino, "Studi sull' *actio exercitoria*," *Riv.
dir. navigaz.* 7 (1941) 7-31; *idem*, "Ancora sull' *actio exercitoria*," *Labeo* 4 (1958)

on a lake, or on a river. It was not necessary for the shipper to be the owner of the ship.[79] The legal remedy given to third contracting parties against the shipper was called *actio exercitoria* and was similar in many ways to the *actio institoria*, which explains why Ulpianus describes the *actio exercitoria* in reference to the *actio institoria*. The same author remarks that there was a higher necessity to give third contracting parties a legal remedy against the principal of a ship-master than against the principal of a business manager (*institor*), because business transactions performed with a shipmaster, usually in overseas locations, could not be postponed long enough to await verification of his status and standing.[80]

The appointment of the shipmaster (*magister navis*) constituted the basis of the liability of the shipper (*exercitor*). The purpose of the appointment usually consisted in transporting goods or passengers for a fixed or negotiated fare/freight, but the contractual arrangement between shipmaster and third contracting parties could take various forms. Other transactions by the shipmaster engaged the liability of the shipper, for instance the purchase of equipment necessary for running the ship, such as rigging, sails, and oars, and of material for repairing it.[81] All obligations incurred in connection with repairs of the ship or maintenance of the crew gave rise to an *actio exercitoria*, because these tasks belonged to the sphere of competence of the shipmaster. By contrast, third contracting parties would have no

---

274-300 (both reprinted in, and cited from, *Diritto privato e società romana* [Rome 1982] 148-70 and 171-99); *idem*, *NNDI* 6 (1960) 1088-92, s.v. *exercitor*; G. Pugliese, "In tema di *actio exercitoria*," *Labeo* 3 (1957) 308-43 (= *Studi F. Messineo* IV [Milan 1959] 287-326); J. Rougé, *Recherches sur l'organisation du commerce maritime en Méditerranée sous l'Empire romain* (Paris 1966) 389-92; K. Wiesmüller, *PW* Suppl. 12 (1970) cols. 365-72, s.v. *exercitor*; B. Sirks, *Food for Rome. The Legal Structure of the Transportation and Processing of Supplies for the Imperial Distributions in Rome and Constantinople* (Amsterdam 1991) 120-23. For a critical review of the texts, cf. G. Longo, *Studi Scherillo* II (1972) 581-603.

[79] Ulpianus (28 *ad ed.*) *Dig.* 14.1.1.15: "...sive is dominus navis sit sive a domino navem per aversionem conduxit vel ad tempus vel in perpetuum." Cf. K. Wiesmüller, *PW* Suppl. 12 (1970) cols. 365-66.

[80] Ulpianus (28 *ad ed.*) *Dig.* 14.1.1 *pr.*: "Utilitatem huius edicti patere nemo est qui ignoret. Nam cum interdum ignari, cuius sint condicionis vel quales, cum magistris propter navigandi necessitatem contrahamus, aequum fuit eum, qui magistrum navi imposuit, teneri, ut tenetur, qui institorem tabernae vel negotio praeposuit, cum sit maior necessitas contrahendi cum magistro quam institore...." In spite of the initial *laudatio edicti* and the references to *necessitas* and *utilitas*, the passage is genuine, cf. G. Longo, *Studi Scherillo* II (1972) 584-86. On the independent origin and similarities of both remedies, cf. below.

[81] Ulpianus (28 *ad ed.*) *Dig.* 14.1.1.3; and Africanus (8 *quaest.*) *Dig.* 14.1.7.

remedy against the shipper if the shipmaster had borrowed money for any purpose independent from the operation of the ship.[82] Africanus even requires from moneylenders that they check that the ship actually needed repairs and that the sum borrowed did not exceed their estimated cost.[83] Failure to do so would have had the effect to rescind the liability of the shipper. However, the moneylender did not have to make sure that the loan was eventually spent on the declared project.

Ulpianus specifies that the status and age of the shipmaster had no bearing on the shipper's liability.[84] According to the same author, third contracting parties had the option of suing either the principal or the agent (cf. below), which implies that by the third century A.D. shipmasters were often of free status (*ingenui* or *liberti*) and independent condition (*sui iuris*).[85]

The same lack of restriction concerning status is attested with regard to the shipper, who could be male or female, dependent or independent, free or slave.[86] There were cases where the shipper was himself an *institor* or an agent with *peculium*. Thus, the shipper was identified only as the one who reaped the profits from the management of the ship.[87]

The shipmaster was entitled to appoint a dependent or an outsider as subagent, whose transactions rendered the principal liable, as long as the latter did not explicitly forbid the appointment.[88] S. Solazzi,

---

[82] Ulpianus (28 *ad ed.*) *Dig.* 14.1.1.7-12, citing Ofilius (second half of first century B.C.), Pegasus, and Pedius (both active in the second half of the first century A.D.). The text is not exempt from interpolations, cf. F. de Martino (1982) [1941] 148-51; and A. Watson, *The Law of Obligations in the Later Roman Republic* (Oxford 1965) 190-91. However, the substance of the text seems to be preserved.

[83] Africanus (8 *quaest.*) *Dig.* 14.1.7 *pr.*

[84] Ulpianus (28 *ad ed.*) *Dig.* 14.1.1.4.

[85] Ulpianus (28 *ad ed.*) *Dig.* 14.1.1.17. About the extension of the *actiones institoria* and *exercitoria* to cases involving agents independent from the principal, cf. below.

[86] Ulpianus (28 *ad ed.*) *Dig.* 14.1.1.15-16.

[87] Ulpianus (28 *ad ed.*) *Dig.* 14.1.1.15: "Exercitorem autem eum dicimus, ad quem obventiones et reditus omnes perveniunt...." Cf. also *Inst. Iust.* 4.7.2.

[88] Ulpianus (28 *ad ed.*) *Dig.* 14.1.1.5: "Magistrum autem accipimus non solum, quem exercitor praeposuit, sed et eum, quem magister: et hoc consultus Iulianus in ignorante exercitore respondit: ceterum si scit et passus est eum in nave magisterio fungi, ipse eum imposuisse videtur. Quae sententia mihi videtur probabilis: omnia enim facta magistri debeo praestare qui eum praeposui, alioquin contrahentes decipientur: et facilius hoc in magistro quam institore admittendum propter utilitatem." Cf. A. Kirschenbaum (1987) 102-03, esp. n. 48. The passage has been considered interpolated, cf. F. de Martino (1982) [1941] 155-57 and [1958] 175-80,

among others, rejects the whole concept of appointment of subagents as post-classical, on the ground that if Iulianus denies the liability of the *exercitor* unaware of the fact that the *magister navis* had appointed a substitute, he cannot accept it in the absence of, or against,
the principal's will.[89] The text of *Dig.* 14.1.1.5 does not say that
Iulianus rejects the principle of the liability of the shipper *ignorans*,
and Solazzi's arguments still do not preclude the validity of a (sub-)
appointment made in accordance with the will (*voluntas*) of the
shipper. Consequently, there is no reason not to admit the validity
of a (sub-)appointment made by the shipmaster with the shipper's
knowledge and consent (*scientia et patientia*), and even without his
knowledge (*ignorantia*).[90]

A similar case occurred when the shipper (*exercitor*) was himself
someone else's dependent. The shipmaster was then in the position
of subagent and third contracting parties could sue the shipper's
principal on account of the transactions performed by either the
shipper or the shipmaster, provided that the principal had commissioned the shipper's involvement in seaborne activities.[91] If the
shipper's principal had not expressed the willingness to have his dependent operate a ship, the shipmaster was acting within the scope

---

but the first sentence is probably genuine, cf. G. Pugliese, *Labeo* 3 (1957) 312-16;
S.E. Wunner (1964) 115-23; and K. Wiesmüller, *PW* Suppl. 12 (1971) cols. 366-
67. Cf. above.

[89] S. Solazzi, "L'età dell' *actio exercitoria*," *Riv. dir. navigaz.* 7 (1941) 185-212 =
Scritti di diritto romano IV (Naples 1963) 243-64, esp. 246-48.

[90] R. Knütel, "Die Haftung für Hilfspersonen im römischen Recht," *ZRG* 100
(1983) 340-443, esp. 437, n. 415 uses this passage to show that Iulianus acknowledges that in some cases equity calls for transgression of the rule "nec factum
servi domino obesse debere nisi hactenus ut ipso careat" (Paulus [6 *ad ed.*] quoting
Sabinus, *Dig.* 2.10.2).

[91] Ulpianus (28 *ad ed.*) *Dig.* 14.1.1.19-20: "Si is, qui navem exercuerit, in aliena potestate erit eiusque voluntate navem exercuerit, quod cum magistro eius
gestum erit, in eum, in cuius potestate is erit qui navem exercuerit, iudicium datur.
20. Licet autem datur actio in eum, cuius in potestate est qui navem exercet, tamen
ita demum datur, si voluntate eius exerceat. Ideo autem ex voluntate in solidum
tenentur qui habent in potestate exercitorem, quia ad summam rem publicam navium exercitio pertinet;" and *idem*, citing Iulianus, *Dig.* 14.1.1.23: "Quamquam
autem, si cum magistro eius gestum sit, dumtaxat polliceatur praetor actionem,
tamen, ut Iulianus quoque scripsit, etiamsi cum ipso exercitore sit contractum,
pater dominusve in solidum tenebitur." The substance of the texts is genuine. Cf.
G. Pugliese, *Labeo* 3 (1957) 321-27 and 333-39; S.E. Wunner (1964) 125-31; G.
Longo, *Studi Scherillo* II (1972) 597-600; K. Wiesmüller, *PW* Suppl. 12 (1970) 370-
71; *contra*, F. de Martino (1982) [1941] 163-65 and 168-70; and [1958] 187-92 and
196-98.

of his own appointment by the shipper; no reference could be made
to the shipper's own appointment by the principal, because appointment and will (*voluntas*) go hand in hand, and the former could not
exist without the latter. Third contracting parties therefore could sue
the principal only to the extent of the shipper's *peculium*. Ulpianus,
following Pomponius, states that it would be unfair to equate mere
knowledge (*nuda scientia*) on the part of the principal with will (*voluntas*), but still refrains from granting a remedy for distribution of the
dependent's *peculium* (*a. tributoria*), as would be expected in the context of the operation of a land based business.[92] By contrast, Paulus
treats both cases alike. When the principal's will was lacking, third
contracting parties could sue him for distribution, provided that he
was aware of his dependent's activity. Otherwise, third contracting
parties had to sue the principal *de peculio*.[93] Finally, if the shipmaster belonged to the *peculium* of the dependent shipper, the shipper's principal was not liable in full, unless he had also commissioned the operation of the ship.[94]

The principal could appoint several shipmasters to a single ship.
Each of these shipmasters was entitled to conduct the same range of
business transactions, unless the principal advised otherwise and
arranged for a division of responsibilities. The advantage of having
several agents in charge of the same ship consisted in reducing the
risk of embezzlement on the part of a single agent by having all
agents check on each other. Ulpianus reports that the terms of the
appointment often specified that contracts would be valid only if the
shipmasters were all present.[95]

---

[92] Ulpianus (28 *ad ed.*), citing Pomponius, *Dig.* 14.1.1.20: "Sed si sciente dumtaxat, non etiam volente cum magistro contractum sit, utrum quasi in volentem
damus actionem in solidum an vero exemplo tributoriae dabimus? In re igitur
dubia melius est verbis edicti servire et neque scientiam solam et nudam patris
dominive in navibus onerare neque in peculiaribus mercibus voluntatem extendere
ad solidi obligationem. Et ita videtur et Pomponius significare, si sit in aliena
postestate, si quidem voluntate gerat, in solidum eum obligari, si minus, in peculium." Cf. above.

[93] Paulus (6 *brev.*) *Dig.* 14.1.6 *pr.*: "Si servus non voluntate domini navem exercuerit, si sciente eo, quasi tributoria, si ignorante, de peculio actio dabitur;" *idem*,
Sent. 2.6; and Ulpianus (14 *ad ed.*) *Dig.* 4.9.3.3. S.E. Wunner (1964) 130-31.

[94] Ulpianus (28 ad ed.) *Dig.* 14.1.1.22. Cf. S.E. Wunner (1964) 114-25; *contra*,
F. de Martino (1982) [1941] 165-66; and [1958] 192-93.

[95] Ulpianus (28 *ad ed.*) *Dig.* 14.1.1.13-14: "Si plures sint magistri non divisis
officiis, quodcumque cum uno gestum erit, obligabit exercitorem: si divisis, ut alter
locando, alter exigendo, pro cuiusque officio obligabitur exercitor. 14. Sed et si sic

Conversely, a shipmaster could be appointed by several shippers bound in a partnership or as joint owners.[96] Each shipper was personally liable in full and could be sued separately by third contracting parties.[97] After discharging the whole debt derived from the shipmaster's contract, the shipper could sue his partner(s) or joint owner(s) with the *actio pro socio* or *communi dividundo*.[98] If the third contracting party was the owner of a slave hired out to a shipper and appointed shipmaster, he could sue the shipper on any contract negotiated with the slave.[99]

Third contracting parties could sue either the principal with the *actio exercitoria*, or the agent with the remedy derived from the contract. For instance, if a shipmaster had operated a ship on a river without the assistance of a pilot and the ship had sunk due to his inability to steer it during a storm, the passengers could sue him on the contract of work (*locatio conductio operis*), probably by analogy with the *Lex Aquilia*. Alternatively, they could sue the shipper with the *actio exercitoria*. If their claim against one was unsuccessful, they could not start litigating against the other, because their claim was then extinguished at the moment of the joinder of issue (*litis contestatio*).[100] This rule has one interesting, though somewhat academic, implication: if the shipper was a slave with *peculium* or *institor servus alienus*, his owner could negotiate a contract with the shipmaster, and later sue the shipmaster or the shipper's principal, but not the shipper, because it would amount to bringing a suit against himself.[101]

Like the *actio institoria*, the *actio exercitoria* is perpetual and is not extinguished by the death of either the shipper or the shipmaster.[102]

The social and economic context in which the other two legal remedies belonging to the category of the *actiones adiecticiae qualitatis* were applied will not concern us in this study. In addition, they have

---

praeposuit, ut plerumque faciunt, ne alter sine altero quid gerat, qui contraxit cum uno sibi imputabit.''

[96] Gaius (9 *ad ed. prov.*) *Dig.* 14.1.2; Ulpianus (28 *ad ed.*) *Dig.* 14.1.1.25 and 14.1.4 *pr.*-2; Paulus (29 *ad ed.*) *Dig.* 14.1.3 and 14.1.6.1.

[97] Ulpianus (28 *ad ed.*) *Dig.* 14.1.1.25; and Gaius (9 *ad ed. prov.*) *Dig.* 14.1.2.

[98] Paulus (6 *brev.*) *Dig.* 14.1.6.1.

[99] Paulus (29 *ad ed.*) *Dig.* 14.1.5 *pr.* On the whole question of the organization of joint seaborne commercial ventures, cf. A. di Porto (1984) 169-204.

[100] Ulpianus (28 *ad ed.*) *Dig.* 14.1.1.17 and 24; and *idem* (32 *ad ed.*) *Dig.* 19.2.13.2. Cf. M. Kaser, *RP* I² (1971) 656-59, esp. 658.

[101] Paulus (29 *ad ed.*) *Dig.* 14.1.5.1.

[102] Ulpianus (29 [28?] *ad ed.*) *Dig.* 14.1.4.4.

formed the subjects of some recent, thorough studies. For these reasons, only a superficial description will be offered here for the sake of comparison.

4. *Actio de in rem verso*

A contract negotiated by a dependent agent acting without specific or general instructions (*iussum* or *praepositio*) could benefit his master/*paterfamilias* without binding him to fulfill the obligations derived from this contract. The benefit taken from the dependent's transaction was similar to unjustified enrichment,[103] and consequently the praetor gave third contracting parties a legal remedy against the principal to the extent of the latter's enrichment, or rather what remained of it at the time of litigation.[104] This remedy, which was perpetual, seems to have been available only when the *peculium* of the dependent was nonexistent, empty, or insufficient. It was exhausted when the third contracting party had brought an *actio de peculio* which resulted successfully in the repayment of the benefit taken.[105]

The juristic discussion related to this type of remedy focuses on the definition of enrichment. For instance, if a dependent made use of unpaid perfumes and ointments for a funeral that the principal was supposed to hold, the latter was viewed as benefiting from the dependent's activity.[106] Similarly, if a dependent used borrowed money to buy food and ordinary clothes for himself, it represented

---

[103] This point is not securely established, cf. M. Kaser, *RP* I^2 (1971) 592-600, esp. 598, n. 51 and 600, with reference to H. Niederländer, *Die Bereicherungshaftung im klassischen Recht* (Böhlau 1953) who rejects the view that the liability *de in rem verso* derives from the *gestio* by the dependent; cf. B. Nicholas, *JRS* 44 (1954) 136-37.

[104] The main sources are Gai., *Inst.* 4.72a-74a; *Dig.* 15.3; Paulus, *Sent.* 2.9; *Cod. Iust.* 4.26; *Inst. Iust.* 4.7. Cf. J.L. Gay, "L'*in rem versum* à l'époque classique," *Varia. Etudes de droit romain* II (Paris 1956) 155-280; G. MacCormack, "The Early History of the *actio de in rem verso* (Alfenus to Labeo)," *Studi Biscardi* II (Milan 1982) 319-39; *idem*, "The Later History of the *actio de in rem verso* (Proculus to Ulpian)," *SDHI* 48 (1982) 318-67.

[105] Ulpianus (29 *ad ed.*), citing Labeo, *Dig.* 15.3.1 *pr.*-1. It appears, on the basis of a couple of passages by Gaius, that the *actio de in rem verso* and the *actio de peculio* could be brought separately, and that the *versio* had priority over the *peculium*, cf. G. MacCormack, *Studi Biscardi* II (1982) 320-21; *idem*, *SDHI* 48 (1982) 330-31, referring to Gaius, *Inst.* 4.74a; *idem* (9 *ad ed. prov.*) *Dig.* 14.5.1; and *idem*, citing Iulianus, *Dig.* 15.1.27 *pr.* (itp.).

[106] Ulpianus (29 *ad ed.*), citing Labeo, *Dig.* 15.3.7.3.

an enrichment for the principal.[107] Ulpianus summarizes the rule as followed:

> We propose as a general rule to consider that the remedy for benefit taken will be granted whenever a slave makes an expenditure to improve or maintain his master's property, in which case a general agent (*procurator*) would be entitled to sue on the mandate or a voluntary administrator on account of unauthorized management (*negotium gestum*).[108]

Pomponius, however, says that ratification by the master/*paterfamilias* of his dependent's transaction was not a necessary condition for the grant of the remedy for benefit taken.[109] Neither was the principal's consent necessary, unless the agent had incurred expenses which the principal was not obliged to pay.[110] Originally, it was irrelevant whether the enrichment was part of the *peculium* or not. As a result, it was more difficult to determine the existence and extent of any enrichment than that of the *peculium*. This may explain why in the classical period a judge would grant recovery under the *actio de peculio*, and only in case of insolvency of the *peculium* would he consider granting recovery under the *actio de in rem verso*.[111]

5. *Actio de peculio*

Dependents were incapable of ownership, and consequently litigation arising from their business transactions—provided that they were valid—could at best result in the grant of an unenforceable

---

[107] Ulpianus (29 *ad ed.*), citing Labeo, *Dig.* 15.3.3.3.

[108] Ulpianus (29 *ad ed.*) *Dig.* 15.3.3.2: "Et regulariter dicimus totiens de in rem verso esse actionem, quibus casibus procurator mandati vel qui negotia gessit negotiorum gestorum haberet actionem quotiensque aliquid consumpsit servus, ut aut meliorem rem dominus habuerit aut non deteriorem." Cf. G. MacCormack, *SDHI* 48 (1982) 348, who considers the text probably genuine; *contra*, A. Watson (1961) 48. Cf. also Africanus (8 *quaest.*) *Dig.* 15.3.17 *pr.*; and MacCormack 363.

[109] Ulpianus (29 *ad ed.*), citing Pomponius, *Dig.* 15.3.5.1.

[110] Ulpianus (29 *ad ed.*), citing Labeo, *Dig.* 15.3.3.6. Gaius (*Inst.* 4.72a) states that the *actio de peculio et de in rem verso* was available when the transaction had been performed without the will and agreement of the principal. This opinion was subject to some exceptions, cf. G. MacCormack, *SDHI* 48 (1982) 329.

[111] The subsidiary character of the *actio de in rem verso* seems well attested in the classical period (Paul [4 *quaest.*], citing Neratius, *Dig.* 15.3.19), but need not be original (Ulpianus [29 *ad ed.*] *Dig.* 15.3.5.2), cf. G. MacCormack, *SDHI* 48 (1982) 342; 345-46; and 360-61.

judgment. Thus, third contracting parties dealing with dependents had no legal protection against either agent or principal until the praetor decided to recognize the juristic existence of fictitious assets (*peculium*) pertaining *de facto* to the dependent, but belonging *de iure* to the principal. Subsequently, third contracting parties were given a legal remedy against the principal, whose liability was limited to a sum equivalent to the value of the dependent's *peculium* at the time of litigation.[112]

Dependents, except for sons, were incapable of making valid legal transactions.[113] But when the principal, male or female,[114] had entrusted his/her dependent, male or female,[115] with a *peculium* (*concessio peculii*) together with the right to administer it freely (*concessio liberae administrationis*),[116] it was understood that the principal had given his/her dependent the capacity to make valid legal transac-

---

[112] The main sources are Gai., *Inst.* 4.72a-74a; *Dig.* 15.1.; *Cod. Theod.* 2.32; *Cod. Iust.* 4.26; *Inst. Iust.* 4.7.4-4c. Cf. G. Micolier, *Pécule et capacité patrimoniale. Etude sur le pécule, dit profectice, depuis l'édit 'de peculio' jusqu'à la fin de l'époque classique* (Lyons 1932); W. von Uxkull-Gyllenband, *PW* 19.1 (1937) cols. 13-16, s.v. *peculium*; I. Buti, *Studi sulla capacità patrimoniale dei servi* (Naples 1976); J.J. Brinkhof, *Een studie over het peculium in het Klassieke Romeinse recht* (Meppel 1978) (non vidi, but cf. P. Apathy, *ZRG* 96 [1979] 398-407); Y. Thomas, "Droits domestiques et droits politiques à Rome. Remarques sur le pécule et les *honores* des fils de famille," *MEFRA* 94 (1982) 527-80; A. Burdese, "Controversie giurisprudenziali in tema di capacità degli schiavi," *Studi Biscardi* I (Milan 1982) 147-80; *idem*, "Considerazioni in tema di peculio c.d. profettizio," *Studi Sanfilippo* I (Milan 1982) 71-111; and L. Amirante, "Lavoro di giuristi sul peculio. Le definizioni da Q. Mucio a Ulpiano," *Studi Sanfilippo* III (1983) 3-15.

[113] M. Kaser, *RP* I[2] (1971) 63-65; 286-88; 343-44; 392-93, n. 26.

[114] Ulpianus (29 *ad ed.*), perhaps following Labeo, *Dig.* 15.1.3.2: "Parvi autem refert, servus quis masculi an mulieris fuerit; nam de peculio et mulier convenietur." This rule applied to the relationship *domina-servus*, and not to the relationship *mater-filius*.

[115] Gaius (9 *ad ed. prov.*) *Dig.* 15.1.27 pr. (itp., but the substance is genuine); Ulpianus (29 *ad ed.*) *Dig.* 15.1.1.2-3: "Verba autem edicti talia sunt: 'Quod cum eo, qui in alterius potestate esset, negotium gestum erit'. De eo loquitur, non de ea: sed tamen et ob eam quae est feminini sexus dabitur ex hoc edicto actio;" and *idem* (29 *ad ed.*) *Dig.* 14.4.5.2. About the *peculium filiae familias* and *peculium uxoris in manu*, cf. M. Kaser, *RP* I[2] (1971) 329, n. 2; and 330, n. 16, with reference to M. García Garrido, *Ius uxorium. El régimen patrimonial de la mujer casada en derecho romano* (Rome/Madrid 1958) 13 ff. and 22 ff. (non vidi).

[116] Ulpianus (29 *ad ed.*) *Dig.* 15.1.7.1: "Ego autem puto non esse opus concedi peculium a domino servum habere, sed non adimi, ut habeat. Alia causa est peculii liberae administrationis: nam haec specialiter concedenda est." The end might be interpolated, but cf. M. Kaser, *RP* I[2] (1971) 287-88, n. 54. The *libera administratio peculii*, first mentioned by Proculus (7 *epist.*) *Dig.* 46.3.84, gives a slave the right to dispose of his *peculium*.

tions. The grant of free administration of the *peculium* was deemed to be tantamount to a general authorization to do business, and the principal's liability was not restricted to transactions related to a specific trade.[117] Thus, the grant of a *peculium* gave an agent more autonomy than his appointment as head of a business. On the other hand, his credit was diminished by the limit set on the liability of the principal.

It seems, however, that the jurists put some restriction on how the *peculium* was to be used. Iulianus, for instance, denies a son-in-power the right to make a deposit or to lend money from his *peculium*, on the ground that his father, by allowing him to administer his *peculium*, did not give him the right to squander it.[118] It is unlikely that this opinion was unanimously accepted, because it would have impaired the capacity of sons-in-power to enter a public career.[119] By contrast, a slave could lend money from his *peculium* as well as from his master's own account with the latter's permission, and the debt could be validly discharged by payment to the slave, even after his manumission or sale.[120] The same discrepancy between son and slave exists concerning borrowing. While slaves *institores* or with *peculium* were usually entitled to take out loans under certain conditions described above, sons-in-power were barred from this type of transaction by a senatorial decree of Vespasianic date, following the reported murder of a *paterfamilias* by his son Macedo under the pressure of his creditors.[121] Besides, the principal's liability could not be limited by the posting of a *proscriptio* forbidding certain, or all, types of transactions with the holder of the *peculium*, unless the latter was also an *institor*. As noted above, the *proscriptio* was used in order to cancel or reduce the scope of the appointment of an agent as head of a business, with the effect of protecting the principal against claims from third contracting parties.[122]

---

[117] Paulus (60 *ad ed.*) *Dig.* 15.1.46.

[118] Ulpianus (29 *ad ed.*), citing Iulianus, *Dig.* 14.6.3.2.

[119] Y. Thomas, *MEFRA* 94 (1982) 535-36.

[120] Alfenus Varus (2 *dig. a Paulo epit.*) *Dig.* 46.3.35.

[121] Ulpianus (29 *ad ed.*) *Dig.* 14.6.1 *pr.*; and M. Kaser, *RP* I[2] (1971) 532. This provision of the senatorial decree did not apply when the son-in-power had been duly appointed for the very purpose of borrowing or lending money, cf. Ulpianus (29 *ad ed.*), following Iulianus, *Dig.* 14.6.7.11; and Y. Thomas, *MEFRA* 94 (1982) 539.

[122] Gaius (9 *ad ed. prov.*) *Dig.* 15.1.29.1: "Etiamsi prohibuerit contrahi cum servo dominus, erit in eum de peculio actio;" and Paulus (4 *ad Plaut.*) *Dig.* 15.1.47

The extent of the liability of the principal was determined by the size of the *peculium* at the time of the judicial decision, after deduction of what the agent owed the principal or his dependents.[123] Thus, the principal clearly had an advantage over the agent's other creditors, because he was liable only for what remained in the *peculium* after deduction of what was owed to him. However, if the principal knew of the type of business activities carried out by his agent and had adopted an attitude of "laissez-faire" (*patientia* as opposed to *voluntas*), he became liable to a suit for distribution (*actio tributoria*) of the stock of the *peculium* (*merx peculiaris*), whereby he was treated as an external creditor. This remedy was given only if the creditors would have obtained less then expected, had they sued the principal on the *actio de peculio*.[124]

If the status of the principal or the agent changed—by transfer, manumission, emancipation, or death—or if the grant of a *peculium* was revoked by the principal, the *actio de peculio* was valid for one year after that,[125] whereas the other *actiones adiecticiae qualitatis* were perpetual. After the agent's manumission or emancipation, the *peculium* was either taken away by the principal or donated to the holder. In the latter case, the rights derived from the administration of the *peculium* had to be transferred to the holder by his former master/ *paterfamilias*.[126]

---

pr.: "Quotiens in taberna ita scriptum fuisset 'cum Ianuario servo meo geri negotium veto', hoc solum consecutum esse dominum constat, ne institoria teneatur, non etiam de peculio."

[123] Ulpianus (29 *ad ed.*) *Dig.* 15.1.30 *pr.* and 15.1.9.2-3, citing Servius.

[124] Ulpianus (29 *ad ed.*) *Dig.* 14.4.1; and Gai., *Inst.* 4.72: "Praeterea tributoria quoque actio in patrem dominumve constituta est, cum filius servusve in peculiari merce sciente patre dominove negotietur. Nam si quid eius rei gratia cum eo contractum fuerit, ita praetor ius dicit, ut quidquid in his mercibus erit quod inde receptum erit, ita pater dominusve inter se, si quid debebitur, et ceteros creditores pro rata portione distribuunt. Et si creditores querantur minus sibi distributum quam oporteret, in id quod deest hanc eis actionem pollicetur, quae, ut diximus, tributoria vocatur." The text is supplemented by *P.Oxy.* XVII 2103 (*fragmenta oxyrhynchitica*). Gaius warned elsewhere (*Inst.* 4.74a) that under certain circumstances the *actio tributoria* might have been less profitable than the *actio de peculio*, because the *actio tributoria* resulted in the division of the *peculium* among creditors, while the *actio de peculio* gave a right on the whole *peculium* to the creditor who brought the suit against the principal. A. Watson (1965) 185 points out that the *actio tributoria* is not attested in the Republican period, but it might of course be much older than the first textual reference to it (Labeo, cited by Ulpianus [29 *ad ed.*] *Dig.* 14.4.5.24; 14.4.7.4; and 14.4.9.2).

[125] Cf. *Dig.* 15.2; M. Kaser, *RP* I² (1971) 343, n. 21; and 607, n. 14.

[126] Paulus (11 *quaest.*) *Dig.* 15.1.53: "Si Sticho peculium cum manumitteretur

The *peculium* was held by the dependent with the consent of his master/*paterfamilias* ("domini permissu"), and was kept under separate account.[127] It could consist of any kind of property, land and movables, underslaves (*vicarii*) and credit.[128] According to Florentinus, the *peculium* was composed of the holder's personal savings, and of all profits made by him and not claimed by his master/*paterfamilias*.[129] It was not necessary for the master/*paterfamilias* to know precisely the content and increment of the *peculium*, as long as it appears that the master would not have objected to it, had he known.[130] The jurists discuss at great length the problems involved in the treatment of assets and liabilities of the *peculium* in case of a suit brought on the *peculium*. When a suit for distribution of the stock-in-trade (*merx peculiaris*) was brought, the holder who was involved in more than one business was considered to have divided his *peculium* into separate economic units (such as a shop or a factory) and distribution should be made according to the specific unit in connection to which the transaction was made. If the stock-in-trade in this particular unit was inferior to the amount of the liability, then remaining assets from other units should be taken into consideration. Only what arose from the stock (goods and the proceeds of their sale, in addition to the tools, equipment, and servile staff) was available for distribution, not the whole *peculium*.[131]

Slaves endowed with a *peculium* could appoint their underslaves (*vicarii*) as business agents (*institores* or *magistri navis*),[132] or grant them a *peculium* of their own. The master was liable on account of their transactions, presumably only to the extent of the *peculium* of the underslave, as if granted by the master himself.[133] In the same way, a principal was liable to a suit for distribution when he knew

---

ademptum non est, videtur concessum: debitores autem convenire nisi mandatis sibi actionibus non potest."

[127] Ulpianus (29 *ad ed.*), citing Tubero through Celsus (6 *dig.*), *Dig.* 15.1.5.4.

[128] Ulpianus (29 *ad ed.*) *Dig.* 15.1.7.4.

[129] Florentinus (11 *inst.*) *Dig.* 15.1.39.

[130] Pomponius (4 *ad Q. Mucium*) *Dig.* 15.1.49 *pr.*

[131] Ulpianus (29 *ad ed.*) *Dig.* 14.4.5.15-17; *idem*, *Dig.* 14.4.5.11 and 13, citing Labeo. Cf. A. di Porto (1984) 257-341.

[132] Ulpianus (28 *ad ed.*) *dig.* 14.1.1.19-20; cf. above.

[133] Celsus (6 *dig.*), following Tubero against Labeo, *Dig.* 15.1.6: "Definitio peculii quam Tubero exposuit, ut Labeo ait, ad vicariorum peculia non pertinet, quod falsum est: nam eo ipso, quod dominus servo peculium constituit, etiam vicario constituisse existimandus est."

that one of his underslaves was engaged in trading, whether the contract from which the third contracting party's claim arose was made
with the holder of the *peculium* or with his underslave *institor*.[134]

When the holder of the *peculium* was a son-in-power, third contracting parties could sue the son for the full debt, or the father to
the extent of the *peculium*. When the agent was a slave with *peculium*,
the third contracting party only held an *actio de peculio* against the
master, because no civil liability arose upon the slave.[135]

This technical survey of the five praetorian remedies available to
third contracting parties to sue principals on account of the contracts
negotiated with their agents illustrates the attention paid by Republican and early Imperial jurists to problems encountered in commercial life and arising from real situations. The level of sophistication
achieved by the Severan period was the result of a long development, the main stages of which will be described in the next section.

C. Historical development

The question of the origin and early development of the *actiones adiecticiae qualitatis* has been for decades a subject of controversy among
legal scholars.[136] Because of the lack of evidence, any theory about
this question is bound to remain speculative, but not necessarily
gratuitous. It seems fair to postulate that the history of indirect agency must follow a logical pattern, on the basis of which it should be
possible to reconstruct the circumstances under which the praetor
introduced these remedies. Because of similarities of form and purpose, the *actiones adiecticiae qualitatis* should be considered as a set of
remedies introduced consecutively rather than simultaneously, and
probably within a relatively short period of time, perhaps over half
a century. It will also be assumed that each of these remedies was
created to supplement, extend, or further define the scope of its fore-
runner(s).

Before the creation of the *actiones adiecticiae qualitatis*, third con-

---

[134] Ulpianus (29 *ad ed.*), citing Pomponius, *Dig.* 14.4.5.1-3: "Item parvi refert,
cum ipso servo contrahatur an cum institore eius."

[135] Ulpianus (63 *ad ed.*) *Dig.* 15.1.44; and *idem* (43 *ad Sab.*) *Dig.* 15.1.41.

[136] Even though the *actio tributoria* is not an *actio adiecticiae qualitatis* (cf. above),
it was included in the same chapter of the perpetual Edict and therefore will be
treated here together with the other five remedies.

tracting parties dealing with a dependent agent had no legal remedies against the master/*paterfamilias*. At the other end of the historical
process, third contracting parties had a choice of remedies not only
against the master/*paterfamilias* of a dependent agent, but also against
the principal of an extraneous agent. One of these remedies applied
to cases where the transaction carried out by the agent had been specifically authorized by the principal (*actio quod iussu*); others applied
to cases where the principal's instructions pertained to activities performed over a period of time and implying sometimes various types
of transactions (*actiones institoria* and *exercitoria*); others still applied to
cases where the involvement of the principal did not exist (*actio de in
rem verso*), or was minimal and consisted in an initial authorization
to do business on an independent basis (*actio de peculio*). The logical
thread that one might expect to recognize in this historical evolution
implies a transition from a restrictive system to a more liberal system. At the beginning, the principal was allowed to retain a tight
control over the transactions carried out by his dependent to the prejudice of the agent's flexibility; later on, the recruitment of agents
outside the inner circle of the extended Roman family was facilitated, and the agent was given more freedom in the conduct of wide-
ranging, loosely-defined business activities.

1. *The origin of the actiones adiecticiae qualitatis*

The conceptual origin of the *actiones adiecticiae qualitatis* is obscure. It
seems possible that the liability of the principal for his dependent's
transactions was conceived as a praetorian extension of his civil
liability for his dependent's delicts.[137] In his commentary on the

---

[137] For the delictual origin of contractual liability in Greek law, in the law of the
papyri, and in Roman law, cf. M. Kaser, *ZRG* 91 (1974) 156, n. 42; 158-60 (with
reference to H.J. Wolff, *ZRG* 74 [1957] 26-72); and 170-72. About the form of the
remedies sanctioning the master's liability for the delicts of his employees, cf.
M. Kaser, *RZ* (1966) 263-64; and *idem*, *RP* I² (1971) 513; and 606, n. 5. These
remedies originated either in civil law (*actiones noxales*, where both *intentio* and *condemnatio* mentioned the defendant's option either of surrendering the dependent to
the plaintiff or of paying him a monetary compensation) or in praetorian law (*actiones in factum* or *in id quod ad eum pervenit*). The rule is expressed by Ulpianus
(67 *ad ed.*) *Dig.* 50.17.149: "ex qua persona quis lucrum capit, eius factum praestare debet," operates in a passage by Labeo/Ulpianus (76 *ad ed.*) *Dig.* 44.4.4.17:
"neque enim esse aequum servi dolum amplius domino nocere, quam <in eo
negotio> in quo opera eius esset usus" (restored by F. Schulz, *ZRG* 33 [1912] 75),
serves to justify the *actiones in factum* (cf. Ulpianus [18 *ad ed.*] *Dig.* 4.9.7 *pr.* and *idem*

praetorian Edict, Ulpianus says that third contracting parties could
sue a shipper for the delicts of all sailors employed on his ship; by
contrast, Ulpianus stressed that the shipper's contractual liability
was restricted to the transactions carried out by the shipmaster
(*magister navis*) only.[138] Ulpianus's statement was meant to clarify a
situation in which third contracting parties were likely to form unrealistic expectations about the contractual liability of the shipper for
transactions carried out by any member of the crew, regardless of
the nature of his position. This ambiguity stems from the wording
of an earlier praetorian edict related to the liability of seamen, innkeepers, and stablekeepers for safekeeping of things deposited with
them.[139] In this edict, seamen were called *nautae*; according to Pomponius, the praetor meant shippers and shipmasters to the exclusion
of the rest of the crew.[140] It is remarkable that, when a dependent
shipmaster had wronged his passengers, his principal became liable
to an *actio in solidum* instead of an *actio noxalis*, provided that he had
actually appointed his dependent as shipmaster. Otherwise, his lia-

---

[28 *ad ed.*] *Dig.* 14.3.1 *pr.*), and contradicts the rule "neque enim debet nocere factum alterius ei qui nihil fecit" (Ulpianus [52 *ad ed.*] *Dig.* 39.1.5.5). Cf. R. Knütel,
"Die Haftung für Hilfspersonen im römischen Recht," *ZRG* 100 (1983) 340-443,
esp. 361-63 and 440-43.

[138] Ulpianus (28 *ad ed.*) *Dig.* 14.1.1.2: "Sed si cum quolibet nautarum sit contractum, non datur actio in exercitorem, quamquam ex delicto cuiusvis eorum, qui
navis navigandae causa in nave sint, detur actio in exercitorem: alia enim est contrahendi causa, alia delinquendi, si quidem qui magistrum praeponit, contrahi
cum eo permittit, qui nautas adhibet, non contrahi cum eis permittit, sed culpa et
dolo carere eos curare debet;" cf. also *idem* (38 *ad ed.*) *Dig.* 47.5.1, about the liability
of shippers (or shipmasters), innkeepers, and liverymen for theft committed by
their employees and permanent residents. Cf. R. Knütel, *ZRG* 100 (1983) 353-54,
who points out that an *actio in factum* was given in addition to the *actio furti*; and
N. Benke, "Zu Papinians *actio ad exemplum institoriae actionis*," *ZRG* 105 (1988) 592-
633, esp. 600-01.

[139] Ulpianus (14 *ad ed.*) *Dig.* 4.9.1 *pr.*: "Ait praetor: 'nautae caupones stabularii quod cuiusque salvum fore receperint nisi restituent, in eos iudicium dabo'."
Cf. M. Kaser, *RP* I² (1971) 585-86. N. Benke, *ZRG* 105 (1988) 607 and n. 74 suggests that Labeo had created an *actio quasi institoria* (*Dig.* 14.3.5.7-10, cf. below) on
the model of the *receptum nautae*, because the situation in this passage supposed a liability for safekeeping (*custodia*) (Gaius [15 *ad ed. prov.*] *Dig.* 4.9.5 *pr.*).

[140] Ulpianus (14 *ad ed.*), citing Pomponius, *Dig.* 4.9.1.2: "Qui sunt igitur, qui
teneantur, videndum est. Ait praetor 'nautae'. Nautam accipere debemus eum qui
navem exercet: quamvis nautae appellantur omnes, qui navis navigandae causa in
nave sint: sed de exercitore solummodo praetor sentit. Nec enim debet, inquit
Pomponius, per remigem aut mesonautam obligari, sed per se vel per navis magistrum: quamquam si ipse alicui e nautis committi iussit, sine dubio debeat obligari."

bility was limited to the extent of the *peculium* of the shipmaster.[141] The wording of the passage by Ulpianus seems to indicate that the original reparation (noxal surrender) was superseded by the obligation to pay a monetary compensation. Thus, the penalty aspect is becoming less visible.

Incidentally, there might be some reminiscence of an assumed noxal origin in Labeo's decision to grant an *actio quasi institoria* against an undertaker (*libitinarius*) whose slave mortician (*pollinctor*) had stripped the body entrusted to him presumably of his clothes and gold teeth, even though the third contracting party could have availed himself—or, could still also avail himself (?)—of an *actio furti et iniuriarum*.[142] In this passage, nothing implies that the third contracting party had contracted with the slave rather than with the undertaker for the preparation of the corpse for the funeral.[143] Labeo also presents a slightly different case: a baker appointed one of his slaves to deliver bread to customers on a daily basis. If the slave did not fulfill his obligations after accepting advance payment

---

[141] Ulpianus (14 *ad ed.*) *Dig.* 4.9.3.3: "Si filius familias aut servus receperit et voluntas patris domini intervenit, in solidum erit conveniendus. Item si servus exercitoris subripuit vel damnum dedit, noxalis actio cessabit, quia ob receptum suo nomine dominus convenitur. Sin vero sine voluntate exerceant, de peculio dabitur."

[142] Ulpianus (28 *ad ed.*), citing Labeo, *Dig.* 14.3.5.8: "Idem ait, si libitinarius servum pollinctorem habuerit isque mortuum spoliaverit, dandam in eum quasi institoriam actionem, quamvis et furti et iniuriarum actio competeret." The passage is considered heavily interpolated by R. Knütel, *ZRG* 100 (1983) 353, n. 45; cf. also P. Angelini, *BIDR* 71 (1968) 235, n. 23; A. Burdese, *BIDR* 74 (1971) 81, n. 53; G. Longo, *Studi Scherillo* II (1972) 613-14; and G. Hamza, *Index* 9 (1980) 227. It is accepted as classical by F. Serrao, *Enciclopedia del diritto* 21 (1971) 831, n. 19, who points out that the slave *pollinctor* was not a *praepositus* and that the liability of the *libitinarius* arises from an unlawful act instead of a contract, and sees in the creation of an *actio utilis* or *quasi institoria* "un'ardita innovazione di Labeo." Similarly, N. Benke, *ZRG* 105 (1988) 597-607, esp. 599 and 601, who considers that the *actio quasi institoria* was created by Labeo to sanction the master's liability in situations falling outside the scope of the *praepositio*.

[143] N. Benke's contention (*ZRG* 105 [1988] 604, n. 60) that *libitinarii* belonged to too high a social stratum to be expected to take part in the management of a funeral company (*libitina*) seems unwarranted, as it rests mainly on the evidence from Petronius, *Sat.* 38.14; and 78.6. Cf., *contra*, Val. Max. 5.2.10; and J.P. Bodel, "Graveyards and Groves: A Study of the *Lex Lucerina*," forthcoming in *AJAH* 10 (1985). For other instances of liability of principals for the delicts of their agents within an enterprise, cf. Ulpianus (28 *ad ed.*) *Dig.* 14.1.1.9 and *Dig.* 14.3.5.15; *idem* (28 *ad Sab.*), quoting Marcellus and Marcus Aurelius against Pomponius, *Dig.* 17.2.23.1 (no compensation of *commoda* and *damna* when the agent was an *institor servus unius ex sociis societati a domino praepositus*); R. Knütel, *ZRG* 100 (1983) 352, n. 43; and 425-28.

and subsequently went bankrupt, the liability of the baker who had authorized the collection of money in prepayment for a sale was not in doubt, but it is not clear whether or not the slave's bankruptcy was fraudulent.[144] In the third case discussed in the same passage by Labeo/Ulpianus, the dependent's delict is well established.[145] Upon his departure for a journey, a launderer (*fullo*) had invited potential customers to do business with his apprentices to whom he had entrusted his workshop with all its equipment.[146] One of the apprentices had made off with the clothes, and the jurists examine the question of the launderer's liability for his employee's delicts. Labeo states that the launderer would not be liable if the apprentice had been appointed in the capacity of *procurator*. However, the principal was declared fully liable if the apprentice had been appointed in the capacity of *institor*. Ulpianus adds that the launderer could be sued on the contract of work (*ex locato*)—but not on the man-

---

[144] Ulpianus (28 *ad ed.*), citing Labeo, *Dig.* 14.3.5.9: "Idem Labeo ait: si quis pistor servum suum solitus fuit in certum locum mittere ad panem vendendum, deinde is pecunia accepta praesenti, ut per dies singulos eis panem praestaret, conturbaverit, dubitari non oportet, quin, si permisit ei ita dari summas, teneri debeat." Cf. N. Benke, *ZRG* 105 (1988) 602-03.

[145] S. Solazzi, "*Procurator* ed *institor* in *D.*14.3.5.10," *SDHI* 9 (1943) 104-13 (= *Scritti di diritto romano* VI [1972] 548-56, esp. 548), where the author says that the use of "teneri" points toward a reference to Labeo's opinion; cf. also N. Benke, *ZRG* 105 (1988) 599.

[146] Ulpianus (28 *ad ed.*) *Dig.* 14.3.5.10: "Sed et cum fullo peregre proficiscens <aliquem> rogasset, ut discipulis suis, quibus tabernam instructam tradiderat, imperaret, post cuius profectionem vestimenta discipulus accepisset et fugisset, (Labeo scripsit) fullonem non teneri, si <discipulus> quasi procurator fuit relictus: sin vero quasi institor, teneri eum. Plane si adfirmaverit mihi recte me credere operariis suis, non institoria, sed ex locato tenebitur." The passage has been considered interpolated, but the substance is intact; cf. P. Angelini, *BIDR* 71 (1968) 236-37; A. Burdese, *BIDR* 74 (1971) 68, n. 23; and G. Longo, *Studi Scherillo* II (1972) 614. An object must be supplied to "rogasset," expressing "any potential customer." *Tradere* could be understood either as the basis of the *praepositio* or as a reference to a different contract (appointment to a procuratorship, mandate, *locatio conductio*). I follow here N. Benke, *ZRG* 105 (1988) 603, nn. 56-58, with parallels. The interpretation of "imperaret"—which has no expressed subject—is undoubtedly "to give order" in the sense of "to enter into a transaction with, to contract with, to do business with" (cf. Varro, *Rust.* 1.16.4; and Alfenus Varus [7 *dig.*] *Dig.* 38.1.26 *pr.*). In this case, the apprentices would be joint managers (*institores*). On the basis of the version in the *Basilica* (*BS* 18.1.5), some authors suggest a different interpretation featuring four characters instead of three: the fuller, the apprentice, the client, and an *institor/procurator* who would be the subject of "imperaret;" cf. S. Solazzi, *Scritti di diritto romano* VI (1972) 548-56; and R. Knütel, *ZRG* 100 (1983) 407-10.

ager's conduct—if he had guaranteed the trustworthiness of his employees.[147]

Noxal liability for two major statutory delicts was laid down in the *XII Tables* (ca. 450 B.C.) and in the *Lex Aquilia* (287 B.C.).[148] If the assumption of a correlation between delictual and contractual liability is correct, it provides a *terminus post quem* for the creation of the *actiones adiecticiae qualitatis*. Further, it is most likely that these remedies were contemporaneous, or slightly posterior, to the introduction of the formulary procedure in the third/second centuries B.C. Since most of these remedies are attested in Republican juristic sources, it can be said that the extension of the delictual liability of the master/*paterfamilias* to the concept of contractual liability of the principal must have occurred during the mid-Republican period. However, there is no evidence for the latter before the middle of the first century B.C.[149]

Some recent studies on the growth-pattern of the praetor's Edict shed some light on the legal environment in which the *actiones adiecticiae qualitatis* were created. J.M. Kelly demonstrates that while most private-law statutes were passed between 286 and 125 B.C., all datable praetorian remedies were created between the last quarter of the second century B.C. and Caesar's time. Thus, there seems to be a dividing line in the history of lawmaking around 125 B.C, perhaps as a consequence of an assumed clause in the *Lex Aebutia* (between 149 and 125) giving the praetor the power to amend the *ius civile*. As Roman praetors had issued edicts and created remedies since the third century, the history of edictal law can be divided into two phases. During the first phase (down to the middle of the second half of the second century B.C.), the praetor aimed at "shoring up" the *ius civile* by giving protection to a wronged party on the basis of his *imperium*. In the second phase, the Edict became "an instrument of open substantive change." According to Kelly, the part of the

---

[147] The second sentence is clearly by Ulpianus rather than Labeo and has been considered classical (cf. S. Solazzi, *Scritti di diritto romano* VI [1972] 553). There is some problem with the opposition *actio institoria* and *actio ex locato*, since the *actio institoria* would in any case be an *actio ex locato*. The distinction may have been between *actio institoria ex locato* and *actio directa ex locato* (cf. Solazzi 554).

[148] *XII Tables* 12.2.a, about theft (*furtum*); Gai., *Inst.* 4.75-76, about damage unjustly inflicted (*damnum iniuria datum*); *Dig.* 9.4. Cf. M. Kaser, *RP* I[2] (1971) 163-65; and 630-33; and A. Watson, *The Law of Obligations in the Later Roman Republic* (Oxford 1965) 234 for the date of the *Lex Aquilia*; and 274-80.

[149] A. Watson (1965) 185.

praetorian Edict representing effective changes in the substantive
law—to which the *actiones adiecticiae qualitatis* belong—seems to have
been incorporated late in the Edict history, i.e. not before the first
century B.C.[150]

A. Watson builds upon Kelly's conclusions and establishes that
the purpose of the praetorian law, starting at the end of the third century B.C., was at first to make "alterations in the measure of dam-
ages." By 160 and until the 140's, the praetors introduced major
changes in the substantive law by creating individual *actiones in factum* (such as the *actio in factum adversus nautas, caupones, stabularios*). By
the third quarter of the second century, and perhaps before in some
cases, the *actiones bonae fidei* (on sales, leases, partnerships, and man-
dates) were available. There is no evidence for any new edict between the time of Plautus and 118, but after that date the praetors
issued several edicts modifying the *ius civile* and creating new remedies and new legal concepts.[151]

Although the dates proposed by Kelly and Watson are only *termini
ante quos*, it should be possible to circumscribe a period during which
the *actiones adiecticiae qualitatis* were created. Since the *Lex Aebutia* is
not securely dated, it is impossible to establish a precise *terminus post
quem* for their creation. The middle of the second century B.C. seems
to be the earliest date acceptable. As the *actio institoria* is mentioned
by Servius Sulpicius Rufus who died in 43 B.C.,[152] the time span
is reduced to approximately one century. It may be worth pointing
out that Servius was the very first jurist to write a commentary on
the praetorian Edict, so that there would be no reason to expect a

---

[150] J.M. Kelly, "The Growth-Pattern of the Praetor's Edict," *IJ* 1 (1966)
341-55, where the author examines Papinianus's statement about the competence
and the functions of praetors as lawmakers (Pap. [2 *def.*] *Dig.* 1.1.7.1: "Ius praetorium est, quod praetores introduxerunt adiuvandi vel supplendi vel corrigendi iuris
civilis gratia propter utilitatem publicam"), which he sees as reflecting the result
of a historical process rather than the original situation.

[151] A. Watson, *Law Making in the Later Roman Republic* (Oxford 1974) 31-62
(= *JRS* 60 [1970] 105-19, slightly revised).

[152] Ulpianus (28 *ad ed.*) *Dig.* 14.3.5.2: "Nam et Servius libro primo ad Brutum
ait, si quid cum insulario gestum sit vel eo, quem quis aedificio praeposuit vel
frumento coemendo, in solidum eum teneri." An indirect allusion is found in a text
by Pomponius (6 *ad Sab.*) *Dig.* 33.7.15 *pr.*: "Si ita testamento scriptum sit: 'quae
tabernarum exercendarum instruendarum pistrini cauponae causa facta parataque
sunt, do lego', his verbis Servius respondit et caballos, qui in pistrinis essent, et
pistores, et in cauponio institores et focariam, mercesque, quae in his tabernis
essent, legatas videri." Cf. below.

quotation from earlier jurists.[153] Further, Ulpianus specifies that Servius's opinion is excerpted from his first book *Ad Brutum* (out of two appended to his *Ad edictum*),[154] which may provide a clue regarding the creation of the *actio institoria*. M. Iunius Brutus was a second-century-B.C. praetor (around 140) and jurist who commented on the *ius civile* in three (or seven) books.[155] Thanks to Cicero, we know that Brutus owned several agricultural estates in Privernum, in the region of Lacus Albanus, and in Tivoli, in addition to a bath establishment. The management of these economic units must have been entrusted either to agents or to lessees.[156] Brutus's interest in estate management surfaces in one of the very few allusions to his legal opinions,[157] and it is possible that his activity as a landowner, magistrate, and jurist lead to the creation of the *actiones adiecticiae qualitatis*.[158]

Another element points towards a late-second-century date for the introduction of the *actiones adiecticiae qualitatis*: as mentioned above, the formula of these remedies was characterized by a transposition of persons from the *intentio* (containing the name of the agent) to the *condemnatio* (containing the name of the principal). Through Gaius, we know of another remedy presenting the same formula, which can be dated on the basis of its name (*Formula Rutiliana*) to 118 B.C.[159]

---

[153] W. Kunkel, *An Introduction to Roman Legal and Constitutional History*[2] (Oxford 1973) 105. Cf. also P. Stein, "The Place of Servius Sulpicius Rufus in the Development of Roman Legal Science," in O. Behrends *et al.* (eds.), *Festschrift F. Wieacker zum 70. Geb.* (Göttingen 1978) 175-84.

[154] Pomponius (*sing. enchir.*) *Dig.* 1.2.2.44. F. Wieacker, *Römische Rechtsgeschichte* (Munich 1988) 602-07, esp. 605, considers that *Ad Brutum Libri II* is the actual title of the commentary on the Edict.

[155] Pomponius (*sing. enchir.*) *Dig.* 1.2.2.39; and Cic. *Brut.* 34.130. F. Wieacker (1988) 542-43.

[156] Cic., *De Or.* 2.55.224 (= *Clu.* 51.140-141). Cf. V.I. Kuziščin, *La grande proprietà agraria nell' Italia romana* (Rome 1984) [1976] 42, nn. 99-100. About managers of agricultural estates, cf. below, Chapter Three; and of baths, cf. below, Chapter Five.

[157] Cic., *Fin.* 1.4.12, about offsprings of slaves attached to an estate, considered as part of the return of this estate.

[158] A. Watson (1974) 51-52 points out that Brutus is known to have expressed opinions on the subject of *usufructus, actio legis Aquiliae, usucapio, postliminium, in diem addictio, furtum, lex Atinia*, and the heir's action on *furtum*, but there is no reference to the praetor's Edict. Cf. O. Lenel, *Palingenesia iuris civilis* I (Leipzig 1889) 77-78. F. Wieacker (1988) 605, n. 65 suggests, however, that Servius's dedication of his commentary to Brutus was politically motivated.

[159] Gai., *Inst.* 4.35. Cf. M. Kaser, *RZ* (1966) 263; and 310-11; and F. Wieacker (1988) 544. About P. Rutilius Rufus, the creator of the *Formula Rutiliana*, and the

It seems likely that all remedies of this type were introduced around the same time.

2. *The chronological order of the introduction of the actiones adiecticiae qualitatis*

In his study of the early history of the *actio de in rem verso*, G. MacCormack writes that, with regard to the relationship of this remedy with the *actio de peculio*, "the praetor is unlikely to have introduced two distinct heads of liability in the same edict at the same time."[160] Therefore, we should think of the *actiones adiecticiae qualitatis* as being created successively.

Which remedy was the oldest? This question can be answered only in a tentative way. E. Costa thinks that the *actio quod iussu* was probably older than the *actiones exercitoria* and *institoria*.[161] His argument is based on a text of Gaius:

> At first, when a transaction had been carried out by an agent with the authorization of the master/*paterfamilias*, the praetor created a remedy for full liability against the latter; and this was right, since the third contracting party trusts the credit of the principal rather than that of the dependent. On the same pattern, the praetor created two other remedies, called *actio exercitoria* and *actio institoria*.[162]

Other texts emphasize this connection between *iussum* and *voluntas* on which the appointment of *institores* stands, and they suggest that *institores* "acted as if they were under the benefit of a *iussum* from their principals."[163] If *iussum* implies *voluntas*, the reverse is not

---

date of his praetorship, cf. F. Münzer, *PW* 1A1 (1914) cols. 1269-80, esp. 1271, s.v. Rutilius no. 321.

[160] G. MacCormack, *Studi Biscardi* II (1982) 324.

[161] E. Costa, *Le azioni exercitoria e institoria* (Parma 1891) 24; cf. also G. Pugliese, *Labeo* 3 (1957) 308, n.1; *contra*, S. Solazzi, *Scritti di diritto romano* IV (1963) 259-62.

[162] Gai., *Inst.* 4.70-71: "Inprimis itaque si iussu patris dominive negotium gestum erit, in solidum praetor actionem in patrem dominumve conparavit; et recte, quia qui ita negotium gerit, magis patris dominive quam filii servive fidem sequitur. (71) Eadem ratione conparavit duas alias actiones, exercitoriam et institoriam." "Inprimis" and "eadem ratione" have been considered interpolated by S. Solazzi, *Scritti di diritto romano* IV (1963) 261-62.

[163] Paulus (4 *ad Plaut.*), citing Iulianus, *Dig.* 12.1.29: "Si institorem servum dominus habuerit, posse dici Iulianus ait etiam condici ei posse, quasi iussu eius contrahatur, a quo praepositus sit." G. and M. Sautel, *Mélange H. Lévy-Bruhl* (1959) 262, n. 5, who consider that the *actio quod iussu* is later than the *actio institoria*, typically label the situation described in this text, where *iussum* is earlier than *praeposi-*

necessarily true, and *voluntas* without *iussum* may represent a more sophisticated ground for liability, thus belonging to a later stage in the development of legal means sanctioning indirect agency. In other words, it is more logical that the Romans accepted at first the principle of the master's liability for specifically authorized transactions performed by his dependent, before extending it to all transactions performed by an appointed manager.[164]

The main objection to Costa's interpretation is that, except for Gaius's text, there is no direct allusion to the use, or even existence, of the *actio quod iussu* during the Republican period.[165] It is true that the silence of our sources is meaningless, because the Republican period has yielded little technical material anyway, especially of the kind that would express the need for a specific remedy. It is nevertheless puzzling to note that the late-Republican jurist Alfenus Varus presents a case where this remedy would have provided an easy, not to say obvious, solution.[166] The omission of the *actio quod iussu* in a case where the master had reportedly given instructions to his slave to buy replacement oxen has been interpreted as an indication that the *actio quod iussu* was still unknown in Alfenus's time.[167] One could object that in this particular case the necessary conditions were not fulfilled for the *actio quod iussu* to be available. There is no indication, for instance, that the master's instruction to his slave had been disclosed to the third contracting party.

---

tio, as "antihistorique." *Cod. Iust.* 4.25.6 (A.D. 294): "Qui secutus domini voluntatem cum servo ipsius habuit contractum, ad instar actionis institoriae recte de solido dominum convenit." Cf. also *Inst. Iust.* 4.7.8: "Illud in summa admonendi sumus id, quod iussu patris dominive contractum fuerit quodque in rem eius versum fuerit, directo quoque posse a patre dominove condici. Tamquam si principaliter cum ipso negotium gestum esset. Ei quoque, qui vel exercitoria vel institoria actione tenetur, directo posse condici placet, quia huius quoque iussu contractum intellegitur."

[164] M. Lemosse, *RD* 62 (1984) 228, n. 12, for whom "l'opinion dominante [represented, for instance, by G. and M. Sautel, *Mél. H. Lévy-Bruhl* (1959) 262] est très douteuse."

[165] The first mention is by Labeo, cited by Ulpianus (29 *ad ed.*) *Dig.* 15.4.1.9. Of course, *iussum* in the sense of special instruction given by a master is attested much earlier (Plaut., *Pseud.* 1092; Cat. *Agr.* 5.3), which does not mean that the master's liability was sanctioned by then.

[166] Alfenus (2 *dig.*) *Dig.* 15.3.16.

[167] A. Watson (1965) 187-88; A. Claus (1973) 76; and G. MacCormack, *Studi Biscardi II* (1982) 327, n. 20. W.W. Buckland, *The Roman Law of Slavery. The Condition of the Slave in Private Law from Augustus to Justinian* (New York 1908) 166-69 shows some uncertainty on this matter.

The absence of early reference to the *actio quod iussu* can be explained in different ways. First, it is possible that the *actio quod iussu* was partly superseded by other remedies at an early date, and thus retained only a subsidiary role, which ensured its survival.[168] A. di Porto convincingly argues that the *iussum* could be used as guarantee in the case of a collective enterprise.[169] Third contracting parties doing business with a *servus communis cum peculio* had an *actio de peculio aut de in rem verso* against each of the slave's joint owners, who were liable to the extent of the slave's *peculium*. If the limited liability of the joint owners seemed to offer insufficient security, third contracting parties could request that one of the owners give a special authorization (*iussum*), thus engaging his own full liability in addition to the limited liability of the other joint owners.

To sum up, Gaius's passage cannot be rejected on textual or logical grounds. This leads me to favor the chronological priority of the *actio quod iussu* over the other *actiones adiecticiae qualitatis*.

Which remedy was introduced next? Modern scholars have attempted to find in the perpetual Edict of the urban praetor, published ca. A.D. 130 by Salvius Iulianus at the request of the emperor Hadrian, a basis to establish the chronological order in which the *actiones adiecticiae qualitatis* had been created. There is no reason to question Lenel's reconstruction.[170] In the perpetual Edict, the respective remedies were arranged in the following order: (1) *actio exercitoria*; (2) *actio institoria*; (3) *actio tributoria*; (4) *actio de peculio*; (5) *actio de in rem verso*; and (6) *actio quod iussu*. This arrangement is reflected by the order of the respective titles dealing with them in the *Digest* and is based on the inscriptions identifying the source of individual excerpts from the *Digest*. For instance, Ulpianus discusses the *actiones exercitoria* and *institoria* in the twenty-eighth book of his commentary *Ad edictum*, and the *actiones tributoria, de peculio, de in rem verso*, and *quod iussu* in the twenty-ninth book. On the other hand, Paulus discusses the *actio exercitoria* in the twenty-ninth book *Ad edictum*, the *actio institoria* in the twenty-ninth and thirtieth books, and the other remedies in the thirtieth book.

The *Digest* also provides some information about the internal

---

[168] The *actio quod iussu* is still mentioned in the *Theodosian Code* (2.31.1 = *Cod. Iust.* 4.26.13, A.D. 422).

[169] A. di Porto (1984) 249-52.

[170] O. Lenel, *Das Edictum Perpetuum*[3] (Leipzig 1927) = *FIRA* I[2], no. 65, pp. 335-89, esp. 355-56.

structure of the perpetual Edict, thus allowing us to reconstruct the place of the respective *actiones adiecticiae qualitatis* in it. Gaius discusses the arrangement of these six remedies in his commentary on the provincial Edict. He describes the *actiones exercitoria, institoria*, and *tributoria*, as "actiones superiores," before discussing the three other remedies granted only when the so-called superior remedies were not available.[171] Another text also shows that all six remedies were arranged in a definite order, as Paulus refers to the *actiones de peculio, de in rem verso*, and *quod iussu* as "inferiora edicta."[172] Since Ulpianus speaks of a "triplex edictum" about these three remedies,[173] it seems logical to assume that the "actiones superiores" were also grouped in a "triplex edictum," although it is not clear what the *actio tributoria* has in common with the *actiones institoria* and *exercitoria*. Further, it is obvious that the formula of the *actio tributoria*,[174] which belongs to the "actiones superiores," presupposes the existence of the *actio de peculio*, which belongs to the "inferioribus edictis." This suggests that the order in which the respective *actiones adiecticiae qualitatis* are listed in the perpetual Edict and discussed in the *Digest* does not reflect the chronological order of their creation. Thus, the order

---

[171] Gaius (9 *ad ed. prov.*) *Dig.* 14.5.1: "Omnia proconsul agit, ut qui contraxit cum eo, qui in aliena potestate sit, etiamsi deficient superiores actiones, id est exercitoria institoria tributoriave, nihilo minus tamen in quantum ex bono et aequo res patitur suum consequatur. Sive enim iussu eius, cuius in nomine iudicium pollicetur: sive non iussu, sed tamen in rem eius versum fuerit, eatenus introducit actionem, quatenus in rem eius versum fuerit: sive neutrum eorum sit, de peculio actionem constituit." Let us note that the order in which the last three remedies are listed by Gaius is the opposite of the order retained by Lenel in his reconstruction of the perpetual Edict.

[172] Paulus (30 *ad ed.*) *Dig.* 14.3.17.1: "Si servum Titii institorem habueris, vel tecum ex hoc edicto vel cum Titio ex inferioribus edictis agere potero."

[173] Ulpianus (29 *ad ed.*) *Dig.* 15.1.1.1: "Est autem triplex hoc edictum: aut enim de peculio aut de in rem verso aut quod iussu hinc oritur actio."

[174] Cf. *FIRA* I², no. 65, p. 355, par. 103: "Qui merce peculiari sciente eo, in cuius potestate erit, negotiabitur, si quid cum eo eius mercis nomine contractum erit, eius, quod ex ea merce erit eove nomine receptum erit, eum, in cuius potestate erit, si quid ei debebitur, cum creditoribus mercis pro rata eius quod cuique debebitur in tributum vocabo." Cf. also Ulpianus (29 *ad ed.*) *Dig.* 14.4.1 *pr.*: "Huius quoque edicti non minima utilitas est, ut dominus, qui alioquin in servi contractibus privilegium habet (quippe cum de peculio dumtaxat teneatur, cuius peculii aestimatio deducto quod domino debetur fit), tamen, si scierit servum peculiari merce negotiari, velut extraneus creditor ex hoc edicto in tributum vocatur." It is not clear to me whether the *merx peculiaris* consists of the running stock only, or includes all assets and liabilities, regardless of the situation of the dependent toward his principal; cf. A. di Porto (1984) 54-57 and 211 ff. who speaks of a "catena di patrimoni separati" and of "un'entità patrimoniale separata dal (*rectius*: entro il) peculio."

in which the six remedies were listed in the perpetual Edict could have been determined by (unspecified) criteria other than chronological, for instance on the basis of their importance in the early second century A.D. Consequently, even a reverse chronological sequence cannot be excluded. This comes as no surprise, since it is well known that even though the praetorian Edict had been little altered during the first century A.D., Iulianus made some significant changes of form, though not of substance, by rewording or rephrasing various sections, and by altering the order of topics.[175]

As noted above, the six remedies could be divided into two groups, based on the extent of the liability of the principal, full or limited. Therefore, the *actio quod iussu* should have been included originally in the same *triplex edictum*—provided that the grouping by three is original, which is dubious—as the other *actiones in solidum* (*exercitoria* and *institoria*). While accepting the possibility of the priority of the *actio quod iussu* over the *actiones exercitoria* and *institoria*, G. Pugliese suggests that the *actio quod iussu* had been transferred into the (second) *edictum triplex* by Iulianus on account of the growing importance of the other remedies.[176]

As to the relationship of the *actio quod iussu* with the *actiones de in rem verso* and *de peculio*, the common denominator between them is that all three were available only when the agent was a dependent of the principal. Gaius records the sequence (1) *actio quod iussu*; (2) *actio de in rem verso*; and (3) *actio de peculio*,[177] although the last two remedies were usually considered together and in the reverse order in the classical period (*actio de peculio vel de in rem verso*).[178] Once more, Gaius's description reflects the historical order, since it seems now established that the *actio de in rem verso* was created independently from, and slightly earlier than, the *actio de peculio*.[179]

The logic behind the creation of the *actiones adiecticiae qualitatis* becomes clearer when one considers that their main purpose was to

---

[175] F. Schulz, *History of Roman Legal Science* (Oxford 1946) 127.

[176] G. Pugliese, *Labeo* 3 (1957) 308, n. 1.

[177] Gaius (9 *ad ed. prov.*) *Dig.* 14.5.1 (cf. above), wrongly considered interpolated by many authors (cf. P. Fabricius [1926] 11, n. 11). Those who reject this passage as interpolated must also reject Marcianus (4 *reg.*) *Dig.* 22.1.32.3 and Ulpianus (29 *ad ed.*) *Dig.* 15.3.5.2.

[178] Gai., *Inst.* 4.74a; *Inst. Iust.* 4.7.4; M. Kaser, *RP* I[2] (1971) 606, n. 7; G. MacCormack, *Studi Biscardi* II (1982) 319-39; and *idem*, *SDHI* 48 (1982) 318-67.

[179] G. MacCormack, *Studi Biscardi* II (1982) 324, who suggests that the creation of the *actio de in rem verso* was connected with the creation of the *condictio*.

facilitate business by allowing people to rely on agents to carry out legal transactions while playing on three variable factors:

(1) the extent of the liability of the principal (liability factor);

(2) the sphere of competence of the agent and the extent of the principal involvement in supervising the activity of the agent (flexibility factor);

and (3) the nature of the relationship between agent and principal (status factor).

The *actio quod iussu*—the priority of which has been postulated above—provides for the full liability of the principal, calls for the strictest control over the activity of the agent, and requires a status of dependency on the part of the agent in relation with the principal. Taking this as a starting point, we have then the choice between three patterns of development:

(a) if the emphasis rested on the liability factor, all legal remedies entailing the principal's full liability must have been created prior to the legal remedies entailing his limited liability, and the chronological order of the creation of the various remedies would be: (1) *actiones quod iussu, institoria* and *exercitoria*; (2) *actiones de in rem verso, de peculio,* and *tributoria* (the order within each group is for now irrelevant);

(b) if the emphasis rested on the flexibility factor, we would expect the same order, since *iussum* and *praepositio* imposed various restrictions on the agent's activity and implied a certain level of control on the part of the principal over his agent's activity. These restrictions no longer exist in the second group, as the principal was liable for any transaction performed by his agent;

(c) if the emphasis rested on the status factor, then the order would be modified to the effect that the *actiones institoria* and *exercitoria* would have been created later than the others, unless we admit that originally, these two remedies (*institoria* and *exercitoria*) were only granted when the agent was a dependent of the principal. P. Fabricius even suggests that the "gewaltfreie Institor" was a creation of the classical jurists, who recommend giving an *actio utilis* to third contracting parties against principal for transactions carried out by extraneous agents.[180] This point will be discussed later on, but it is sensible to surmise that the *actiones institoria* and *exercitoria* underwent an evolution whereby the position of agent, first reserved to members of

---

[180] P. Fabricius (1926) 30-32.

the household, was subsequently open to outsiders. It remains to be established when and under what circumstances this reform took place.

To return to the early history of the *actiones adiecticiae qualitatis*, I shall suggest, on the basis of the arguments developed in the preceding paragraphs, that the most likely chronological order of creation was (1) *actio quod iussu*; (2) *actiones institoria* and *exercitoria* (cf. below); (3) *actio de in rem verso*; (4) *actio de peculio*; and finally (5) *actio tributoria*. This hypothesis is consistent with Ulpianus's remark that the Roman praetor chose to attend first to those contracts that gave rise to a remedy carrying full liability on the part of the principal before turning to those that gave rise to a remedy on the *peculium*. In this passage, he refers to the original order of the edict, and not to the actual form of the perpetual Edict, to which he switches in the next passage.[181]

3. *The relationship between actio institoria and actio exercitoria*

In the previous section, *actio institoria* and *actio exercitoria* have been treated together. It is necessary at this point to determine which one was created first. The answer to this question is affected by one's overall view of the Roman economy of the mid-Republican period. As noted above, modern scholars seem to have been almost unanimously in favor of the priority of the *actio exercitoria*.[182] The main arguments used to support this thesis are the following:

(1) the *actio exercitoria* was described before the *actio institoria* in the perpetual Edict;

---

[181] Ulpianus (29 *ad ed.*) *Dig.* 15.1.1 *pr.*-1: "Ordinarium praetor arbitratus est prius eos contractus exponere eorum qui alienae potestati subiecti sunt, qui in solidum tribuunt actionem, sic deinde ad hunc pervenire , ubi de peculio datur actio. (1) Est autem triplex hoc edictum: aut enim de peculio aut de in rem verso aut quod iussu hinc oritur actio." The main problem with this text is that the *actio quod iussu* should have been treated with the first group of remedies. Therefore, it is necessary to admit that the two excerpts (*pr.* and 1) are not logically connected. The order in which all three remedies are listed in the latter excerpt reflects the subsidiary nature of both the *actio de in rem verso* and the *actio quod iussu* in reference to the *actio de peculio* in Iulianus's time.

[182] A. Kirschenbaum (1987) 94-96, with references to E. Costa (1891) 31-36; P. Fabricius (1926) 24-25; P. Huvelin, *Etudes d'histoire du droit commercial romain* (Paris 1929) 177-83; S. Solazzi, *Scritti di diritto romano* IV (1963) 243-64, who lists, 243, n. 1, the position of previous authors on the subject; cf. also A. Watson (1965) 191, n. 2; and A. Claus (1973) 74-83.

(2) the *actio exercitoria* is more sophisticated than the *actio institoria*;

(3) the *actio exercitoria* is similar to the *actio institoria* in that a ship-master is not different from a business manager, suggesting that if the *actio institoria* were older, the *actio exercitoria* would have been superfluous;

(4) the name of the *actio institoria* is surprising because it refers to the agent, whereas one should expect a reference to the principal, whose liability was at stake. The inadequacy of the term would be a sign that the *actio institoria* is a later, somewhat clumsy, addition to the *actio exercitoria*;

(5) the economic development of Rome and Italy after the Second Punic War, characterized by the soaring importance of seaborne trade, provided the momentum for the creation of the praetorian remedies. Borrowing from Greek maritime laws, the peregrine praetor would have dealt first with shipmasters, before turning his attention to business managers.

The first point has been dealt with in the previous section, where it has been shown that classical and post-classical jurists discuss the *actiones adiecticiae qualitatis* in the order selected by Salvius Iulianus in the final draft of the perpetual Edict, which does not reflect the chronological order of the creation of the respective remedies. P. Huvelin and S. Solazzi illustrate this fact with the case of the *bonorum possessio contra tabulas* (*Dig.* 37.4 and 5) and *secundum tabulas* (*Dig.* 37.11), the former being mentioned first in the Edict because it was more "useful and practical" than the latter, although there is no doubt that the *bonorum possessio secundum tabulas* was created before the *bonorum possessio contra tabulas*.[183] The same explanation may apply to the place of the *actio exercitoria* with regard to the *actio institoria* in the perpetual Edict.[184]

The second point is equally unconvincing. It is true that the scope of the *actio exercitoria*, as reflected in the *Digest*, is wider than the scope of the *actio institoria*. In the first title (14.1), some technical problems concerning the application of this remedy were regarded as deser-

---

[183] P. Huvelin (1929) 182; and S. Solazzi, *Scritti di diritto romano* IV (1963) 244, n. 8.

[184] The practical priority of the *actio exercitoria* as opposed to the historical priority of the *actio institoria* is highlighted by Ulpianus (28 *ad ed.*) *Dig.* 14.1.1 *pr.*: "aequum fuit eum, qui magistrum navi imposuit, teneri, ut tenetur, qui institorem tabernae vel negotio praeposuit, cum sit maior necessitas contrahendi cum magistro quam institore."

ving a detailed discussion, while there is no parallel in the second
title (14.3). This discrepancy, however, might be ascribed to the
method of the Compilers, or to the fact that people involved in seaborne trade ended up requiring a more elaborate system of protection. As Solazzi himself points out, this would have been a good
motive for the creation of the *actio exercitoria* to compensate and supplement the lack of flexibility of the *actio institoria*.[185]

The third point is closely related to the second, because it rests on
the same texts by Ulpianus (*Dig.* 14.1.1.5 and 20). Solazzi, who considers the texts interpolated, concludes that

> they prove that the liability of a shipper was not more rigorous than
> that of a principal operating a business. The standards of liability were
> the same for both remedies. If the *actio institoria* had been introduced
> earlier, the praetor would have saved himself the trouble of creating
> the *actio exercitoria*, because the *praepositio* was a very large concept also
> applicable to seaborne trade.[186]

The problem with such a view is that it rests on the debatable assumption that the process of interpolation changed the substance (as
well as the form) of the passage in such a way that it meant something very different from what the authors originally intended. This
assumption seems unwarranted to me, and I consider it very likely
that the *actio exercitoria* represented indeed an improvement over the
actio institoria in terms of its adequacy with regard to the specificity
of the problems associated with seaborne trade.

The fourth point represents at first sight a real puzzle. The adjective *institoria* seems to refer to the agent, while the corresponding
word *exercitoria* refers to the principal. How can this semantic discrepancy in the terminology be explained? It is unlikely that the praetor would have been content with using an inappropriate term—or
at least a term acknowledged as conceptually inconsistent with that
designating the twin remedy—to describe the *actio institoria* as opposed to the *actio exercitoria*. It is contrived to argue that there is no

---

[185] S. Solazzi, *Scritti di diritto romano* IV (1963) 245, n. 13. Other passages have
been interpreted as suggesting that the *actio institoria* was formed on the model of
the *actio exercitoria* ("exemplo actionis exercitoriae," cf. Ulpianus [28 *ad ed.*] *Dig.*
14.3.7.1 and 14.3.13.2), but since elsewhere the *actio exercitoria* is set in contrast to
the *actio institoria* (Ulpianus [28 *ad ed.*] *Dig.* 14.1.1 *pr.*; 14.1.1.5; 14.1.1.20), the argument has little value. Besides, the former series of texts can be explained by the
order in which the two remedies were listed and discussed in the perpetual Edict.
[186] S. Solazzi, *Scritti di diritto romano* IV (1963) 249.

word in Latin to designate the principal operating a *taberna* or *officina*, because it would have been possible to call both remedies *actiones exercitoriae*, in view of the fact that the word *exercitor* originally refers to any kind of businessman.[187] The addition of a qualifying label—such as *institoris* or *de institore*—to specify that the remedy was a variant of the original *actio exercitoria* would have been more acceptable than using an incorrect, and otherwise rare, word.[188]

The solution to this puzzle seems to lie elsewhere, for instance in the meaning of the word *institor*. In Chapter One, I pointed out that *institores* in the literary sources are never represented as agents, but always as small, seemingly independent businessmen.[189] This usage is best illustrated by the scholiast of Horace's *Epodes*, who sets *institores* and *exercitores* on equal ground.[190] *Institores* are not considered as agents, and the distinction between the two categories was based on the type of business they engaged in (land based *vs.* seaborne trade). By contrast, *institores* in the legal sources are always identified as appointed agents (*praepositi*),[191] although some cases remain ambiguous. Labeo, for instance, says that the shopkeeper who dispatched his slave abroad to purchase goods for his own supply will be held liable "loco institoris."[192] In this passage "loco" can be

---

[187] Ulpianus (4 *ad ed.*) *Dig.* 2.13.4 *pr.*: "Praetor ait: 'Argentariae mensae exercitores rationem, quae ad se pertinet, edent adiecto die et consule'" (= *FIRA* I², no. 65, section 3, par. 9a); *idem* (38 *ad ed.*) *Dig.* 47.5.1 *pr.*: "In eos, qui naves cauponas stabula exercebunt, si quid a quoquo eorum quosve ibi habebunt furtum factum esse dicetur, iudicium datur, sive furtum ope consilio exercitoris factum sit, sive eorum cuius, qui in ea navi navigandi causa esset;" *idem* (1 *ad leg. Iul. et Pap.*) *Dig.* 23.2.43.9: "Si qua cauponam exercens in ea corpora quaestuaria habeat, ..." Paulus, *Sent.* 2.31.16: "Quaecumque in caupona vel in meritorio stabulo diversoriove perierint, in exercitores eorum furti actio competit." Cf. *TLL* 5.2 (1953) 1389-90, section 2 ("qui exsequitur, factitat negotium"), a. *exercitor navis*; b. *exercitor aliorum negotiorum.* Even though neither the noun nor the adjective—in this particular acceptation—are found in any text earlier than Gaius, it was obviously used in the praetorian Edict, and therefore belongs to the Republican period.

[188] The adjective *institorius* is not used in Classical Latin, except in the legal sources. The neutral *institorium* ("business") in Suet. *Nero* 27.3 constitutes a unique, relatively late case.

[189] This fact has already been noticed by E. Costa (1891) 35.

[190] ΣHor., *Epod.* 17.20: "Duo sunt genera negotiatorum: institores et exercitores."

[191] Gai., *Inst.* 4.71: "Idem autem institoria vocatur, quia qui tabernae (aut cuilibet negotiationi) praeponitur, institor appellatur;" and Ulpianus (28 *ad ed.*) *Dig.* 14.3.5 *pr.*: "Cuicumque igitur negotio praepositus sit, institor recte appellabitur."

[192] Ulpianus (28 *ad ed.*), citing Labeo, *Dig.* 14.3.5.7: "Sed et si tabernarius servum suum peregre mitteret ad merces comparandas et sibi mittendas, loco insti-

understood either as "instead of" or as "as if he were in the legal situation of." In the first case, "institor" refers to the slave dispatched abroad, whereas in the second case, "institor" refers to the "tabernarius," i.e. the principal. A similar ambiguity is found in a text by Paulus, where trainers in charge of a workshop or store are held fully liable for the contracts of their apprentices.[193] What is remarkable is that the remedy is given "in magistros vel institores," where the word "institores" clearly designates the principals, unless the apprentices acted as subagents. If "institores" referred to "discipuli" Paulus would have directed the remedy "in magistros *aut* institores." Finally, Papinianus presents the case of a slave who had committed himself to pay someone else's debt, although he had been appointed for the specific purpose of lending money. The jurist rightly decides that the principal should not be held liable "ut institor." The text as it stands in the manuscript clearly refers to the principal as "institor" and consequently has been corrected by modern commentators. In view of the interpretation presented here, namely that *institor* does not invariably refers to a business manager, this correction is uncalled-for.[194]

From a linguistic point of view, *institor* is formed on the verb *insistere* (rather than *instare*), which has the double meaning "to stand in *or* on" and "to establish someone in a certain position."[195] It is clear that in no case *institor* should be made the equivalent of a passive past participle, referring to "one who has been established." Most recently, M. Fruyt studied the semantic development of words ending with the syllable *-tor* and came to the conclusion that they

---

toris habendum Labeo scripsit." Cf. also Paulus (1 *decr.*) *Dig.* 14.5.8, where the principal is liable "nomine institoris."

[193] Paulus, *Sent.* 2.8.3: "Quod cum discipulis eorum, qui officinis tabernis praesunt contractum est, in magistros vel institores tabernae in solidum actio datur." The text may be interpolated ("vel institores").

[194] Papinianus (3 *resp.*) *Dig.* 14.3.19.3: "Servus pecuniis tantum faenerandis praepositus per intercessionem eas alienum suscipiens ut [institorem] < institor > dominum in solidum iure praetorio non adstringit."

[195] Cf. *Oxford Latin Dictionary*, fasc. 4 (1973) 929, s.v. *institor*; and A. Ernout–A. Meillet, *Dictionnaire étymologique de la langue latine*[4] (Paris 1959) 319, s.v. *institor* "celui qui s'établit, s'installe avec son étalage." By contrast, A. Walde–J.B. Hofmann, *Lateinisches etymologisches Wörterbuch* I[5] (Heidelberg 1982) 707, s.v. *instita*, favor a derivation from *insto* through *in-stator*; cf. also *ibidem* II 597, s.v. *insto*; and F. Gaffiot, *Dictionnaire illustré latin-francais* (Paris 1934) 833, s.v. *institor*. Two ancient writers (Ulpianus and Salonius, cf. below) rest their definition on etymological grounds and trace the origin of the word *institor* to the verb *instare* rather than *insistere*.

were the result of a twofold process.[196] Through the process of *lexi-calisation*, these words designate persons in reference to their trade, profession, or social functions, thus undergoing a semantic specification and acquiring meanings more remote from that of the verb from which they stem. Through the process of *grammaticalisation*, these words are used as substitutes for the missing form of the active past participle of the corresponding verb: the person is assigned the role of first acting character ("premier actant") of the original verb. Thus, the word *institor* designates on one hand a specific type of businessman, and on the other the person who established himself or another at the head of a business. This is quite consistent with Ulpianus's definition, which emphasizes only the fact that an *institor* runs a *negotium*, without reference to his function of agent or independent businessman.[197] Likewise, the fifth-century bishop Salonius considers that an *institor* is a businessman who puts his energy into increasing his profit.[198]

In sum, I would suggest that at the time of the creation of the *actio institoria* in the mid-Republican period, *institores* were mainly independent businessmen. As the praetor decided that the transactions of their dependents would make them fully liable under certain circumstances, the remedy granted to third contracting parties was named after the principal whose liability was at stake, as is the case for the twin remedy, the *actio exercitoria*. As time went on, the word *institor* took a derogatory social flavor and ended up designating almost exclusively the agent *praepositus*, often a slave, a freedman, or a free person of low station in life. Such was the usage adopted by the classical Roman jurists.[199] If this explanation concerning the name of the *actio institoria* is correct, then the argument whereby the peculiarity and inadequacy of the name of this remedy are proof of a later creation than the *actio exercitoria*[200] does not stand.

---

[196] M. Fruyt, "La plurivalence des noms d'agents latins en -tor: lexique et sémantique," *Latomus* 49 (1990) 59-70 says that "les noms en -tor constituent, en réalité, une pluralité de classes lexicales s'étageant en un *continuum* entre une lexicalisation et une grammaticalisation."

[197] Ulpianus (28 *ad ed.*) *Dig.* 14.3.3: "Institor appellatus est ex eo, quod negotio gerendo *instet*."

[198] Salonius, *In Proverbia Salomonis* 31.14 (*PL* 53.990 B): "Institor dicitur negotiator, propterea quod semper *instat* ut acquirat et multiplicet merces et lucra sua."

[199] Gai., *Inst.* 4.71: "Ideo autem institoria vocatur, quia qui tabernae praeponitur institor appellatur." Cf. also Ulpianus (28 *ad ed.*) *Dig.* 14.3.5 *pr.*, and Paulus (*sing. de var. lect.*) *Dig.* 14.3.18.

[200] S. Solazzi, *Scritti di diritto romano* IV (1963) 250-51.

The fifth point rests on a myth. It is pointless to argue at great length that a development in seaborne trade in the second century B.C. would have been accompanied, or preceded, by a similar or even greater development in local and regional production and trade.[201] In any case, Plautus shows that agents have been employed both in land based enterprises and in seaborne trade much earlier than the time of the introduction of the *actiones adiecticiae qualitatis*.[202] As will be suggested in the following chapters, there are good reasons to believe that the law of indirect agency was developed in response to changes in the pattern of production in by far the largest sector of the Roman economy, i.e. agriculture and the manufacturing activities connected with it. As for the appealing theory that the Roman praetor may have been influenced by existing provisions of Greek maritime laws, comparable to the Rhodian Law on jettison (*Dig.* 14.2), the lack of evidence on this point confines it to the state of mere conjecture.[203] Besides, if one accepts the conclusion reached above that the *actiones adiecticiae qualitatis* were not introduced before the third or fourth quarter of the second century, it seems unlikely that the Romans would have borrowed any legal institution from a people with whom they had been in a state of cold war for one or two generations.[204] If there was indeed a Greek connection behind the introduction of the *actiones adiecticiae qualitatis*, it must have been with Delos, where an important community of Roman and Italian businessmen had been established for some time. As these businessmen had retained personal and economic ties with the Italian mainland, where their relatives or business contacts controlled parts of the centers of agricultural and industrial production, it is possible that the influence of Greek laws, provided that it ever existed, would have affected land based activities no less than seaborne trade.

Therefore, I believe that it can be suggested, against a widely ac-

---

[201] This point has been noted by P. Huvelin (1929) 181, cited by A. Claus (1973) 82.

[202] Cf. Chapter One (introduction), about *vilici, atrienses, procuratores*, and *lapicidae* in Plautus. In *Mercator*, Charinus acts as shipmaster on behalf of his father, cf. Y. Thomas, "Droits domestiques et droits politiques à Rome. Remarques sur le pécule et les *honores* des fils de famille," *MEFRA* 94 (1982) 527-80, esp. 543-44.

[203] A. Claus (1973) 79-81, citing E. Seidl, *Römisches Privatrecht*[2] (Cologne/Berlin 1963) 43.

[204] A.N. Sherwin-White, *Roman Foreign Policy in the East (168 B.C. to A.D. 1)* (Norman, OK 1984) 30-36.

cepted opinion, that the *actio institoria* was introduced somewhat earlier than the *actio exercitoria*. This suggestion is, coincidentally, supported by the *termini ante quos*, which, *per se*, do not prove anything: the earliest juristic opinion about the *actio institoria* is by Servius Sulpicius Rufus, who died in 43 B.C. (*Dig.* 14.3.5.1), whereas the earliest reference to the *actio exercitoria* is by Servius's student, A. Ofilius (*Dig.* 14.1.1.9).[205] Further, it is perhaps no coincidence that it is in reference to the *actio institoria* that Ulpianus and Paulus twice record that, with regard to fairness, the praetor sanctioned the contractual liability of the principal for the transactions of his agent from which he benefited.[206] This interpretation is consistent with the hypothesis that the *actio exercitoria* became more important in the Imperial period, hence the order in which both remedies lie in the perpetual Edict.

4. The extension of the actio institoria to agents outside the circle of the Roman family

It has been suggested above that the *actio institoria/exercitoria* was originally granted only when the agent was a dependent (*servus, filius familias*, etc.) of the principal. This is only conjectural, because it is clear that by the middle of the second century A.D. this condition of status was no longer relevant.[207] It is not clear when the remedy became available to third contracting parties dealing with free agents. A. Watson, following M. Kaser, argues against P. Fabricius that the inclusion of free agents must predate the second century

---

[205] Both are quoted by Ulpianus (28 *ad ed.*). Cf. E. Costa (1891) 33.

[206] Ulpianus (28 *ad ed.*) *Dig.* 14.3.1: "Aequum praetori visum est, sicut commoda sentimus ex actu institorum, ita etiam obligari nos ex contractibus ipsorum et conveniri;" and Paulus, *Sent.* 2.8.1: "Sicut commoda sentimus ex actu praepositi institoris, ita et incommoda sentire debemus." S. Solazzi, *Scritti di diritto romano* IV (1963) 251 rejects both texts as interpolated.

[207] Gai., *Inst.* 4.71: "Institoria vero formula tum locum habet, cum quis tabernae aut cuilibet negotiationi filium servumve aut quemlibet extraneum sive servum sive liberum praeposuerit,..." P. Fabricius (1926) 7 dismisses "aut...liberum" as a gloss; cf. also Ulpianus (28 *ad ed.*) *Dig.* 14.3.7.1; and Paulus,*Sent.* 2.8.2. The situation of freed (or emancipated) *institores* and of *servi alieni* was similar to that of free *institores*, since all were contractual agents (cf. below); cf. also Ulpianus (28 *ad ed.*) *Dig.* 14.3.11.8; Iulianus (11 *dig.*) *Dig.* 14.3.12; Paulus (30 *ad ed.*) *Dig.* 14.3.17.1; Papinianus (3 *resp.*) *Dig.* 14.3.19.1 and (11 *quaest.*) *Dig.* 26.7.37.1; Scavola (5 *dig.*) *Dig.* 14.3.20 and (11 *dig.*) *Dig.* 26.7.58 *pr.*; cf. also G. Hamza, *AUB (iur.)* 25 (1983) 101, n. 68.

A.D.[208] These authors, however, provide no further information as to whether or not the *actiones institoria* and *exercitoria* were granted immediately from the time of their creation in cases involving extraneous agents.[209] If a change actually took place, it is not clear when and under which circumstances it occurred.

Two considerations must be kept in mind. First, the extension of the availability of the *actio institoria/exercitoria* to situations where the agent was an outsider became a necessary consequence of the evolution of the very institutions on which the system originally rested, i.e. slavery and the unity of the Roman family. The social and economic rise of Roman freedmen and the increasing number of emancipations of sons-in-power elicited a shift of competent economic agents from the status of dependents to that of independent businessmen.[210] Second, it must have been desirable for all parties involved, i.e. principals and third contracting parties, to enlarge the pool of potential agents while retaining the same conditions of credit. It is possible that free extraneous agents appeared first in the context of the operation of a ship.[211] Because of the similarity between the two remedies, it is likely that any development on one side would be followed shortly by an adjustment on the other.

The sources do not indicate when the transactions performed by extraneous agents first made their principal liable to a remedy *in soli-*

---

[208] A. Watson (1965) 192, n. 1; M. Kaser, *RP* I² (1971) 608, n. 27; against, P. Fabricius (1926) *passim*.

[209] A negative answer is given by A. di Porto (1984) 24; 37-42, citing previous literature in n. 12; and 177; cf. A. Bürge, *ZRG* 105 (1988) 856-57; and 863.

[210] P. Garnsey, "Independent Freedmen and the Economy of Roman Italy under the Principate," *Klio* 63 (1981) 359-71, esp. 364-65; J.A. Crook, *Law and Life of Rome, 90 B.C. –A.D. 212* (Ithaca, NY 1967) 109-10 tentatively suggests that emancipation in the Republican period was still considered a penalty for misbehavior. This applies directly to those propertied classes involved in economic operations requiring the intervention of agents; cf. also D. Daube, *Roman Law: Linguistic, Social and Philosophical Aspects* (Edinburgh 1969) 83; Y. Thomas, *MEFRA* 94 (1982) 556 ff.; *contra*, J.A. Crook, "*Patria Potestas,*" *CQ* 17 (1967) 113-22, esp. 120 thinks that cases of emancipation became more and more common in the late Republic. This trend was certainly strengthened in the reign of Vespasian, when the *Senatusconsultum Macedonianum* (*Dig.* 14.6) barred sons-in-power from taking out loans. At a later time, the ban was softened, for instance when sons-in-power were involved in the collection of taxes (Ulpianus [29 *ad ed.*] *Dig.* 14.6.3.1) or when they were acting with the expressed authorization of their father (Ulpianus [29 *ad ed.*] *Dig.* 14.6.7.15)—by the third century, knowledge and tolerance on the part of the principal was sufficient to validate the loan (Paulus [4 *resp.*] *Dig.* 14.6.16).

[211] G. Hamza, *AUB (iur.)* 25 (1983) 93-94.

dum. For our purpose, it is not important whether this remedy was an *actio directa*, applicable to all *praepositi* indiscriminately, or an *actio utilis*, with a modified formula extending the remedy to cases not originally covered by the *actio directa*, because the practical effects would be the same.[212] In both cases, freedmen, *servi alieni*, and free-born, could step into the shoes of business agents, a position which had been up to this point restricted to slaves and dependents belonging to the *familia* of the principal.

Almost three centuries may have elapsed between the time of the introduction of the remedy by the praetor and the time of Iulianus or Gaius, when extraneous *institores* are unambiguously attested. In a recent article, K. Visky points out that, in the legal sources, freedmen are almost never presented in the capacity of *institores*, and concludes from it that the appointment of freedmen as *institores* must have been rare. According to Visky, the scarcity of freed *institores* was a consequence of the employment of freedmen on the basis of their obligations toward their former masters, derived from their *officium*.[213] This explanation is irrelevant, because, as will be demonstrated later on, the liability of the principal for his agent's transactions was independent from the type of legal relationship existing between them.

In order to establish whether the appointment of free *institores* constituted an option commonly resorted to by businessmen before the time of Iulianus, we have to search through the non-legal—literary and epigraphical—sources of the late Republican and early Imperial periods for occurrences of independent people advertising in non-ambiguous terms their link to a principal and their position of *praepositi*. As will be seen in the following chapters, this is no easy task. To provide one single example, Cicero touches on the subject of subordinates in a discussion of the interdict *unde vi*. The interdict had been given to his client, A. Licinius Caecina, after he had been denied access to some disputed property. Cicero reminds the judges of the meaning of the terms of the interdict "unde tu aut familia aut procurator":

---

[212] P. Fabricius (1926) 18-20 uses the evidence from the Byzantine scholiasts to reconstruct the position of classical jurists on this point and concludes that, before Iustinianus, only an *actio utilis* was given against the principal. Fabricius (21-23) identifies two cases in the *Digest* (Iulianus [11 *dig.*] *Dig.* 14.3.12 and Papinianus [3 *resp.*] *Dig.* 14.3.19 *pr.*) where an *actio institoria utilis* (in the sense of fictitious, according to Lenel, cited by Fabricius 21, n. 1) was given on the ground that the agent was independent from the principal. This is not the only possible explanation.

[213] K. Visky, "L'affranchi comme *institor*," *BIDR* 83 (1980) 207-20.

It does not matter, insofar as equity is concerned, whether there was
one or several slaves. It makes no difference in law whether I have
been expelled by your *procurator*—a man who, according to the terms
of the law, administers the whole property of a citizen absent from
Italy or busy serving the state, who behaves almost as if he were the
owner, and who acts as the legal representative of someone else—or
by your farmer, your neighbor, your client, your freedman, or whoever committed such a violent eviction at your request and in your behalf. (58) Therefore, if equity always keeps the same standing when
it comes to restoring someone who had been violently forced out,
provided that the concept of equity is clear, it is pointless to argue
about the meaning of words and terms. You must re-establish my
rights if I have been expelled by your freedman, even though he is not
one of your agents appointed to oversee your affairs, none the less
than if it had been the deed of your *procurator*. And I do not mean that
all people appointed to take care of one's affairs should be called
procuratores, but it is not relevant to dwell on this point here.[214]

The passage is ambiguous, and consequently, has been interpreted
in opposite ways. A. Watson considers it as an unmistakable reference to free(d) *institores* and rejects Fabricius's interpretation that the
freedman *praepositus* was a *procurator*.[215] The passage remains ultimately inconclusive.

Cicero provides other instances of businessmen involved in transactions on behalf of others. The best known case is that of M. Scaptius and P. Matinius who lent Brutus's money to the city of Salamis,
Cyprus in the 50's B.C. and subsequently tried to collect usurious
interests. This case does not provide any evidence for our investigation, because neither Scaptius nor Matinius were business managers

---

[214] Cic., *Caecin.* 20.57-58: "Non enim alia causa est aequitatis in uno servo et
in pluribus; non alia ratio iuris in hoc genere dumtaxat, utrum me tuus procurator
deiecerit, is qui legitime procurator dicitur, omnium rerum eius qui in Italia non
sit absitve rei publicae causa, quasi quidam paene dominus, hoc est alieni iuris
vicarius, an tuus colonus aut vicinus aut cliens aut libertus aut quivis qui illam vim
deiectionemque tuo rogatu aut tuo nomine fecerit. (58) Qua re, si ad eum restituen-
dum qui vi deiectus est eandem vim habet aequitatis ratio, ea intellecta, certe nihil
ad rem pertinet quae verborum vis sit ac nominum. *Tam restitues si tuus me libertus
deiecerit nulli tuo praepositus negotio, quam si procurator deiecerit*; non quo omnes sint
procuratores qui aliquid nostri negoti gerunt, sed quod id in hac re quaeri nihil atti-
net" (with my emphasis).
[215] A. Watson (1965) 192, n. 1; *contra*, P. Fabricius (1926) 32 "wird doch auch
der Prokurator technisch als *praepositus* bezeichnet," with reference to Scaevola
(27 *dig.*) *Dig.* 20.4.21.1 ("'procurator exactioni [marmorum] praepositus" who
"ad lapidum venditionem officium suum extendit") and Iulianus (54 *dig.*) *Dig.*
46.3.34.3 (*omnibus negotiis praepositus*). Cf. also below, about Papinianus (3 *resp.*)
Dig. 14.3.19 *pr.*

in the sense of agents appointed to the head of an enterprise.[216] Further, Cicero explicitly describes them as *procuratores*.[217]

More interesting is the case of Quintus Cicero's *vilicus*, Nicephorus,[218] who will be discussed in the next chapter. For the moment, our investigation about the employment of free *institores* before the second century A.D. must remain inconclusive.

5. *Locus emendi vendendive*

In the first chapter, I alluded to a possible change in the rule regarding the setting of the activity of *institores*. It is necessary to return now to this issue and to examine the economic and legal significance of the commercial facilities in enterprises run by business managers. When a landowner wanted his agent to take responsibility for carrying out agricultural work, he would determine which part of his estates he would entrust to him, what type of crop he would expect him to grow, and for what purpose. Similarly, a potter planning to open a subsidiary workshop in another province would have to decide where he would send his deputy and what type of articles he would like him to produce. In both cases, the principal had to decide on a location and on a general strategy for the enterprise.

The makeup of the enterprise was defined by the type of premises (*fundus, hortus, figlinae, officina, taberna, caupona, mensa, statio, mansio, mutatio, deversorium, insula, domus, horreum, balneum, pistrinum*, etc.) in which the business manager would carry out his activities. A ship (*navis*) was just another kind of enterprise and was not treated differently. A *vilicus* who had been appointed to the head of an agricultural estate in a wine-growing area would be expected to engage in wine-growing, wine-making, and perhaps wine-selling, including various operations connected with this trade, such as the provision of adequate containers, tools, and manpower. On the other hand, he was not automatically allowed to engage in moneylending. An *officinator* in charge of a brickyard was expected to organize the production of bricks and other types of building material, perhaps even of other types of clay articles, but it would have been inappropriate for him

---

[216] Cic., *Att.* 5.21.10-13; 6.1.5-7; 6.2.7-9; 6.3.5-7 (51 B.C.). Cf. J. Andreau, *La vie financière dans le monde romain* (Rome 1987) 435.

[217] Cic., *Att.* 6.1.4: "qui in regno rem Bruti procurabant."

[218] Cic., *QFr.* 3.1 (54 B.C.).

to keep a restaurant or a brothel in some part of the concern, unless he was specifically appointed to do so (double *praepositio*). This point is important, as people living near subsistence level have a tendency toward diversification of their economic activities.[219] It also explains why the Roman jurists were so concerned with establishing the scope of the appointment in order to determine the liability of the principal. This could be done on the basis of the charter of appointment (*lex praepositionis*) and on the basis of the structure of the premises.

The appointment of a manager to the head of a specific store or workshop enabled the principal to keep an eye on the activity of his agent. It also provided a guarantee for parties doing business with him. Anyone who went through the experience of buying a telephone in New York City knows the difference between a transaction conducted on the sidewalk of 14th Street and the purchase of a similar device at Bloomingdale's. The manager of this store knows that he can sell a telephone at a certain price, whereas no one would accept to pay even one fourth of this price on the street. In case of dissatisfaction with the quality of the product, the customer could expect to obtain redress from the department store, but would probably consider it useless to argue with the peddler if he chanced to run into him again. This basic economic reckoning was undoubtedly familiar to Roman businessmen and consumers.

In Roman law, a third contracting party who had successfully brought a suit against the agent or his principal would be given a condemnatory judgement, specifying the amount of the compensation to which he was entitled. If he did not receive his due within thirty days, he would bring an *actio iudicati* for the execution of the judgement. The magistrate would then pronounce the *addictio*, and the plaintiff would immediately proceed with the execution on the property of the defendant (*missio in possessionem* and *venditio bonorum*).[220] The plaintiff would obtain redress only if the defendant owned some property to be seized. At this point, it made a significant difference whether or not the defendant (agent or principal) was operating a shop, or was at least tied to a piece of real estate.

In Rome, the *tabernarii* conducted their business in shops (*tabernae*) located on privately-owned or state-owned property (streets, public

---

[219] Cf. Chapters Three and Four.
[220] M. Kaser, *RZ* (1966) 296-312.

places, *fora* and *saepta*).[221] In the latter case, neither the land nor the building located on it could be mortgaged to a third contracting party, because of the rule that every product or increment belongs to the owner of the soil.[222] The shopkeeper (*superficiarius*) owned (a) the right to use the space; (b) the material, tools, equipment, and stock kept inside the shop; and (c) the servile staff operating it. This asset was liable to be seized or given as security.[223] Hence the importance of providing a legal definition of what belonged to the shop and what did not:

> When a debtor mortgaged a shop to his creditor, the question arose whether the pledge was void or whether the stock contained inside the shop was considered mortgaged. And if the debtor sold this stock over a period of time, bought replacement, and carried it inside the shop before he died, could the creditor bring a suit on the mortgage and claim everything that was found inside the shop with regard to the replacement of the stock? He replied that what was found inside the shop at the time of the debtor's death would be considered mortgaged.[224]

In this context it was vital for the jurists to come up with a universally accepted definition of what was considered a *taberna*. Ulpianus defines it as follows: "the term *taberna* is used about any building which is not fit for dwelling. The word stems from the fact that a *taberna* is walled with slabs (*tabulae*)."[225] This definition focuses on the specification of spatial limits, but does not deal with the purpose

---

[221] H. Wagner, "Zur wirtschaftlichen und rechtlichen Bedeutung der Tabernen," *Studi Biscardi* III (Milan 1982) 391-422, who collects and discusses all the evidence used in this section. Cf. also V. Gassner, "Zur Terminologie der Kauflädn im Lateinischen," *MBAH* 3 (1984) 108-15.

[222] Gai., *Inst.* 2.73: "...superficies solo cedit."

[223] Ulpianus (44 *ad Sab.*) *Dig.* 18.1.32: "Qui tabernas argentarias vel ceteras quae in solo publico sunt vendit, non solum, sed ius vendit, cum istae tabernae publicae sunt, quarum usus ad privatos pertinet." M. Kaser, *RP* I² (1971) 456 considers this point as controversial.

[224] Scaevola (27 *dig.*) *Dig.* 20.1.34 *pr.*: "Cum tabernam debitor creditori pignori dederit, quaesitum est, utrum eo facto nihil egerit an tabernae appellatione merces, quae in ea erant, obligasse videa[n]tur? et si eas merces per tempora distraxerit et alias comparaverit easque in eam tabernam intulerit et decesserit, an omnia quae ibi deprehenduntur creditor hypothecaria actione petere possit, cum et mercium species mutatae sint et res aliae illatae? respondit: ea, quae mortis tempore debitoris in taberna inventa sunt, pignori obligata esse videntur."

[225] Ulpianus (28 *ad ed.*) *Dig.* 50.16.183: "'Tabernae' appellatio declarat omne aedificium <non> utile ad habitandum [non] ex eo quod tabulis cluditur." The correction was proposed by Th. Mommsen.

of the facility and its scope. It can apply to any type of enterprise, but also to premises without economic purpose. Further precisions are required and provided by the same jurist: "This is our understanding that an equipped *taberna* comprises all things and people suitable for its operation."[226] The content of every shop was thus determined by the nature of the activity carried out there.[227] The managers themselves belonged to the enterprise and were transferred with it.[228] Consequently, the execution on the property of the principal in result of a suit brought on the *actio institoria* had a flavor of noxal surrender (cf. above).

In Roman times, an enterprise was an economic unit oriented toward the production of goods or services, and was composed of one or several persons using capital in order to make a profit, or at least to provide for the needs of the entrepreneur. This capital included a place and means of production, a staff, and raw material. It was either owned by the entrepreneur or taken on lease. In the latter case, it was necessary to determine who supplied what, and we have some evidence that the Roman jurists tried to set forth clear legal standards for farm leases at an early stage. It is likely that similar principles were applied to other forms of commercial leases.[229] Besides, the legacy of premises on which enterprises were established gave rise to a sophisticated jurisprudence, starting in the

---

[226] Ulpianus (28 *ad ed.*) *Dig.* 50.16.185: "'Instructam' autem tabernam sic accipiemus, quae et rebus et hominibus ad negotiationem paratis constat."

[227] Neratius (2 *resp.*) *Dig.* 33.7.23: "Cum quaeratur, quod sit tabernae instrumentum, interesse, quod genus negotiationis in ea exerceri solitum sit." Cf. H. Wagner, *Studi Biscardi* III (1982) 401-02.

[228] Pomponius (6 *ad Sab.*), quoting Servius, *Dig.* 33.7.15 *pr.*: "Si ita testamento scriptum sit: 'quae tabernarum exercendarum instruendarum pistrini cauponae causa facta parataque sunt, do lego', his verbis Servius respondit et caballos, qui in pistrinis essent, et pistores, et in cauponio institores et focariam, mercesque, quae in his tabernis essent, legatas videri." In the *Formula Baetica* (*FIRA* III², no. 92, pp. 295-97), the slave Midas is transferred together with the *fundus Baianus* to which he is attached. Cf. also Paulus (4 *ad Sab.*), citing Neratius, *Dig.* 33.7.13; Papinianus (7 *resp.*) *Dig.* 32.91.2; and Scaevola (22 *dig.*) *Dig.* 33.7.7. Cf. E.M. Staerman–M.K. Trofimova, *La schiavitú nell'Italia imperiale* (Rome 1975) 78. *Contra*, Alfenus Varus, cited and rejected by Ulpianus (20 *ad Sab.*) *Dig.* 33.7.12.2, considers that no living being (*animal*, a category including slaves) could be part of the equipment.

[229] B.W. Frier, "Law, Technology, and Social Change. The Equipping of Italian Farm Tenancies," *ZRG* 96 (1979) 204-28, based on the study of Ulpianus (32 *ad ed.*), quoting a letter from L. Neratius Priscus to Titius Aristo, *Dig.* 19.2.19.2. I do not see why Frier doubts that shop leases would be treated like farm leases (216-17, n. 66).

Republican period onwards and aimed at defining the makeup of each economic unit in terms of staff, livestock, tools, and raw material. As could be expected, the most extensively discussed type of enterprise is the agricultural estate.[230] The economic unit is indifferently referred to as *fundus, villa, ager, praedia, saltus, pascua,* and *prata.* According to Sabinus, the staff is composed of two groups of persons, those who work the land and those who supervise them.[231] The size and level of specialization of the staff varies accordingly with the size and structure of the enterprise. It is understood that some members of the staff may not be working on the premises. This is the case when the manager is temporarily on a business trip, or when some of the workers have been sent away to get supplementary training, or have been temporarily removed for whatever reason.[232] Conversely, some of the people living on the premises may not be included in the staff. Underslaves (*vicarii*) are normally excluded, as are craftsmen attached to a villa whose services bring their master a yearly salary.[233] The equipment (*instrumentum*) of the enterprise consists of those items without which the purpose of the enterprise could not be achieved. It does not include the fixtures, because they are part of the premises.[234] The equipment of an economic unit is limited to the bare minimum, and is sometimes shared with other units. In this case, the owner freely decides which unit is dominant in comparison with the others.[235]

A business (*negotiatio*) could be divided into several units of production/distribution (branches or outlets). Ulpianus considers that they should be regarded as separate managerial units with distinct accounts.[236] Conversely, two or more businesses could be carried

---

[230] Excerpts of this jurisprudence are preserved in the *Digest* (33.7). Cf. A. Steinwenter, *Fundus cum instrumento* (Vienna/Leipzig 1942); and below, Chapter Three.

[231] Ulpianus (20 *ad Sab.*), quoting Sabinus (*Ad Vit.*), *Dig.* 33.7.8 *pr.*: ''...veluti homines qui agrum colunt, et qui eos exercent praepositive sunt is, quorum in numero sunt vilici et monitores.''

[232] Papinianus, quoted by Ulpianus (20 *ad Sab.*) *Dig.* 33.7.12.38; Scaevola (3 *resp.*) *Dig.* 33.7.20.4 and 6; and *idem* (6 *dig.*) *Dig.* 33.7.27.1.

[233] Celsus, quoted by Ulpianus (20 *ad Sab.*) *Dig.* 33.7.12.44; and Paulus (13 *resp.*) *Dig.* 33.7.19.1.

[234] Pomponius (1 *fideicom.*) *Dig.* 33.7.21: ''...quaecumque infixa (adfixa) inaedificataque sunt...ut partes aedificiorum esse videantur.''

[235] Ulpianus (20 *ad Sab.*) *Dig.* 33.7.12.14.

[236] Ulpianus (29 *ad ed.*) *Dig.* 14.4.5.16: ''Sed si duas tabernas eiusdem negotiationis exercuit et ego fui tabernae verbi gratia quam ad Bucinum habuit ratioci-

out within the same premises by the same manager(s). If the principal was sued for distribution of the stock (*merx peculiaris*), the creditors of each business were treated separately and had access only to that part of the equipment directly related to the business they were involved in.[237]

The concern of classical jurists with the definition of shop or farm equipment tends to obscure the fact that a significant part of business transactions was carried out in places where little or no real guarantee could be offered to third contracting parties. The business transactions of shipmasters, for instance, suffered somewhat from the fact that ships are transient, and that the mobility of agents was an obstacle to a proper assessment of their condition and credit.[238] The advantage and necessity of doing business through agents forced third contracting parties to ease their expectation in relation to the security provided by the association of agents with a fixed place of activity, and it seems that progressively the *actio institoria* was given in cases involving transactions performed by anybody, regardless of the localization—or localizability—of the appointment.[239] The detailed history of this evolution cannot be traced, but a working hypothesis will be presented in the next chapter in connection with the rise of *actores*.

D. RELATIONSHIP BETWEEN PRINCIPAL AND AGENT

The relationship between principal and agent was determined by several factors: (a) the legal status of the parties, in particular of the agent; (b) the social situation of the parties toward each other; (c) the gratuitous or onerous nature of the relationship; and (d) the willingness of each party to form a relationship of agency.[240]

---

nator, alius eius quam trans Tiberim, aequissimum puto separatim tributionem faciendam, ne ex alterius re merceve alii indemnes fiant, alii damnum sentiant.''

[237] Ulpianus (29 *ad ed.*) *Dig.* 14.4.5.15: ''Si plures habuit servus creditores, sed quosdam in mercibus certis, an omnes in isdem confundendi erunt et omnes in tributum vocandi? Ut puta duas negotiationes exercebat, puta sagariam et linteariam, et separatos habuit creditores. Puto separatim eos in tributum vocari: unusquisque enim eorum merci magis quam ipsi credidit.''

[238] Ulpianus (28 *ad ed.*) *Dig.* 14.1.1 *pr.* Cf. above.

[239] Paulus (*sing. de var. lect.*) *Dig.* 14.3.18: ''Institor est, qui tabernae locove ad emendum vendendumve praeponitur quique sine loco ad eundem actum praeponitur.''

[240] F. Serrao, *Enciclopedia del diritto* 21 (1971) 832.

1. Non-contractual relationships (potestas, manus)

The legal capacity to own property and to make contracts was a prerequisite for people who wanted to rely on business agents. If this condition was not fulfilled, for instance when the principal was independent and did not enjoy the right to enter into valid legal transactions in Roman law (*commercium*), the transaction would be legally void if the agent was a dependent of the principal. If the agent was independent, he alone would be liable to an *actio directa*. If the principal was himself dependent, any remedy arising from transactions performed by his agent would be given against the principal's master/*paterfamilias*.[241]

Let us assume from now on that this condition of status was fulfilled, namely that the principal was a free adult Roman citizen independent from parental power. If the agent was a dependent of the principal, either a relative (son, daughter, wife *in manu*, or any descendant through males) or a slave (or a person *in mancipio*), the agency relationship rested on the power of the head of the family (*manus* or *potestas*), and the legal capacity of the agent was directly derived from that of the principal. Their relationship was non-contractual, and disagreements arising between them did not give rise to a remedy and could not be settled in court. It was merely a family matter: the Roman legal system had no bearing on—and no interest in—the issue. However, any transaction between principal and agent could give rise on either side to natural obligations, which could have some consequences after the agent's emancipation or manumission. This is probably the reason why some master-slave relationships are sometimes described in legal terms.[242] Then, the contract between master and slave—or father and son-in-power—

---

[241] Ulpianus (28 *ad ed.*) *Dig.* 14.1.1.19: "Si is, qui navem exercuerit, in aliena potestate erit eiusque voluntate navem exercuerit, quod cum magistro eius gestum erit, in eum, in cuius potestate is erit qui navem exercuerit, iudicium datur." Cf. also *ibidem*, *Dig.* 14.1.1.20-23 and *idem* (29 *ad ed.*) *Dig.* 14.4.5.1; and A. di Porto (1984) 257-341.

[242] An example of such relationship is provided by Alfenus Varus (2 *dig.*) *Dig.* 15.3.16: "Quidam fundum colendum servo suo locavit et boves ei dederat...." A. Watson (1965) 186 explains this text by saying that the sort of commercial transaction existing between master and slave would not have been possible, had not the slave had a *peculium*. As we have seen above, the *peculium* of the slave was an entity that was distinct from the *res familiaris* of the master, in relation to which the *peculium* could be creditor or debitor, cf. I. Buti (1976) 131-38. This point will be discussed in the next chapters.

was void and did not give grounds for a suit at law.[243] Such contracts were fictitious, because the *peculium* entrusted to a slave (*servus quasi colonus* and others) did not bestow on him a personal legal capacity distinct from his master's.

If the agent was an extraneous slave (*servus alienus*), his relationship toward the principal was determined by contract or quasi-contract between the principal and the slave's owner. All rights and liabilities acquired by the slave in his dealing as agent belonged to his master, who transmitted them to the principal in accordance with the contractual arrangement. Disagreement between the principal and the slave's owner were settled through litigation, each party having a remedy on the contract on which the relationship was based (stipulation, mandate, hire, unauthorized administration).

If the agent was independent, the relationship between principal and agent was likewise based on a contractual arrangement. Each party to the contract had obligations and rights toward the other, and disputes were settled through litigation by the means of remedies based on the contract (cf. below).

2. Operae libertorum

When the agent was a freedman, his relationship toward the principal might rest upon his pledge to perform labor services (*operae*) for his former master, whether he worked for him or for a third party at the request of the former master.[244] The obligation to perform *operae* arose from an oath sworn before manumission and repeated afterwards. This obligation was actionable in law. It is not clear how often this type of social bond formed the basis of agency relationships: J.A. Crook, for instance, claims that freedmen performing

---

[243] A. Watson, *The Contract of Mandate in Roman Law* (Oxford 1961) 65 rightly states that a son-in-power could not bring a remedy against his *paterfamilias* and vice versa and that "there can be no valid mandate between a father and a son in his *potestas*. This, in fact, is a particular case, based on the principle that sons and slaves are extensions of the *paterfamilias*." Cf. also D. Daube, "Actions between *pater familias* and *filius familias* with *peculium castrense*," *Studi E. Albertario* I (Milan 1950) 433-74.

[244] The main sources are *Dig.* 38.1; *Cod. Iust.* 6.3. Cf. M. Kaser, *RP* I[2] (1971) 299-301; and W. Waldstein, *Operae libertorum. Untersuchungen zur Dienstpflicht freigelassener Sklaven* (Wiesbaden/Stuttgart 1986). About the power retained by the former master over his freedmen, cf. M.A. Levi, "*Liberi in manu*," *Labeo* 22 (1976) 73-80.

operae are attested working for their patron as bailiffs and *exercitores*.[245]

However, one should point out that *operae* normally consisted of a limited number of entire workdays that could not be subdivided into shorter periods.[246] This provision, as well as other restrictions concerning the type of services that could be requested from freedmen, may have prevented patrons from using their rights to their freedmen's *operae* as a basis for permanent agency. It is possible that originally, in the absence of praetorian regulation, former masters were exacting from their freedmen the performance of services on a more regular basis.[247] The classical jurists, however, seem to have been rather flexible about the enforcement of these restrictions: Celsus, for instance, acknowledges the validity of a freedman's commitment to perform services for a period of one thousand days.[248]

Another obstacle to the employment of agents performing *operae* arose from the fact, reported by Iavolenus, that services should be performed where the patron usually lives.[249] The purpose of the rule was evidently to protect freedmen from being sent away to the middle of nowhere, but could clearly be invoked by freedmen living far away from their former master in order to escape from their duty. Since one of the main reasons for relying on agents to perform legal transactions was the expected absence of the principal, it made little sense to employ freedmen whose services could be used only where the principal stayed. However, the situation was different if the appointment of the agent was prompted by the unwillingness of the principal to be personally involved on account of the demeaning nature of the business.

These obstacles, however, were more theoretical than real. Agency could work effectively only if both agent and principal agreed to the relationship. Then, the agent could waive his rights concerning the performance of his labor services.

---

[245] J.A. Crook, *Law and Life of Rome, 90 B.C. –A.D. 212* (Ithaca, NY 1967) 191, without providing any evidence.

[246] Pomponius (6 *ad Sab.*) *Dig.* 38.1.3. Cf. W. Waldstein (1986) 209-14.

[247] Ulpianus (38 *ad ed.*) *Dig.* 38.1.2 *pr.*

[248] Ulpianus (38 *ad ed.*), citing Celsus, *Dig.* 38.1.15.1. Cf. W. Waldstein (1986) 308 ff.; and 380.

[249] Iavolenus (6 *ex Cass.*) *Dig.* 38.1.21.

3. Contractual relationships

In the discussion about the technicalities of the *actio exercitoria*, Ulpianus points out that a shipper had no legal remedy against third contracting parties who had negotiated a contract with his independent
shipmaster. Ulpianus argues that the principal could avail himself
of the *actio ex locato* or *mandati* to compel the shipmaster to transfer
to him the remedies arising from the transaction. The choice between the two remedies rested upon the nature—onerous or gratuitous—of the relationship between principal and agent.[250] Likewise, if the agent was an extraneous slave (*servus alienus*), the principal
could sue the slave's master on the same contracts—hire or mandate—in order to force him to transfer the remedy which would entitle him to bring a suit against third contracting parties for the
agent's transactions.[251]

It may have happened that there was no preestablished contractual relationship between the principal and the person acting as
agent. This was particularly the case when the agent took the initiative of administering the affairs of the principal (*negotium gestum*), insofar as this initiative was ratified later by the principal, or did not
meet any opposition or complaint on his part once he became aware
of it. Ulpianus says that the principal, who had no remedy against
third contracting parties, could sue the agent—provided that he was
not one of his dependents—or the agent's owner on the basis of his
unauthorized administration.[252]

Thus, any transaction could be performed by the agent either as
a favor to the principal or in exchange for a fixed compensation
(*merces*). In the first case, the relationship between independent

---

[250] Ulpianus (28 *ad ed.*) *Dig.* 14.1.1.18: "Sed ex contrario exercenti navem adversus eos, qui cum magistro contraxerunt, actio < nem > (*Mommsen*) non pollicetur, quia non eodem auxilio indigebat, sed aut ex locato cum magistro, si mercede operam ei exhibet, aut si gratuitam, mandati agere potest."

[251] Paulus (29 *ad ed.*) *Dig.* 14.1.5 *pr.*: "Ex locato tamen mecum ages, quod
operas servi mei conduxeris, quia et si cum alio contraxisset, ageres mecum, ut actiones, quas eo nomine habui, tibi praestarem, quemadmodum cum libero, si quidem conduxisses, experieris: quod si gratuitae operae fuerint, mandati ages." Cf.
also following note.

[252] Ulpianus (28 *ad ed.*) *Dig.* 14.3.1: "... sed non idem facit circa eum qui institorem praeposuit, ut experiri possit: sed si quidem servum proprium institorem
habuit, potest esse securus adquisitis sibi actionibus: si autem vel alienum servum
vel etiam hominem liberum, actione deficietur: ipsum tamen institorem vel dominum eius convenire poterit vel mandati vel negotiorum gestorum."

agent and principal was governed by the law of mandate or unauthorized administration; in the second case, it was governed by
the law of hire.

a. *mandate and procuratio*

Like other consensual contracts giving rise to a claim based on the
good faith of the parties (*bonae fidei iudicium*), the contract of mandate
was introduced probably in the second century B.C.[253] It was based
upon the intention of the parties to enter into a legal relationship and
upon their agreement as to the object of the contract. Its origin lay
in the fulfillment of duties connected with friendship. Consequently,
the service done by the mandatary was necessarily free of charge and
could not result in worsening the condition of the mandator.[254] As
a rule, the contract was void if it benefited the mandatary only, to
the exclusion of the mandator, because it amounted to nothing more
than mere advice (*consilium*). Thus, the contract had to benefit either
the mandator or a third party (or both). According to H.T. Klami
"the contract of mandate was a kind of intermediary form between
non-contractual services and *locatio conductio*."[255]

A breach of contract and other legal disputes originating in the
contract gave rise to an *actio mandati directa* (given to the mandator,
for instance for the assignment of the mandatary's remedies),[256]
and to an *actio mandati contraria* (given to the mandatary, for instance
for the reimbursement of expenses incurred in good faith in carrying
out the mandate).[257] In both cases, the defendant, if condemned,
was branded with *infamia*.[258]

The conclusion of the contract of mandate did not require a
particular form. The agreement of the parties could be expressed

---

[253] The main sources are Gai., *Inst.* 3.155-162; *Dig.* 17.1; Paulus, *Sent.* 1.3 and
2.15; *Cod. Iust.* 4.35; *Inst. Iust.* 3.26. Cf. A. Watson, *The Contract of Mandate in
Roman Law* (Oxford 1961); *idem* (1965) 147-56; M. Kaser, *RP* I² (1971) 577-80,
with more bibliography.

[254] Paulus (32 *ad ed.*) *Dig.* 17.1.1.4 and 17.1.3 *pr.* A similar provision applied
in the case of a *procurator*, cf. Paulus (54 *ad ed.*) *Dig.* 3.3.49.

[255] H.T. Klami, "*Mandatum* and Labour," *ZRG* 106 (1989) 575-86, esp. 576.

[256] Ulpianus (23 *ad ed.*) *Dig.* 17.1.43; and Paulus (5 *ad Plaut.*) *Dig.* 17.1.45 *pr.*

[257] Gaius (9 [10?] *ad ed. prov.*) *Dig.* 17.1.27.4.

[258] B. Albanese, "*Iudicium contrarium* e *ignominia* nel mandato," *Iura* 21 (1970)
1-51; G. MacCormack, "The Liability of the Mandatary," *Labeo* 18 (1972)
156-72; W. Litewski, "La responsabilité du mandataire," *Index* 13 (1983-84)
106-39.

through the utterance or writing of any word ("rogo," "volo," "mando," etc.) by the mandator, and through its acceptance by the mandatary. The presence of the parties was not even required, since Paulus says that the contract could be entered into through a messenger or a letter.[259] If the parties failed to reach an explicit agreement about the nature and the purpose of the mandate, there was no contract, and therefore no remedy on the mandate for either party. The absence of a bilateral agreement, however, did not preclude a legal relationship from arising between the parties, who could then avail themselves of a remedy for unauthorized administration (*actio negotiorum gestorum*), unless the principal had opposed any interference by the would-be agent.[260] The scope (*fines* and *forma*) of the mandate had to be scrupulously observed and not departed from, otherwise the mandatary was liable toward the mandator for not carrying out the task that he had undertaken.[261] The mandate was extinguished by the withdrawal or death of one of the parties before its inception.[262] Once started, the mandate had to be fulfilled, and the remedy given to or against the heir of either party.[263]

A particular situation existed when the mandatary was a *procurator* in charge of administering the affairs of the principal/mandator[264] or of conducting a lawsuit in his behalf (*ad litem*).[265] As Ulpianus puts it, "it is of the utmost necessity for those people who are un-

---

[259] Paulus (32 *ad ed.*) *Dig.* 17.1.1.2. The same is true about *procurator*, cf. Ulpianus (9 *ad ed.*) *Dig.* 3.3.1.1.

[260] Paulus (9 *ad ed.*) *Dig.* 17.1.40. Cf. below.

[261] Paulus (32 *ad ed.*) *Dig.* 17.1.5 *pr.*; and *idem* (74 *ad ed.*) *Dig.* 17.1.46.1.

[262] Paulus (32 *ad ed.*), quoting Iulianus, *Dig.* 17.1.26 *pr.*; and Gaius (9 *ad ed. prov.*) *Dig.* 17.1.27.3. Cf. P. Meylan, "Révocation et renonciation du mandat en droit romain classique," *Studi G. Grosso* I (Turin 1968) 463-82.

[263] Paulus (4 *quaest.*) *Dig.* 17.1.58 *pr.*

[264] Ulpianus (9 *ad ed.*) *Dig.* 3.3.1 *pr.*: "Procurator est qui aliena negotia mandatu domini administrat." Cf. also Ulpianus (31 *ad ed.*), citing Iulianus, *Dig.* 17.1.6.6; and Papinianus (3 *resp.*) *Dig.* 17.1.7, etc. On the *procurator*, cf. A. Watson (1961) 36-60; and *idem* (1965) 193-206; O. Behrends, "Die Prokuratur des klassischen römischen Zivilrechts," *ZRG* 88 (1971) 215-99; P. Angelini, *Il procurator* (Milan 1971); and M. Kaser, *ZRG* 91 (1974) 186-202, who suggests (188, n. 152) that *Dig.* 3.3.1 *pr.* may be genuine.

[265] Ulpianus (31 *ad ed.*) *Dig.* 17.1.8. Most of what is said in *Dig.* 3.3 refers to the *procurator ad litem*, but since its classical origin is no longer to be questioned (cf. A. Watson [1961] 56-60), it can be surmised that in many aspects the other kinds of *procuratores* were treated in the same way.

willing or unable to attend to their own affairs to rely on a *procurator* so as to be represented by an agent as plaintiff or defendant in court."[266]

It would be wrong to equate *procurator* and mandatary, at least before the classical period,[267] because there were cases where the *procurator* was a paid employee or was acting in his own interest.[268] In other cases where a *procurator* was involved in litigation in someone else's behalf, he was acting without mandate.[269] Consequently, the *procurator* had to guarantee that his principal would ratify his acts, hence the rule "ratification equals mandate."[270] A. Watson convincingly demonstrates that *procuratio* and *mandatum* were equated only in the second century A.D. after a long historical evolution, and that they had started as two different institutions. At an earlier stage, the relationship between principal and *procurator* was governed by the remedy for unauthorized administration, and was almost certainly not gratuitous. Originally, the *procurator* was normally a former slave of the principal, and because of his inferior social status, his agreement to the relationship was not instrumental.[271] On the other hand, the *procurator* had a wider power of administration than the mandatary, because of his tie to the principal's household. For instance, the *procurator* had the capacity to acquire possession for his principal earlier than the mandatary (cf. above) and was subjected to a different standard of liability (*dolus* and *culpa*).[272]

---

266 Ulpianus (9 *ad ed.*) *Dig.* 3.3.1.2.

267 A. Watson (1961) 43-44 shows that Papinianus was the first jurist to consistently treat mandate and *procuratio* as the same thing, cf. (3 *resp.*) *Dig.* 3.3.68; (1 *resp.*) *Dig.* 17.1.55; (3 *resp.*) *Dig.* 17.1.56.4; (7 *resp.*) *Dig.* 34.3.23; (2 *def.*) *Dig.* 41.2.49.2; and (12 *resp.*) *Dig.* 46.8.3 *pr.* About the historical development of the *procurator*, cf. J.H. Michel, "Quelques observations sur l'évolution du procurateur en droit romain," *Etudes J. Macqueron* (Aix-en-Provence 1970) 515-27; and M. Kaser, *RP* I² (1971) 265-66.

268 Ulpianus (31 *ad ed.*), discussing Labeo's opinion, *Dig.* 17.1.10.9; and Paulus (8 *ad ed.*) *Dig.* 3.3.42.2. This text obviously refers to a *procurator ad litem*, but by the third century A.D. the *procuratio omnium rerum* (Paulus [3 *ad ed.*] *Dig.* 2.13.9 *pr.* [itp?]) and *unius rei* (Africanus [8 *quaest.*] *Dig.* 47.2.62(61).5 [itp?]) gave rise to an *actio mandati*; cf. A. Watson (1961) 39-41; 45-46; 51; and 55.

269 Ulpianus (9 *ad ed.*) *Dig.* 3.3.35 *pr.*

270 Ulpianus (30 *ad Sab.*) *Dig.* 46.3.12.4: "rati enim habitio mandato comparatur;" *idem* (9 *ad ed.*) *Dig.* 3.3.39.1; *idem* (10 *ad ed.*), citing Pedius, *Dig.* 3.5.5(6).11(9): "Sed ratihabitio fecit tuum negotium;" and Scaevola (1 *quaest.*), against Pomponius, *Dig.* 3.5.8(9).

271 Celsus (38 *dig.*) *Dig.* 17.1.50 *pr.* Cf. also M. Kaser, *RP* I² (1971) 587.

272 A. Watson (1961) 7-9; 37-39; and 202-11. Cf. also P. Apathy, "*Procurator* und *solutio*," *ZRG* 96 (1979) 65-88.

A *procurator* could take care of all his principal's affairs (*procurator omnium rerum*); this was probably the earliest type of *procuratio*.[273] Otherwise, he could carry out a single (type of) transaction (*procurator unius rei*). Pomponius records that some jurists did not consider this second type of agent as *procurator*, which suggests that there might have been originally a more drastic contradistinction between *procurator* (as a long term general agent) and mandatary (as an occasional agent).[274]

There were some restrictions pertaining to the appointment of a *procurator*. In public affairs, for instance, the *actor civitatis* was not entitled to appoint a *procurator*.[275] The reason for this is probably that public *actores* were direct representatives of the community and of its officials (*administratores rerum civitatis*), and that there was no reason to allow them to delegate the very tasks for which they had been themselves appointed.[276]

The *procurator* entrusted with unrestricted power of administration was entitled to exact and make payments, and to perform novations and exchanges of things.[277] A. Watson states that "it is generally agreed that in classical law the procurator had power to alienate his principal's property without special authorization and that the texts which restrict this power have been interpolated."[278] However, some restrictions existed or were possibly introduced after the classical period. In accordance with the rule that agents could not make the position of their principal worse, the *procurator* was barred from transferring the principal's property, except for fruits and other perishable items, unless he had been given a special mandate to do so.[279]

---

[273] A. Watson (1965) 193-98 shows that the function was given legal recognition by the time of the *Lex agraria* of 111 B.C. (*FIRA* I[2], no. 8, line 69, pp. 115-16). Cic., *Caecin.* 20.57 provides the earliest definition: "is qui legitime procurator dicitur, omnium rerum eius, qui in Italia non sit absitve rei publicae causa, quasi quidam paene dominus, hoc est alieni iuris vicarius." A. Watson (1961) 6-7 rightly considers it as too narrow.

[274] Ulpianus (9 *ad ed.*), citing Pomponius, *Dig.* 3.3.1.1.

[275] Ulpianus (4 *opin.*) *Dig.* 3.3.74.

[276] Paulus (1 *manual.*) *Dig.* 3.4.10.

[277] Paulus (71 *ad ed.*) *Dig.* 3.3.58; and *idem* (10 *ad Plaut.*) *Dig.* 3.3.59.

[278] A. Watson (1965) 203-06, with a discussion of the only Republican text (Paul [3 *epit. Alf. dig.*], with reference to Alfenus, *Dig.* 5.4.9). Cf. above.

[279] Modestinus (6 *diff.*) *Dig.* 3.3.63. Cf. M. Kaser, *RP* I[2] (1971) 266, n. 47; *idem*, *RP* II[2] (1975) 101, n. 8; *idem*, *ZRG* 91 (1974) 188, n. 154. A. Watson (1961) 50 points out that the fragment was "regarded as a mass of interpolations," but cautions that modern authors advocating this position have gone too far.

Originally, a strict legal distinction existed between *procuratores* and *institores*. In reference to their respective economic functions, *procuratores* were normally not appointed to the head of an enterprise, and therefore had wider powers of administration than *institores*. This translates in terms of social status by the fact that *procuratores* usually ranked higher than *institores*. We have even seen that the latter could be appointed by the former.[280] As a result of some obscure historical development, probably linked with the extension of the *actiones institoria* and *exercitoria* to cases involving extraneous agents, this legal and social distinction seems to have lost its significance by the early third century A.D. Papinianus was the first to recognize the propriety of granting an *actio utilis ad exemplum institoriae* in a case involving a *procurator* appointed by his principal for the purpose of borrowing money. The mandate to carry out a specific transaction was additional to the procuratorship, and the liability for the transactions conducted by the *procurator* within the scope of this special appointment lay with both the *procurator* and his principal.[281] The final stage was reached with the promulgation of an imperial rescript in A.D. 294, which possibly widened the scope of validity of the *actio institoria* to cases where the transaction was carried out by a mere mandatary, who was not even a *procurator*.[282] Thus, it seems that *praepositio* and mandate ended up having the same legal effect. How-

---

[280] Ulpianus (28 *ad ed.*) *Dig.* 14.3.5.18; and Paulus (30 *ad ed.*) *Dig.* 14.3.6.

[281] Papinianus (3 *resp.*) *Dig.* 14.3.19 *pr.*: "In eum, qui mutuis accipiendis pecuniis procuratorem praeposuit, utilis ad exemplum institoriae dabitur actio: quod aeque faciendum erit et si procurator solvendo sit, qui stipulanti pecuniam promisit" (the last sentence is probably a post-classical addition, cf. A. Burdese, *BIDR* 74 [1971] 64). This innovation by Papinianus is cited twice by Ulpianus (31 *ad ed.*) *Dig.* 17.1.10.5 and (32 *ad ed.*) *Dig.* 19.1.13.25 (both genuine according to M. Kaser, *ZRG* 94 [1971] 196, n. 187). Cf. also Papinianus (2 *resp.*) *Dig.* 3.5.30(31) *pr.*: "Liberto vel amico mandavit pecuniam accipere mutuam: cuius litteras creditor secutus contraxit et fideiussor intervenit: etiamsi pecunia non sit in rem eius versa, tamen dabitur in eum negotiorum gestorum actio creditori vel fideiussori, scilicet ad exemplum institoriae actionis" (both A. Burdese [p. 75] and F. Serrao, *ED* 21 [1971] 831, n. 17 suggest to read at the beginning "liberto procuratori domi-nus. . . ."). On the *actio quasi institoria*, cf. N. Benke, "Zu Papinians *actio ad exemplum institoriae actionis*," *ZRG* 105 (1988) 592-633, who cites the previous bibliography.

[282] *Cod. Iust.* 4.25.5: "Si mutuam pecuniam accipere Demetriano Domitianus mandavit et hoc posse probare confidis, ad exemplum institoriae eundem Domitia-num apud competentem iudicem potes convenire;" *contra*, G. Hamza, "Fragen der gewillkürten Stellvertretung im römischen Recht," *AUB (iur.)* 25 (1983) 89-107, esp. 104, who considers that Demetrianus was undoubtedly a *procurator*. M. Kaser, *RP* I² (1975) 107, n. 55 leaves the question open.

ever, in the absence of specific mandate, the *procurator* remained liable for his own transactions, and no remedy would be given against the principal.[283]

b. *unauthorized administration (negotium gestum)*

If someone had managed the affairs of an absentee without his request, permission, and knowledge, the praetor gave the unauthorized administrator a remedy against the absentee for any expenditure and obligation he had incurred in the furtherance of the absentee's interests.[284] Conversely, the absentee was given a remedy against the unauthorized administrator of his affairs to force him to give an account of his activity and to condemn him for not taking the appropriate steps or for keeping a transaction fee.[285] This remedy was called *actio (directa* or *contraria) negotiorum gestorum* and was concerned mainly—if not only—with the fraud of one of the parties.[286] The standard of liability of the administrator, however, seems to have been his *diligentia*, and Pomponius states that the administrator would have to answer for his negligence (*culpa*) and his fraud (*dolus*), while Proculus even included liability for accident (*casus*).[287]

Like the contract of mandate, the unauthorized administration had to be gratuitous, otherwise the unauthorized administrator was regarded as taking care of his own business. If the principal had benefited from the transactions of an unauthorized administrator, the latter had a remedy against him for the amount of his enrichment.[288] Besides, the gratuitous character of the relationship be-

---

[283] Ulpianus (28 *ad ed.*), quoting Labeo, *Dig.* 14.3.5.10: "...fullonem non teneri, si quasi procurator fuit relictus: sin vero quasi institor, teneri eum." S. Solazzi, "*Procurator* ed *institor* in *D.*14.3.5.10," *SDHI* 9 (1943) 104-13 (= *Scritti di diritto romano* VI [Naples 1972] 548-56).

[284] The main sources are *Dig.* 3.5; Paulus, *Sent.* 1.4; *Cod. Iust.* 2.18; *Inst. Iust.* 3.27.1. Cf. A. Watson (1965) 206-07; M. Kaser *RP* I² (1971) 586-90; H.H. Seiler, *Der Tatbestand der negotiorum gestio im römischen Recht* (Cologne/Böhlau 1968) (with the review by T. Mayer-Maly, "Probleme der *negotiorum gestio*," *ZRG* 86 [1969] 416-35); *idem*, "Zur Haftung des auftraglosen Geschäftsführers im römischen Recht," in D. Medicus–H.H. Seiler (eds.), *Studien zum römischen Recht M. Kaser zum 65. Geb. gewidmet* (Berlin 1973) 195-208; and *idem*, "Bereicherung und *negotiorum gestio*," in H.P. Benöhr *et al.* (eds.), *Iuris Professio* (Vienna/Cologne/Graz 1986) 245-57.

[285] Gaius (3 *ad ed. prov.*) *Dig.* 3.5.2.

[286] Ulpianus (10 *ad ed.*), citing Labeo, *Dig.* 3.5.3.9.

[287] Ulpianus (10 *ad ed.*) *Dig.* 3.5.5(6).14(12); and Pomponius (21 *ad Q. Mucium*), citing Proculus, *Dig.* 3.5.10(11).

[288] Ulpianus (10 *ad ed.*), citing Labeo, *Dig.* 3.5.5.5(3).

REPLY CARD / ORDER FORM

Please send me the following books:

Qty.	ISBN	Author	Title

Name: _____

_____

Address: _____

_____

City / State: _____

_____

Zipcode / Country: _____

_____

Date / Signature:

❏ I enclose a cheque
❏ Send me an invoice
❏ Charge my credit card
   ❏ Access
   ❏ Eurocard
   ❏ Mastercard
   ❏ VISA
   ❏ Diners Club
   ❏ American Express

card no.

Expiry date ____/____

TUTA SUB AEGIDE PALLAS · 1683 ·

Congratulations on your choice and thank you for purchasing our publication. If you wish to be kept informed about our new publications in your field of interest, we would kindly ask you to tick the boxes for all the subjects on which you wish to receive our catalogues and brochures. We look forward to serving you and to hearing from you again.

- ☐ Ancient Judaism and Christian Origins
- ☐ Ancient Near East / Egypt
- ☐ Biblical Studies
- ☐ Central, South & SE Asia
- ☐ Christianity
- ☐ Classical Studies
- ☐ History
- ☐ Islamic Studies / Middle East
- ☐ Literature and Linguistics
- ☐ Philosophy
- ☐ Religious Studies
- ☐ Sociology
- ☐ All Categories

Place stamp here

SEND TO:

E · J · B R I L L

P.O.BOX 9000

2300 PA LEIDEN

HOLLAND

tween principal and administrator is underlined by the requirement that even fraudulent claims made by the administrator had to be transferred to the principal.[289]

On the other hand, the unauthorized administrator was entitled to receive full compensation for his expenses, including the interests that could have been received on the money spent on the principal's business.[290] Compensatory payments were limited to what ought to be spent, and were not expected to match unnecessary expenditures on the part of the administrator.[291]

Unauthorized administration is comparable to procuratorship in that the performance of a number of transactions could give rise to a single obligation, unless the administrator had the intention to remove himself from the situation upon completion of each of them. The administrator's will (*voluntas*) could repeatedly induce him to take care of someone else's affairs, and thus, each occasion would give rise to a new obligation, in the same way as a *procurator omnium rerum* would be held under a general obligation, while a *procurator unius rei* would be held liable individually for each of the transactions he had been entrusted with.[292]

If a free person acting in the genuine belief that he was a slave performed a transaction on someone else's behalf, he had a remedy for unauthorized administration against his assumed principal. Thus, the remedy was available when the agent had given the principal a sum of money raised as a loan, unless the money had been used to reimburse the creditor.[293] Conversely, Labeo says that if a principal had given a mandate to a man who genuinely thought that he was the mandator's slave (*homo liber bona fide serviens*), this man was not held liable on the contract of mandate, because his performance was secured through compulsion. But he was liable to a remedy for unauthorized administration brought by the principal, because the intention (*affectio*) of the agent was not in doubt.[294]

A remedy for unauthorized administration was given by analogy with the *actio institoria* against a mandator to the creditor and/or

---

[289] Ulpianus (10 *ad ed.*) *Dig.* 3.5.7(8).1.

[290] Paulus (2 *ad Nerat.*) *Dig.* 3.5.18(19).4.

[291] Paulus (27 *ad ed.*) *Dig.* 3.5.24(25).

[292] Paulus (7 *ad Plaut.*) *Dig.* 3.5.15(16).

[293] Ulpianus (10 *ad ed.*), perhaps following Labeo, *Dig.* 3.5.5.7(5); and Paulus (4 *quaest.*) *Dig.* 3.5.35(36).

[294] Paulus (2 *ad Nerat.*), citing Labeo, *Dig.* 3.5.18(19).2.

guarantor of a loan made out to a freedman (*procurator*) or friend acting on the basis of a mandate.[295] In this case, the mandator was considered as the principal, the mandatary/debtor as the agent (*quasi institor*), and the creditor and guarantor as the third contracting party.[296] The remedy is labelled ''ad exemplum institoriae actionis'' because the mandate consisted of a single transaction.[297]

c. *lease and hire (locatio conductio)*
Locatio conductio as a consensual contract goes back at least to the time of Quintus Mucius Scaevola (cos. 95 B.C.),[298] and perhaps as early as the time of Plautus (*Aul.* 455-457) or Cato (*Agr.* 144-145).[299] It is not clear when and in which order the different types of *locatio conductio* were created, but legal scholars seem to agree upon a date as early as—if not earlier than—the introduction of the mandate, i.e. in the second half of the second century B.C.[300]

The most important feature of this type of contract was the agreement of the parties about the rent/salary/reward (*merces*), paid usually in money,[301] in exchange for job opportunity (*opus faciendum*), for services (*operae*), or for the temporary use of some definite commo-

---

[295] Papinianus (2 *resp.*) *Dig.* 3.5.30(31) *pr.* Cf. above.

[296] Ulpianus (28 *ad ed.*) *Dig.* 14.3.5.16: ''Item fideiussori, qui pro institore intervenerit, institoria competit. . . .''

[297] A. Watson (1961) 81. The mandate to accept a loan was equivalent to a *praepositio* (Ulpianus [31 *ad ed.*], citing Papinianus, *Dig.* 17.1.10.5, cf. above). Cf. also N. Benke, *ZRG* 105 (1988) 611-21, esp. 613-14, n. 107. The text by Papinianus (2 *resp.*) *Dig.* 3.5.30(31) *pr.* presents major difficulties of interpretation, and the passage ''vel fideiussor, scilicet ad exemplum institoriae actionis'' has been considered interpolated on the basis of the comparison with Papinianus (3 *resp.*) *Dig.* 14.3.19 *pr.* and Ulpianus (32 *ad ed.*), citing Papinianus, *Dig.* 19.1.13.25.

[298] Cic. *Off.* 3.17.70; and *Nat. D.* 3.30.74.

[299] The main sources are Gai., *Inst.* 3.142-147; *Dig.* 19.2; Paulus, *Sent.* 2.18; *Cod. Iust.* 4.65; *Inst. Iust.* 3.24. Cf. A. Watson (1965) 100-24; M. Kaser, *RP* I² (1971) 562-72; I. Molnár, ''Object of locatio conductio,'' *BIDR* 85 (1982) 127-42; *idem*, ''Subjekte der locatio-conductio,'' *Studi Sanfilippo* II (Milan 1982) 413-30; *idem*, ''Verantwortung und Gefahrtragung bei der locatio-conductio zur Zeit des Prinzipats,'' *ANRW* II.14 (1982) 583-680.

[300] A. Watson (1961) 9-10 favors the following chronological order: *locatio conductio operis faciendi* (first developed in state contracts); *locatio conductio operarum*; and *locatio conductio rei*. Cf. also P. Leuregans, ''L'origine administrative du terme *locatio* dans la *locatio-conductio* romaine,'' *Eos* 65 (1977) 303-22, with a good collection of the evidence.

[301] The *merces* was paid in kind in a few types of transactions (*negotia partiaria*) involving work to be done or services, where the remuneration amounted to a share in the product or produce, cf. A. Watson (1965) 101-05.

dity or facility (*res*). In the context of contractual agency, the contract could be concluded between the principal and the agent—in which case the object of the contract would be the services of the agent—or between the principal and the agent's owner—in which case the object of the contract was the agent himself (*servus alienus mercennarius*) and his services.[302] Since the manager (*institor, vilicus,* or *actor*) was normally part of the equipment of an economic or managerial unit (*fundus, taberna, officina,* etc.), whoever rented such a unit had a contractual relationship with the agent's owner.[303] Alternatively, the principal/lessee could also appoint his own manager.

As an employee of the principal, the agent worked for a salary. His functions were specified in the part of the contract called *lex locationis*. His title (*locator operarum, conductor, redemptor, manceps, colonus, mercennarius, procurator, institor,* but not *mandatarius*) defined his legal position toward the principal and determined the extent of the latter's liability for his transactions. The principal was held fully liable only if he had appointed the hired employee as *institor*. If third contracting parties chose to sue the agent or the agent's master (if the agent was a *servus alienus*) rather than the principal, the agent or the agent's master had in turn a remedy on the contract of lease and hire against the principal. Conversely, since all claims arising from the transactions negotiated by the hired agent belonged to the agent himself (or to his master), the principal had a remedy on the contract of lease and hire against the agent (or his master) in order to obtain the remedies arisen from the transactions of the agent.

If the agent was established at the head of a business and received a fee for operating it, he was held liable for the risk of safekeeping

---

[302] Ulpianus (28 *ad ed.*) *Dig.* 14.3.11.8: "Si a servo tuo operas vicarii eius conduxero et eum merci meae institorem fecero isque tibi mercem vendiderit, emptio est: nam cum dominus a servo emit, est emptio, licet non sit dominus obligatus, usque adeo, ut etiam pro emptore et possidere et usucapere dominus possit;" and Iulianus (11 *dig.*) *Dig.* 14.3.12: "et ideo utilis institoria actio adversus me tibi competet, mihi vero adversus te vel de peculio dispensatoris, si ex conducto agere velim, vel de peculio vicarii, quod ei mercem vendendam mandaverim: pretiumque, quo emisti, in rem tuam versum videri poterit eo, quod debitor servi tui factus esses." About the validity of the sale by the slave *praepositus* to his master (different from the principal), cf. I. Buti (1976) 107-08, n. 80, quoting S. Riccobono and referring to *ratio naturalis* as opposed to *ratio civilis*. In my opinion, the sale is valid because the legal capacity of the slave is an extension of the legal capacity of the principal, which supersedes that of the master.

[303] Pomponius (6 *ad Sab.*), quoting Servius, *Dig.* 33.7.15 *pr.*; Scaevola (22 *dig.*) *Dig.* 33.7.7; and Papinianus (7 *resp.*) *Dig.* 32.91.4. Cf. above.

the facilities and the material entrusted to him.[304] If the agent was
a *servus alienus* and stole from his principal or caused him a loss, the
principal could sue the agent's master with a noxal remedy, but not
on the contract of hire.[305]

E. Conclusion

Due to its extreme formalism rooted in the archaic period, Roman
law lacked the concept of direct agency. Short of reversing this situation, the praetor responded to the needs of businesspeople by creating a legal system based on existing structures of Roman society
(slavery and the unitary character of the family), with advantages
similar to those which direct agency would have offered. This solution provided the elite with a way of skirting the social prohibition
against becoming personally involved in business ventures, as had
been enacted through statutory law in the late third century B.C.[306]
In addition, it established the legal basis of a managerial system
which made possible and profitable the extension—both in terms of
geographical location and scale—and the diversification of business
enterprises.

The system introduced by the praetor consisted in a set of six legal
remedies (*actiones adiecticiae qualitatis* and *actio tributoria*) given to third
contracting parties against the principal of the agent with whom the
transaction had been entered into. The liability of the principal was
complementary to that of the agent whose social status or economic
condition would make any legal proceedings or subsequent execution on his property worthless. The nature of the relationship—non-
contractual, quasi-contractual, or contractual—between principal
and agent was instrumental only insofar as it served as a basis for
determining how the rights arising from the transaction and belonging to the agent could and should be transferred to the principal.

The contractual liability of the principal originated with the con-

---

[304] Gaius (5 *ad ed. prov.*) *Dig.* 19.2.40; and Labeo (*post.* 5 *a Iavol. epit.*) *Dig.*
19.2.60.9.

[305] Paulus (22 *ad ed.*) *Dig.* 19.2.45. In early classical law the slave's master was
not liable for the *culpa* of his hired-out slave, cf. Labeo (*post.* 5 *a Iavol. epit.*) *Dig.*
19.2.60.7; and A. Watson (1965) 72 and 119, on the basis of the situation in the
law of sale. This situation changed in late classical law, cf. Ulpianus (32 *ad ed.*) *Dig.*
19.2.11 *pr.*

[306] *Lex Claudia* of 218 B.C. (Liv. 21.63.3; and Cic., *2Verr.* 5.18.45), supplemented by a *Lex Iulia* of 59 B.C. (Scaevola [3 *reg.*] *Dig.* 50.5.3).

cept of civil liability for the delicts of one's dependents. The principal's liability resulted (1) from his own enrichment derived from the transaction carried out by the agent; (2) from his commissioning the agent by granting him the free administration of a *peculium* or by appointing him to the head of a managerial unit (estate, workshop, store, or ship). The basis of the principal's liability determined its extent, which was either limited to his actual enrichment (*versum in rem*) or to the size of the agent's *peculium*, or unlimited.

The six remedies were not introduced at one single time, but as the result of a historical evolution. Each remedy presumably represented an improvement, an extension, a refinement, or a specification by comparison to the previous situation. The chronological order in which these remedies were introduced appears to be (1) *actio quod iussu*; (2) *actio institoria*; (3) *actio exercitoria*; (4) *actio de in rem verso*; (5) *actio de peculio*; and (6) *actio tributoria*, with the possibility that (2) and (3) came last or were the object of reforms at a later date during the first century B.C. or A.D. A newly introduced remedy did not totally supersede the older ones, although it seems likely that the *actio quod iussu* became practically subsidiary with the passage of time.

In classical Roman law, only the *actiones institoria* and *exercitoria* were not restricted to cases where the agent was a dependent of the principal. Therefore, these two remedies became more popular with businessmen who benefited from the possibility of relying on free(d) people. The emphasis in the legal sources on dependent *institores* suggests that both remedies were at first restricted to cases involving transactions performed by dependent agents, slaves or relatives (*alieni iuris*). Extraneous *institores* are attested by the middle of the second century A.D. in the legal sources, but they may have appeared as early as the Republican period, although the evidence for these is scant and inconclusive. The relationship between principal and extraneous agent was governed by the law of mandate, unauthorized administration, or hire and lease. Freedmen may have acted as business managers within the scope of the *operae* which they pledged to perform for their master at the time of manumission.

The appointment of an agent to the head of a managerial unit helped define the types of transactions for which the principal would be held liable. The piece of real estate and the premises in which the agent carried out the activity to which he had been appointed served as a security towards third contracting parties. On occasions, however, it proved impractical to tie down agents in a narrowly-defined establishment, and the classical jurists ended up regarding as *institor* anyone who had been appointed to perform some business activity on a regular basis, even without assigned location. Due to the scarcity of the evidence, this development is difficult to trace.

The purpose of the next three chapters is to examine the social and economic context from which this legal system was born and in which it was subsequently applied and developed. It is necessary to remark that although the role of *institores* in the economic life of the Roman empire is well documented, there is no evidence outside of the legal sources for the application of the *actio institoria*. Consequently, one cannot be sure that these legal instruments were used as described in the *Digest*, and one should perhaps allow for differences according to the place, time, type of business, and people involved. The relation between law and practice in ancient times is rather elusive.

CHAPTER THREE

MANAGERS OF AGRICULTURAL ESTATES

A. ITALIAN AGRICULTURE IN THE MID-REPUBLICAN PERIOD

The ancient Roman economy was always oriented mainly, though perhaps less and less exclusively, toward agriculture. Landowning as a source of wealth and as a form of investment was considered socially respectable because of its traditional roots. Moreover, agriculture was recognized as an economically safe pursuit, in contrast with commercial ventures in general, although the latter were admittedly more lucrative.[1] Even those who, like Cato the Elder, invested their money into seaborne trade posed as defenders of traditional values and retained a significant part of their assets in landholding.[2]

It is fair to postulate that the primacy of agriculture in the ancient economy bore on the historical development of Roman legal institutions, and in particular of Roman praetorian law, which stems from litigation connected with real-life situations. Consequently, it seems reasonable to look for the roots of the Roman system of indirect agency in a rural setting and to focus first on the management of agricultural estates. As the achievement of self-sufficiency seems to have been a constant primary goal of both subsistence farming and the market-oriented villa economy, *villae* and *fundi* served as the setting of a broad range of trades. Therefore, it will be necessary to examine in the next chapter the role of business managers in the exploitation of other natural resources, such as clay or quarries, and the manufacturing activities carried out on farmsteads.

1. *Patterns of landholding*

In Roman Italy during the Republican period, unavoidable shifts in the distribution of wealth led to changes in patterns of landholding. The main features of these transformations are the following:

---

[1] For instance, Cato, *Agr.* pref.; Hor., *Carm.* 1.1.17-18; Mart. 4.37; Gell., *NA* 15.1.

[2] Plut., *Cat. Mai.* 21.5-6; cf. A.E. Astin, *Cato the Censor* (Oxford 1978) 240-66; and 319-23.

– the concentration of agricultural estates in the hands of a more restricted class of wealthy landowners, although occasional assignations or redistributions of land tried to counter this trend;

– the scattering of their properties through different areas sometimes located far away from one another;

– the diversification of crops and profitable activities carried out on farmsteads, linked to an increasing division of labor;

– the widespread reliance on tenants, stewards, bailiffs, and overseers;[3]

– and the more extensive use of slave labor, temporarily supplemented by hired workers (free or slave) for ploughing, hoeing, and harvesting.[4] This general view of the development of Roman

---

[3] For the sake of clarity, I make a distinction between steward, bailiff, and overseer, even though they are often considered as exchangeable terms by modern translators of ancient texts. I use "steward" to translate *procurator*, "bailiff" or "reeve" to translate *vilicus*, and "overseer" or "foreman" to translate *praefectus, monitor*, and *magister*. I have tried thus to be consistent with the use of these terms in a medieval context, following the usage adopted, for instance, by D. Oschinsky, *Walter of Henley and Other Treatises on Estate Management and Accounting* (Oxford 1971). The terminology used in reference to the antebellum American plantation system distinguishes between steward, overseer, and driver; cf. W. K. Scarborough, *The Overseer. Plantation Management in the Old South*[2] (Athens, GA 1984). Both the English and the American systems present major differences in comparison with the Roman system, first of all because, in the Anglo-Saxon cases, all stewards and the majority of overseers stemmed from the upper classes (legal practitioners in medieval England, and landowners in Colonial America), and received a salary. By contrast, Roman managers were in most cases promoted slaves or freedmen whose position could be revoked at will. In the American case, the situation is complicated by the racial factor.

[4] Cato, *Agr.* 4.2. For supplementary work as part of labor services, cf. J. Percival, "Seigneurial Aspects of Late Roman Estate Management," *EHR* 84 (1969) 449-73, esp. 459-65 with second-century A.D. evidence from Africa (*CIL* VIII 25902, A.D. 116-117; 14428, A.D. 181; 10570, A.D. 180-183), fourth-century evidence about Illyricum (*Cod. Iust.* 11.53.1.1, A.D. 371), and sixth-century evidence from the region of Ravenna in northern Italy (*P. Ital.* 3). Columella's allusions (*Rust.* 1.7.1 and 11.1.14) are admittedly more controversial; St. John Chrysostom, *Hom. in Matth.* 61.3, sounds unequivocal to me. The scarcity of material has led modern scholars to the conclusion that labor services similar to those attested in the early Middle Ages were exceptional in antiquity, cf. C.R. Whittaker, "Circe's Pigs: From Slavery to Serfdom in the Later Roman World," in M.I. Finley (ed.), *Classical Slavery* (London 1987) 88-122, esp. 93. The silence of the sources is perhaps due to the nature of the material, and in any case arguments from silence are weak. One should not discount the possibility of local variations and other forms of pressure on the part of large landowners in order to exact labor services from the local peasantry. Cf. L. Foxhall, "The Dependent Tenant: Land Leasing and Labour in Italy and Greece," *JRS* 80 (1990) 97-114. V.I. Kuziščin, *La grande proprietà agraria nell'Italia romana* (Rome 1984) (first published in Russian in 1976) 235 interestingly

agriculture has been widely accepted, but needs to be qualified, in particular with regard to regional and chronological variations.[5]

In all parts of the Roman Empire the land fell into one of the following categories of property: public land; city land; temple land (which is rarely attested in the western part of the Empire), and church land in the Christian period; imperial land; and private land.[6] Land passed from one category to another through confiscation, restoration, gift, assignment, sale, marriage, or inheritance. The evidence suggests that in the late Republican and early Imperial periods transfers of land from one category to another and, within the same category, from one owner to another occurred very frequently.[7] Such changes would have been damaging to the productivity of agricultural land, had not some continuity been ensured at the management level.

2. Absentee landownership

The people who owned the land did not necessarily cultivate it. In the archaic period, landowners were more likely to be personally in-

---

suggests that the passage from tenancy to sharecropping attested by the early second century A.D. (Pliny, *Ep.* 9.37.3) may have contributed to worsen the situation of *coloni* with regard to labor services.

[5] R. MacMullen, *Roman Social Relations* (New Haven/London 1974) 3-6; 20-22; and 38; P.W. de Neeve, *Colonus. Private Farm-tenancy in Roman Italy during the Republic and the Early Empire* (Amsterdam 1984). A set of regional studies has been published in A. Giardina–A. Schiavone (eds.), *Società romana e produzione schiavistica* (Bari 1981), esp. vol. 1, for Italy; in A. Giardina (ed.), *Società romana e impero tardoantico* (Rome/Bari 1986) and *ANRW* II.1, 3, and 4 (1974 and 1975) for the provinces of the Roman Empire. Regional surveys are discussed by K. Greene, *The Archaeology of the Roman Economy* (Berkeley/L.A. 1986) 88-89 and 98-141; cf. also the review articles by D.W. Rathbone, in *JRS* 73 (1983) 160-68; C. Wickham, in *JRS* 78 (1988) 183-93; and N. Purcell, *ibidem* 194-98.

[6] For the difference between each category, cf. R.P. Duncan-Jones, "Some Configurations of Landholding in the Roman Empire," in Finley (1976) 7-33, in part. 7-12, now updated in R.P. Duncan-Jones, *Structure and Scale in the Roman Economy* (Cambridge 1990) 121-42. By the early third century A.D., the distinction between the first two categories was blurred; cf. Ulpianus (10 *ad ed.*) *Dig.* 50.16.15, who insists on the proper use of "publicus" as pertaining to the Roman state and not to a city; and F. Millar, *PBSR* 52 (1984) 133.

[7] For instance Cic., *Caecin.* 4.12-6.17; and Plin., *Ep.* 7.11.1 and 6; and 7.14. Cf. E. Rawson, "The Ciceronian Aristocracy and its Properties," in Finley (1976) 85-102, esp. 86; and J. Andreau, "Les financiers romains entre la ville et la campagne," in P. Leveau (ed.), *L'origine des richesses dépensées dans la ville antique* (Aix-en-Provence 1985) 177-96, esp. 186-87. This view has been qualified by S. Treggiari, "Sentiment and Property: Some Roman Attitudes," in A. Parel–T. Flanagan (eds.), *Theories of Property. Aristotle to the Present* (Calgary 1979) 53-85, esp. 57-62.

volved in farming than later. The stories depicting the members of
the Roman elite tilling their ancestors' land, alone or with the help
of other people (neighbors, hired labor, or dependents), may represent a literary *cliché*, but its historical roots cannot be disputed since
such a pattern of landholding remained frequent throughout the
Roman period.[8] However, there is no reason to think that the process of dissociation of landownership and farming was unknown at
an early date: the Roman law of property gave absolute ownership
to the head of the family, who often must have been unfit for the
harshness of farmwork by reason of age, health, or gender.[9] Absentee landownership, however, is often linked to three well-attested
phenomena:

– the increased involvement of the landowning population in
military and political activities;

– the development of cities and the connected—cause or consequence—drift of country dwellers to urban areas;

– and the growth in size of agricultural estates.

---

[8] Some recent archaeological surveys have shown that small-scale farming continued to be important in Italy until the second century A.D. at least; cf. J.M.
Frayn, *Subsistence Farming in Roman Italy* (London 1979) 29; and P.W. de Neeve,
Colonus (1984), *passim* (reviewed by B.W. Frier, *ZRG* 100 [1983] 671-76). One can
argue, however, that the archaeological evidence is unlikely to show the difference
between estates run by independent peasants and those cultivated by tenants or
bailiffs. R.P. Duncan-Jones, in Finley (1976) 22 uses epigraphical evidence, such
as land registers, to demonstrate that in the regions where the spectrum of agrarian
wealth is the broadest, small landholdings are more numerous.

[9] Women were *sui juris* when no male relative (father, husband, brother, son)
was left to be *pater familias*. Female landowners are frequently attested in Greek and
Latin literature and in inscriptions during the Imperial period; cf. S. Dixon, "Polybius on Women and Property," *AJP* 106 (1985) 147-70, whose opinion (p. 157) I
share: "It is evident that, once her husband's death rendered her *sui juris*, a woman
owned property, made wills, and created obligations.... In neither period [IInd
and Ist centuries B.C.] does the tutor seem to have presented any effective bar to
the woman's activities." In the provinces during the Imperial period, the picture
might be distorted by the fact that men had a strong interest in registering their
property in their wives' name, since women were usually not liable for compulsory
public services: according to Ulpianus (2 *opinionum*) *Dig.* 50.4.3.3, "corporalia
munera feminis ipse sexus denegat." Admittedly, women could be forced to perform *honores*, *munera personalia*, and *munera patrimoniorum*, although this could be a
third-century development (*Cod.Iust.* 10.64.1, 244-249; and 10.42.9, 284-305).
Still, this fact does not account for every case in which a woman is found owning
property; cf. D. Hobson, "Women as Property Owners in Roman Egypt," *TAPhA*
113 (1983) 311-21. Cf. *AE* 1961, no. 175; *CIL* VI 758? *CIL* VI 9986 (= *CIL* XI
4422); *CIL* VI 9989 (= *ILS* 7370); *AE* 1966, no. 106; *CIL* IX 3103? *CIL* IX 3446;
CIL X 4917? *CIL* X 8217 (= *ILS* 3523)? *CIL* XIV 2751? Cf. also below, *actores*
whose principals were women.

Due to the lack of reliable evidence, it is difficult to trace the origin of these phenomena, but they were undoubtedly well under way at the beginning of the second century B.C.[10]

The threefold historical development described below affected only part of the rural population. It is not important for my purpose to determine what percentage of landowners switched from direct farming to absentee landownership: their number proved to be large enough to call for the development of alternative systems of management. What is more important is that these landowners belonged to a social stratum most likely to leave a mark in the literary, legal, and epigraphical sources, though there is a risk that this social group might be overestimated by modern historians for this very reason. Further, the Latin agronomists shamelessly and endlessly whine over what they see as ill-inspired and unwelcome changes in response to which they wrote their treatises on agriculture.[11]

a. military and political activities of landowners

In the early Republic, the Roman army was made up of farmers who were rich enough to qualify for enrollment in the centuriate organization. Personal or family wealth, in the form of landed property, was instrumental in determining in which unit a citizen was expected to serve, and hence, how much political power he would enjoy. The richer a citizen, the more likely he would be to stay away from his estate. Short campaigns conducted in the vicinity of Rome did not affect agricultural activities, but the development of siege-warfare and the involvement of Rome in Mediterranean politics brought radical changes in the life of farmers-soldiers. Livy's description of the siege of Veii[12] suggests that cultivators were kept away from their farms for long periods already at the beginning of the fourth century B.C. Such a change in warfare was certainly facilitated by the growing availability of substitute manpower, such as slavery.[13]

---

[10] M. Rostovtzeff, *The Social and Economic History of the Roman Empire*[2] (Oxford 1957) 13-19 and 33.

[11] P.A. Brunt, *JRS* 62 (1972) 153-58, esp. 154-55, reviewing K.D. White, *Roman Farming* (London 1970), discusses the attitude of the elite toward farming (as opposed to landowning).

[12] Livy 5.1-22.

[13] W.V. Harris, "Roman Warfare in the Economic and Social Context of the Fourth Century B.C.," in W. Eder (ed.), *Staat und Staatlichkeit in der frühen römischen Republik* (Stuttgart 1990) 494-510, esp. 499 and 507. Harris rightly surmises that

Absentee landowners appointed managers to take care of their estate in their absence. Once in a while, they would show up at the farmstead to make sure that business was conducted as expected. In the *Captivi*, a Latin comedy written around the turn of the third to the second century B.C., Plautus mentions that during certain periods of the year a recess in public affairs was pronounced so that people could go to the country to take care of their possessions.[14]

The first "historical" occurrence of a *vilicus* belongs to the third century B.C. The anecdote, which is reported with some significant discrepancies by several Latin authors of the Augustan and early Imperial periods (Livy, Valerius Maximus, Seneca, and Frontinus), may be mostly fictitious, but it contains plausible elements that deserve our attention. In 255 B.C., as he was successfully campaigning against the Carthaginians in Africa, the Roman general Atilius Regulus wrote to the senate to ask for an honorable discharge. To justify his request, Regulus argued that the manager of his Pupinian estate had died and that some of the farm equipment had been subsequently stolen. The senate refused to give him a leave of absence, but promised to take care of the matter. Our sources specify that the estate consisted of seven *iugera*, which is probably an exaggeration aimed at emphasizing Regulus's modesty. One man could easily perform the agricultural work, and this accounts for the fact that Regulus apparently did not own any slave and had to hire a *mercennarius* as *vilicus*. Seneca's and Frontinus's reports, though they differ on a significant detail—the death or flight of the manager—are probably more accurate than the others, who tried to conflate the two versions. The question consists in deciding whether the *mercennarius/-ii* who left ("discessit/-erunt") conceals in fact a hired *vilicus* who died ("decessit"). The size of the estate—provided that the data recorded in the sources are reliable—makes it unlikely that more than one person was employed to cultivate it.[15]

---

the availability of "a large and well organized body of non-citizen labour" accounted for a change in the organization of the Roman Republican army from a citizen militia to "a strategically more flexible force which could stay in the field for months on end, and do so year after year." He dates this change to the period between the 350's and the 290's, which coincides with the abolition of debt-bondage (*nexum*, cf. below).

[14] Plaut., *Capt.* 78 ff.

[15] I provide the relevant texts (with my emphasis) in the chronological order in which they were written:

  – Livy, *Per.* 18: "Atilius Regulus . . ., cum aliquot proeliis bene adversus Car-

E. Maróti dismisses the whole story as anachronistic and argues that the *vilicus* mentioned by Valerius Maximus, Pliny the Elder, and Frontinus could not correspond to the type of manager described by Cato, because "Regulus could not have needed such an overseer, as he did not cultivate intensive farming for the market: no author mentions any other slave working in his farmstead but the *vilicus*." On the basis of this debatable statement, Maróti concludes that the appearance of the *vilicus* must have followed the growth of the villa phenomenon.[16]

b. *vilicus system and villa economy*
Maróti, like many other modern historians, links the *vilicus* system with a plantation-type mode of production based on slave labor and commonly called "slave mode of production." This view rests on two misconceptions. First, the etymological association of the word *vil(l)icus* with the word *villa* lead many scholars to the conclusion that the *vilicus* system should be understood only in connection with a

---

thaginienses pugnasset, successorque ei a senatu prospere bellum gerenti non mitteretur, id ipsum per litteras ad senatum scriptas questus est, in quibus inter causas petendi successoris erat quod agellus eius *a mercennariis* desertus esset."

– Val.Max. 4.4.6: "...Atilius Regulus ... consulibus scripsit *vilicum* in agello, quem septem iugerum in Pupinia habebat, mortuum esse, occasionemque nanctum *mercennarium* amoto inde rustico instrumento discessisse, ideoque petere ut sibi successor mitteretur, ne deserto agro non esset unde uxor ac liberi sui alerentur. Quae postquam senatus a consulibus accepit, et agrum Atili ilico colendum locari et alimenta coniugi eius ac liberis praeberi resque, quas amiserat, redimi publice iussit."

– Sen., *Helv.* 12.5: "Atilius Regulus, cum Poenos in Africa funderet, ad senatum scripsit *mercennarium* suum discessisse et ab eo desertum esse rus, quod senatui publice curari, dum abesset Regulus, placuit. Fuitne tanti servum non habere, ut *colonus* eius populus Romanus esset?"

– Frontin., *Str.* 4.3.3: "Atilius Regulus, cum summis rebus praefuisset, adeo pauper fuit, ut se coniugem liberosque tolleraret agello, qui colebatur per unum *vilicum*: cuius audita morte scripsit senatui de successore, destitutis rebus obitu servi necessariam esse praesentiam suam." Cf. also Pliny, *HN* 18.39; Apul., *Apol.* 18.11; *Auctor de viris illustribus* 40; Dio Cass., Book 11, frg. 43.20.

[16] E. Maróti, "The *vilicus* and the Villa-system in Ancient Italy," *Oikumene* 1 (1976) 109-24, esp. 112-13. The whole paper is articulated on the premise that "the appearance of the *vilicus* became timely in ancient Italy, when—alongside the self-supplying small-peasant farms based on polyculture—there appeared the intensive agricultural economic units called into existence to produce some especially lucrative products (such as wine, oil, fruit and vegetables) that establish close contact with the market" (p. 111). Cf. also M. Rostovtzeff, *SEHRE*[2] (1957) 30, who assimilates the *vilicus* system with the slave mode of production, which he considers derived from a Hellenistic pattern.

certain type of rural or suburban establishment, the development of
which took place in the first half of the second century B.C. around
the Bay of Naples and is known to us through archaeological remains and literary descriptions. This architectural development reflects a social phenomenon as well as an economic mutation.[17]
However, it is quite likely that long before the development of the
so-called "villa economy" there were some kinds of architectural
structures that the Romans designated by the term *villa*. Early villas
were certainly owned by the wealthiest, the poor living in mere
tuguria.[18]

The second misconception rests on the belief that Cato's *vilicus* is
the archetype of the Roman bailiff throughout Roman history, without taking into consideration that the system described by Cato was
already the result of a long historical development. We can surmise
that the concept of a manager set up at the head of an agricultural
unit is certainly older than the so-called villa phenomenon and the
plantation-type estate familiar to Cato. In addition, both the epigraphical and literary evidence provide a distorted picture of agricultural estates run by bailiffs, because extant sources tend to record
only large and prosperous estates. Most of the time the scale of the

---

[17] E. Maróti, *Oikumene* 1 (1976) 112-13. On the villa phenomenon, cf. J.H.
D'Arms, *The Romans on the Bay of Naples* (Cambridge, MA 1970) and *idem*, *Commerce
and Social Standing in Ancient Rome* (Cambridge, MA 1981) 72-96; and G. Pucci,
"Schiavitù romana nelle campagne. Il sistema della villa nell'Italia centrale," in
A. Carandini *et al.* (eds.), *Settefinestre. Una villa schiavistica nell'Etruria romana* I
(Modena 1985) 15-21. The etymology of the word *vilicus* is discussed by Varro:
"Vilicus agri colendi causa constitutus atque appellatus a villa, quod ab eo in eam
convehuntur fructus et evehuntur, cum veneunt" (*Rust.* 1.2.14). References to villas and *vilici* in Plautus are not rare, cf. *Merc.* 277-278; *Cas. passim*; *Poen.* 170;
Mostell. 68; *Tri.* 508 and 542, etc. The first references in Livy to a *villa* occur in
2.23.5 and 2.26.1 and 3: the owner of the villa was a centurion who went into debt
and became *nexus* around 495 B.C. The other references to early villas are related
to the razzias perpetrated by the Romans in the Sabine country in 470 B.C. (Livy
2.62.4: *villae et vici*) and in the Faliscan country in 394 B.C. (Livy 5.26.4). I see
no reason to dismiss as anachronistic the use of the term *villa* by Livy in reference
to early Republican farms. This is not to say that these early villas have any connection with the social phenomenon described by D'Arms.

[18] Livy (3.26.7-9) illustrates the low social level of people living in *tuguria* by
describing the simplicity of L. Quinctius Cincinnatus, who reportedly lived off four
iugera of land located on the right bank of the Tiber River. His poverty, however,
was the result of the penalty paid a few years earlier (461 B.C.) on behalf of his son
Caeso and was therefore exceptional (Livy 3.13). Spurius Ligustinus, the veteran
centurion who pronounced a famous speech in 171 B.C., was even worse off: his
plot was as small as one *iugerum*. He also lived in a *tugurium* (Livy 42.34.2).

concern and the type of management remain unknown. On the basis of the available material one has to admit that the type of management of an estate can be inferred neither from the size of the estate and of its staff, nor from the kinds of crops produced on it.[19] In my opinion, there is no connection between type of management and capital investment: mixed farming and cash crops called for fully equipped estates, which assumedly yielded a higher rent and therefore could not be afforded by poor tenants, but it would be wrong to see tenants as belonging to a homogeneous, impoverished class of farmers.[20]

To return to Regulus's story, I think that no historical considerations permit us to reject it as implausible. The authors who reported it may differ on some points, but they do not seem to have been troubled in the least by the fact that a small plot had been entrusted to a *vilicus* during the landowner's absence. There is no doubt that in the following century and a half until the Marian reforms Roman imperialism made the practice of setting up managers on agricultural estates more common, but when difficulties arose, most landowners on duty could not count on the Roman People to take over the management of their farms.

c. *urbanization of Roman society*

Absentee landownership became also more common as a broader range of the population became aware of, and aspired to, the leisure and amenities of urban life in contrast with the hardships and toils of the country.[21] In addition to that, many farmers were forced out of their ancestral land. As a result of both desired and forced migration from country to towns, the extension of urban areas made fewer agricultural lands accessible by foot to city-dwellers, and the gap between urban and rural population grew wider. Plautus shows that a lower-middle-class landowner like Lysidamus, who wanted to live in town, had to rely on a bailiff for the operation of his farm, because

---

[19] Some modern scholars have tried to demonstrate that tenancy was more convenient for grain cultivation, while the *vilicus* system would have been better fitted for the cultivation of cash-crops (wine, oil), which requires a larger capital investment. Cf. for instance P.W. de Neeve, *Colonus* (1984) 92-95.

[20] Ulpianus (32 *ad ed.*), quoting a letter from L. Neratius to T. Aristo, *Dig.* 19.2.19.2; cf. B.W. Frier, "Law, Technology, and Social Change. The Equipping of Italian Farm Tenancies," *ZRG* 96 (1979) 204-28.

[21] R. MacMullen, *RSR* (1974) 15.

the distance separating the town from the villa was great.[22] Two centuries later, Columella recommends to prospective buyers that they purchase a suburban villa. The vicinity of the town—where the landowner was expected to live—would make his visits to his estate easier and therefore more frequent. As a result, he could expect a better management on the part of his bailiff and a higher return from his investment.[23]

d. *growth of large estates*

The building up of large estates called for new forms of management. When and how the creation of estates too large to be farmed by one family took place is a much debated question that cannot be discussed here.[24] Even if one considers the tradition about the Licinian-Sextian law limiting the size of occupancy of public land to 500 *iugera* as an anachronism reflecting the Gracchan legislation, it is enough to state that by the beginning of the second century B.C. large estates must have been fairly common.[25] Cato, who wrote in the first half of the second century, discusses for the sake of example a vineyard of 100 *iugera* or an olive-grove of 240 *iugera*.[26] These figures are discussed by Varro who does not discard them as unreasonable or exceptional.[27] They possibly reflect the size of some of Cato's personal properties and correspond to an average managerial unit.[28] Columella mentions an estate of 200 *iugera* of arable

---

[22] Plaut., *Cas.* 420: "Scin tu rus hinc esse ad villam longe quo ducat?" In Plaut., *Tri.* 508, Lesbonicus, undoubtedly a city-dweller, admits that he owns an "ager sub urbe" exploited by Syrian slaves (542). Theopropides, whose main household is in town, owns a villa in the countryside ("ruri") which he left in the care of his slave Grumio while spending three years in Egypt on a business trip (Plaut., *Mostell.* 1 ff.; 62; 68; and 440).

[23] Columella, *Rust.* 1.1.19.

[24] V.I. Kuziščin (1984) [1976] 8 describes a *latifundium* as a big agricultural enterprise, organized as a single centralized managerial unit, extended over a wide area (1,000 *iugera* or more), and cultivated mostly by slaves, with a specific internal organization. According to this scholar, this type of estate was the result of a long historical process, culminating in the first century A.D., whereby rich landowners who had bought disjuncted estates tended to consolidate their assets by buying neighboring properties (with reference to Petron., *Sat.* 48.2-3; and Pliny, *Ep.* 3.19.1).

[25] On the availability of public land and how the rich benefited from it, cf. W.V. Harris (1990) 503, who points out that the senators who served on the commission presiding over the creation of colonies legally took part of the land for themselves or assigned it to their friends.

[26] Cato, *Agr.* 10-13.

[27] Varro, *Rust.* 1.18-19.

[28] V.I. Kuziščin (1984) [1976] 28-29 plausibly suggests that the vineyard and

land, which he uses as a basis for computation of labor-input in grain and vegetable production.[29]

In spite of the figures found in agricultural treatises, we have very little information about what should have been the average size of agricultural estates at any given period and in any given area. One can expect a great variety of sizes. The attempt to define a minimum size, based on the calculation of the basic needs of a small household, would be distorted by the fact that it is likely that small landholders were relying on other resources, like fishing, hunting, fruit-picking, or temporary work—not necessarily related to agriculture—to support their family. The other end of the spectrum lies somewhere in the hundreds of thousands of *iugera*, as we know, for instance, that a late Republican senator, L. Domitius Ahenobarbus, could plausibly afford to promise 40 *iugera* per man to some thirty cohorts. We are also told that a freedman under Augustus could boast about using 3,600 pairs of oxen on his estate, or that half of the province of Africa was owned by six landowners at the time of Nero.[30]

e. *managerial units and units of production*
Even though ancient writers failed to develop a theory of optimum size for agricultural holdings, landowners had to figure out what was most practical in terms of management. We possess some incidental information about sizes and prices of estates across the Empire in later times. As might be expected, the figures vary greatly, so that it seems impossible to draw any general conclusions from them.[31] It is clear that for practical reasons large estates must have been divided into managerial units, the size of which must be comprised within a certain range.[32] Archaeological surveys are useless for this

the olive-grove constituted two separate managerial units, located in two different areas.

[29] Columella, *Rust.* 2.12.7. Elsewhere, the same author denounces large estates, and recommends to prospective buyers to show moderation "ne maiorem (agrum) quam ratio calculorum patitur emere velint;" cf. *Rust.* 1.3.8-13.

[30] P.A. Brunt, "Two Great Roman Landowners," *Latomus* 34 (1975) 619-35, based on Caesar, *BCiv.* 1.17.3; Pliny, *HN* 33.135 (cf. below); and Pliny, *HN* 18.35.

[31] R.P. Duncan-Jones, *The Economy of the Roman Empire: Quantitative Studies*[2] (Cambridge 1982) 323-26.

[32] B.W. Frier, *ZRG* 96 (1979) 214, nn. 51-52 suggests a range between 50 and 250 *iugera* (= 12.6 and 63 ha). Large estates were often the result of successive purchases of contiguous plots. What looks like a *latifundium* was not necessarily managed differently from a collection of estates; cf. V.I. Kuziščin (1984) [1976] 77.

matter, because managerial units do not always coincide with units of production: Horace's estate, for instance, was made of six units of production, but formed only one managerial unit.[33]

The division of large and middle-sized estates into several managerial units brought in a new class of middlemen responsible for supervising the management of single units. The lower level of management seems to have been the *fundus*. B.W. Frier suggests that "the area of the *fundus* was more or less the amount of land that could be conveniently cultivated, out of the villa, by a single operator-manager plus a complement of permanently assigned slaves (assisted now and again by hirelings)."[34] The *fundus* can be described as a managerial unit that often corresponded to a unit of production, or economic unit.[35] The discussion about the precise meaning of these concepts has been recently reviewed by P.W. de Neeve,[36] who came to the following conclusions: the available evidence suggests that a *fundus* was an administrative unit, the extent and purpose of which was determined by the owner;[37] the value of the *fundus* had to be estimated, registered in tables, and transcribed in the *forma* for fiscal purposes; the yields (*reditus*) were registered under one heading in the account books (*rationes*) of the owner, and it does not matter whether the *fundus* was partitioned or was part of a larger economic unit.[38] A *fundus* was identified by the name of its

---

[33] Hor., *Epist.* 1.14; and *Sat.* 2.7.117-118 (cf. below). R.P. Duncan-Jones, in Finley (1976) 7-33, esp. 12-18, shows that large estates were made of components, the average size of which remained relatively small and depended on the type of activities (agricultural concerns being smaller than pastures). He compares some figures related to the Ligures Baebiani (A.D. 101), Veleia (A.D. 102/113), Volcei (A.D. 307), Lamasba/Numidia (A.D. 218/222), Magnesia-on-the-Maeander, and Hermopolis in Egypt (both in the fourth century). On Horace's estate, cf. *Epist.* 1.14 and below.

[34] B.W. Frier, *ZRG* 96 (1979) 214.

[35] A. Steinwenter, *Fundus cum instrumento* (Leipzig/Vienna 1942) 10-24.

[36] P.W. de Neeve, "Fundus as Economic Unit," *RHD* 52 (1984) 3-19.

[37] Ulpianus (69 *ad ed.*) *Dig.* 50.16.60 *pr.*: "'Locus' est non fundus, sed portio aliqua fundi: 'fundus' autem integrum aliquid est. Et plerumque sine villa 'locum' accipimus: ceterum adeo opinio nostra et constitutio locum a fundo separat, ut et modicus locus possit fundus dici, si fundi animo eum habuimus. Non etiam magnitudo locum a fundo separat, sed nostra affectio: et quaelibet portio fundi poterit fundus dici, si iam hoc constituerimus. Nec non et fundus locus constitui potest: nam si eum alii adiunxerimus fundo, locus fundi efficietur."

[38] Ulpianus (3 *de cens.*) *Dig.* 50.15.4 *pr.*: "Forma censuali cavetur, ut agri sic in censum referantur. Nomen fundi cuiusque: et in qua civitate et in quo pago sit: et quos duos vicinos proximos habeat. Et arvum, quod in decem annos proximos satum erit, quot iugerum sit: vinea quot vites habeat: olivae quot iugerum et quot

present or past owner(s), by its manager, by its location in a *civitas* and *pagus*, and by its relation to neighboring estates (*adfines*).[39]

B. Systems of management

1. *Tenancy or agency*

When a landowner was unable or unwilling to cultivate parts of his estates, he had several options. He could sell or abandon the land. If he wished to keep it in his ownership, he could lease some plots to tenant-farmers (*conductores* or *coloni*) from whom he would periodically collect a rent in cash or in kind, fixed or proportional to the size of the crop (sharecropping). In this case, he had no say in the management of the enterprise. The tenant could either sublet the land or cultivate it himself, alone or with the help of a rural household. This system will be referred to as tenancy.

Another option, available both to landowners and to chief-lessees (*conductores*), was to establish a bailiff (*vilicus*) in charge of an estate. The *vilicus* either worked the land himself or supervised the work of a rural household (*familia rustica*) in accordance with the instructions of the landowner who remained interested in the good management of the enterprise. Landowners and chief-lessees collected the proceeds from the activities of the *vilicus*, but had to pay for all operating expenses while securing the manager's cooperation and diligence with some kind of incentive, most often of economic nature. This system will be referred to as *vilicus* system or agency.

The difference between tenancy and agency is not so clear-cut as it appears at first sight. The late-second-century-A.D. jurist Q. Cervidius Scaevola unambiguously indicates that both tenants (*conductores*) and farm managers (*vilici*) were paying some type of rent (*pen-*

---

arbores habeant: pratum, quod intra decem annos proximos sectum erit, quot iugerum: pascua quot iugerum esse videantur: item silvae caeduae. Omnia ipse qui defert aestimet.'' Actual examples are found in the *Tabulae* of Veleia (*CIL* XI 1147 = *ILS* 6675) and of the Ligures Baebiani (*CIL* IX 1455 = *ILS* 6509).

[39] Scaevola (17 *dig.*) *Dig.* 32.35.1: ''Sempronio ita legavit: 'Sempronius sumito praedia mea omnia, quae sunt usque ad praedium, quod vocatur Gaas, finibus Galatiae, sub cura vilici Primi, ita ut haec omnia instructa sunt'. Quaesitum est, cum in eodem confinio praediorum unum sit praedium non Galatiae, sed Cappadociae finibus, sub cura tamen eiusdem vilici, an etiam id praedium cum ceteris ad Sempronium pertineat. Respondit et hoc deberi.''

siones).[40] If this passage reflects a common practice, it shows that landowners choosing between tenancy and agency were guided by various factors, but not necessarily by the extent, nature, or form of payment of the income derived from the estate.

Absentee landowners and farmers, either tenants or bailiffs, were bound by some type of legal relationship. When both sides enjoyed full legal capacity to make a contract in Roman law and were willing to establish a legal relationship, they could choose between lease/ hire (*locatio conductio*), mandate (*mandatum*), or procuratorship (*procuratio*). If the circumstances did not permit the parties to conclude a contract based on mutual agreement (*consensus*), the farmer who took the initiative to manage another person's estate was made accountable for, and enjoyed the rights pertaining to, his unauthorized administration (*negotium gestum*). By contrast, those farmers who lacked a full legal capacity could be tied to their landowners by a socio-legal bond based on their status of dependency: they were slaves, descendants-in-power (*alieni iuris*), freedmen, clients, or bondmen (*nexi*). Even though this last type of social bond was statutorily abolished in the late fourth-century B.C., the measure fell short of its purpose, and *nexi* were replaced by a new category called *addicti*, whose status of dependency was determined by judicial decision.[41] Varro mentions *obaerarii* in the section dealing with the role of free men in agriculture, reporting that in his time they were most numerous in Asia, Egypt, and Illyricum.[42] There is little evidence that they existed in Italy. Incidentally, one should point out that Varro's assertion about their frequency in Egypt is not supported by papyrological evidence, which raises some questions about the overall validity of the statement. The whole passage

---

[40] Scaevola (24 *dig.*) *Dig.* 40.7.40.5: "Item quaero, an eorum quoque nomine ratio haberi debeat, quod neque a conductoribus praediorum neque a vilicis pensiones exegerit et insuper etiam promutuum eis dederit." This point will be further discussed later on.

[41] On the whole question of the personal status of insolvent debtors during the Republican period, cf. G. MacCormack, "*Nexi, judicati*, and *addicti* in Livy," *ZRG* 84 (1967) 350-55; *idem*, "The Lex Poetelia Papiria," *Labeo* 19 (1973) 306-17; and L. Peppe, *Studi sull'esecuzione personale* I (Milan 1981). The late-fourth-century statute is the *Lex Poetelia Papiria*, dated to 326 B.C. by Livy (8.28) and to 313 by Varro (*Ling.* 7.105).

[42] Varro, *Rust.* 1.17.2; cf. also E. Lo Cascio, "*Oberarii (obaerati)*. La nozione della dipendenza in Varrone," *Index* 11 (1982) 265-84; and J. Ramin-P. Veyne, "Droit romain et société: les hommes qui passent pour esclaves et l'esclavage volontaire," *Historia* 30 (1981) 472-97, esp. 486-87.

might be nothing but an antiquarian digression and distortion with no historical significance, since *nexi/addicti/obaerarii* do not appear anywhere else but in the works of antiquarians.[43]

2. *Vilicus system and slave mode of production*

It is important to stress that the choice between agency and tenancy is not connected with the employment of slaves *vs.* free labor. Even though the evidence is not so abundant as expected, there is no doubt that tenants could, and did, employ slave labor.[44] These slaves were either part of the equipment (provided by the lessor) or of the increment (provided by the lessee).[45] On the other hand, the story of Regulus according to Frontinus shows that *vilici* were not necessarily at the head of a rural household. Similar cases are rarely attested, because small enterprises are unlikely to be recorded in our sources. In the late Republican and early Imperial periods, the two

---

[43] The antiquarian character of Varro, *Rust.* 1.17.2: "iique quos obaerarios nostri vocitarunt et etiam nunc sunt in Asia atque Aegypto et in Illyrico complures" is emphasized by the comparison with *Ling.* 7.105: "Liber qui suas operas in servitutem pro pecunia quam debebat <dabat> dum solveret, nexus vocatur, ut ab aere obaeratus." First- and second-century-A.D. antiquarians were obviously fond of this topic: some contemporary historical event, phenomenon, or controversy might lurk in the background (cf. Columella, *Rust.* 1.3.12; Quint., *Inst.* 7.3.26; Gell., *NA* 20.1.42-52; Festus, 165 Müller; Gai., *Inst.* 3.199).

[44] Ulpianus (20 *ad Sab.*), citing Labeo and Pegasus, *Dig.* 33.7.12.3, speaking of a *servus quasi colonus* (cf. below): "...etiamsi solitus fuerat et familiae imperare." Cf. V.I. Kuziščin (1984) [1976] 31, n. 58 and 237. Columella, *Rust.* 1.7.3, refers to a tenant (*colonus*) living in town and running his farm "per familiam." This passage illustrates the difference between chief-lessee and tenant-farmer; cf. also Pliny, *Ep.* 3.19; Ulpianus (18 *ad ed.*), quoting Proculus, *Dig.* 9.2.27.11 (= *Coll.* 12.7.9) and quoting Neratius, *Dig.* 9.2.27.9 (= *Coll.* 12.7.7) = *FIRA* II² 575. Some epigraphical evidence is cited by D.P. Kehoe, *Chiron* 18 (1988) 18, n. 10 (*CIL* IX 3674-3675 [= *ILS* 7455-7455a]; and *CIL* IX 5659), to which one can add an interesting tile inscription (on two columns) from Erlach (Upper Germania): MATERNVS / MACCIVS / GRATVS // POSSESSIO / DIROGIS / GRATI / SER(vu)S / MASSO / FECIT, cf. R. Laur-Belart, *JBM* 34 (1954) 164-65 and *JSGU* 44 (1954) 111-12, cited by N. Brockmeyer, *AncSoc* 6 (1975) 211-28, esp. 222. Masso, Gratus's slave, was working in a tile factory located on Dirox's estate. It is possible that Gratus was a joint-tenant (together with Maternus and Maccius) of Dirox. Cf. now R. Frei-Stolba, *AS* 3 (1980) 103-05.

[45] B.W. Frier, *ZRG* 96 (1979) 218, nn. 73-75, citing Labeo, quoted by Ulpianus (17 *ad Sab.*) *Dig.* 7.8.12.6, and Pliny, *Ep.* 3.19.2 to illustrate the first case; and Alfenus (3 *dig. a Paulo epit.*) *Dig.* 19.2.30.4, Proculus and Neratius, quoted by Ulpianus (18 *ad ed.*) *Dig.* 9.2.27.9 and 11, and Iulianus (49 *dig.*) *Dig.* 43.33.1 *pr.* to illustrate the second case. Frier also points out that in Cato's agricultural contracts (*Agr.* 144-150), livestock and labor are provided by the (*red*)*emptor*.

best-represented types of estate management were either personal
management by small- and middle-scale tenant-farmers who paid
rent on the land to the landowner or to his steward (*procurator/actor*),
or the so-called "slave mode of production" featuring a certain—
often large—number of slaves under the command of a bailiff. But
once again, *vilicus* system does not imply slave mode of production,
and vice-versa. Inferring the existence of either institution from the
evidence pertaining to the other amounts to, at best, a plausible assumption.

The selection of a type of management was determined by various
factors. It could be a matter of personal prejudice or inclination,
family tradition, local custom, historical and social context, economic and political considerations, etc. As might be expected, the
sources are rather laconic about the reasons why one system was to
be preferred to the other. The Latin agronomists focus on the economic aspect, but they sound as if they were more interested in containing potential destruction on the part of the manager and the
hands—out of neglect or malfeasance—than in maximizing their
profit. This attitude shows that landowners were highly concerned
about the consequences of a possible cessation of agricultural work,
and with any kind of mishandling of the crops and of the farm
equipment.

The negative views expressed by the agronomists about the *vilicus*
system in connection with the slave mode of production cannot be
accepted uncritically, because, in spite of their reservations about
the reliability of *vilici* and slave labor in general, they dwell on the
subject of agency much longer than on tenancy. This is, however,
no evidence for the respective success of the two systems, for treatises on agriculture were written for inexperienced landowners who,
I would suggest, had some difficulty in keeping up with their managers.[46]

3. Agency vs. tenancy during the Imperial period: decline or stability?

Whether absentee landowners showed a preference for one system
over the other is difficult to assert. The debate among modern scho-

---

[46] N. Purcell, "Wine and Wealth in Ancient Italy," *JRS* 75 (1985) 1-19, esp.
5 and 8, suggests that Cato's and Virgil's treatises were clearly addressed to *vilici*,
and through them to the municipal elite rather than to the senatorial nobility. Cf.
below.

lars on the comparative practicality and popularity of tenancy and agency is heated, and the secondary literature supporting each side is enormous and often ideologically biased. As mentioned above, modern historians often identify the *vilicus* system with the slave mode of production featuring a massive use of slave labor on plantation-type estates.[47] Such a connection is undoubtedly correct in some instances, but is by no means necessary, and consequently, the evidence on which the discussion is based remains ultimately inconclusive. In addition, several literary and epigraphical texts show that in many cases agency existed side-by-side with tenancy and independent smallholdings, and that the various systems of management supplemented each other.

a. *vilicus system in the early Principate*
Not long after Varro wrote his treatise on agriculture with its detailed description of the *vilicus* system, the poet Horace was given an estate in the Sabine country on which he employed five free tenants and a small rural household composed of nine slaves. Horace's *vilicus* formerly belonged to an urban household and had apparently no training in agriculture.[48] What is noticeable in this case is that the *vilicus* supervised both the slaves and the tenants.

On January 27, 8 B.C. a freedman named C. Caecilius Isidorus, possibly a member of the notorious family of the Metelli, made his will in which he listed the extent of his wealth: 4,116 slaves, 3,600 pair of oxen, a herd of 257,000, and 60,000,000 sestertii in cash, out of which 1,100,000 were alloted for his funeral. P.A. Brunt's astute calculation reveals that the number of oxen, considered as farm equipment, would suffice for ca. 360,000 *iugera* of arable land, whereas the herd would require ca. 771,000 *iugera* of pasture land. Brunt points out that "at the ratio of one slave to every 15 or 20 *jugera*, his (= Isidorus's) whole *familia* could have cultivated no more than 62-82,000 *jugera*. And yet…the greater number of his slaves were probably in other employment, or in the case of many children, in none." Brunt's conclusion is that only a small part of Isidorus's

---

[47] Cf. above and V.I. Kuziščin (1984) [1976] 86.

[48] Horace, *Epist.* 1.14.14, calls him a *mediastinus* ("common drudge"). For the size of the *familia rustica*, cf. *Sat.* 2.7.117-18. Horace approved the use of slaves in agriculture and trade (*Epist.* 1.16.70-72); cf. J.E. Skydsgaard, *JRS* 61 (1971) 277; and M. Rostovtzeff, *SEHRE*² (1957) 59-61, who qualifies Horace's estate as being of "intermediate size."

estate was cultivated by slaves, who, according to a sensible though gratuitous assumption, were subordinated to a *vilicus*. The rest of the land must have been leased out to tenants or worked by free laborers (*operarii*). This case suggests that when the slave mode of production was supposed to be at its peak some great landowners were reluctant to rely exclusively on slave labor.[49] In this case, there is no way to say whether hired labor was preferred to tenancy. A factor that might have influenced Isidorus's options was a law of Caesar stipulating that one third of herdsmen in Italy had to be freeborn adults,[50] so that the slaves mentioned in Isidorus's will are more likely to have been employed in cultivation than in cattle grazing.

A century later, Pliny the Younger is known to have relied on tenants to farm his estates. Pliny was considering the merger of two neighboring estates of significant sizes in Tifernum Tiberinum. The original estate, which had been hitherto cultivated by slaves, was to be administered together with the prospective one by a *procurator* and *actores*, and leased out to tenants (*coloni*). The main function of *procurator* and *actores* probably consisted in collecting the rent and exercising a general supervision. Pliny was planning to equip the tenants of the prospective estate with new slaves of good quality, which proves that tenancy and slave mode of production were not exclusive of each other.[51]

A harder point to decide is whether or not Pliny kept part of his Tuscan estate under direct management. Pliny's interest in agriculture was limited, as he reports how glad he was to be able to rely on his urban slaves for the organization of the farmwork at harvest

---

[49] P.A. Brunt, *Latomus* 35 (1974) 619-35, using the evidence provided by Pliny, *HN* 33.135: "C. Asinio Gallo C. Marcio Censorino cos. a.d. VI Kal. Febr. C. Caecilius C.l. Isidorus testamento suo edixit, quamvis multa bello civili perdidisset, tamen relinquere servorum IIII CXVI, iuga boum III DC, reliqui pecoris CCLVII, in numerato HS |DC|, funerari se iussit HS |XI|." It does not matter for my purpose whether Brunt's calculations are accurate, or whether, as he himself suggests, arable land and pasture partly overlap. The point is to demonstrate that the number of slaves boasted by Isidorus is far inferior to the number required by the size of his estate, estimated on the basis of the available traction equipment (oxen), provided that all oxen were indeed used only for ploughing, and not for other tasks, such as hauling heavy material (stone or marble from quarries, or timber).

[50] Suet., *Iul.* 42.1: "neve ii, qui pecuariam facerent, minus tertia parte puberum ingenuorum inter pastores haberent." Cf. also Appian, *BCiv.* 1.1.8 about a similar provision existing at the time of the Gracchi.

[51] Plin., *Ep.* 3.19.2; cf. A.N. Sherwin-White, *The Letters of Pliny: A Historical and Social Commentary* (Oxford 1966) 254.

time, thus allowing him to devote his time to his favorite intellectual pursuits.[52] Pliny probably alludes to something more specific than the general administration of his properties as a whole, but the management of the plot kept under direct control may have been entrusted to a *vilicus*, although it is striking that the title is never used in Pliny's *Letters*. *Vilicus* management is perhaps implied in the context of *Ep.* 8.2, where Pliny reports that he had sold the vintage to wine dealers. It has been argued, however, that the crop sold by Pliny was the produce of the rents collected in kind after the temporary crisis in A.D. 107, which forced him to reconsider the system of tenancy applied until then and to switch to sharecropping.[53] A.N. Sherwin-White has tried to discard this interpretation on the basis of the quantities involved and of the most likely date of *Ep.* 8.2 (107 rather than 108 or later), but his arguments are not cogent.[54] Whether or not Pliny employed tenants and a *vilicus* on the same estate remains unclear. In some other cases, it is difficult to determine what type of management Pliny had in mind. In one letter, he writes about his effort to find a strong man to cultivate Calpurnius Fabatus's Villa Camilla in Campania.[55] Elsewhere, he thanks one Verus for taking over his nurse's mismanaged farm.[56] Tenants and *vilici* are possible in either case.[57]

---

[52] Pliny, *Ep.* 9.20. V.I. Kuziščin (1984) [1976] 216-50 argues that Pliny was in fact very much involved in the management of his landed properties. D.P. Kehoe, "Approaches to Economic Problems in the Letters of Pliny the Younger. The Question of Risk in Agriculture," *ANRW* II.33.1 (1989) 555-90, esp. 565-66 and 578 suggests that the "urbani" in *Ep.* 9.20.2 were not slaves attached to Pliny's urban household, but the same *negotiatores* as referred to in *Ep.* 8.2., who, Kehoes argues, belonged to a lower class than Pliny and supervised the *rustici*; in the same sense, P.W. de Neeve, "A Roman Landowner and his Estates: Pliny the Younger," *Athenaeum* 78 (1990) 363-402, esp. 378, with reference to Cato's *redemptor* in *Agr.* 146-148.

[53] Pliny, *Ep.* 9.37.

[54] A.N. Sherwin-White (1966) 448-50, discussing V.A. Sirago's suggestion (*L'Italia agraria sotto Traiano* [Louvain 1958] 118) and arguing that a) the proceeds of the rents should be much bigger than the quantity mentioned by Pliny, which corresponds to the produce of an estate of around 17 "Roman acres" (= *iugera*?) (against Kehoe [1989] 576-77); b) the letter belongs to a group including 9.16 and 9.20 and is probably to be dated to the fall of 107, although a later date cannot be excluded (*ibid.* 500).

[55] Pliny, *Ep.* 6.30. Calpurnius Fabatus was the grand-father of Pliny's wife, cf. A.N. Sherwin-White (1966) 71.

[56] Pliny, *Ep.* 6.3.

[57] On Pliny's estates management, cf. also G.B. Ford, jr., "The Letters of Pliny the Younger as Evidence of Agrarian Conditions in the Principate of Trajan,"

Tenants and bailiffs are found working side-by-side on private and imperial estates in various parts of the empire.[58] An interesting case is recorded on an inscription found near Monte Testaccio in Rome. Three *vilici* and a group of individuals (*plebs*) attached to the *Praedia Galbana* formed a religious college of sixty members and set up an inscription to the *numen* of the imperial House, to Aesculapius, and to the Good Health of the emperor in a place assigned by an imperial *procurator*. Some of the names refer to free men, but it is not clear whether the members of the *plebs* were independent tenants or belonged to one of the rural households headed by the bailiffs.[59]

Another example is provided by two lead tablets found in a grave near Pola, in Histria. They bear the names of free *coloni* and of slaves, *dispensatores* and former *dispensatores*, one *vilicus* (or former *vilicus* "qui vilicavit"), one *adiutor coloni*, and (*quasi*) *coloni*. The archaeological context points toward an early-second-century-A.D.

Helikon 5 (1965) 381-89; R. Martin, "Pline le Jeune et les problèmes économiques de son temps," *REA* 69 (1967) 62-97; D. Kehoe, "Allocation of Risk and Investment on the Estates of Pliny the Younger," *Chiron* 18 (1988) 15-42; *idem*, *Management and Investment on Estates in Roman Egypt During the Early Empire* (Bonn 1992); P. Rosafio, *Studies in the Roman Colonate* (Diss. Cambridge 1991) 104-26, published in a revised form in *ARID* 22 (1993) 67-79.

[58] Sen., *Ep.* 123.2: "Non habet panem meus pistor; sed habet vilicus, sed habet atriensis, sed habet colonus." Mart. 2.11.9; and 3.58.20, 29-31, and 33-40. Cf. P. Rosafio (1991) 44-71, esp. 47. This was already the case in the late Republican period, as Caesar reports (*BCiv.* 1.34.2) how L. Domitius Ahenobarbus (cos. 54) could man seven ships with his own slaves, freedmen, and tenants. These were probably employed on his estates located in the territory of Cosa (*CIL* XI 2638); cf. J. Carlsen, "Considerations on Cosa and Ager Cosanus," *ARID* 13 (1984) 49-58, esp. 54.

[59] *CIL* VI 30983 (= *ILS* 3840): "Numini domus Aug. sacrum / Aesculapio et Saluti Aug. collegium salutar[ ] / loco adsignato ab proc(uratore) patr(imonii) Cae(saris) N(ostri) a solo [ ] / fecerunt Felix ver(na), Aspergus Regianus, Vindex / ver(na), vilici pr(a)ediorum Galbanorum, et plebs / imm(o) Actalius Ianuarius, Ulpius Sextianus, Cluturius Secundus,..." (+ 53 other names); both editions have no comma between Aspergus and Regianus, so that we have to understand that Aspergus Regianus was a slave (or less plausibly a freedman) whose former owner was a certain Regius. How he managed to pass into the emperor's property is a matter of guess. G. Boulvert, *Domestique et fonctionnaire sous le Haut-Empire romain. La condition de l'affranchi et de l'esclave des princes* (Paris 1974) 52 points out that the phenomenon of slaves bearing a double name, one of which finishing with -ianus, is not attested after the time of Hadrian. D.J. Crawford, "Imperial Estates," in Finley (1976) 44, adds a comma and counts four bailiffs of slave status, which is possible. For the emperor as landowner, relying on his slaves and freedmen, cf. M. Rostovtzeff, *SEHRE*² (1957) 54-55.

date, and imperial estates are attested in the region by other inscriptions.[60]

The epigraphical evidence for *vilici* in charge of agricultural estates in Italy is abundant. It is enough to say that there is no noticeable geographical concentration in those areas where the villa economy is best documented by archaeological evidence. Let us note, however, that out of more than 200 *vilici* recorded in Italian and Sicilian inscriptions, only ca. 5% were explicitly connected with agricultural estates (*praedia, fundus, locus, saltus*, etc.), while another 3% were in charge of suburban estates or gardens (*horti*). It is probable that a large proportion of the *vilici* whose functions are unspecified in the inscriptions were also in charge of agricultural estates.

To conclude this section, it is necessary to mention a famous document which admittedly does not belong to the geographical area chosen for this study, but which sheds light on the administration of imperial estates. This document, so-called *Lex colonis fundi Villae Magnae data ad exemplum legis Mancianae*, is a Latin inscription, dated to A.D. 116/117 and found in Henchir Mettich (Africa). It reveals interesting details concerning the organization of the management of an imperial estate located in the Bagradas Valley. The Fiscus, represented by imperial *procuratores*, contracted with private individuals (*conductores*) for the right to collect the rents from tenant farmers (*coloni*) who cultivated the land. Parts of the estate, however, were cultivated under the management of bailiffs (*vilici*). It is not clear whether these *vilici* were appointed by the chief-lessees or by the landowner, i.e. the emperor represented by his *procuratores*. The text refers to "conductoribus vilicisve do/minorum eius f(undi)" in III.19-20 and to "conductores vilici{s}ve eor[um]" in IV.15, an ambiguous phrase which could be part of a general formula (i.e. "whichever").[61] The hands are called *coloni, coloni inquilini*,

---

[60] *Inscr.It.* X,1 592a and b (= *AE* 1906, no. 100) mentions "...Lucifer disp(ensator), Lucifer adiutor coloni, Vitalis disp(ensator),...Anconius qui vilicavit,...Trophimus qui dispensavit, ...Viator colonus, ..." next to a list of people (farmers?) with *duo nomina*. The vicinity of imperial estates is illustrated by *Inscr.It.* X,1 593; cf. also *Inscr.It.* X,1 599; X,2 222; and 229. The date of the inscription is provided by the presence of Trajanic and Hadrianic coins in the grave.

[61] This point has been suggested to me by Prof. J.P. Bodel and is corroborated by some papyrological evidence, cf. H. Harrauer–P.J. Sijpesteijn, "Ein neues Dokument zu Roms Indienhandel. P.Vindob. G40822," *AAWW* 122 (1985) 124-55, with reference to ἐπίτροποι ἤ φροντισταί. J. Carlsen, "Estate Management

stipendiarii, and *servi*. It is impossible to say how these workers were distributed among chief-lessees and bailiffs. The state of preservation of the inscription and the content itself leave many questions unsolved, such as the identity of the *domini* who are mentioned in a rather impersonal way. If the application of the Mancian Law was not restricted to imperial estates, the authors of the letter quoted in the inscription, i.e. the imperial *procuratores*, may have been quoting an original, therefore non-specific, version of the enactment.[62] This interpretation would also account for the use of the plural to designate landowners, chief-lessees, and bailiffs, although it is possible to find several *vilici* or *conductores* on the same estate.

b. *vilicus system and the alleged decline of slavery*

Some scholars consider the reign of Trajan as a turning point in the history of Italian agriculture. The change in agricultural practice would have been caused by a drastic shift in foreign policy by the imperial government, whereby more than five centuries of conquest were followed by a period of internal consolidation of the Empire. One consequence of this change would have been a shortage of prisoners of war, followed by the gradual decline of the slave mode

---

in Roman North Africa. Transformation or Continuity?'' in A. Mastino (ed.), *L'Africa romana* VIII (Sassari 1991) 625-37, esp. 626 points out that the phrase may recall the original *Lex Manciana*.

[62] *CIL* VIII 25902 (= *FIRA* I², no. 100), col. IV, lines 22-35: ''ne quis conductor vilicusv[e colonu]m in[q]uilinu[m eius] / f(undi) <amplius quam ter binas praestare praecipiat>, coloni qui intra f(undum) Vill(a)e Magn[(a)e sive Mapp]ali(a)e Sig(a)e ha[bit]/abunt dominis aut conduct[oribus vilicisve eorum] in assem [q]/[u]o<t>annis in hominibus [singulis in aratio]nes oper/as n(umero) II et in messem op[eras n(umero) II et cuiusqu]e generi[s] / [s]ingulas operas bin[as] p[r(a)estare debebun]t. colon[i] / inquilini eius f(undi) [int]ra [pr(idie) kal(endas) primas cuiusque] anni n/omina sua con[duc]tor[ibus vilicisve i]n custo/dias singulas qu[as in agris pr(a)estare debent nomi]nent, / ratam seorsum [+ - 20 seor]sum. / stipendiaror[um qui intra f(undum) Vill(a)e Magn(a)e sive M]appa/li(a)e Sig(a)e habitabu[nt, nomina sua nominent in custodias q]uas c/onductoribus vil[icisve eius f(undi) pr(a)estare deben]t. cust/odias f(undi) servis dominic[is + - 20] est.'' I quote the text from D.P. Kehoe, ''Lease Regulations for Imperial Estates in North Africa,'' *ZPE* 56 (1984) 193-219; and *ZPE* 59 (1985) 151-72; *idem, The Economics of Agriculture on Roman Imperial Estates in North Africa* (*Hypomnemata* 89, Göttingen 1988), where the author thinks (45, n. 25) that *inquilini* were resident tenants (= *coloni inquilini*) owing *operae* and *custodiae* to the chief-lessee; cf. also P. Rosafio, ''*Inquilini*,'' *Opus* 3 (1984) 121-31; about *stipendiarii*, cf. Kehoe (1988) 46-47, n. 28, who suggests that they were either wage-laborers or *coloni* who cultivated the *ager stipendiarius*, a category of land located outside the imperial estate and subject to provincial land-tax (*stipendium*).

of production and of the *vilicus* system in the context of the villa economy, which left room for the expansion of free tenancies.[63] This view is not supported by the literary and epigraphical evidence. Further, we cannot expect the phenomenon of decline to be recorded in the types of documents which have survived. Slaves were probably used in agriculture throughout antiquity and even in the early Middle Ages, even though the proportion of slaves to free men may have gone through long-term variations.[64] It is possible that tenancy became increasingly common, but this would be hard to demonstrate and would not prevent the *vilicus* system from holding on until the very end of the Roman Empire.[65] The Middle Ages adopted it, like many other Roman institutions, while adapting it to changing circumstances and conditions.[66]

Let us first point out that some of the inscriptions mentioning

---

[63] This view was expressed long ago by M. Weber and M.I. Rostovtzeff, and adopted by V.A. Sirago, *L'Italia agraria sotto Traiano* (Louvain 1958); and G.B. Ford, jr., *Helikon* 5 (1965) 381-89. A different view has been proposed more recently by R. MacMullen, "Late Roman Slavery," *Historia* 36 (1987) 359-82, according to whom slaves had never been widely used in agriculture, at least in the provinces, during the Imperial period; *contra*, R. Samson, "Rural Slavery, Inscriptions, Archaeology and Marx," *Historia* 38 (1989) 99-110.

[64] This is not the place for a lengthy refutation of a widely supported thesis. M.I. Finley, who at first thought that "agricultural slavery was far more common than most modern writers allow," changed his mind in the second edition of *The Ancient Economy* (1985) 179-80; cf. also *ibidem* 71 and 223, n. 18; and C.R. Whittaker, "Labour Supply in the Later Roman Empire," *Opus* 1 (1982) 171-79, esp. 174. A few literary references to chattel slavery from the second to the fifth century should invite to exert caution on this issue (Apul., *Apol.* 93.3-4; Ath. 6.104-105 [272 e – 273 c]; *Vita Melaniae* [L] 1.18 = *AB* 8 [1889] 33). Cf. A.H.M. Jones, *The Later Roman Empire, 284-602. A Social, Economic, and Administrative Survey* (Norman, OK 1964) 787; 793; and 1325, n. 53; and P. Bonnassie, "Survie et extinction du régime esclavagiste dans l'Occident du haut moyen âge (IVe-XIe s.)," *Cahiers de civilisation médiévale* 28 (1985) 307-43.

[65] A.H.M. Jones, *LRE* (1964) 793 suggests that the slaves attested in Asia Minor in fewer numbers than free *coloni* were probably "*vilici* or bailiffs, who supervised the free tenants."

[66] J. Percival, "*P.Ital.* 3 and Roman Estate Management," *Hommages à M. Renard* II (Brussels 1969) 607-15; and *idem*, "Seigneurial Aspects of Late Roman Estate Management," *EHR* 84 (1969) 449-73. Missing links in terminology—medieval administrators are usually called *iudices, maiores,* or *bailivi*—are not significant (p. 450). According to Percival, there was no necessary interdependency in antiquity between the part of an estate administered by a *vilicus* and the plots let out to tenants, whereas in the medieval period demesne and tenures formed a more closely tied unit. That the nature of the relationship between demesne and tenure changed as early as during the Roman period does not affect the point demonstrated here (450-459).

agricultural *vilici* belong to the second and early third centuries A.D. The bailiff Victor was in charge of the *Praedia Maeciana* and made a dedication to Mithra and his priest on April 7 of the year A.D. 154 or 177.[67] Another inscription dated to A.D. 205 and found in Ostia mentions a slave bred in the imperial House in the capacity of bailiff of the *Praedia Rusticeliana*.[68] Many inscriptions belong undoubtedly to the late second and early third centuries. In the following period *vilici* become even scarcer in our sources, but do not disappear completely. This apparent decline may be accounted for by the changing nature of the material.

The evidence is often elliptic. An interesting document has been unearthed in the *tepidarium* of a Roman villa at Varignano in Southern Liguria (*Regio* IX). It is a marble slab, dated to the second or third century, which has been interpreted as the accounts of tenants of public land belonging to the colony of Luna. The accounts comprise at least five entries, the first one referring to the rent paid by one Ecloga. The following entries contain no names, but the recorded sums of money are of similar range (20-30 *nummi*). According to the editor of the inscription, Ecloga was a tenant (*conductrix*). Her name, however, suggests that she was a female slave, and she might have been the manager (*vilica*) of the estate on which the inscription was found. Ecloga could also have been a slave-tenant, but her position in the list and the fact that only her name is recorded set her apart from the anonymous payers listed in the other entries of the account, bestowing on her a special role.[69] Admittedly, *vilicae* are rarely recorded in inscriptions, and they have been generally considered as the wives of *vilici*.[70] It is true that in one inscription from Noricum the *vilica* is the wife of an *actor*, but since *actor* and *vilicus* usually represent two different levels of management (cf. below), the inscription can be used as evidence of a *vilica* at the head of a managerial unit.[71] In a few other cases, the *vilica* may have been a

---

[67] *CIL* VI 745.

[68] *CIL* XIV 4570 (= *AE* 1922, no. 93).

[69] *AE* 1976, no. 229 (*Regio* IX). The structure of the inscription is similar to that of *P.Ital.* 3 discussed below. Cf. A. Bertino, in A. Frova (ed.), *Archeologia in Liguria. Scavi e scoperte 1967-1975* (Genova 1976) 61-78, esp. 75 and fig. 86, p. 68.

[70] Columella, *Rust.* Book 12; and Scaevola (4 *resp.*) *Dig.* 40.5.41.15. Cf. W. Scheidel, "Feldarbeit von Frauen in der antiken Landwirtschaft," *Gymnasium* 97 (1990) 405-31, esp. 410. Some cases are admittedly ambiguous, cf. for instance Mart. 1.55.11-12; and 10.48.7-20; and Juv. 11.64-76.

[71] *CIL* III 5616. There is only one epigraphical occurrence of an *actrix* (*CIL* XI 1730).

female manager, since Ulpianus explicitly says that business managers could be of either gender.[72]

In order to substantiate the claim that the *vilicus* system did not fade away with the alleged decline of slavery in the second century A.D., it is necessary to review the later evidence in which *vilici* are attested. There is no evidence from Italy for bailiffs on agricultural estates in the second half of the third century nor in the first half of the fourth century.[73] This vacuum can be ascribed to changing epigraphic habits, and to the nature of the legal and literary sources. The *Theodosian Code*, which contains a few references to *procuratores* and *actores*,[74] refers only once to a *vilicus* whose function was not even concerned with agriculture.[75]

In a letter addressed to his friend Paulinus of Nola, Ausonius complains about the incompetence of his *vilicus*, named Philo. The consul of A.D. 379 criticizes his agent for neglecting the farmwork on his Lucaniacan estate near Bordeaux, for engaging in commercial activities in the countryside, and for spending time visiting his *inquilini*.[76] The nature and extent of Philo's functions are not clear, because Ausonius first speaks of him as a former steward ("procuratoris quondam mei"). Philo had purchased and stored foodstuff in Paulinus's Hebromagum estate, and was plannning to ship it to Ausonius's estate at a later time in order to relieve its personnel from the threat of a temporary food shortage. Ausonius was obviously displeased with his manager's performance on this particular occasion and with his competence in general. His disappointment stemmed from the fact that he expected Philo to pay a closer attention to farmwork, whereas the manager "loathed the name of bailiff" and turned to business activities.[77] Ausonius mocks Philo's claim to the title of ἐπίτροπος (*procurator*):[78]

---

[72] Ulpianus (28 *ad ed.*) *Dig.* 14.3.7.1. *CIL* V 7348; *CIL* IX 163 (?); *CIL* XI 356 (?); and 871; *CIL* XV 6905; *CIL* VIII 5384 (= 17500 = *ILAlg* I 323, imperial *vilica* under or before Claudius, Calama/Numidia); and *AE* 1927, no. 50 (Brestowetz, Bulgaria). Cf. J. Carlsen, "The *vilica* and Roman Estate Management," in H. Sancisi-Weerdenburg *et al.* (eds.), *De agricultura. In memoriam P. W. de Neeve* (Amsterdam 1993) 197-205.

[73] A late-third-century reference is found in the *Sententiae Pauli* 3.6.35.

[74] *Cod. Theod.* 12.1.6 (A.D. 319); 11.7.6 (A.D. 349); and 2.30-32 (A.D. 422).

[75] *Vilicus* as manager of an urban house, cf. *Cod. Theod.* 16.5.36.1 (A.D. 399).

[76] Auson., *Ep.* 22 = 26 (LCL).

[77] Auson., *Ep.* 22.14: "nomen perosus vilici" and 22-24: "negotiari maluit / mercatur <et> quo <vult> foro venalium / mutatur ad Graecam fidem."

[78] This equivalence is valid for the Roman period only. By contrast, in classical

> Philo, who was once the bailiff of my estates, or, as he claims, my steward—this Greek believes that he might elicit some glory from a title that smacks of Dorian—obnoxiously solicits as a favor the object of my plea, which I reluctantly set out to reveal.[79]

It is likely that Philo had started his career in the capacity of *vilicus*, and had been subsequently promoted to the position of *procurator*, being then in charge of the whole of Ausonius's scattered estates.[80]

While recording in a literary form his disappointment concerning his agent's services, Ausonius uses a combination of rare Latin words borrowed from Plautus's play *Pseudolus*, trusting that his reader would be familiar with its content.[81] In Plautus's play, the slave Pseudolus tries to pose as the agent of a pimp in order to collect a sum of money in payment for a female slave from the buyer's agent. The latter, named Harpax, who has been instructed to pay the money either to the pimp himself or to his agent (*atriensis*), inquires about Pseudolus's identity and position. Pseudolus answers that he is a *procurator*—a blatant lie—and that he gives orders to the *atriensis*, which is theoretically correct. Harpax then asks about Pseudolus's legal status, and is told that he is still a slave. This answer raises

---

Greece, the position of an ἐπίτροπος was similar to that of the Roman *vilicus*; cf. Xen., *Oec. passim*; Columella, *Rust.* 11.1.5 (with reference to Xenophon's work, 12.3-4); Cic., *Off.* 2.18.64 (with reference to Theophrastus recording a fifth-century Athenian case). This point has been brought to my attention by Mr. J.M. Jorquera Nieto. By the second-century B.C. farm managers are called οἰκονόμοι: cf. for instance the slave Athenion who played a leading role in the second slave revolt in Sicily (Diod. Sic. 36.5). The third-century-A.D. agronomist Florentinus, however, considers these two titles as synonymous (*Geop.* 2.44: περὶ τοῦ ἐν τῷ ἀγρῷ ἐπιτρόπου ἢ οἰκονόμου).

[79] Auson., *Ep.* 22.1-6: "Philo, meis qui vilicatus praediis, / ut ipse vult, ἐπίτροπος, / (nam gloriosum Graeculus nomen putat, / quod sermo fucat Dorius) / suis querellis adserit nostras preces, / quas ipse lentus prosequor."

[80] On Ausonius's landed property, cf. R. Etienne"Ausone, propriétaire terrien et le problème du *latifundium* au IVe siècle ap. J.-C.," in M. Christol *et al.* (eds.), *Institutions, société et vie politique dans l'empire romain au IVe siècle après J.-C.* (Rome 1992) 305-11, who points out that Ausonius's estates should be referred to as *lati fundi* rather than *latifundia*. P. Bistaudeau, "A la recherche des villas d'Ausone," *Caesarodunum* 15 bis (1980) 477-87, lists (486) the few locatable urban and rural properties of Ausonius and describes them as the components of a "fortune relativement modeste": an urban house in Bordeaux; a villa near Cognac (= *fundus Lucanus* or *Lucaniacus*); an estate at Bazas; some land in the country of Buch and at Rom, south-west of Poitiers.

[81] Auson., *Ep.* 22.20: "promusque quam condus magis," which is reminiscent of Plaut., *Pseud.* 608: "condus, promus sum, procurator peni." Ausonius quotes a line from the same play in the preface of the same letter. *Promus* refers to a distributor of provisions, who is subordinated to the bailiff in Varro, *Rust.* 1.16.5; and Columella, *Rust.* 12.3.9; cf. K.D. White (1970) 381.

Harpax's suspicion, and accordingly he refuses to pay him the money. Later on, Pseudolus changes his story and pretends that, being in charge of his master's patrimony and acting as bookkeeper, he is entitled to make and accept payments. Harpax finally entrusts him with the document and token proving the validity of the contract. It is clear that Ausonius's literary allusion was aimed at emphasizing the pretension of his agent with reference to his position of *procurator*.

Ausonius's pun, however, should be read in its historical context. First, the distinction between steward and bailiff was sometimes meaningless, since the former could assume the direct management of an estate (*procurator* acting *vilicus*).[82] Second, as a result of Papinianus's extension of the *actio institoria* to cases involving transactions performed by *procuratores*, the social and legal differences between *procuratores* and *vilici* became blurred.[83] From this point of view, Ausonius's *Epistle* 22 (26) does not tell much about the survival of the *vilicus* system in late antiquity.

More is to be gained from the correspondence of Symmachus. proconsul of Africa in 373, Urban Prefect in 384 and 385, and finally consul in 391, Symmachus owned land in Italy, Sicily, and Mauretania Caesarensis, and is a good representative of the landowning upper class in the fourth century. He incidentally tells us that he employed *vilici* and *coloni* on his estate in Tivoli, and *actores* and *conductores* on more distant estates, for instance in Sicily.[84]

---

[82] American history provides an interesting comparative case: in 1841, A. Nicol, who was the steward of R.B. Bolling's Sandy Point Estate (Charles City County, Virginia), took over the direct management of 7,000 acres with the assistance of two deputies. This was an innovation on the part of Nicol, since it is known that up to 1840, the estate was divided into four farming units under the managements of separate overseers. Nicol's reform was meant to diminish the "expenses, inconvenience and frequent misunderstandings incident to [the previous] arrangement." Cf. A. Nicol, "Note on the Sandy Point Estate," *Farmers' Register* 9 (June 1841) 343, quoted by W.K. Scarborough, *The Overseer. Plantation Management in the Old South*[2] (Athens, GA 1984) 161.

[83] Papinianus (3 *resp.*) *Dig.* 14.3.19 *pr.*, etc. (cf. above, Chapter Two). The idea of the declining social status of *procuratores* in late antiquity has been discussed by G. Hamza, "Fragen der gewillkürten Stellvertretung im römischen Recht," *AUB (iur.)* 25 (1983) 89-107, esp. 101-05, with reference to *Cod. Theod.* 4.12.5 (362), where *actores* and *procuratores* are counted among people of servile condition; cf. also *Cod. Theod.* 9.29.2.

[84] Symmachus, *Ep.* 6.81 (*vilici* and *coloni*); 5.87; 9.6; 9.15; 9.52; and 9.130 (*actores* and *conductores*). D. Vera, "Strutture agrarie e strutture patrimoniali nella tarda antichità: l'aristocrazia romana fra agricoltura e commercio," *Opus* 2 (1983)

By contrast with his predecessors and models, Palladius, a late-fourth- or fifth-century agricultural writer, does not devote a lengthy and detailed discussion to the topic of management and work force. Although his work might include references to earlier practices, it seems unlikely that the little information he chose to incorporate in his treatise was obsolete and irrelevant to his readers. He deals with practical details, such as the measures to be taken by the *dominus* or the *procurator* to prevent thefts by workmen.[85] The bailiff or overseer (*praesul agri*) is a slave,[86] and the *rustici* are free workers who seem to have emigrated from the city to the countryside.[87]

Palladius provides direct evidence for tenancy by advising against the lease of plots to neighbors, either landowners (*domini*) or tenant-farmers (*coloni*).[88] Agency, on the other hand, is more elusive. Palladius mentions once a *procurator* and once an *agri praesul*, but the exact functions of both remain unclear. E. Frézouls recently pointed out that the confinement to Book I of the mention of both functions is explained by the fact that Palladius's work was aimed at a twofold audience: Book I was intended for the landowner, and the rest of the work was intended for the actual cultivators. Book I then would deal with the questions that were of primary interest to the landowner, i.e., the configuration of the estate and its management. Palladius records two intermediate hierarchic positions between landowner and the hands (*rustici*) and these positions correspond to the classical model (*procurator-vilicus*). In the fifth century, landowners were more likely to live on the estate than in an earlier period, and the *agri praesul* was probably more involved in the actual farmwork than the classical *vilicus*. Thus, the *agri praesul* was perhaps more an overseer than a bailiff, his status of legal representative being of secondary importance in the management of the estate.[89]

489-533; *idem*, "Simmaco e le sue proprietà: struttura e funzionamento di un patrimonio aristocratico del quarto secolo d.C.," in F. Paschoud (ed.), *Colloque genevois sur Symmaque* (Paris 1986) 231-76.

[85] Palladius, *Rust.* 1.36.
[86] Palladius, *Rust.* 1.6.18.
[87] Palladius, *Rust.* 1.6.2.
[88] Palladius, *Rust.* 1.6.6.
[89] E. Frézouls, "La vie rurale au Bas-Empire d'après l'oeuvre de Palladius," *Ktèma* 5 (1980) 193-210, esp. 207-10; W. Kaltenstadler, "Arbeits- und Führungs-kräfte im *Opus Agriculturae* von Palladius," *Klio* 66 (1984) 223-29; *idem*, "Betriebs-organisation und betriebswirtschaftliche Fragen in *Opus Agriculturae* von Palladius," in H. Kalcyk–B. Gullath–A. Graeber (eds.), *Studien zur alten Geschichte S.*

Finally, a Latin roll from the Vatican Library (*P. Ital.* 3), dated to the middle of the sixth century, preserves a large fragment of a "Gestaprotokoll" (proceedings of activities) of the Church of Ravenna, the form of which prefigures the Carolingian polyptychs. This document was probably written in the wake of the reorganization of the Church properties after the war against the Goths and records various deliveries in money and in kind. The second column pertains to an estate located in the territory of Padua and contains ten entries. The first entry lists the payment of three *solidi*, 2 *tremisses*, 3 *siliquae*, in addition to the delivery of 8 hens, 80 eggs, and 70 pounds of honey, made by the *vilicus* Maximus who was in charge of the *Saltus Erudianus*. The following entries (2 to 8) list payments and deliveries made by *coloni* for their respective *coloniae*, even though some of these were not cultivated (*in sentibus*) at the time when the document was written. Entries 9 and 10 contain no names of cultivators, but concern two *paludes* (swamps) that seem to have been used as pasture land.[90] The *Saltus Erudianus* was divided into two parts; one was managed by the *vilicus* Maximus, and the other by a group of *coloni*, since entry no. 2 refers to a *colonia supra scripta*. It is remarkable that the payments made by the tenants and the *vilicus* fall within a limited range, which indicates that the plots were of broadly similar sizes, estimated by L. Cracco Ruggini around 4 or 5 *iugera*.[91]

The combination of the *vilicus* system and free tenancy (demesne/

Lauffer zum 70. Geb. (*Historia* 2, Rome 1986) 501-57; and L. Cracco Ruggini, "Vicende rurali dell'Italia antica," *RSI* 76 (1964) 261-86, who points out, however, that in Italy towns remained important for a longer time than in the rest of the empire, so that Italian landowners continued to live in town and to rely on managers to take care of their estates (p. 267, n. 14).

[90] The *paludes* near Ravenna were famous for their fertility, cf. Polyb. 3.88; Cato, cited by Varro, *Rust.* 1.2.7; and Strab. 5.4.2 (241) and 5.1.7 (214). A. Tchernia, *Le vin de l'Italie romaine* (Rome 1986) 111, n. 210; 185; and 224, stresses the quality of the vineyards.

[91] J.-O. Tjäder, *Die nichtliterarischen lateinischen Papyri Italiens aus der Zeit 445-700* I (Lund 1955); J. Percival, *EHR* 84 (1969) 449-73; and *idem, Hommages à M. Renard* II (Brussels 1969) 607-15. Percival thinks that the name *Saltus Erudianus* applies to the whole estate, including demesne and tenures (*coloniae*) (p. 609, n. 2) and that the *colonia* in entry no. 2 "was almost certainly carved out of the original demesne, thus lowering the amount of dues required of that demesne and at the same time relieving it of the need for outside help in its working" (609), with reference to A.H.M. Jones, *LRE* (1964) 805-06. L. Cracco Ruggini, *RSI* 76 (1964) 283-84 points out that "i villici della Chiesa Ravennate—al contrario di quelli delle grandi proprietà laiche, soprattutto nell'Italia Centro-Meridionale—appaiono ridotti a un livello modestissimo, del tutto analogo a quello dei coloni" and that "pare, infatti, che in età longobarda boschi e pascoli occupassero in prevalenza la parte

tenure) was flourishing in the Middle Ages up to the Early Modern period. Numerous examples could be cited, from the Abbot Irminon's estate at St. Germain des Prés at the time of Charlemagne, to the Manors of Adam de Stratton in Wiltshire in the late thirteenth century, and to the Cloister of Diessen in seventeenth-century Germany.[92]

C. Social and economic aspects of the vilicus system

In contrast to a widely accepted theory, the evidence suggests that the *vilicus* system did not undergo an irreversible decline starting in the second century A.D. It appears that its existence did not depend on the slave mode of production—in the sense of massive use of slave labor on plantation-like estates—and that, when attested, it was used in combination with tenancy. That apparent continuity can be ascribed to various social and economic factors.

1. *Legal status of farm managers*

M.I. Finley has argued (a) that the slave mode of production survived because of a chronic shortage of tenant-farmers;[93] (b) that there was "no significant managerial difference, for absentee land-

---

indominicata delle tenute, mentre nel massaricio trovavano posto per lo più la terre arative" (p. 286).

[92] B. Fois Ennas, *Il 'Capitulare de Villis'*, (Milan 1981); A. Longnon, *Polyptique de l'Abbaye de Saint-Germain des Prés rédigé au temps de l'abbé Irminon*, 2 vols. (Paris 1886-1895); R.B. Pugh (ed.), *Court Rolls of the Wiltshire Manors of Adam de Stratton (1275-1288)* (*Wiltshire Record Society* 24, 1968 (1970)); W. Reittorner von Schöllnach, *Die Oekonomie des Klosters Diessen: das Compendium Oeconomicum von 1642*, edited by P. Fried and H. Haushofer (*Quellen und Forschungen zur Agrargeschichte* 27, Stuttgart 1974). A classic and still up-to-date study of the exploitation of large ecclesiastical estates from the ninth to the twelfth century, with details on the changing role of *vilici* and their like, is found in Ch.-E. Perrin, *Recherches sur la seigneurie rurale en Lorraine d'après les plus anciens censiers* (Paris 1935). Cf. also J. Durliat, *Les finances publiques de Dioclétien aux Carolingiens (284-889)* (Siegmaringen 1990), esp. 155; 213; 258, n. 41; and 272, n. 143. About the survival of the *vilicus* system in medieval England, cf. T.F.T. Plucknett, *The Medieval Bailiff* (*The Creighton Lecture in History*, London 1954) and H.S. Bennett, "The Reeve and the Manor in the Fourteenth Century," *EHR* 41 (1926) 358-65.

[93] "Penuria colonorum" is first mentioned by Pliny, *Ep.* 3.19.7 (cf. also *Ep.* 7.30.3 and 9.37.1-3), and often repeated in Africa in a later period, cf. Lactantius, *De Mort. Pers.* 7.3 (early fourth century); *Nov. Val.* 13.8 (445); and A. Carandini, "Produzione agricola e produzione ceramica nell'Africa di età imperiale. Appunti sull'economia della Zeugitana e della Bezacena," *Studi Miscellanei* 15 (1970) 95-122, esp. 104.

lords, between tenancies and slave-operated estates under *vilici*";
and (c) that the choice between the two systems depended not on
"the notion of comparative profitability", but on the respective
availability of free or slave labor.[94] The second statement in Finley's interpretation is absolutely correct, except for the fact that it
assumes a necessary connection between *vilicus* system and slave
mode of production. The first and third parts are unsatisfactory, because Finley left out part of the evidence.

a. *slave tenants*
There was no connection between the type of management chosen
by a landowner and the legal status of the work force employed on
the estate. In other words, it is not necessarily true that a large supply of slaves would contribute to spreading the *vilicus* system, while
free workers would automatically be employed as tenant-farmers.
We know that the Republican jurists created the concept of slave
tenant or *servus quasi colonus*, providing Roman landowners with a
managerial system that combined the advantages of free tenancy
with the availability of slave labor. The farmer was not part of the
farm equipment,[95] paid a rent, and enjoyed a great deal of autonomy in the management of his farm. The master collected the rent
and remained in control of the estate, being entitled to remove a
careless or incompetent manager without breaking the lease before
its term. *Servi quasi coloni* are attested in the inscriptions, for instance
in the lead tablets of Polla cited above, but it is impossible to estimate
how common they were.[96]

---

[94] M.I. Finley, "Private Farm Tenancy in Italy before Diocletian," in Finley
(1976) 103-21.

[95] Ulpianus (20 *ad Sab.*), citing Labeo and Pegasus, *Dig.* 33.7.12.3: "Quaeritur,
an servus, qui quasi colonus in agro erat, instrumento legato contineatur. Et Labeo
et Pegasus recte negaverunt, quia non pro instrumento in fundo fuerat."

[96] G. Giliberti, *Servus quasi colonus: forme non tradizionali di organizzazione del lavoro
nella società romana* (Naples 1981), esp. 92, n. 22, citing some epigraphical evidence:
CIL VI 9276 (= *ILS* 7453, *fundus Marianus*, near Rome); *CIL* IX 3674-3675 (=
ILS 7455-7455a, *fundus Tironianus* in Pescinae); *CIL* V 8190; and *CIL* X 7957; to
which one can add *AE* 1913, no. 210 (Crotone); *Inscr.It.* X, 2 222 and 229 (Paren-
tum/Histria). Cf. also B.W. Frier, *ZRG* 100 (1983) 667-71 (review of Giliberti's
book); P. Veyne, "Le dossier des esclaves-colons romains," *RH* 265 (1981) 3-25;
C.R. Whittaker, "Circe's Pigs: From Slavery to Serfdom in the Later Roman
World," in M.I. Finley (ed.), *Classical Slavery* (London 1987) 88-94; and W.
Scheidel, "Skaven und Freigelassene als Pächter und ihre ökonomische Funktion
in der römischen Landwirtschaft (Colonus-Studien III)," in H. Sancisi-Weerdenburg *et al.* (eds.), *De agricultura. In memoriam P.W. de Neeve* (Amsterdam 1993)
182-96.

b. *vilici paying rent*

Vilici, like *coloni*, could be required to pay a rent in kind or in money. This is indicated repeatedly by the late-second-century-A.D. jurist Q. Cervidius Scaevola, who unambiguously states that rent (*pensiones*) was collected from both *conductores praediorum* and from *vilici*,[97] and who includes in the farm equipment the arrears of both *vilici* and *coloni*, along with the servile household and the livestock.[98] This is also confirmed by non-legal evidence. We have seen above the *vilicus* Maximus paying both money and farm products in sixth-century Ravenna.[99] Martial and Juvenal are proud to be able to serve their guests the products of their suburban estates collected by a prosperous *vilica*.[100] The surplus was probably sold on the market. Whether the manager was expected to deliver all of the proceeds of his/her activity or only a fixed part was probably a matter of personal arrangement with the principal.

A problem arises from another text by Scaevola, who examines whether or not a slave cultivating a plot of land and holding a large sum of money (rent in arrears or *peculium*) should be relinquished to a legatee as part of the farm equipment.[101] Scaevola compares two different types of slave managers. On one hand, the slave pays a rent (*merces* or *pensionis certa quantitas*), is treated like an *extraneus colonus*, and is not part of the farm equipment; as mentioned above, this type of farmer was called *servus quasi colonus*. On the other hand, the slave is appointed by his master (*fide dominica*) to cultivate the land and is part of the farm equipment.[102] This type of manager was called *vilicus*, and it is remarkable that Scaevola does not use this term. According to Scaevola, the distinction between the two types of managers rests on whether or not they were acting *fide dominica*, i.e. whether or not they had been appointed by their master/landowner

---

[97] Scaevola (24 *dig.*) *Dig.* 40.7.40.5.

[98] Scaevola (3 *resp.*) *Dig.* 33.7.20.3: "Praedia ut instructa sunt cum dotibus et reliquis colonorum et vilicorum et mancipiis et pecore omni legavit et peculiis et cum actore."

[99] *P.Ital.* 3, col. II, first entry. Cf. above.

[100] Mart. 1.55.11-12; and 10.48.7-20; Juv. 11.64-76. These products could also be considered as gifts instead of rent.

[101] Scaevola (3 *resp.*) *Dig.* 33.7.20.1: "Quaesitum est, an Stichus servus, qui praedium unum ex his coluit et reliquatus est amplam summam ex causa fideicommissi Seio debeatur. Respondit, si non fide dominica, sed mercede, ut extranei coloni solent, fundum coluisset, non deberi."

[102] *Dig.* 33.7; and *CIL* II 5406 (= 5042 = *FIRA* III², no. 92). Cf. Chapter Two.

to the position of manager of an agricultural estate. When the slave was not appointed, he was not a *vilicus*, but belonged to a different category of manager, for instance a slave with *peculium* or a *servus quasi colonus*. The latter category was best defined by the fact that the manager was paying rent in the technical, i.e. legal sense.

This passage is cited by Paulus in the context of a discussion about the place of the *vilicus* (as opposed to other kinds of slave managers) in the farm equipment.[103] In contrast to Scaevola, Paulus ends up comparing two types of *vilici* and puts more emphasis on the question of the rent. In Paulus's view, the payment of the rent and the appointment are both determining factors to establish whether or not a farm manager is part of the farm equipment, and they are mutually exclusive. This apparent contradiction between the two jurists results from the fact that they discuss different issues.

Alternatively, *vilici* could rent an additional plot of land from their landowner, and manage it side-by-side with the estate entrusted to them, but on a different basis (i.e. as *coloni* or *servi quasi coloni*). There is no direct evidence supporting that hypothesis.

In conclusion, *vilici* paying some kind of rent must have been common, which implies that the question of the manager's autonomy did not necessarily bear on the profitability of the estate.

c. *legal status of vilici*

The alleged decline of slavery in the Imperial period is unlikely to have affected the role of *vilici* in agriculture, because the *vilicus* system was not necessarily associated with the slave mode of production. Slave labor was an ordinary feature of both agency and tenancy, and a hypothetical shortage of slaves is unlikely to have caused a general switch from one managerial system to the other. Even though a prosopographical survey shows that Italian *vilici* were mostly slaves, servile condition was not a requirement during the Principate, because *vilici* were business managers and belonged to the category of *institores*.[104] The inscriptions and the literary sources record a few free(d) *vilici*, and there is no reason to think that *vilici* formed a subcategory with its own characteristics.

---

[103] Paulus (2 *ad Vit.*) *Dig.* 33.7.18.4: "Cum de vilico quaereretur et an instrumento inesset et dubitaretur, Scaevola consultus respondit, si non pensionis certa quantitate, sed fide dominica coleretur, deberi."

[104] Paulus (29 *ad ed.*) *Dig.* 14.3.16; and Ulpianus (28 *ad ed.*) *Dig.* 14.3.7.1. Cf. Chapter One and below.

On the basis of the scarce evidence about non-slave *vilici*, some recent studies conclude that freeborn *vilici* are never attested, and that manumitted *vilici* are found only in two inscriptions.[105] The first one was found in Tralles (Caria) and was dedicated by one Thalamus, most certainly a slave, to his *vilicus* Cn. Vergilius Nyrius, freedman of one Cn. Vergilius.[106] It seems possible that the stone-cutter made a mistake in writing "villico" instead of "villicus"—in which case the *vilicus* would have been Thalamus himself—although the reflective pronoun "su[o]" indicates that the *vilicus* was the recipient of the dedication. The other inscription has been found in Atina (Italy, *Regio* I) and commemorates the fourteen-year long management of C. Obinius Epicadus, freedman of one C. Obinius, and of Trebia Aphrodisia, a freedwoman and possibly Epicadus's wife.[107] However, nothing indicates that the couple was still in activity at the time of the dedication of the inscription. Manumission may have been granted upon retirement.

In spite of the uncertainty about the latter instance, there is no doubt that active *vilici* were sometimes manumitted slaves or freeborn individuals. A few other instances illustrate this point. Two inscriptions found in Capua (*Regio* I) record manumitted *vilici*. The first honors one Brittius Alexander and his spouse Brittia Apamia, both former slaves of one M. Brittius.[108] The second example records one M. En(nius) Elp(idus), whose reconstructed title of *v(ilicus) anato(cismi)* points toward moneylending activities and whose name suggests free(d) status.[109] Further, one among very few private *vilici* attested in Northern Italy was named Tellius Censorinus and was perhaps a manumitted or freeborn manager.[110] The dates of these last two examples are uncertain. Finally, there are two pos-

---

[105] R. Beare, "Were Bailiffs Ever Free Born?" *CQ* 28 (1978) 398-401. Cf. also W. Scheidel, "Free-born and Manumitted Bailiffs in the Graeco-Roman World," *CQ* 40 (1990) 591-93.

[106] *CIL* III 7147: "[C]n. Vergilio / Cn. l(iberto) Nurio / [T]halamus villico / su[o] constituit."

[107] *CIL* X 5081 (= *ILS* 7372): "C. Obinius C. l(ibertus) / Epicadus / Trebia (Gaiae) l(iberta) Aprodisia / hic vilicarunt / annos XIIII."

[108] *AE* 1980, no. 229: "[-B]rittius M(arci) l(ibertus) / [Ale]xander vilicus / et Brittia M(arci) l(iberta) / Apamia."

[109] *AE* 1980, no. 230. The reconstruction by S. Panciera, *Epigraphica* 22 (1960) 20-36, esp. 34 is debatable, since there is no parallel example.

[110] *CIL* V 7739 (near La Spezia, *Regio* IX): "Tellius Censorinus / vilicus Compitum / aram munus Laribus / d. suo / l. m." The *nomen* Tellius is not attested elsewhere, and is perhaps a mistake for <G>ellius.

sible instances from Gallia Belgica. One inscription records one Q. Titius, who was the *vilicus* of Tib. Iulius Tiberinus, *duumvir* of the Nervii. On the basis of the names of both agent and principal, the former seems to have no connection with the latter.[111] In another inscription, the *vilicus* Celsus is introduced as the patron of a freed-woman (Camama), which seems to indicate that he was himself of free status.[112] This list could be extended by including a few imperial *vilici*, who, it is worth noticing, seem even more likely to be non-slave than private managers.[113]

Why were Italian *vilici* mostly slaves? The answer to this question may lurk in the well-known fact that slaves usually acquired some experience in the fields while growing up[114] and sometimes even received an education paid for by their masters as a form of investment. This remark, however, applies to freedmen as well. Why then did not most slave *vilici* obtain their freedom, since the prospect of being manumited should have served as a strong incentive for them to be loyal and efficient?[115] One famous case shows that some *vilici* were fortunate enough to be manumitted. When the fictional character Trimalchio was still a slave, he was relegated from his position of *dispensator* in his master's urban household to a *vilicatio* in the country after being suspected of having a sexual relationship with his master's wife.[116] Trimalchio held the position of bailiff only for a

---

[111] *CIL* XIII 3572 (Bagacum): "Tib. Iul(io) Tibe/rino IIvir(o) / Ner(viorum) Q. Titius / vilicus lict(or?)."

[112] *CIL* XIII 4352 (from the region of the Mediomatrici): "[D(is)] M(anibus) / Cam[–]a Celsi vil(ici?) / lib(erta) Ianuariae filiae / annorum XVII."

[113] *CIL* VI 532; 7528; 9089; 9984 [public]; *AE* 1987, no. 188 (all from Rome). P.R.C. Weaver, *Familia Caesaris* (Cambridge 1972) 5 considers that imperial *vilici* working on imperial estates were administrative servants and "can scarcely be said to belong to a familia rustica" because of their privileged status within Roman society. This might be true from a social point of view, but it does not affect their legal position nor their functions as agents of the emperor as a private landowner.

[114] Columella, *Rust.* 11.1.7: "Quare, sicut dixi, docendus, et a pueritia rusticis operibus edurandus, multisque prius experimentis inspiciendus erit futurus villicus,..."

[115] A good slave *vilicus* could indeed be promoted to higher functions (position of *procurator?*), cf. NT, *Matth.* 24.45-47. S. Treggiari, *Roman Freedmen during the Late Republic* (Oxford 1969) 106 points out that the agronomists neglect to mention manumission as an incentive or a reward for good *vilici*.

[116] Petron., *Sat.* 69.3. The episode of the *dispensator* caught while having sexual intercourse with his mistress is echoed with a more tragic and probably more realistic outcome in *Sat.* 45.7-8, where the *dispensator* Glycon was sent to the beasts in the amphitheater. The *relegatio* consisted in both a social demotion (*dispensatores* ranked higher than *vilici*) and a geographical displacement from urban to rural setting.

short while until he regained his master's favor to be subsequently manumitted and promoted to his glorious fate of *nouveau riche*. Interestingly, Trimalchio made no allusion to this stage of his career in his funeral inscription.[117] Previous occupations were unlikely to be advertised on tombstones, especially if the commemorated person had climbed up the social ladder and wanted his lowly past to be forgotten. An exception is provided by a retired public *vilicus*, once in charge of the treasury of the *municipium* of Patavium, who had become a farmer and advertised his career change on an altar dedicated to Priapus.[118] The dedicator of the inscription thought that his previous position was prestigious enough to be worth recording. Other managers of agricultural estates may not have shared his pride.

Besides, non-slave managers may have snubbed the title of *vilicus* because of its servile flavor, and consequently it may have become a habit to avoid it in referring to them. Such was perhaps the case of the freedman Acilius Sthenelus, whose revolutionary technique in wine growing allowed him to quadruple in ten years the value of the land entrusted to his care.[119] Sthenelus was active during the reign of Claudius and worked for the famous grammarian Q. Remmius Palaemon, himself a freedman who reportedly made a fortune in education and in the garment industry.[120] The suburban estate managed by Sthenelus on behalf of Palaemon was located in the vicinity of Nomentum in a depressed area known for the poor quality of its land. It is remarkable that Sthenelus owned another estate of 60 *iugera* in Nomentum, which he cultivated with the same suc-

---

On the basis of some recent studies, Trimalchio's early career can be outlined as follows: after arriving in Italy as a small boy, he was his master's pet (*delicium*) until the age of 14; then he learnt basic arithmetic and became a *dispensator* (*Sat.* 29.4); while holding this position, he was temporarily sent to an agricultural estate; cf. J. Bodel, *Phoenix* 43 (1989) 72-74, partly following M.D. Reeve, *Phoenix* 39 (1985) 378-79, against T. Wade Richardson, *Phoenix* 40 (1986) 201.

[117] Petron., *Sat.* 71.12.

[118] *CIL* V 2803 (*Regio* X): "Villicus aerari quondam nunc cultor agelli / haec tibi perspectus templa Priape dico / pro quibus officieis si fas est sancte paciscor / adsiduus custos ruris ut esse vellis / improbus ut si quis nostrum violabit agellum / hunc tu sed tento scis puto quod sequitur."

[119] Pliny, *HN* 14.49-51.

[120] Suet., *Gramm.* 23 reports that Palaemon was making 400,000 sestertii a year out of his school alone, to which should be added the profits drawn from his cloth workshops ("cum et officinas promercalium vestium exerceret") and from his agricultural estates.

cess.[121] The only author who records the manager of Palaemon's estate is Pliny the Elder, who refers to Sthenelus's activity as *opera* (singular) or *cura*, while ironically calling the principal *agricola*. Sthenelus was either a *procurator* or, more likely, a *vilicus*, since Palaemon's Nomentanum estate formed a single managerial unit, its size being estimated between 166 and 360 *iugera* on the basis of the purchase price of the land (600,000 sestertii) and on the basis of its exceptional yield (worth 400,000 sertertii).[122]

It is always difficult to differentiate *procuratores* and non-slave *vilici*. Cicero plays with this ambiguity in his defense of Sex. Roscius Amerinus, charged with patricide in 80 B.C.[123] The prosecutor contended that the defendant was in unfriendly terms with his father who, out of hostility, had relegated him to the country and appointed him to the infamous position of *vilicus*.[124] By contrast, Cicero tries to demonstrate that it was common for municipal landowners to entrust their sons with the administration of their estates, and goes on arguing that, in the defendant's case, his father not only appointed him as estate manager, but also allowed him to keep for himself the produce of some *fundi*.[125] The father owned thirteen estates in Ameria (Umbria) along the Tiber,[126] and it is not clear whether the son was in charge of a single *fundus* (which would bolster the prosecutor's case) or of the whole property (which would stress the trustworthiness of Cicero's client). Neither party seemed able to

---

[121] Pliny, *HN* 14.48. This story, however, could be the result of a duplication by Pliny the Elder, caused by irreconcilable variants in his sources (for instance, the size of the estate). It is also possible that the order was chronologically reversed, and that Sthenelus acquired his plot after managing Palaemon's estate.

[122] J. André, *Pline L'Ancien, Histoire naturelle, Livre XIV* (Ed. Budé, Paris 1958) 94-95 (= 166 *iugera*); and R.P. Duncan-Jones (1982) 46-47 (= "not less than 360 *iugera*"); and 324-25. The latter figure sounds more credible, considering the bad condition of the estate at the time of its purchase by Palaemon.

[123] Cic., *Rosc. Amer.* 15.42-18.52. Cf. Y. Thomas, "Droits domestiques et droits politiques à Rome. Remarques sur le pécule et les *honores* des fils de famille," *MEFRA* 94 (1982) 527-80, esp. 546-47.

[124] Cic., *Rosc. Amer.* 15.42: "hunc in praedia rustica relegarat;" and *ibidem* 18.50: "etenim qui praeesse agro colendo flagitium putes, . . ." For the meaning of *agro colendo praeesse* or *praeponere*, cf. Paulus, *Sent.* 2.8.2; and Ulpianus (28 *ad ed.*), citing Labeo, *Dig.* 14.3.5.2.

[125] Cic., *Rosc. Amer.* 15.44: ". . . hunc non modo colendis praediis praefuisse sed certis fundis patre vivo frui solitum esse . . ." The appointment is derived from the father's decision (*ibid.* 17.48: "hoc patrum voluntate liberi faciunt"); cf. also *ibid.* 7.18.

[126] Cic., *Rosc. Amer.* 7.20.

produce a decisive argument about this point, and this part of the
speech must have contributed little to Cicero's eventual victory. It
is, however, quite possible that Sex. Roscius was a freeborn *vilicus*
in his father's power. We have seen in the previous chapter that the
legal position of a son-in-power was similar to that of a slave.

The non-slave status of other *vilici* may escape notice, for instance
because of the lack of explicit reference in the texts recording them,
and because they are not referred to by *duo* or *tria nomina*.[127] This
might be the case of Nicephorus, the *vilicus* of Cicero's brother. Principal and agent had made a contract of work for the construction of
minor additions to the former's villa at Laterium for the sum of
16,000 sestertii. A *locatio conductio operis* requires a contractual capacity on both sides, which a slave agent enjoyed, except when dealing
with his own master.[128] In addition, Cicero refers to Quintus's instruction to Nicephorus as *mandatum* instead of *iussum*. The word is
obviously used in a non-technical sense—*locatio conductio* and *mandatum* are mutually exclusive—but it emphasizes the existence of a consensual contract established between principal and agent. The use
of *mandare* is not conclusive in itself, but in two other Ciceronian
passages the technical meaning of the word is emphasized.[129] If
Nicephorus was a slave, he could have been a *mercennarius* working
independently on behalf of an unspecifed master (χωρὶς οἰκῶν), like
the slave Cillo in the same letter, who was responsible for an irriga-
tion project at Quintus's house at Bovianum.[130] The issue is impor-

---

[127] Freedmen started using *tria nomina* around 106 B.C., cf. A.E. Gordon, "On
the First Appearance of the *cognomen* in Latin Inscriptions of Freedmen," *Univ. of
Calif. Publ. in Class. Philol.* (1935) 151-58.

[128] Cic., *QFr.* 3.1.5 (54 B.C.); cf. S. Treggiari, *RFLR* (1969) 107. The only
case where a contract between a slave and his master was valid was when the
slave was someone else's agent (*institor mercennarius*), cf. Ulpianus (28 *ad ed.*) *Dig.*
14.3.11.8; and Iulianus (11 *dig.*) *Dig.* 14.3.12. O. Lenel, *Das Edictum Perpetuum*[3]
(Leipzig 1927) 261-62 suggests that the master would have been given an *actio institoria utilis* ("si liber esset ex iure Quiritium") against the principal.

[129] Cic., *De Or.* 1.58.249: "...si mandandum aliquid procuratori de agri cultura aut imperandum vilico est;" and Cic., *Rosc. Am.* 38.111-39.115, with a discussion of the degrading effect of the *actio mandati*. About the non-technical use of *mandare* and *mandatum* in literary sources, cf. A. Watson, *Contract of Mandate in Roman
Law* (Oxford 1961) 11-16 (in Plautus), including *mandata* given by freeborn to their
slaves (p. 12, n. 3, with reference to Plautus, *Amph.* 338; *Asin.* 121; *Capt.* 343; *Epid.*
46 and 90; *Mostell.* 25; and *Poe.* 129). Cf. also M. Just, "Ansätze zur Ansches-
vollmacht im römischen Recht," in *Festschrift für K.H. Neumayer zum 65. Geburtstag*
(Baden-Baden 1985) 355-87, esp. 380, discussing the interpolation of a passage by
Paulus (1 *decret.*) *Dig.* 14.5.8.

[130] Cic. *QFr.* 3.1.3; cf. S. Treggiari, *RFLR* (1969) 99. S. Martin, *The Roman*

tant, because if Nicephorus was indeed a freedman or a *servus alienus*, he could be the earliest occurrence of a contractual agent whose transactions would have given rise to an *actio institoria* against the principal.[131]

It is admittedly hazardous to determine a person's status on the basis of his/her name, even though it is often the only way to do so. As mentioned above, even slaves could use *duo nomina*. Often, freedmen adopted as a *cognomen* or *agnomen* (second *cognomen*) a name ending in -*ianus* derived from their former master's *nomen* or *cognomen*. This occurs rarely in the first century A.D., but more often later on; chances are that we are then dealing with members of the imperial household. Slaves and equestrian *procuratores* sometimes did so as well.[132] Thus, it is possible, yet unwarranted, that the *vilicus* Sergil*ianus* who dedicated an altar to Diana Lucifera Augusta in Montana (Moesia) was the freedman of a member of the *gens Sergilia*.[133] Cases where the name was formed on a *cognomen* are even more elusive: we know, for instance, a *vilicus* named Scaurianus—after the *cognomen* Scaurus—but the rest of the inscription explicitly indicates that he was an imperial slave active in Dacia.[134]

This tombstone, however, may provide a clue to explain the scarcity of manumitted *vilici*: Scaurianus died at age 23. As mentioned above, Trimalchio must have been around 20, if not younger, when he was sent to the country. It is possible that *vilici* were commonly appointed in their youth, as suggested by the jurist Gaius who reports that "most people appoint youngsters in the position of business managers."[135] Because of the Aelian Sentian Law (A.D. 4)

Jurists and the Organization of Private Building in the Late Republic and Early Empire (Brussels 1989) 55, n. 53 thinks that Nicephorus was almost certainly a slave with *peculium*. If she is right, it implies that the contract between Nicephorus and his master gave rise to an *obligatio naturalis*, but the concept is not attested sofar before the time of Augustus or even Nero; cf. I. Buti, *Studi sulla capacità patrimoniale dei servi* (Naples 1976) 265-75; and R. Vigneron, *BIDR* 23 (1981) 287-88.

[131] Cf. Chapter Two.

[132] P.R.C. Weaver (1972) 87-92 and 212-23.

[133] *AE* 1985, no. 737.

[134] *AE* 1956, no. 209 (= *CIL* III 1610).

[135] Gaius (9 *ad ed. prov.*) *Dig.* 14.3.8: "Nam et plerique pueros puellasque tabernis praeponunt," probably applicable to other types of economic activities, including farm or workshop management; cf. below (*vilicus* as *institor*), Chapter Four, and my paper, "Workshop Managers," in W.V. Harris (ed.), *The Inscribed Economy* (1993) 171-81, esp. 180. In *Dig.* 14.3, the word *taberna* represents any kind of *locus emendi vendendive*.

which set drastic restrictions on manumissions of slaves under the age of 30,[136]—and the current opinion is that manumission before 30 were not common[137]—young *vilici* had to wait a long time before fulfilling their dream of freedom. Many never reached the age limit. Among them, Narcissus, who died at age 25 while working for T. Titucius Florianus and Teia Galla in Venafrum (*Regio* I), expressed his sorrow and resignation in a verse epitaph probably set up by his master:

> The law denied me the benefit of a deserved freedom because of my youth, but an untimely death gave it back to me for ever.[138]

The effect of the Aelian Sentian Law combined with the low life expectancy of people in ancient Rome in general, and of slaves in particular, may have deprived many a diligent *vilicus* of what would have been a normal expectation: freedom as a reward for good services.

---

[136] Gai., *Inst.* 1.18-19: "Quod autem de aetate servi requiritur, lege Aelia Sentia introductum est. Nam ea lex minores XXX annorum servos non aliter voluit manumissos cives Romanos fieri quam si vindicta, apud consilium iusta causa manumissionis adprobata, liberati fuerint. Iusta autem causa manumissionis est veluti si quis filium filiamve aut fratrem sororemve naturalem, aut alumnum aut paedagogum, aut servum procuratoris habendi gratia, aut ancillam matrimonii causa apud consilium manumittat." On the manumission of slaves under 30 and the *Lex Aelia Sentia*, cf. de Zulueta's commentary on Gaius 1.18ff.; P. Angelini, *Il procurator* (Milan 1971) 86-87; M. Kaser, *Das römische Privatrecht* I² (Munich 1971) 297. The problem of the appointment of a *procurator* as a *iusta causa* did not receive the attention it deserves. Perhaps *institores* and *vilici* were not important enough to be included in the provision. I would rather suggest that their servile status was no obstacle and was even convenient: the status of Iunian Latin was perhaps thought to affect the credit of freedmen, even though they had the *ius commercii*. Of related interest is a passage by Ulpianus (*Reg.* 1.12 = *FIRA* II², p. 263) recording a different provision of the Aelian Sentian Law according to which slaves under 30 who were manumitted by the rod (*vindicta*) without the approval of a private council automatically became imperial slaves.

[137] P. Garnsey, "Independent Freedmen and the Economy of Roman Italy under the Principate," *Klio* 63 (1981) 359-71, esp. 361-62, following K. Hopkins, *Conquerors and Slaves* (Cambridge 1978); and W.V. Harris, "Toward a Study of the Roman Slave Trade," *MAAR* 36 (1980) 117-40; *contra*, G. Alföldy, "Die Freilassung von Sklaven und die Struktur der Sklaverei in der römischen Kaiserzeit," *RSA* 2 (1972) 97-129; and P.R.C. Weaver, "Children of Freedmen (and Freedwomen)," in B. Rawson (ed.), *Marriage, Divorce, and Children in Ancient Rome* (Oxford 1991) 166-90, esp. 182-89, who suggests that many slaves were manumitted to become Iunian Latin.

[138] *CIL* X 4917 (= *Anthol.Lat.* 2.2 = *Carm.Epigr.* [ed. Bücheler 1897] 468, no. 1015): "Debita libertas iuveni mihi lege negata / morte immatura reddita perpetua est."

Thus, hidden status, short life expectancy, and legal barriers may partly account for the scarcity of freedmen and freeborn among known Italian *vilici*. However, none of these arguments is totally convincing, and it remains unclear why landowners were obviously reluctant to appoint freeborn or manumitted *vilici*, since there was no legal obstacle to do so. While some *vilici* must have moved on to new positions before or at the time of manumission, it is surprising to note that many slave *vilici* recorded on tombstones died at an old age, or at least after 30.[139] If these slaves could retain their position for a long time, they must have done a decent job. This was obviously not a good enough reason to manumit them, and it is safe to assert that slave *vilici* seem to have never lost their appeal to landowners.

To sum up, the respective availability of slave and free labor is not sufficient to account for the choice between tenancy and the *vilicus* system, for Roman law did not prevent slaves from being tenants or non-slaves from being *vilici*. A survey of the epigraphical material concerning *vilici* in Italy and Sicily shows that less than ten percent of all *vilici* can reasonably be considered as freedmen, and none as freeborn. Considering that manumitted *vilici* were more likely to record their exceptional status, it seems logical to assume that the majority of instances with no status indication refer to slaves rather than freedmen. For the same reason, freed *vilici* may be overrepresented in inscriptions in comparison with their frequency in real life. Thus, it is obvious that even though landowners were not compelled to choose their bailiffs among their slaves, they elected to do so for practical reasons. In addition, it appears that bailiffs rarely remained in the same position after manumission. The reasons behind this preference for slave *vilici* are not entirely clear.

---

[139] *CIL* VI 8684 (the parents of the *vilicus* Auximus died at 87 (mother) and 85 (father), which suggests that Auximus was at least in his 40's (provided that the figures are reliable); *AE* 1929, no. 155 (Athictus, imperial *vilicus*, died at 31); *CIL* VI 37828 (an imperial *vilicus* who died at age 32); *CIL* XI 1751 (a public *vilicus* from Volaterra (VII) died at age 44); *CIL* X 7041 (Gallicanus in charge of an agricultural estate in Sicily died at 45); *CIL* VI 8495 (Sabbio, an imperial *vilicus* in charge of an aqueduct, had lived 24 years with his concubine when he dedicated the inscription); *AE* 1955, no. 205 (an imperial *vilicus* in charge of a *statio* for the collection of customs dues died at 64); *CIL* VI 8676 (Flavius, an imperial *vilicus* in charge of the Neronian baths, had lived with his concubine for 40 years; there is a slight chance that he was a freedman); *AE* 1989, no. 195 (a *vilicus* possibly in charge of an agricultural estate near Brindisi died at age 120, but the figure (CXX) must be wrong and should be read 70 (LXX). Cf. also *CIL* XIV 199 (a freed *vilicus* in charge of a *praetorium* died at age 40).

2. *The economic aspect of the vilicus system*

Tenancy and *vilicus* system are attested side-by-side in the same geographical areas and in the same periods. M. Rostovtzeff mentions that the *vilicus* system—combined with the slave mode of production—was common in Latium, Campania, and Etruria, and basically all over Central and Southern Italy, while small landowners who became *coloni* from the time of Augustus onward were mostly found in Etruria, Umbria, Picenum, and in the Po Valley; other regions, such as Apulia, Samnium, Latium, Sicily, Sardinia, and Corsica consisted mostly of pasture land.[140] The epigraphical evidence for Italian *vilici*, though biased toward the area around the city of Rome, leaves the question of geographical distribution of *vilici* open, as it is often unclear whether a *vilicus* was in charge of an agricultural estate or of some other type of enterprise. This indicates that neither mode of cultivation was so convenient and advantageous as to supersede the other. This fact can be interpreted in three different ways.

a. *profitability of agency vs. tenancy*

There was probably no significant difference in terms of productivity and cost-efficiency between agency and tenancy, and if there was any, it was not necessarily the landowner's main concern. Both systems could rely on slave labor, even though it is possible that most tenants had few or no dependents to help them cultivate their plot. In both systems, the landowner had to provide and repair the farm equipment, and collected his share of the profits, in the form of rent or crops (or the proceeds of their sale). Judging from the New Testament and from the writings of Columella, Pliny the Younger, and Symmachus, this process sometimes entailed a great deal of frustration.[141] Moreover, it seems that failure to pay the rent did not usually result in eviction from the land. The smooth and successful collection of the return from an agricultural estate depended less on the type of management than on the pressure that a landowner could exert on his tenant/manager, and ultimately on the latter's ability to pay.

---

[140] M. Rostovtzeff, *SEHRE*[2] (1957) 61-63.
[141] For instance, NT, *Matth.* 21.33-41; Columella, *Rust.* 1.7.2-4; Pliny, *Ep.* 9.37; Symmachus, *Ep.* 5.87; 9.6; and 9.15.

One could argue that tenants might have kept a larger share of the profit than *vilici*. As we have no information concerning the ratio of rent to productivity in Roman Italy, it is difficult to estimate how profitable tenancy was to the landowner. Pliny's letters, however, show that in his case the profit to be made was less important than the steadiness of the income and the uninterrupted cultivation of his estates.[142]

b. *reliability of vilici*

Agency and tenancy must each have had their pluses and minuses, and could be more or less attractive according to the circumstances. The agronomists insist that the *vilicus* system requires more supervision on the part of the landowner than tenancy. This attitude is biased, and rests on the double assumption that tenants are, by nature, more responsible farmers than *vilici*, and that the latter invariably try to cheat their landowners and to abuse the workers for their own benefit. Columella, however, indicates that tenancy required an active supervision on the part of the landowner, lest the land be neglected or abandoned. The stakes were so high that landowners were advised to regard the continuous exploitation of leased plots as more important than the regular payment of the rent.[143] In addition, Roman moralists expect slave employees to engage in all kinds of passive and active resistance.[144] Such actions and attitudes on the part of slaves undoubtedly occurred,[145] but both the primary evidence and the historical probability point toward a different reality. A few inscriptions dated to the Imperial period were set up by grateful masters who praise the loyalty of their managers.[146] Other

---

[142] D. Kehoe, *Chiron* 18 (1988) 15-42; and P.W. de Neeve, *Athenaeum* 78 (1990) 363-402.

[143] Columella, *Rust.* 1.7.1: "Avarius opus exigat quam pensiones."

[144] Positive opinions about slave labor are rare in literary sources, cf. Pliny, *Ep.* 3.19.7; cf. V.I. Kuziščin (1984) [1976] 229 and 243-44. I have not seen C. Castello, "Sui rapporti tra *dominus* e *vilicus* desunti dal *de agricultura* di Catone," *Atti del Seminario romanistico internazionale* (Perugia 1972) 76-140.

[145] K.R. Bradley, "*Servus Onerosus*: Roman Law and the Troublesome Slave," *Slavery & Abolition* 11 (1990) 135-57, with some remarks on the stereotyped aspects of literary sources (140, and 154, n. 18).

[146] *CIL* VI 9989 (= *ILS* 7370, Rome): "Sabiniano vilico et homini bono et [f]idelissimo;" *CIL* XI 1751 (a public *vilicus* from Volaterra, *Regio* VII, honored by a decree of the local council carried out by a questor); *CIL* X 7041 (= *ILS* 7371, Catinia/Sicily): "Gallicano fidelissimo, qui fuit vilicus Afinianis (praediis);" *CIL* XIV 469 (= *ILS* 7376, Ostia): "Cerdontis actor(is) fidelissimi;" *CIL* VI 9119 (=

inscriptions show the affection and gratefulness of managers toward their principal.[147] Significantly, Plautus names the bailiff of one of his characters Pistus (in Greek, "loyal, conscientious") and there is no reason to see any joke or irony in his choice.[148] The *cognomen* itself is not rare in Latin inscriptions, especially among freedmen. Columella urges landowners to test the loyalty and good dispositions of would-be *vilici* at an early age as a necessary corollary of their technical training.[149] One could argue that the evidence cited here is either exceptional or stereotyped, but, on the other hand, Ausonius and Symmachus, who voice their disappointment in their *vilici*, were clearly expressing the prejudices of the elite. In either case it is difficult to generalize, but these documents reflect a certain degree of social peace.

A similar bias against estate managers is observed in other historical contexts. In the Southern states of antebellum America, the evidence about the overseer system reflects the planters' frustrations and prejudices, and conveys the impression that overseers were generally unreliable. It is remarkable then that a planter from Green Hill, Tennessee, A.T. Goodloe, expressed in the *Southern Cultivator* (no. 18, September 1860, p. 287) his amazement concerning the view commonly held among his fellow planters that overseeing was "a calling unfit to be followed by a man who possesses any gentlemanly principles, or has respectable parentage." Occasionally, some planter would speak in defense of overseers. James Barbour, President of the Agricultural Society of Albemarle County, Virginia and future Secretary of War in the Cabinet of John Quincy Adams,

---

CIL XIV 2301, Ager Albanus/Latium): "Iunio actori fidelissimo;" Lucil., *frg.* 581-582 Krenkel; Cic., *QFr.* 3.1.5; cf. E. Maróti, *Oikumene* 1 (1976) 109-24, esp. 122, nn. 76-82, to which one can add *CIL* VIII 2767, an inscription from Lambaesis (Numidia) set up by one Iulius Sabinianus, a military tribune of the third legion Augusta, in memory of Hyacinthus, his *epistates fidelissimus adque optime meritus*. An *epistates* was a kind of manager (Cato, *Agr.* 56).

[147] These dedications were made by *actores*/πραγματευταί, but not by *vilici*: *CIL* XIII 6730 (= *ILS* 4615, Moguntiacum/Upper Germania); *IGRR* III 1434 (A.D. 115, Kytorios/Pontos); *IGRR* IV 152 (II A.D., Cyzicus/Mysia); *AE* 1955, no. 80 (A.D. 230's, Lambaesis/Numidia); *AE* 1968, no. 109 (III A.D., Latina or Satricum/*Regio* I).

[148] Plaut., *Merc.* 277-278. Compare with Apul., *Met.* 2.26, where the *actor* is called Philodespotus.

[149] Columella, *Rust.* 11.1.7: "multisque prius experimentis inspiciendus erit futurus villicus, nec solum an perdidicerit disciplinam ruris, sed an etiam domino fidem ac benevolentiam exhibeat, sine quibus nihil prodest villici summa scientia."

reportedly said at a meeting of the Society on November 8, 1825 that "undue prejudices are indulged against this class of people. That such a class is necessary to the state of society, their existence and employment unquestionably prove. A prejudice against that which is indispensable cannot be defended on rational grounds." Such testimonies, as well as the account of individual careers, induced a leading authority on American overseers to conclude that "in the final analysis, [it] seems warranted that, within the limitations imposed by their background and by the vast responsibilities with which they were burdened, the majority of southern overseers performed their duties with commendable energy, efficiency, and competence."[150] The same judgement probably applies to the *vilicus* system in the Roman Empire.

Vilici formed a select group of privileged slaves and were therefore more likely to be induced by social or economic incentives to side with landowners, keeping the behavior of their subordinates under control, and taking good care of the equipment. Harshness on the part of the bailiff towards the hands was expected, and when fairness was applied it did not go unnoticed: the *familia rustica* attached to the estate of one Plautius at Teate Marrucinorum (*Regio* IV) set up a tombstone to commemorate the restraint of its *vilicus* Hippocrates.[151] Conniving between *vilici* and landowners is supported by comparative historical cases; in nazi concentration camps during World War II, the capos, recruited among inmates, often played into the hands of their torturers out of fear, ambition, or instinct of self-preservation.[152]

One of the advantages of having *vilici* in various places throughout the country consisted in that landowners could employ them as agents to conduct business on their behalf within the adjustable limits of their appointment. Then, the purpose of the *vilicus* system was fulfilled only if no continuous supervision on the part of the landowner or his representative (*procurator*) was needed. One can wonder how often Julius Caesar could and would have stopped by to check the management of his *vilicus* Diogenes, who operated in

---

[150] W.K. Scarborough, *The Overseer. Plantation Management in the Old South*[2] (Athens, GA 1984) 129-30 and 201.

[151] *CIL* IX 3028 (= *ILS* 7367): "...quibus imperavit modeste."

[152] A satirical view of such behavior is presented in a movie by L. Wertmüller, *Pasqualino Settebellezze* (It., 1975).

Transalpine Gaul in 61 B.C. Nevertheless, he certainly considered him loyal enough to be entrusted with the delicate mission of hiding some slaves who, he feared, would contribute to create a major polit-ical embarrassment if they were to be questioned under torture by the magistrates in charge of investigating Clodius's profanation of the mysteries of Bona Dea.[153]

c. *complementarity of agency and tenancy*

Agency and tenancy supplemented each other to be fully effective or to suit the landowner's expectation. As the *vilicus* system is usually associated with the villa economy, it should be possible to determine the compared profitability of different labor systems on the basis of the reconstruction of the overall economic structure of a given area, taking into consideration the archaeological data.

A single case study should suffice to demonstrate why the two sys-tems of management were considered complementary. Some recent attempts have been made to calculate the size of the work force in relation to the total production of the estate attached to the villa of Settefinestre. The villa is located in the Valle d'Oro in Southern Etruria, three kilometers from the town of Cosa. One of the excava-tors, A. Carandini, reconstructed the organizational structure of the villa, as an hypothesis based on the combined data provided by the Latin agronomists and the archaeological remains.[154] The villa at

---

[153] This little known story is recorded in the *Schol. Bob. in Ciceronis in Clodium et Curionem orationem*, frg. 27a (ed. T. Stangl, pp. 90-91): "Praetextuntur argumenta quibus incestum P.Clodii potuerit facillime probari, nisi pecunia intercessisset. Nam C. Caesar pontifex diebus illis repudiarat uxorem; feminae quoque quae illi sacrificio interfuerant de interventu virili testimonium dixerant; servi etiam, cum peterentur in quaestionem, alienati fuerant et in diversas provincias ab domino missi; quinque et enim servi, in quos maxime suspicio congruebat, partim missi sunt ad Appium Claudium, qui frater eiusdem Clodii fuerat et in Graecia tunc age-bat, partim ad vilicum Diogenem nomine, qui trans Alpis morabatur." About the reliability of the Bobbio scholiast, cf. E. Badian, "Marius' Villas: The Testimony of the Slave and the Knave," *JRS* 63 (1973) 121-32, esp. 125-30. The implication of the fact that Caesar owned, rented, or possessed (cf. Gaius, *Inst.* 2.7 and 31; and Paulus [2 *de cens.*] *Dig.* 50.15.8.1) some land in Transalpine Gaul (probably Nar-bonensis) before the conquest of the 50's has not been given the attention it deserves. P. Moreau, *Clodia religio. Un procès politique en 61 avant J.-C.* (Paris 1982) 198 interprets the passage as referring to Clodius's slaves, bailiff, and estate.

[154] A. Carandini, "Il vigneto e la villa del fondo di Settefinestre nel Cosano: un caso di produzione agricola per il mercato transmarino," *MAAR* 36 (1980) 1-10; *idem*, in A. Carandini *et al.* (eds.), *Settefinestre: Una villa schiavistica nell'Etruria romana* I (Modena 1985); *idem*, *Schiavi in Italia. Gli strumenti pensanti dei Romani fra tarda Repubblica e medio Impero* (Roma 1988) 19-224.

Settefinestre was one among eleven known villas in the Valle d'Oro engaged in the production of wine for seaborne trade. One can assume that mixed farming was practiced to support the staff of the villa. According to Carandini, the estate, estimated at ca. 500 *iugera*, was divided into a vineyard (200 *iugera*), woodland (30 *iugera*), and agricultural land and pasture (270 *iugera*). The rural household was composed of one *vilicus* and his concubine (*vilica*), 11 slaves for the cultivation of agricultural land, and between 23 and 32 slaves for the cultivation of the vineyard and for wine-production, which makes a total of 36-45 people achieving self-sufficiency and producing some 4,260 amphorae (= 111,612 liters) of wine a year.[155] According to Carandini, these numbers are consistent with the archaeological data, namely the number of *cellae* identified as slave quarters and the volume of grapes that could be processed in the three *torcularia* discovered in the villa. The proceeds of the wine export are estimated at almost 64,000 sestertii, which represents a yearly profit of about 1,500 sestertii per slave.

Carandini's model may be debatable on many points, but it suggests that the slave mode of production was, theoretically, very profitable. If the model is realistic and was reproduced in each of the eleven identified villas of the Valle d'Oro, the region would indeed present the feature recorded by Tiberius Gracchus during his trip to Spain in 137 B.C., when he first took notice of the absence of citizen-farmers and the prominence of foreign slaves in the position of cultivators and shepherds.[156]

The main problem with this model is that it does not take into account seasonal variations of labor input into wine-making. The vintage period probably required much more than 45 workers to carry out the operations on an estate of this size. During this period, the landowner or his *vilicus* must have hired supplementary workers. Since the harvest of grapes allows for almost no anticipation or postponement without subsequent loss in quantity or quality of the

---

[155] On the occupation density of slave quarters, cf. N. Purcell, *JRS* 78 (1988) 197-98 (review of Tchernia [1986] and of Carandini *et al.* [1985]).

[156] Plut., *Ti.Gracch.* 8; and Appian, *BCiv.* 1.1.7-8. V.I. Kuziščin (1984) [1976] 62-68 and other scholars before him convincingly argue that both Appian's and Plutarch's accounts are anachronistic and reflect conditions existing in the late first century A.D. Others think that the statement is authentic, but amounts to a voluntary historical distortion used as political propaganda; cf. D.B. Nagle, "The Etruscan Journey of T. Gracchus," *Historia* 25 (1976) 487-89.

production, neighboring estate had the same needs in extra labor
at the same time, and manpower shortages were likely to occur,
unless a good supply of workers was available in the vicinity. The
proximity of the town of Cosa, only three kilometers away from
Settefinestre, could provide part of the required additional labor,
and in fact a drift from the town to the countryside is attested in the
last quarter of the second century and in the first quarter of the first
century B.C.[157] It is not specifically related to the villa of Settefinestre, which was built in the middle of the first century B.C., but
one cannot infer from that that there was no agricultural concern on
the same site before the construction of the villa. If the town had
been too far away, temporary labor would have had to come from
another source.[158]

If one looks at the map surveying the agricultural facilities of the
Ager Cosanus, one notices a considerable number of secondary buildings which are not accounted for in Carandini's reconstruction.[159]
Besides, one has to allow for possible wooden structures, used either
as houses, stables, or storage spaces, which would have left no archaeological remains. Small landholders, either independent farmers
or tenants, could provide supplementary hired labor and, theoretically, compulsory service. This might have been the solution to temporary manpower shortages in large slave-staffed villas. Small landholders could provide supplementary labor only if they were not
engaged in the same type of production or if they were chronically
underemployed because of the small size of their plot.

---

[157] D. Manacorda, "The *Ager Cosanus* and the Production of the Amphorae of
Sestius: New Evidence and a Reassessment," *JRS* 68 (1978) 122-31, esp. 130; *idem*,
"L'*Ager Cosanus* tra tarda Repubblica e Impero: forme di produzione e assetto della
proprietà," *MAAR* 36 (1980) 173-84; *idem*, "Produzione agricola, produzione ceramica e proprietari nell' *Ager Cosanus* nel I° a.C.," *SRPS* II (1981) 3-54.

[158] M. Rostovtzeff, *SEHRE*² (1957) 63 points out that large villas in Apulia,
Calabria, Etruria, Sardinia, and Africa were often surrounded by villages (*vici*) in-
habited by wage laborers and slaves. For the complementarity of slave labor and
transient workers, cf. Apul., *Apol.* 17.1.

[159] M. Grazia Celuzza–E. Regoli, "Gli insediamenti nella Valle d'Oro e il
fondo di Settefinestre," in A. Carandini *et al.* (1985) 48-59, esp. 52 report that these
secondary buildings were built in the second century B.C. and that most of them
were abandoned in the second half of the first century B.C. Those remaining in activity were rare and very poor. J. Carlsen, *ARID* 13 (1984) 50-51 remarks that the
interpretation of the archaeological evidence from the *Ager Cosanus* has been influenced by the opposite ideology (liberalistic *vs.* marxist approach) of the two
teams of excavators at work there (an American team lead by S.L. Dyson, and an
Italo-British team lead by A. Carandini *et al.*). Cf. also S.L. Dyson, "Some Reflections on the Archaeology of Southern Etruria," *JFA* 8 (1981) 79-83, esp. 81-83.

D.W. Rathbone showed the theoretical improbability of the absence of small holdings in the *Ager Cosanus*, and calculated that the employment of mixed labor was twice as profitable as slave labor.[160] This explains why the small peasantry survived the rise of the slave mode of production. But were it only a matter of profitability, such a rise would not have been possible, since Rathbone's calculations show that *métayage* and the exclusive input of free labor in *vilicus*-managed farms would have been even more profitable than mixed labor.

What is surprising is that, even though free labor must have been available outside, the owner of the villa considered it appropriate to build extended slave quarters (provided that the identification of the excavated facilities is correct) precisely when wine-production was supposed to be in its decline (Flavian period). What is even more surprising is that, in spite of this decline—admittedly slow—the villa continued to prosper for a century (until the end of the Antonine period). During this period, the *pars rustica* of the villa took more and more importance (especially in the Trajanic period).[161]

As a tentative explanation, one may suggest that the staff of the villa of Settefinestre was not involved only, or even mainly, in agriculture. It is well known that during the late Republican period the vicinity of the harbor of Cosa was the site of the production of amphorae of the Dressel 1 and 2-4 types. The stamp of many of the Dr. 1 amphorae bears the name of Sestius, a family of landowners, wine-producers, manufacturers, or merchants otherwise well attested in the first century B.C.[162] Even though the production of the

---

[160] D.W. Rathbone, "The Development of Agriculture in the *Ager Cosanus* during the Roman Republic: Problems of Evidence and Interpretation," *JRS* 71 (1981) 10-23, esp. 21 for the existence of smallholdings; and 14-15 for the comparative profitability of various labor systems on the basis of the data provided by the ancient agronomists. Cf. also W. Scheidel, "Zur Lohnarbeit bei Columella," *Tyche* 4 (1989) 139-46.

[161] A. Carandini, *MAAR* 36 (1980) and (1985) 138-85 (= [1988] 109-224); A. Tchernia (1986) 269, following D. Manacorda, *MAAR* 36 (1980). The assumption of a decline in wine-production is based on the disappearance of Dr. 1 and 2-4 amphorae. As Tchernia has shown (*ibidem* 162-66), this assumption is highly questionable. The first-century-A.D. crisis in Italian agriculture has been cogently dismissed by N. Purcell, "Wine and Wealth in Ancient Italy," *JRS* 75 (1985) 1-25; and J.R. Patterson, "Crisis: What Crisis? Rural Change and Urban Development in Imperial Apennine Italy," *PBSR* 42 (1987) 115-46.

[162] D. Manacorda, *JRS* 68 (1978) 129 n. 22, citing E.L. Will. Cicero mentions one Publius Sestius, praetor in 54 B.C., who owned some property at Cosa (*Att.*

Sestian amphorae cannot be assigned to the villa of Settefinestre,
one may speculate that the staff of the villa was also involved in non-
agricultural activities. It is known that ancient legal writers were
aware that some economic activities conducted on agricultural estates were more profitable than mixed farming. For instance, Ulpianus records the case of an usufructuary farmer who converted part
of his estate into a quarry, a clay bed, or a sand pit. Others would
go into mining.[163]

At Settefinestre, tile and brick production could be thought of as
possible alternatives, but these industries were commonly practiced
on a seasonal basis, which seems to overlap the vintage time.[164]
However, the seasonability of ceramic and brick/tile production is a
controllable factor, adjustable as needed. Some villas were equipped
with sheds on pillars, open on each side, where the process of drying

---

15.27.1). His son, L. Sestius Quirinalis, was *consul suffectus* in 23 B.C.; tiles with
the latter's stamp have been found (*CIL* XV 1445, Rome); cf. also E.L. Will, "The
Sestius Amphoras: A Reappraisal," *JFA* 6 (1979) 339-50; J.H. D'Arms, *CSSAR*
(1981) 55-62 rightly argues that the manufacturer of the Cosan amphorae was L.
Sestius, the father of Cicero's friend, who abstained from pursuing a political career
(Cic., *Sest.* 3.6); and D. Manacorda, *SRPS* II (1981) 28-36.

[163] Ulpianus (18 *ad Sab.*) *Dig.* 7.1.13.5: "Inde est quaesitum, an lapidicinas vel
cretifodinas vel harenifodinas ipse instituere possit: et ego puto etiam ipsum instituere posse, si non agri partem necessariam huic rei occupaturus est. Proinde
venas quoque lapidicinarum et huiusmodi metallorum inquirere poterit: ergo et
auri et argenti et sulpuris et aeris et ferri et ceterorum fodinas vel quas pater familias
instituit exercere poterit vel ipse instituere, si nihil agriculturae nocebit. Et si forte
in hoc quod instituit plus reditus sit quam in vineis vel arbustis vel olivetis quae
fuerunt, forsitan etiam haec deicere poterit, si quidem ei permittitur meliorare
proprietatem." Cf. also Ulpianus (35 *ad ed.*) *Dig.* 27.9.3.6 and 5 *pr.*; and A. Steinwenter (1942) 63.

[164] H. Bloch, "*Consules suffecti* on Roman Brick Stamps," *CP* 39 (1944) 254-55;
cf. below Chapter Four. This fits well with Labeo's example of a landowner having
potters on his estate whom he employs for most of the year at farmwork, cf. Iavolenus (2 *ex posterioribus Labeonis*) *Dig.* 33.7.25.1. However, the season for brickmaking might be longer than is generally assumed: *AE* 1982, no. 843 (Moesia) provides a mark stamped on a brick before firing. The stamp is dated to the day before
the Kalends of March. It is not the place to discuss in detail the various possibilities
encountered in pottery-making. However, D.P.S Peacock, *Pottery in the Roman
World: An Ethnoarchaeological Approach* (London/New York 1982) presents modern
cases across the area covered by the Roman Empire which show that (a) pottery-
making could start months before the time of firing (p. 14); (b) pottery-making was
often, but not necessarily, a seasonal female activity (p. 17): the brick factory
located on the estate of Ashburnham employed male potters all year round, sun-
drying of the clay and of the brick being replaced by storage under protecting hacks
(pp. 46-50). Internally-situated kilns had the advantage of providing a heated
storage space which freed the workers from the necessity of relying on the sun to
proceed with the production (p. 30).

before firing could take place even in the winter.[165] Another important activity connected with the town of Cosa was the fish industry.
Located near the harbor was a fish-farm that required a large labor
force to operate water-lifting machinery, and to build and maintain
the facilities. The same staff could also be involved in fish processing. It has been suggested that the Sestii were involved in the
commerce of fish sauce, but strong evidence is still missing.[166] Such
an industry would have called for subsidiaries producing containers,
and would have required a network of distribution. Even though the
fisheries of Cosa were probably not connected with the villa of
Settefinestre, it shows that non-agricultural jobs were available in
the area.

Underemployment in agriculture affected not only slave-owners
in Roman times, but also small landholders. Columella already
recognizes the necessity to plan the farmwork over a period of 250
days, including 45 days of rain and 30 days of rest after sowing.[167]
The rest of the year, a little less than four months, was to be used
for all kinds of useful tasks, such as hauling hay, forage, and manure,
or engaging in short-term crops.[168] If bad weather was contrary to

---

[165] For instance, at the Roman villa dell'argine d'Agosta in Emilia Romagna,
in the Valle del Mezzano, in the vicinity of Padova, in activity from the first century
B.C. to the fourth century A.D., cf. G. Uggeri, "Un insediamento romano a carattere industriale," *Musei Ferraresi* 3 (1973) 174-86, esp. 175. A somewhat different
structure has been excavated at Pizzica, near Metaponto, where a brick factory
(IV-I B.C.) comprised a large covered space near the kiln where the moulded bricks
and tiles were kept before firing and the finished products stored before transport
to the final destination; cf. J. Carter, "Rural Architecture and Ceramic Industry
at Metaponto, Italy, 350-50 B.C.," in A. McWhirr (ed.), *Roman Brick and Tile*
(Oxford 1979) 45-64, esp. 57. Cf. also previous note.

[166] A.M. McCann, "The Portus Cosanus: A Center of Trade in the Late
Republic," *RCRF* 25/26 (1987) 21-70, esp. 32-33 (Fig. 15) and 39-40, mentions
an amphora from the Athenian Agora (Ath. Ag. Excavation P 6867), of a type identified as containing fish sauce, bearing no stamp but a red painted inscription
CO/SES. It is dated to the very end of the second century B.C. and is unique. Cf.
also R.I. Curtis, *Garum and Salsamenta. Production and Commerce in Materia Medica*
(Leiden 1991) 87.

[167] Columella, *Rust.* 2.12.8-9. Let us note, however, that labor input in olive
cultivation peaks in the wintertime, a marked difference with wheat or wine
production.

[168] Cato, *Agr.* 2.3-4 describes the work to be done during rainy days and holidays; cf. K.D. White, "The Productivity of Labour in Roman Agriculture," *Antiquity* 39 (1965) 102-07, esp. 103-04. In medieval England in the last quarter of the
thirteenth century, Walter of Henley, a former bailiff, allows for only eight weeks
off for holidays and other "desturbances" (30), cf. D. Oschinsky, *Walter of Henley
and Other Treatises on Estate Management and Accounting* (Oxford 1971) 315. For the re-

agricultural—and, to some extent, industrial—production, it had the immediate effect of filling the waterways which were used to transport the production of the villa to the market-place. Pliny the Younger, who owned a villa at Tifernum Tiberinum some 150 miles north from Rome, says that the Tiber was navigable only in the winter and spring, at which time the produce was conveyed to Rome.[169] If part of the work force attached to the villa was under-employed at this time of the year, it could be assigned to the task of loading, sailing, unloading, storing, and selling the goods, both agricultural and artisanal/industrial, produced during the rest of the year. This would explain why the equipment of the villa included the material, containers and vehicles, necessary to carry the products of the farm to the market.[170] Finally, the servile staff of the villa could be rented out to independent entrepreneurs on a temporary basis. Ulpianus considers that these workers are nonetheless part of the farm equipment.[171]

To sum up: absentee landowners relied on a mixed work force under the leadership of the *vilicus* who coordinated the respective input of skilled and unskilled labor. Temporary shortages of manpower could be balanced by hiring wage laborers in order to keep the level of seasonal underemployement of the villa staff at the lowest level year round. The availability of temporary wage laborers depended on the existence of small plots worked by independent farmers or tenants, whose activities were somewhat different from that performed on the estate managed by the *vilicus*. Thus, a diversification of activities was imposed upon the managers of such estates.[172] The system was most efficient if it required minimum supervision on the part of the landowner.

---

maining forty-four weeks, ploughmen were supposed to be constantly employed.

[169] Plin., *Ep.* 5.6.12.

[170] Ulpianus (20 *ad Sab.*) *Dig.* 33.7.12.1: "Sed et ea, quae exportandorum fructuum causa parantur, instrumenti esse constat, veluti iumenta et vehicula et naves et cuppae et culei."

[171] Ulpianus (20 *ad Sab.*) *Dig.* 33.7.12.8: "Servi, si aliqua parte anni per eos ager colitur, aliqua parte in mercedem mittuntur, nihilo minus instrumento continentur."

[172] *Coloni* could also be involved in non-agricultural activities, cf. Ulpianus (18 *ad ed.*), citing Proculus and Neratius, *Dig.* 9.2.27.9 and 11 (about a slave *fornicarius* who belonged to a *colonus* and whose negligence had caused a fire). Cf. also *Cod. Theod.* 13.1.10 (A.D. 374, concerning the *collatio lustralis*); and A. Carandini, *Studi Miscellanei* 15 (1970) 116-19.

D. *VILICI* AS BUSINESS MANAGERS

Discussing the difference between agriculture and grazing, C. Licinius Stolo remarks that distinct managers are appointed to take care of either sector: the bailiff (*vilicus*) and the chief herdsman (*magister pecoris*).[173] The choice of the terminology used by Varro ("praeponuntur") is hardly a coincidence, as Columella also recommends the appointment of a mature person to the position of bailiff, specifying that the *vilicus* would be in charge of the *fundus* and would command a *familia*.[174] These two texts demonstrate that *vilici* were *praepositi*, i.e. *institores* in the juristic sense of the term (cf. Chapters One and Two).

Major differences of functions could exist among *vilici* in charge of agricultural estates. These differences arose from the scale and structure of the managerial unit, but also from the entrepreneurial strategy of the landowner. The jurist Paulus is aware of this fact when he denies the *actio institoria* against the principal of a *vilicus* who has been appointed for the sole purpose of collecting the produce of the soil. This type of *vilicus* is best represented in the literary sources by Regulus's story (cf. above). There is hardly any doubt that the *vilicus* had been hired primarily as a farmer. Since Regulus's plot was too small to require extra labor input and to yield any marketable surplus, the appointment entailed no business activity. On the other hand, Paulus knows that in real life many *vilici* were involved in more sophisticated and lucrative pursuits, in connection with which they were required to make all sorts of contracts on behalf of their absentee landowner. Under these circumstances, Paulus acknowledges, as Labeo and Ulpianus had done before him, that the principal should be held fully liable for the contracts negotiated by his *vilicus* within the scope of his appointment.[175]

---

[173] Varro, *Rust.* 1.2.14: "Quocirca principes qui utrique rei praeponuntur vocabulis quoque sunt diversi, quod unus vocatur vilicus, alter magister pecoris. Vilicus agri colendi causa constitutus (est)." About *magister pecoris*, cf. below.

[174] Columella, *Rust.* 11.1.3: "Villicum fundo familiaeque praeponi convenit aetatis nec primae nec ultimae."

[175] Paulus (29 *ad ed.*) *Dig.* 14.3.16: "Si cum vilico alicuius contractum sit, non datur in dominum actio, quia vilicus propter fructus percipiendos, non propter quaestum praeponitur. Si tamen vilicum distrahendis quoque mercibus praepositum habuero, non erit iniquum exemplo institoriae actionem in me competere;" and *idem, Sent.* 2.8.2: "Si quis pecuniae fenerandae agroque colendo, condendis vendendisque frugibus praepositus est, ex eo nomine quod cum illo contractum est in solidum fundi dominus obligatur: nec interest, servus an liber sit." The latter

In their descriptions of the duties of the *vilicus*, the agronomists dwell on the organization of agricultural work. This aspect has been the subject of many learned books and articles on Roman farming and need not be discussed here.[176] Besides, the ancient sources contain numerous incidental allusions to various managerial tasks that the bailiff was supposed to perform:

- keeping track of the yields of all products;[177]

- recording all tasks performed on the estate or outside by any member of the household;[178]

- registering all transactions involving cash, grain, wine, oil, fodder, etc;[179]

- selling surpluses of oil, wine, grain, wool, hides, and everything that was deemed superfluous—or simply marketable—such as old and sick slaves or animals, worn-out tools, etc.;[180]

- buying farm equipment, slaves, tools, draft animals, seeds, fodder, etc.;[181]

---

text echoes Labeo, quoted by Ulpianus (28 *ad ed.*) *Dig.* 14.3.5.2: "Labeo scripsit, si quis pecuniis faenerandis, agris colendis, mercaturis redempturisque faciendis praeposuerit, in solidum eum teneri." On these texts and their interpretation, cf. A. di Porto, *Impresa collettiva e schiavo 'manager' in Roma antica (II sec. a.C. –II sec. d.C.)* (Milan 1984) 72-83; and *idem*, "Impresa agricola ed attività collegate nell'economia della *villa*. Alcune tendenze organizzative" in *Sodalitas. Scritti in onore di A. Guarino* VII (Naples 1984) 3235-77, esp. 3238, n. 12; 3248; 3254, n. 51bis; and 3263 ff., rightly criticized by T.J. Chiusi, "Landwirtschaftliche Tätigkeit und *actio institoria*," *ZRG* 108 (1991) 155-86; and by A. Bürge, *ZRG* 105 (1988) 856-65, esp. 861-62. Cf. also above, Chapter One.

[176] W.E. Heitland, *Agricola. A Study of Agriculture and Rustic Life in the Graeco-Roman World from the Point of View of Labour* (Cambridge 1921); K.D. White, *Roman Farming* (London 1970); W. Kaltenstadler, *Arbeitsorganisation und Führungssystem bei den römischen Agrarschriftstellern (Cato, Varro, Columella)* (Stuttgart 1978); D. Flach, *Römische Agrargeschichte* (Munich 1990); and the forthcoming book by J. Carlsen, *Vilicus. A Study in Roman Estate Management.*

[177] Cato, *Agr.* 2.1.

[178] Cato, *Agr.* 2.2: "ad rationem operum (*including* opera publica) operarumque vilicum revoca."

[179] Cato, *Agr.* 2.5. Record-keeping is attested in Apul., *Apol.* 87.7.

[180] The sale of surpluses was part of the six-stage agricultural process described by C. Licinius Stolo (one of the characters in Varro's treatise): preparation of the land; planting; cultivation; harvesting; storing; and marketing (Varro, *Rust.* 1.27.4). Trade with neighbouring communities (towns, villages, and other villas) included sale of surpluses, such as props, poles, and reeds, and purchase of necessary items (Varro, *Rust.* 1.16.3). In addition, some products were made on the farmstead and sold outside. Varro (*Rust.* 1.22.1) lists hampers, baskets, threshing-sledges, fans, and rakes, in addition to articles made of withes, wood, hemp, flax, rush, palm fibre, and bulrush. Cf. also Chapter Four, about the production of clay artifacts.

[181] Columella, *Rust.* 11.1.23: "Non urbem, non ullas nundinas nisi vendendae

– dealing with securities and credit, even though the agronomists urge landowners to keep this type of activity under personal
control;[182]
  – hiring additional workers to perform specific tasks;[183]
  – letting contracts for work to be done (cf. below).
The managerial functions were the source of considerable power for
the *vilicus*, and the basis of patronage in the countryside.[184] In
Cato's time, farm management already entailed many business
transactions. Construction work, lime burning on shares, and other
tasks were contracted out. Mills, wine- and oil-presses were purchased outside, and it was necessary to contract to have them built,
transported to the farmstead, and assembled. Arrangements were
made for olive picking and for milling. Olives were sold on the tree
and grapes on the vine, often with delayed payment. The wine was
sold in jars. In the context of wine and grain production, it was common to rent agricultural land to sharecroppers. In the context of
animal husbandry, it was necessary to sell the increase of the flock,

---

aut emendae rei necessariae causa, frequentaverit.'' Cf. also *ibid.* 1.8.6; and Chariton of Aphrodisias, *Chaereas and Callirhoe* 1.12-14, discussed below, in the general
conclusion to this book.
    [182] Cato, *Agr.* 2.6: ''Quae satis accipiunda sint, satis accipiantur;'' and 5.3:
''Iniussu domini credat nemini: quod dominus crediderit, exigat;'' cf. also Florentinus, *Geop.* 2.44.3-4. Trimalchio had an *actuarius* read in front of him the ''nomina
vilicorum'' representing arrears of rent or debts incurred by bailiffs towards either
their master or third contracting parties (Petron., *Sat.* 53.10). The *kalendarium* or
register of loans was kept by a ''servus kalendario praepositus'' who could be the
vilicus himself (*CIL* III 4152 = *ILS* 7119, a public *vilicus* in charge of the ''kalendarium Septimianum'' of the colony of Savaria/Pannonia) or another agent (*actor*, *dispensator*, *praepositus*); cf. G. Giliberti, *Legatum kalendarii* (Naples 1984) 71-100. Sen.,
Ep. 14.18, in which a *dominus* turned into a *procurator* ''rationes accipit, forum con-
terit, kalendarium versat'', is no evidence for a ''procurator kalendarii'', as he
supervises the agent in charge of it.
    [183] Cato, *Agr.* 2.4-7; and 5.4: *operarii*, *mercennarii*, *politores* (for no more than a
day). Cato also reports (*Agr.* 13.1; and 66-67) that three watchmen (two freeborn
and one slave) and a ladler (*capulator*) were hired at the time of the pressing; cf. also
Columella, *Rust.* 3.13.11-13; and 3.21.10. Hired laborers performed heavy and
dangerous operations (Varro, *Rust.* 1.17.2) and skilled work: artisans (*artifices,
medici, fullones, fabri*) were often hired on a yearly basis; *contra*, *P. Oxy.* LI 3641 (A.D.
544), a contract of work made between a millstone-cutter and Flavius Apion II,
consul and landowner at Oxyrhynchus, through his administrator (διὰ Μηνᾶ
οἰκέτου), for the duration of the millstone-cutter's life. The situation was different
in villas located far away from urban centers: artisans were kept on the farmstead
under the control of the *vilicus* (Varro, *Rust.* 1.16.4-5).
    [184] L. Foxhall, *JRS* 80 (1990) 103, citing parallels in nineteenth-century Sicily
and in contemporary Andalousia.

and to lease winter pasture.[185] It is true that Cato never says explicitly that the *vilicus* should negotiate these contracts himself, which would have contradicted his stand on the question of personal involvement of landowners in the management of their estates. There is no doubt, however, that Cato had *vilici* in mind as the audience of his treatise, as he exceptionally addresses them directly in the chapter immediately preceding the description of various contracts of work.[186] In any case, the distance separating city-dwelling landowners from their scattered estates, the growing involvement of these landowners in other pursuits, and the development of diversified activities in the context of the villa economy, made delegation desirable and even necessary at an early date, certainly by the second century B.C.

Searching for contractors, negotiating the contracts, overseeing their execution, calculating the laborers' remuneration, the *vilicus* must have had little time to take part in the actual farmwork. The reliance on oral arrangements forced him to be present for each transaction wherever it took place. When the size and the complexity of the economic structure of the estate made it necessary, foremen (*praefecti*, *magistri singulorum officiorum*, *epistatai*, and *monitores*) could take care of the technical direction of the farmwork.

If we look at the occupations of *vilici* in the literary sources, we notice that we rarely find them out in the fields, a fact that caused some dismay among the agronomists: Columella obsessively writes that the *vilicus* should focus on the organization of the agricultural work, lest he become a *negotiator*.[187] We are not told what business, except flirting, brought the *vilicus* to town in Plautus's comedy *Casina*, but no excuse was given to explain why he was wandering away from his farmstead. His rival would have rather seen him stay in the country.[188] It is true that the needs of the plot may have brought

---

[185] Cato, *Agr.* 14-16; 20-22; 136; and 144-150.

[186] Cato, *Agr.* 143.1-2: "Vilicae quae sunt officia, curato faciat. Si eam *tibi* dederit dominus uxorem, ea esto contentus. Ea *te* metuat facito... Cibum *tibi* et familiae curet uti coctum habeat" (with my emphasis). Cf. N. Purcell, *JRS* 75 (1985) 5.

[187] Columella, *Rust.* 11.1.24: "Pecuniam domini neque in pecore nec in aliis rebus promercalibus occupet. Haec enim res avocat villici curam, et eum negotiatorem potius facit quam agricolam, nec umquam sinit eum cum rationibus domini paria facere; sed ubi nummum est numeratio, res pro nummis ostenditur."

[188] Plaut., *Cas.* 98-103: (Chalinus) "quid in urbe reptas, vilice haud magni preti?" / (Olympio): "Lubet." (Chalinus): "Quin ruri es in praefectura tua? / quin

Plautus's *vilici* to town more often than usual, but we also see one of them being sent by his master to a distant place in order to buy a pair of plough-broken oxen.[189] Cicero presents Atticus's bailiff as a moneylender,[190] and his brother's *vilicus* Nicephorus as a building contractor.[191] Suetonius reports that the future emperor Claudius allowed his bailiff to manage a tavern, in which other agricultural workers were employed.[192] Finally, we read in Apuleius's *Metamorphoses* the atrocious punishment of a *vilicus* whose sexual misconduct had lead his pregnant concubine to commit suicide. As a result of this, his angry master had him covered with honey and devoured by ants. He was an innkeeper.[193]

The inscriptions and the jurists record private *vilici* as superintendents of urban houses, as keepers of gardens or suburban estates (*horti*), and as moneylenders.[194] Private *vilici* also show up at the head of various workshops and mines, as managers of amphitheaters or circus factions, and as collectors of various taxes.[195] There is

---

potius quod legatum est tibi negotium, / id curas atque urbanis rebus te apstines? / huc mihi venisti sponsam praereptum meam. / Abi rus, abi dierectus tuam in provinciam." The *vilicus* reveals that he has appointed a substitute to take care of his *praefectura* during his absence from the farmstead: "Praefeci ruri recte qui curet tamen" (*Cas.* 105).

[189] Plaut., *Per.* 259-260. Sagaristio is not called *vilicus*, but it is likely that some experience in agriculture was required in order to carry out a transaction of this type. Besides, Sagaristio seems to have had a *peculium*, which makes him a privileged slave. Cf. J.-C. Dumont, *Servus. Rome et l'esclavage sous la République* (Rome 1987) 462-63.

[190] Cic., *Att.* 11.13.4 (47 B.C.): "Itaque tum et a tuo vilico sumpsimus et aliunde mutuati sumus cum Quintus queritur per litteras sibi nos nihil dedisse, qui neque ab illo rogati sumus neque ipsi eam pecuniam asperimus."

[191] Cic., *QFr.* 3.1.5. Cf. above.

[192] Suet., *Claud.* 38.2: "... senatorem...relegavit, quod...hic in aedilitate inquilinos praediorum suorum, contra vetitum cocta vendentes, multasset vilicumque intervenientem flagellasset." The bequest of a *fundus* (or *praediolum*) *cum taberna* is discussed by Scaevola (17 *dig.*) *Dig.* 32.35.2 and (19 *dig.*) *Dig.* 32.38.5.

[193] Apul., *Met.* 8.22.

[194] **Urban houses**: *CIL* VI 9483; Juv. 3.195; Mart. 12.32.23; *Cod. Theod.* 16.5.36.1 (A.D. 399);
  gardens/suburban estates: *CIL* VI 623; 9472; 9990; 9990a; 9991;
  moneylending: *AE* 1980, no. 230.

[195] **Amphorae**: *AE* 1927, no. 7 (Augusta Raurica) (?); *AE* 1952, no. 93 (London) (?). Cf. Chapter Four;
  lead pipes: *CIL* XI 725; 731-736; 1320; *CIL* X 3967 (perhaps mint manager). Cf. Chapter Five and my paper "Workshop Managers," in W.V. Harris (ed.), *The Inscribed Economy* (1993) 175-78.
  mines and metal workshops: *CIL* III 13239 and 13240 (Dalmatia); *AE* 1958, no. 64 (Dalmatia, A.D. 228); *AE* 1973, nos. 411-414 (Dalmatia, A.D. 201-229).
  amphitheaters: *CIL* VI 10163 (= *ILS* 5155). Cf. Chapter Five.

even one instance of a *vilicus navis*, probably to be understood as the equivalent of a *magister navis* (shipmaster).[196] Public and imperial *vilici* are found in many areas of administration, in charge of gardens, woodlands, granaries, markets, buildings, libraries, baths, mines, workshops, aqueducts, tax collection, and public finances.[197]

---

circus factions: *CIL* VI 10046. Cf. Chapter Five.

tax collection: *CIL* VI 779; *CIL* IX 4681 (= *ILS* 1865); *CIL* X 3964 (= *ILS* 1875); *CIL* X 7347; *CIL* XI 5032; *CIL* V 810; 820; 1864; 7264; 7852 (= *ILS* 1854); 8650; *AE* 1934, no. 234; *AE* 1959, no. 261; *AE* 1975, no. 202; *CIL* II 1742 (Gades); *CIL* II 2214 (Cordoba); *CIL* XIII 1130 (Poitiers); *AE* 1899, nos. 74-77 (Poetovio); *CIL* III 5121 (= *ILS* 1857, Pannonia); *CIL* III 4288 (= *ILS* 1861, Brigetio/Pannonia); *CIL* III 751 (= 7434 = *ILS* 1855, Nicopolis/Moesia); *AE* 1894, no. 32 (Vratnik); *AE* 1895, no. 45 (Moesia); *CIL* III 447 (= *ILS* 1862, Miletus); *AE* 1979, no. 610 (Iasus); *BCH* 10 (1886) 267 (Iasus); *CIL* III 7153 (Iasus, A.D. 26); *CIL* VIII 1128 (= *ILS* 1873, Carthage); *AE* 1923, no. 22 (Thuburbo Maius); *AE* 1942-43, no. 63 (Setif). Cf. Chapter Five.

[196] *CIL* XII 2379 (Between Vienna and Aoste, Gallia Narbonensis).

[197] **Gardens/suburban estates**: *CIL* VI 8669;

woodlands: R. Meiggs, *Roman Ostia*² (Oxford 1973) 343;

granaries: *CIL* VI 4226; 30855; 36786; *AE* 1937, no. 61; *AE* 1904, no. 180 (Moguntiacum, Germania);

markets: *CIL* XI 1231 (*macellum*);

imperial houses: *CIL* VI 8650; 8655; *CIL* XIV 199; *CIL* X 6637; and 6638;

public buildings: *CIL* VI 37175 (*saepta*);

libraries: *CIL* VI 2347; 4435; 8744; *AE* 1959, no. 300; *CIL* XIV 196. Cf. Chapter Five;

baths: *CIL* VI 8676; 8679; *AE* 1924, no. 105; *MAAR* 10 (1932) 73. Cf. Chapter Five;

mines: *CIL* III 7837 (Ampelum/Dacia, II/III); *AE* 1908, no. 233 (Vipasca, Lusitania);

lead pipes: *AE* 1946, no. 136 (v. plombariorum). Cf. Chapter Five;

aqueducts: *CIL* VI 8495; 8496; 33732; 33733. Cf. Chapter Five;

tax collection: *CIL* V 7211; *AE* 1955, no. 205; *AE* 1954, no. 194 (Nice); *AE* 1897, no. 4; *AE* 1945, no. 123 (St. Maurice, Valais); *CIL* XIII 7215 (Moguntiacum, Germania); *CIL* III 13239; 13240; *AE* 1938, no. 154 (Poetovio); *AE* 1952, no. 192 (Aquae Bassianae? A.D. 206); *AE* 1958, no. 64 (Dalmatia); *AE* 1973, no. 411-414 (Dalmatia); *AE* 1981, no. 24 (Poetovio, A.D. 225); *CIL* III 1351 (= 7853 = *ILS* 1860, Micia and Pons Augusti, Dacia); *CIL* III 8042 (Celeiu on the Danube); *CIL* III 752 (= 7435 = *ILS* 1856, Nicopolis/Moesia); *CIL* III 555 (= 7287 = *ILS* 1867, Athens); *CIL* VIII 12134 (Bisica); *AE* 1925, no. 73 (Cuicul); *AE* 1926, no. 164 (= *AE* 1954, no. 20, Leptis Magna); *AE* 1952, no. 62 (Leptis Magna); *AE* 1950, no. 256 (Lisbon). Cf. Chapter Five;

public finances: *CIL* XIV 255; *CIL* IX 59; 472; *AE* 1985, no. 314; *CIL* XI 6073 (*vilicus ab alimentis*); 1751; *CIL* V 737; 2803; 4503; 5858; *CIL* III 4152 (Savaria/Pannonia, "Col(oniae) Sav(ariae) vil(icus) kal(endarii) Septimiani"); R.P. Duncan-Jones, *Structure and Scale in the Roman Economy* (Cambridge 1990) 182, n. 56, suggests that "Onesimus vilicus Cuiculitanorum" (*BCTH* [1917] 346, no. 76, Cuicul/Numidia, not reported in *AE*) was responsible for running the town's estates, but it seems more likely that municipal *vilici* were in charge of public finances or buildings, as city land was rarely under direct management.

This lengthy list demonstrates that *vilici* were considered managers *par excellence*. Insofar as they were appointed to the head of a managerial unit, they were fully covered by their principal, whose credit significantly enhanced their reliability as contracting parties and their efficiency as managers. The land or other types of premises of which they were in charge was regarded as adequate security by those who entered into contractual relationship with them.[198] If all types of business managers were called *vilici*, it explains why *institores* are rarely represented in literary and epigraphical sources, in contrast to their importance in the *Digest*: in view of the social prejudice that the Roman elite affected towards trade and commerce, the word *institor* was used as a term of abuse or as a purely legal term. By contrast, *vilici* were spared the shame because of their connection to the land, a feature that made them more respectable. And they turn up by the hundreds in preserved Latin inscriptions.

E. Farm workers and the chain of command

1. *The hands* (familia rustica)

In the villa economy, the farmwork and other tasks connected with the estate were carried out by workers, free or slave, subordinated to the *vilicus* and living in the villa or its vicinity. Even though the managerial and business activities in which *vilici* engaged, as well as the size of some estates, called for a hierarchic organization of the staff and for an increasing division of labor, Regulus's story shows that a large and specialized rural household was by no means a necessary feature of the *vilicus* system. The archaeological remains of Roman villas often show structures which have been identified as slave quarters. From them, modern scholars have tried to reconstruct the size and structure of the rural household. Such reconstructions are often problematic, for it is not sure that the inhabitants of these quarters were slaves, and not free *inquilini* or temporary workers. We do not know either the density of occupation of these cells,

---

[198] Real estate was regarded as a valuable security. This is illustrated by the meaning of the term "praedium", formed on "praes" = (1) pledge given by a guarantor (Varro, *Ling*. 5.40; Plaut., *Truc*. 214; Cato, *Orat*. 118; *CIL* I² 585.46 and 698.1.7); and (2) estate (Cato, *Agr*. 1; Plautus, *Stich*. 203). Cf. T. Helen, *Organization of Roman Brick Production in the First and Second Centuries A.D.* (Helsinki 1975) 38.

nor can we be sure that they were not also partly used as stables. Such an hypothesis would help solve the problem of the *embarras d'esclaves* quartered at Settefinestre.[199]

a. *division of labor*

Within the villa, the division of labor was never absolute. Among the various agricultural tasks very few required any specific training that could not be learned on the job. Thus, skilled workers (potters, cattle drivers, wine tasters, etc.) who were underemployed at one time could be put to work in a different area under the supervision of a fellow worker or of a squad leader.

The type of estate described by the Latin agronomists was oriented toward mixed farming: the agricultural production consisted of grain and cash crops (wine, olives, vegetables, and fruits). Cattle raising, apiculture, and woodcutting[200] could play an important role in the economic life of a villa. They should not be underestimated on the ground that the production was not meant for mass export in identifiable containers, but was often consumed on the estate to support the household.

As suggested above, part of the labor force could be employed in the exploitation of other natural resources found on the land attached to the estate, in particular clay, stone, metals, wood, withe, salt, etc. The workers could also be involved in processing and manufacturing goods, milling flour and baking bread, shearing, carding and weaving wool, sewing garments and shoes, repairing

---

[199] N. Purcell, *JRS* 78 (1988) 197 (= review of Carandini *et al.* [1985]). Sometimes, the find of implements contributes to our understanding of how the various parts of a villa were used; cf. M. Rostovtzeff, *SEHRE*² (1957) 64 and fig. X.2, featuring iron stock found in the villa of Gragnano near Pompeii and used to restrain slaves.

[200] An imperial *vilicus saltuariorum*, recorded in an inscription from Ostia, was in charge of an estate where the exploitation of woodland constituted the main activity, cf. R. Meiggs, *Roman Ostia*² (Oxford 1973) 343 and *idem*, *Trees and Timber in the Ancient Mediterranean World* (Oxford 1982) 330. Meiggs suggests that these *saltuarii* were employed on the imperial Laurentine estate. Inscriptions set up by *saltuarii* are not rare, which possibly indicates that they held a privileged position among other workers in the rural household; cf. especially *CIL* IX 3386 (= *ILS* 5542, Capestranum in the Ager Vestinorum) where an *ingenuus* and a *libertinus* dedicated a portico erected "ex pec(unia) saltuar(iorum)," which reveals the existence of economic means and perhaps of a social organization (*collegium saltuariorum*). Like *vilici*, *saltuarii* commonly made dedications to the god Silvanus; cf. *CIL* V 2383; *CIL* IX 3421; *CIL* X 3522; *AE* 1938, no. 168; and G. Ramilli, "Un *saltuarius* in una epigrafe dell'agro Bresciano," *Suppl. ai Comment. dell'Ateneo di Brescia* (1975) 77-88.

tools and carts, and providing lodging, food, fodder, fresh horses, and draft animals to travelers.[201] Hunting, fishing, picking, and gathering formed a significant source of supply in subsistence farming.[202] Since larger estates also tried to achieve near self-sufficiency while producing for the market, part of the staff had to be distracted from the main production to carry out these activities,[203] and one sector of the villa economy must have been organized along the same lines as smaller farms. A few slaves provided the rural household with logistical support under the supervision of the wife of the *vilicus*. Her functions are described in Book 12 of Columella's treatise.[204]

b. *magister pecoris*

Varro divides the rural household into two sectors: one was formed by the staff occupied in arable farming, wine growing, and/or olive cultivation under the supervision of the *vilicus*; the other was composed of the *pastores* who looked after the livestock under the leadership of a chief herdsman (*magister pecoris*).[205] Accordingly, the *ma-*

---

[201] Varro, according to a later compilator, advised his reader to keep potters in the villa, for clay was available almost everywhere (*Geoponika* 2.49). The same author (*Rust.* 1.2.22-23) reports that the Sasernas regarded the management of clay pits (*fig(i)linae*), mines (*argentifodinae* + *alia metalla*), and quarries (*lapidicinae* + *harenariae*) as activities connected with agriculture. According to them, a villa located near a road could offer facilities to travelers (*tabernae deversoriae*). Columella, *Rust.* 1.5.7 voices his concern that such a villa would suffer from depredation and corruption caused by travelers.

[202] J.M. Frayn, *Subsistence Farming in Roman Italy* (London 1979) 57-72 (= *JRS* 65 [1975] 32-39).

[203] Varro, *Rust.* 3.3.4. Fowlers, hunters, and fishermen were in charge of supplying certain products that would otherwise have to be purchased from outside. But Varro is talking here of luxury goods deemed indispensable only by a small fringe of the population.

[204] The concubine of the *vilicus* is called *vilica* in agricultural treatises (cf. above); R. Martin, "*Familia rustica*: les esclaves chez les agronomes latins," *Actes du colloque 1972 sur l'esclavage* (*Annales littéraires de l'Université de Besançon* 163, Paris 1974) 267-97, esp. 276-77.

[205] Varro, *Rust.* 1.2.14. The evidence for *magistri pecoris* is rather scarce: Cic., *2Verr.* 5.7.16-17; Varro, *Rust.* 2.3.9; 2.5.18; 2.10.10; Columella, *Rust.* 7.3.16. A recently published inscription from Sicily records a Nabatean slave, named Abdalas, who died at a very old age, since he reportedly held for 80 years—an obvious exaggeration—the functions of "magister magnus ovium" of Domitian's wife, Domitia Domitiani, landowner in the Abruzzi, at Baiae, in Sicily, and in Phrygia, and owner of important *figlinae*; cf. G. Salmeri, "Un *magister ovium* di Domizia Longina in Sicilia," *ASNP* 14 (1984) 13-23 (= *AE* 1985, no. 483, Ramacca, near Morgantina, first part of second century A.D.); and J. Carlsen, "*Magister Pecoris*. The Nomenclature and Qualifications of the Chief Herdsman in Roman Pasturage," *ARID* 20 (1991) 57-64. It is possible that the imperial *vilicus saltuariorum* mentioned

gister pecoris kept separate accounts and was required to be literate,
a pious wish expressed by Varro, but unlikely to be always fulfilled.[206] The scale of the herd would be determinant in setting the
level of skills (accounting, veterinary knowledge) required of the
staff. A division of the household between cultivation and animal
breeding was due to the practice of transhumance or to the distance
separating pastures (hills) from the farmstead (valleys, costal areas).
Further, as large herds were vulnerable to epidemics, it made sense
to divide them into smaller bands.[207] It does not necessarily follow
that each of these smaller bands formed a separate managerial unit.
The ratio of herdsmen to heads must have varied according to the
owner.[208]

The *magister pecoris* was probably a type of *institor*, since he is
described as *praepositus* by C. Licinius Stolo.[209] As pasture land was
often located in the hills, it was natural for the *magister pecoris* to spend
part of the year away from the farmstead.[210] Consequently, his
credit and the limits of his contractual capacity were more difficult
to check. Thus, it is possible that already at an early date chief herdsmen held as *peculium* part of the capital entrusted to them. This *peculium*, which strengthened their credit in transactions with third contracting parties, contained a few heads and some assistant herdsmen
(*vicarii* or *servi peculiares*). A text by Varro seems to support this interpretation, as it is considered relevant to specify that, in case of
purchase of a slave herdsman, the *peculium* follows the slave, unless
a different agreement has been explicitly reached between buyer and
seller.[211] When the *magister pecoris* was a freedman or a freeborn, he
had a full legal capacity on his own, but his transactions still made

---

above was the equivalent of a *magister pecoris*, although it seems more plausible to
regard him as a forester. On the relationship between specialized pastoralism and
the market-economy, cf. G. Barker, "The Archaeology of the Italian Shepherd,"
PCPhS 215 (n.s. 35) (1989) 1-19, esp. 11-14.

[206] Varro, *Rust.* 2.10.10.

[207] Varro, *Rust.* 2.1.24; 2.2.20 (reporting practices common among sheep
breeders in Epirus, although "nulli enim huius moduli naturales"); 2.3.9-10
(about a practice adopted by goat breeders in Cisalpine Gaul); 2.4.22 (pigs); and
2.5.18 (cows). Cf. V.I. Kuziščin (1984) [1976] 19-20.

[208] Varro, *Rust.* 2.10.10-11.

[209] Varro, *Rust.* 1.2.14: "Principes qui utrique rei (= pastioni aut agri culturae) praeponuntur vocabulis quoque sunt diversi, quod unus vocatur vilicus,
alter magister pecoris." Cf. above.

[210] Varro, *Rust.* 2.10.2 and 6.

[211] Varro, *Rust.* 2.10.5.

his employer fully liable. A law of Julius Caesar requiring that one third of all herdsmen be freeborn adults could be used as evidence for an early extension of the application of the *actio institoria* to cases involving extraneous agents. However, actual instances of non-slave herdsmen are rare.[212]

One can wonder under which circumstances the *magister pecoris* would be expected to negotiate contracts in the context of his professional activity? The tending of livestock consists mainly in providing the herd with fodder and water (input), and in processing and marketing its produce, i.e. offspring, meat, milk and its derivatives, and hides (output). The availability of the input and the quantity of the output were determined by factors beyond the control of herdsmen, such as the weather, market conditions, and the fecundity and productivity of the herds. These factors could be affected by storms, gluts or shortages, epidemics, and other acts of God. In modern times, Swiss peasants in mountain regions respond to such variables by adjusting periodically, sometimes seasonally, the size and the nature of their livestock. The breeding of bull-calves and heifers for their meat is sometimes more profitable than milk-producing cows, and vice versa. Temporary surpluses of fodder or pasture permit to host a few heads of cattle belonging to a neighbor. Such arrangements give rise to numerous, sometimes complicated business transactions which cattle raisers are required to negotiate.[213] In Roman Italy, the *magister pecoris* could be expected to negotiate passage rights during the period of transhumance, to lease pasture land from or to other people, to purchase, sell, and barter livestock, and to buy, sell, hire, or rent out herdsmen. It should be noted that the transfer of ownership of large animals and slaves required a formal conveyance (*mancipatio*) in order to validate the transaction. Slave *magistri pecoris* were legally not qualified to do so, and this is perhaps the reason why Varro, through his character Cossinius, recommends that a double guarantee be provided by the buyer of a slave herdsman when the transfer is not done by *mancipatio*.[214]

---

[212] Suet., *Iul.* 42.1: "neve ii, qui pecuariam facerent, minus tertia parte puberum ingenuorum inter pastores haberent." Cf. J. Carlsen, *ARID* 20 (1991) 59-60, citing, for instance, *CIL* XIII 7070. Cf. above, and Chapter Two.

[213] This information was obtained while holding summer jobs in the country in the 1970's. I thank P. Calame (Les Planchettes/NE) and G. Nef (Hemberg/SG) and their families for teaching me various aspects of subsistence and mixed farming carried out with a minimum degree of mechanization.

[214] Varro, *Rust.* 2.10.5, after listing six methods for the acquisition of ownership.

c. *squads and squad leaders*

The structure of a rural household has been rightly compared to a
military unit.[215] When the size and the economic structure of the
estate required a numerous work force, the hands (*servi rustici, soluti*
or *vincti*) were organized in squads of six to ten men (*classes, decuriae*)
commanded by foremen (*monitores, magistri, praefecti*).[216] The third-
century-A.D. agricultural writer Florentinus specifies that gangs
should include "ten or six laborers," but not fewer, because it would
require too many foremen (ἐφεστῶτες, ἐπιστατοῦντες) to organize
and supervise their work. It is necessary that all gangs be composed
of the same number of laborers, so that the work progressed at the
same pace, the most vigorous slaves imposing their rhythm on the
laziest ones.[217] An obvious advantage of the division of the work
force into small units was that it stimulated competition between
squads within the rural household. This point will be discussed further in the section dealing with the organization of mints.[218]

The foremen were subordinated to the *vilicus* and selected among
the older, better, and more educated slaves. They were offered various economic and social privileges.[219] For instance, they received a
peculium and a mate as an incentive to be honest, fair, and efficient.
Thus, Varro advises landowners to consult and treat them with
respect, and recommends that they be given a food and clothing
allowance, exemption from work, and permission to graze some cattle on their own as part of their *peculium*.[220]

d. *mediastini and skilled workers*

In addition to unskilled workers (*mediastini*), the rural household included a limited number of specialists, probably of higher status and

---

[215] R. Martin, *Actes du colloque 1972 sur l'esclavage* (1974) 285, following Columella, *Rust.* 11.1.17. Military features in the organization of a *familia rustica* may
have originated with the practice of assigning land to army veterans. The *agrimen-
sores* report that from Cesar's time onward whole units remained grouped together;
cf. V.I. Kuziščin (1984) [1976] 154-56.

[216] Columella, *Rust.* 1.9.7: "quod is numeri modus in opere commodissime
custodiretur, nec praeeuntis monitoris diligentiam multitudo confunderet."

[217] *Geoponika* 2.45.

[218] Cf. Chapter Five.

[219] Varro, *Rust.* 1.17.4: "Qui praesint esse oportere, qui litteris atque aliqua
sint humanitate imbuti, frugi, aetate maiore quam operarios, quos dixi. Facilius
enim iis quam qui minore natu sunt dicto audientes."

[220] Varro, *Rust.* 1.17.5-7.

therefore not part of the squads. To return to the comparison with the organization of army units, skilled workers could be considered as the equivalent of military *immunes*. In the case of craftsmen (*artifices, fabri*), only rich villas could afford to keep them on the farmstead on a regular basis. Smaller farms turned to traveling artisans, shared the cost of their services with neighbors, or had them come on request from nearby towns.[221] Varro writes about the necessity to have smiths (χαλκεῖς), carpenters (τέκτονες), and potters (κεραμεῖς) attached to the villa to permit a diversification of production.[222] It is remarkable that those artisans, as well as other hired laborers, free or slave, living on the farmstead, were considered in law as members of the household ("loco servorum") and subordinated to the *vilicus*.[223]

The description of the life of an actual rural household has never been written or has not been preserved in the extant sources. The picture that we get from the agronomists (Cato to Columella) and from the jurists (Alfenus Varus to Ulpianus) possibly reflects the ideal of theoretical writers. They, however, were likely to have been personally acquainted with agricultural life. Cato presents the staff of an estate oriented toward the production of olive oil and wine. His primary interest lies in the economically optimum size of the work force combined with the most efficient division of labor. To equip an olive-grove of 240 *iugera*, he recommends to employ one *vilicus*, one housekeeper (*vilica*), five laborers (*operarii*), three teamsters

---

[221] Varro, *Rust.* 1.16.4-5: "...quam partem lati fundi divites domesticae copiae mandare solent." Others *artifices, medici, fullones,* and *fabri* could be hired on a yearly basis. The situation was different in villas located at some distance from urban centers.

[222] Varro, cited in *Geoponika* 2.49.

[223] Ulpianus (69 *ad ed.*) *Dig.* 43.16.1.18: "Familiae appellatione et eos, quos loco servorum habemus, contineri oportere dicendum est" and 20: "Si filius familias vel mercennarius vi deiecerit, utile interdictum (de vi et de vi armata) competit." Cf. K.D. White (1970) 347-48, citing J.A. Crook, *Law and Life of Rome* (Ithaca, NY 1967) 196. Cf. also Ulpianus (17 *ad Sab.*) *Dig.* 7.8.2 and 4; Paulus (3 *ad Vit.*) *Dig.* 7.8.3; *idem* (*lib. sing. de poen. pagan.*) *Dig.* 47.2.90(89); *idem, Sent.* 2.18.1; and Marcianus (2 *de publ. iud.*) *Dig.* 48.19.11.1. Cf. F.M. de Robertis, "I lavoratori liberi nelle *familiae* aziendali romane," *SDHI* 24 (1958) 269-78; *idem,* "*Locatio operarum* e status del lavoratore," *SDHI* 27 (1961) 19-45; *idem, Lavoro e lavoratori nel mondo romano* (Bari 1963); *contra,* D. Nörr, "Zur sozialen und rechtlichen Bewertung der freien Arbeit in Rom," *ZRG* 82 (1965) 67-105; J. Ramin – P. Veyne, "Droit romain et société: les hommes qui passent pour esclaves et l'esclavage volontaire," *Historia* 30 (1981) 472-97, esp. 482; and E. Maróti, "Die Rolle der freien Arbeitskraft in der Villa-Wirtschaft im Zeitalter der Republik," *AArchHung* 32 (1989) 95-110.

(*bubulci*), one muleteer (*asinarius*), one swineherd (*subulcus*), and one shepherd (*opilio*), a total of 13 persons. The staff of a vineyard of 100 *iugera* should comprise one *vilicus*, one housekeeper, ten laborers, one teamster, one muleteer, one willow worker (*salictarius*), and one swineherd, a total of 16 persons. Varro's and Columella's descriptions of the size and composition of the rural household are based on Cato's and the Sasernas' treatises.[224]

The Augustan jurist Alfenus Varus provides a detailed description of the composition of what he considers a typical *familia rustica*. In a discussion of a provision of the censorial rule governing the payment of customs dues (*portorium*) in the harbor of Sicily, whereby dues should not be collected on slaves brought home for the personal use of the owner, Alfenus wonders whether or not the law applies to the case of a *familia rustica*. Incidentally, he lists as members of a rural household bookkeepers, superintendents of apartment-buildings, bailiffs, butlers, weavers, and field-workers.[225] The presence of *dispensatores* (cf. below) and *insularii* in the list leads me to surmise that the type of *fundus* that Alfenus Varus had in mind is probably a suburban estate, whose owner belonged to the elite and could afford to keep a large household.[226] Labeo and Pegasus, in their discussion on the composition of the farm equipment (*instrumentum*), also review the staff of a rural household. They list foresters (*saltuarii*), bakers (*pistores*), barbers (*tonsores*), masons (*fabri*), female cooks and housemaids, millers (*molitores*), kitchen maids (*focariae*), housekeepers (*vilicae*), woolmakers (*lanificae*), and fullers (*fullones*). Ulpianus adds comptrollers (*cellararii*), doormen (*ostiarii*), muleteers (*muliones*), hunters (*venatores*), and game tracers (*vestigatores*).[227]

---

[224] Varro, *Rust.* 1.17-18 and *passim*; Columella, *Rust. passim*, esp. in Books 1 and 11.

[225] Alfenus Varus (7 *Dig.*) *Dig.* 50.16.203: "In lege censoria portus Siciliae ita scriptum erat: 'servos, quos domum quis ducet suo usu, pro is portorium ne dato.' Quaerebatur, si quis a Sicilia servos Romam mitteret fundi instruendi causa, utrum pro his hominibus portorium dare deberet nec ne... Utrum *dispensatores, insularii, vilici, atrienses, textores, operarii quoque rustici*, qui agrorum colendorum causa haberentur, ex quibus agris pater familias fructus caperet, quibus se toleraret, omnes denique servos, quos quisque emisset, ut ipse haberet atque eis ad aliquam rem uteretur, neque ideo emisset, ut venderet?"

[226] On the staff of a *villa urbana*, cf. H. Mielsch, *Die römische Villa. Architektur und Lebensform* (Munich 1987) 133-34. Cf., however, Paulus (*sing. de instr. signif.*) *Dig.* 32.99.

[227] Ulpianus (20 *ad Sab.*) *Dig.* 33.7.12.4-6, citing Labeo, Neratius, and Trebatius; and *Dig.* 33.7.12.9 and 12. K.D. White (1970) 355-56 and 377-83 provides a complete list of persons employed on agricultural estates, with a definition of their

Papinianus also includes the *actor*, even though, as an agent, he was likely to be absent on a mission at some distance from the farm.[228]

As the classical jurists cite the opinions of earlier authors (Alfenus Varus and Trebatius), it seems that the process of specialization within the rural household had reached an advanced stage by the late Republican period at the latest. This applies at least to a certain type of villa, the owners of which were rich and educated enough to secure the help of legal practitioners when problems arose in connection with transfer of property by sale or inheritance. The passages by Labeo, Pegasus, Papinianus, and Ulpianus are all excerpted from *Dig.* 33.7, a title devoted entirely to the bequest of farm equipment. Disputes concerning the definition of that category of goods gave rise to a series of legal opinions devised by expert lawyers in response to consultations by parties involved in litigation.

2. The managerial staff

a. procuratores

Landowners who had several estates leased to tenants or managed by *vilici* and who did not want to spend their time touring their farms to control their management and collect the rents needed to rely on general agents or stewards (*procuratores*). In the Republican and early Imperial periods, *procuratores* held large powers of administration and were expected to keep detailed written accounts.[229] They ranked higher than *vilici*, and they did not belong to the category of *institores*, since they were not appointed to the head of a managerial unit. Consequently, the contracts negotiated by them did not en-

---

respective functions based on mostly literary and legal evidence. Cf. also R.J. Buck, *Agriculture and Agricultural Practices in Roman Law* (Wiesbaden 1983).

[228] Ulpianus (20 *ad Sab.*), citing Papinianus, *Dig.* 33.7.12.38: "Idem respondit praediis instructis legatis actorem ex his in provinciam missum, ut ordinatis negotiis ad pristinum actum rediret, legato praediorum cedere, quamvis nondum redierit." Cf. below.

[229] Petron., *Sat.* 30.1. A. Watson, *Contract of Mandate in Roman Law* (Oxford 1961) 8 states that a *procurator*—in contrast with a mandatary—was subject to giving an account of his administration to his principal. It is remarkable, however, that in medieval England, stewards (*seneschals*), who by the thirteenth century were commonly highly literate, never kept accounts themselves, but assisted auditors in checking the accounts presented by their subordinates—bailiffs or reeves—against the "extent" or survey drawn up at the beginning of their tenure; cf. C. Noke, "Accounting for Bailiffship in Thirteenth[-]Century England," *Accounting and Business Research* 42 (1981) 137-51.

gage the liability of their employers.[230] It is important to note that not all *procuratores* were involved in the administration of agricultural estates.

The *procurator* was already a familiar character in the time of Plautus,[231] but is absent from Cato's treatise. An ambiguous reference in the Agrarian Law of 111 B.C. presents the representative of some potential land purchaser in Africa as *procurator*.[232] Later on, Cicero provides a narrow definition of *procurator* as the person who "administers all the property of a citizen absent from Italy or busy serving the state, behaving almost as if he were the owner, and acting as the legal representative of someone else."[233] Neither of these conditions seems to have been fulfilled by one M. Tullius who owned an estate composed of several villas in the territory of Thurium in the 70's B.C. Yet, Cicero reports that his client had sent written instructions to his *procurator* and to his *vilicus* in charge of his estate on the occasion of a land dispute which ended up in bloodshed.[234] Cicero himself had his Cuman estate managed by *vilici* and *procuratores*, but it is not clear whether he refers to the same type of general agent well attested in a later period, or to some type of overseer subordinated to the *vilicus*.[235] In the same sense, Varro's only reference to a *procurator* is non-technical, and shows no connection with the general administration of agricultural estates.[236] By the time of Columella, however, the *procurator* had become a necessary

---

[230] J.H. D'Arms, *CSSAR* (1981) 143. Cf. above, Chapter Two.

[231] Plaut., *Pseud.* 607-10. Cf. above, Chapter One.

[232] *FIRA* I², no. 8, par. 69, pp. 115-16: "...tum tantundem modum agri ei, quoi ita emptum esse comperiet[ur, emptorive ei]us *pro curatoreve eius* heredive quoius eorum de eo agro, quei ager in Africa est, pro eo agro IIvir reddito;..."

[233] Cic., *Caecin.* 20.57: "... is qui legitime procurator dicitur, omnium rerum eius qui in Italia non sit absitve rei publicae causa, quasi quidam paene dominus, hoc est alieni iuris vicarius,..." Cf. P. Angelini, *Il procurator* (Milan 1971) 65-67 and above, Chapter Two.

[234] Cic., *Tull.* 7.17: "Mittit ad procuratorem litteras et ad vilicum Tullius [...]."

[235] Cic., *Att.* 14.16.1 (44 B.C.): "Conscendens ab hortis Cluvianis in phaselum epicopum has dedi litteras, cum Piliae nostrae villam ad Lucrinum, vilicos, procuratores tradidissem." The same ambiguity remains in Ps.-Quint., *Decl. min.* 345.10, where rich people are said to "familiam per procuratores continere."

[236] Varro, *Rust.* 3.6.3, about a peacock keeper. This is probably also the case in Petron., *Sat.* 96.4-97.1: Bargates, "procurator insulae", is probably a slave as he speaks of his "contubernalis" (although it is possible that only she was a slave); besides, the *procurator* receiving accounts in the *triclinium* (*Sat.* 30.1) might be the same person as Cinnamus, referred to as *dispensator* in the rest of the chapter; cf. G. Giliberti (1984) 27-28, n. 63.

feature of the hierarchic structure of the villa economy: landowners were instructed by the agronomists to let him stay in private quarters located above the entrance—and above the room of the *vilicus*—so that he could control the comings and goings of the *familia*, and watch over the cabinet where iron tools were stored.[237] Both efficiency and security were enhanced by this arrangement, and there are reasons to believe that Columella's advice was followed: in a villa located in the vicinity of Boscoreale and destroyed in A.D. 79, the seal of Thallus, the *procurator* of one Asellius, was found in one of the entrance rooms.[238]

Only freeborn or manumitted *procuratores* are recorded in the sources, and this is consistent with the provision of the Aelian Sentian Law, whereby a slave could by exception be manumitted before the age of 30 if the purpose of the manumission was to appoint him as a *procurator*.[239] Cicero was aware of the difference of status between *procurator* and *vilicus*, as he has one of his characters, the orator M. Antonius, correctly state that the instructions given to a *procurator* were the object of a *mandatum*, whereas a *vilicus* received orders.[240]

Landowners could entrust the general administration of their affairs either to one or to several persons. Thus, stewards were either *procuratores omnium rerum* or *procuratores unius rei*. *Procuratores* could be assigned a geographical area or a specific type of activity (agriculture, customs dues, libraries, baths, etc.). As landed properties tended to spread over wider and wider geographical areas, landown-

---

[237] Columella, *Rust.* 1.6.7: "Vilico iuxta ianuam fiat habitatio, ut intrantium exeuntiumque conspectum habeat, procuratori supra ianuam ob easdem causas; et is tamen vilicum observet ex vicino, sitque utrique proximum horreum, quo conferatur omne rusticum instrumentum, et intra id ipsum clausus locus, quo ferramenta recondantur." Other features in the physical arrangement of the villa were inspired by the necessity to facilitate the supervision of the work by the *procurator*; cf. Columella, *Rust.* 1.6.23; and Palladius, *Rust.* 1.36.1.

[238] *Not.Scav.* 1921, p. 428 (retrograde): THALLI / ASEL(li) PRO(curatoris).

[239] Gai., *Inst.* 1.18-19: "...apud consilium iusta causa manumissionis adprobata... servum procuratoris habendi gratia...." Cf. A. Watson (1961) 9, n. 1; S. Treggiari, *RFLR* (1969) 150-53; and P. Angelini (1971) 13-14, n. 59, who notes that the evidence used to demonstrate the opposite view is ultimately inconclusive. Fourth- and fifth-century legal evidence reflects changing conditions; cf. *Cod. Theod.* 4.12.5; 12.1.179; 16.5.65.3; *Mai.Nov.* 7; and G. Hamza, *AUB (iur.)* 25 (1983) 89-107, esp. 97-106, where the author emphasizes the decline in status of *procuratores*. Cf. above.

[240] Cic., *De Or.* 1.58.249: "si qui fundus inspiciendus aut si mandandum aliquid procuratori de agri cultura aut imperandum vilico est, ..." The dramatic date is set in the 90's B.C.

ers became increasingly dependent on a host of *procuratores* assisted
by a managerial staff composed of *actores* (for rural properties) or *dispensatores* (for urban properties).[241]

b. *actores*

Actores (πραγματευταί) are not attested in the sources before the first
century A.D. and are still quite common in the fourth and fifth centuries.[242] Even though *actores* are very well represented in epigraphical and legal sources, it is not always clear to what extent their
functions differed from that of *procuratores*, *dispensatores*, and *vilici*. In
several cases *actores* are found in an agricultural context, although in
most cases the evidence does not provide any information about the
nature of their occupation. Since non-agricultural *actores* would be
more likely to record the field in which they worked as a sign of social
privilege, many of those inscriptions recording *actores* without field
specification should be regarded as referring to agricultural agents.
We do not know to what percentage of *actores* this hypothesis applies.[243] Those who were not employed in agriculture were attached

---

[241] Pomponius (6 *ad Sab.*) *Dig.* 34.2.1 *pr.*: ''...detractis...et ei adsignatis, cui
specialiter legata sunt, reliquum alteri debetur...Idem urbanis servis tibi legatis,
si mihi dispensator legatus sit.'' G. Bloch, *Dar.-Sag.* 2 (1892) 280-86, s.v. *dispensator*; cf. below. This rule is not absolute, cf. for instance Pomponius (6 *ad Sab.*) *Dig.*
50.16.166 *pr.*: '' 'Urbana familia' et 'rustica' non loco, sed genere distinguitur:
potest enim aliquis dispensator non esse servorum urbanorum numero: veluti is,
qui rusticarum rerum rationes dispendet ibique habitet;'' Paulus (*sing. de instr. signif.*) *Dig.* 32.99; and *Inscr.It.* X,1 592a and b (= *AE* 1906, no. 100). The epigraphical material provides a better basis for a definition, and it shows that *dispensatores*
were clerical employees attached to various areas of administration while *actores*
rarely bear any qualifying label and were attached to a person rather than to a
specific department. Prof. J.P. Bodel pointed out to me that a similar distinction
is attested for personal attendants of magistrates (*accensi* as opposed to *apparitores*),
cf. N. Purcell, ''The *apparitores*: A Study in Social Mobility,'' *PBSR* 51 (1983)
125-73, esp. 127 and 140.

[242] I know of no Republican *actor* either in inscriptions—which are in any case
rarely datable—or in legal or literary sources, whereas Republican *vilici*, *dispensatores*, and *procuratores* are common, at least in the last two categories of sources. For
late antiquity, cf. *AE* 1912, no. 256 (Fondi, A.D. 337); *CIL* XI 2997 (Ager Viterbiensis, IV); *CIL* VIII 25817 (= *AE* 1978, no. 880, Furnos Minus, Afr. Proc., IV);
Cod.Iust. 3.26.9 (A.D. 365); *Cod.Theod.* 2.30.2; 2.31.1; and 2.32.1 (all in 422);
Cod.Iust. 11.72 (A.D. 426); Symmachus, *Ep.* 5.87; 9.6; 9.15; 9.52; and 9.130;
August., *Ep.* 24* and 247; *Ep. ad Salvium* 4 (Maktar, Afr. Proc., early V); cf. C.
Lepelley, *AntAfr.* 25 (1989) 240-51. The African material is discussed by J. Carlsen,
''Estate Management in Roman North Africa. Transformation or Continuity?'' in
A. Mastino (ed.), *L'Africa romana* VIII (Sassari 1991) 632-36.

[243] The same could be assumed for *vilici*. For *actores* attached to an estate, cf.

to private businessmen who purchased various concessions from the state,[244] in particular the right to collect taxes.[245] Other *actores* were employed in the imperial administration.[246] A few documents record *actores* as agents of families,[247] corporate bodies, religious associations, temples, public services, or collectivities.[248] These *actores*

CIL V 5005 (Tridentum, early III "actor praediorum Tublinatium"); *AE* 1982, no. 401 (Tridentum, πραγματευτὴς τῆς χώρας ᾿Αντιοχέων); *CIL* VI 721 = 30820 ("actor praediorum Romanianorum"); *CIL* VI 8683 (imperial "exactor (?) praediorum Lucilianorum"); *CIL* X 6592 ("actor et agricola"); *CIL* XII 2250 (Gratianopolis/Narb., "actor huius loci"); *CIL* XIII 2243 (Lugdunum, "actor praed[i]orum horum"); *CIL* XIII 2533 (Ambarri, near Lugd., "actor fundi Ammatiaci b(onorum) F[l]avi Stratonis"); *CIL* VIII 19328 (Numidia, "in his praediis . . ."); *AE* 1906, no. 11 (Henchir/Afr.Proc.); *AE* 1906, no. 30 (Ephesus, IV A.D., "restitu[end]i et ministrandi idem reditus (fundi) ab act[oribus pr]ibatae (*sic*) rei nostrae"); Scaevola (3 *resp.*) *Dig.* 33.7.20.3 ("praedia ut instructa sunt cum dotibus et reliquis colonorum et vilicorum et mancipiis et pecore omni legavit et peculis et cum actore"); *actor* married to a *vilica*: *CIL* III 5616 (Noricum). Three inscriptions refer to *actores* attached to an urban (?) house, cf. *CIL* VI 9124 ("actor domo Veronae"); *AE* 1964, no. 87 ("d(omus) d(ivinae) actor" or "domus D(omitianae) actor"); *CIL* XI 1730 ("actrix c(onsularis) domus"); *Cod.Iust.* 2.12 (13).16 (A.D. 293).

244 Cf. Chapter Five; *CIL* X 1913 (Puteoli, "act(or) ferr(ariarum)"); *AE* 1967, no. 388 = *AE* 1957, no. 273 (Dacia, "actor conductoris pascui et salinarum"); *AE* 1937, no. 141 (Pannonia, "actor conductoris salinarum"); *CIL* II 5181 = *ILS* 6891 = *FIRA* I², no. 105 (*Lex metalli Vipascensis*/Lusit., II, "conductor socius actorve" for various concessions, such as collecting taxes on sales, auctioneering, managing baths, shoemaking, barbering, fulling, quarrying and digging).

245 Cf. Chapter Five; *CIL* VI 8591 (imperial freedman "actor XXXX Gal."); *CIL* X 7225 (Lilybaeum, "act(or) port(orii) Lilybit[a]ni"); *CIL* VI 38003 ("act(or) vic(esimae hereditatium?")); *P.Ross.Georg.* II 26 (A.D. 160, *XX her.*); *AE* 1930, no. 87 (Ephesus, *vicesima libertatis*); *AE* 1947, no. 180 (Palmyra, A.D. 174, *a. mancipis quartae merc(aturae* or *-ium adventiciarum*) = τεταρτώνου πραγματευτὴς ἴδιος).

246 *CIL* XI 4427 (Ameria, "actor Imp. Commodi Aug. N."); *CIL* VI 8688 (imperial freedman "actor ad Castor et ad loricata(m) ad auctoritatem"), cf. G. Boulvert, *Esclaves et affranchis impériaux sous le Haut-Empire romain. Rôle politique et administratif* (Naples 1970) 69-70, n. 381; *CIL* IV 3728 = 31046 ("actores de foro suario"), who may not have been imperial servants; *CIL* VI 8673 (imperial freedman "ex act(ore? or exactor?) hort(orum) Servi(lianorum)"); *CIL* VI 8850 (imperial "actor a frumento"); Suet., *Dom.* 11.1 ("actor summarum"); *Cod.Iust.* 3.26.9 (365); and *ibidem* 11.72 (426).

247 For agents of joint owners who were members of the same family, cf. *CIL* VI 9112; *CIL* VI 9115; *CIL* XI 1952 (Perusia); *CIL* XI 2997 (Ager Viterbiensis, IV).

248 M. Wlassak-P. Habel, *PW* 1 (1893) cols. 326-30, s.v. *actor*; E. de Ruggiero, *Diz.Epigr.* 1 (1895) s.v. *actor*, 68-70; and G.N. Olcott, *Thesaurus Linguae Latinae Epigraphicae* I (Rome 1904) 64-65, s.v. *actor*.
   religious associations: Gaius (3 *ad ed. prov.*) *Dig.* 3.4.1.1; Ulpian (5 *ad ed.*) *Dig.* 2.4.10.4; and *idem* (39 *ad ed.*) *Dig.* 37.1.3.4;
   temples: *CIL* XI 2686; and *CIL* VIII 15894;
   social security (*alimenta*): *CIL* IX 5859.

may have played above all a judicial role (= *defensores*, *syndici*, etc.) and therefore should not be considered as business managers.

In the second century A.D., *actores* are often attested in the capacity of business agents involved in seaborne trade. They were active either in seaports (like the Peiraeus), or aboard a ship. One Myrinos was the agent of Claudia Bassa and traveled as far as Germania. One Bosiconius sailed around the ports of the North Sea. Finally, one Aurelius Statianus dedicated an inscription to *Deus Aeternus* in Novae (Lower Moesia) to express his gratefulness after escaping some unspecified danger in connection with the sea.[249]

Actores were appointed (*praepositi*) for the purpose of carrying out specific tasks, and therefore should be counted among *institutores*.[250] On occasion, our sources show them dealing with financial matters, in particular collecting payments, handling cash, and keeping accounts. They were assisted in this task by *adiutores* belonging to their *peculium* (*vicarii*).[251] *Actores* collected rents from *conductores*, *coloni*, and perhaps *vilici*, and lent them money (*promutuum*), for instance

---

public collectivities: *CIL* X 4904; *CIL* XI 2714 (Volsinii, "r(ei) p(ublicae) (or p(rivatae)?) act(or)"); *CIL* IX 2827 (low ranking magistrate: "M. Paquius Aulanius actor municipi Histoniensium," dated to the first century A.D.); *AE* 1938, no. 53 (Macedonia, *a. coloniae*); *AE* 1986, no. 333, col. LXX (*actores municipum* in the *Lex Irnitana*); *CIL* VI 31807 ("act(or) r[ei publicae] Calenorum"); *CIL* VI 33823; Pliny, *Ep.* 7.18.2 (Comum); Tac. *Ann.* 2.30 (A.D. 16); and *ibidem* 3.67 (A.D. 22), etc.; cf. W. Eder, *Servitus Publica* (Wiesbaden 1980) 79-80, who suggests that free(d) public *actores* did not appear before the second century A.D. for legal reasons. This is at best a *terminus ante quem* (cf. Chapter Two). In the third century, this type of function (*actus rei publicae*) often fell to slaves, and could not be imposed on free(d) persons, cf. *Cod. Iust.* 11.37; and F. Jacques, *Le privilège de liberté* (Paris 1984) 315-16.

[249] *SIG* 865 (ca. 161); *SIG* 1229 (= *IGRR* IV 186); M. Hassall, "Britain and the Rhine Provinces: Epigraphic Evidence for Roman Trade," in J. du Plat Taylor – H. Cleere (eds.), *Roman Shipping and Trade: Britain and the Rhine Provinces* (London 1978) 41-48, esp. 43, table I, no. 14 ("actor navis Flori Severi;" cf. Chapter Four); *AE* 1989, no. 635 ("acto[r] pericu[l]o maris lib[e]ratus ex voto promis[s]o r(estituit)"). Compare with *CIL* XII 2379 (between Vienna and Aoste, Gallia Narbonensis) recording a *vilicus navis* on the Rhone River. On this aspect, cf. J. Rougé, *Recherches sur l'organisation du commerce maritime en Méditerranée sous l'Empire romain* (Paris 1966) 284-87.

[250] Paulus (71 *ad ed.*) *Dig.* 44.4.5.3: "Actoris, qui exigendis pecuniis praepositus est, etiam posterior dolus domino nocet;" Scaevola (24 *dig.*) *Dig.* 40.7.40.4: "Item quaero, an ea, quae exacta sunt per adiutores eius (actoris) neque kalendario illata sunt aut fraudulenter acta, huic adscribi possint, cum esset his praepositus;" Gaius (*sing. ad form. hyp.*) *Dig.* 20.6.7.1 is probably interpolated, cf. A. Burdese, *Autorizzazione ad alienare in diritto romano* (Turin 1950) 26.

[251] *CIL* V, *Suppl.* 239 (Aquileia/*Regio* X).

in the form of uncollected arrears.[252] The cash flowing in could be reinvested or used to make payments on behalf of the principal. Payments made to and by a slave *actor* were valid and extinguished the principal's credit/debt.[253] In his capacity of accountant, the *actor* was in charge of the *kalendarium*, a book in which he registered revenues (rents, payments of either interest or capital) and expenses (payments, loans, and arrears).[254] The principal was supposed to sign it periodically after checking it.[255] Scaevola discusses the case of an *actor* manumitted by will (*testamento*) with the condition that he first submit the accounts of his activity (*actus*).[256]

Actores were handling large sums in cash, and are sometimes depicted as cashiers. After accepting the job of protecting a corpse overnight against preying Thessalian witches, Lucius, the hero of Apuleius's *Metamorphoses*, expected to receive the promised award of 1,000 sestertii from the *actor* Philodespotus, acting on the order of his mistress, the unfortunate widow.[257] Domitius Zosimus, a freedman of Domitius Terentianus, who bore the title of "act(or) in rat(ioni-

---

[252] Scaevola (24 *dig.*) *Dig.* 40.7.40.5; Papinianus (7 *resp.*) *Dig.* 32.91 *pr.*; Paulus (2 *decret.*) *Dig.* 32.97. The title of *actor* is sometimes omitted in the sources; cf. Ulpianus (41 *ad Sab.*) *Dig.* 46.3.18: "Si quis servo pecuniis exigendis praeposito solvisset..." and Paulus (1 *decret.*) *Dig.* 14.5.8: "Titianus Primus praeposuerat servum mutuis pecuniis dandis et pignoribus accipiendis...."

[253] Marcianus (*sing. ad hyp. form.*) *Dig.* 46.3.49: "tutori quoque si soluta sit pecunia vel curatori vel procuratori vel cuilibet successori vel servo actori, proficiet ei solutio;" Paulus (71 *ad ed.*) *Dig.* 44.4.5.3; Papinianus (8 *quaest.*) *Dig.* 46.3.94.3 (as long as the payment was made out to a creditor of the *dominus*); cf. A. Burdese (1950) 26-28, who thinks that *actores* were not entitled to transfer property until a late date; cf. *Cod. Iust.* 2.12.16 (293): "Procuratorem vel actorem praedii, si non specialiter distrahendi mandatum accepit, ius rerum dominii vendendi non habere certum ac manifestum est. Unde si non ex voluntate domini vendentibus his fundum comparasti, pervides improbum tuum desiderium esse dominium ex huiusmodi emptione tibi concedi desiderantis." The prohibition, however, concerns specifically the sale of the estate which provides the basis of the *praepositio*, and it is likely that *actores* could sell the produce of the estate and even parts of the equipment without specific instructions before that date.

[254] G. Giliberti (1984). It is not clear whether *actor* and *cellararius* performed the same functions. Ulpianus (20 *ad Sab.*) *Dig.* 33.7.12.9 describes the latter as "praepositus ut rationes salvae sint." He might have been a controller. Cf. *CIL* VI 33747 (line 4); and Plaut., *Capt.* 895.

[255] Iulianus (39 *dig.*) *Dig.* 34.3.12.

[256] Scaevola (24 *dig.*) *Dig.* 40.7.40.3-7. Cf. also Ulpianus (19 *ad ed.*), quoting Pomponius, *Dig.* 10.2.8 *pr.* (in case of division of an estate after the owner's death, the bequeathed *actor* is not to be handed over to the legatee before he has presented his accounts described as "authenticae rationes").

[257] Apul., *Met.* 2.26.3.

bus)," probably paid with his master's money for the restoration of a monument that he supervised.[258] In the capacity of administrators, bookkeepers and treasurers, *actores* had plenty of opportunity to cheat their master, and it is no coincidence that a Roman jurist used the case of an *actor* altering his master's accounts to illustrate his point about corrupted slaves.[259] Good faith on the part of the manager was always expected and sometimes acknowledged.[260] Conversely, drastic punishment was meted out to those who succumbed to the temptation: according to Suetonius, Domitian caught his *actor summarum* red-handed and had him crucified.[261]

Actores were instrumental in the good management of estates. In the early third century, the emperors Septimius Severus and Caracalla enacted that the sale or manumission by imperial procurators of *actores* attached to estates that had passed into imperial property would be void.[262] This rule was a tacit acknowledgement that an estate was worth what its manager was able and willing to get from it. If *actores* were not there to collect the rents paid by imperial tenants, the revenues of the imperial treasury dwindled.

The difference between *actor* and *vilicus* is not always clearly established.[263] Columella alludes to the risks of collusion between *actor* and the *familia* aimed at cheating the master. Since the purpose of Columella's passage is the description of the functions of the *vilicus*, it seems that in that particular case *actor* equals *vilicus*.[264] Elsewhere, Columella speaks about the female companion to be assigned to the *vilicus* in order to keep him at home and to assist him in his task. The next sentence refers to Columella's wish—a *topos* among agrono-

---

[258] *CIL* V 8237 (Aquileia/*Regio* X, A.D. 244).

[259] Ulpianus (23 *ad ed.*) *Dig.* 11.3.1.5: "vel si actori suasit verbis sive pretio, ut rationes dominicas intercideret adulteraret vel etiam ut rationem sibi commissam turbaret."

[260] *CIL* V 1035 (Aquileia) recording an "actor bonae fidei."

[261] Suet., *Dom.* 11.1. Compare with Ps.-Quint., *Decl. min.* 353, the subject of which is "dispensatores torti."

[262] Marcianus (3 *inst.*) *Dig.* 49.14.30; Modestinus (5 *reg.*) *Dig.* 49.14.8; Hermogenianus (6 *iur. epit.*) *Dig.* 49.14.46.7.

[263] K.D. White (1970) 379 suggests that an *actor* was "(a) general agent acting on behalf of the owner; (b) spec. (i) = *vilicus*, steward, bailiff; (ii) manager, distinct from the *vilicus* (esp. in legal texts), where the term supersedes that of *vilicus* in many passages;" A.-N. Sherwin-White, *The Letters of Pliny* (Oxford 1966) 254, on *Ep.* 3.19.2, notes that "the term *actor* is used for any type of agricultural manager, including even *vilicus*."

[264] Columella, *Rust.* 1.7.7.

mists—that the *vilicus* would refrain from engaging in non-agricultural activities. The expression *idem actor* is used for the sake of stylistic variation and undoubtedly refers to the *vilicus*.[265] The term *actor* is also used in a non-technical way in another passage, where Columella points out that it is to the owner's advantage to have the *vilica* sew clothes for privileged slaves.[266] This group includes the *vilicus* and the foremen.

By contrast, Scaevola discusses the case of a debtor whose estates were mortgaged and who entrusted his *actor* with a plot of land.[267] It is uncertain whether the *vilicus* Stichus mentioned in the same passage is the same slave as the *actor*, in which case he would be an "acting *vilicus*." Elsewhere, the same author clearly makes a distinction between *vilicus* and *actor*, while specifiying that both were part of the *instrumentum*: the *vilicus* should be in charge of the *res rusticae* and the *actor* of the *rationes fundi*.[268] Scaevola's view about the chain of command in agricultural enterprises is best illustrated by a text in which the jurist discusses the concept of farm equipment: "So-and-so bequeathed his estates with what constituted then its equipment, i.e. dowries, arrears of tenants and bailiffs, slaves and all the livestock, together with the *peculia* and the *actor*."[269] In all these passages, *actor* and *vilicus* are clearly distinguished. The coexistence on the same estate of an *actor* and a *vilicus* is attested in one inscription from Altmünster (Noricum).[270] The *vilicus* Lupus set up a monument to commemorate his father-in-law, the *actor* Probinus, who died at age 40, and in memory of his wife Ursa (Probinus's daughter). In conclusion, the combination of legal and epigraphical evidence tends to suggest that Columella's usage of the term "actor", usually cited to

---

[265] Columella, *Rust.* 1.8.5: "eidemque actori praecipiendum est, ne convictum cum domestico multoque minus cum extero habeat."

[266] Columella, *Rust.* 12.3.6: "actoribus et aliis in honore servulis."

[267] Scaevola (5 *resp.*) *Dig.* 20.1.32.

[268] Scaevola (14 *dig.*) *Dig.* 34.4.31 *pr.*, where both functions are exceptionally carried out by the same slave. A. Burdese (1950) 31 thinks that in both passages *actor* and *vilicus* are one and the same person. Several texts indicate that the *actor* was part of the *instrumentum*; cf. also Ulpianus (20 *ad Sab.*), quoting Papinianus, *Dig.* 33.7.12.38; Scaevola (3 *resp.*) *Dig.* 33.7.20.4; and Paulus, *Sent.* 3.6.48 (probably interpolated, cf. A. Steinwenter [1942] 78).

[269] Scaevola (3 *resp.*) *Dig.* 33.7.20.3: "praedia ut instructa sunt cum dotibus et reliquis *colonorum* et *vilicorum* et mancipiis et pecore omni legavit et peculis et cum *actore*."

[270] *CIL* III 5622.

show that *actor* and *vilicus* filled the same position in farm management, is not technical.

Whereas *vilici* were usually appointed to a single managerial unit, *actores* could be in charge of the financial administration of several units.[271] Consequently, *actores* may not have been so closely tied to the land as *vilici*. In addition, *actores* appeared in a later period than *vilici* and may have taken over some of the functions originally carried out by *vilici*.[272] If the first occurrences of *actores* followed shortly the creation of the position, it is to be dated probably in the first century A.D. and may reflect a new stage in the history of Roman farming, characterized by an increased division of labor imposed by the scattering of properties and by the appearance of large estates (*latifundia*).[273] The appearance of the *actor* as a type of *institor* may also correspond to a significant change in the law governing indirect agency. Since the Republican period, third contracting parties had an *actio institoria* to sue the principal of the agent with whom they had made a contract. This legal remedy may originally have been available only when the agent was established as manager of some real estate (*fundus*) or building (*taberna*, *officina*). This condition may have been strictly enforced in the early history of the *actio institoria*, and tended to be overlooked in a later period, a sign that the system worked smoothly. As a result, the trustworthiness of the agent depended less and less on the security provided by the real estate value and equipment of the premises where the economic activity took place. This development bears witness to the practicality and adjustability of praetorian law: over the years, the *actio institoria* had proved suitable to protect the interest of all parties, and therefore was made available in less closely-defined types of situations.

The position of *actor* ranked fairly high on the list of privileged positions open to slaves. Career patterns were not strictly established. The sources record the case of an *actor* who had been formerly a *vilicus* or a *dispensator*, of a *dispensator* who had been formerly an *actor*,

---

[271] Pliny, *Ep.* 3.19.2.

[272] This is suggested by Horace, who reports (*Epist.* 1.14 and *Sat.* 2.7.117-118) that his *vilicus* was supervising a small servile household and a few free tenant-farmers (cf. above).

[273] V.I. Kuziščin (1984) [1976] 247-50. There is no doubt that scattered properties existed earlier, but the impressionistic evidence adduced by Kuziščin suggests that the phenomenon increased dramatically around the time when *actores* are first attested in the inscriptions.

and of *dispensatores* who had been promoted from the position of *vilici*. These cases show, however, that *actores* and *dispensatores* ranked above *vilici*.[274] An interesting case is that of the slave Sagaris, who shows up in two inscriptions from Venusia (*Regio* II), once as οἰκο-νόμος and once as *actor*. The relative chronology of the two depends on the meaning of οἰκονόμος; if it is the equivalent of *vilicus*, then the Greek inscription is certainly earlier than the Latin one; other-wise, the relative chronology remains uncertain.[275] Finally, an unique case of social promotion and personal loyalty was brought to us by the chance recovery of two inscriptions pertaining to the same person: one Salvianus is first attested as *vilicus portorii Illyrici* at Celeiu (Dacia) under Commodus, and later as *dispensator rationis extraordinariae provinciae Asiae* at Ephesus. In both positions, he was subordinated to the same *procurator*.[276] These two examples demon-strate that promoted *vilici* could follow two different career tracks, becoming either *actores* or *dispensatores*.

Most *actores*, like most *vilici*, were male slaves. Only one woman is recorded in this position.[277] Examples of freedmen and even free-born *actores* are rare, but not abnormal.[278] This is not to say that

---

[274] Cases of promotion from one function to another are not frequent; cf. *AE* 1972, no. 759 (Setif, "actor qui vilic(avit?)"); *AE* 1942-1943, no. 61 (Setif, "actor ex disp(ensatore)"); *CIL* IX 4186 (Amiternum/*Regio* IV, "dispensator ex ac-tor(e)"). Cf. also NT, *Matth.* 24.45-47, where the faithful slave is at first in charge of the household (ἐπὶ τῆς οἰκετείας) and is later entrusted with all his master's properties (ἐπὶ πᾶσιν τοῖς ὑπάρχουσιν αὐτοῦ), possibly a promotion from *vilicus* to *procurator*. More problematic are the inscriptions mentioning *exactores* (*CIL* VI 8673; 8683; and 8697a). Do they refer to retired *actores* (*ex actore*) or to a different function, such as tax collector? Cf. E. de Ruggiero, *Diz.Epigr.* 2 (1912) 2176-78, s.v. *exactor*. P. Habel, *PW* 1 (1893) col. 330 argues that in many cases *actor* and *exactor* refer to the same position (with reference to *CIL* III 349; *CIL* VI 42 [cf. Chapter Five]; *CIL* VI 8434; 8697a; and 9381-9383; *CIL* IX 4186; *CIL* X 3732; and 3907; and *CIL* XII 3070).

[275] *IGRR* I 464; and *CIL* IX 425 (= *ILS* 3197). Cf. Chapter One.

[276] *CIL* III 8042; and *CIL* III 6575 (= 7127 = *ILS* 1421); cf. also *CIL* VI 278 ("disp(ensator) qui ante vilicus huius loci (fuit)").

[277] There is no doubt about the gender of the character, cf. *CIL* XI 1730 (Florentia, "actrix c(onsularis) domus").

[278] The legal status of *actores* is in most cases unspecified; cf. *CIL* VI 8688 (first century A.D., imperial freedman); *CIL* VI 8591 (imperial freedman in charge of tax collection, II/III); *AE* 1968, no. 109 (Satricum, III, *libertus*); *CIL* V 8237 (Aquileia, 244); *AE* 1937, no. 141 (Pannonia, *libertus*); *CIL* IX 2827 (Buca, second half of I? *ingenuus*); *AE* 1978, no. 880 (= *CIL* VIII 25817, *ingenuus?*); and *AE* 1989, no. 635 (Lower Moesia). The cases of *CIL* VI 8673, *CIL* IX 2123, and 6083, no. 49 are dubious. Cf. also Iulianus (39 *dig.*) *Dig.* 34.3.12 (where the *actor* reportedly kept his functions after manumission); and W. Scheidel, *CQ* 40 (1990) 591-93.

deserving *actores* were denied the prospect of manumission, only that once freed they were unlikely to retain their position.[279] Landowners obviously considered slave *actores* more useful or more suitable than free(d) *actores*, since Ulpianus reports that some people were selling themselves into slavery to find employment as *actores*, or to share in the price of the sale.[280] This is precisely how Pallas, Claudius's or Nero's freedman, started his enormously successful career, selling himself into slavery "ad actum administrandum."[281] It also shows that the function of *actor* carried some prestige and could be rewarding. From the point of view of the agent, the position was attractive because it gave him access to a substantial sum of money in cash. Besides, the agent was very mobile, shuttling from country to town, where he could spend part of his time conducting business on account of his master and taking care of his own interests.[282] As middleman between his master, the staff of the agricultural estates, and people doing business with his master, the *actor* was able to collect tips, and to exert control over the activities of the community in which he lived and operated.[283] Thus, he could af-

---

[279] Scaevola (24 *dig.*) *Dig.* 40.5.19 *pr.* (after manumission the *actor* cannot be compelled to present the accounts he kept while he was still a slave); *idem* (22 *dig.*) *Dig.* 32.41.2; *idem* (24 *dig.*) *Dig.* 40.7.40.3-8; and Paulus (2 *decret.*) *Dig.* 32.97.

[280] Ulpianus (10 *ad Sab.*) *Dig.* 28.3.6.5: "ad actum gerendum pretiumve participandum." Cf. C.R. Whittaker, "Circe's Pigs . . . ," in M.I. Finley (ed.), *Classical Slavery* (1987) 109; and C. Lepelley, "Liberté, colonat et esclavage d'après la Lettre 24*: la juridiction épiscopale *'de liberali causa'*," in *Les Lettres de Saint Augustin découvertes par J. Divjak* (Paris 1983) 329-42, esp. 335 ff. W.V. Harris, "Towards a Study of the Roman Slave Trade," *MAAR* 36 (1980) 117-40, esp. 124, and n. 75, considers that self-enslavement accounted for a tiny part of the slave supply (Petron., *Sat.* 57.4; Dio Chrys. 15.23, which Harris takes as metaphorical; and Marcianus [1 *inst.*] *Dig.* 1.5.5.1). Cf. also J. Ramin–P. Veyne, *Historia* 30 (1981) 472-97, esp. 488 and 493-97.

[281] Stat., *Silv.* 3.3.60; Tac., *Ann.* 12.53; cf. J. Ramin–P. Veyne, *Historia* 30 (1981) 496-97.

[282] On the mobility of *actores* as business managers, cf. Ulpianus (20 *ad Sab.*) *Dig.* 33.7.12.38, who indicates that *actores* were sent on business trips not necessarily connected with the management of an agricultural estate; and Scaevola (3 *resp.*) *Dig.* 33.7.20.4 (". . .cum actor non in praediis, sed in civitate moratus sit").

[283] R. MacMullen, *Corruption and the Decline of Rome* (New Haven/London 1988) 125 and 258, n. 5, citing Juv. 3.188 and Amm. Marc. 14.6.15, with other references in R. MacMullen, *RSR* (1974) 197, n. 78 (Lucian, *Merc. Cond.* 14 and 37; Fronto, *Ep.* 4.5; Hor., *Sat.* 1.9.57). For *actores* controlling local markets, cf. B.D. Shaw, "Rural Markets in North Africa and the Political Economy of the Roman Empire," *AntAfr.* 17 (1981) 37-83; and J. Carlsen, *Africa romana* VIII (1991) 636. Compare with *CIL* XI 1231 (Placentia/*Regio* VIII, s(*ervus*) vil(*icus*) *macelli* of the colony).

ford to keep a retinue and worked at building a private fortune to be enjoyed after his eventual manumission.[284] Several *actores* had the leisure or the energy to cumulate their functions and to make use of their special qualifications, such as literacy or agricultural skill.[285]

Italian *actores* recorded in Latin inscriptions were often employed by female principals, and in that respect *actores* seem to have been in a different situation from *vilici*.[286] As there is no apparent chronological difference in the epigraphical evidence illustrating the two categories of agents, this peculiarity may be ascribed to the type of work performed by *actores*, or to some other unknown reason. In addition, the number of references to *actores* on stamps (amphorae, tiles, seals) is much higher than for *vilici*.[287] This detail is perhaps significant and will be further discussed in the next chapter.

As indicated in the case of *procuratores* and *vilici*, it was probably common for rich landowners to rely on several *actores* to take care

---

[284] Slave *actores* could have *vicarii*, cf. *CIL* V 5318; *CIL* V, Suppl. 239 (= *adiutor*); and Scaevola (5 *resp.*) *Dig.* 20.1.32. On the *peculium* of *actores*, cf. Scaevola (24 *dig.*) *Dig.* 40.7.40.3; Papinianus (5 *resp.*) *Dig.* 26.7.39.18 ("Quod de peculio servi actoris . . .").

[285] It is likely that both functions were assumed simultaneously, cf. *CIL* VI 9130 ("not(arius) et act(or)"); *AE* 1955, no. 80 (Lambaesis/Numidia, "actor et notarius"); *CIL* VI 31652 ("act(or) ark(arius)"); *CIL* X 6592 (Velitrae/*Regio* I, "actori et agricolae optimo"). Whether the *actor* Trophimus was himself one of the shopkeepers (*canabarii*) or whether he merely collected revenues from them is unclear, cf. *CIL* XIII 6730 (Moguntiacum/Upper Germania).

[286] Cf., for instance, *CIL* VI 41 (I); *CIL* VI 272; *CIL* VI 365 and 366; *CIL* VI 8696 (imperial slave?); *CIL* VI 8850 (imperial "actor a frumento"); *CIL* VI 9118; *CIL* VI 9125 and 9127 (two different *actores* of the same *domina*); *CIL* VI 33827 (?); *AE* 1964, no. 94 (II); *CIL* IX 322 (Cannae?); *CIL* IX 6083, no. 48 (Larinum, seal); *CIL* IX 6083, no. 130 (Aeclanum, seal); *CIL* X 1909 (Puteoli); *CIL* X 285 (Tegianum); *CIL* XV 1049 (Rome) = *CIL* X 8046, no. 5 (Caralitanus/Sard., tile); *CIL* XI 6076 (Urvinum Mataurense, late III); *CIL* XI 3732 = *CIL* VI 585 (Lorium, II); *CIL* XI 2686 (Volsinii); *AE* 1985, no. 189 (Ostia); *CIL* XIV 2251 (Ager Albanus); *CIL* XIV 2301 (Ager Albanus); *AE* 1983, no. 874 (Ulpiana/Moesia); and Apul., *Met.* 2.26.

[287] *AE* 1984, no. 56 (Rome, after 123, tile); *CIL* XV 1049 (Rome, tile) = *CIL* X 8046, no. 5 (Caralitanus/Sard.); *CIL* IX 6083, no. 48 (Larinum, seal); *CIL* IX 6083, no. 49 (Aeclanum, seal); *CIL* IX 6083, no. 130 (Aeclanum, seal); *CIL* IX 6083, no. 43 (Antinum, seal); *CIL* IX 6083, no. 111 (Stempeda, seal); *CIL* IX 6083, no. 124 (Colonia Giliti or Tegoliti?); *CIL* IX 6083, no. 163 (Palata, seal); *CIL* X 8059, no. 29 (Neapolis, seal); *CIL* X 8059, no. 135 (Sardinia, seal). *CIL* IV 6499 (amphora stamp) should perhaps be discarded, since the restitution "[ac]tor" is questionable in view of the early date of the archaeological context (late I B.C.) and of the absence of parallel instances of *actores* on amphorae.

of their business, especially when their estates were widely scattered.[288] *Actores* held a middle position between *procuratores* and *vilici*, but the nature of their relationship with either group remains unclear.

c. *dispensatores*

The position of *dispensatores* was comparable in many ways to that of *vilici* or *actores*.[289] The jurists, however, never mention the *praepositio* of a *dispensator*. One single inscription from Pannonia records one *dispensator rationis* as *praepositus arcae*, but the two functions may have been complementary.[290] Besides, some circumstancial evidence suggests that *dispensatores* did not belong to the category of *institores*: Gaius says that *dispensatores* were slaves left in charge of handling cash.[291] Thus, the legal position of *dispensatores* rested on their master's consent (*permissus domini*), while the legal position of *institores* rested on the principal's will (*voluntas*) expressed through the appointment (*praepositio*) of the agent to the head of a managerial unit. Pomponius remarks that only the transactions performed by agents in accordance with their principals' will would make the latter fully liable. Short of that, the liability of the principal would be

---

[288] Valerius Agathopous Meliteus, who was possibly the *procurator* of Herodes Atticus, had 27 πραγματευταί who were active at Peiraeus, the commercial port of Athens, cf. *SIG* 856 (ca. 161). Several *actores* are also mentioned by Pliny, *Ep.* 3.19.2; Scaevola (24 *dig.*) *Dig.* 40.7.40.7; Symmachus, *Ep.* 5.87; 9.6; 9.15; 9.52; 9.130; and by the anonymous author of the *Ep. ad Salvium* (*AntAfr.* 25 [1989] 240-41 and 245). The two *actores* of Valeria Polla (*CIL* VI 9125 and 9127) may have been active either successively or simultaneously.

[289] W. Liebenam, *PW* 5 (1903) 1189-98; J. Muñiz Coello, "*Officium dispensatoris*," *Gerion* 7 (1989) 107-19, based on the study of 235 inscriptions from all over the Empire; and J. Carlsen, "*Dispensatores* in Roman North Africa," in A. Mastino (ed.), *L'Africa romana* IX (Sassari 1992) 97-104. The Greek translation is οἰκονόμος (cf. Chapter One, and *CIL* III 333 = *IGRR* III 25 (Bithynia) and *SB* VI 9248 (Egypt)), which stands also on occasions for *vilicus* (*CIL* III 447, Miletus, *portorium*, bilingual), but not for *actor* (*IGRR* I 464, Venusia, the same man as in *CIL* IX 425, Venusia): these two inscriptions probably reflect two different moments in the life of Sagaris; cf. L. Robert, *Études anatoliennes* (Paris 1937) 310; *idem*, *Hellenica* X (Paris 1955) 83, n. 3; and A. Swiderek, *Cd'E* 45 (1970) 157-60.

[290] *CIL* III 4049 (Poetovio/Upper Pannonia), which records one "Ono[...] Aug(usti) n(ostri) d[ispensator] rationis p(rae)p(ositus) arcae." G. Boulvert (1970) 429, n. 318 considers that the *dispensator rationis* in charge of an *arca* was assisted by *arcarii*.

[291] Gaius, *Inst.* 1.122: "unde servi quibus permittitur administratio pecuniae dispensatores appellati sunt".

limited to the extent of the *peculium*.[292] It is then no coincidence that the late Republican jurist Tubero regards the same *permissus domini* as the legal basis of a slave's *peculium*.[293]

In our sources, *dispensatores* are always slaves and because slaves had no legal personality, all payments received by them were automatically credited to their master.[294] Although most of the evidence focuses on *dispensatores* as the receiving end of transactions, there is no doubt that they also made out payments, as their title suggests. Gaius, for instance, indicates that the parties to a contract by stipulation had to give formal notice to their respective *dispensatores* for every payment made (and received) in their absence, lest the stipulation be void. This formal notice was tantamount to a *iussum*. As a result, the transaction performed by the *dispensator* was valid and binding, and his master was fully liable.[295] By acting through *iussum* instead of *praepositio*, the principal retained a tighter control over an economically sensitive operation, namely the handling of cash. G. Boulvert points out that some sources show imperial *dispensatores* making contracts on behalf of the imperial treasury (*fiscus*), and he

---

[292] Ulpianus (28 *ad ed.*), quoting Pomponius, *Dig.* 14.1.1.20: "Et ita videtur et Pomponius significare, si sit in aliena potestate, si quidem voluntate gerat, in solidum eum obligari, si minus, in peculium." In this context, Ulpianus discusses the liability of the *dominus/paterfamilias* of an *exercitor*-in-power who had appointed a *magister navis*. While the rest of the passage may show signs of interpolation, this sentence seems genuine.

[293] Ulpianus (29 *ad ed.*), quoting Tubero through Celsus (6 *dig.*), *Dig.* 15.1.5.4: "Quod servus domini permissu separatum a rationibus dominicis habet." On the concept of *permissus domini*, cf. A di Porto, *Impresa collettiva e schiavo 'manager' in Roma antica (II sec. a.C. –II sec. d.C.)* (Milan 1984) 278 ff.

[294] G. Boulvert (1970) 430, n. 28. G. Bloch, *Dar.-Sag.* 2 (1892) 280-286, s.v. *dispensator* thinks that while *dispensatores* were most commonly slaves, there were a few exceptional freedmen or freeborn. The only possible case of a freed *dispensator* known to me is recorded in a badly damaged Latin inscription from Lower Moesia (*CIL* III 14427).

[295] Gaius (2 *de verb. oblig.*) *Dig.* 45.1.141.4: "Si inter eos, qui Romae sunt, talis fiat stipulatio: 'hodie Carthagine dare spondes?' quidam putant non semper videri impossibilem causam stipulationi contineri, quia possit contingere, ut tam stipulator quam promissor ante aliquod tempus suo quisque dispensatori notum fecerit in eum diem futuram stipulationem ac demandasset promissor quidem suo dispensatori, ut daret, stipulator autem suo, ut acciperet: quod si ita factum fuerit, poterit valere stipulatio." The word *iussum* is admittedly not used, but it is worth stressing that only the paying party gives instruction to the effect that payment be made ("demandasset") while both parties notify ("notum fecerit") their respective *dispensator*. Since the third contracting party—who was asking the question—was taking part in the *stipulatio*, there was no need for the *iussum* to be addressed to the receiving *dispensator* as well.

correctly assumes that in such cases the intervention of an imperial *procurator* was necessary.[296] The same is true about Ps.-Quintilian's contention that rich landowners lent money through their *dispensatores*.[297] In conclusion, it is fair to assume that each time a *dispensator* entered a contract on behalf of his master, he did so upon request (*iussum*) from the master himself or from his *procurator*.

Dispensatores could also have some legal capacity on their own if they had a *peculium*. Since *dispensatores* rank high in the servile hierarchy and since it was essential that they remain trustworthy, they must have fared rather well in this respect.[298] Some of the *dispensatores* recorded in the literary and epigraphical sources were notorious for accumulating gigantic *peculia*. Musicus Scurranus, who held the title of *dispensator ad fiscum Gallicum provinciae Lugdunensis* under Tiberius, used to travel with his own doctor, banker, business manager, etc. among his *vicarii*. He certainly belonged to the top layer of his class, and perhaps of Roman society altogether.[299] The transactions performed by such *dispensatores* made their masters liable to an *actio de peculio* instead of an *actio institoria*.[300]

For *dispensatores*, unlike *vilici* and *actores*, manumission represented the end of a career. In accordance with equity, however, a payment made by an ignorant debtor to a *dispensator* who had been manumitted or removed from office was considered valid, in spite of the fact that "stricta iuris ratione" payment to a third party does not extinguish a debt.[301] In case of manumission, the former master had an *actio negotiorum gestorum* or *mandati* against his former *dispensator* to get his money back.[302] Had the *dispensator* been a type of *institor*, manumission would not affect his ability to carry out his job, since the legal status (*libertus* or *servus*) of the *institor* after his initial appoint-

---

[296] G. Boulvert (1970) 432-33 points out that the contractual capacity of imperial *dispensatores*, like that of other slaves attached to the *fiscus*, was limited, cf. *Frg. de iure fisci* 6: "Edicto divi Traiani cavetur, ne qui provincialium cum servis fiscalibus contrahant nisi absignante [*or* adsignante] procuratore;" and 21 (= *FIRA* II², pp. 627-30); *Cod.Iust.* 2.36.1 (A.D. 200).

[297] Ps.-Quint., *Decl. min.* 345.10: "...per dispensatores faeneratis...."

[298] Ulpianus (8 *ad Plaut.*) *Dig.* 46.3.62: "Dispensatorem meum testamento liberum esse iussi et peculium ei legavi...." Cf. also Plin., *HN* 7.128; and *ibidem* 33.145.

[299] *CIL* VI 5197 (= *ILS* 1514).

[300] Iulianus (11 *dig.*) *Dig.* 14.3.12.

[301] Gai., *Inst.* 3.160; and Paulus (9 *ad ed.*) *Dig.* 46.3.51.

[302] Ulpianus (8 *ad Plaut.*) *Dig.* 46.3.62.

ment was irrelevant.[303] *Dispensatores* did not enjoy the same type of legal capacity as *actores* in spite of their equality of rank, because the former usually worked in the proximity of the *dominus* or his *procurator*. This factor implied a significant difference in the nature of their respective functions.[304]

F. Conclusion

In consequence of various social and economic developments, the traditional citizen-farmers of Early Rome were partly replaced by absentee landowners who had their land leased out to tenants or managed by *vilici*. The choice between the two systems was probably not determined, as is often surmised, by the availability of free vs. slave labor or by their compared profitability. Both tenant-farmers (*coloni*) and *vilici* could oversee a servile or mixed rural household (*familia rustica*). A survey of the literary and epigraphical sources suggests that tenancy and *vilicus* system existed side-by-side, and that the legal status of the managers was no barrier to either track. As slave labor was considered—and has been shown to be—most efficient when supplemented by temporary hired labor, it is likely that the *vilicus* found his *raison d'être* in the time-consuming job of coordinating the farmwork by balancing the needs of labor at different times of the year, hiring additional hands, and negotiating contracts for the execution of certain tasks. In addition, he may have been involved in the marketing of surpluses, even more so when the villa economy became oriented toward the production of cash crops and non-agricultural goods. His position of dependence in relation to his master and his appointment as manager of an economic unit, consisting of real estate (*fundus*) equipped with adequate staff (*familia rustica*), livestock, tools, materiel, and furnished facilities (*instrumentum*), bestowed unto him a legal capacity with which he could play the role of economic agent in spite of the deficiencies of the Roman law of persons and obligations, and notwithstanding the deep-rooted prejudices of the Roman elite against petty tradesmen. The literary and legal texts referring to *vilici* in the Republican

---

[303] Ulpianus (28 *ad ed.*) *Dig.* 14.3.7.1.

[304] N. Vulic, *Diz.Epigr.* 2 (1922) 1920-1923, s.v. *dispensator*, mentions *dispensatores* attached to gardens, imperial suburban villas, the postal service (*a iumentis*), the mint (*ratio monetae*), the office of public works, the circus, the fleet, the corn supply, granaries, and the collection of various revenues.

period present them invariably in an agricultural setting, which induces me to postulate that the *vilicus* system was first developed in agriculture. This hypothesis is also supported by the etymology of the term *vilicus*. The later evidence shows that the system apparently worked well and soon outreached the boundaries of agricultural estates to become a sort of standard system of management.

The evidence suggests that the *vilicus* system remained alive throughout Roman history down to the early Middle Ages and was probably not affected by the possible—though hypothetical—fluctuations of ancient slavery. Even the decline of the villa economy in the second century A.D. cannot be shown to have had an adverse effect on this system of management. A good example is provided by the Roman villa at Contrada Mirabile (Mazara del Vallo/Sicily) which was destroyed by fire between A.D. 150 and 180. Although the villa was never rebuilt, its archaeological remains show unmistakable signs of continuing agricultural activity until the fifth century. The excavators conclude that ''there is no certain *a priori* link between the abandonment of the villas as even temporary residences of their owners and the dissolution of their apparently productive economy: wheat cultivation, with slaves or free labour overseen by a *vilicus* or *conductor* could, and probably did, continue.''[305]

One of the drawbacks of the system consisted in the lack of mobility on the part of the *vilicus*. Communication between estate managers and landowners could, and often did, pass through the intermediary of a general agent, the *procurator*. By the first century A.D. a new character shows up in the literary, legal, and epigraphical sources, i.e. the *actor*, whose legal capacity was also based on his appointment (*praepositio*) by the principal/landowner. His bond to the land was looser, and his geographic mobility enhanced. *Vilicus* and *actor* coexisted from then on, and the latter might have eclipsed the former in the legal sources in later antiquity, when the concept of direct agency, short of being accepted by the jurists, raised less and less suspicion in practical situations.

How the *vilicus* system was extended to other areas of private and public life will be discussed in the following chapters.

---

[305] E. Fentress–D. Kennit–I. Valenti, ''A Sicilian Villa and its Landscape (Contrada Mirabile, Mazara del Vallo 1988),'' *Opus* 5 (1986) [1990] 75-95, esp. 85-86. The point is that production continued seemingly unaffected by the destruction of the villa as a luxurious or simply comfortable residence, therefore occupied by well-to-do owners.

CHAPTER FOUR

PRODUCTION AND DISTRIBUTION OF CLAY ARTIFACTS

A. INFRASTRUCTURE

In Italy during the Republican and early Imperial periods, artifacts were commonly produced within the household or in small workshops appended to stores where independent craftsmen sold their finished products on a local scale.[1] The production was intended to satisfy local consumption, which explains why it was carried out in such small units of production. Under these conditions, there was little need for agency, division of labor, and specialization.

Regional exports, however, must have started early. In Cato's list of favorite shopping centers, the landowner is invited to buy tools, equipment, containers, and garments in various towns of Latium, Campania and even Lucania.[2] The cost of transport and installation of a mill bought at Suessa to a farmstead near Venafrum amounted to 72 sestertii, including the wages of six men for six days. By way of comparison, the freight from Pompeii would have been 280 sestertii.[3] If the production of small towns like Pompeii, Suessa, etc. was supposed to satisfy the demand of a regional market, one should expect the size or the number of these units of production to grow accordingly. Because of the slow growth of the industrial sector in antiquity, small and medium-sized workshops were never replaced by large factories.[4]

---

[1] M. Rostovtzeff, *The Social and Economic History of the Roman Empire*[2] (Oxford 1957) 550-51, n. 25, reports that in Pompeii the first workshops attached to private houses date to the second century B.C. (House of Pansa): a small factory was combined with a retail shop (local trade). By contrast, the archaeological evidence from Ostia points toward larger establishments producing for exports (*ibid.* 73 and 567-68, nn. 36-37). A typical small workshop in Pompeii is described by G. Cerulli Irelli, "Officina di lucerne fittili a Pompei," in *L'instrumentum domesticum di Ercolaneo e Pompei nella prima età imperiale* (Rome 1977) 53-72, where the production of lamps was only one of several economic activities performed on a regular basis. Other low-cost clay artifacts were produced according to an established rotation.

[2] Cato, *Agr.* 135.1-3.

[3] Cato, *Agr.* 22.3-4.

[4] M. Rostovtzeff, *SEHRE*[2] (1957) 36.

Some artifacts were indeed produced on a larger scale, in establishments employing numbers of workers. One thinks primarily of the clay industry, which produced various types of building materials, such as bricks and tiles, disposable or reusable containers, such as amphorae and *dolia*, and artifacts of daily use, such as tableware and lamps. The mass production of glass, metal, and stone objects was carried out along the same lines. Due to the size of the production and the extent of the distribution of these artifacts, the organizational structure of these industries was undoubtedly different from that used in small, local enterprises. In its most extreme form, the whole economic process would splinter either vertically (with marketing gaining independence from manufacturing) or horizontally (with the opening of branch factories and outlets), or both ways. When this phenomenon occurred, entrepreneurs had to rely on agents and middlemen.

One important feature of craftsmanship, not peculiar to the Roman world, and well attested in a wide range of artistic activities and crafts, is that artists and artisans tend to claim credit for their work by signing their products, which enables customers and later historians to identify the origin of many artifacts.[5] This point is verified by the thousands of stamped and painted signatures on clay artifacts. Signatures also appeared on less resistant materials, such as wood or glass, and even on perishable commodities, such as bread.[6] Pliny the Younger reports that his gardener used to clip box shrubs into the shape of letters which represented the names—probably in an abbreviated form—of both the artisan and his master.[7] The problem with such signatures is that they rarely provide any information about the craftsmen's legal status, social condition, or professional situation. When the name itself points toward a servile origin, it is often impossible to distinguish slaves from freedmen. Besides, the role of the masters/patrons in the manufacturing pro-

---

[5] G. Siebert, "Signatures d'artistes, d'artisans et de fabricants dans l'antiquité classique," *Ktèma* 3 (1978) 111-31; and D. Manacorda, "Appunti sulla bollatura in età romana," in W.V. Harris (ed.), *The Inscribed Economy: Production and Distribution in the Roman Empire in the Light of instrumentum domesticum* (*JRA* Suppl. 6, Ann Arbor 1993) 37-54.

[6] *CIL* X 8058, no. 18 (Herculaneum); *CIL* XIII 6935 (Moguntiacum). Cf. D. Manacorda, in W.V. Harris (ed.), *The Inscribed Economy* (1993) 45.

[7] Plin., *Ep.* 5.6.35: "Alibi pratulum, alibi ipsa buxus intervenit in formas mille descripta, litteras interdum, quae modo nomen domini dicunt modo artificis."

cess remains unclear in most cases, to the point that there is often no way to tell whether the slave/freedman is an employee or an independent entrepreneur. The signatures are found on various parts of the artifact, they display various shapes (circular, bilinear, unilinear) and internal structures (phrase, single or several names), and are more or less abbreviated. Room is left for a wide array of interpretations, none of which are universally valid and/or verifiable.

The purpose of this chapter is to examine the organization of certain types of workshops producing clay artifacts, and the subsequent marketing of this production. The choice of this sector of the Roman economy for a series of case studies does not reflect the importance of the clay industry in the ancient economy. In that regard, a larger part of the non-agricultural work force was employed in the textile industry.[8] What is unique in the case of the clay industry is that both the manufacturing process and the final products have left plenty of traces in the form of archaeological material, such as kilns, sheds, moulds, tools, scores of completely preserved artifacts, and sherds. This enormous quantity of archaeological remains forms the main evidence for the study of ancient trade. The point is to determine whether archaeology can fill some of the blanks in the written sources. Be it said at the outset: I found only scarce evidence pointing indisputably toward the role of agents, in contrast with independent businessmen or contractors, in any of the occupations described below. There is a lot of room, however, for the potential activity of *institores* or slaves with *peculium* at almost any stage and in any area, and my purpose is to demonstrate how nicely *institores* would fit in the picture based on current interpretations of the archaeological material. Consequently, I consider fruitless and misleading any attempt at quantifying the respective importance of agents, contractors, and independent businessmen involved in Roman industrial production and trade.[9] More relevant is the identif-

---

[8] D.P.S Peacock, *Pottery in the Roman World: An Ethnoarchaeological Approach* (London/New York 1982) 115; J.-P. Morel, ''Aspects de l'artisanat dans la Grande Grèce romaine,'' in *La Magna Grecia nell'età romana. Atti del XV convegno . . . (Taranto, 5-10 ott. 1975)* (Naples 1976) 263-324, esp. 287, with evidence from Roman Egypt and Classical Athens.

[9] Along the same lines, M. Rostovtzeff, *SEHRE*[2] (1957) 190, speaking about the involvement of the municipal middle-class in trading, warns that ''we shall never be able to say how many shops were owned by this petty *bourgeoisie* and how many were run by slaves and freedmen (*institores*) for the members of the municipal aristocracy.''

cation and analysis of factors that may have influenced entrepreneurs facing the choice between various forms of industrial and
commercial organization.

1. *Industrial production and the villa economy*

The production of clay artifacts was carried out in both urban and
rural contexts. The higher the input of clay into the final product,
the closer to the clay beds the workshop would have to be located.
This is the reason why dolia, amphorae, bricks, and tiles were likely
to be produced in suburban or rural workshops, while tableware
(especially the finest kinds) and lamps rather belonged to an urban
context. Conversely, the input of craftsmanship differed widely
from one sector of the clay industry to the other. It would have been
economically senseless to waste the talent and expertise of a specialized mould designer by employing him in other unrelated activities,
whereas it mattered little if a brickmaker or even a common potter
was assigned to agricultural works for extended periods of time.[10]

It is hard to assess to what extent the production of clay artifacts
was integrated in the villa economy, but we have seen in the preceding chapter that the Latin agronomists regarded industrial activities
as a natural complement to agriculture.[11] The Sasernas, cited by
Varro, considered the exploitation of clay beds as part of the agricultural process, because of the profits that landowners could derive
from it.[12] It is generally assumed that the clay was, under normal
circumstances, used within a reasonable distance from the clay bed,
but there is some evidence that high quality clay was sometimes
transported and stored in amphorae.[13] The farmstead was a con-

---

[10] Iavolenus (2 *ex post. Lab.*), quoting Labeo, *Dig.* 33.7.25.1: "Quidam cum in
fundo figlinas haberet, figulorum opera maiore parte anni ad opus rusticum utebatur, deinde eius fundi instrumentum legaverat. Labeo Trebatius non videri figulos in instrumento fundi esse." On this text and the connection between agricultural and industrial production, cf. A. di Porto, "Impresa agricola ed attività
collegate nell'economia della *villa*. Alcune tendenze organizzative," *Sodalitas. Scritti
in onore di A. Guarino* VII (Naples 1984) 3235-77, esp. 3244-47.

[11] M. Rostovzeff, *SEHRE*[2] (Oxford 1957) 175; and 617-18, n. 40.

[12] Varro, *Rust.* 1.2.22-23.

[13] M.H. Callender, *Roman Amphorae with Index of Stamps* (London 1965) 37-41
("Amphora-borne commodities") mentions the exceptional find in Turin of
1,350,000 amphorae (I suspect a misprint in the original report by H. Dressel,
BCAR 7 [1879] 193) piled up in two layers and filled with "finely washed and
levigated clay."

venient setting, because it could provide labor and facilities for the manufacture of clay artifacts, as a result of the seasonal unemployment inherent to Mediterranean agriculture (cf. Chapter Three).

The connection between industrial and agricultural activities is supported by epigraphical and legal evidence. In the *Tabula Veleiensis* (Trajanic period), one estate was registered as "fundus Iulianus cum figlinis" and another as "saltus Avega Veccius Debeli cum figlinis."[14] By comparison, the late-second-century-A.D. jurist Q. Cervidius Scaevola mentions the bequest of a "fundus/praediolum cum taberna." The *taberna* could be either a restaurant/bar, a repair shop, or a store where the production of the local workshop was sold to travelers and neighbors.[15] Tile and brick stamps often contain an indication of origin, which makes it possible to identify the owner of the estate where the clay was produced. The following standard stamp is found on a tile made ca. A.D. 138: EX PR(aediis) DOMI-TIAE LVCILLAE EX FIG(linis) DOMIT(itianis) / MINORI-B(ibus) OP(us) DOL(iare) AELI ALE/XANDRI.[16] The stamp indicates that the tile was made on the estate (*praedia*) of Domitia Lucilla, out of clay coming from a particular clay district or brick-yard (*figlinae*), by the entrepreneur, workshop manager (*officinator*), or potter (P.) Aelius Alexander, or by one of his anonymous workers, if he had any. More will be said on this particular industry and on the specific meaning of *figlinae* later on. Around the same period, the jurist L. Neratius Priscus, whose familiarity with rural situations is well documented, cites the case of a tenant-farmer (*colonus*) whose slave left in charge of a kiln (*forn*[*i*] < *a* > *carius*) had inadvertently fallen asleep while on duty, thus causing a fire that destroyed the villa rented by his master.[17] Finally, the jurist Paulus examines the case of servitudes imposed upon the usufructuary exploitation of an estate, and contends that the production of vases, amphorae, jars, and tiles in *figlinae* should not be restricted, regard-

---

[14] *CIL* XI 1147, II, 14, 89; and 47 (*Regio* VIII).

[15] Scaevola (17 *dig.*) *Dig.* 32.35.2 and *idem* (19 *dig.*) *Dig.* 32.38.5.

[16] *CIL* XV 171.

[17] Ulpianus (18 *ad ed.*), quoting Neratius, *Dig.* 9.2.27.9 (= *Coll.* 12.7.7, *FIRA* II[2] p. 575): "Si fornicarius servus coloni ad fornacem obdormisset et villa fuerit exusta,..." Admittedly, the *fornax* could also be used to heat baths or to bake bread, cf. Paulus (2 *ad Vit.*) *Dig.* 33.7.14, about a *forn*[*i*] < *a* > *cator* attached to a *balnearium*. On Neratius's agricultural knowledge, cf. B.W. Frier, "Law, Technology, and Social Change. The Equipping of Italian Farm Tenancies," *ZRG* 96 (1979) 204-28.

less of whether it was intended to satisfy the needs of the estate or to be exported.[18]

All these rather incidental remarks are confirmed by the archaeological remains of some villas where signs of industrial activities are still visible. At Russi (*Regio* VIII, between Faenza and Rimini), the excavators found a kiln dated to the post-Trajanic era. The inland location of the villa was no obstacle to the export of the production, since waterways connected the villa with the neighboring town of Ravenna.[19] Elsewhere in Emilia Romagna, the remains of a villa in activity from the first century B.C. to the fourth century A.D. show traces of sheds or lean-tos supported by pillars, which have been interpreted as drying areas for bricks and tiles before firing. The villa was located near the *Via Popillia*, built in 132 B.C., and on a canal (*Fossa Augusta*) connected with the main waterways (*Fossae Flavia* and *Claudia*) linking Ravenna and Altinum.[20] Another industrial concern has been identified in the same region: it includes a levigation tank, two kilns, and a drying area. Two amphorae (Dr. 2-4), fourteen coins (from Augustus to the fourth century), a few sherds of fine pottery (North-Italic, from the late first century B.C. to the first century A.D.), some late lamps, a large number of sherds of coarse pottery (first and second century A.D.), and numerous tiles bearing the rectangular or *in planta pedis* stamp of T. Apusius Ampliatus point toward the activity of a local manufacturer in activity during the reigns of Augustus and Tiberius, or perhaps even later.[21]

---

[18] Paulus (15 *ad Plaut.*) *Dig.* 8.3.6 *pr.*: "Veluti si figlinas haberet, in quibus ea vasa fierent, quibus fructus eius fundi exportarentur (sicut in quibusdam fit, ut amphoris vinum evehatur aut ut dolia fiant), vel tegulae vel ad villam aedificandam. Sed si, ut vasa venirent, figlinae exercerentur, usus fructus erit." Cf. A. di Porto, *Sodalitas* VII (1984) 3246-47.

[19] R. Chevallier, *La romanisation de la Celtique du Pô* (Paris/Rome 1983) 162-64, nn. 21-22; and 263. On waterways (*fossae*) in the Po Valley, cf. G. Uggeri, "La navigazione interna della Cisalpina in età romana," *AAAd* 29 (1987) 305-54; and *idem*, "Aspetti archeologici della navigazione nella Cisalpina," *AAAd* 36 (1990) 175-96.

[20] G. Uggeri, "Un insediamento romano a carattere industriale (relazione preliminare degli scavi sull'argine d'Agosta, 1971-1973)," *Musei Ferraresi* 3 (1973) 174-86.

[21] D. Cavazzoni, "Un complesso produttivo fittile di età romana a Santo Marino (Poggio Berni [provincia di Forlì]). Relazione topografica preliminare," *StudRomagn* 34 (1983) 67-85. The site is located in a rural environment 18 km away from Rimini. The stamps display the following variants: VSI A; or T AMPLIATI; or APVSI AMPLIATI; or T APVSI AMPLIAT. Other stamps have been found there: BALBI AEMILII (second century A.D.).

Other examples exist, but it is remarkable that kilns actually found near a villa are not so numerous as could be expected.[22] This is probably due to the fact that kilns and workshops were often located at some distance from the farmstead for reasons of convenience and security. A good example is provided by two kilns recently excavated near Torrita di Siena (Central Etruria). The vicinity of the Clanis river—navigable into the Tiber—and of a relay station (*Mansio Manliana*) situated on a passing road (*Via Cassia*) between two important towns (Arretium and Clusium) provided ideal conditions for the marketing of the production. A villa was located on a higher hill nearby. The dump attached to the workshop shows that the production was composed of various items (terra sigillata, bricks, tiles, and perhaps clay pipes and Dr. 2-4 amphorae). Terra sigillata and amphorae were probably fired in kiln A, while bricks and tiles were sent to kiln B. A series of stamps (*tabula ansata* or *in planta pedis*) on terra sigillata and on bricks bear the name of C. Umbricius Cordus (*CVArr* 468). Less common are the stamps of L. Umbricius Hospes (*CVArr* 2440) and Camurius (*CVArr* 397).[23]

In such rural enterprises, the owner or manager (*conductor, colonus,* or *vilicus*) of the farmstead could run both the industrial and the agricultural production as one or two managerial units, or he could lease out one sector to a (sub)contractor or to a (sub)tenant, or appoint a (sub)agent (*institor* or *subvilicus*) to be in charge of it.[24]

2. *Nucleated industries*

Centers of production, whatever their size, required a limited initial investment in tools and facilities. The most sophisticated—and therefore most expensive—item used in the clay industry was un-

---

[22] D.P.S Peacock–D.F. Williams, *Amphorae and the Roman Economy* (London/ New York 1986) 68-71 (= gazetteer of kiln sites in Italy, linked with amphora production); N. Cuomo di Caprio, "Proposta di classificazione delle fornaci per ceramica e laterizi nell'area italiana dalla preistoria a tutta l'epoca romana," *Sibrium* 11 (1971-1972) 371-461, esp. 443-61; and V. Righini, "Officine artigianali e nuclei industriali nella villa romana," in *La Villa Romana, Giornata di Studi, Russi, 10 maggio 1970* (Faenza 1971) 29-36.

[23] G. Pucci, "A Sigillata Kiln in Valdichiana (Central Etruria)," *RCRF* 27/28 (1990) 15-23, who comments that it is quite uncommon to have the combination of three types of products in the same workshop.

[24] About the legal aspect of double appointment, cf. my paper "Workshop Managers," in W.V. Harris (ed.), *The Inscribed Economy* (1993) 171-81, esp. 175-78.

doubtedly the kiln, but even individual potters producing on a small
scale could have their own firing place. The raw material consisted
mainly of three relatively common items, clay, water, and firewood.
The fact that qualities of clay could vary greatly and that firewood
was scarce in some regions may have conditioned the location and
organization of such industries. Their supply necessitated some kind
of logistical apparatus and may have motivated the occasional creation of nucleated industries, where independent potters shared the
same kiln, in the proximity of good clay beds. In La Graufesenque
(Aveyron/Gaul), the find of separation rings with various marks and
some 213 account lists dated to the Neronian and Flavian periods attest the existence of a complex organization in the terra sigillata industry.[25] If this hypothetical cooperation among potters did not extend over the stage of the firing, it was somewhat limited in time and
certainly seasonal, because it is unlikely that more than ten or fifteen
batches of ca. 30,000 vases could be fired within a year.[26] As simi-

---

[25] Rings of separation are mentioned by J.-P. Jacob–H. Leredde, "Un aspect
de l'organisation des centres de production céramique: le mythe du 'cartel'",
RCRF 21/22 (1982) 89-94, who do not provide any reference. About account lists,
cf. A. Oxé, "Die Töpferrechnungen von der Graufesenque," *BJ* 130 (1925) 38-99,
esp. 41 and 65-68 (names of potters linked with the Gallic words "duci" or "toni"
or "eti"); P.M. Duval–R. Marichal, "Un 'compte d'enfournement' inédit de La
Graufesenque," *Mélanges d'archéologie et d'histoire offerts à A. Piganiol* III (Paris 1966)
1341-52; R. Marichal, "Quelques graffites inédits de la Graufesenque (Aveyron)," *CRAI* (1971) 188-212, esp. 207: "Les bordereaux d'enfournement prouvent
l'existence d'une coopération entre les potiers, on y constate de véritables associations, on y voit figurer des *cassidani* ou 'surveillants', les historiens parlent de *collegium*, de 'coopérative de production', de 'cartel', ce qui suppose au moins un rudi-
ment de comptabilité, des règlements de comptes périodiques; ainsi s'expliquerait
la cuisson des comptes des esclaves d'Atelia" (cf. below); *idem*, "Nouveaux graffites
de la Graufesenque," *REA* 76 (1974) 85-110 and 266-99, in part. 90, n. 1 with
bibliography about the *cas(s)idani*; *idem*, *CRAI* (1981) 244-72, esp. 264-70, where
the author proposes a new interpretation of *casidanus* (= *flamen*), perhaps as a way
to date the batch (*furnus* or *tuθos* or *autagis*) or in reference with a five-year contract
concluded between the kiln operator and the potters; cf. also C. Delplace, "Les
potiers dans la société et l'économie de l'Italie et de la Gaule au Ier siècle av. et
au Ier siècle ap. J.-C.," *Ktèma* 3 (1978) 55-76, esp. 63-70, who considers (67) the
casidanus as "un contrôleur chargé du contrôle fournée-bordereau" and the *flamen*
as "un contrôleur chargé de vérifier la température du four dans le but d'éviter tout
accident de cuisson;" both the *casidanus* and the *flamen* are chosen among the potters
who deliver their goods to be fired, which points toward a sort of self-management;
J.-P. Jacob, *Le monde des céramistes gallo-romains. Esquisse d'une problématique économique, sociale et juridique* (Thèse pour le Doctorat d'Etat en Histoire du Droit et des
Faits Sociaux, Dijon 1981) (non vidi); and now, R. Marichal, *Les graffites de La
Graufesenque* (*Gallia* Suppl. 47, Paris 1988).
[26] R. Marichal, *CRAI* (1981) 259; and 267-70.

lar accounts have been found in other locations, it seems possible to extrapolate from the Gallic evidence for, at least, Italy, and perhaps for some other Western provinces.[27] It is, however, difficult to estimate the importance of communal firing in any period and at any given place.

In most cases, it is impossible to determine the identity of the kiln's owner. The owner of an agricultural estate may have rented out his kiln to the neighboring community, in the same way as he would have rented his mill, baking oven, baths, shops, or any other means of production or facility.[28] One Republican inscription records the possible gift of a tile factory (?) by a landowner, Cn. Domitius M.f. Calvinus, to his tenants.[29] One should, however, refrain from proposing a general model whereby wealthy landowners would have controlled the means of production in a capitalistic fashion. Such an economic structure belongs rather to medieval seigneurial organization.

A group of independent potters could also jointly hire or appoint a specialist to take care of the kiln operation. The legal position of such an operator would vary from case to case. He could be hired or appointed by one of the potters, who would then subcontract his services to other potters. He could also be employed by the whole group united in a partnership (*societas*). Finally, if he was a slave manager, he could be jointly owned (as *servus communis*) by his employers.[30] Again, this type of arrangement did not necessarily

---

[27] A. Oxé, *BJ* 130 (1925) 51-52 cites texts from Arezzo (*CIL* XI 6702, nos. 1-5); Horta (Italy, *CIL* XI 6702, no. 23a); Montans (Southern Gaul, *CIL* XIII 10017, no. 46); Blickweiler (O. Bohn, *Germania* 7 [1923] 64-68; cf. now R. Marichal [1988] 260-62); and Rheinzabern (Ludowici, *Rheinzabern Töpfer* I and II [1901-1904 and 1901-1905]). Cf. also D.P.S. Peacock (1982) 125-26. G. Pucci, in E. Ettlinger *et al.*, *Conspectus formarum terrae sigillatae italico modo confectae* (Bonn 1990) 14-15 reports the find at Isola di Migliarino (7 km north of Pisa) of a plate signed by one SEX(tus) M(urrius) F(estus) with an illegible graffito on its inside bottom part, which could be interpreted as another such account.

[28] The evidence for such practices is rare, cf. Columella, *Rust.* 1.6.21: "Circa villam deinceps haec esse oportebit: furnum et pistrinum, quantum futurus numerus colonorum postulaverit;" *CIL* VIII 14428; 14457; and 16411; and perhaps Ulpianus (28 *ad ed.*), quoting Neratius, *Dig.* 9.2.27.9. Cf. J. Percival, "Seigneurial Aspects of Late Roman Estate Management," *EHR* 84 (1969) 456, nn. 7-8.

[29] *ILLRP* 430 (Circeii/Tarracina, Latium) (= *CIL* X 5314 = 8043): [Cn. Do]MITIVS M.F. / [C]ALVINVS / [co]LONEIS DEDIT. The editors (*ILLRP*, p. 430, and *CIL* X, p. 998) suggest that the object of "dedit" was perhaps some *figlinae* belonging to Cn. Domitius Calvinus. Similar tiles were found in Pompeii and Naples.

[30] A. di Porto, *Impresa collettiva e schiavo 'manager' in Roma antica* (Milan 1984);

imply that the cooperation between potters extended further than
the kiln operation. A combination of joint management of the kiln
(in ownership or leasing) and subcontracting to outsiders was of
course possible. More will be said about contracting potters in the
section on amphorae (cf. below).

To improve the efficiency of the kiln operator, the employer(s)
could give him some autonomy in the organization of his job. In
the capacity of indirect agent appointed by the kiln owner(s)/potters
for a specific purpose, the kiln operator was likely to negotiate contracts with outsiders, in order to hire assistants, buy fuel, and perhaps sell the production to customers, consumers or traders. In La
Graufesenque, a woman named Atelia is known to have rented six
of her slaves to one entrepreneur or to a consortium of potters. The
account (*diurnum*), written before firing on the inside of a plate, lists
various tasks performed by each of the slaves between July 22 and
August 23 of an unknown year (in the first century A.D.). The
slaves were assigned to various workplaces (entries phrased with *ad*
+ accusative) or had to perform specific tasks (entries with an accusative alone), such as collecting clay ("argilam"), gathering construction material or firewood (? "materiem erige(n)da(m)"),
polishing (? "ad samiandum"), and transporting and marketing the
products ("mercatu(m)").[31] The verso of the Ateleia inscription

P. Bürgin, "Figuli im römischen Recht," *RCRF* 23/24 (1984) 123-27, esp. 126;
G. Prachner, *Die Sklaven und Freigelassenen im arretinischen Sigillatagewerbe* (Wiesbaden
1980), esp. 172 (*CVArr* 2392-2393, partnership or joint ownership of C. Umbricius
Philologus and L. Avillius Sura), 202, n. 64, and 209 (*CVArr* 1838 = 2311:
GRATVS SOCIOR(um); or 2310: GRATVS VIBIOR(um), possibly the same
potter; *CVArr* 2046: CINNA(mus) G(aii) L(ucii) TITI(orum); *CVArr* 1007-1009:
CHRESTVS PANTAGATVS QVARTIO RASINI MEMMI = three slaves be-
longing to two owners); cf. *CVArr*, p. XXVIII; pp. 43-44; and pp. 89-90 (Ateius's
partnerships).
[31] R. Marichal, *CRAI* (1971) 188-212, esp. 193-201; *idem*, *REA* 76 (1974) 85-
110 and 266-99, esp. 266-77; and *idem* (1988) 226-28. The inscription (25B = 169),
to my knowledge never recorded in *AE*, reads (recto = interior): "[?]a ATELIAE
puerorum ex XI August[is /] in X K(alendas) Septe(m)bres / [SE]CVNDVS,
AGILEIVS dies XIIII s(emis) ar[gilam /[?] dierum XXX, IIII ad Capuries, XI
[/ CA]LISTVS / [O]NESIMVS ad Sabros III, ad Crau[cinam /] ad Craucinam
III it ONESIMVS[/ mat]eriem erigenda I / [?] dierum XXX / [?]ae III CA-
LISTVS ad samiandum [/]...EOS, VIGEDOS III mercatu a[d /]s materi^em
erige(n)dam [/] argilam III di[es /] [/]s ad a[?]...." and (verso = exterior):
"mulio CANDIDI VRI d(ies) XXV / ad ar[gilam?] / ad m[ercatum?] / ad Sabr[os]
...." Marichal points out (193) that Atelia could be either a man or a woman, but
M. Lejeune (commenting on Marichal's paper, *CRAI* 1971, 208 ff) favors the latter
possibility for linguistic reasons. This inscription, however, does not allow us to

mentions the service of a muleteer (*mulio*) who was the slave of one Candidus, himself the son or slave of one Urus. This document shows that slaves belonging to various masters were involved in the enterprise. If this hypothesis is correct, contracts of hire were concluded between the kiln operator or his employer(s) on one side, and Atelia, Candidus, Urus, or any other master on the other. The purpose of this contract was to provide the kiln operator with whatever manpower (*mercennarii*) was required to enable him to keep the kiln in activity. Other possibilities, however, are not excluded. Incidentally, it is interesting that even in a provincial setting such as La Graufesenque labor contracts were established in accordance with Roman law. A fragment found recently presents the same form as standardized legal documents attested elsewere across the empire.[32]

Finally, it is worth mentioning that even nucleated concerns could have offshoots. When business opportunities were discovered in the vicinity of a center of production, a few independent potters could join together to take advantage of the new market and relocate, at least on a temporary basis. Thus, it appears that a group of potters from Montans in Southern Gaul operated a workshop at Valery (Tarn) on a seasonal basis.[33] Such workshops are called "satellite-workshops," as they always retain their link with the original center of production.

---

determine the legal status of potters at La Graufesenque, because (a) Atelia was not necessarily a potter herself (at least her stamp has not been found so far); and (b) the use of slaves by the kiln operator or any potter does not preclude him from being a slave himself, because slaves could have *vicarii* and *mercennarii* (against M. Lejeune, who mistakenly asserts (209) that "il ne saurait y avoir d'esclaves d'esclaves"). On the organization of the pottery industry in La Graufesenque, cf. K. Strobel, "Einige Bemerkungen zu den historisch-archäologischen Grundlagen einer Neuformulierung der Sigillatenchronologie für Germanien und Rätien und zu wirtschaftsgeschichtlichen Aspekten der römischen Keramikindustrie," *MBAH* 6 (1987) 75-115, esp. 100-13.

[32] R. Marichal, *CRAI* (1981) 266 and 272, publishing an incomplete sale document (graffito made before firing) found in 1980 in the dump of the Flavian kiln. It reads: "...]uanto oppa[.../ ...]emit hominem [.../ ...s]ive is quo alio nom[ine est ...]." Cf. also R. Marichal (1988) 243, no. 211, who dates the fragment to A.D. 80-120, and provides as parallel *FIRA* III² no. 88 (A.D. 142, triptych from Transylvania): "Dasius Breucus emit mancipioque accepit puerum Apalaustum, sive is quo alio nomine est, ..." Marichal (1981) mentions the existence of another sherd (origin not specified) presenting the word SPONSALIA.

[33] T. Martin, "L'atelier de Valery (Tarn): ses rapports avec ceux de Montans," *Figlina* 1 (1976) 1-12, esp. 7-10.

3. Channels of distribution

When production was too abundant to be absorbed by local consumption, the manufacturers had to organize the distribution of their goods, again individually or collectively, sometimes over long distances. They could rely on their own agents, slaves or freedmen, or deal with independent tradesmen, *mercatores* or *negotiatores*. The difference between the two categories was a matter of scale and diversity of interests—and therefore a matter of respectability. Both groups provided basically the same types of services.[34] Traders could be personally engaged in trade or provide financial support for operations actually carried out by others, contractors or agents, dependents or hired employees.[35] Modern historians usually associate the reliance on agents with important people involved in large-scale operation. This might be a reasonable assumption in some cases, but it should not necessarily be so. Florus and Severus, whose ship was operated by the *actor* Bosiconius,[36] were involved in trade between Britain and Lower Germania sometime between ca. 190 and 227. There is no evidence that they owned more than this one ship and that they were doing anything more than shipping commodities from one place to another. In the capacity of *actor navis*, Bosiconius was the agent of a partnership between two people (or a *servus communis*).[37] This joint venture suggests that neither of the shippers was financially strong enough to equip a ship on his own, or that both felt the necessity to decrease the impact that a potential loss of the

---

[34] J.H. D'Arms, *Commerce and Social Standing in Ancient Rome* (Cambridge, MA 1981) 24-25, quoting (n. 21) Cic., *Planc.* 26.64: "negotiatoribus comis, mercatoribus iustus;" and (n. 24) *CIL* X 1797 (Augustan age): "mercatores qui Alexandr. Asiai Syriai negotiantur." *Mercatores* were people of low station in life, while *negotiatores* (or "qui negotiantur") were members of the upper classes (equestrian or senatorial order).

[35] J. Rougé, *Recherches sur l'organisation du commerce maritime en Méditerranée sous l'Empire romain* (Paris 1966) 269-321, esp. 274-87.

[36] The inscription (not recorded in *AE*) reads: "Bosiconius actor navis Flori (et) Severi;" cf. M. Hassall, "Britain and the Rhine Provinces: Epigraphic Evidence for Roman Trade," in J. du Plat Taylor–H. Cleere (eds.), *Roman Shipping and Trade: Britain and the Rhine Provinces* (London 1978) 43, table I, no. 14 (citing J.E. Bogaers, "Nehalennia en de epigrafische gegevens," in P. Stuart–J.E. Bogaers, *Deae Nehalenniae—Gids bij de tentoonstelling Nehalennia de Zeeuwse godin, Zeeland in de Romeinse tijd, Romeinse monumenten uit de Oosterschelde* [Middelburg/Leiden 1971] 33-43, esp. 39 [non vidi]).

[37] Since the *cognomen* Florus is more common than the *nomen* Florius, I suggest that Bosiconius was the agent of two persons rather than one.

ship would have on their financial assets.[38] M. Hassall, however, suggests that

> Shipping, too, will have been in the hands of both individual *nautae* and small *societates*. The smaller shipowners or the active members of partnerships will have operated their own vessels, but the larger owners will have employed *actores navium*, agents to represent them on board ship...*Actores* may also have been employed by the larger companies of *negotiatores*, although it is likely that most of the dedications at the two Dutch sites [= Domburg and Colijnsplaat] were made by merchants or shippers rather than their agents.[39]

Occasional epigraphical references to *negotiatores cretarii* (or *artis cretariae*) offer a glimpse of the phenomenon, but it is difficult to recognize the ramifications of their networks and the full range of their activities. Sometimes, merchants dedicated inscriptions in which they recorded their place of origin, or the markets that they used to supply.[40] *Negotiatores cretarii*, however, are attested only in the Northern provinces in the late second and early third centuries, and we do not know how to distinguish distributors of clay artifacts from other businessmen in other regions and in earlier times.[41] Most of them

---

[38] Compare with Cato the Elder's practice (reported by Plut., *Cat.Mai.* 21.5-6) of taking only a share in companies involved in seaborne trade. The operation was entirely financed by Cato, who lent money to his partners. Like Florus and Severus, he was represented by an agent, his freedman Quintio, who traveled on the ship. Cf. J.H. D'Arms, *CSSAR* (1981) 39-40.

[39] M. Hassall (1978) 45-46.

[40] J.E. Bogaers, "Foreign Affairs," in B. Hartley – J. Wacher (eds.), *Rome and her Northern Provinces* (Gloucester 1983) 13-32; *idem* – P. Stuart, "Augusta Raurica und die Dea Nehalennia," *JAK* 1 (1980) 49-58.

[41] For *negotiatores cretarii* or *negotiatores artis cretariae*, cf. *CIL* XIII 1798 (Lyons); *CIL* XIII 1906 (Lyons); *CIL* XIII 2033 (Lyons); *CIL* XIII 6366 (Rottenburg, A.D. 225); *CIL* XIII 8793 (Domburg), also attested in an inscription from the newly found temple of Dea Nehalennia at Colijnsplaat, dated 190-227 (= *AE* 1973, no. 370); *CIL* XIII 8350 (Cologne); *CIL* XIII 8224 (Cologne); *CIL* XIII 4336 (Metz); *CIL* XIII 6524 (Lorch); *CIL* XIII 7228 (Mainz); *CIL* XIII 7300 (Cassel); *CIL* XIII 7588 (Wiesbaden); *BRGK* 27 (1937) 104, no. 188 (= ? *AE* 1931, no. 27, Bonn); and *BRGK* 40 (1950) 124, no. 3 (Trier); *CIL* III 5833 (Augsburg). Cf. also M. Hassall (1978) 41-48, esp. 44-45, according to whom *negotiatores cretarii* were trading in tableware (terra sigillata) as well as clay figurines, and might have formed guilds or companies; O. Schlippschuh, *Die Händler im römischen Kaiserreich in Gallien, Germanien und den Donau Provinzen, Rätien, Noricum und Pannonien* (Amsterdam 1974, repr. with additions in 1987) 60-64, and 213-15, nn. 340-60; P.S. Middleton, "Army Supply in Roman Gaul. An Hypothesis for Roman Britain," in B.C. Burnham – H.B. Johnson (eds.), *Invasion and Response: The Case of Roman Britain* (Oxford 1979) 81-97, esp. 85; K. Greene, *The Archaeology of the Roman Economy* (Berkeley/L.A. 1986) 166-67; D.P.S. Peacock (1982) 158-59; G. Pucci, "Pottery and

certainly also traded in other commodities, since it was easier, more efficient, and more cost-effective to load a ship with goods of various shapes and weights.

Wholesale traders supplied local retailers, either shopkeepers (*tabernarii*) or peddlers (*circitores*). Some of these were independent merchants, others could be the distributors' agents. Some wooden tablets found in Lothbury (London) and dating from the reign of Domitian come from the archive of a businessman and present one Crescens, possibly a slave, as debtor of the holder of the tablet. Another document alludes to a *taberna*, a ship, and the grant of permission (= *iussum* or *praepositio*?) in the context of a sale, but the text is illegible in many parts and prevents a complete understanding of the transaction.[42]

Traders could deal with several producers. A wooden box found in Pompeii and containing unused earthenware of various origins illustrates the involvement of middlemen in the distribution of clay artifacts in Italy in the first century A.D. The crate was filled with ninety stamped bowls made in Southern Gaul and thirty-seven lamps produced by various Italian firms (Strobilus, Communis, Echio, and Fortis). The package must have been put together somewhere in Italy before it was sent to Pompeii.[43]

It has been argued that some major manufacturers, acting individually or in trusts, secured delimited areas where commercial competition was defused or eliminated.[44] This kind of commercial practice is known to exist, as D.P.S. Peacock cites a case from modern Corsica, where potters—or the distributors of their pro-

---

Trade in the Roman Period," in P. Garnsey *et al.* (eds.), *Trade in the Ancient Economy* (Berkeley/L.A. 1983) 105-17; G. Raepsaet, "Aspects de l'organisation du commerce de la céramique sigillée dans le Nord de la Gaule au IIe [et IIIe] siècle[s] de notre ère, I: Les données matérielles," *MBAH* 6 (1987) 1-27; and "II: Négociants et transporteurs. La géographie des activités commerciales," *MBAH* 7 (1988) 45-69 (with M.-Th. Raepsaet-Charlier).

[42] R.G. Collingwood–M.V. Taylor, "Roman Britain in 1930," *JRS* 21 (1931) 247. The date (Domitianic) is given by the first tablet (= a); the text of the second tablet (= b) reads "quam pecuniam petisionis item / scriptis solvere mihi debebit Cres/cens isve ad quem ea res per/tinebit . . . ris primis/. . .ss. . .t;" and the text of the third tablet (= c) reads ". . .rem vendidisse . . ./ex taberna sua . . ./. . .navem faci/endam et permissionem dedisse/. . .clavi faciendi."

[43] D. Atkinson, "A Hoard of Samian Ware from Pompeii," *JRS* 4 (1914) 27-64. The stamps on the bowls record the name of the potters (for instance, OFMOM for Mommo), and the diameter. Cf. *ILS* 8605.

[44] C. Goudineau, "Céramique arétine à reliefs de Bolsena," *MEFR* 80 (1968) 167-200, esp. 184-86; *idem, Bolsena IV. La céramique arétine lisse. Fouilles de l'Ecole Française de Rome à Bolsena (Poggio Moschini) 1962-1967* (Paris 1968) 348-69.

ducts—seem to have carefully avoided competition by establishing local monopolies.[45] C. Goudineau points out that the stamps found on the site of Bolsena permit to identify the production of the well-known Arretine potters Rasinius, Tetteius, and the Perennii, whereas other important contemporary manufacturers, such as Cornelius, C. and L. Annius, Publius, and L. Pomponius Pisanus are conspicuously absent. The cooperation between potters could have started with sharing some of the means of production, and was made possible by the lack of external competition. Such agreements were bound to be short-lived: signs of decline of the Arretine pottery industry are visible as early as A.D. 15, with the appearance of the stamps *in planta pedis* (cf. below) which Goudineau interprets as an effort by Arretine potters to fight external competition through the adoption of a new common trademark.

The absence of products of well-known potters on a site relatively close to Arezzo is admittedly surprising, but it does not necessarily imply that Arretine manufacturers ever managed to divide among themselves exclusive "zones d'influences." First, as Goudineau himself notes, only a small percentage of the fine ware was signed, and the production of other potters might be concealed in the mass of anonymous sherds. Further, one should take into consideration the possibility of non-economic factors in the process of distribution, such as personal connections of manufacturers or traders, or preferred routes of merchants, without overemphasizing the deliberate nature of the phenomenon. There is no sign of overproduction during the Augustan period, and this may be ascribed to the fact that some potters could, and chose to, export their production to the provinces. Thanks to a network of dynamic traders, it was possible to take advantage of a developing and juicy provincial market, part of which was constituted by the Roman army. This strategy was more profitable than to engage in a price war at home. Stiffer competition may have arisen slightly later, which undoubtedly affected the relationship between potters. Pliny the Elder was familiar with magical practices resorted to by potters: their purpose was to destroy their competitors' production during firing with the help of an array of curses and spells.[46] If Pliny's allusion has any historical basis, it

---

[45] D.P.S. Peacock (1982) 18.

[46] Pliny, *HN* 28.19: "multi figlinarum opera rumpi credunt tali modo (= deprecationibus, defixionibus, incantamentis)." Cf. J.G. Gager (ed.), *Curse Tablets and Binding Spells from the Ancient World* (Oxford 1992) 151-74, esp. 153-54 and 162, with similar material from Archaic and Classical Greece.

might reflect the economic situation in the middle of the first century A.D., when provincial manufacturers had displaced Italian potters and restricted the latter's share of the Gallic/Germanic markets.

The possibility of temporary cooperation between potters or traders does not necessarily imply that the clay industry was dominated by trusts.[47] Some degree of economic concentration was occasionally achieved. W.V. Harris points out that the oligopolistic nature of the lamp industry in the first century A.D. is illustrated by the fact that "in most places the vast majority of signed lamps exhibit common marks which are also known from far distant sites."[48] However, such phenomena would have had a limited impact, as numerous instances show that the products of large firms never succeeded in totally displacing local production. In Southern Italy in the second century B.C., a black-glazed pottery was produced by scores of small workshops and distributed within a limited area, side-by-side with the widely-distributed Campanian A pottery.[49] The situation was similar for the lamp industry: the finds of moulds and workshops as well as the distribution of marks show that numerous small workshops of limited range could coexist with a few major firms.[50]

The mere quantity of artifacts produced by some firms, the range of their distribution, and the estimated duration of the activity of these firms suggest that the names appearing in the stamps could represent rich and powerful entrepreneurs who were unlikely to take part in the actual manufacturing process. It is therefore plausible that they were relying on agents working as workshop managers. Besides, mass production entailed problems of marketing which could be solved through decentralization of the production and by opening subsidiary workshops located closer to new markets. This type of measure had the advantage of lowering the costs of transportation. In addition, the producers were able to respond faster to market fluctuations by adjusting the quantity and/or the quality of their

---

[47] J.-P. Jacob–H. Leredde, *RCRF* 21/22 (1982) 89-94, esp. 92-93, dismissing the interpretation of the marks *in planta pedis* as the sign of a concerted effort by some potters to fight external competition; and D.P.S. Peacock (1982) 120-21.

[48] W.V. Harris, *JRS* 70 (1980) 129.

[49] J.-P. Morel, "Aspects de l'artisanat dans la Grande-Grèce romaine," in *La Magna Grecia nell'età romana. Atti del XV convegno di Studi sulla Magna Grecia (Taranto 5-10 ottobre 1975)* (Naples 1976) 263-324, esp. 280-81; and 286.

[50] J-P. Morel, *ibid.* 281, and n. 25, based mostly on unpublished material.

production. The literary and legal sources contain a few allusions to fictional or actual situations where business was conducted abroad through slaves and freedmen.[51] Since the law governing indirect agency was appropriate to deal with this type of situation, it is sensible to look for traces of the involvement of business managers (*institores*, *officinatores*, *vilici*, *actores*, etc.) in the production and distribution of clay artifacts.

This chapter will focus on four categories of goods, and study the role of business agents in the whole process, from the clay bed to the market. The first two sections will deal with clay artifacts produced mainly in the context of the villa economy, namely the production of building material, in particular bricks and tiles, and the production of amphorae and *dolia* as containers of agricultural products. The last two sections will focus on the production and distribution of artifacts produced mostly, but not exclusively, in urban workshops, namely Arretine pottery (terra sigillata) and terracotta lamps. In each section, the specific nature of the material will be used to illustrate a particular aspect of the clay industry. Thus, the relationship between landowners and manufacturers will be examined in the section about bricks and tiles; the relationship between manufacturers and distributors in the section on amphorae; the epigraphical structure of the stamps and the use of chemical or physical means in identifying branch workshops in the section on terra sigillata; and the question of export of finished products and moulds in the section on terracotta lamps. Whether or not the conclusions reached in one case can be extrapolated to the others is admittedly debatable, but the main purpose of this chapter is to demonstrate the probable complementarity of various types of material.

B. Bricks and tiles

Because of the massive input of clay necessary for brick and tile production, brickyards were usually located in the country, on the site of clay beds and in the vicinity of convenient roads and waterways. The main question to be examined is whether or not the own-

---

[51] For instance, Gaius (1 *rerum cottid. sive aureorum*) *Dig.* 40.9.10: "Saepe enim de facultatibus suis amplius, quam in his est, sperant homines. Quod frequenter acccidit his, qui transmarinas negotiationes et aliis regionibus, quam in quibus ipsi morantur, per servos atque libertos exercent." Cf. Chapter Two.

ers of the land on which the clay beds were located were involved in the manufacturing process, and, if they were not, to what extent they remained in control of the brickyards (clay beds and workshops) and of the distribution networks. The responses to these questions depend on the identification of the persons represented in brick and tile stamps, on the interpretation of their other components, and on the general assessment of the function of the stamps.

1. *Historical outline*

While fired tiles were already produced throughout Italy during the Republican period,[52] Roman bricks, down to the time of Vitruvius (ca. 15 B.C.), were usually sun dried. The change from sun dried to fired bricks must have occurred soon after that date and was probably connected with the building policy pursued by the Julio-Claudian emperors. Fired bricks are more resistant than sun dried bricks, as heat treatment (firing) provokes chemical and physical changes in the clay. In terms of production, fired bricks were more convenient than sun dried bricks, because they could be made year-around, faster, and on a larger scale. The shift from one technique to the other had the indirect consequence of providing modern historians with a mass of new documents in the form of brick and tile stamps, which yield some valuable information on the organization of the brick and tile industry.

The brick industry took off during the reign of Augustus, and was concentrated in the area around Rome. One of the earliest large brickyards located outside of Latium was the *figlinae Pansianae*, the production of which is attested in Northern Italy from ca. 43 B.C. until the Flavian period. The factory was at first privately owned, and later became imperial property.[53] The Roman brick industry peaked during the second century A.D., may have declined in the

---

[52] On the intensification of the building industry during the Republican period, cf. M.J. Strazzulla, "Le produzioni [terrecotte architettoniche] dal IV al I A.C.," *SRPS* II (1981) 187-207; S. Tortorella, "Le lastre Campana," *SRPS* II (1981) 219-35; and F. Coarelli's remark following M. Steinby's article "I senatori e l'industria laterizia urbana," *Tituli* 4 (1982) 227-37.

[53] *ILS* 8648a-h; etc. R. Matijasic, "Cronografia dei bolli laterizi della figlina Pansiana nelle regioni adriatiche," *MEFRA* 95 (1983) 961-95; G. Uggeri, *La romanizzazione dell'antico delta padano* (Ferrara 1975) 135-54; and M. Rostovtzeff, *SEHRE*² (1957) 611, n. 26.

third century, and shows signs of prosperity in the fourth century and beyond.[54]

2. *The structure of tile and brick stamps*

Most of the evidence about the organization of the brick and tile industry is provided by the artifacts themselves, in particular from the signatures stamped by the manufacturers on a certain percentage of their products.[55] Signatures are more common on tiles than on bricks, but the reason for this is unclear. During the first phase of the history of fired brick and tile production (from the first to the early third century) the internal structure of the stamps changed. First-century stamps are shorter, and therefore more elliptic, than second-century stamps. As the latter usually convey more information, they will be used here to determine the relationship between the persons mentioned on them.

The most elaborate tile and brick stamps contain, in various orders, five bits of information:

(a) the name of the owner of the land where the clay was collected (EX PR(aediis) DOMITIAE LVCILLAE);

(b) the name of the person in charge of the production (OP(us) DOL(iare) AELI ALEXANDRI, or EX OF(ficina) MYR(ini), or EX CONDVC(tione) PVBLICIAES QVINTIN(ae), or Q VOL-VSI BENEDICTI CONDVCTORIS);

(c) the name of the clay bed from which the clay originated, or of the brickyard in which the brick/tile was produced (EX FIG(linis) DOMIT(ianis) MINORIB(us), or DE LIC(inianis));

(d) a consular date (SQVILLA ET TITIANO COS); and

(e) the type of artifacts (TEG(u)L(a) SECIPEDALE (= sesqui-pedalis) DOLIARIS).

Not one single stamp presents all these elements together, but various combinations of some of them are attested.[56] Only the first three categories will be examined here.

---

[54] M. Steinby, "L'industria laterizia di Roma nel tardo-impero," in A. Giardina (ed.), *Società romana e impero tardo-antico* II (Roma/Bari 1986) 99-164 (hereafter *SRIT*).

[55] G. Brodribb, "Markings on Tile and Brick," in A. McWhirr (ed.), *Roman Brick and Tile: Studies in Manufacture, Distribution and Use in the Western Empire* (Oxford 1979) 211-21.

[56] *CIL* XV 40; 171; 277; 650a; 761; 2414; and *CIL* XI 6683.

a. *nomenclature*

It is obvious that two groups of people are represented in stamps. One group is composed of *domini* (landowners), i.e. the people who owned the estate from which the clay was extracted and upon which the brickyard was located. The other group includes the *officinatores* (entrepreneurs or workshop managers), i.e. the people who produced the bricks. The term *officinator* indifferently applies to a small potter working alone or with a few assistants, as well as to the director of one or several factories employing scores of workers. In order to understand the nature of the relationship between *dominus* and *officinator*, it is necessary to identify the individuals mentioned in either function in the stamps and to determine to which social group they belonged. Some of the characters recorded in brick stamps are known to us through other sources, but most of them, especially those who belonged to the category of *officinatores*, appear only in the stamps.

Roman nomenclature provides some clues about social status. Unfortunately, the identification of people appearing in the stamps is often hampered by the abbreviated form of their name, the reconstruction of which is rarely secure.[57] In addition, when the abbreviated names of several persons are juxtaposed, it is difficult to establish which letter refers to whom. Finally, it is not even clear whether any individual letter represents a *praenomen*, a *nomen gentilicium*, or a *cognomen*, since people were usually referred to by either one or several names (*duo* or *tria nomina*). No consistency was observed in the stamps in this regard. The association *nomen* + *cognomen* was used to designate not only one branch of a family, but also women, who bore no *praenomen*. Two-letter stamps could represent any combination of *praenomen* + *nomen* or *cognomen*, or *nomen* + *cognomen*. Four- or five-letter stamps could represent brothers.

Cognomina existed at an early date, but down to the first century A.D. they were not necessary;[58] from the second century A.D. onward, their absence was unusual. In the Imperial period, while only

---

[57] T.P. Wiseman, "Tile-stamps and Roman Nomenclature," in A. McWhirr (ed.), *Roman Brick and Tile* (Oxford 1979) 221-30, comparing abbreviated names on tile stamps with abbreviated names on coins (moneyers) and amphorae (cf. below); and I. Calabi Limentani, *Epigrafia Latina*⁴ (Milan 1991) 135-48.

[58] I. Calabi Limentani (1991) 137-38; and A.E. Gordon, "On the First Appearance of the *cognomen* in Latin Inscriptions of Freedmen," *Univ. of Calif. Publ. in Class. Philol.* (1935) 151-58 (around 106 B.C.).

freeborn and freedmen were referred to by *tria nomina*, a single name (usually a *cognomen*) could designate people of any social status. Freedmen usually adopted the *praenomen* and *nomen* of their former master and used their slave name as *cognomen*.

Slaves are usually referred to in connection with the name of their master in the genitive case. A. Oxé summarizes the development of slave nomenclature in the Republican and early Imperial periods as follows:

– names composed of the master's *praenomen* in the genitive case and the ending *-por* (from *puer*) are found only in the literary sources (for instance, "Lucipor" = **Form I**);

– in the earliest monumental inscriptions (250-100 B.C.), slaves are referred to by their personal name (*cognomen*, such as "Eros, Primus, Fidelis," etc.), followed by (a) the *nomen* of their master in the same case (used as an adjective, such as "Aurelius"); (b) the master's abbreviated *praenomen* (meant to be in the genitive case, "L(uci)"); and (c) the label of slavery (*s(ervus)*) (for instance, "Eros Aurelius L(uci) s(ervus)" = **Form II**);

– in the first century B.C. (from Sulla to the end of the Republic), the master's *nomen* lost its function of adjective and became a genitive agreeing with the *praenomen* that follows (for instance, "Eros Aureli L(uci) s(ervus)" = **Form III**);

– under Julius Caesar and Augustus, the master's *praenomen* and the label of slavery were dropped, and the slave was referred to by his personal name followed by his master's *nomen* in the genitive case (for instance, "Eros Aureli" = **Form IV**);

– during the Imperial period, one finds four variants of **Form IV**, with the the normal form featuring the slave's personal name followed by his master's *praenomen* and *nomen*, with or without the label of slavery (for instance, "Eros L(uci) Aureli (servus) *or* ser(vus)" = **Form V**); or

– the slave's personal name followed by his master's *tria nomina*, with or without the label of slavery (for instance, "Eros L. Aureli Cottae (servus) *or* ser(vus)" = **Form VI**); or

– the slave's personal name followed by his master's *cognomen*, without the label of slavery (for instance, "Eros Cottae" = **Form VII**); or

– the slave's personal name followed by his master's *nomen* and *cognomen*, without the label of slavery (for instance, "Eros Aureli Cottae" = **Form VIII**).[59]

---

[59] A. Oxé, "Zur älteren Nomenklatur der römischen Sklaven," *RhM* 59 (1904)

More important, Oxé tentatively mentions another type of slave nomenclature (**Form IX**), which he regards as post-Augustan and typical of stamped signatures. This form features the master's name (*nomen*, or *praenomen* + *nomen*, or *tria nomina*) in the genitive case followed by the slave's personal name, in the nominative or genitive case (for instance, "Aureli Ero(ti)s" or L(uci) Aureli Ero(ti)s" or "L(uci) Aureli Cottae Ero(ti)s" = **Form IX**).[60] Oxé admits that he could not find one single unquestionable instance of this pattern among early pottery stamps. He also warns that it cannot be excluded in the later period, for which he also cites evidence from monumental inscriptions.[61] As Oxé points out, this pattern was perhaps reserved for freedmen. Be that as it may, **Form IX** could be used to emphasize the relationship between *servus/libertus* and *dominus/patronus*, in order to advertise a relationship between agent and principal. In this case, the legal status of the agent had little relevance. This point will be discussed further on while dealing with the structure of the stamps on other clay artifacts. In conclusion, one should keep in mind that it is always difficult, not to say impossible, to determine the status of people on the basis of their name only, because the names of slaves and freedmen could be formed on the same pattern.

b. *dominus and officinator*

Brick stamps display various patterns. First-century stamps are shorter and less explicit than second-century stamps, because they usually contain only one name referring to some unknown character. It is uncertain whether single-name stamps represent (a) the owner of the land in which the clay bed, or brickyard, was located, or (b) the manufacturer of the brick (provided, of course, that they were not one and the same person). By contrast, second-century stamps contain a set of two names (therefore they are called binominal), one of which often refers to the higher stratum of Roman socie-

---

108-40. Cf. also J.-C. Dumont, "Le gentilice: nom de citoyen ou d'esclave?" *Ktèma* 6 (1981) 105-14.

[60] A. Oxé, *RhM* 59 (1904) 135-40.

[61] A. Oxé, *RhM* 59 (1904) 139-40, citing *CIL* II 2093 (Iliberris/Baetica, A.D. 26): "L. Valeri Laeti / (et) M. Valeri Vetusti / libertus Verna / (et) M. Valeri Vetusti / Prima Vernae ux(or) / v(otum) s(olverunt) l(aeti) m(erito) Saluti" etc.; *CIL* III 3141 (Apsoros Island/Dalmatia); and *CIL* XII 4068 (Near Nîmes/Narbonensis).

ty, i.e. the senatorial aristocracy or the imperial family. The names in the other group usually reflect a much lower social stratum and are thought to be similar, in many cases, to the names read on first-century stamps. The discrepancy in social status between the two groups has been interpreted in the past as evidence for increasing concentration of ownership and management of the brick industry akin to what was thought to have occurred in landownership, with the passage from small landholdings to *latifundia*, resulting, in the final stage, in an imperial monopoly. This thesis, defended by H. Dressel, H. Bloch, and others, has been questioned by T. Helen on the basis of his interpretation of some 9,000 stamps from Ostia, in addition to Roman stamps collected in *CIL* XV.[62]

As second-century stamps are binominal and therefore more explicit, it is necessary to consider first what information they can yield before inquiring whether the conclusions drawn from them shed some light on the interpretation of first-century stamps.

The first category of names, most often in the genitive case introduced by the expression "ex praediis" or "ex figlinis," refers to the owner of the land (*dominus/domina*) where the clay bed or brick-yard (*figlinae*) was located. Among the group studied by Helen, we find—excluding the emperors—150 persons in all, among whom there are 54 senators, 7 members of the equestrian order, 43 women, and, a noticeable exception, one imperial slave.[63]

---

[62] T. Helen, *Organization of Roman Brick Production in the First and Second Centuries A.D.* (Helsinki 1975) 13. The material used in the rest of this section has been published by J. Suolahti, M. Steinby, *et al.*, *Lateres Signati Ostienses* (Rome 1978), thereafter abbreviated *LSO*. Earlier publications of Roman brick stamps are by H. Dressel in *CIL* XV,1; H. Bloch, "The Roman Brick-stamps not Published in Volume XV, 1 of *CIL*," *HSPh* 56/57 (1947) 1-128 (= *S*); and M. Steinby, "Appendice a *CIL* XV,1," *BCAR* 86 (1978/79) 55-88. The *indices* to these collections have been published by H. Bloch, "Supplement to Volume XV,1 of *CIL* Including Complete Indices to the Roman Brick Stamps," *HSPh* 58/59 (1948) 1-104; and M. Steinby, *Indici complementari ai bolli doliari urbani (CIL XV,1)* (Rome 1987). H. Bloch, *I bolli laterizi e la storia edilizia romana* (Rome 1947) (= *BCAR* 64 [1936] 141-225; 65 [1937] 83-187; 66 [1938] 61-221) remains the basic study of brick stamps, supplemented by M. Steinby, "La cronologia delle *figlinae* doliari urbane dalla fine dell'età repubblicana fino all'inizio del III secolo," *BCAR* 84 (1974-1975) 7-132; and *eadem*, *PW* Suppl. 15 (1978) cols. 1489-1531, s.v. *Ziegelstempel von Rom und Umgebung*. An updated discussion of the brick industry by M. Steinby will be published in a forthcoming issue of *JRS*.

[63] T. Helen (1975) 22-23 and 94. The only *dominus* who can be surely identified as a slave is represented in stamps dated to 123, cf. *CIL* XV 810a-b (= *LSO* 678-679): DOL EX FIG ANTEROTIS CAES N SER / PAETINO ET APRO-

The second category of names, either in the nominative case followed by an expressed or implied "fecit" or "officinator," or in the genitive case introduced by the word "ex officina" or "opus doliare," represents 355 persons in all, including at least one member of the equestrian order,[64] 20 women, and a majority of freedmen and slaves.[65] It is remarkable that *officinatores* often remained attached to *figlinae* which were transferred from one *dominus* to the other.[66]

Helen considers the presence of women among *officinatores* as a sign that *officinatores* were usually free entrepreneurs—similar to *conductores* in agriculture, mining, or tax collection—rather than business managers physically involved in the production.[67] This assumption may be correct, but one ought to stress that it is nothing more than a *petitio principii* based on the biased idea that women were not to be entrusted with managerial responsibilities or physical labor. Women are well attested as potters, and Roman law explicitly allowed them to play the role of business managers.[68] An interesting, though isolated, piece of evidence concerning the physical involvement of young women in tile production in the Republican period may strengthen this point.[69] A bilingual inscription from

---

NIAN / COS. Anteros may have held the *figlinae* as part of his *peculium*. As no other name is mentioned in these stamps it might be that Anteros was both the holder of the land and the producer of the bricks. Cf. also P. Setälä, *Private domini in Roman Brick Stamps of the Empire* (Helsinki 1977) 59; *CIL* XV 1063 (discussed below); and *S* 537 (where the *dominus* is an *arcarius dispensatoris*, hence probably a slave). M. Steinby, *PW* Suppl. 15 (1978) cols. 1519-24, counts 181 private *domini*, including 47 women and 67 senators.

[64] *CIL* XV 526 (= *LSO* 463): OPVS DOL IVLI THEODOTI EQ R FIG / SAL EX P FL TITIANI C V. Cf. *PIR* IV², no. 599; and M. Steinby, *PW* Suppl. 15 (1978) col. 1517.

[65] T. Helen (1975) 23. M. Steinby, *PW* Suppl. 15 (1978) cols. 1516-19, counts 1325 names (1076 with *nomen*, and 249 with *cognomen* only).

[66] M. Steinby, *PW* Suppl. 15 (1978) col. 1519. *Figlinae* changed hands very often. For instance, the *figlinae Publilianae* were transferred five times between ca. 120 and 217; and the *figlinae Tonneianae* were owned by seven different *domini* from the time of Vespasian until ca. 150 (Steinby [1978] cols. 1520-21).

[67] T. Helen (1975) 112-13.

[68] Ulpianus (28 *ad ed.*) *Dig.* 14.3.7.1: "Parvi autem refert, quis sit institor, masculus an femina, liber an servus, proprius vel alienus." Cf. below in the section on terra sigillata.

[69] A. La Regina, "Rivista di epigrafia italica," *SE* 44 (1976) 284-88; M. Lejeune, *ibid.* 290-91; M.J. Strazzulla, "Le produzioni [terrecotte architettoniche] dal IV al I A.C.," *SRPS* II (1981) 187-207; J.-P. Morel, "Les producteurs de biens artisanaux en Italie à la fin de la République," in *Les bourgeoisies municipales italiennes aux IIe et Ier siècles av. J.-C.* (Paris/Naples 1983) 21-39, esp. 28, n. 52; and my paper

Pietrabbondante (Samnium), written on a tile by two different hands, displays two short texts, one in Oscan and the other in Latin:

a)   *HN SATTIIEIS DETFRI*
            SEGANATTED PLAVTAD

b)   HERENNEIS AMICA
            SIGNAVIT QANDO
            PONEBAMVS TEGILA.

The text, written before firing, is dated to the first decade of the first century B.C. and records the signatures of two female slaves, Amica and Detfri (or Deftri = the "kneader"), who belonged to one tile-maker named Herennius Sattius, a member of a *gens* well represented in Campania and Samnium during the Imperial period.[70] The size of two sets of footprints impressed on the tile suggests that the two girls were about 12 year old, which should be considered as a minimum age.[71] Well-documented nineteenth- and early-twentieth-century attitudes of adult Italians toward children and child labor lend some credence to the assumption that teenagers in Roman times engaged in hard work and were entrusted with positions of responsibility.[72] The jurist Gaius reports that it was frequent to appoint youngsters as store managers,[73] and there is no reason why it should be different with other types of managerial

---

"Workshop Managers," in W.V. Harris (ed.), *The Inscribed Economy* (1993) 180, nn. 63-64.

[70] Cf. *CIL* X 1272 (Nola); *CIL* X 5204 (Casinum); *CIL* IX 1588 (Beneventum); etc. Cf. *CIL* IX *indices.*

[71] Such evidence for age is rather fragile, as adults can also have very small feet. Because of the combination of two different sets of footprints of similar sizes on the tile from Pietrabbondante, the possibility that the two women were nevertheless grown-up is fairly remote. Footprints are also found on inscriptions exhibited at the entrance of the Church of San Silvestro in Rome, and in the archaeological museum at Ostia.

[72] A very young child entrusted with the technical aspect of film projection is the subject of the movie *Cinema Paradiso* (It., 1989), directed by G. Tornatore. In modern times, child labor was first regulated in Lombardo Veneto in 1843: the law prohibited the employment of children below age 9, and limited the duration of a workday to 10 hours for children from age 9 to 12, and to 12 hours for children from age 12 to 14. This law was rescinded in 1884, but new limitations were imposed by the government Giolitti (prohibition of night shifts, and imposition of shorter shifts); cf. R. Lill, *Geschichte Italiens in der Neuzeit*[4] (Darmstadt 1988) 147-48; 213; and 249.

[73] Gaius (9 *ad ed. prov.*) *Dig.* 14.3.8: "Nam et plerique pueros puellasque tabernis praeponunt."

units, such as workshops. The surprising fact that the two girls were
literate could indicate that they were more than mere handworkers;
they probably belonged to the clerical staff or were joint-managers
of the workshop.[74] This inscription does not prove that all women
officinatores were *institores*, but should warn us against the common
assumption that women could not be involved in industrial activities
in Roman Italy.

A similar document sheds light on the internal structure of a tile
factory in Southern Italy. An inscribed tile was found on a tomb at
Pellaro near Reggio Calabria. The archaeological context is somewhat confused, but clearly sets a *terminus post quem* in the second century B.C.[75] The Greek text, composed of four parts, was written
before firing. The main text records, in large letters, one Cleme(n)s,
slave of one Alfius Primio. Three secondary inscriptions, in smaller
letters, may be due to the hand of one of the potters employed in
the workshop. The writer identifies himself as Anthus Reginus, or
Anthus of Reggio, and addresses some derogatory comments to a
few other characters named Hermeros, Soterichus, and Primigenius
(?), whom he calls "bald," "effeminate," "pseudo-potter," or
"bad investment."[76] The editors propose an ingenious interpretation of Αἰσωπιτάνα κεραμίς, which they read as the tile that lives
near Aesop, hence a speaking tile. An alternative, simpler solution
would be to consider Aesopitana as a female potter, a κεραμίς being
to a κεραμεύς what a βασιλίς was to a βασιλεύς. To sum up,
Cleme(n)s could have been the slave manager of a tile factory belonging to Alfius Primio. The staff was composed of male and female
slaves, with the addition of at least one outsider (Anthus), who was

[74] W.V. Harris, *Ancient Literacy* (Cambridge, MA 1989) 197-206, esp. 199:
"Italy had a corps of literate slaves who supervised the work of others." Harris does
not refer to the inscription from Pietrabbondante, but to the scratchings made in
the channel of an aqueduct near Tarentum by the foreman (?) of a work crew to
record the names of workers present on certain days. This interpretation fits well
with the evidence from agricultural writers (Harris 256).
[75] E. Lattanzi–M. Letizia Lazzarini–F. Mosino, "La tegola di Pellaro (Reggio Calabria)," *PP* 44 (1989) 286-310, esp. 286-94 mention the nearby find of an
early circular kiln and of bronze coins of Augustus, and the presence of amphora
sherds (III/II B.C.) and coins from the mint of Reggio (perhaps II B.C.) next to
the skeleton of the deceased person.
[76] The text reads: (a) ΚΛΗΜΗΣ ᾿ΑΛΦΙΟΥ | ΠΡΙΜΙΩΝΟΣ ΔΟΥΛΟΣ. (b) Ἄνθου
{ΡΗ} Ῥηγείνου χείρ· κεραμεὺς Ἑρμέρως Φάλακρε χαῖρε, Σωτήριχε κίναιδε, ψευ-
δοκαμινάρι Πριμογένη μάλημπτε· Αἰσωπιτάνα κεραμίς. (c) Πριμιγένη ΩΘΙΤΑ (?) τῷ
μαλήνπτῳ ΚΑΤΤΑΓ (?) γάρ ἐστι. (d) Πριμο.

far from enthusiastic about his fellow workers. One of them (Primigenius) was possibly a specialist in charge of operating the kiln (κάμινος). Such was the possible life and organization of a workshop in the first century B.C., representing a local industry which became famous enough to be mentioned one century later by Pliny the Elder.[77]

To return to the organization of the Roman brick industry, Helen shows that only 17.2 % of all *officinatores* seem to have been dependent (freedmen or slaves) of the *dominus/-a* mentioned in the same stamps. While these dependent *officinatores* are very likely to have been agents of the *dominus*, it does not imply that all other *officinatores* (more than 80 %) were contractors.[78] In the two groups, only 19 % of all names are *cognomina* alone, which indicates, according to Helen, that less than 19 % of the people mentioned in brick stamps were slaves, because some of these isolated *cognomina* undoubtedly refer to freeborn, even senatorial persons.[79] This assumption is unwarranted, since, as suggested above and in the following sections, what is usually regarded as *tria nomina* signatures can in some cases be read as the combination of a *praenomen* + *nomen* in the genitive case (sometimes abbreviated) representing the principal or at least the owner of the slave whose *cognomen*—in the nominative or the genitive case—had been misidentified as the third part of the name (= Oxé, **Form IX**). Stamps of the Republican and early Imperial periods often bear a signature composed of *duo nomina* (*praenomen* and *nomen* in the genitive case) with a consular date.[80] They undoubtedly refer to the owner of the brickyard. By the time of Augustus, the stamps became more and more binominal, *officinator* and *dominus* being referred to by one, two, or three names in the genitive case.[81] In a

---

[77] Pliny, *HN* 35.165. Cf. E. Lattanzi *et al.*, *PP* 44 (1989) 306-08, favor a date in the late first century B.C. or early first century A.D. on the basis of the Romanized context (Latin names and words, for instance, *malemptus*) and the absence of *praenomen* for Alfius Primio, a phenomenon which became common only in the second century A.D. They also suggest that Alfius Primio owned a villa in the vicinity, but this remains a mere hypothesis. In this case, Clemens could have been a *vilicus*; cf. R. Gordon, *JRS* 83 (1993) 152, n. 350.

[78] T. Helen (1975) 103-09; and 130, mentioning only *locatio conductio* and *usus fructus*, cf. Paulus (15 *ad Plaut.*) *Dig.* 8.3.6. *Officinatores* who were not dependents of the *dominus* could nevertheless be appointed business managers (cf. Chapter Two).

[79] T. Helen (1975) 23-24.

[80] *ILLRP* 1151-1170 (= *CIL* XI 6673, nos. 1-6, 11, and 21 = *ILS* 8646a-h).

[81] For instance, the products of the *figlinae* owned by C. Asinius Pollio (cos. A.D. 23) are signed by various *officinatores*, all of free status, cf. *CIL* XV 2231-2234

later period, the uncertainty about the order in which the names should be read is increased by the circular form of brick stamps.[82] For instance, the stamp C CALPETAN / CRESCENTIS is extant on a variety of products (*dolium, pelvis*, brick). It is uncertain whether we are dealing with one person, C. Calpetanus Crescens, or with two persons, i.e. a slave/freedman named Crescens working for one C. Calpetanus.[83] An *officinator* with the same name is attested in other stamps as CRESCEN / C CALPETA / LIVIANI and as CRESCENTIS / C CALP FAVORIS.[84] The name Crescens is too common to permit any safe conclusion, and it is not sure whether the first Crescens was the same person as the slave of C. Calpetanus Livianus at Pompeii before 79, or of C. Calpetanus Favor in Rome in the early second century A.D. Further, Crescens may have been manumitted at some point and thereafter was known as C. Calpetanus Crescens. It is also possible that Crescens started as *officinator* and ultimately became *dominus*.

Slave *officinatores* are sometimes identified in the stamps by an indication of status and/or by an unmistakable reference to their owners.[85] Dionysius was a slave of Domitia Lucilla, and advertised his status on the bricks he made in a brickyard located on an estate belonging to his *domina*.[86] In his capacity of *officinator*, Dionysius was perhaps an *institor* or a *servus cum peculio* who remained active during more than a decade (123-134). It is worth noticing that he was not the only *officinator* employed in the brickyard located on the property of Domitia Lucilla, which means that brickyards (*figlinae*) were certainly divided into workshops (*officinae*). Other slaves, freedmen, and freeborn employed by Domitia Lucilla may have been actively involved in brick production at the same time as Dionysius, but they

---

(= *ILS* 8649a-d): (a). . . ASIN POLL; (b) TEG(ula) C COSCONI / (ex) FIG(linis) ASIN POLL; (c) N DECEITI / TEG(u)LA / (ex) FIG(linis) ASIN POLL; and (d) Q LEPIDI HILARI / (ex) F(iglinis) AS POL.

[82] T. Helen (1975) 31-35.

[83] *CIL* XV 901; *S* 243; and *S* 273.

[84] *CIL* X 8048, no. 3 (on a *pelvis* from Pompeii = *S* 475); *CIL* XV 2422 (*pelvis* and amphora from Rome). T. Helen (1975) 28; 30; and 141, where it is suggested that there are two or three persons of the same name in the stamps, which is quite possible.

[85] According to T. Helen (1975) 35, n. 3, this is especially true in early stamps.

[86] *CIL* XV 1020 (= *LSO* 788): OP DOL EX PR DOM LVC DIONYS LVC / PAETIN ET APRO COS (A.D. 123); and *CIL* XV 1030a (= *LSO* 796): EX FIG DOM LVC O D DION DOM LV SE / SERVIANO III ET VARO COS (A.D. 134).

were probably working in different workshops or even in different brickyards.[87]

In some cases, the master of the slave *officinator* was obviously different from the owner of the brickyard (*figlinae*). For instance, Mercurius was the slave of Tib. Claudius Quinquatralis, and signed the bricks produced on the estate of Lucilla Veri, probably between 145 and 155.[88] Mercurius was probably a *mercennarius* (in the sense of a slave rented out by his master) employed as manager of the *officina* by Lucilla Veri. Tib. Claudius Quinquatralis had other slaves signing bricks in the position of *officinatores*; one was named Epagathus.[89] In addition, we know that Tib. Claudius Quinquatralis was himself an *officinator* of the same *domina*, from the time she called herself Domitia Lucilla (before 145)[90] almost until her death after 155.[91] If Mercurius, Epagathus, and the other slaves were workshop managers, they could have been appointed either by the *domina* or by Tib. Claudius Quinquatralis. In the latter case, the slaves were either the agents or the subagents of Tib. Claudius Quinquatralis, depending on his legal relationship with the *domina* (independent contractor or business manager).

As Helen points out, *domini* and *officinatores* formed two mutually exclusive groups, in the sense that *officinatores* rarely became *domini*.[92] The nature of the relationship between the two groups is difficult to establish. Were *officinatores* agents of the *domini* of the land where the *figlinae* were located, or were they lessees of the brick-

---

[87] *LSO* 778-833. Cf. also M. Steinby, *PW* Suppl. 15 (1978) cols. 1498-1500, who remarks that decorative seals (*signa*), which tend to supersede the stamps in the early third century, remained with the *figlinae/officinae* and were not kept either by the *dominus* or by the *officinator*. One can consider that they were part of the workshop equipment (*instrumentum*). Cf. Chapter Two.

[88] *CIL* XV 1077a and 1078 (= *LSO* 836-837).

[89] *CIL* XV 1073-1076 (= *LSO* 833-835).

[90] *CIL* XV 1069a and b (= *LSO* 827-828); and *CIL* XV 1071b (= *LSO* 831).

[91] *CIL* XV 1072 (= *LSO* 832), unless AB CL QVIN should be read AB(ascantus) CL(audi) QVIN(ti). The use of the preposition *ab* is common.

[92] T. Helen (1975) 91. The same author cites (p. 131) as a noticeable exception one Vismatius Successus, who was known as *officinator* of the *figlinae Tempesinae* owned by Calpurnia Secunda (M. Steinby, *MAL* 17 [1974] 98, no. 4) before becoming the owner of the brickyard (*CIL* XV 1518-1526); cf. P. Setälä (1977) 202-03. Other cases are mentioned by Helen, who rightly points out that the names might refer to homonymous people; cf. P. Setälä (1977) 50; and 140-41. Cf. also M. Steinby, *PW* Suppl. 15 (1978) col. 1513, who reports that one C. Satrinius was the *officinator* of the *figlinae Marcianae* in the first century A.D., and that a stamp (*S* 372) identifies one C. Satrinius Priscus as *dominus* of unspecified *figlinae*.

.

yards, including clay beds and workshops? In spite of the fact that some families of *officinatores* were involved in the brick industry for generations—the C. Calpetani are attested "in unbroken series" from the early first century A.D. to the beginning of the third century[93]—there is little evidence that *officinae* were owned by *officinatores*. As a result of long-term undisturbed possession, they might have owned the facilities (building(s) and/or the kiln), while renting the clay beds or contracting for some work to be done.[94]

In some cases, there is no doubt that *officinatores* were appointed business managers. The slave Earinus, who signed bricks and tiles in his capacity of *actor* of Lucilla Veri,[95] appears on other stamps as an agent of Domitia Lucilla or working in the brickyard owned by his mistress (Domitia P.f. Lucilla Minor, known both as Domitia Lucilla and Lucilla Veri).[96] One should perhaps also count as *actor* one Glyptus who signed his products EX FIG Q CASS CAECIL SALAR / AGIT GLYPT CALP.[97] A more puzzling instance is provided by the stamps of Primus, slave *p(rae)p(ositus)* (?) of C. Nunnidius Fortunatus, an *officinator* otherwise well-known at Ostia.[98] Although the abbreviation PP for *praepositus* is well attested in Latin inscriptions,[99] the stamp would be unique in specifying the nature

---

[93] T. Helen (1975) 125.

[94] On the protection of the right of the *superficiarius* through the grant of *interdicta*, cf. Ulpianus (70 *ad ed.*) *Dig.* 43.18.1.1 and Paulus (44 *ad ed.*) *Dig.* 39.2.18.4. Cf. M. Kaser, *Das römische Privatrecht* I² (Munich 1971) 456.

[95] *CIL* XV 1049 (= *LSO* 808); and *CIL* X 8046, no. 5 (on a tile found in Sardinia); cf. also *CIL* XV 1050 (= *LSO* 809). Other *actores* are mentioned (a) on a tile found in Astutum/Sicily (*CIL* X 8045, no. 12): CEL NIGR MAIO / L MINICI NATALI[s] EULALVS ACTOR EI[us]; the principal lived under Trajan and had links with Africa (cf. *CIL* VIII 2478); and (b) on a tile from Rome made by one Soterichus in the *figlinae Brutianae*, owned by T. Statilius Maximus, after 123 (*AE* 1984, no. 56): BRVTIAN(a tegula) / SOTERICHI / T STAT MAX / ACT(or). For other cases where the *officinator* was the slave of the *dominus*, cf. *CIL* XV 198 (= *S* 48 and 280); and *AE* 1911, no. 196 (= *CIL* XIV 5308, no. 27, Ostia): BASSVS L IVLI HERM / OFFICINATOR.

[96] *CIL* XV 1047-1048 (= *LSO* 806-807). Cf. P. Setälä (1977) 107-08. Domitia P.f. Lucilla Minor used the name Lucilla Veri between 145 and 155. The identification of Earinus's *domina* remains uncertain, because it is also possible that Domitia Lucilla in *CIL* XV 1048 was Domitia Cn.f. Lucilla Maior, the mother of Domitia Lucilla Minor, and that Earinus served both successively.

[97] *CIL* XV 517. Cf. M. Steinby, *PW* Suppl. 15 (1978) col. 1501.

[98] *CIL* XV 862 (= *LSO* 712): C NVNN FORT PRIM / PP. Cf. T. Helen (1975) 123-24; and 137, n. 89, with reference to H. Thylander, *Inscriptions du port d'Ostie* (Lund 1952) A 74.

[99] The abbreviation *pp* for *praepositus* is warranted by a series of three inscriptions from Rome recording *praepositi cellariorum*: *CIL* VI 8745 ("Aur. Germanicus

of the appointment. In addition, part of the text may be missing. In any case, even though Primus is likely to have been an *institor*, we do not know who was the owner of the land where the brickyard was located: C. Nunnidius Fortunatus is a likely candidate. Finally, a few stamps record that the brick/tile was made "sub cura alicuius," which possibly refers to the activity of a *curator*, or of a business manager, such as a *vilicus*.[100]

There are other cases where the relationship between landowner and entrepreneur was undoubtedly contractual. In one stamp, the last part of the first line refers to a *conductor* (Cethes(?)) to whom an *officinator* (Trophimas) was subordinated. Trophimas may have been the business manager of Cethes(?), but the relationship between *dominus* (the emperor) and *conductor* (Cethes(?)) was defined by the law of hire and lease.[101] *Conductores* are mentioned in a few other stamps.[102] In the *Tabula Veleiensis* (Trajanic), the "fundus Iulianus" is pledged "cum figlinis et colonis VIIII." The text does not say, however, that each of the nine tenants attached to the estate was in charge of one unit of production, and the type of management of the brickyard remains unknown.[103]

Aug. lib. p.p. cellaris"); *CIL* VI 8746 ("T. Aelius Aug. lib. M[?] praepositus cellario[rum]"); and *CIL* VI 8747 ("Trophimus Aug. lib. p.p. c.l""). Cf. also *ILS* V, p. 782.

[100] *CIL* XV 363; and 1434-1438 (Hadrianic). Cf. M. Steinby, *PW* Suppl. 15 (1978) col. 1501. For *curatores* supervising the production of stamped material, compare with *fistula* stamps, cf. C. Bruun, *The Water Supply of Ancient Rome. A Study of Roman Imperial Administration* (Helsinki 1991). "Sub cura vilici" is used with regard to the management of an agricultural estate by Scaevola (17 *dig.*) *Dig.* 32.35.1. One *officinator* of the *figlinae Sulpicianae*, who was identified as a member of the *gens Villia*, could in fact be a *vilicus*; cf. *CIL* XV 560 (A.D. 123): APR ET PAE COS / EX F A V ALEX S; *CIL* XV 561: VILLI ALEXANDRI / SVLPICES; *CIL* XV 562 (A.D. 134): SERVIANO III COS / EX F VIL AVG SVLPIC; *CIL* XV 593 (Hadrianic): C VILLI CRES SVL; and *S.* 18 (A.D. 134): BRVTIAN EX FIG / T S SEVERI EX PR / NON IVL SER / VIL VLP P.

[101] *CIL* XV 390: DE F CAES N PAG STEL DE CON CETHES / EX OFIC TROPHIMATIS. Cf. T. Helen (1975) 92.

[102] *CIL* XV 545 (= *LSO* 477-480): EX FIGILINI CAESARI CON MARCI<O> / FYRMI SUBORTANI. In a later period, Marcius Fyrmus took over the production on the estate of Titia Quartilla (*CIL* XV 1478), for whom another *conductor*, Domitius Ision, worked in the same year (123) (*CIL* XV 1477); cf. P. Setälä (1977) 192-93. Cf. also *CIL* XV 542; 643: DE FIG PEDANIES QVINTILLAE CONDV / C LABERIVS ZOSIMV; 761 (= *ILS* 8663): OPVS DOLIARE EX PRAEDIS D N EX C/ONDVC PVBLICIAES QVINTIN; *CIL* XI 6683 (= 8106 = *ILS* 8666, Viterbum): EX PREDIS L AELI VERI FIGLIN/AS MARTINIANAS Q / VOLVSI BENE/DICTI CONDV/CTORIS; and T. Helen (1975) 97; and 132, n. 2.

[103] *CIL* XI 1147 (col. II.89). *Contra*, F. Mayet, "Les *figlinae* dans les marques

Officinatores may have been independent from *domini*, because quite a few *officinatores* are attested in stamps of more than one *dominus*.[104] It can be argued, however, that these *officinatores* were transferred from one brickyard to the other, or that they were active as managers of several workshops at the same time. The flexibility of the job market, combined with the chances of transfer of property, should account for most of these movements.

M. Steinby points out that the stamps were no labels of quality, and suggests that they contained an abridged version of the contract binding *officinatores* and *domini*: the legal relationship between the two parties would have been based on a contract of work (*locatio conductio operis faciendi*), as the reference to *opus doliare* (or *opus figlinum*) suggests. Accordingly, the stamps list the names of the parties, the object of the contract (*opus*), and the place where the work was supposed to be carried out (*figlinae*).[105] This ingenious interpretation of the stamps, however, meets two difficulties. First, one necessary element of the contract, i.e. the monetary compensation (*merces*) agreed upon by the parties, is always missing from the stamps.[106] Second, the contract of work has the *locator* (= *dominus*) placing out a job to be done, namely the production of building material, supplying the *conductor/redemptor* (= *officinator*) with the basic raw material (clay, perhaps also water and firewood), and paying the *merces* to the entrepreneur. The finished products belonged to the *dominus*, and this explains why the products of several *figlinae* owned by the same *dominus* are regularly found together as part of the same building.[107] It seems, however, that it was common in the brick and tile industry for the *dominus* to also own the means of production,

---

d'amphores Dressel 20 de Bétique," *REA* 88 (1986) 285-305, esp. 287-88, who claims that "il est évident que le *fundus Iulianus* comprenait des glaisières, puisque l'on y a créé neuf *figlinae* avec des colons, c'est-à-dire neuf établissements de production."

[104] T. Helen (1975) 116-18; and 139-50.

[105] M. Steinby, "I senatori e l'industria laterizia urbana," *Tituli* 4 (1982) 227-37, esp. 232-33: "Vi sono tutte le componenti essenziali del contratto fra *locator* e *conductor*...I bolli si possono quindi leggere come una versione abbreviata del contratto;" *eadem*, *SRIT* II (1986) 100; 106-07; and 149-50.

[106] Gai., *Inst.* 3.142: "Locatio autem et conductio similibus regulis constituitur; nisi enim merces certa statuta sit, non videtur locatio et conductio contrahi." Iavolenus (11 *epist.*) *Dig.* 19.2.51.1: "Locavi opus faciendum ita, ut pro opere redemptori certam mercedem in dies singulos darem." Cf. M. Kaser, *RP* I[2] (1971) 571, n. 87.

[107] M. Steinby, *PW* Suppl. 15 (1978) col. 1513.

i.e. the brickyard, composed of drying sheds, kilns, and temporary storage space. This is illustrated by the phrase EX FIG + name in the genitive case, provided that the term *figlinae* represents more than the clay bed. Thus, the contract between *dominus* and *officinator* resembles a labor contract (*locatio conductio operarum*), whereby the *officinator* provided no more than his technical and managerial skills. The difference between labor contract and contract of work depended on the degree of control that the *dominus* wanted to exercise over the manufacturing process, and how much interest he had in the good management of the brickyard.[108] It should be noted, however, that a labor contract was excluded when the *officinator* was called a *conductor* in the stamps (cf. above), because, in labor contracts, the *conductor* is the party who hires the services (*operas*) of.the *officinator* (= *locator*). One could also argue that the contract between *dominus* and *officinator* was a *locatio conductio rei*, the object of the contract being the *figlinae*, i.e. the brickyard including the means of production and the clay beds. In that case, the finished products belonged to the *officinator*, and the *dominus* had no interest and no say in the management of the brickyard. In conclusion, if the stamps indeed reflect a contract of work, as Steinby suggests, the *officinator* should be seen as providing the means of production, which he either owned or leased from the *dominus* under a separate contract. Alternatively, ownership of the finished products by the *dominus* may point toward direct management, the *officinator* being appointed to the management of the brickyard, either as a dependent or as an employee of the *dominus*. Some practical examples will be examined in the section on amphorae.

According to Steinby, brick and tile stamps were meant to permit a comparison between the levels of production of several *officinae* operating side-by-side. The consular date and the name of the *officinator* would have enabled the *dominus* to ascertain the yearly production achieved in each workshop. We know that a single worker was able to produce more than 220 tiles a day. This quantity must have represented the minimum daily requirement at a tilery near Siscia (Upper Pannonia). A team of four brickmakers, who perhaps worked in the same managerial unit (hence the sum of the total production at the end of the account), recorded their daily production on a

---

[108] B. Nicholas, *An Introduction to Roman Law* (Oxford 1962) 183.

tile.[109] On one particular day, all workers produced the same number of tiles, but such homogeneity in productivity was not always achieved. In another similar document, two workers out of four failed to meet the assigned quota.[110] While Artemas is recorded as missing 21 tiles to achieve the minimum requirement (MIN XXI), Iustinus produced only 137 tiles. The lack of any explicit account for his shortcoming suggests that he may have been working part-time. In any case, considering the quantity of bricks or tiles produced by a workshop of similar size, it is difficult to see how the stamps, which do not appear on all products, would have facilitated the yearly accounting.

The suggestion that the stamps served a legal purpose can be pressed further. Not only *domini*, but also consumers had an interest in keeping track of the origin of the production, especially if the manufacturer/supplier was a dependent of the landowner. The practice of stamping could have been imposed, in an indirect way, of course, on the manufacturer by the customer with the idea that sloppy quality of the product would entail a civil suit (*actio empti*, *institoria*, etc.) to be brought against the *officinator*, if he was an independent entrepreneur or a contractual business manager, or against the landowner if he was the principal of the *officinator*. The identification on the product of the people responsible for its quality was an important guarantee. It does not preclude us from considering the practice of stamping tiles and bricks as reflecting a bilateral arrangement between *dominus* and *officinator*, whereby the *dominus* would have been compelled to accept civil liability for the quality of the product and for the fulfillment of any contract concluded between the *officinator* and a third contracting party, while retaining control over the production and its proceeds. Landowners, manufacturers, and consumers were all likely to benefit from such an arrangement.

---

[109] *CIL* III 11381 (= *ILS* 8675a): KAL IVLIS / SEVERVS CCXX, / FORTIS CCXX, / CANDIDVS CCXX / FELICIO CCXX, / IN VNO DCCCLXXX. The unit of production was called *navale* (*CIL* III 11382 = *ILS* 8675c), and was perhaps overseen by a military *optio navaliorum* (*CIL* XIII 6714, Moguntiacum, A.D. 185 = *ILS* 2435). The Pannonian evidence discussed here shows that the members of the team changed over time, and that a team could be split between two units of production, cf. *CIL* III 11382: III KAL AVGVSTAS / SEVERVS ET CANDIDVS / IN HOC NAVALI / CCCLXXX / ARTEMAS ET EVLYME/ NVS IN ALIO NAVALI / CCCLXXX.

[110] *CIL* III 11385 (= *ILS* 8675b): XIII K OCT / FORTIS CCXXII, / CANDIDVS CCXXV, / IVSTINVS CXXXVII, / ARTEMAS CLXXXXVIIII, / MIN XXI. Cf. also R. Frei-Stolba, *AS* 3 (1980) 103-05, esp. nn. 9-12.

It is clear from the evidence discussed above that it is impossible to select one mode of production as more common than the other. *Officinatores* were at times tenants, contractors, usufructuary, or business managers. Nothing compelled the *domini* to stick to one system of management, as J. Andreau remarks:

> la facilité avec laquelle un propriétaire pouvait passer de l'exploitation directe (médiatisée par la présence de *vilici*) au fermage, ou du fermage à l'exploitation directe, aide à comprendre pourquoi les textes et les inscriptions (qu'il s'agisse de terres, de commerce ou de fabrication de briques et tuiles) s'abstiennent de définir les divers rôles en présence... Et les marques de briques de la région romaine sont rédigées de telle sorte qu'il est possible de les interpréter, soit en termes de fermage et de rente foncière, soit en termes d'entreprises directes et de profits industriels.[111]

Even though the nature of the extant evidence does not provide a clear picture of the organization of the Roman brick industry, it is worth noticing that the variety of patterns of production proposed by Andreau is well documented in fifteenth-century England. Then, brickyards were either permanent, semi-permanent, or temporary, privately or publicly owned, and operated by corporations that sometimes owned the kiln but not the brickyard. Various types of management are attested.[112] In Hull in 1422-1423, one John Drinkdale was employed, perhaps on a contractual basis, by a public corporation that operated the municipal brickyard. Drinkdale is known to have been assisted by other employees (*servientes sui*). Firing was, however, entrusted to an independent worker, Willelmo Scotter ("pro combustione dictatum ustrinarum in grosso liiis. iiid"). Scotter unfortunatly spoiled a batch and was replaced by one Robert Puttock, a more experienced brickmaker, who ultimately

---

[111] J. Andreau, "Les financiers romains entre la ville et la campagne," in *L'origine des richesses dépensées* (Aix-en-Provence 1985) 177-96, esp. 186; cf. also *idem*, *Annales (ESC)* 37 (1982) 923-25, esp. 924: "Les relations économiques entre le propriétaire et le 'deuxième homme' ont certainement emprunté plusieurs formes, et non pas une seule, comme le croit Helen, et comme l'ont cru presque tous les spécialistes d'épigraphie doliaire." A similar view is adopted by J.P. Bodel, *Roman Brick Stamps in the Kelsey Museum* (Ann Arbor 1983) 3-4. In a personal letter, Prof. Bodel remarks that "the stamps must have served a specific purpose for whomever they were intended. Rather, it [= the ability of the *dominus* to switch from one system to the other] explains why so many diverse modern models can fit most of the evidence, and why none fits all of it."

[112] T.P. Smith, *The Medieval Brickmaking Industry in England, 1400-1450* (London 1985), esp. chapter 8, pp. 60-70 ("Organization of the industry, 1400-1450").

took over the entire operation of the brickyard, with the assistance of Drinkdale.[113] A mixed system is also attested in tilemaking in a manorial context. Some court rolls (*compoti*) record the yearly rents paid in cash and in kind by lessees (5-12 year contracts) to the bailiff in charge of the manorial tile kiln of Moulsham (Chelmsford, Essex), owned by Westminster Abbey and active since 1373 (until the 16th century). From 1427 on, the bailiff's accounts always list the same entry with the name of "John Scheryng," which suggests that the tilery was operated by the agents of one family.[114]

c. *figlinae and officinae*

One of the most important contributions made by Helen bears on the meaning of *figlinae*.[115] Helen notes that the word *figlinae* (or *praedia* in the second century) is often accompanied by an adjective, for instance *figlinae Marcianae* or *Domitianae*. The same adjectives can be found qualifying other words, such as *opus (doliare)* or *tegula*. Such combinations (noun + adjective) allow identification of the geographical origin of the clay, an important factor in establishing the quality of the product. Thus, the name of the *figlinae* would have served as "quality mark," whereas the names of the *dominus* and *officinator* would have served as "trademark." Both terms are admittedly inadequate in a Roman context, because the products of the same *figlinae* could be, and are known to have been, of varying qualities, and because the authenticity of craftsmanship was not protected by law.[116] Quality marks do not provide any information *ipso facto* concerning the owner, unless a name in the genitive form is appended to it, which is not attested before the second century A.D. Thus, the *figlinae Caepionianae*, which were located on the left bank of the Tiber near Orte, are known to have been owned first by Plotia Isaurica, C. Curiatius Cosanus, and perhaps Arria Fadilla, then by the last two mentioned and Ti. Tutinius Sentius Satrinus, and final-

---

[113] T.P. Smith (1985) 63, based on F.W. Brooks, "A Medieval Brick-Yard at Hull," *JBAA* (3rd series) 4 (1939) 151-74.

[114] P.J. Drury, "The Production of Brick and Tile in Medieval England," in D.W. Crossley (ed.), *Medieval Industry* (London 1981) 126-42. Cf. also J. Stopford, "The Organization of the Medieval Tile Industry," *Oxford Journal of Archaeology* 11 (1992) 341-63, illustrating the various models proposed by D.P.S. Peacock (1982).

[115] T. Helen (1975) 33-88.

[116] The scope of the Roman law of forgery did not include trademarks, cf. F. Marino, "Appunti sulla falsificazione del marchio nel diritto romano," *ZRG* 105 (1988) 771-75.

ly by the son (the future Antoninus Pius) and the daughter of Arria Fadilla.[117] Although it would be normal to think of a partnership,[118] this evidence may also suggest that the *figlinae* were owned *pro parte* by the owners of adjacent estates. This can be verified through the study of the chemical and mineralogical composition of the clay by a method using wavelength-dispersive X-ray fluorescence. The conclusions from a study of the material found in the Villa of the Quintilii (Via Appia, Antonine period) indicate that the products of the same *figlinae* stamped by different *domini* have the same chemical composition.[119]

On the other hand, a single *dominus/domina* may have owned more than one clay bed/brickyard at the same time: between 115 and 141 Flavia Seia Isaurica owned the *figlinae Aristianae, Fabianae, Caelianae, Publilianae, Tonneianae* and *Tur*(?),[120] which were located on separate estates. Consequently, Helen concludes that the word *figlinae* does not represent a unit of production, but a clay district, by contrast with *officina* which represents the actual unit of production.[121]

---

[117] *S.* 239 (and pp. 13-16). Cf. M. Steinby, *BCAR* 84 (1974-1975) 30-33; T. Helen (1975) 76-82, following H. Bloch; and P. Setälä (1977) 62-64; and 260. M. Steinby drew my attention to the fact that Arria Fadilla took over from Plotia Isaurica, and that the *figlinae Caepionianae* had only two owners.

[118] Partnerships, either of *domini* or of *officinatores*, are well attested, cf. T. Helen (1975) 113-15, with reference to *CIL* XV 88-89; 205; 363; 367; 370; 626; 1079; 1147; 2174; *S* 33; and 69 (= 286). In the case of *societates* of *officinatores*, the partners were often members of the same household, sometimes married couples or fellow slaves. The *officinator* could also be a slave jointly owned by two or more people who were not partners, cf. A. di Porto (1984).

[119] G. Olcese, "Archeologia e archeometria dei laterizi bollati urbani: primi risultati e prospettive di ricerca," in W.V. Harris (ed.), *The Inscribed Economy* (1993) 121-28, comparing the products of the *figlinae Domitianae* (*minores* and *maiores*) and those signed by the Domitii.

[120] T. Helen (1975) 57, with reference to *CIL* XV 11-12; 207-210; 421; 651; and 674. Cf. P. Setälä (1977) 119-21, with additional references.

[121] T. Helen (1975) 75 acknowledges the difficulty to fit such stamps as *CIL* XV 1063 in his theory: OP DOL EX P DOM LVC EX / FIG QVARTIONIS where Quartio, who is evidently a slave of Domitia Lucilla (cf. *CIL* XV 1064 = *LSO* 821: EX FIGLINIS LVCILLAES / QVARTIONIS; and M. Steinby, *MAL* 17 [1974] 101, no. 9: QVARTIONI OPVS FIG / EX PR DOM LV), seems to have "owned" the *figlinae*. Unless Quartio was granted at one point the possession of the *figlinae* as part of his *peculium*, one should accept Helen's suggestion that we are dealing with a maker's mistake or that *figlinae* "gradually assumed the meaning of *officina*;" cf. also F. Mayet, *REA* 88 (1986) 285-305. Helen (*op. cit.* 37) mistakenly states that the word *figlina(e)* is found only in brick stamps, and never on other clay artifacts. In fact, the word is also used in amphora stamps (cf. below, Callender's categories 6, 7, and 9 and Mayet). According to Dressel (*CIL* XV, p. 4), *figlinae*

The word *figlinae* is commonly used in the plural to designate one clay district and could include several *officinae*, in the same way as an estate could be composed of several *fundi*. Perhaps as a result of the reform of the imperial sector of the brick industry by the emperor Aurelian (270-275), the terminology changed in the late third and early fourth centuries. *Figlinae* were called *officinae*, while earlier *officinae* became *stationes*.[122] The new *officinae* were directed by a *magister*,[123] which lead M. Steinby to suggest that second-century-A.D. *figlinae* were more than clay districts, and should be considered as an administrative unit directed by the *officinator*.[124]

F. Mayet, however, suggests that a single *officina* could be attached to more than one brickyard.[125] As this author provides no evidence to support her statement, we have to guess that she probably means that the same *officinatores*—or at least the bearers of the same name—appear in stamps connected with various brickyards or in conjunction with several *domini*. It cannot be established, however, that all the stamps referring to such *officinatores* had been produced simultaneously, and it could be argued that some *officinatores* were undoubtedly big entrepreneurs who could contract with several landowners at the same time, the actual management of the production being left to agents or foremen. In any case, there is no cogent evidence of one *officina* spreading over more than one clay district at the same time.

3. *The organization of the industry*

a. *subsidiary workshops*
In Italy, the evidence for subsidiary workshops is scarce. M. Rostovzeff reports that the important industrial complex of Vibius

---

are production units divided into several *officinae* (similarity with the organization of the mint, cf. *CIL* XIV 1878 and below, Chapter Five).

[122] *CIL* XV 1712: DE STATIONE SVRRENTINI. In some *officinae*, up to 8 *stationes* are attested, cf. *CIL* XV 548; 1549; 1567; 1568; 1550; 1551 (*stationes* V-VI are never attested). M. Steinby, *PW* Suppl. 15 (1978) 1502; and *eadem*, *SRIT* II (1986) 110; 117-18; and 156-57.

[123] *CIL* XV 1612 (Constantinianic): EX OFF IOVIA MAG VITALIAN; *S* 614: FORTVNATVS SEVERIANI MAG; and *S* 615 (= *CIL* XV 1710): MARTINVS SEVERIANI MAG. M. Steinby, *SRIT* II (1986) 125-26; and 150. A new brick stamp from Lower Pannonia, dated to the time of Valentinian I, reads CABALLVM MARINIANO / VRSICINO MAGISTRO (*AE* 1988, no. 939).

[124] M. Steinby, *SRIT* II (1986) 156-57.

[125] F. Mayet, *REA* 88 (1986) 289.

Pansa in Northern Italy seems to have had a branch near Ter-geste.[126] A better example is provided by one A. Decius Alpinus who produced bricks, tiles, and hypocaust pipes in Gaul under the reign of Antoninus Pius, and who was perhaps related to Q. Decius Alpinus, *quattuorvir* in Vienna and *curator* of the *nautae* of the *Lacus Lemanus*. A. Decius Alpinus started his activity near Vienna. His stamps, bearing his name alone, are found in the Hautes-Alpes. At some point, he had his slave Clarianus as an assistant or agent. The stamps read first CLARIANVS / A DECI ALPINI or CLA-RIANVM ADA. Later on, the name of Alpinus disappears, and the stamps read CLARIANVS. In the middle of the second century, the prosperity of his business induced Clarianus to open a subsidiary workshop near Vaison, where the stamps read CLARIANA. The distribution of Clarianus's products covered the Rhône valley from the Jura to the Bouches-du-Rhône.[127]

By comparison, it can be demonstrated through petrological studies that branches were also established by prosperous entre-preneurs in medieval England: the owner(s) of a tilery located in the Severn Valley established a subsidiary kiln at some distance, per-haps on a temporary basis, to supply some Welsh sites, as a variant for itinerant industry.[128]

b. *influence of negotiatores upon the production*
Another interesting feature of the medieval brick industry consists in the role of architects in controlling brick production, by commis-sioning specific types of bricks and by sometimes cutting their own moulds. One can wonder whether it should not be informative to look at the Roman brick and tile industry from the demand side as well as from the supply side.[129] Such an approach could provide an

---

[126] M. Rostovtzeff, *SEHRE*² (1957) 611, n. 26, with references.

[127] *CIL* XII 5679, nos. 19-25; and *CIL* XIII 12721-12724. Cf. M. Verguet, "La marque de Clarianus sur briques, tuiles et tuyaux d'hypocauste. Epoque des Antonins," *RAE* 25 (1974) 239-44.

[128] P.J. Drury (1981) 132, citing a lecture given by A. Vince at the Cambridge Tile Seminar in November 1978.

[129] Brickmaking on order is the subject of Iavolenus's response (11 *epist.*) *Dig.* 18.1.65: "Convenit mihi tecum, ut certum numerum tegularum mihi dares certo pretio quod ut faceres: utrum emptio sit an locatio? respondit, si ex meo fundo tegu-las tibi factas ut darem convenit, emptionem puto esse, non conductionem: totiens enim conductio alicuius rei est, quotiens materia, in qua aliquid praestatur, in eodem statu eiusdem manet: quotiens vero et immutatur et alienatur, emptio magis quam locatio intellegi debet." For parallels in the building industry and others, cf.

explanation for a series of stamps referring to a *neg(otiator)* or *neg(otiatrix)*, which perhaps imply that the *officinator* was also in charge of the distribution, or was an agent of the distributor.[130] For instance, Aemilia Severa, who was the owner of the *figlinae Publilianae* in the Severan period, entrusted the operation of the *officina* to a female *negotiatrix* named Iunia Antonia.[131] The stamp, however, provides no information about the nature of the relationship between *domina* and *negotiatrix*, and it is not even sure that the latter was directly involved in the process of production. We will see further on how traders sometimes tried to be in control of the manufacturing process of amphorae.

Helen argues that often manufacturers and consumers had no contact with each other.[132] The basis for this assertion is that some buildings contained stamps from several workshops and that the products of one workshop could be disseminated over a very wide area comprising sometimes two or more provinces. This view implies the existence of a complex system of distribution, probably organized by private *negotiatores*.

There is almost no evidence about channels of distribution of building material. In spite of the high cost of transportation, heavy artifacts, such as bricks, tiles, and mortaria manufactured in Northern Italy were distributed all over Dalmatia.[133] Roman bricks and tiles are also found in Northern Africa.[134] It is possible that build-

---

S.M. Martin, *The Roman Jurists and the Organization of Private Building in the Late Republic and Early Empire* (Brussels 1989) 33-38.

[130] *CIL* XV 415-419 (= *ILS* 8661a-e); 430-432; 649; 879; and *S* 105. Cf. T. Helen (1975) 92 and 131, n. 7 (with reference to Shtaerman [1964] 82). All such stamps are dated to the Severan period. Cf. P. Setälä (1977) 50; 129; and 154. M. Steinby, "La diffusione dell' opus doliare urbano," *SRPS* II (1981) 237-45, esp. 239 thinks that the references to *negotiatores*, *horrea*, and *portus* in the stamps point toward the existence of a well organized trade, although she admits that the relationship between distribution and production is unclear.

[131] *CIL* XV 430 (= *LSO* 399): OP DOL EX FIG PVB DE PR AEM SEVE / NEG IVNIAES ANTONIAES.

[132] T. Helen (1975) 20.

[133] M. Buora, "Sul commercio dei laterizi tra Aquileia e la Dalmazia," *AAAd* 26 (1985) 209-26; and M. Steinby, *SRPS* II (1981) 237-45.

[134] M. Steinby, *PW* Suppl. 15 (1978) col. 1493; *eadem*, *SRPS* II (1981) 243. The majority (7/10) of the stamps on Roman material found outside Italy is post-Trajanic. Cf. also R. Tomber, "Evidence for Long-distance Commerce: Imported Bricks and Tiles at Carthage," *RCRF* 25/26 (1987) 161-74, who concludes, on the basis of unstamped material from Carthage submitted to petrological analysis, that ballast was often made of saleable cargo, with a greater resale value than sand or stone.

ing material was used as ballast on ships, which explains why the distribution of Italian building material remained mostly limited to coastal areas. However, the high stowage factor (or low cargo density) of clay artifacts probably made their use as ballast less appealing to shippers, provided, of course, that other options were available to them.[135] Occasionally, second-century-A.D. shipwrecks (Ile de Frioule, near Marseilles, or off Cape Andreas, Cyprus) reveal that tiles could form the only cargo, although mixed cargoes were the rule.[136] An alternative explanation could lie in the economic situation in Central Italy in the late second century A.D.: the combination of a declining demand for building material in Rome and a lingering agricultural crisis compelled landowners and manufacturers to keep the brick and tile production at its previous level and to export it to more distant markets in order to avoid bankruptcy. This remedy had a limited, temporary effect, and the area where bricks and tiles used to be produced nevertheless witnessed the gradual abandonment of villae.[137] Ultimately, only the emperors and those who were close to the imperial family were strong enough to continue their industrial activity.

c. *municipal and military factories*

Private landowners and the imperial family were not the only ones to own and operate brickyards. There is some evidence, both epigraphical and ethnoarchaeological, that some towns signed bricks and tiles produced in public workshops.[138] The exploitation of these workshops was let by municipal magistrates (*duoviri* or *curatores*) to an entrepreneur (*manceps, conductor,* or *redemptor*) with a five-year contract, like other state or municipal contracts. Alternatively, the management could be entrusted to an agent (public *vilicus, actor,* or

---

[135] S. McGrail, "The Shipment of Traded Goods and of Ballast in Antiquity," *Oxford Journal of Archaeology* 8 (1989) 353-58, with a table of comparative stowage factors (356) of goods commonly transported by ship (does not include bricks): tiles have a much higher stowage factor (2.13-2.27 m³/tonne) than, for instance, tin ingots (0.22-0.28), sand (0.53-0.56), water (1.00), and, surprisingly, even earthenware in crates (1.70-2.13).

[136] R. Tomber, *RCRF* 25/26 (1987) 161-74.

[137] M. Steinby, *Tituli* 4 (1982) 235.

[138] D.P.S. Peacock (1982) 150-51, citing examples from England. Compare with the production of lead pipes in municipal workshops, cf. *CIL* XV 7235a-b (Rome = *ILS* 8695a-b); *CIL* XI 3155a-b (Falerium); *Not.Scav.* 1894, p. 408 (Canusium); *CIL* IX 343 (Canusium); *CIL* XI 3817 (Veii) (= *ILS* 8702-8704).

institor), assisted by a team of public servants (*familia publica*), private slaves, or hired employees.[139] The coexistence of these two systems of management is attested in other areas of public administration, and will be discussed in the following chapter.

Finally, there is some evidence that the Roman army was also producing building material on its own. Many stamps show the number of the legion or the signature of the fleet to which the workshop was attached.[140] A couple of inscriptions shed some light on the organization of the production. At Dobreta (Dacia) in the first half of the third century A.D., a soldier attached to the first cohort of archers was the manager (*magister*) of a military workshop in which sixty soldiers were employed.[141] Another *magister figulorum* is recorded at Holdeurn (Holland).[142]

Military workshops could be staffed with outsiders, in some cases civilians. A stamp of the third or fourth century found near Krefeld in Germany shows that the works were located outside the military camp, in the *canabae*. The civilian who signed the tile was perhaps an agent hired by the army or a worker (imperial slave or *mercennarius*) acting under military supervision.[143] The army may have

---

[139] Usually, the stamps do not provide any clue about the system of management of the *officina*, cf. *CIL* XIV 4090, no. 1: REI PVB<1>ICAE / TVSCVLA-NOR(um). Cf. also *CIL* XV 7; and *CIL* XI 6675, no. 1 (Arretium): [R] P COL FID. A municipal *curator* oversaw the production of tiles or bricks needed to repair some public building, cf. *CIL* XIV 4091, no. 9; and *CIL* XV 2297 (Praeneste): C VOLVNTILIVS Q F VARVS / IIVIR ITER(um) CVR(ator) AED(ium) SACR(arum).

[140] Cf. for instance, *CIL* III 6489 and 11349 (near Lauriacum/Noricum): FIGVLINAS IVENSIANAS LEG(io) I NOR(icorum). Compare with the production of lead pipes in workshops operated by praetorian guards, cf. *CIL* XV 7237; 7240; 7242; 7244-7245 (= *ILS* 8697-8700).

[141] D.P.S. Peacock (1982) 143, citing M. Macrea, "Note au sujet des briqueteries en Dacie," *Dacia* 11-12 (1947) 275-80 (non vidi). *AE* 1939, no. 19 (= *IDR* II 107): "Aurelius Me/rcurius milis c[ohor-]/tis I sagitt[ariorum] in / figlinis magis/ter super mi/lites LX. scripsit / Aurelius Iulianus / milis co[ho]rtis prima(e)." The editor of *IDR* points out that the figure in line 6 might be IX and translates it as if he had read XX. This inscription is therefore poor evidence for the size of the workshop.

[142] D.P.S. Peacock (1982) 143, with reference to J.H. Holwerda–W.C. Braat, *De Holdeurn bij Berg en Dal: centrum van pannenbakkerij en aardewerkindustrie in den Romeinschen tijd* (*Oud Med Suppl. of N.R.* 26, 1946) (non vidi). The inscription is not recorded in *AE. Magistri* on brick stamps of a later period are fairly common, cf. *AE* 1954, no. 15; *AE* 1955, no. 16; and *AE* 1988, no. 939 (Ursicinus and Bonus, fourth century). Cf. above.

[143] D.P.S. Peacock (1982) 143, citing H. von Petrikovits, "Ein Ziegelstempel der Cohors II. Varcianorum aus Gelduba-Gellep," *BJ* 154 (1954) 137-45. *AE*

occasionally sold surpluses of building material to civilians, or to veterans or soldiers investing their savings in real estate. It has been argued, however, that military workshops did not produce more than what was needed by the army, as logistical officers preferred to rely on private enterprise. Military production occurred mostly in the period immediately following the establishment of a military unit in a non-Romanized area, and probably declined with the arrival of civilian producers and traders. The competition between the army and private producers for the military market must have been only occasional and temporary.[144] Sales were probably made by the officer or the agent in charge of the workshop(s), or by some higher officer in charge of logistics. The legal situation of the manager was similar to that of representatives of the Roman state or municipal administration. This aspect will be examined in the following chapter. The phenomenon described above, whereby the military took over functions usually reserved to civilians, became important at the beginning of the third century. Where private entrepreneurs would have employed *institores* as managers of a workshop (*officina*), the Roman army appointed officers as *praepositi* and *magistri*.

4. *Conclusion*

Second-century-A.D. brick stamps from the region of Rome can be used as evidence for the study of the organization of the brick and tile industry. Owners of clay beds/brickyards (*figlinae*), and operators of the units of production (*officinae*) are well represented. The first group (*domini*) included many members of the upper classes, which is not surprising considering the proximity of the capital. By tradition and by law, the senatorial order invested heavily in Italian land. The picture could be fairly different in other parts of Italy, but the connection of the brick industry with the villa economy would make it a typical preserve of the upper classes. The evidence concerning the production of the *figlinae Pansianae* in Northern Italy points toward the same situation. The second group (*officinatores*) was composed of people of lower status than *domini*. It is unclear whether or not *officinatores* were personally and physically involved in the process of manufacturing. The nature of the relationship be-

---

1955, no. 38: SCES IN KAN(abis) L(egionis I Minerviae?) / COH(ortis) II VARC(ianorum) C(ivium) R[omanorum).

[144] G. von Bülow, "Militärische und zivile Keramikproduktion in den römischen Provinzen am Rhein und an der oberen Donau," *Klio* 57 (1975) 233-40.

tween *officinatores* and *domini* remains most of the time elusive. The stamps possibly contain an abridged version of the contract established between *dominus* and *officinator* regarding the production. The type of contract depended on who owned the means of production, and who kept the finished products. The three forms of *locatio conductio* (*operis faciendi*, *operarum*, and *rei*) seem to have been used. The presence of women among *officinatores* does not preclude the possibility that they were commonly supervising the work, as contractors or agents of the *domini*.

Wholesale traders, or even architects, may have had a hand in the brick industry in the same way as traders and shippers may have controlled the production of amphorae (cf. below). Conversely, there is some evidence that building contractors were relying on several suppliers for the construction of one building. The group of *domini* need not be homogeneous, and various combinations are possible.

The building activity of municipalities and the Roman army during the Principate resulted in the involvement of representatives or units of these collectivities in the brick industry. The organization of brickyards under municipal, state, or military control does not seem to have differed from private ones.

C. AMPHORAE

The production and distribution of amphorae involve problems which are substantially different from those raised in connection with the other types of clay artifacts studied in this chapter, because, as containers of wines, oil and olives, fish sauces and salted fish, fruits, vegetables, honey, ointments and medical products, occasionally grains, and even refined clay,[145] their marketing value and trade patterns were accessory to, and therefore determined by, that of their content.[146]

---

[145] M.H. Callender, *Roman Amphorae with Index of Stamps* (London 1965) 37-41 ("Amphora-borne commodities"). A. Tchernia, reviewing Callender's book in *JS* (Oct.-Dec. 1967) 216-34, esp. 225-26, excludes grains, at least as original content. According to Iulianus (6 *ex Min.*) *Dig.* 50.16.206, *dolia*, *seriae*, and *amphorae* were to be considered *vasa vinaria* only if they contained wine, and it is understood that they could be used for other purposes, "veluti si frumentum in his addatur." Amphorae were also used as urns for burial after cremation, cf. G. Calza, *La necropoli del Porto de Roma nell'Isola Sacra* (Rome 1940).

[146] This section owes much to the work of D. Manacorda, "Le anfore dell'Italia repubblicana: aspetti economici e sociali," in *Amphores romaines et histoire écono-*

1. *Amphorae as products and containers*

The typological classification established by Dressel in his edition of *CIL* XV (2.1) in 1899 and constantly refined since then is of primary importance for historians of the Roman economy, because it allows them to determine, with variable degrees of probability, the provenance, date, and content of amphorae independently from the existence, preservation, and legibility of inscriptions usually uncovered on them.[147] For instance, Dr. 1 amphorae are known to have been made in Central Italy during the last century of the Republican period and to have been filled with Italian wine.[148] Unfortunately, our understanding of the organization of the amphora industry and trade, and of the people involved in it did not benefit much from the progress accomplished in the study of amphora types. However, some names can be associated on more secure grounds with the production and trade of some amphora-borne commodities, although the hypothesis that a certain type of amphora always contained the same commodity is not proven, but constitutes only a likely working hypothesis.[149]

Amphorae were meant to be discarded after being emptied of their original content, but it often happened that they were reused for the storage or transport of different commodities.[150] Amphorae are often associated with retail trade, and for the storage or bulk packaging of amphora-borne commodities other kinds of containers, such as clay jars (*dolia*), leather containers, and wooden barrels are thought to have been commonly used in the early Empire. The first of these three categories may be used to supplement the epi-

---

mique (Rome 1989) 443-67, where the author developed views already outlined in "Schiavo 'manager' e anfore romane: a proposito dei rapporti tra archeologia e storia del diritto," *Opus* 4 (1985) 141-51.

[147] An updated treatment of the question is presented by D.P.S. Peacock–D.F. Williams, *Amphorae and the Roman Economy* (London/New York 1986).

[148] A. Tchernia, *Le vin de l'Italie romaine* (Rome 1986) 42-47 dates the beginning of their production between 145 and 135 B.C.

[149] A. Tchernia, *JS* (Oct.-Dec. 1967) 226 considers this assumption an "a priori logique" and an "hypothèse de travail vraisemblable."

[150] J. van der Werff, "Sekundäre Graffiti auf römischen Amphoren," *AKB* 19 (1989) 361-76, points out that secondary graffiti on oil amphorae (Dr. 20 from Baetica, ca. 100-175; and Pélichet 47 from Southern Gaul, ca. 71-104) found in Gaul and in Germania (*CIL* XIII 10003, nos. 18-151) can be interpreted as evidence for the reuse of containers in the context of local trade. The secondary content (wheat, flour, or beans) seems to have been measured in *modii/sextarii* (instead of *librae*), hence the discrepancy between the figures recorded in primary (= *tituli picti*, cf. below) and secondary graffiti, respectively.

graphical evidence preserved on amphorae. One should keep in
mind, however, that *dolia* were used longer than amphorae, and had
a different purpose. They were not always meant to circulate, as
they were used as equipment for wine-making. They can be used,
however, to illustrate the relationship between the people who made
them and those who used them, provided that these two categories
did not necessarily overlap.

These preliminary remarks should serve as a reminder that the
production and distribution of amphorae differ from other clay artifacts: after the first stage of manufacture, the container was filled
and became accessory to its content,[151] a fact that can be expected
to bear on the organization of the amphora industry. The production of the containers, and the relationship between the person in
charge of this process with the people who filled, transported, and
distributed them at a later stage, will be the main focus of this
section.

The production of amphorae is archaeologically documented by
the refuse found in the vicinity of excavated kilns. This type of evidence, however, tells little about the actual organization of the
manufacturing process. The Roman jurists incidentally touch upon
the subject of packaging, in particular when they try to determine
who should supply individual items of farm equipment, but they
have little to say about personnel. Therefore, the study of the organization of the production, use, and distribution of amphorae is based
mainly on the examination of three categories of inscriptions
preserved on various parts of the amphora (or *dolium*). The first
category is made of stamps (signatures) located on or below the rim,
on the neck, handle or spike; the second category is made of painted
inscriptions (*tituli picti*) drawn on the body; and the third category
consists of marks impressed on the stoppers. Those three types of
inscriptions correspond to various moments in the life of an amphora.

2. *Stamped signatures: the making of the container*

a. *types of signatures*

The stamp (signature) was impressed in the clay before firing and

---

[151] Celsus, quoted by Ulpianus (23 *ad Sab.*) *Dig.* 33.6.3.1: "... non quia pars
sunt vini vasa, quemadmodum emblemata argenti (scyphorum forte vel speculi),
sed quia credibile est mentem testantis eam esse, ut voluerit accessioni esse vino
amphoras." Cf. D. Manacorda (1989) 450, n. 27.

therefore is probably connected with the process of manufacturing the container, regardless of its future content and destination. M.H. Callender analyzes the signatures preserved on amphorae with regard to their social significance and distinguishes thirteen different types of signatures:

(1) imperial stamps, displaying the abbreviated name of an emperor or just an imperial title (IMP), and often including the name of a slave (e.g., Callender, no. 1810f: IMPE VECT ANCHA and no. 1810g: IMP CLYME), whom Callender identifies as the *vilicus* in charge of the estate where the amphora was made or used;

(2) senatorial stamps, consisting of the *tria nomina* of a known member of the senatorial order;

(3) *tria nomina* (non-senatorial);

(4) *tria nomina*, with the name of a slave or freedman, possibly a *vilicus* (e.g., Callender, no. 855: EVTSTERPS [= EVT(yches) (C) STER(tini) P(aullini) S(ervus)]);

(5) *tria nomina*, with a toponym;

(6) *tria nomina*, with the name of a brickyard (*figlinae*) (e.g., Callender, no. 18: FIGLIN ACIRGI M S MAVRI);

(7) *figlinae* (e.g., Callender, no. 637);

(8) firms (partnerships);

(9) firms, with a name of *figlinae*;

(10) single names, written out in full, either in the nominative or in the genitive case;

(11) two-letter stamps;

(12) single-letter stamps;

(13) symbols.[152]

According to Callender, the type of the stamp is likely to have some bearing on the probable date, but the evidence provided by the stamps recorded on other clay artifacts does not seem to support this hypothesis.[153] This list suggests that, for reason of social status, some of the people whose names have been identified in amphora

---

[152] M.H. Callender (1965) XXVI-XXVII. Cf. also D. Manacorda–C. Panella, "Anfore," in W.V. Harris (ed.), *The Inscribed Economy* (1993) 55-64; and D. Manacorda, "Produzione agricola, produzione ceramica e proprietà nella Calabria romana tardo-repubblicana: L'epigrafia delle anfore," in *Epigrafia della produzione e della distribuzione. VIIe rencontre de l'Ecole Française de Rome, 5-6 juin 1992* (Preatti, pp. 15-24).

[153] A. Tchernia, *JS* (1967) 224-25. An exception is provided by brick and tile stamps, which can be dated on the basis of their form and content, cf. M. Steinby, *PW* Suppl. 15 (1978) cols. 1495-1505.

stamps were probably not involved at all, at least personally, in the physical process of manufacture.[154] Thus, some of the stamps must represent the owners or lessees of the estate, clay bed, or workshop where a significant stage of the production took place, namely the extraction of the clay, or the whole process of manufacture of the amphora. The relationship between estate (*fundus*, *praedia*), clay bed/brickyard (*figlinae*), and workshop (*officina*) is probably similar to the situation found in the context of the brick industry.

b. *diversification and integration*
The manufacturer of amphorae could be a potter who specialized in this kind of artifact and sold them to producers or traders of amphora-borne commodities. If the demand was too small or seasonal, this potter could decide to diversify his production by producing other kinds of clay artifacts, such as bricks and tiles, tableware, or lamps. Thus, his economic interests would be independent from those of the producer/trader of the commodities, to the extent that changes in the demand of amphorae, due to production crisis in agriculture or competition by other potters, could be compensated by increasing the production of other artifacts.

On the other hand, the manufacturer of amphorae could be part of a more or less integrated economic system, whereby containers and content would be produced and distributed by the same person or company. Profits and losses in one sector could compensate or absorb those of another sector. In a system plagued by manpower shortages, but also liable to important seasonal variations in employment level, integrated enterprises, within which temporary transfer of labor from one sector to the other did not affect the overall production, were undoubtedly appealing to those who had economic ambitions and the means to do business on a large scale.

---

[154] D. Manacorda (1989) 450-51: "Dai dati a disposizione sembra che i nomi di ingenui che compaiono sui contenitori indichino personaggi di un livello sociale elevato, non semplici *figuli*, ma i proprietari (o i responsabili) delle *figlinae*, se non del *fundus* in cui queste dovessero trovarsi. Più incerta è invece la interpretazione dei bolli con nomi servili, che talora accompagnano o sostituiscono quelli con nomi di ingenui. Si definiscono talora questi personaggi quali *officinatores*, con una denominazione che sembra descrivere la funzione piuttosto che interpretarla all'interno di uno schema di rapporti giuridici ed economici." D.P.S. Peacock–D.F. Williams (1986) 9-10 express their doubt about the interpretation of the stamp as marks of potters: "the balance of opinion at the moment is in favour of the stamps representing the estate owners rather than their subservient potters."

In view of the hypothesis presented in the previous section concerning the role of *negotiatores* in the production of building material, one must consider whether amphora stamps could represent the demand side. The user would have ordered a certain number of new (empty) amphorae to be made, which he would have subsequently filled with some commodity produced, purchased, or collected by him. Because of the lack of evidence, no certainty can be reached on this point. The comparison with signatures on terra sigillata and lamps, which clearly represent the manufacturer, speaks against the latter hypothesis. In addition, the current interpretation of painted inscriptions and stopper stamps seems to preclude such an interpretation (cf. below).

Considering that the stamps refer to someone involved in the production of the containers, it is not surprising to note that the same people were possibly engaged in the production of both terra sigillata vessels and amphorae. E.L. Will points out that, despite the risk of homonymy resulting from the fact that slaves' names were not numerous and owners' names were rather common, similarities in letter-shapes with striking variations in size point toward the conclusion that stamps on first-century-B.C. and A.D. amphorae and terra sigillata may refer to the same people.[155] The most striking example is found at Cosa, where the Sestii stamped amphorae and terra sigillata vessels in the first century B.C. before engaging in tilemaking (cf. Chapter Three) and perhaps in the production of fish sauce. The distribution of Arretine wares bearing Sestius's marks points toward the existence of two branches, one in Rome and another one in Arezzo.[156] A later example is that of the Umbricii

---

[155] E.L. Will, "Ähnlichkeiten zwischen Stempeln auf Amphoren und auf arretinischen Gefässen," *RCRF* 23/24 (1984) 9-11.

[156] On the Sestii, cf. Callender (1965) no. 1599; A. Oxé – H. Comfort, *Corpus Vasorum Arretinorum* (Bonn 1968) = *CVArr* 1792-1819; E.L Will, "The Sestius Amphoras: A Reappraisal," *JFA* 6 (1979) 339-50, who mentions (348, n. 28) the find of new tiles stamped by Sestius in the Ager Cosanus, to be added to the Roman ones (*CIL* XV 1444-1445); D. Manacorda, "Produzione agricola, produzione ceramica e proprietari nell'ager Cosanus nel I a.C.," *SRPS* II (1981) 3-54, esp. 33-34, referring to a brick from Carthage (*CIL* VIII 22362, no. 80) and Rome (*CIL* XV 529-540; *S* 443; and M. Steinby, *BCAR* 84 [1974-75] 87f.), and to some (Augustan or Tiberian) tile stamp of P. Sextius (= Sestius?) Quirinalis found in Luni (M.P. Rossignani, *Scavi di Luni* II [Rome 1977] 314, CM 5520, tav. 173, 9); and J.H. D'Arms, *Commerce and Social Standing in Ancient Rome* (Cambridge, MA 1981) 55-62, esp. 59, n. 41. Garum production is suggested by an isolated red painted inscription (CO/SES) on an unstamped Dr. 1 C amphora from the Athenian Agora (P 6867); cf. E.L. Will, *JFA* 6 (1979) 346-47, n. 25, fig. 5; A.M. McCann, "The Portus

Scauri, whose amphorae (Dr. 2-4, and Dr. 6 + unknown type) are attested in the Greek East from the middle of the first century B.C. Established first in the region of Pompeii, the Umbricii started diversifying their activities and expanded all over Italy, their many branches gaining fame for their Arretine wares and their varieties of fish sauce (cf. below).[157] One can surmise that both the Sestii and the Umbricii Scauri were presiding over economic concerns large enough to fill their own amphorae with their own products.[158]

c. *workshop managers*
Slave names occasionally appear in the stamps, for instance in Callender's categories (1) and (4).[159] It is quite likely that slaves and/or hired workers were also involved in the production of amphorae bearing other types of stamps. D. Manacorda rightly suggests that, considering the scale of the production, the servile names on the stamps should represent more than mere potters.[160] If these slave names refer to business managers (*institores*), Callender's assumption that they were *vilici* makes sense, although the scope of their *praepositio* might have been limited to the brickyard (*figlinae*) or workshop (*officina*) in which they operated, another *vilicus* being in charge of the agricultural sector of the villa.[161] It should be stressed

---

Cosanus: A Center of Trade in the Late Republic," *RCRF* 25/26 (1987) 21-70, esp. 32-33, fig. 15, and 40-42; and E.L. Will, in A.M. McCann *et al.*, *The Roman Port and Fishery of Cosa: A Center of Ancient Trade* (Princeton 1987) 202-14.

[157] On the Umbricii Scauri, cf. *CVArr* 2384-2459; and C. Zaccaria, "Per una prosopografia dei personaggi menzionati sui bolli delle anfore romane dell'Italia nordorientale," *Amphores romaines et histoire économique* (Rome 1989) 469-88, esp. 477, n. 59, who cautions against possible cases of homonymy.

[158] N. Purcell, "Wine and Wealth in Ancient Italy," *JRS* 75 (1985) 1-19, esp. 5, n. 18 remarks that there is little evidence showing that manufacturers of amphorae and wine producers overlapped before the first century A.D.

[159] D. Manacorda (1989) 451, n. 34, discusses the stamps SOCRAT CRAS, representing a slave named Socrates of the Republican statesman Crassus, which are attested at Reggio Emilia, Tarentum, and Carthage. Cf. also the stamps CTESO, DASI, CΩTERIX, associated with the name of one Aninius on amphorae from Brundisium; GORGIA, LEONTISCVS, PERDICAS, associated with the name of one Vehilius; and AEN, LVC, MAR, METR, PIL who were called BETIL(ieni) M(arci) S(ervi) (references in Manacorda [1989], 453, nn. 38-39). Other examples are attested all over Italy, cf. Manacorda (1989) 454 ff.

[160] D. Manacorda (1989) 456; *idem, Opus* 4 (1985) 145-46, where the author points out that some slaves obviously occupied a prominent position in comparison to others whose names are also found in the stamps. The relationship could be that of a *servus ordinarius* (with *peculium*) with respect to *vicarii*, or *institor/vilicus* with respect to the servile staff employed in the workshop.

[161] Cf. my paper "Workshop Managers," in W.V. Harris (ed.), *The Inscribed Economy* (1993) 173-75.

also that there is not a single amphora stamp on which the titles of *vilicus* or *actor* are associated with any name,[162] but we have seen that *actores* occasionally show up on tile stamps and pottery.[163]

From a legal point of view, a *vilicus* could be in charge of both the farmstead (agricultural sector) and the workshop (industrial sector). The staff of both units of production either belonged to a single managerial unit, or were kept separate. In the latter case, the *vilicus* could carry out the double appointment, or delegate the management of one sector to a subagent. The scale of the production was instrumental in determining whether or not the exploitation of the *figlinae* should be considered as part of the villa economy, or as a separate industry attached to the *fundus* for practical reasons. The late-first-century-A.D. jurist Iavolenus Priscus records that the Augustan jurists Labeo and Trebatius excluded potters from the farm equipment, i.e. from the managerial unit formed by the agricultural sector of the villa, even though these potters may have been involved in agricultural work during most of the year. The Roman jurists took a stand on this issue probably because it was a sensitive, undecided matter, and it is not unreasonable to think that Labeo and Trebatius might have been challenged by some other legal scholar of the time.[164]

D. Manacorda points out that in some cases the names of two slaves were found together on stamps bearing the signature of an identifiable member of the elite, one Sulpicius Galba (SVLP). Thus, in the shipwrecks of Dramont A and of S. Severa, BAC is associated with either EVTA or OPEL, and PILIP with either DAM or

---

[162] There is the dubious case of the late-first-century-B.C. Νεικασίου ᾿Αγρ(ίπ-που) [ac]tor (*CIL* IV 6499) from the villa of Agrippa Postumus at Boscotrecase, but the restoration proposed by Della Corte and accepted by Rostovtzeff seems highly questionable, as it would represent an isolated, early example of a title that is otherwise not attested before the middle of the first century A.D. Cf. Della Corte, *Not. Scav.* (1922) 459ff; M. Rostovtzeff, *SEHRE*² (1957) 552-53, n. 26, no. 31; and *CIL* IV 6995-6997, where the same name is associated with the title of διο(πεν-σάτωρ?).

[163] Cf. above, *CIL* X 8045, no. 12 (Astutum/Sicily); *CIL* XV 1049 (Rome) (= *CIL* X 8046, no. 5, Sardinia); and below, *CIL* X 8056, no. 154 (Soluntum/Sicily).

[164] Iavolenus (2 *ex post. Lab.*) *Dig.* 33.7.25.1: "Quidam cum in fundo figlinas haberet, figulorum opera maiore parte anni ad opus rusticum utebatur, deinde eius fundi instrumentum legaverat. Labeo Trebatius non videri figulos in instrumento fundi esse." A. di Porto, *Sodalitas* VII (1984) 3244-46 says that Labeo's and Trebatius's opinion reflects the managerial autonomy ("autonomia organizzativa" or "impreditoriale") of the *figlinae* from the *fundus*.

HERM.[165] These stamps suggest that one of the Sulpicii owned an estate and had entrusted it to a *vilicus* or a slave with *peculium*. The production of amphorae was carried out by an *officinator/institor*, appointed by the landowner or by the slave manager. Such a scheme was possible, in accordance with the rule stipulating that business managers were entitled to appoint a subagent as long as the principal knew and approved the appointment.[166] Subagents are sometimes attested in the inscriptions as *subvilici*.[167] The *officinator* appointed by the *vilicus* could be a *vicarius* of the *vilicus*, a member of the *familia rustica*, or an outsider.

Amphora stamps provide some evidence about collective enterprises in amphora production. As this practice will be described in the section on terra sigillata, the discussion can be reduced here to a few remarks. A slave name followed by a *gentilicium* in the plural genitive (for instance, ORESTE LENTVLO(rum)) is the most simple example. D. Manacorda mentions a puzzling case of an amphora bearing two different stamps, one on each handle: (a) ORESTE LENTVLO; and (b) PHILONIC APPVLEI.[168] A possible explanation is that both *officinatores* belonged to two different masters, but it is not possible to ascertain whether the partnership was set up by the *domini* or by the *officinatores*. Manacorda suggests that such a practice reflects a division of labor within the enterprise, but one could envision several workshop managers sharing responsibilities.[169]

In most cases, one can surmise that the slaves who appear in amphora stamps were workshop managers or mere potters. The case

---

[165] D. Manacorda (1989) 454, n. 42; and 457-58, nn. 48-49.

[166] Ulpianus (29 *ad ed.*) *Dig.* 14.1.1.5 and 14.1.1.20, cf. Chapters One and Two. In both passages, the restrictions concerning *institores* bear on the issue of the master's knowledge and acceptance of the secondary appointment and of the extent of his liability, and not on the issue of the overall validity of the appointment of a subagent. In the second passage, the *exercitor* is not an *institor*, but a dependent with *peculium*. Cf. A. Kirschenbaum, *Sons, Slaves and Freedmen in Roman Commerce* (Jerusalem/Washington 1987) 101-03, esp. n. 48; A. Carandini, ''L'economia italica fra tarda repubblica e medio impero considerata dal punto di vista di una merce: il vino,'' in *Amphores romaines et histoire économique* (Rome 1989) 505-21, esp. 508, following A. di Porto.

[167] *CIL* VI 9991; *CIL* X 6638; and *Eph. Ep.* VII 1248.

[168] D. Manacorda (1989) 458-60.

[169] Ulpianus (28 *ad ed.*) *Dig.* 14.1.1.13: ''Si plures sint magistri non divisis officiis, quodcumque cum uno gestum erit, obligabit exercitorem: si divisis, ut alter locando, alter exigendo, pro cuiusque officio obligabitur exercitor,'' provided that the rule applied to *institores* as well.

of Tarula, Sulla's slave, whom Sallust cites together with his colleague Scyrtus as the main beneficiaries of the proscriptions, suggests that slaves attested in amphora stamps were no small fries.[170]
In this particular instance, I suspect that Tarula was a *servus cum
peculio* whose interest in agriculture and clay industry was fairly remote, and who might appear here in the capacity of principal rather
than workshop manager.[171]

d. *contractors*

When the facilities were not operated by the owner himself (or herself),[172] they were either entrusted to an agent or rented out. The
latter practice is thought to be attested in some third-century-A.D.
papyri, the specificity of which requires a short discussion in spite
of my initial commitment not to bring in papyrological evidence
from Roman Egypt.[173] In 243, two female landowners, Aurelia
Leontarous and Aurelia Plousia, acting through their guardian or
procurator (διὰ τοῦ ἐπιτρόπου),[174] leased a potter's workshop attached to an estate located in the village of Senepta in the Oxyrhyn-
chite nome.[175] The contract was made for a period of two years
with one Aurelius Paesis, who was a newly enfranchised Roman

---

[170] D. Manacorda (1989) 458, connects a stamp from Brundisium (TARVLAE
SVLLAE L, published by the same author in "Per uno studio dei centri produttori
delle anfore brindisine" in *I Convegno di studi sulla Puglia romana (Mesagne 1986)*
[Mesagne 1988] 91-108, esp. nn. 40-41 [non vidi]) with the text of the *Oratio Lepidi*
in the Corpus Sallustianum (*Hist.* 1.55.21). The identification is certain, because
the name is rare.

[171] A. di Porto (1984) 257-341 discusses a two-level structure of management
where a *servus cum peculio* has *vicarii* in charge of managerial units.

[172] Women are not common in amphora stamps. A famous example is that of
Calvia Crispinilla, Nero's lover (Tac., *Hist.* 1.73 and Dio Cass. 60.12.3), who
signed Dr. 2-4 and 6 B (= Baldacci III, for oil) amphorae in Northern Italy and
Histria (*CIL* V 8110, no. 207; 8112, nos. 24-25 and 139; *CIL* XV 3381 etc.; cf. M.H.
Callender (1965) no. 231?; J. Paterson, " 'Salvation from the Sea': Amphorae and
Trade in the Roman World," *JRS* 72 (1982) 146-57, esp. 154; F. Tassaux, "Lae-
canii. Recherches sur une famille sénatoriale d'Istrie," *MEFRA* 94 (1982) 227-69,
esp. 263; and A. Tchernia (1986) 133, n. 25, and 252. C. Zaccaria (1989) 471-72,
and 475, n. 39, warns against a possible confusion with the stamps of the Tullii
Crispini. Crispinilla also appears in tile stamps all over Histria, cf. Zaccaria 477.

[173] H. Cockle, "Pottery Manufacture in Roman Egypt: A New Papyrus," *JRS*
71 (1981) 87-97. The papyri have since been published as *P.Oxy.* L 3595-3597. Cf.
also K. Strobel, *MBAH* 6 (1987) 91-97.

[174] G. Hamza, "Zur Frage der Stellvertretung im Willen anhand der *P.Amh.*
90 und *P.Oxy.* 501," *AUB* (*iur.*) 30 (1988/89) 55-65, esp. 57-62. Cf. also above,
Chapter Three.

[175] *P.Oxy.* L 3595.

citizen and a professional potter from the same village. The landladies agreed to supply the potter with facilities (including store
rooms, kiln, potter's wheel, and other equipment) and raw material
(including clay and firewood). The contract (ἐπιδοχή) stipulated
that Aurelius Paesis would bring his own assistants and would
deliver to the landladies a certain number of pitched jars of various
sizes by the early summer of each year, for which he would receive
a fixed price in money and in kind (wine). The landladies reserved
the right to buy any additional container produced in the workshop.
Such contracts are rarely attested before the late second century
A.D.[176] It is not clear whether we are dealing in this case with

    (a) a contract of lease (*locatio conductio rei*), whereby the lessor lets
the lessee use an equipped workshop for his own benefit in exchange
for a fixed rent in money;

    (b) a contract of work (*locatio conductio operis (faciendi)*), whereby
the landlord (*locator*) provides a contractor with raw material and a
salary in exchange for a certain task to be performed; or

    (c) a labor contract (*locatio conductio operarum*), whereby a worker
(*locator*) hires his services to an employer (*conductor*).[177] The last option seems unlikely, because the contract stipulates that the potter
could produce for his own profit, in case the landladies did no want
to buy the surplus of the production. In addition, the premises were
definitely under the control of the potter. Thus, Aurelius Paesis was
probably a contractor rather than a contractual business manager,
the landladies having no say in the management of the enterprise.

---

[176] *P. Mert.* II 76 (Oxy., 181) is a contract of lease (μίσθωσις) according to
which the rent was to be paid in money. The lessee rents part of a workshop from
three or four joint lessors, but assumes a complete responsibility for its management
(lines 8-10): . . . [τὸ ὑπάρχον αὐτοῖς] | ἐπ' ἀμφόδου Ἡρῴου κεραμ[είου μέρος καὶ τὴν
πρὸς] | πᾶν οἰκονομίαν μέρους τ[οῦ] ἐργ[α]σ[τηρίου τούτου]. *P. Tebt.* II 342 (Tebty-
nis, late second century) is too badly damaged to determine to what category of contract the document belongs.

[177] J. Hengstl, "Einige juristische Bemerkungen zu drei Töpferei-Mieturkunden," *Studi Biscardi* IV (Milan 1983) 663-73, esp. 668, considers that the three
documents record a variant of a contract of work, and cites (p. 670) other types of
mixed forms of *locatio conductio* in the context of brick production in the Ptolemaic
period, cf. *PSI* dem. IX 1002 (252/51 B.C.) and *P. Cair. Zen.* I 59 133 (256 B.C.).
L. Amirante, *BIDR* 62 (1959) 9-111 and *Labeo* 13 (1967) 49-60, who argues for a
late emergence of *locatio conductio operis* for manufacture, is rightly refuted by M.
Kaser, *Iura* 11 (1960) 229-34. Cf. also S.M. Martin, *The Roman Jurists and the Organization of Private Building in the Late Republic and Early Empire* (Brussels 1989) 36-37,
n. 63.

It is noticeable that in two similar documents,[178] the contracting potter, Claudianus, was a dependent (κεραμεὺς οἰνικοῦ κεράμου ἴδιος Εὐδαίμονος) of one of his employers/landlords, Septimius Eudaimon, gymnasiarch and councillor in Oxyrhynchus and a man of considerable wealth. Thus, Claudianus fell into the category of slaves paying their masters a share of their earnings (ἀποφοραί).[179] The potter was bound to Septimius Eudaimon and his sister, Aurelia Apia, by a fictitious contractual relationship. As already mentioned above (cf. Chapter Three) slaves could not enter a legal, valid contract with their own master, even though they had some legal autonomy based on the grant of a *peculium*. The juristic personality of a *servus cum peculio* was confused with that of his master, while the *peculium* constituted a distinct entity within the master's property (*ratio dominica*). This type of pseudo-contract gave rise, at best, to natural obligations.[180]

It is not clear whether or not people like Aurelius Paesis or Claudianus were personally involved in the manufacturing process. Another papyrus contains a note sent by probably the same Claudianus[181] to one of his assistants requesting the delivery of a certain number of jars to a customer. This may suggest that Claudianus was assuming only a coordinating and supervisory role.[182]

To sum up, the person in charge of the manufacture of amphorae could be the landowner himself, a contractor, or either's agent. In the context of the brick and tile industry, the term *officinator* refers either to an agent or to an entrepreneur under contract with the owner of the *figlinae*; similarly, amphora stamps may represent either the owner or the operator (principal or agent) of the workshop. In the event that landowners, contractors, and traders belonged to the upper social stratum, it is likely that all of them were content

---

[178] *P. Oxy.* L 3596 (between 219 and 255); and *P. Oxy.* L 3597 (A.D. 260).

[179] *P. Oxy.* L 3597, line 15: ...ἀφ'ὧν ὑπολογοῦνται ὑπὲρ μὲν ἀποφορῶν μου τοῦ Κλαυδιανοῦ δραχμαὶ ἑπτακόσιαι... and H. Cockle's commentary. Cf. I. Bieżuńska-Małowist, "Les esclaves payant l'ἀποφορά dans l'Egypte gréco-romaine," *JJP* 15 (1965) 65-72.

[180] I. Buti, *Studi sulla capacità patrimoniale dei servi* (Naples 1976) 74 ff and 211 ff points out that slaves could be debtors of their masters, but it is not necessarily the result of a contract between them (for instance, if someone makes a payment to the slave with *peculium* with the intention of paying the master).

[181] H. Cockle, *JRS* 71 (1981) 92.

[182] *P. Oxy.* XXXI 2616 (after 244-249). The identification of both potters is proposed by H. Cockle, *JRS* 71 (1981) 92.

with exercising a supervisory role at best, or merely with providing their employees with financial support and warranty. Thus, D.J. Mattingly notes that "the fact that the stamps on Tripolitanian amphorae often seem to represent the abbreviated *tria nomina* of major aristocratic figures reinforces the view that rural production was dominated by the urban elite through large-scale landholdings and that they had some sort of dominant control of surplus production."[183]

e. *amphorae in the villa economy*
There is some archaeological evidence for the production of amphorae as part of the villa economy. According to D.P.S. Peacock, the Tripolitanian amphorae produced at the Roman villa of Aïn Scersciara in North Africa provide the first firm material evidence of a connection between agricultural exploitation and amphora manufacture. It is quite likely that a similar situation existed in many other places, in particular in Italy at Mondragone and Albinia, in connection with brickmaking and other types of pottery production.[184] For specifics, we have to look at some typical representatives of a class of large landowners with extended interests. Such was the case of C. Laecanius Bassus, a landowner attested in the first century A.D. in the region of Pola or Tergeste.[185] This man is perhaps to be identified with the consul of A.D. 40 or his son (consul in 64). He is represented on Dr. 2-4 wine-amphorae and on Dr. 6 B (= Baldacci III) oil-amphorae. One workshop of his has been located at Fasana, 8 km north of Pola, where a significant deposit of amphorae has been recovered. This workshop is thought to have produced bricks, tiles, pipes, pearls (?), coarse pottery, lamps, *dolia*, amphorae, and stoppers.[186]

---

[183] D.J. Mattingly, "Oil for Export? A Comparison of Libyan, Spanish and Tunisian Olive Oil Production in the Roman Empire," *JRA* 1 (1988) 33-56, esp. 38.

[184] D.P.S. Peacock (1982) 130; cf. also D.P.S. Peacock–D.F. Williams (1986) 68-71.

[185] *CIL* V 698.

[186] M. Rostovtzeff, *SEHRE*² (1957) 235-37 and 611, n. 26; *AE* 1911, no. 31; M.H. Callender (1965) 103, no. 365; J. Paterson, *JRS* 72 (1982) 154; F. Tassaux, *MEFRA* 94 (1982) 253; and A. Tchernia (1986) 133, n. 26.

f. *main factory and subsidiary workshops*

The products of the *figlinae* of the Laecanii Bassi raise some questions concerning the personnel employed in it. In a study of the stamps on Dr. 2-4 and Dr. 6 B (= Baldacci III) amphorae, F. Tassaux counts some twenty-nine names of slaves attached to the workshop, whom he identifies as *vilici* or *officinatores*.[187] The production did not last very long before it was taken over by the emperor, during or shortly after the reign of Nero. The transfer of property is perhaps visible in two stamps in which the same slave Clymenus is first associated with Laecanius, and then with the emperor.[188] If one allows for a period of production of three or four decades and assumes that each of the twenty-nine slaves was successively in charge of the workshop at Fasana, the average career of a single *vilicus/officinator* would have been rather short in comparison with the figures provided by epitaphs of *vilici* (cf. Chapter Three). Should we conclude from this fact that the slaves represented on amphora stamps were potters working side-by-side in the same workshop, or *institores* in charge of one of several branch workshops active at the same time? Since F. Tassaux suggests that Laecanius took over existing workshops (for instance, those of M. Aurelius Iustus and Pollio), the dynamism of the enterprise may have called for a decentralization of the production. This hypothesis may be strengthened by the discovery of another amphora deposit at the Villa of Val Catena (near Brioni Grande), and by the find of numerous brick stamps at Pola, Tergeste, and Brioni.[189]

g. *principal and agent in the stamps*

The structure of some of the stamps of C. Laecanius Bassus calls for some remarks. Along the same lines as the hypothesis presented above concerning slave nomenclature in brick and tile stamps (based

---

[187] F. Tassaux, *MEFRA* 94 (1982) 254-57, with the list of slaves 255-56; for instance, *CIL* XV 3477 (Rome); *CIL* V, *Suppl.* 1077, no. 88 (Aquileia); *CIL* V 8112, nos. 52-53 (Vercelli); *CIL* III 6007, no. 5; 12010, no. 1; 14371, no. 4 (Noricum) etc. The number of slaves is not exceptional by comparison with the terra sigillata industry. The mark EBIDIVS or EBIDIENVS is associated with some twenty slave names, cf. C. Zaccaria (1989) 474, with reference to P. Gardellini, *Bolli laterizi e servi figuli della officina ebidiena* (Rovigo 1932) (non vidi).

[188] F. Tassaux, *MEFRA* 94 (1982) 260 and 262, with reference to *CIL* V 8112, no. 52 (Vercelli): C LAE BA / CLYMEN; and *CIL* V 8112, no. 6 (Vercelli): IMP / CLYME.

[189] F. Tassaux, *MEFRA* 94 (1982) 251 and 253-54.

on Oxé's **Form IX**), there is no doubt that C LAEC(anii) BAS(si) / CLARVS refers to a slave (or freedman) of C. Laecanius Bassus named Clarus, whose function was related to the manufacture of the amphora.[190] In this stamp, the name of the principal in the genitive case unambiguously precedes the name of the slave in the nominative case. The stamp is slightly abbreviated, but the name of the principal appears in the *tria nomina* form. There is little doubt about the status of Clarus: he was a dependent, most likely a slave, of C. Laecanius Bassus. If the principal had been referred to in the *duo nomina* form in the genitive case, the stamp could have been read C(ai) LAECANI / CLARVS or C(aius) LAECANI(us) / CLARVS, in which case chances are great that he would have been identified as a freedman of C. Laecanius Bassus. Thus, some stamps found at Aquileia and in Noricum present the variants C LAEK / FELIX and C LAEK BAS / FELIX SER,[191] and there is no cogent reason why we are to believe that these variants necessarily represent two different stages in the life of Felix. Consequently, the legal status of those involved in amphora production cannot be determined on the basis of their name, because it is theoretically possible that some of the stamps containing abbreviated *tria nomina* represent two persons instead of one. This hypothesis—which will be hard to verify—is attractive when the *cognomen* has a servile flavor and is written on a separate line.

One example will suffice to illustrate the possible implication of such an hypothesis. In a recent study of the distribution of the stamp Q NINNI / SECVNDI and its variant Q N SEC on amphorae and tiles in Cisalpine Gaul and along the Adriatic, M.-B. Carre points out that even though the *gens Ninnia* is well known at Capua in the Republican period and in northern Samnium in the first two centuries of the Empire, not one Q. Ninnius Secundus is attested.[192] The *praenomen* Quintus, however, is attested among the members of

[190] Callender, no. 365; and *CIL* XV 3477.
[191] *CIL* V, Suppl. 1077, nos. 88b and c (= *ILS* 8572d and e): C LAEK / FELIX and C LAEK BAS / FELIX SER; and *CIL* III 6007, no. 5 (Helenenberg, Carinthia): C LAEC BASSI on one handle, and FELIX SER on the other.
[192] M.-B. Carre, "Les amphores de la Cisalpine et de l'Adriatique au début de l'empire," *MEFRA* 97 (1985) 207-45, esp. 235-41, with a collection of 6 amphora stamps from the Museum of Aquileia, one from Concordia (*CIL* V, *Suppl.* 1077, no. 104), one from Rome (*CIL* XV 3494), and one tile found on the border between Samnium and Picenum (*CIL* IX 6078, no. 204).

the *gens* and belonged to no less a figure than Q. Ninnius Hasta, the suffect consul of A.D. 88 or to his son, ordinary consul in 114 and proconsul of Africa in 128/129.[193] The *cognomen* Secundus is most common among slaves and freedmen, even though it is also used by freeborn. Thus, it is theoretically possible that Secundus who signed amphorae was a dependent of the senator and was active at the end of the first century A.D. as the change from Dr. 6 to flat-bottomed type suggests. If the connection between Secundus and Q. Ninnius Hasta could be established, Secundus, whose status is uncertain and, in fact, irrelevant, could have been working as an agent (*vilicus, actor, institor,* or *procurator*) of Q. Ninnius Hasta rather than as an independent entrepreneur (*servus cum peculio* or independent freedman). In my opinion, this form of stamp (Oxé, **Form IX**) underlines the relationship between principal and agent in the amphora industry without providing any clue about the agent's status.

h. *users of amphorae: producers or traders?*

If the products of Aurelius Paesis or Claudianus had been preserved, how would they be signed? The stamp would most likely contain the name of the potter, and perhaps also the name of the landowners. In this case, the owners of the workshop would coincide with the users of the containers, and probably with the producers of the content. Considering that amphora-borne commodities (agricultural products and processed food) were sometimes transported in bulk containers, both producers of the content and distributors could have an interest in owning or renting a workshop run by a contractor or a manager. If it was possible to determine on a case-by-case basis who needed to be supplied with amphorae, the logistical aspects of amphora production and trade would be easier to grasp.

Winegrowers and producers of other staples acquired through purchase or collection the number of amphorae and *dolia* they needed every year to store and package their production. Alternatively, the producers sold their products in bulk to wholesale traders, who would then have to acquire amphorae and fill them. Thus, the first-century-A.D. jurist Proculus maintains, against Trebatius, that a

---

[193] *PIR*[2] V.3 (1987) 360-61, nos. 100-101; on Q. Ninnii in *Regio* IV, cf. *CIL* IX 3024 (Teate Marrucinorum, Q. Ninnius Q.f. Arn( ) Oppianicus); *CIL* IX 3358 (Pinna, Ninnia Q.f. Primilla); and *CIL* IX 3858 (Supinum, Q. Ninnius Q.l. Strenuus).

legacy of wine included retail (*vasa vinaria*, i.e. *amphorae* + *cadi*) as well as bulk containers (*dolia*):

> We fill up *amphorae* and *cadi* with wine, and let it sit until it is tasted for consumption. And there is no doubt that this wine is sold with its container. We keep wine in *dolia* for a different purpose, either to fill *amphorae* and *cadi* at a later stage or to sell it without the jars (*dolia*).[194]

It is not clear whether Proculus means a winegrower or a wine trader. Provided that production and distribution were not carried out by the same person, it seems that both producers and traders were regular customers of amphora manufacturers. Celsus and Ulpianus make a distinction between storage (*dolia* and sometimes *cuppae*), transport (*utres* and *cullei*), and retail containers (*amphorae*, *cadi*, and *cuppulae*). Only the latter category was considered an *accessio* to the wine.[195] Insofar as a producer was not involved in retail trade, he had no use for transport or retail containers, which were provided by wine traders. Varro says that in Apulia, traders were known to keep trains of pack animals (donkeys) to carry wine, oil, grains, and other products to the sea in special containers ("asellis dossuariis").[196] This seems to indicate that the wine was not poured into amphorae by the producers.

For half a century between Augustus and Nero, some ships importing Spanish wine to Italy were loaded with both *dolia* and amphorae (Dr. 2-4). The *dolia* were part of the fixture of the ship. It is remarkable that out of seven shipwrecks where the phenomenon is attested,[197] six contained *dolia* signed by the same family, the

---

[194] Proculus (2 *epist.*) *Dig.* 33.6.15: "Vinum enim in amphoras et cados hac mente diffundimus, ut in his sit, donec usus causa probetur, et scilicet id vendimus cum his amphoris et cadis: in dolia autem alia mente coicimus, scilicet ut ex his postea vel in amphoras et cados diffundamus vel sine ipsis doliis veneat."

[195] Ulpianus (23 *ad Sab.*) *Dig.* 33.6.3.1, citing Celsus, and Proculus (2 *epist.*) *Dig.* 33.6.15. A. Tchernia (1986) 39 uses both passages to illustrate how wine could be sold at retail directly from the *dolia*, without being put into amphorae, and transported in animal skins (*utres* and *cullei*) on a regional scale, as shown in Pompeian paintings (*Dar.-Sag. I*, fig. 286) and on a sarcophagus (*Dar.-Sag. V*, fig. 7514). For the transport of wine in wineskin or hide (ἀσκός), cf. Philostr., *VA* 1.40.

[196] Varro, *Rust.* 2.6.5. A. Tchernia (1986) 39, n. 127.

[197] A. Hesnard – M.B. Carre, *Archaeonautica* 8 (1988) 149-54 list the shipwrecks of Petit Congloué (Marseilles), La Garoube (Antibes), Grand Ribaud D (Hyères, Var), Ile Rousse (Corsica), Diano Marina (Liguria), Ladispoli (Etruria), and Gulf of Baratti (Populonia). They are described by M. Corsi-Sciallano – B. Liou, "Les épaves de Tarraconaise à chargement d'amphores Dr. 2-4," *Archaeonautica* 5 (1985).

Pirani, attested in the late Republican period in the region of Minturnae.[198] The *gentilicium* is rare enough to make the connection absolutely certain. In the shipwreck Grand Ribaud D, dated to the last decade of the first century B.C. and bound from Campania to Spain and Southern Gaul, one of the *dolia* was stamped C PIRANVS / SOTERICVS F. In another shipwreck (Diano Marina) dated to the middle of the first century A.D. one *dolium* is signed by two representatives of the same family, C PIRANVS / PRIMVS FEC and C PIRANVS / PHILOMVSVS F.[199] It is possible that Sotericus, Primus, and Philomusus, were the owners or managers (even joint-managers in the second case) of a workshop producing containers. They must have had a special relationship with the audacious shippers who were ready to sacrifice the security of traditional cargoes of amphorae (in two or three layers) to maximize their profits by transporting a larger quantity of wine on each trip.[200] Because of the the risk of wreck in case of breakage, the experiment seems to have been short-lived, but it had been important enough to leave some trace in the legal sources.[201] Such ships would unload their cargo in *horrea* equipped with *dolia*, like those found in Ostia.[202] The wine would then reach the consumer in locally-made amphorae, or in other perishable or reused containers, thus eliminating the need for the production of amphorae at the place of origin of the content. This phenomenon may have affected a significant share of the market.

---

[198] A woman, Pirana, and her slaves are recorded in *ILLRP* 738; 740-741; and 743.

[199] *AE* 1986, no. 239. Cf. also F. Pellarés, "Il relitto di Diano Marina nel commercio vinicolo antico," in *El vi a l'antiguitat. Economia, producció i comerç al Mediterrani occidental. Actes del 1 colloqui d'arqueologia romana* (Badalona 1987) 298-305 (non vidi).

[200] A. Hesnard–M.B. Carre, *Archaeonautica* 8 (1988) 149-54 calculate that the weight ratio of container/content, which had already improved from 1 to 0.6 with the shift from Dr. 1 to Dr. 2-4 amphorae, went down to 0.25 with the use of *dolia*. Thus, it was possible to multiply the quantity of wine transported in *dolia* by 1.2 to 1.7 (according to the number of layers of amphorae used in comparison).

[201] Paulus (40 *ad Sab.*) *Dig.* 47.2.21.5, about the theft of bulk commodities in storage: "Et quid si cisterna vini sit, quid dicet? aut aquae cisterna? quid deinde si nave vinaria (ut sunt multae, in quas vinum effunditur), quid dicemus de eo, qui vinum hausit? an totius oneris fur sit? et magis est, ut et hic non totius dicamus." Cf. J. Paterson, "Roman Tankers," *LCM* 13 (1988) 62.

[202] A. Hesnard–M.B. Carre, *Archaeonautica* 8 (1988) 149-54 point out that such facilities are rarely preserved, and list instance in Massilia, Salone, and Histria Pontica. They are also mentioned by Paulus (6 *resp.*) *Dig.* 18.1.76 *pr.* ("dolia in horreis defossa").

The control over the manufacture of containers probably shifted back and forth between producers and traders/shippers. In the *Ager Falernus*, the change from Dr. 1 to Dr. 2-4 amphorae in the first century B.C. was followed by a possible change in the pattern of distribution. As P. Arthur notes:

> That a move of kiln sites inland during the first century A.D. may have been part of a trend could be indicated by the presence of inland kiln sites which produced Dr. 2-4 in other areas such as Sutri, in Southern Etruria, and in the Melfa area of the Liri valley. It may have been that the wine was no longer transported from the *fundi* to the 'packaging sites' along the coast, perhaps in large animal skins mounted on carts, but was fed directly into the amphorae on the various agricultural estates for a more restricted market.[203]

This interpretation is supported by the presence of paved roads in the vicinity of the inland kilns. The chief consumers of Falernian wine in the early Empire might have been the members of the upper classes, including the imperial family, who owned properties in Southern Latium and Campania. The distribution could have been carried out by farm managers (*vilici*), regional (*actores*) or general agents (*procuratores*), possibly off market (gift, exchange, or internal consumption).

The passage by Proculus cited above provides a clue for what happened when traders (*negotiatores*) were buying the crops in bulk before the harvest.[204] No ancient text records who paid for the amphorae, but the jurists say that *dolia* used for storage were part of the *instrumentum* of a *fundus*.[205] It has been argued that the silence of the Roman jurists on this point can be explained by the fact that *negotiatores* were supposed to bring their own amphorae, even though they

---

[203] P. Arthur, "Roman Amphorae and the *Ager Falernus* under the Empire," *PBSR* 50 (1982) 22-33, esp. 31-33.

[204] This situation was not exceptional, as it is already described by Cato in his *De Agricultura* (146-148), writing about the terms for the sale of olives on the tree, grapes on the vine, and wine in jars (*in doliis*), and more than two centuries and half later by Pliny the Younger. The latter reported to his friend Calvisius Rufus that the dealers who had bid enthusiastically for the wine crop, forecasting interesting profits as a result of rising prices, had incurred some losses as the harvest turned out to be larger than expected, thus bringing down the price of wine on the market (*Ep.* 8.2.1, Tifernum, 107?): "vendideram vindemias certatim negotiatoribus ementibus, invitabat pretium et quod tunc et quod fore videbatur. spes fefellit."

[205] In addition to the texts cited above, cf. Ulpianus (32 *ad ed.*) *Dig.* 19.2.19.2, citing a letter of Neratius to Aristo, and B.W. Frier, "Law, Technology, and Social Change: the Equipping of Italian Farm Tenancies," *ZRG* 96 (1979) 204-28.

could use the facilities of the landowner for storage and processing of the crops.[206] According to the circumstances, both producers of staples and traders might have had an interest in controlling the production of containers. Thus, both groups were likely to buy or rent a workshop which they entrusted to an agent or to a contractor. In my opinion, not enough attention has been paid to the fact that *officinatores* might have been employed by traders. This would explain why and how amphorae became so standardized, the traders laying down the norms in amphora production to suit their own requirements.[207]

Negotiatores could buy the containers they needed from a local manufacturer.[208] The *negotiator* L. Antonius Epaphroditus, represented in the shipwreck Saint-Gervais 3, was shipping the products of two different estates packed in amphorae originating from two different *figlinae*. That the oil was poured into the amphorae at the site of the workshop is suggested by the fact that the same *ponderator*, Anicetus, signed the amphorae containing the produce of both estates. If the *negotiator* was responsible for the manufacturing of amphorae, the name in the stamp should match the name in one of the entries (β) of the painted inscriptions (*tituli picti*, cf. below). Such instances are unknown to me.[209]

i. *purpose of the stamps*

There seems to be no agreement on the question of the purpose of the stamps. The following stamp has been found on a *dolium* of Republican date found in Orvieto: FIG L TETTI BALBI / ANTI-

---

[206] J. Paterson, *JRS* 72 (1982) 155-56, with reference to R. Yaron, "Sale of Wine," in D. Daube (ed.), *Studies in the Roman Law of Sale dedicated to the memory of F. de Zulueta* (Oxford 1959) 71-77, esp. 77. Most relevant legal texts deal with transactions involving the sale of wine in *dolia*, sometimes in amphorae, to *negotiatores*.

[207] This has been suggested, for instance, by J. Paterson, *JRS* 78 (1988) 243, who says that *negotiatores* and *navicularii* "were among the principal customers of the potteries."

[208] B. Liou, "Les amphores à huile de l'épave Saint-Gervais 3 à Fos-sur-mer: premières observations sur les inscriptions peintes," in J.M. Blázquez Martínez (ed.), *Producción y comercio del aceite en la antigüedad* (Madrid 1980) 161-75, esp. 174.

[209] E. Rodriguez-Almeida, "Bolli anforari del Monte Testaccio, introducción," *BCAR* 84 (1974-1975) 119-248, esp. 219 points out that among the sherds found on Monte Testaccio, some *figlinae* (e.g., *fig. saxoferreo*) were represented on both stamps and *tituli picti* (*CIL* XV 4171 and 3167). But as we are dealing with entry δ instead of β (cf. below), the correspondence is not relevant for identifying *negotiatores* as manufacturers of amphorae.

OC(hus) TOS(si) SEX(ti).[210] Antiochus, a slave owned by one Sex. Tossius (or jointly owned by one Tossius and one Sextius), was the manager (*officinator?*) or employee of a workshop attached to a clay bed/brickyard belonging to L. Tettius Balbus.[211] Sex. Tossius may have rented the clay bed or the workshop from L. Tettius Balbus. An alternative interpretation would be that Antiochus had been hired as *mercennarius* by L. Tettius Balbus. Antiochus was probably a professional workshop manager who supplied containers to his principal, and possibly to other producers or traders of agricultural products.

Why did Antiochus or his principal consider it necessary to sign the products of the workshop? The answer to this question will remain tentative. Many facts speak against the interpretation of stamps as advertising labels: the quality of the signatures, their location on amphorae, and their absence on a significant number of amphorae would make little sense if the only purpose of the stamps was to advertise the product (content or container). As A. Tchernia once suggested, it is more likely that the stamps served as a mark of control: in case of breakage of a whole batch of containers due to low quality, the owner (producer or trader) of the content could hold the manufacturer of the container liable for the loss of his product.[212] The absence of stamps from many—perhaps a majority of—amphorae is no objection to this theory, because legal action was unlikely to be taken in case of individual or minor breakage. Selective stamping would allow for effective identification of the origin of, and responsibility for, a faulty batch. In our particular instance, a *negotiator* would have an *actio institoria* against the principal to obtain a full

---

[210] *CIL* XI 6691, no. 32 (= *ILLRP* 1241 = *CIL* I² 2351). A. Oxé, *RhM* 59 (1904) 126 states that the slave nomenclature in this stamp (= his **Form III**, cf. above, in the previous section) is rare on *dolia*.

[211] J. Paterson, *JRS* 72 (1982) 155: "The simplest and most probable hypothesis is that the stamps represent the owners of the *figlina* which made the amphorae or the slaves or freed *officinatores* who worked for them." M. Steinby kindly informed me that the Tettii also produced bricks and tiles. So did the Tossii, cf. *ILLRP* 1176 (tile).

[212] A. Tchernia, *JS* (Oct.-Dec. 1967) 231: "Le contenu seul importe, et les timbres ne se justifient que si l'atelier dépend d'un domaine qui profite de ses ventes d'amphores pour faire connaître du même coup son existence en tant que producteur agricole...Rien n'interdit au contraire qu'elles représentent simplement les noms des propriétaires d'ateliers céramiques indépendants," thus allowing wine traders, for instance, to control the quality of packaging. On the function of the stamps as labels of guarantee, cf. D. Manacorda (1989) 449.

monetary compensation for the damage incurred as a result of the lousy work done by his agent Antiochus.

3. Painted inscriptions: the marketing of the content

The second type of epigraphical evidence found on amphorae is more explicit, but unfortunately also more ephemeral: *tituli picti*, best represented on Dr. 19 and 20 oil-amphorae imported from Spain, have drawn less attention than stamps, but are of primary importance to understand the origin and distribution of the content. Many are found in shipwrecks in Southern Gaul or in the refuse of Monte Testaccio (Rome). The latter collection stretches from the age of Augustus until 260 and presents a somewhat standardized form.[213]

a. *five-level structure of tituli picti*

The most detailed painted inscriptions usually contain five entries (α-ε), the first three being located one below the other on the upper part of the body, and the last two near the handle:

(α) shows a figure representing the weight of the empty container in pounds;

(β) records a name (*tria nomina*) thought to represent the merchant rather than the shipper handling the consignment.[214] As the oil

---

[213] On painted inscriptions in general, cf. P. Remark, *De amphorarum inscriptionibus Latinis quaestiones selectae* (Diss. Bonn 1912); M.H. Callender (1965) 20-22; F. Zevi, "Appunti sulle anfore romane," *ArchClass* 18 (1966) 208-47; D. Colls *et al.*, "L'épave Port-Vendres II et le commerce de la Bétique à l'époque de Claude" *Archaeonautica* 1 (1977) 93-103; R.I. Curtis, *AncSoc* 15-17 (1984-1986) 209-28, esp. 210-11, n. 4-5; D.P.S. Peacock–D.F. Williams (1986) 13-14. *Tituli picti* are also found on Italian amphorae, but they are reputed to be less complex (cf. below).

[214] T. Frank, "Notes on Roman Commerce," *JRS* 27 (1937) 72-79; E. Rodriguez-Almeida, "Monte Testaccio: I *mercatores* dell'olio della Betica," *MEFRA* 91 (1979) 873-975; *idem*, "Vicissitudini nella gestione del commercio dell'olio betico da Vespasiano a Severo Alessandro," *MAAR* 36 (1980) 277-90, esp. 278-79; *idem*, "Altri *mercatores* dell'olio betico," *DArch* 1 (3rd series) (1983) 79-86. The name was originally thought to represent the producer of the content of the amphora: D. Colls *et al.*, *Archaeonautica* 1 (1977) 100 consider that the names in β and δ represent the same person, namely the owner of the estate and distributor; D.P.S. Peacock–D.F. Williams (1986) 13 see in entry β of the *tituli picti* a mention of the *navicularius*; B. Liou–J.-M. Gassend, "L'épave Saint-Gervais 3 à Fos-sur-mer (milieu du IIᵉ siècle ap. J.-C.). Inscriptions peintes sur amphores de Bétique. Vestiges de la coque," *Archaeonautica* 10 (1990) 157-264, esp. 198-209, favor the interpretation of *mercatores* over *negotiatores*. The organization of the Spanish oil trade was complex, as suggested by the difficulty that modern scholars meet in inter-

trade from Spain became an imperial monopoly in the third century A.D., the name was then replaced by the inscription "fisci rationis patrimonii provinciae Baeticae" (or "Tarraconensis");

(γ) provides the weight of the full vessel;

(δ) is more complex, as it may consist of several lines, in various orders, including

(a) a crossed R (= *receptum* or *recensitum*) or a symbol meaning *arca* ("treasury") next to two figures representing the value and the content of the container, meaning that it has been checked by an agent of the *portorium*, and the name of the town where the control was carried out;[215]

(b) the name of the estate or locality, where the products (content) originated;

(c) a name in the genitive case, which may represent the owner of the estate or his agent;[216]

(d) the name of the employee in charge of supervising the loading of the ship (if *acc, acp*, or *act* are to be interpreted as *acceptor*), of registering their weight (*ponderator*), and of filling out the tag (*scriptor*). In the third century it bears a control mark from imperial *actores*;

(e) a consular date;

---

preting such functions as that of *diffusores*: A. Tchernia, "D. Caecilius Hospitalis et M. Iulius Hermesianus," in J.M. Blázquez Martínez (ed.), *Producción y comercio del aceite en la antigüedad* (Madrid 1980) 155-60 and S. Panciera, "*Olearii*," *MAAR* 36 (1980) 235-50, both favor a meaning close to that of *negotiator, mercator*, or *navicularius; contra*, M.-F. Loyzance, "A propos de Marcus Cassius Sempronianus Olisiponensis, *diffusor olearius*," *REA* 88 (1986) 273-84, following R. Thouvenot, suggests that they were specialists in charge of decanting liquids into amphorae and checking the quality, playing a intermediary role between producers and traders; P. Le Roux, "L'huile de Bétique et le prince sur un itinéraire annonaire," *REA* 88 (1986) 247-71 considers them as intermediaries between wholesale traders (*negotiatores*) and retailers (*mercatores*); and E. Rodriguez-Almeida, *BCAR* 92 (1987-88) 299-306, considers that there is no difference in the inscriptions between *diffusores, negotiatores*, and *mercatores olearii*, but that these are distinct from *navicularii*. All known *diffusores* are freeborn or freedmen, and they might have played only a supervisory role.

[215] D. Colls *et al., Archaeonautica* 1 (1977) 93-103 reject T. Frank's interpretation (in *AJP* 57 [1936] 87-90) of δ as a reference to the *portorium*.

[216] H. Dressel, in *CIL* XV, p. 563, thought of an *actor* or *procurator*. Cf. also T. Frank, *JRS* 27 (1937) 72. The person could be a woman, cf. E. Rodriguez-Almeida, "El Monte Testaccio, hoy: Nuevos testimonios epigráficos," J.M. Blázquez Martínez (ed.), *Producción y comercio del aceite en la antigüedad* (Madrid 1980) 57-100, esp. 71-73. Cf. also B. Liou – A. Tchernia, "L'interpretation des inscriptions sur les amphores Dr. 20," in *Epigrafia della produzione e della distribuzione. VIIe rencontre de l'Ecole Française de Rome, 5-6 juin 1992* (Preatti, pp. 73-82).

(ε) consists of a figure thought to have some relevance for loading on the ship or arrangement in storage rooms (*horrea*).[217]

b. *institores in the fish sauce industry*
There are but a few cases where painted inscriptions record the activity of possible *institores*. Numerous amphorae from Pompeii and Herculaneum, Southern Spain, and other Western provinces display labels advertising their content as fish sauce (*garum, hallex, muria, liquamen*) of various qualities (*flos, optimum, primum, excellens, castum, etc.*). Among the producers and merchants of fish sauce at Pompeii, A. Umbricius Scaurus, a member of the local elite, was one of the most active.[218] He is known to have secured the assistance of several family members, freedmen, and slaves.[219] His containers (mostly *urcei* of Pompeian form VI) were possibly produced by his agent(s), although one cannot exclude that he bought them from independent manufacturers.[220] In some *tituli picti*, the product identification is followed by his name in the genitive case (A VMBRICI SCAVRI, or only SCAVRI), and it is clear that he produced various sorts of fish sauce.[221]

Some painted inscriptions display the expression EX OFFICINA of so-and-so, combined with several names (in the genitive case), that of Scaurus himself and that of some of his slaves or freedmen, Abascantus and Agathopus.[222] It indicates that A. Umbricius Scau-

---

[217] E. Rodriguez-Almeida, in J.M. Blázquez Martínez (ed.) (1980) 58-59.

[218] *CIL* X 1024 (= *ILS* 6366); and perhaps Petron., *Sat.* 77.5. Cf. J. Andreau, *Les affaires de Monsieur Jucundus* (Rome 1974) 296-98; R.I. Curtis, "A Personalized Floor Mosaic from Pompeii," *AJA* 88 (1984) 557-66; *idem*, "Product Identification and Advertising on Roman Commercial Amphorae," *AncSoc* 15-17 (1984-1986) 209-28, esp. 214, 220, n. 41, and 225; *idem*, "A. Umbricius Scaurus of Pompeii," in *Studia Pompeiana e Classica in Honor of W.F. Jashemski* (New York 1988) 19-50; and *idem, Garum and Salsamenta. Production and Commerce in Materia Medica* (Leiden 1991) 157-58.

[219] R.I. Curtis, *AncSoc* 15-17 (1984-1986) 225 reports that the name of A. Umbricius Scaurus "or the name of one of his slaves, freedmen, or family members appears on 28.6 percent of all extent fish sauce containers found in Pompeii and Herculaneum."

[220] The *tituli picti* used in this section are found on containers bearing (presumably) no stamped signatures. Stamps of the Umbricii are rarely reported. Cf. M.H. Callender (1965) no. 1748 (Modena): VMBRICIV.

[221] R.I. Curtis, *AncSoc* 15-17 (1984-1986) 209-28, esp. 224-26, with the evidence cited nn. 62-67. Cf. also Curtis (1991) 148-58 (about producers and merchants), and 197-200 (= Curtis [1988] 37-39), whose interpretation of the names in *tituli picti* is slightly different from the one presented here.

[222] *CIL* IV 5689 (= *ILS* 8599a): G(ari) F(los) SCOMBR(i) / OPTIMVM / EX

rus operated at least three factories or workshops, but it is not known whether they were active at the same time.[223]

Another element found in some painted inscriptions is the name of one of A. Umbricius Scaurus's relatives or dependents, male or female, in the ablative case preceded by the preposition *ab*.[224] Curtis identifies these characters as the "consignors" of the container, and the phrase seems indeed to refer to the distributors of the content. From the extant evidence, it appears that Scaurus's fish sauce was distributed by his dependents in several outlets, one of which, at least, was managed by a female *institor*. Distribution was also carried out by people not necessarily connected with Scaurus's family. Thus, some containers filled with Scaurus's fish sauce bear the label of one imperial freedman named Martialis.[225]

It is likely that Abascantus and Agathopus, who are both known to have been in charge of an *officina*, were the same people as the ones who consigned amphorae. That the two formulae (EX OFFICINA + name in the genitive case, and AB + name in the ablative case) refer to two distinct operations is shown by the occurrence of both formulae side-by-side in the same *titulus* (cf. previous note), but it remains uncertain whether both positions were held simultaneously or consecutively. One finds also the combination AB + ablative and DE + ablative: G F SCOMBR / SCAVRI / AB AGATHOPO DE / CLAVDIO EVLOGO, although another *titulus* may suggest that

OFFICINA / A VMBRICI ABASCANTI; *CIL* IV 5694 (= *ILS* 8599b): G F SCOMBR / SCAVRI / EX OFFICINA SCAVRI (cf. also *CIL* IV 2572(?); 2574-2575; 2577; and 9406); *CIL* IV 5690 (= *ILS* 8599c): G F SCOMBR / SCA-VRI / EX OFFICINA AGATHOPI (cf. also *CIL* IV 2580 = 5691; 7110; and 9403-9405). Cf. R.I. Curtis, *AncSoc* 15-17 (1984-1986) 225, n. 67.

[223] R.I. Curtis, *AncSoc* 15-17 (1984-86) 226 remarks that the *titulus CIL* IV 5689 (= *ILS* 8599a), which he translates "the flower of garum, made from the mackerel, a product of Scaurus, from the shop of Agathopus," has named "the product, declared its high quality, disclosed its ingredients, identified the ultimate owner of the product, and given the name of the distributor, a sort of subsidiary of the owner." In my opinion, the *officina* is the place of production of the fish sauce, hence a branch factory, and not necessarily a retail shop.

[224] Eutyches: *CIL* IV 2576 (G F SCOMBR / SCAVRI / AB EVTYCHE SCAVRI). Abascantus: *CIL* IV 5671; and 5685. Stlabor(?): *CIL* IV 5686. Martialis: *CIL* IV 9406. Agathopus: *CIL* IV 6921; and 9418. Fortunata: *CIL* IV 5661; and 5674 (perhaps also 5670; 5696-5697; 5711; 5723; and 10262). Cf. also R.I. Curtis, *AncSoc* 15-17 (1984-1986) 225, n. 66.

[225] *CIL* IV 9406: G F SCOMBR / SCAVRI / EX OFFICINA SCAVRI / AB MARTIALE AVG L, where the editor suggests that a verb such as "missus" is implied. Cf. also R.I. Curtis, *Studia Pompeiana* ... (1988) 44-45, n. 60.

DE should be understood as a spurious ending of the Greek name
'Αγαθόπους, -oδoς: LIQVAMEN / OPTIMVM / CLAVDIO
EVLOGO / AB VMBRICIO AGATHOPODE.[226] This would
mean that Claudius Eulogus was the recipient of a shipment made
by Umbricius Agathopus, but a scribal mistake (inversion of lines
3 and 4) seems more likely. A comparative study of the use of the
prepositions *ab*, *ex*, and *de* in painted inscriptions and stamps related
to various types of clay artifacts might yield some interesting results.

Finally, there is one case where the agent of A. Umbricius Scaurus signs with his initial only: LIQ / A VMBRICI SCAVRI / A V
C. It is likely that the agent (producer or distributor) was a freedman
called A. Umbricius C(?).[227]

The concern of which A. Umbricius Scaurus was the director provides an excellent example of an integrated enterprise. One sector
was responsible for the production of various kinds of fish sauce,
another for the packaging, and a third one for the distribution of the
product in retail shops. Both production and distribution were carried out in more than one managerial unit. As the cases of Abascantus and Agathopus show, it was possible for a competent manager
to be in charge of more than one sector, or to be transferred from
one to another.

4. *Stopper marks: the transport of the product*

The third type of epigraphical evidence related to amphorae is found
on stoppers. Filled amphorae were closed with a cork bung sealed
with pozzolana and stamped. It is the current opinion that the marks
found on stoppers refer to the trader (*mercator* or *negotiator*)[228] or to
the shipper (*navicularius*),[229] although both functions could very well

---

[226] *CIL* IV 6921 and 9418, where the editor suggests that "missum" is implied
after CLAVDIO EVLOGO.

[227] *CIL* IV 5705, where the same *titulus* appears both on the neck and on the
body of the container.

[228] J. Paterson, *JRS* 72 (1982) 156: "A number of stoppers for the necks of amphorae have survived and occasionally names appear on them. Such names are
most likely those of the *negotiator*;" cf. also D.P.S. Peacock–D.F. Williams (1986)
11-12 (*negotiator*, possibly of low rank) and 50-51 (merchant who bought the amphorae).

[229] A. Tchernia (1986) 119 "armateur et négociant;" A. Hesnard–P.A. Gianfrotta, "Les bouchons d'amphores en pouzzolane," *Amphores romaines et histoire
économique* (Rome 1989) 393-441, esp. 398-99, do not decide between *navicularii* and
mercatores.

be assumed by the same people.[230] The basis for this interpretation of stoppers is provided by the similarity observed in some shipwrecks between names, geometrical designs, with or without isolated letters, and symbols (star, trident, etc.) found on both anchors and stoppers. More suggestive still is the find of a seal matrix and pozzolana in a shipwreck, which indicates that the sealing of amphorae took place onboard, probably at the time of loading.[231] This would be congruent with the fact, observed by D.J. Mattingly, that in Spain Dr. 20 amphorae were produced no further than one or two kilometers away from the waterways, which implies that only the oil intended for the market was stored in amphorae and that this process was carried out near the place where the amphorae were loaded onto riverboats.[232]

An interesting document found in Egypt points toward the involvement of imperial slaves in long-distance trade. The stopper bears the Greek mark ΚΕΡΕ.ΟΝΙΟΣ ΣΕΒ ΑΠΕΛΕΤΘ and was regarded as evidence for ''an imperial freedman's activity in charge of a wine-producing establishment which shipped to Quseir'' and as ''the first clear proof that one of these [wine-producing imperial estates in Egypt] was headed by an imperial freedman.''[233] If one accepts the view that stoppers represent shippers or traders, this imperial freedman was in charge of a shipping company, which would be no surprise in a port town like Quseir. It does not necessarily im-

---

[230] For instance, the equestrian C. Sentius Regulianus was a *diffusor olearius ex Baetica*, a *negotiator vinarius Lugudunensis in canabis consistens*, and a *nauta Araricus* (*CIL* VI 29722 = *ILS* 7490, Rome, second century); P. Olitius Apollonius, from Colonia Narbonensis, was a *navicularius* of the said *colonia* under the reign of Antoninus Pius (*CIL* XII 4406) and a *negotiator olearius* found in line β of some *tituli picti* from the Testaccio (*CIL* XV 3974-3976); and L. Hilarianus Cinnamus from Lugdunum was both a *nauta Rhodanicus Rhodano navigans* and a *negotiator* [*vin*]*arius* (*CIL* XIII 1996 = *ILS* 7031, Lyons, late second/early third century); cf. P. Le Roux, *REA* 88 (1986) 270, nos. 8, 12, and 14; and *CIL* XIII 1954 and 1966 (= *ILS* 7028 and 7030).

[231] A. Hesnard–P.A. Gianfrotta (1989) 393-441, esp. 393-98: ''Les trois arguments nous semblent sans ambiguïté: le remplissage et le bouchage des amphores sont effectués sous le contrôle de celui qui prend livraison du vin, sur les ports d'embarquements, et qui accompagne sa cargaison à bord.'' Cf. also A. Tchernia (1986) 119, n. 237.

[232] D.J. Mattingly, *JRA* 1 (1988) 42-43. Cf. also K. Strobel, *MBAH* 6 (1987) 97-100.

[233] R.S. Bagnall, in D.S. Whitcomb–J.H. Johnson (eds.), *Quseir al-Qadim 1978. Preliminary Report* (Cairo 1979) 243-44, who mentions another plug with the name of one Titus Flavius . .allis, ''perhaps also a freedman (of one of the Flavian emperors).''

ply that this imperial freedman was acting in the capacity of agent of the emperor. The involvement of members of the imperial household in long-distance trade left some traces in the region of the Bay of Naples (Pompeii and Puteoli).[234]

a. *shippers vs. traders vs. producers and manufacturers?*
Instances of single amphorae for which all three types of epigraphical evidence have been preserved and identified are unknown to me. This may be ascribed to the fact that the number of recovered *tituli picti* and stoppers is small compared to the number of amphora stamps, and that they are not yet readily available in published corpora. As no correspondence has been noticed between stamps, *tituli picti*, and stopper marks, it is likely that trade and shipping of amphora-borne commodities were most of the time carried out by different people, who were themselves apparently independent from producers and manufacturers.

First, manufacturers/producers and traders were independent from one another. Tassaux observed that the diffusion of the stamps of Laecanius on Dr. 2-4 is most intense in Noricum, where not one of the ninety known members of the *gens* is recorded.[235] This means perhaps that the Laecanii relied on other people for the distribution of their agricultural surpluses, an hypothesis which would support A. Tchernia's statement that "pour le moment, les données de l'épigraphie des amphores tendent plutôt à maintenir la séparation au moins nominale entre la production et le négoce."[236]

Second, manufacturers/producers and shippers were independent from one another. Although P. Sestius and L. Lentulus Crus are known to have owned ships in the late Republican period, the amphorae found in the shipwreck of the Grand Congloué (stamped with the mark SESTIVS) were sealed with stoppers marked L TITIVS C F, and those found in the shipwreck A at Cape Dramont

---

[234] M. Crawford, "Economia imperiale e commercio estero," *Tecnologia, economia e società nel mondo romano* (Como 1980) 207-17, esp. 215-17, with reference to *AE* 1973, no. 157 (Agro Murecine, Pompeii, A.D. 51) recording the obligation to pay a large sum of money to an imperial slave.

[235] F. Tassaux, *MEFRA* 94 (1982) 257-60. The stamps of the Laecanii have been found at Fasana, Val San Pietro, Val Catena, Pola, Aquileia, Concordia, Padua, Cremona, Milan, Vercelli, Turin, Tortona, Rome, on the Magdalensberg, at Ptuj, Emona, Aguntum, Zollfeld, and Szombathely; cf. C. Zaccaria (1989) 479, n. 66, with bibliography.

[236] A. Tchernia (1986) 119; and J. Paterson, *JRS* 72 (1982) 154-55.

(stamped with the mark LENTVLVS CRVS) were sealed with
stoppers marked SEX ARRIVS, a name found also on one anchor
in the same shipwreck.[237]

Third, traders and shippers were independent from one another,
as shown by Labeo's and Paulus's allusion to a merchant hiring (or
chartering) a ship at a flat rate (*aversio*) for the transport of amphorae.[238] The lack of consensus among modern historians concerning the identification of people referred to in stopper marks suggests, as noted above, that the functions of trader and shipper may
have sometimes been performed by the same people.

b. *agents of traders and shippers*

A. Hesnard and P.A. Gianfrotta remark that the obscurity of the
names found on stoppers implies a low social station for those they
represent, mostly freeborn and freedmen. Slaves are conspicuously absent: there is only one occurrence (B26) of a slave named
PHILEMO on an amphora marked PHILO on the rim. Manacorda has another instance, dating perhaps from the Republican
period: DIPILVS N(aevi?) L(uci?) S(ervus).[239] This is no proof,
however, that slaves were not entrusted with the task of shipping
amphora-borne commodities; but it might simply suggest that the
marks on the stoppers refer to the principal rather than to the agent,
or that agent shippers were often freeborn or freedmen. I have suggested in Chapter Two that the extension of the *actio institoria* to extraneous agents (independent or slave) might have been borrowed
from the *actio exercitoria*. This change may be ascribed to the fact that
it was more difficult to check the status and credit of a shipmaster
than of a business manager,[240] and for this reason the *actio exercitoria*

---

[237] A. Tchernia (1986) 118-19, citing C. Santamaria, "Nouvelles recherches
sur l'épave A du Cap Dramont. Qui était l'armateur du navire?," *Annales du Sud-
Est Varois* 7 (1982) 7-9. According to E.L. Will, *JFA* 6 (1979) 349, the Sestii might
have had some "shipping interest, or at least 'naval capabilities'" as suggested by
Cicero's remark in 44 B.C. about the "navigia luculenta . . . Sestii" (*Att.* 16.4.4);
cf. also D. Manacorda, *SRPS II* (1981) 28-36. One Titia L.f. is attested in Cosa
(*CIL* XI 2630).

[238] Labeo (1 *pithanon a Paulo epitomarum*) *Dig.* 14.2.10.2: "Si conduxisti navem
amphorarum duo milium et ibi amphoras portasti, pro duobus milibus amphorarum pretium debes. (Paulus): immo si aversione navis conducta est, pro duobus
milibus debetur merces: si pro numero impositarum amphorarum merces constituta est, contra se habet: nam pro tot amphoris pretium debes, quot portasti."

[239] D. Manacorda (1989) 462, n. 78, citing *CIL* I^2 2341, now at Ostia.

[240] Ulpianus (28 *ad ed.*) *Dig.* 14.1.1.1: "Utilitatem huius edicti patere nemo est

had to be granted more freely than the *actio institoria*. The conspicuous majority of freed and freeborn shipmasters in our sources can be interpreted as both the cause and the consequence of such a development of the legal system.

Evidence for agents of *negotiatores* or *navicularii* is scarce,[241] and this fact might be ascribed to the desire on the part of some members of the senatorial order not to advertise their involvement in marketing and shipping amphora-borne commodities. Whereas we can have a glimpse of possible slave *institores* on the basis of amphora stamps, there is no way we can even estimate who among known *mercatores*, *negotiatores*, and *navicularii* were doing business through agents, or were acting as agents, and for whom.[242]

Evidence for women *negotiatrices*[243] and shippers[244] in the oil and

---

qui ignoret. Nam cum interdum ignari, cuius sint condicionis vel quales, cum magistris propter navigandi necessitatem contrahamus, aequum fuit eum, qui magistrum navi imposuit, teneri, ut tenetur, qui institorem tabernae vel negotio praeposuit, cum sit maior necessitas contrahendi cum magistro quam institore. Quippe res patitur, ut de condicione quis institoris dispiciat et sic contrahat: in navis magistro non ita, nam interdum locus tempus non patitur plenius deliberandi consilium.''

[241] J. Rougé, *ROCMMER* (1966) 234-38 cites as the only valuable inscription recording a *magister navis* a Pompeian text (*AE* 1951, no. 165) found on a small amphora containing a sample sent by an African landowner through a mandatary, M. Lartidius Vitalis from Cape Bon, Tunisia (= domo Clupeis), on the ship of one C. Umbr(icius) Ampiocus, and in the care of the *magister* P. Pompilius Saturus. It is interesting to note that the *magister* was not a slave, which suggests that the *actio exercitoria* was extended to cases involving agents of free status already by the second half of the first century A.D. Cf. also *Not.Scav.* 1905, p. 257 (= *CIL* IV 5894, Add. p. 725), where only the names of the shipowners are known; *CIL* III 3 (Lustri, Crete, Trajanic), a dedication by a freedman *tabellarius* (Epictetus) set up by the freeborn pilot ("curam agente operis Dionysio Sostrati filio Alexandrino gubernatore") of a ship ("parasemo Isopharia") owned by one T. Claudius Theon; as the *magister navis* is usually distinct from the pilot, I consider it likely that Epictetus was the agent in charge of the ship; cf. Rougé 260. The only additional inscription known to me comes from Vettona (Italy, *Regio* VI) and is much damaged, cf. *CIL* XI 5183: "Priamus Mar(ci?) / s<er>rus magist<er> / navium" (the editor reads "siivus magistii").

[242] J. Rougé, "Droit romain et sources de richesses non foncières," in *L'origine des richesses dépensées dans la ville antique* (Aix-en-Provence 1985) 161-75, esp. 167, where the author mentions that in Arelate the *navicularii* were *praepositi* of great families of landowners. Cf. M. Christol, *Latomus* 31 (1971) 643-63 and *Provence historique* 32 (1982) 5-14.

[243] *AE* 1973, no. 71 (Rome, first half of II); *CIL* XV 3729 (Testaccio, 149); *CIL* XV 3845-3847 (Orti Torlonia, 191); *CIL* XV 3960-3961 (Testaccio, ca. 149). S. Panciera, "*Olearii*," *MAAR* 36 (1980) 244-45 has other unpublished examples. Cf. also P. Le Roux, *REA* 88 (1986) 267.

[244] *AE* 1930, no. 53 (Medamoud on the Red Sea): Λητωῖ θεᾷ μεγίστῃ / Αἰλία

wine trade strengthens the possibility that traders and shippers were often represented by *vilici, actores,* and *institores*,[245] although we have seen that women could be agents as well as principals.

The discrepancy in terms of social status between the people whose names show up in amphora stamps[246] and those attested in the *tituli picti* and stopper marks may indicate that the *plebiscitum Claudianum* of 218 B.C. and the provisions of the *Lex Iulia de repetundis* of 59 B.C. were still enforced as late as the second century A.D.[247] It is impossible to ascertain whether the *negotiatores* and the *navicularii* attested on amphorae were independent economic agents, or mere straw men covering up the commercial activities of the senatorial nobility, or people of free status, but more or less socially dependent on a patron, a relative, or a "friend."[248]

Ἰσίδωρα καὶ Αἰλία/ Ὀλυμπιὰς ματρῶναι / στολᾶται ναύκληροι κα[ὶ / ἔμπο]ροι ἐρυθραϊκαὶ ἄμ[α / . . . Ἀ]πολλιναρίῳ / ἐπάρχ[ῳ . . .] Ὀλυμ/πιάδος κα[ὶ . . .] / ἀμφο-τέρων [. . .] / ἀνέθηκαν [. . .]. Cf. J. Rougé, *ROCMMER* (1966) 335, n. 1.

[245] Cf. the case of Bosiconius, "actor navis Flori (et) Severi" (cf. M. Hassall [1978] 43, table I, no. 14), and that of the *vilicus navis* operating on the Rhone River (*CIL* XII 2379, Gallia Narbonensis, between Vienna and Augusta Praetoria, II/III). Cf. also the case of Myrinos, πραγματευτής of Claudia Bassa, who travelled widely during 35 years (rather than until the age of 35, φορικὰ χρήματα πράξας ἔτη λε', *IGRR* IV 186 = *SIG* 1229). About *magistri navis*, ναύκληροι, *nauclerus*, and προναύκληροι, cf. J. Rougé, *ROCMMER* (1966) 234-45. D.P.S. Peacock–D.F. Williams (1986) stress the fact that those *negotiatores* and *navicularii* recorded in inscriptions and literary texts are usually the financial backers of commercial enterprises, which means that the operations are likely to have been carried out by agents.

[246] In the earlier stage (second century B.C.), the names on stamps referred to freeborn of no outstanding social condition or status, cf. D. Manacorda (1989) 446. Later on, names of people belonging to the senatorial aristocracy were more common, cf. J. Paterson, *JRS* 72 (1982) 156. Members of the equestrian order and municipal aristocracies are well represented. The higher the status of the owner/lessee of a workshop, the more likely the possibility that he/she was relying on *institores*.

[247] J.H. D'Arms, *CSSAR* (1981) 5; 31-39; and 153, citing Scaevola (3 *reg.*) *Dig.* 50.5.3: "His, qui naves marinas fabricaverunt et ad annonam populi Romani praefuerint non minores quinquaginta milium modiorum aut plures singulas non minores decem milium modiorum, donec hae naves navigant aut aliae in earum locum, muneris publici vacatio praestatur ob navem. Senatores autem hanc vacationem habere non possunt, quod nec habere illis navem ex lege Iulia repetundarum licet;" and Paulus, *Sent.* (*Frg. Leid.*, ed. G.G. Archi *et al.*, 1956, p. 5) §3: "Senatores parentesve eorum, in quorum potestate sunt, vectigalia publica condu-cere, navem in quaestum habere equosve curules praebendos suscipere prohiben-tur: idque factum repetundarum lege vindicatur."

[248] About freedmen working as agents of their patrons, cf. Plut., *Cato Maior* 21; Gaius (1 *rerum cottidianorum vel aureorum*) *Dig.* 40.9.10; and Scaevola (11 *dig.*) *Dig.* 26.7.58 *pr.* Cf. D. Manacorda (1989) 461.

5. *Conclusion*

Amphorae, in contrast with building material, tableware, and lamps, were used as containers and therefore submitted to different factors in the process of manufacturing and distribution. The production of amphorae was conditioned by the combined requirements of the producers, traders, and shippers of the goods (mostly wine, oil, and fish sauce) they contained. Each of the four categories of economic participants involved in the trade of amphora-borne commodities is represented in one of the three types of inscriptions preserved on amphorae.

The stamps (signature) refer to the manufacturers—owners of the firms and/or their agents. All social strata are represented, from the emperor down to obscure people of uncertain status and slaves. The production of amphorae was sometimes conducted in the context of the villa economy. Cases where a landowner—through his *vilicus*, a subagent appointed by the latter, or a manager/potter appointed or hired by the landowner and working independently from the bailiff—would have produced the containers in which he would market his agricultural production must have been fairly common (cf. the cases of the Sestii and of the Umbricii Scauri), but the archaeological and epigraphical evidence for this phenomenon is not as abundant as could be expected. The structure of the stamps calls for the same remark as those expounded in the preceding section, namely that what appears to be the *tria nomina* of a freedman could conceal the combination of the names of a principal and his agent (cf. the case of the agent of C. Laecanius Bassus).

For wholesale trade the containers seem to have been usually provided by the trader rather than by the producer of the content. Then, the production of amphorae could have been entrusted to local potters under contract or to the trader's agent in charge of such facilities near the place of shipping.

The purpose of the stamps seems to have been the same as the one proposed in the context of the brick and tile industry. Thus, the person referred to in the stamps would have been liable for the quality of the container.

The most detailed written evidence on amphorae comes from the painted inscriptions, which provide information about the nature, weight, and origin of the content, the identity of the trader and of the employee(s) supervising shipping formalities, the date of the shipment, and some storage code.

Stopper marks represent the shipper or his agent, as the sealing of amphorae was completed at the time and place of shipping. Slave shippers are very rare, but the scantiness of the evidence gives little value to such a statement. Free(d) *magistri navium* can be confused with *exercitores*, and the provision of the *Lex Claudia*, still enforced during the Principate according to the legal sources, probably accounts for the complete silence of our sources about connections between ship operators and their financial backers.

The absence of links in the epigraphical evidence between the various categories of people engaged in the production, trade, and transport of amphora-borne commodities points against the vertical concentration of business activities within the hands of a few magnates, but one cannot exclude the existence of concealed cases of legal or social dependency between seemingly independent people.[249]

D. POTTERY (TERRA SIGILLATA)

1. *Historical outline*

During the Republican period, the so-called Campanian pottery underwent an evolution toward mass production, standardization, simplification of decoration, and disappearance of signatures, which makes it impossible for us to reconstruct the organization of the industry. J.-P. Morel speculates that, as far as the post-Hannibalic-War Campanian A pottery was concerned, the anonymous producers must have had very few contacts, if any, with the consumers, because, according to him, the distribution was carried out by middlemen.[250] Thus, the anonymity of the market and its growing size called for the mass production of standardized wares made by potters working in larger production units than earlier.

---

[249] D. Manacorda, *Opus* 4 (1985) 142, following A. di Porto, *Sodalitas* VII (1984) 3256, thinks that many landowners were trying to retain control over the sale of the products of their farms by organizing their processing and transport to the marketplace. This may be correct insofar as the marketing did not imply oversea shipment.

[250] J.-P. Morel, "La produzione della ceramica campana. Aspetti economici e sociali," *SRPS* II (1981) 81-97, esp. 93. The involvement of middlemen is inferred mainly from a text of Diodorus Siculus (5.13) that applies to iron work in Puteoli and from two allusions in Sallust (*Iug.* 21.2 and 26.3) about the role of *negotiatores* in Numidia in the late second century B.C, where Campanian A pottery was massively exported.

As mentioned in the introduction to this chapter, small workshops supplying local markets provide an unlikely setting for the appointment of business managers. The evolution described in the preceding paragraph created a new situation which prepared the way for the introduction of new forms of management. The emergence of larger units of production was followed by a typological change to Campanian B and C and Arretine black-glazed pottery during the second century B.C. The reappearance of the signatures was combined with the potters' growing awareness of market conditions. Producers and traders tried to reach farther markets inland and overseas, and transfers of workshops occurred more and more often. Insofar as some major firms managed to retain, at least temporarily, their Italian bases while conquering provincial markets, the conditions became ideal for the development of agency in the pottery industry.

In a recent and comprehensive study of the development of trade and economic activities in the Po Valley, R. Chevallier described a recurrent pattern of development common to both Etrusco-Campanian pottery and terra sigillata. In the first case, the diffusion of pottery antedates the conquest of Cisalpine Gaul in the second century B.C. In the aftermath of the military occupation, branch workshops were opened and simultaneously local potters started producing imitations. Consequently, areas of exportation went through periods of economic and demographic growth which resulted in the creation of local enterprises ultimately superseding those from which the techniques of production had been learned. The same phenomenon started all over again with the next area of expansion.[251]

This phenomenon is best attested for the production and distribution of Italian-type terra sigillata, also called Samian or Arretine ware.[252] An early example is provided by the potter C. Aco who, in

---

[251] R. Chevallier, *La romanisation de la Celtique du Pô* (Paris/Rome 1983) 266-67, and nn. 397-401 for the bibliography: "la décentralisation d'une même production, évidente d'après les différents types d'argiles, visait à diminuer les frais de transport" and 273-74: "(les zones d'exportation,) douées, à un certain stade de développement, de plus de vitalité démographique et économique, produisent à leur tour, aux dépens des régions qui les ont initiées, en vertu de cette loi économique qui veut que les centres de fabrication cherchent à se rapprocher des lieux de consommation."

[252] E. Ettlinger *et al.*, *Conspectus formarum terrae sigillatae italico modo confectae* (Bonn 1990) (here after *Conspectus* [1990]). Cf. also M. and P. Vauthey, "Les courants artistiques et économiques de l'industrie céramique dans l'Antiquité

the second half of the first century B.C., worked near Comum or Cremona. His production was sold in Northern Italy (Upper Po Valley), and exported to Gaul, Upper Germania, Raetia, Noricum, and Pannonia. At one point, his agents seem to have controlled other centers of production in Ravenna, Faenza, and perhaps also Abano and Aquileia. Later, he even established a branch workshop in Lyons, which he possibly entrusted to a slave *institor/officinator*, to take advantage of the Gallic markets. Still active in A.D. 15, C. Aco is known to have employed slaves and freedmen (Diophanes, Aescinus, Antiochus, Gratus, and the most active of them, Aco Acastus) who were using decorative stamps (*poinçons*) and moulds imported from Arezzo. The contacts between Italian main workshops and provincial branches seem to have remained active for a while.[253]

In a later period, some potters located in Raetia (Westendorf and Pfaffenhofen) stamped the label PRO or PROV on the outside bottom of their products (Dragendorff 32 and 37), which has been interpreted as the abbreviation of PROVINCIALIS (*officina*).[254] If this interpretation were correct, it would suggest that Italian origin did not constitute a fashionable must in the mind of the consumers who purchased Arretine-like terra sigillata, and that provincial products were not necessarily of lower quality. This would be confirmed by the development of Gallic production centers. In the early first century A.D., local Gaulish potters started imitating the Italian style of products imported or made by Italian potters in branch workshops. The resulting overproduction forced Italian potters to relocate upstream along the Saône, probably under Tiberius or Claudius. Later in the first century A.D., Arretine potters were completely

---

d'Arezzo aux confins de l'Empire à travers la Gaule romaine," *RACF* 12 (1973) 115-26; L. Mazzeo Saracino, *EAA, Atlante delle forme ceramiche* II (1985) 175-280 ("Terra sigillata nord-italica"); and G. Pucci, *ibid.* 359-406 ("Terra sigillata italica"), esp. 368-71 ("Problema delle succursali").

[253] R. Chevallier (1983) 268-69; M. Vegas, "Aco-Becher," *RCRF* 11/12 (1969-1970) 107-24; J. and A. Lasfargues–H. Vertet, "L'atelier de potiers augustéen de la Muette à Lyon," *Notes d'épigraphie et d'archéologie lyonnaises* (Lyons 1976) 61-80; C.M. Wells, "L'implantation des ateliers de céramique sigillée en Gaule. Problématique de la recherche," *Figlina* 2 (1977) 1-11; and M.-P. Lavizzari Pedrazzini, "Artigianato colto e di tradizione ellenistica nella transpadana di età augustea. La ceramica 'tipo Aco'," *RCRF* 25/26 (1987) 255-80, esp. 255-56.

[254] M. and P. Vauthey, *RACF* 12 (1973) 123, citing H.-J. Kellner, "Warum signierte PRO(VINCIALIS)?" *RCRFCommunicationes* 2 (1969) 47-49, no. 10. The vases are also signed HELENIVS or RIPANVS. On double signatures, cf. below.

superseded by provincial competitors. It seems, however, that the mark PROVINCIALIS should be interpreted differently (cf. below).

2. *Pattern of expansion of major Italian firms*

Aco's firm found its interprovincial vocation at an early date. Other firms developed at a slower pace or retained their Italian base for a longer period. Even then, decentralization was not out of question.

Around the same period or slightly later than Aco (in the 30's or 20's B.C.), the Ligurian potter L. Sarius, with the assistance of his slave and later freedman Surus, started producing terra sigillata near Pavia, Brescia, or Bologna. Their production is also attested in Giubiasco, Concordia, and Aquileia. In some other places, stamps bearing the name of other slaves of Sarius (Tyrsus, Celer, Crestus, Felix) suggest that the famous potter had perhaps established branch workshops in Mantova, Rimini, Aquileia, Veleia, and Giulanova.[255] The signatures show the name of the slave in the nominative or genitive form, followed by the name of the master in the genitive form (*nomen* only, or *praenomen* plus *nomen*).[256] The existence of a Southern Italian branch is possibly illustrated by the find of a cup stamped SARIVS L L SVRVS in the wreck of a ship presumably bound from the Adriatic coast to the Aegean.[257]

---

[255] C. Goudineau, "Un nouveau vase de L. Sarius Surus," *MEFRA* 80 (1968) 527-45; and R. Chevallier (1983) 269. On branch industries in the Po Valley, cf. E. Ettlinger, *Conspectus* (1990) 5, reporting the existence of branch workshops in the Po Valley by A.D. 20, the production of which was signed by C. Sertorius, A. Sestius, and A. Titius; and S. Zabehlicky-Scheffenegger, "Frühe padanische Filialen einiger Töpfereien," *RCRF* 29/30 (1991) 95-104.

[256] For instance, CELER SARI or CRESTI L SARI. Cf. also *CIL* XI 6700, no. 576 (Ocriculum): T(?) SARI; *ibid.*, no. 577 a and b (Volaterra): L(ucius) SAR(i or -ius) C(ai) L(uci) L(ibertus) SVRVS; and SVRVS SARI L(uci) S(ervus); *ibid.*, no. 578 (Arimini): TYRSV(s) SARI L(uci) S(ervus); *ibid.*, no. 579 (Rimini): CELER SARI; *ibid.*, no. 580 (Rimini and Veleia): FELIX SARI; *CIL* V 8115, no. 108 (Genua): C(?) SARI; cf. *CVArr* 1665-1666.

[257] A. Freschi, "Il relitto A delle Tre Senghe (Isole Tremiti). – Relazione preliminare 1981-1982," in *Archaeologia subacquea* (*BA* Suppl. 4, Rome 1982 [1983]) 89-100, esp. 100. The location of a branch in Apulia and the export to the East of Surus's production is hypothetical, as it rests on the assumption that the location of the shipwreck off the Tremiti Islands (Diomedeae) was on a route followed by ships transporting Lamboglia 2 wine-amphorae from Apulia to the East. But as A. Tchernia (1986) 53-56 points out, Lamboglia 2 amphorae were also produced further north. Thus, it is possible that this particular ship had set out from Rimini or Ravenna rather than from Apulia, and that it was bound to Southern Italy or even Rome.

a. *archaeological evidence for workshops*

It is clear that the existence of a workshop (main or subsidiary) cannot be inferred from the find of a stamp. Only a concentration of the same stamps within a given area, not necessarily to the exclusion of other locations, suggests that they were perhaps produced locally, hence the importance of maps of distribution.[258] The only reliable type of evidence for the identification of a workshop consists in the find of a dumping site, where the refuse is composed of defective or unfinished stamped pottery, in the best cases located in the vicinity of a kiln. Very few assemblages of this type have been discovered. Recently, the workshop and kiln of C. Umbricius Cordus was found between Arezzo and Chiusi, in Central Etruria.[259] Another case is provided by the kiln found on the Ianiculum in Rome, with refuse stamped OPPI or C O(ppius) R(estitutus), a well-known lamp-maker whose products are found in great numbers in Italy, North Africa, Spain, Sardinia, Gallia Narbonensis, and even in the Northern provinces.[260]

The most famous instance, however, is that of the Arretine potter Cn. Ateius.[261] The stamps found among the refuse dumped near his workshop in Arezzo, identified in 1954,[262] show that Ateius was at first working alone or, at least, that his possible assistants were not autonomous enough to sign their products. On the other hand, the stamps found all over Italy and the Western provinces show that Ateius was assisted, perhaps at a later stage, by several slaves or freedmen, and by the latters' slaves.[263] The nature of the link between Ateius and his personnel remains unclear, because the form and purpose of the stamps resist any definitive explanation. In addition, no modern scholar has attempted to establish a relative chro-

---

[258] S. von Schnurbein, *Conspectus* (1990) 22 mentions the possibility of branch workshops under Augustus or Tiberius in Southern Gaul (Narbonne, Bram, Aspiran, Jonquières/Saint Saturnin) on the basis of correspondences of potters' names, which might be purely coincidental.

[259] G. Pucci, "A Sigillata Kiln in Valdichiana (Central Etruria)," *RCRF* 27/28 (1990) 15-23.

[260] Mentioned by E.W. Haley, "The Lamp Manufacturer Gaius Iunius Draco," *MBAH* 9 (1990) 1-12, esp. 3.

[261] The best up-to-date discussion of Ateius's personnel is found in G. Prachner, *Die Sklaven und Freigelassenen im arretinischen Sigillatagewerbe* (Wiesbaden 1980) 26-36. Cf. *CIL* XI 6700, nos. 100-107, etc; and *CVArr* 144-186.

[262] G. Maetzke, "Notizie sulla esplorazione dello scarico della fornace di CN. ATEIVS in Arezzo," *RCRF* 2 (1959) 25-27.

[263] For instance, *CVArr* 174: PHIL(omus)VS / CN ATEI SALVI.

nology of the signatures on the basis of the typology of the wares on which they are preserved. Consequently, it is still difficult to exploit to a full extent the wealth of information contained in the stamps, with all their variants, in order to trace the development of the production of each individual represented in them. The comparison between the respective patterns of distribution of the products of individual potters of the *familia* Ateii (or *gens* Ateia) seems to point toward a certain level of economic independence among the potters of the same group. Whether or not these potters remained legally, socially, or economically tied to their master/patron is debatable. Both slaves (with *peculium*) and freedmen could have an independent activity, and consequently could be found in the position of either entrepreneurs or workshop managers.

b. *branch workshops*
The localization and identification of workshops is facilitated by the finds of moulds. Such is the case of a workshop owned by one N. Naevius in Cumae, where three moulds were discovered.[264] They bear a stamp in *tabula ansata* which reads N NAEVI / HILAR (or N N H, or H N N).[265] The presence of a workshop in Cumae is not surprising, since several literary sources record an active ceramic industry there in the late Republic and early Empire.[266] The production of Naevius is well attested elsewhere in Campania, in particular in Puteoli, where some 300 sherds and 60 stamps suggest the presence of another workshop. While some of the decorative elements of the moulds from Cumae are unique, one decorative stamp (*poinçon*) was used in both workshops. It seems that Naevius started in Cumae and subsequently opened a branch workshop in Puteoli, which produced for overseas export. Significantly, the signatures most commonly attested on Naevius's vessels are composed of two stamps, one bearing the name of the owner in the genitive (NAEVI) and another bearing a slave name.[267] Naevius's production is found at Haltern, which points toward a late Augustan date. It was

---

[264] G. Soricelli, "Un'officina di N. Naevius Hilarus a Cuma," *ArchClass* 34 (1982) 190-95. Stamps of the Naevii are collected in *CVArr* 1080-1110.

[265] *CVArr* 1083a-g. The stamp of Hilarus alone is also attested, cf. *CVArr* 1084.

[266] G. Soricelli, *ArchClass* 34 (1982) 190-92, with reference to Varro, Tibullus, Apicius, Statius, and Martial. Cf. also Pliny, *HN* 35.165 (about ceramic production in Rhegium and Cumae).

[267] *CVArr* 1080. They are very common on vases and moulds in Puteoli.

still in use in Pompeii in A.D. 79, which implies that the production must have lasted until the end of the reign of Claudius or even later.

The existence of workshops can sometimes be inferred from the pattern of distribution of the products signed by a specific potter. The potter Comitialis is well attested in Westendorf, probably in the second century A.D. His products exhibit a combination of two stamps COMITIALIS and CSSER (or CSSEROT).[268] The finds of products signed by the same Comitialis in Niederbieber and in Württemberg, where the products of Westendorf seem never to have reached, point toward the existence of a workshop in Rheinzabern. This hypothesis is strengthened by the fact that the stamps of Comitialis from Rheinzabern and Westendorf seem to be contemporary.[269]

As for Ateius's concern, four workshops have been identified so far: Arezzo, Pisa, Lyons, and perhaps La Graufesenque (Aveyron), and more might be found in the future. The first workshop produced mostly for the Italian market, the second for export overseas, and the third and fourth for export to the Rhine markets.[270] The existence of various branches has been established on the basis of the chemical analysis of 68 sherds of pottery found in Gaul. Seven sherds have a lower content of TiO_2 (titanium dioxide) than the rest, and provide evidence for a workshop in Lyons. Out of the remaining 61 Italian sherds, 55 have a higher content of K_2O (potassium oxide) than Arretine pottery, which suggests the existence of another Italian workshop, located in Pisa. It has been speculated that Ateius first opened a branch workshop in Pisa to conquer overseas markets (including Southern Italy), and then in Lyons to conquer the Rhine area, thus setting a pattern followed by other potters.[271]

---

[268] H.-J. Kellner, *RCRFCommunicationes* 2.10 (1969) 47, postulating that the first signature ("im Bildfeld") represents the entrepreneur or potter, while the second signature ("am Rand" or "am Boden") could refer to an agent or subcontractor.

[269] G. von Bülow, "Militärische und zivile Keramikproduktion in den römischen Provinzen am Rhein und an der oberen Donau," *Klio* 57 (1975) 233-40, esp. 235, n. 16, and 236.

[270] On the Pisan workshop, cf. P. Taponeco Marchini, "La fabbrica pisana di Ateio," *Antichità Pisane* 1 (1974) 3-9.

[271] M. Picon *et al.*, "Recherches sur les céramiques d'Ateius trouvées en Gaule," *RCRF* 14/15 (1972/1973) 128-35. This method has become increasingly sophisticated in the last twenty years, cf. G. Schneider, "X-ray Fluorescence and the Production and Distribution of Terra Sigillata and Firmalampen," in W.V.

Similar conclusions have been reached through a different method, based on Neutron Activation Analysis (NAA), measuring a wide array of elements (ca. 50) with good accuracy (average precision ca. 2 %):

> Pottery with the Ateius signature has been shown to have the same chemical composition pattern as many pottery rejects found near kilns in the large complex of workshops of La Montée de la Muette in Lyons. We believe this indicates definitely that the great pottery-making firm in Arezzo, Ateius, had a branch workshop in Lyons around 10 B.C. This branch was probably opened with experienced workers and equipment from Arezzo in order to shorten the distance to the new markets of Gaul and the Germanic border legions.[272]

The presence of a workshop of Ateius in La Graufesenque has been established on the basis of the find of one (!) sherd among the refuse of a kiln.[273] The validity of such an isolated piece of evidence is questionable.

Despite these pioneering attempts, it remains difficult to draw any definite conclusion on the basis of the distribution of stamps because in most cases the dearth of chemical analysis prevents us from determining what was produced where and when. For instance, it is not known whether all Ateius's workshops were active at the same time, or whether these workshops correspond to successive stages in the career of one craftsman. Furthermore, there is no way to estimate the quality and quantity of the output for each workshop respectively.

Harris (ed.), *The Inscribed Economy* (1993) 129-37, using wavelength-dispersive X-ray fluorescence (focusing on 16 to 25 elements) to determine the provenance of pottery found in Rheinzabern, in particular for the products of two potters from Arezzo, L. Gellius Quadratus and L. Sempronius Hilarus, who seem to have had a branch in Lyons. G. Schneider – B. Hoffmann, "Chemische Zusammensetzung italischer Sigillata," *Conspectus* (1990) 32 report that out of the stamped pottery found in Haltern (abandoned ca. A.D. 9), 48 % of the material was produced in Lyons, 36 % in Pisa, and only 2 % in Arezzo.

[272] F. Wiedemann *et al.*, "A Lyons Branch of the Pottery-making Firm of Ateius of Arezzo," *Archaeometry* 17 (1975) 45-59, esp. 58 (quotation). On NAA potentials and limitations, cf. now the paper by J.T. Peña, "Two Studies of the Provenience of Roman Pottery Through Neutron Activation Analysis," in W.V. Harris (ed.), *The Inscribed Economy* (1993) 107-20.

[273] R. Marichal, "Nouvelles fouilles et nouveaux graffites de la Graufesenque," *CRAI* (1981) 251. G. Schneider – B. Hoffmann, *Conspectus* (1990) 32 add five fragments of locally-produced artifacts with dubious stamps ("mit zweifelhaften Ateius-Stempeln").

c. variations in patterns of distribution of finished products
Several members of the Ateius concern seem to have operated in the
region of Pisa during the same period,[274] but their products followed different patterns of distribution. Whether they belonged to
the same workshop with separate units of production or to distinct
ones is unclear. E. Ettlinger compares the respective ratios of stamps
found within two wide areas, the Mediterranean basin and the
Gallic/Germanic provinces.[275] An independent study has shown
that the whole production was divided into three groups. The first
is represented mainly in Italy and in the Western provinces (signed
by Eros, Euhodus, Euryalus, Mahes, Plocamus, Rufus (?), Salvius,
Tetius (?), Xanthus and Zoilus); the second is represented in Italy,
Spain and North Africa, but not in the Gallic and Germanic provinces (signed by Amaranthus, Dei(us) Di(on), Germulus, and Phil-
(omusus), but most names are abbreviated); and the third is represented only in Germania and, exceptionally, in Gaul (signed by
Albanus, Crestus, (Stab)ili(o), Primigenius, Germanio(?), Hilarus,
Narcissus, and Otonius(?), in addition to the product of the partnerships formed by Crestus and Euhodus, Mahes and Zoilus, and Xanthus and Zoilus).[276] The tentative result of Ettlinger's survey suggests that the potters identified as freedmen are better represented
in the Mediterranean region, while the potters identified as slaves
produced wares mostly found in the Gallic/Germanic provinces.
Her study rests on the questionable assumption that the form of
names in the stamps provides a secure basis for the identification of
individual potter's status.

The pattern recognized by Ettlinger is best attested for other contemporary potters who did not belong to Ateius's clan. Thus, the
freedman A. Vibius Scrotula (producing from ca. 30 until 10 B.C.)
and his slave Diomedes (ca. 25 – 5 B.C.) are represented respectively
by 114 and 29 stamps in the Mediterranean basin vs. 34 and 41 in
the Gallic/Germanic provinces. T. Rufrenus (ca. 10 B.C. – A.D. 20)

---

[274] T.O. Jefferson – G.B. Dannell – D. Williams, "The Production and Distribution of *terra sigillata* in the Area of Pisa, Italy," in A.C and A.S. Anderson (eds.),
Roman Pottery Research in Britain and North-West Europe (Oxford 1981) 161-71, about
the discovery of kilns and workshops operated by Ateius, Hilarus, Mahes, and
Xoilus between 15 B.C. and A.D. 25. D. Williams reports (169-70), however, that
the petrological analysis of eight sherds shows that seven of them might not be of
Pisan origin.
[275] E. Ettlinger, "How was Arretine Ware Sold," *RCRF* 25/26 (1987) 5-19.
[276] G. Prachner (1980) 31.

and his slave Rufio (ca. 10 B.C. – A.D. 7) are represented respectively by 80 and 34 vs. 9 and 45. The potter Sex. Avilius (ca. A.D. 2 – 24), represented by 113 stamps in the Mediterranean basin vs. 44 in the Gallic/Germanic provinces, had a slave Mena (ca. A.D. 2 – 13) in Lyons, whose stamps (17) are only found in the Gallic provinces, with one exception in Rome. The case of L. Tettius Samia (ca. 20 – 3 B.C.) and his slave Crito (ca. 15 – 5 B.C.), with respectively ca. 200 and 8, vs. ca. 187 and 26, is less spectacular, because of the discrepancy in quantity between master's and slave's production.[277]

Ettlinger's study of Ateius's exports from Pisa reveals that the ATEIVS signature (ca. 11 B.C. – A.D. 22) is found on 381 (+ ?) sherds in the Mediterranean basin and 1,061 (+ ?) in the Gallic/ Germanic provinces. This in itself is not revealing because any potter belonging to the *familia* of Ateius could have signed with the name of the firm only. Ateius's agents or workers Euhodus (ca. 5 B.C. – A.D. 25), Mahes (ca. 5 B.C. – A.D. 15), Xanthus (ca. 5 B.C. – A.D. 27) and Zoilus (ca. 2 B.C. – A.D. 30) are represented respectively by 37, 36, 91, and 122 stamps in the Mediterranean basin vs. 92, 122, 464, and 94 in the Gallic/Germanic provinces (cf. below for specifics). The conclusion to be drawn from Ettlinger's study is that it is possible that freedmen or freeborn were in charge of Italian workshops producing high quality and finely decorated wares for the Italian and Mediterranean markets, while slave potters or managers belonged to workshops—in Italy or in Gaul—producing coarser wares for the Northern markets.[278]

That the pattern of distribution may have changed at the time of manumission is also illustrated, for instance, by the production of a later potter attached to Ateius's concern, Cn. Ateius Amaranthus,[279] whose workshop was located in Tuscany and who started producing as a slave around A.D. 10. His pottery was exported to Spain (Ampurias, Merida), Lyons, Cologne, and London. Ten years later, just after he had adopted the signature *in planta pedis*, i.e. encompassed in a foot-shaped cartouche, he was manumitted and started producing plates which were exported to Carthagena and

---

[277] E. Ettlinger, *RCRF* 25/26 (1987) 15-16. All dates are approximated on the basis of Ettlinger's tables.

[278] E. Ettlinger, *RCRF* 25/26 (1987) 13-16.

[279] *CVArr* 153 and 154.

sold in Italy.[280] If this particular example represents a trend, it
shows that Ateius's potters were ready to abandon the Northern
markets, perhaps as a result of the growing competition of Gallic
potters.

In an earlier study, E. Ettlinger sketches a set of maps of distribution of the products of Euhodus, Mahes, Xanthus and Zoilus,
from which she concludes that each potter belonged to a separate
workshop working apparently independently from the others and
that the production signed with the name of the firm (CN ATEI +
cognomen of the potter) is earlier than the production signed with the
potter's *cognomen* only. The latter type is distributed mainly in Gaul
and in Germania. The assumption that the signature with *cognomen*
alone (e.g., XANTHVS) refers to a later stage in the life of the
potter (after manumission) than a signature with *tria nomina* (e.g.,
CN(aeus) ATEI(us) XANTHVS) or *duo nomina* in the genitive and
cognomen in the nominative (e.g., CN(aei) ATEI XANTHVS) in-
dicating the identity of the slave's owner or agent's principal is based
on the occurrence of the marks with *cognomen* alone *in planta pedis*,
a form of stamp which became common after A.D. 15 or 20.[281] If
Ettlinger's theory is correct, the stamps with CN ATEI + *cognomen*
clearly emphasize the link between the worker/manager and his
master/patron/principal, no matter how one interprets the form CN
ATEI. It could be argued, however, that the use of the *cognomen*
alone is a sign of servile status, which a newly manumitted potter
would try to put behind him by adopting the *tria nomina*, thus implying that the sequence adopted by Ettlinger should be reversed.[282]

---

[280] H. Comfort, "Late Ateius Signatures," *RCRF* 4 (1962) 5-25, esp. 6-8. On
the evolution of stamp shapes, cf. P.M. Kenrick, "Potters' Stamps," *Conspectus*
(1990) 147-48, discussing stamps applied radially; larger, two-line stamps; circular
stamps; trefoil or quatrefoil; *tabella ansata*; *in planta pedis* (from A.D. 15 or 20); and
crescent shape (late Italian, I/II A.D.).

[281] E. Ettlinger, "Vorbemerkungen zu einer Diskussion des Ateius-Problems,"
RCRF 4 (1962) 27-44. Cf. also R. Chevallier, *Les potiers antiques (monde romain)*
(*Caesarodunum* Suppl. 60, Tours 1990) 7: "Le génitif d'appartenance, comme ATEI
XANTHI se lit: vase fait par Xanthus, esclave d'Ateius. Quand Xanthus signe
seul, c'est qu'il a été affranchi, cas fréquent pour les noms d'origine grecque."

[282] C. Delplace, "Les potiers dans la société et l'économie de l'Italie et de la
Gaule au Ier siècle av. et au Ier siècle ap. J.-C.," *Ktèma* 3 (1978) 55-76, esp. 58,
considers the most likely sequence to be *cognomen* alone first, then *tria nomina* as a
proof of manumission. E.W. Haley, *MBAH* 9 (1990) 8: "It is evident that the mark
OPPI is a predecessor of C OPPI RES" based on the evidence from two shipwrecks
(Culip IV and Culip I).

A comparison with the figures provided by G. Prachner raises some questions about the basis of Ettlinger's theory: for instance, CN ATEI AMARANT is attested on 8 stamps *in planta pedis* (*i.p.p.*) out of 11, while AMAR is represented on only 1 stamp *i.p.p.* out of 8.[283] CN ATEI / EVHODI is attested on 7 stamps *i.p.p.* out of 73 stamps, while EVHODI is also attested on 7 (?) stamps *i.p.p.* out of 58 stamps.[284] CN ATEI / MA(h)ES (or CN ATEI / MAHETIS) and MAHES (or MAHETIS) are represented on respectively 53 (?) and 116 stamps, none of them *i.p.p.*.[285] By contrast, Ettlinger's hypothesis is confirmed in the case of CN ATEI / XANTHI, with 126 stamps, none of them *i.p.p.*, while 50 or more out of 428 (?) stamps signed XANTHI are found *i.p.p.*[286] The same remark applies to the case of CN ATEI / ZOILI with none of the 40 stamps *i.p.p.*, while 36 (?) out of 175 stamps signed ZOILI or SOILI are reported *i.p.p.*.[287] These figures are likely to be modified by future discovery, and the whole demonstration may crumble as a result. My personal opinion leans toward Ettlinger's theory, although I suspect that ancient potters were not necessarily always consistent and systematic in the choice of the form of their signature.

3. The structure of the stamps

a. nomenclature in pottery stamps

As we have seen in the case of bricks, tiles, and amphorae, potters' stamps are notoriously ambiguous: the *praenomen* is usually abbreviated and the *gentilicium* could be read as an abbreviated nominative (ATEI(us)) or as a regular genitive. For instance, we know of several variants of the stamp bearing the name of Cn. Ateius Hilarus: ATEI / HILARI; CN ATEI / HILARVS; CN ATEI / HILARI; and CN ATEIVS / HILARVS.[288] Whether or not these variants reflect an actual progression in this potter's career, from the status of slave working with his master or operating a workshop on his behalf to that of independent freedman, is difficult to ascertain. For each of

---

[283] *CVArr* 153-154.
[284] *CVArr* 160-161.
[285] *CVArr* 168-169.
[286] *CVArr* 176-177.
[287] *CVArr* 180-181. G. Prachner (1980) 26-29.
[288] *CVArr* 166.

the variants it remains unclear whether we are dealing with a free-born/freedman called Cn. Ateius Hilarus, or with the slave/freed-man Hilarus of Cn. Ateius.[289] Ascription of libertine status to the potters who adopted such signatures is unwarranted, because there is no way to determine whether the signature stands for CN(aeus) ATEI(us) HILARVS (or the same in the genitive form) or whether the *cognomen* is independent from the *praenomen* and *gentilicium*. In that case, the stamp should be read CN(aei) ATEI (servus) HILARVS or (*ex officina*) CN(aei) ATEI, HILARVS (*fecit*), or finally (*ex officina*) CN(aei) ATEI, (*opus*) HILARI.[290]

The reading of stamps proposed here, whereby two persons are referred to, seems sometimes inescapable. Ceramics found in Rome and Arezzo were produced by one A. Titius who signed A TITI / FIGVL. Some of his stamps, however, include a third line with the mention ARRET, which has been interpreted as a reference to the place of origin (= *Arretio* or *Arretii*).[291] In view of the rarity of such usage, it seems more logical to understand ARRET as the abbreviated form of a name, Arretius, who would have been an employee of A. Titius.[292] Another illustration is provided by one manufacturer named L. Gellius, who had a workshop in Arezzo producing terra sigillata signed with a variety of stamps. One type of stamp features two names: L SEMPR / L GELLI. The chemical analysis of samples of the whole production indicates that artifacts signed with this particular stamp were produced in Lyons.[293] S. Zabehlicky-

---

[289] S. Treggiari, *Roman Freedmen during the Late Republic* (Oxford 1969) 92, n. 3.

[290] Cf. above, and A. Oxé, *RhM* 59 (1904) 135-140 (= **Form IX**).

[291] *CIL* XV 5649a-c and *CIL* XI 6700, no. 688: A TITI / FIGVL / ARRET; *CIL* XV 5649d-l: A TITI / FIGVL; *CIL* XV 5649m-o: A TITI (= *ILS* 8603). Dessau points out that A. Titius would be the only potter to provide an indication of provenance in his stamps (with the exception of *CIL* III 14215, no. 14 (Silistria, Lower Moesia): FILEMON / ARETIO FEC, where the signature is scratched—not stamped—on the rim of the vessel).

[292] According to the index of *CIL* VI, the *cognomen* Arretius is not rare. The *cognomen* Arretinus is not attested in Rome, but there are several Arret(?), and one Claudia Arretin(a) at Brixia, cf. *CIL* V 4405 (= *ILS* 6721a). Cf. also *CIL* X 8056, no. 1 (Puteoli and Catina): ARRETI or ARRE.

[293] G. Schneider–E. Wirz, "Chemical Answers to Archaeological Questions–Roman Terracotta Lamps as Documents of Economic History," *Doc. et Trav. IGAL* 15 (1991) 13. Cf. also S. Zabehlicky-Scheffenegger, *L. GELLIVS–Versuch einer Töpfermonographie mit einem Beitrag zu den Ergebnissen der chemischen Analysen von G. Schneider und R.C.V. Hancock* (forthcoming), the outline of which is already presented in *eadem*, "Die Geschäfte des Herrn Lucius G.–ein Arbeitsbericht," *RCRF* 21/22 (1982) 105-15; and G. Schneider–B. Hoffmann, "Chemische Zusammen-

Schaffenegger suggests that the earlier stamps feature the names of both L. Gellius and L Sempronius in either order (L GELLI / L SEMPR or L SEMPR / L GELLI), and that L. Gellius appears alone in later stamps *in planta pedis*. It could be argued that the two potters were partners. If it was possible, however, to demonstrate that both workshops in Arezzo and Lyons were active contemporaneously, one could suggest that L. Sempronius was a workshop manager working for L. Gellius (or vice versa). These stamps demonstrate the validity of the theory of binominal stamps on terra sigillata.[294]

In this context, one should keep in mind that epigraphical habits contemporary with terra sigillata stamps point toward a reference to two persons rather than one. In monumental inscriptions down to the Augustan period, it was common for freeborn to omit their *cognomen* (if they had one) from their signatures.[295] This may not be the case of freedmen, who seem to have adopted the use of the cognomen around 106 B.C.[296] While the use of *duo nomina* is most common in early inscriptions, it is only during the first century A.D. that the *tria nomina* became fashionable, and perhaps only during the second century that it became normal to refer to people by their *tria nomina*. Military inscriptions show that the practice of using the *tria nomina* instead of *praenomen* + *nomen* developed mostly after A.D. 42,[297] and Pliny the Younger used *nomen* + *cognomen* or *praenomen* + *nomen* to refer to a new character, but never the *tria nomina*.[298]

---

setzung italischer Sigillata," *Conspectus* (1990) 27-36, with detailed analysis (by X-Ray Fluorescence and Neutron Activation) of Gellius's production from Arezzo and Lyons.

[294] Binominal stamps are well identified in brick and tile stamps, cf. above. Cf. also, for the sake of comparison, the series of three bread seals found in Moguntiacum (Upper Germania, *CIL* XIII 6935b-d): the owner/principal in all three cases is a *centurio* named Caecilius (*praenomen* and *cognomen* are unknown), and the bakery managers are named Sabineus, Musentius, and Metonius. Musentius bears the title of *adiutor*.

[295] E. Ettlinger, *Conspectus* (1990) 5 points out that the oldest stamps on tableware from Arezzo often consist of two single letters. Even when *praenomen* and *nomen* are written in full, the *cognomen* is left out.

[296] A.E. Gordon, "On the First Appearance of the *cognomen* in Latin Inscriptions of Freedmen," *Univ. of Calif. Publ. in Class. Philol.* (1935) 151-58.

[297] H. Comfort, *CVArr* p. XXXI.

[298] A.N. Sherwin-White, *The Letters of Pliny: A Historical and Social Commentary* (Oxford 1966) 113. This point might not be relevant for nomenclature in inscriptions, as it may reflect the idiosyncratic habit of Pliny, who should be compared to other literary writers, especially Cicero in his correspondence.

Therefore, it is possible that the buyer of Arretine tableware in the time of Augustus would have regarded the stamps as referring to two different persons, one referred to by his *praenomen* and *gentilicium*, the other by his *cognomen*.

It has been usually assumed, on the basis of monumental inscriptions, that a slave would be referred to by his *cognomen* followed by the name (*praenomen*, and/or *gentilicium*, and/or *cognomen*) of his master in the genitive case, for instance, HILARVS CN ATEI (servus). In monumental inscriptions, the order in which the respective names appear seem to have been standardized in the form slave's name first, master's name second. This is not the case in more casual inscriptions such as stamps on clay artifacts. This fact, which has been surprisingly overlooked by archaeologists and epigraphists,[299] is documented by numerous examples. Among the potters belonging to the firm of L. Umbricius Scaurus, we find one Aeschines who signed L VMBRICI / SCAVRI AE(schines),[300] one Artemo who signed L VMBRICI / SCAVRI ART(emo), etc.[301] More interesting is the case of Icarus, who signed indifferently SCAVR / ICAR,[302] ICARVS / L VMBR(ici),[303] or L VMBRICI / SCAVRI IC(arus).[304] In the same way, Rufio signed indifferently RVFIO / L VMBR(ici),[305] or L VMBRICI / RVFIO.[306] In spite of the fact that the form with *tria nomina* was not necessarily expected in the first century A.D. to designate the principal, the stamps often display the name of the principal with *tria nomina* before the agent's *cognomen*, thus avoiding the ambiguity that makes it so difficult for modern scholars to determine the status of the person(s) referred to.

The workers' servile status is not explicitly indicated in the stamps, except in a few cases to be discussed later on. The shape of

---

[299] Cf. now G. Pucci, "I bolli sulle terra sigillata fra epigrafia e storia economica," in W.V. Harris (ed.), *The Inscribed Economy* (1993) 73-79, esp. 77: "Nella ceramica a vernice rossa italica abbiamo, fino al 15, quasi tutte le combinazioni possibili, con abbondanza di nomi di schiavi preceduti o seguiti da prenome e gentilizio del *dominus* (meno numerosi i bolli di liberti)."

[300] *CVArr* 2409.

[301] *CVArr* 2410. Cf. also *CVArr* 2412: L VMBRICI SCAVRI / NO(thus) STA(tu liber?) (cf. below); *CVArr* 2413: L VMBRICI / SCAVRI ZET(us); and *CVArr* 2418-2459.

[302] *CVArr* 2406.

[303] *CVArr* 2441.

[304] *CVArr* 2411.

[305] *CVArr* 2450.

[306] *CVArr* 2451.

many stamps adds to the difficulty of decoding the name(s) they contain: the names are written on two lines and it is not always clear whether or not the second line was meant to represent a different person from the first line. As we have seen in the section on bricks and tiles, the problem is even more acute with circular stamps, because sometimes there is no way to tell in which order the names were supposed to be read. The conclusion to be drawn from these remarks is that in most cases we remain unable to identify the social status of those who signed terra sigillata vessels, and therefore any statement to the effect that the production of Arretine pottery was mostly carried out by freedmen rather than by slaves should be regarded as lacking a firm textual basis.[307]

The social status of the workmen who produced and sometimes signed the terra sigillata pottery is most often uncertain and rarely explicitly stated. We have seen that Surus, slave and freedman of L. Sarius, used to advertise his status on his stamps with the adjunction of an S or L standing for *servus* or *libertus*.[308] Other similar instances are rare.[309] A few stamps might refer to *statuliberi* (conditionally manumitted slaves).[310]

H. Comfort once suggested that

---

[307] J.H. D'Arms, *CSSAR* (1981) 164, for instance, considers the potters Ateii to be comparable to other families involved in "far-flung independent business enterprises," like the Sex. Fadii or the Barbii, "who are freeborn, politically powerful, with geographically extended and well-organized shipping concerns."

[308] *CVArr* 1665-1666.

[309] The only other instances known to me are *CVArr* 133: DAMAS AR(i) Q.S.; *CVArr* 647 (= 1625 = 2428): EROS / V L S, standing for V(mbrici?) or V(erna?) L(uci) S(ervus), or something else; *CVArr* 1647: FAVSTVS SALINATORIAE SER(vus); *CVArr* 157: CN ATEI / CN L DEI(phobus); *CVArr* 168, no. 34: CN ATEI CN / L MAHES (dubious).

[310] *CVArr* 2040: DIODO / TIT STA, who is otherwise known (*CVArr* 2041) as C TITI / DIODOR; *CVArr* 2042: HERMI / TITI STA, who also signed (*CVArr* 2024) C TITI / HERM; *CVArr* 2044: PRIMIG / TITI ST, perhaps the same as *CVArr* 2128: PRIMIGE / NI L TITI; and *CVArr* 2412: L VM SC / NO STA, identified as L. Umbrici Scauri No(thus?) (cf. above). Cf. G. Prachner (1980) 151, n. 1; 168; and 208-09. A doubt remains as to whether this interpretation of STA( ) is correct, since *statuliberi* are not common in the inscriptions, cf. *ILS* 8269 (= *Not.Scav.* 1898, p. 192, Cumae): "...qui testamento statu libertatis relicti essent." For legal opinions, cf. Gaius, *Inst.* 2.200 and *Dig.* 40.7. Cf. G. Fabre, *Libertus* (Rome 1981) 29-33; and P. Garnsey, "Independent Freedmen and the Economy of Roman Italy under the Principate," *Klio* 63 (1981) 362, with reference to H. Kupiszewski, "Des remarques sur les *statuliberi* en droit romain classique," in I. Bieżuńska-Małowist–J. Kolendo (eds.), *Actes du colloque sur l'esclavage, Nieborow 2-6 XII 1975* (Warsaw 1979) 227-38.

most gentile names are adjectives in -*ius*, but until the time of Augustus the ordinary man did not customarily pronounce his name in the full nominative form in -*ius*, but in the form in -*i* which was the commonest in daily life. Stamps reading Atei or Cn. Atei, . . . for instance, can represent either the genitive or the vocative (= nominative). Indeed, nominative forms in -*ius* or -*iu(s)* are so uncommon that in the case of Atei or Cn. Atei standing alone it must be the vocative-nominative that is intended.[311]

This statement is debatable, to say the least, as many instances of stamps in which the nominative in -*ius* is spelled out demonstrate.[312]

b. *women as potters (or managers) and firm owners*

To support his theory about the use of the vocative, Comfort cites two stamps which, according to him, display an unambiguous vocative: ATTICE / P CORNE,[313] and ATTICE / C TELLI.[314] Comfort understands ATTICE as the vocative of Atticus, which is grammatically correct. It probably did not escape him that Attice is the transliteration of the female Greek name Ἀττική, which is not uncommon in inscriptions.[315] Female potters were not so exceptional as to make the vocative-theory compelling.[316] If the interpretation presented here is correct, it does not mean that these women were necessarily mere workers employed in a workshop. Women, like

---

[311] H. Comfort, *CVArr* (1968) XXVII.

[312] *CVArr* 166: CN ATEIVS / HILARVS. Cf. also *CVArr* 37; 42; 45; 46; 241; 274; 302; 315; 316; 448; 473; 543; 548; 589; 730; 818; 1015; 1641, etc. The attempt to interpret a stamp such as L ALFI / VS FEC (*CVArr* 46) as L(ucius) ALFI(us)/ V(ilicus) S(ervus) FEC(it) is unconvincing, because there is no explicit reference to *vilici* in pottery stamps. R. Chevallier, *Les potiers antiques (monde romain)* (*Caesarodunum* Suppl. 60, Tours 1990) 3-4 suggests that *vilici* were in charge of pottery production, which is a likely though unverifiable hypothesis.

[313] *CVArr* 487.

[314] *CVArr* 1915.

[315] *IGRR* IV 710 (= *CIL* III 7047, Synnadis/Asia, bilingual). Cf. also G. Prachner (1980) 130.

[316] Other stamps may refer to a female potter or manager, cf. *CVArr* 374: MAMA / CALIDI; *CVArr* 375: MASA / CALIDI; *CVArr* 387: SASA CA/LIDI or SASA STRI / CALDI; *CVArr* 525: PHILE / P COR; *CVArr* 1702: PROCHNE / SAVFEI; *CVArr* 1968-1975: SAMIA / L TETTI (and variants), although in this case a male potter is more likely; *CVArr* 1985 (?): PRIMA / L TETTI; *CVArr* 1988: SARI(va) / L TETTI (and variants). Cf. G. Prachner (1980) 53-55; 66-67; 130; and 135-37; C. Delplace, *Ktèma* 3 (1978) 60-61. It is remarkable that in all those cases the name of the principal/master/owner follows the name of the potter/manager.

men, could fill the role of branch manager, as Ulpianus states that in Roman law

> it matters little who is business manager, whether it is a man or a woman, a free person or a slave, the latter belonging either to the principal or to someone else. In the same way, the gender of whoever makes the appointment is not relevant: if it is a woman, the *actio institoria* is valid in accordance with the pattern established by the *actio exercitoria*, and if the person she appoints is a woman, she will also be personally liable. And if the appointee is a daughter-in-power or a female slave, the *actio institoria* is available.[317]

Thus, it is not abnormal either to find women as factory owners.[318] The pottery stamps suggest that the social reality of the first centuries B.C. and A.D. was in agreement with the juristic opinion expressed two hundred years later.

c. stamps as evidence for the internal organization of workshops

Names on the stamps admittedly tell little about the social status and economic function of their bearer, but it seems reasonable to assert that "only the more important members of the staff would attain the distinction of stamping the product with their own name. In many cases, this means that the name is that of the owner or contractor, in others it will be a foreman or designer whose name has come down to us."[319] This remark brings us to the question of the internal organization and size of the workshops. C. Delplace considers that

---

[317] Ulpianus (29 *ad ed.*) *Dig.* 14.3.7.1: "Parvi autem refert, quis sit institor, masculus an femina, liber an servus proprius vel alienus. Item quisquis praeposuit: nam et si mulier praeposuit, competit institoria exemplo exercitoriae actionis et si mulier sit praeposita, tenebitur etiam ipsa. Sed et si filia familias sit vel ancilla praeposita, competit institoria actio;" and Gaius (9 *ad ed. prov.*) *Dig.* 14.3.8: "Nam et plerique pueros puellasque tabernis praeponunt." Cf. above, the section about brick and tile industry.

[318] *CVArr* 76: SECVNDVS / [. . .]IAE (= Anniae?); *CVArr* 1647: FAVSTVS / SALINATOR / SER(?)IAE (= SALINATORIAE?); *CVArr* 1850: BLANDVS / STATILIAE; *CVArr* 1851: CANOPVS / STATILIAE S(ervus). H. Comfort, in *CVArr* XXVIII, considers that such stamps as *CVArr* 786: HERTORIA; *CVArr* 1023: METILIAN(a); *CVArr* 1545: RVFIO / RASINIAE, like *CVArr* 1565: DE RASTICANIS refer to the *figlinae*, following the model of tile stamps, cf. *CIL* XV 309: DE MARCIANIS, etc. Cf. G. Prachner (1980) 210, n. 105, who rejects Comfort's interpretation of *CVArr* 1647 as representing a woman's name on the basis that Salinatoria being built on the male agent's *cognomen* Salinator should refer to the *figlinae* to which the slave Faustus would have been attached, probably as part of the *instrumentum* ("Inventar"). Cf. also C. Delplace, *Ktèma* 3 (1978) 60.

[319] S. Treggiari, *RFLR* (1969) 91.

large workshops were organized along the same lines as agricultural estates, with a pyramidal hierarchic structure.[320] This is a reasonable hypothesis, demonstrable in other types of managerial or production units (for instance, mints), but there is hardly any evidence to support it in the context of ceramic production.

Exceptionally, a signature contains an elliptic reference to the position of the potter/manager within the firm. Diomedes, slave or freedman of one of the Vibii,[321] signed some of his stamps DIOMED / VIBI ⊂ or ⊃ and DIOMED / VIBI PR, which have been interpreted as *contrascriptor* (or *contrascriba*) and PR(ocurator), respectively.[322] Such reconstructions of these abbreviations are possible, but not entirely warranted. PR could stand for PR(aepositus), although epigraphical usage would favor in this case the abbreviation PP. The stamps do not say whether Diomedes was working for Vibius or for himself, and whether or not his titles are connected with his industrial activity. One can imagine that in the position of *contrascriptor* (a slave in charge of controlling the accounts) and *procurator* (always a freedman entrusted with the administration of someone's affairs) Diomedes might have enjoyed some economic autonomy and owned (or leased) a pottery, in which he was employing a few slaves. Otherwise, as a slave or a freedman, he could have been appointed *institor/officinator* to run his master's/patron's workshop. In any case, Diomedes's signature is exceptional and probably idiosyncratic. It may reflect Diomedes's pride about his social promotion from slave potter or even assistant to the position of agent in charge of his patron's business interest.[323]

In some cases, the signature specifies the function of the signing worker within the workshop. A few stamps on decorated vases found in Gallia Narbonensis explicitly refer to the owner or maker of the matrix of some kind of decorative element used for pottery: FELICIS CERA or CERA FELICIS.[324] Besides, a late stamp from Africa

---

[320] C. Delplace, *Ktèma* 3 (1978) 61.

[321] *CVArr* 2347: A VIBI / DIOME.

[322] *CVArr* 2343-2345. Cf. G. Prachner (1980) 156-59; and 206. According to C. Delplace, *Ktèma* 3 (1978) 61, the three terms designate "le représentant, le mandataire du propriétaire ou du maître-potier de l'atelier, à la fois administrateur et contrôleur." I doubt that both functions would be performed by the same person.

[323] G. Prachner (1980) 156-59, who unconvincingly argues that Diomedes could have been a *procurator* before manumission. There is no evidence supporting this assertion, as the chronology of the stamps is not strictly established.

[324] *CIL* XII 5687, nos. 9; 17; and 18a-c (= *ILS* 8606c and d). Cf. also 8606a (APOLLINAR(is) / CERA); b ([Ap]OLLINARIS CERA); and e (LATIN[i] / CERA).

(exact origin unknown) on a sherd of red pottery reads: EX OFICI-
NA (*sic*) QVOD/VVLTDEI TZACONIS / CRESCE(n)S PVGIL/
VM FECIT. Thus, the worker Crescens, who was attached to a
workshop belonging to one Quodvultdeus Tzaco, takes credit for
making a tool (*poinçon*).[325] These instances illustrate the fact that
stamped signatures may refer to specialized part makers instead of
workshop owners or managers.

4. *The organization of the industry*

a. *size and importance of firms*
The relative size or importance of any firm can be estimated by the
overall duration of its activity, the range of its diffusion, and the number of people whose signatures are associated with it. G. Prachner,
for instance, concludes that Cn. Ateius's *familia* was prosperous during at least 35 to 40 years, thanks to its domination of the Rhine market. One late member of the group, Cn. Ateius Arretinus, may even
have been active as late as the 60's,[326] thus extending the period of
activity of the Ateii over more than eighty years.

The stamps preserve the names of the slaves and freedmen attached to the main firms and the quantity of those which have been
catalogued (2,600 in *CVArr*) is large enough to provide a data bank
unlikely to be invalidated by further discoveries. The large-scale
producers are P. Cornelius, who is represented by sixty-five persons;
Rasinius, with sixty persons; L. Titius with more than fifty-three
persons, etc.[327] As G. Pucci points out, these figures are meaningless, since we do not know whether the signatures represent potters,
foremen, workshop managers, or factory owners. One can compare
the organization of Arretine firms, in which dozens of workers were
involved, with the Gallic pottery industry. In Lezoux, for instance,
the largest firm was that of Cinnamus, whose bowls exhibit only
seven different signatures. These names could represent Cinnamus's

---

[325] *AE* 1989, no. 832 (fifth or sixth century). Cf. J.W. Salomonson, "Litterae
Africanae. Ein Tonfragment mit kursiver lateinischer Inschrift in der archäologischen Sammlung der Utrechter Universität," in J. den Boeft–A.H.M. Kessels
(eds.), *Actus. Studies in honor of H.L.W. Nelson* (Utrecht 1982) 343-93.

[326] *CVArr* 151. H. Comfort, *RCRF* 4 (1962) 8-9.

[327] I borrow these figures from G. Prachner (1980) *passim*. Cf. also G. Pucci,
"La produzione della ceramica aretina. Note sull' 'industria' nella prima età
imperiale," *DArch* 7 (1973) 255-93, esp. 266-70.

workers or agents, or even independent craftsmen who had purchased Cinnamus's moulds.[328]

D.P.S. Peacock brings another element into the discussion: the
archaeological remains of identified kilns. The size of the levigation
tanks of the potter Perennius, which could hold some 10,000 gal-
lons, points toward very large units of production that imply some
degree of division of labor and of specialization.[329] Peacock's view
is admittedly impressionistic, but the archaeological material on
which he relies fits nicely the picture provided by the study of pottery
stamps.

b. *collective enterprises or partnerships*

On occasion, Ateius himself and another potter, ATEI / TETI,[330]
or two of Ateius's slaves/freedmen are attested jointly in stamps. G.
Prachner thinks that such associations were of short duration, as it
appears that in all cases pairs of partners soon split and started operating independent workshops, possibly in different locations.[331] An
interesting case, perhaps connected with temporary association, is
provided by one Stabilio, whose signature indicates that he was at
times working for three different Ateii.[332] It is admittedly difficult
to interpret the first stamp, because of its poor state of preservation.
The other stamps may theoretically refer to two homonymous
slaves. If not, various interpretations are possible: Stabilio could
have been sold, donated, or bequeathed by one owner to another;
he could also have worked at times for only one of his joint owners.[333] Otherwise, it may be that Stabilio was owned by one of the
two freedmen before they set up their partnership, and went to the
other after they dissolved it or after the death of one of them. Finally,
Stabilio could belong, as part of the *instrumentum*, to a single workshop which passed from one freedman to the other.[334]

---

[328] D.P.S. Peacock (1982) 123, citing J.A. Stanfield–G. Simpson, *Central Gaulish Potters* (London 1958).

[329] D.P.S. Peacock (1982) 122.

[330] *CVArr* 175.

[331] *CVArr* 182: ATEI CREST / ET EVHODI (or variants); *CVArr* 183: ATEI
MAHE(tis) / ET ZOELI; *CVArr* 186: XANTH(i) SOILI. Cf. G. Prachner (1980)
32.

[332] *CVArr* 162: (Stab)ILI(o) / (Atei?) EVHOD; *CVArr* 184: MAHETIS
STABILIO; *CVArr* 185: ZOILI / STABILIO.

[333] G. Prachner (1980) 32.

[334] On the composition of the *instrumentum* of a managerial unit (*fundus, taberna,
officina, statio*, etc.), cf. Chapter Two.

c. *transfers of moulds and decorative stamps (poinçons)*

When a new workshop was opened, the owner or branch manager could bring with him some of the moulds he used in his previous position. For instance, a slave *institor/officinator* sent to Gaul or to the Rhine border to start a subsidiary workshop would transfer there moulds made and perhaps already used for a while in the main Italian factory. This practice is attested in La Muette at Lyons, where chemical analysis of Ateius's moulds showed that their content of titanium dioxide and magnesium oxide points toward an Italian origin.[335] One has to remember, however, that a manumitted slave could also take away with him any part of his *peculium* that his former master did not claim for himself. Then, the question arises whether moulds and *poinçons* were part of the *instrumentum* of the workshop or belonged to the slave's *peculium*. Both solutions are possible. Consequently, the find of a mould made in Italy in a workshop in Gaul is no cogent evidence for branch workshop.

The signatures found on tableware could represent any stage of a threefold process, starting with the making of decorative *poinçons*, continuing with the making of moulds, and finishing with the making of the vessel. These three stages could be carried out independently from one another. Moulds and *poinçons* could travel widely and be objects of trade. Consequently, the actual maker of a vessel could have no connection whatsoever with the workshop where the mould originated.[336] Therefore, it is important to figure out to which stage any stamped signature belongs.

5. *Purpose of the stamps*

As mentioned above, the interpretation of the stamps is far from being simple and straightforward. They could represent the men who made the vessel, or the proprietors of the firms. Other types of signatures clearly represent the makers of the moulds or *poinçons*, or

---

[335] M. Picon–J. Lasfargues, "Transfert de moules entre les ateliers d'Arezzo et ceux de Lyon," *RAE* 25 (1974) 61-69; and M. Picon–J. Garmier, "Un atelier d'Ateius à Lyon," *ibidem*, 71-76. The analysis of Ateius's production, not limited to moulds, focused on seven different chemical components.

[336] S. Treggiari, *RFLR* (1969) 91; B. Hofmann, "Marques de potiers, de producteurs de moules et de fabriquants de poinçons," *RCRFCommunicationes* 2.11 (1970) 61-62; and G. Pucci, "La ceramica italica (terra sigillata)," *SRPS* II (1981) 99-121, esp. 115, showing that the same *poinçon* was used by Xanthus, a potter attached to Ateius's concern, and by L. Rasinius Pisanus.

some bowl finishers (who added the footstand). Sometimes, it is obvious that a mark refers to one particular operation, for instance when the name appears in cursive script below the decoration or on the plain rim band (Dragendorff 30 or 37).[337] The presence of several stamps of different types on a single vessel points toward a division of labor, but it is not clear whether potters, makers of moulds and *poinçons*, and other specialists were independent from one another or belonged to the same workshop.[338]

Pottery stamps present various forms, and it is not easy to ascertain whether the difference between these forms was significant. In a recent report on an on-going study of ca. 4,800 stamped sherds found at Vechten (Netherlands), M. Polak identifies six types of stamps: (a-c) stamps containing the words *officina*, *fecit*, or *manu*; (d-e) stamps featuring names in the nominative or genitive forms: (f) others. The vessels were made in La Graufesenque between the early first century A.D. and the Flavian period. The preliminary conclusions drawn from the study of this material suggest that the potters whose stamps feature the word *fecit* or *manu*, or a name in the nominative form are modestly represented at Vechten and would therefore be small producers. At the other end of the spectrum, the potters whose stamps regularly display the word *officina* are better represented at Vechten and consequently would have been attached to larger units of production. The stamps composed of a name in the genitive form are inconclusive. On the basis of this analysis, Polak speculates that large workshops became more and more important at La Graufesenque around the middle of the first century A.D.[339] More work is needed to confirm or invalidate this theory in the context of pottery production in Gaul in this period, but it seems already possible to assert that such conclusions would not apply to other types of material (bricks, tiles, amphorae, lamps, and lead pipes) produced in Italy in the late Republican and early Imperial periods.

The very purpose of the stamps is puzzling. The assumption that

---

[337] D.P.S. Peacock (1982) 124; B. Hofmann, "Les relations entre potiers, fabricants de moules et artistes producteurs de poinçons," *RCRF* 13 (1971) 5-20, esp. 7 and 12-13, n. 7, considers that a mark on the rim represents the signature of the potter.

[338] C. Delplace, *Ktèma* 3 (1978) 71, n. 104 (with reference to B. Hofmann [1971] 5-20) and 73 (with reference to M. Lutz, *L'atelier de Saturninus et de Satto à Mittelbronn (Moselle)* [Paris 1970] 192-94).

[339] M. Polak, "Some Observations on the Production of Terra Sigillata at La Graufesenque," *AKB* 19 (1989) 145-54.

stamps were meant for consumers in order to enable them to identify the producer of a good is not always valid, because it is not exceptional for a signature to be invisible to the consumer. For instance, the signature PRIMI found on the footstand of a vase of Sarius-type from the Magdalensberg was stamped on the part of the stand that would be pieced together with the body of the vase.[340] Primus was certainly a worker specialized in the production of footstands; the signature on his products is probably not to be compared with signatures thought to represent the owner of the firm or his representative. The same is true of the signature PROV(incialis) on a Dragendorff 37 bowl found at Pfaffenhofen. The stamp was covered before firing, which indicates that Provincialis was a potter in charge of making the core of the vessel, which was subsequently finished and signed anew by one RIP[an]VS, a well-known potter of Westendorf.[341]

The use of abbreviated signatures, monograms, and symbols, clearly points toward the same fact.[342] Some kinds of signatures could have an internal function that remains unexplainable to us. The fact that some wares bear more than one signature supports the hypothesis of division of labor within a single workshop or among several ones. E. Schindler-Kaudelka is among those who suggest that big firms would deliver semi-finished products to smaller, possibly independent, workshops, but once again the evidence is inconclusive.

There is no reason why the person referred to in the stamps in the genitive form next to a slave's name should be considered the owner of this slave. This person could be the owner or lessee of the workshop, and the stamp should then be read: (ex officina) MAHETIS STABILIO (fecit), the legal relationship between Mahes and Stabilio being explained in terms of employer/employee or principal/

---

[340] E. Schindler-Kaudelka, "Zur Bedeutung der Signaturen auf norditalischer Reliefkeramik," in E. Weber–G. Dobesch (eds.), *Römische Geschichte, Altertumskunde und Epigraphik. Festschrift für A. Betz zur Vollendung seines 80. Lebensjahres* (Vienna 1985) 557-64 (citing G. Ulbert).

[341] H.-J. Kellner, *RCRFCommunicationes* 2.10 (1969) 47-49, and *ibid.* 2.12 (1971) 74-75. It is unclear to me why Kellner attributes this bowl to the workshop of Helenius.

[342] J.-P. Morel, "Les producteurs de biens artisanaux en Italie à la fin de la République," in *Les bourgeoisies municipales italiennes aux IIe et Ier siècles av. J.-C.* (Paris/Naples 1983) 21-39, esp. 23. Symbols on clay artifacts are discussed below, in the section on lamps.

agent. Stabilio could be owned either by Mahes or by a third party, in which case he would be a *mercennarius*. Regardless of whether the name in the genitive case refers to the owner, principal, or employer (*conductor servi* or *conductor operarum servi*) of the slave—and a single person could, and probably commonly did, play all three roles—it seems almost necessary to postulate that the meaning of the stamps was straightforward for whomsoever they were addressed to. If they were in any degree confusing, they would miss their point and therefore be useless. In my opinion, the stamps served as a label of guarantee. By identifying the person ultimately liable for the quality of the product and his/her principal, it enabled a dissatisfied buyer to bring a law suit against the producer (agent or principal). Unfortunately, there is no evidence, as far as I know, for litigation connected with pottery-making.

6. *Conclusion*

In the second century B.C., the emergence of larger units of production in the ceramic industry was made possible by the existence of a quantitatively growing, yet qualitatively less-demanding, market. This phenomenon, combined with the intervention of developing networks of distribution, provided adequate conditions for the introduction of managerial innovations in this increasingly concentrated sector of the economy. The result seems to have been a rise of the production, soon to be followed by stiffer competition and the necessity for both producers and distributors to respond to market conditions in a more personalized manner, through diversification of the products, distant exports, or relocation of the centers of production closer to the consumers. This may have been done mainly through transfers of workshops or the opening of branches.

Exports preceded the conquest, but the pacification of the western provinces induced dynamic entrepreneurs to take advantage of the new conditions created by this historical development by establishing branch workshops in areas where the army provided numerous consumers of manufactured goods with adequate purchasing power. The mobility of the army during the phase of expansion of the empire called for a relative mobility of the centers of production.[343]

---

[343] E. Ettlinger, *RCRF* 25/26 (1987) 5-8 notes that maps of distribution of the earliest Arretine stamps (of A. Titius and Sex. Annius, ca. 30 B.C. – A.D. 20) show

The success of Italian-based entrepreneurs, such as Aco, L. Surus, or Cn. Ateius, is illustrated by the wide distribution of their products made in the few identified—and numerous surmised—branch workshops located at first in neighboring regions and ultimately in more distant provinces. The high standard of quality brought by transient potters or dispatched agents may have played a significant part in securing the reputation of provincial products that soon superseded Italian pottery, first in remote areas, and to some extent also in Italy proper, by the middle of the first century A.D.[344]

Apart from a few account-lists scratched on plates and discovered here and there, potters' stamps constitute the main written evidence for the organization of the industry. They should not be used as a basis for the identification of the potter's status, but as evidence for a relationship between principal/employer and agent/employee. Their reading is ambiguous, and a new approach to the interpretation of the names should be adopted in view of the nomenclature used in inscriptions down to the Augustan period. The structure of the stamps written on two lines leads me to propose the following reading: "(from the workshop of) X, Y (made it)," which corresponds to "Y, who belongs to, or works, for X, is responsible for the production of this item." Consequently, the names which have been taken to represent freedmen on the basis of the *tria nomina*—an interpretation which is undoubtedly correct in some cases—should be subjected to a critical review. The names in the stamps can represent owners, managers, ranking staff members, or designers. Exceptionally, the stamps contain some veiled indication of status or evidence for partnerships of potters. One of the possible purposes of the stamps is to advertise the origin of the products in order to make the producers (agent and/or principal) of faulty artifacts liable to a legal action on the part of the consumer.

The importance of individual enterprises can be measured by the number of people signing their products and by the length of time during which their activity is recorded. The size of a workshop is more difficult to establish, unless adequate archaeological data, such as levigation tanks, kilns, or drying areas, are available.

Considering the evidence as a whole, it seems that Ateius and his

---

that the trade in Arretine ware followed the movement of the legions, from Spain to the Rhine.

[344] M. Rostovtzeff, *SEHRE*[2] (1957) 94; and 575, n. 13.

peers were for quite a while successful entrepreneurs who trained
and set up their employees in similar business enterprises, sharing
moulds and *poinçons* with them. Some of these employees obtained
their manumission and continued in the same line of business either
as agents or as competitors of their patron. G. Prachner, who be-
lieves in the possibility of telling apart freedmen from slaves in the
stamps, states that among all known Ateius's potters fifteen are attested only as freedmen and four only as slaves.[345] He also speculates that Ateius sent his freedmen to the provinces as branch managers, with the authority to run the workshop and the capacity to
form partnership. Those managers took credit for their activity by
signing their products. This would account for the continuous activity of some firms over a long period of time, which does not necessarily imply that the trade promoted the entrepreneurs to the ranks
of the wealthy. Even though some names are found in many locations across the Western provinces and in various chronological contexts, it is not enough to assume the existence of a well-to-do bourgeoisie involved in ceramic production.

The above considerations have been based on the examination of
the stamps and their distribution. More could be learned from a systematic study of typological variations within each potter's production as they could reflect the practice of different workshops.[346] The
picture is complicated by the fact that potters are known to have
been quite mobile, and what could be considered as a branch workshop might simply be the new location of the center of production
of a potter previously connected with a different place.

Finally, it should be stressed that this type of evidence is scarcer
in the East. H. Comfort once said that the opening of branch factories was a sign of vitality absent from the East, where "independent 'little men' rather than overseas representatives of large Italian
concerns" were expected.[347]

---

[345] G. Prachner (1980) 36.

[346] C.M. Wells, "Manufacture, Distribution and Date: Some Methodological
Considerations on the Dating of Augustan Terra Sigillata," *RCRF* 17/18 (1977)
132-40, esp. 133.

[347] H. Comfort, in T. Frank, *ESAR* V (1940) 188-94, esp. 194. The only stamp
known to me which might point toward the activity (production or distribution) of
a branch manager comes from Asia Minor (*CVArr* 2132: PVDE(n)S / L TITI).

E. Terracotta Lamps

1. *Historical outline*

The production and marketing of terracotta lamps present basically the same problems as those dealt with in connection with terra sigillata. The manufacturing stage requires the combination of cheap and almost ubiquitous raw material (clay, wood, water), storage room and kiln, and limited skill on the part of the worker. The product, in its simplest form, was affected by variations in craftsmanship and could be improved by the addition of various artistic decoration to the effect that the consumer in an adequately-provided market could choose between well-differentiated products. Even in the case of lamps of the highest quality, the use of moulds in the manufacturing process would ensure that mass production would not necessarily be sacrificed to aesthetic refinements.

Lamps, like terra sigillata vessels, often bear stamps on their outside bottom part,[348] so that much of what has been said in the previous section about pottery stamps applies to lamps as well and will not be repeated here. For both categories, stamps first appear—or reappear—around 50 B.C.[349] The lamps studied in this section belong roughly to the same period as the signed terra sigillata vessels, but the boom in the lamp industry and trade occurred slightly later. The evidence provided by those lamps which originated in Italy and are attested in several provinces permits us to follow the development of Italian manufacturing organization during a period when Italian producers of terra sigillata were already losing control over provincial markets.[350]

---

[348] Catalogue by L. Mercando, *EAA* Suppl. 1970 (1973) 419-42, s.v. *lucerna*.

[349] J.-P. Morel, "Les producteurs de biens artisanaux en Italie à la fin de la République," in *Les bourgeoisies municipales italiennes aux IIe et Ier siècles av. J.-C.* (Paris/Naples 1983) 34. W.V. Harris, "Roman Terracotta Lamps: The Organization of an Industry," *JRS* 70 (1980) 126-45, esp. 128 allows for a later date ("20s B.C., or perhaps slightly earlier, but it was only in the last years of the first century A.D. that signed lamps reached something like their full geographical range"); C. Pavolini, "Le lucerne nell'Italia romana," *SRPS* II (1981) 139-84, esp. 152-53, with the example of the North Italian production of C VIBI / TIBVR (or TIBVR / C VIBI) (= *CIL* V 8114, no. 130), dated to 100-50 B.C., found at Aquileia and on the Magdalensberg, perhaps associated with a *gens* Vibia attested in Arezzo (cf. Pavolini's appendix 181).

[350] The historical development of Roman lamps is described by C. Pavolini, "Le lucerne romane fra il III sec. A.C. e il III sec. D.C.," in P. Lévêque–J.-P. Morel (eds.), *Céramiques hellénistiques et romaines* II (Paris 1987) 139-65.

2. *Italian factory lamps (Firmalampen)*

A significant proportion of preserved lamps bear the makers' names in Greek or in Latin, hence the label of "factory lamps" (*Firmalampen*) attributed to them. According to their pattern of distribution, it is possible to distinguish four groups:[351] the first two groups include brands which were distributed on a local or regional basis. The third and fourth groups include marks found in several provinces: Group III, which will be the focus of this section, is centered in Northern Italy and covers most of the Northern provinces. The marks feature the producer's *cognomen* alone in the genitive form (e.g., PHOETASPI). Group IV is centered in Central and Southern Italy and spread around the Western Mediterranean. The marks contain the producer's name with *tria nomina* in the genitive form (e.g., C OPPI RES(tituti)). It is difficult to explain the difference in stamp form between the two groups, which overlap in some places. The stamps do not convey any message about the social status of the persons they represent, but it is remarkable that the lamps of Group IV, which are conspicuous by the richer decorative motifs exhibited on the top of the lid, follow a different pattern of distribution from those of Group III. It seems unlikely that the difference between the two forms of stamp reflects a variation in the organization of the industry.[352] It is possible, however, that each group stems from an independent tradition.

3. *Patterns of distribution*

W.V. Harris presents some statistical data concerning the distribution of factory lamps belonging to Groups III and IV.[353] In Group III, the commonest mark is that of FORTIS which was found in

---

[351] I am summarizing here the conclusions reached by W.V. Harris, *JRS* 70 (1980) 126-45. An up-to-date bibliography is provided by D.M. Bailey, "Lamps Metal, Lamps Clay: A Decade of Publications," *JRA* 4 (1991) 51-62. The standard catalogue of lamps, unfortunately short on provenances, is by D.M. Bailey, *A Catalogue of the Lamps in the British Museum* I-III (London 1975-1988).

[352] C. Pavolini, "I bolli sulle lucerne fittili delle officine centro-italiche," in W.V. Harris (ed.), *The Inscribed Economy* (1993) 65-71 mentions that from the period 80-120 until the third century the stamps exhibit (a) *tria nomina*; (b) *cognomina*; and (c) *duo nomina* (*praenomen* + *nomen*, or *nomen* + *cognomen*), all three groups in the genitive form.

[353] W.V. Harris, *JRS* 70 (1980) 130. C. Pavolini, in *Céramiques hellénistiques et romaines* II (1987) 144-45, is critical of Harris's interpretation of Group IV.

great numbers (in the hundreds) in Northern Italy, Switzerland, Pannonia, Dalmatia, Dacia, as well as in the Germanic and Gallic provinces. The FORTIS lamps are found more sporadically in Central Italy and appear to have found their way to Spain or North Africa only exceptionally and not necessarily in connection with long-distance or large-scale trade. A similar pattern of distribution is attested for the marks ATIMETI, CRESCE(nti)S, PHOETASPI, STROBILI, and VIBIANI. These marks are combined with various types of lamps (in particular Loeschcke IX and X),[354] but the lack of information available in modern catalogues on this particular aspect makes it difficult to draw any conclusion from it. Harris points out that type diversity is less significant for *Firmalampen* than for *Bildlampen* (figured lamps), for which up to twelve types are known in connection with the same mark.[355]

On the basis of this material, the main questions to be addressed are: (a) were all lamps bearing the same mark and found in several provinces manufactured in one factory, located in Italy or elsewhere, and then exported? (b) if the answer to this first question turns out to be at least partially negative, then were the provincial workshops subsidiary ones, i.e. operated by the agents of the owner of the main factory, or were they independent workshops producing unauthorized copies? and (c) was there any other alternative? One can imagine, for instance, that some well-known potters transferred their workshop from Italy to some provincial location—and several successive movements are possible, especially if those potters are involved in the supplying of a Roman legion. Another possibility would be that a slave/freedman/employee of the owner of the main factory left with a small capital (*peculium*) to start an independent workshop; however, the concept of independent local potters operating under patent would be anachronistic.[356]

The answer to these questions need not be simple, and it is fair to suspect that all the practices listed in the previous paragraph coincided in some areas. Some regional trends can be identified. In a

---

[354] The typology was established by S. Loeschcke, *Lampen aus Vindonissa. Ein Beitrag zur Geschichte von Vindonissa und des antiken Beleuchtungswesens* (Zurich 1919). According to H. Menzel, *EAA* 4 (1961) 707-18, s.v. *lucerne*, esp. 713, Loeschcke X was created by Fortis around A.D. 100 and was manufactured into the third century.

[355] W.V. Harris, *JRS* 70 (1980) 131. For a definition of these terms, cf. *ibid.* 127.

[356] M. Rostovtzeff, *SEHRE²* (1957) 173-74.

study of Roman lamps of Carthage, J. Deneauve notices a decline
in quality in the second half of the first century A.D. and a tendency
toward simplification. The conquest and Romanization of the
provinces provided favorable circumstances for exports from Italy,
soon to be challenged by local products and imitations, resulting in
the gradual disappearance of Italian makers' marks in the second
century, at least in North Africa. Deneauve distinguishes four stages
of development: the first stage was characterized by significant exports from Italy to North Africa (late Republican period to second
century A.D.) of lamps which increasingly bear marks, some of
them encompassed in a foot-print (*in planta pedis*); the second stage
saw the opening of new workshops, some of them in Africa (such as
the *officina Pullaenorum*), perhaps in connection with the exploitation
of large estates by Romanized provincials whose social rise is attested in the second century; the third stage started with the appearance
of specifically African types, derived from Italian lamps, made for
instance by M. Novius Iustus, a famous producer who might have
started in Italy in the first century A.D. and who is thought to have
established branch workshops in the provinces, attested both in
Hadrumetum (find of kiln refuse) and in Montans;[357] and the
fourth stage consisted in making new moulds from actual lamps (*surmoulage*) in secondary workshops producing very simple artifacts.[358]
These four stages might have developed concurrently, at least from
the beginning of the second century.

a. *exports*

The question of exports has to be examined first. Harris, who is
most skeptical about the economic rationality of exporting low-price

---

[357] J. Deneauve, *Les lampes .de Carthages* (Paris 1969) 86, with a reference to
A. Truillot, *BCTH* (1941-1942) 282 ff. for "la découverte d'un dépôt de ratés de
cuisson à Hadrumète." According to W.V. Harris, *JRS* 70 (1980) 132, nn. 39-41
and D.M. Bailey (1980) 90, there is no evidence that M. Novius Iustus ever
produced in Italy (cf. also *BMQ* 36 [1971-72] 104). For lamps made by M. Novius
Iustus and L. Munatius Threptus in adjacent kilns at Montans in Gaul, cf. T.
Martin, "Fouilles de Montans. Notes préliminaires sur les résultats de la campagne 1975," *Figlina* 2 (1977) 51-78, who points out (62), however, that all lamps
signed by L. Munatius Threptus found in Montans are imitations ("surmoulage"). Martin thinks (76-77, n. 35) that Threptus worked in Campania in the late
first or early second century. His products are well attested in Southern Italy and
in North Africa, but rare in Gaul.

[358] J. Deneauve (1969) 83-86 ("Origine et évolution de la production. Les
marques").

items, recognizes that lamps were sometimes exported over long distances. For instance, a cargo of lamps manufactured somewhere in Italy in the 40's A.D.—or possibly under the reign of Nero—by the potter C. Clodius was found on the shore of the Balearic Islands, in the wreck of a ship bound to Spain. The load consisted of at least ninety lamps with a mark *in planta pedis*, but the number might in fact be much larger. Interestingly, they belong to four distinct typological groups and bear various decorative motifs. Each prototype is represented by two to seven copies from the same mould. It illustrates the diversity of the production of the potter Clodius, which is so far only rarely represented elsewhere: three lamps bearing his mark were found in Rome,[359] and individual examples exist also in museum collections in Tunis, Sevilla, and Cyprus, which is not to say that they were found in the vicinity. One can infer from this very thin distribution that Clodius manufactured lamps during a short period of time and on a rather moderate scale. That did not stop him from reaching markets overseas.[360] The low cost of sea transportation made it possible and economically sensible. We do not know whether the ship which transported these lamps was operated by Clodius's agent (*magister navis*) or by an independent shipper.

b. *impracticality of land transportation*
Harris regards as unlikely the transport of lamps overland for commercial purposes, because of the assumed high cost of land transportation in antiquity. In these costs one should include (a) the initial investment, maintenance, and replacement of the personnel (*muliones*, etc.), animals (donkeys, oxen, etc.), and material (carts, crates, boxes, etc.) necessary for the transport of goods; (b) the fees collected by middlemen in charge of transportation, temporary storage, and wholesale and retail distribution, expenses that were lower when the operation was carried out by the producers' agents; (c) the customs dues (*portoria*, between 2.5 and 5% of the value of the goods) collected at provincial borders by contractors or agents of

---

[359] *CIL* XV 6375, nos. 1-3.

[360] C. Domergue, "Un envoi de lampes du potier Gaius Clodius," *MCV* 2 (1966) 5-40, esp. 7 and 14-19, cited by W.V. Harris, *JRS* 70 (1980) 135, n. 70. Harris stresses the relatively early date of this shipment in the history of signed lamps, implying that what was done in the 40's A.D. does not necessarily fit a later period. D.M. Bailey (1980) 92-93 provides additional material which might support a later date for Clodius's production.

the imperial administration;[361] and (d) the losses due to breakage. Consequently, the market price in the provinces of lamps made in Italy would have been too high to compete with the presumably low price of local products and, in any case, the margin of profit of Italian manufacturers would have been considerably reduced.[362] On the basis of these considerations, Harris suggests that Italian factory owners had little choice but to open branch factories near the centers of consumption. The main evidence in support of this hypothesis is provided by the legal remedy (*actio institoria*) created by the Republican praetor and granted to businessmen entering into commercial transactions with authorized, i.e. appointed, agents.

The lack of reliable data on prices of lamps and costs of transportation makes it impossible to calculate the comparative profitability of branch workshops *vs.* exports. Even though one should beware of underestimating the capacity of transportation by cart or pack animal,[363] the availability of river transportation,[364] and the practi-

---

[361] If the export of lamps was intended to supply the Roman legions—each soldier carried a lamp as part of his personal equipment—the merchants carrying out the shipping were exempted from such excises, cf. Paulus (5 *sent.*) *Dig.* 39.4.9.7 (= *Sent.* 5.1a.8), cf. C.R. Whittaker, "Trade and the Aristocracy in the Roman Empire," *Opus* 4 (1985) 49-75, esp. 55-57.

[362] W.V. Harris, *JRS* 70 (1980) 133-35: "In practice lamps are not at all likely to have been carried even a hundred miles unless there was an assured market at the other end of the journey, a market large enough to be profitable but also backward enough to lack qualified potters of its own."

[363] D.M. Bailey, "The Roman Terracotta Lamp Industry. Another View About Exports," in T. Oziol and R. Rebuffat (eds.), *Les lampes de terre cuite en Méditerranée* (Lyons 1987) 59-63, esp. 60-61; P. Procaccini, "Ancora a proposito dell''industria' delle lucerne nell'impero romano. Note in margine ad un recente studio di storia economica," in L. Gasperini (ed.), *Scritti in memoria di F. Grosso* (Rome 1981) 507-21, esp. 517-18; and R. Duncan-Jones, *Structure and Scale in the Roman Economy* (Cambridge 1990) 48-58, esp. 49, who points out that ten lamps would occupy more or less the same space as a modius of wheat and would not be worth much less. Some scholars have recently argued that land transport sometimes presented advantages over water transport, because the former could be carried out year-round and was relatively safe with regard to accidents; cf. D.V. Sippel, "Some Observations on the Means and Cost of the Transport of Bulk Commodities in the Late Republic and Early Empire," *AncW* 16 (1987) 35-45; A. Deman, "Réflexions sur la navigation fluviale dans l'Antiquité," in T. Hackens–P. Marchetti (eds.), *Histoire économique de l'Antiquité* (Louvain 1987) 79-106, esp. 83; G. Raepsaet, *MBAH* 6 (1987) 1-27, esp. 19-23 (about the distribution of ceramics in Northern Gaul by land transport).

[364] G. Uggeri, "La navigazione interna della Cisalpina in età romana," *AAAd* 29 (1987) 305-54; and W.V. Harris, "Trade and the River Po: A Problem in the Economic History of the Roman Empire," in J.-Fr. Bergier (ed.), *Montagnes, fleuves, forêts dans l'histoire* (St. Katharinen 1989) 123-33. The case of Pannonia,

cality of supplementary cargoes (at least waterborne),[365] Harris's hypothesis is sensible. However, even though branch workshops run by *institores* might have been common, they remain entirely hypothetical. As D.M. Bailey rightly puts it, "the facts are unknown, the ramifications so complex and the possibilities so endless, that it will never be established what really happened Empire-wide."[366] But sound skepticism is not inconsistent with cautious speculation, and Harris's model is worth considering.

4. Branch workshops

Since there is little doubt that, as Bailey and others contend,[367]

---

where a high percentage of Group III lamps are preserved (989 lamps or more according to Harris [1980] 130), is telling. A. Tchernia, *Le vin de l'Italie romaine* (Rome 1986) 170-71 points out that only "soixante milles" (= "only about fifty miles" in Harris [1980] 136, n. 76) of easy road (Strabo 7.5.2 [314] and 4.6.10 [207]) separated Aquileia from Nauportus (a river-port on the road to Emona, where activity is attested already in the middle of the first century B.C.), from where goods could be transported by boat to the River Sava and then to the Danube across Pannonia and Upper Moesia. Another easy stretch would bring them from Celeia to a tributary of the Drava. The wine trade from Italy that supplied the Roman legions and Italians established in the Danube provinces might have provided the momentum for the export of Italian-made lamps transported as supplementary cargo.

[365] C.R. Whittaker, *Opus* 4 (1985) 54-55; and R. Duncan-Jones (1990) 49: "Traders whose ships carried foodstuffs in one direction still needed goods for the return voyage, and could not necessarily fill their holds with high-priced luxury goods."

[366] D.M. Bailey (1987) 62 points out that "there are many examples of lamps bearing the names of Italian or African makers, found in provincial areas and which were undoubtedly made in those provincial areas," citing (n. 12) as examples the lamps of the Italian maker L. Munatius Threptus and of the African M. Novius Iustus (cf. above). The same author acknowledges the existence of branch workshops for the mark PHOETASPI in Italy and Egypt, ROMANESIS in Cnidus and Dalmatia (unless the latter location was a place of export—it has been demonstrated since then that the ROMANESIS lamps were produced in Cnidus or Miletus), and FAVSTI in Egypt and at Petra (*Greek and Roman Pottery Lamps* [London 1963] 24). C. Pavolini, in W.V. Harris (ed.), *The Inscribed Economy* (1993) 65-71 speaks, in the context of the organization of the industry in Central Italy, of " 'catene' di officine collegate fra loro, e gestite da più liberti per conto di un unico *patronus*."

[367] R. Duncan-Jones (1990) 49 refers to the distribution of modest African tableware in most of the empire in late antiquity to demonstrate the validity of the export theory. E.W. Haley, "The Lamp Manufacturer Gaius Iunius Draco," *MBAH* 9 (1990) 1-12, esp. 10, cites as evidence for large-scale seaborne traffic in lamps a shipwreck off Puteoli containing 4,000 lamps (cf. D.J.L. Gibbins, *International Journal of Nautical Archaeology and Underwater Exploration* 18 [1989] 20 [non vidi]). G. Schneider–E. Wirz, "Chemical Answers to Archaeological Questions— Roman Terracotta Lamps as Documents of Economic History," *Doc. et Trav. IGAL*

lamps were indeed exported in massive quantities in all provinces of the Empire, the practicality of the model of branch workshops favored by Harris must be accounted for with a different explanation. The reasons why Italian manufacturers might have thought suitable to open subsidiary workshops in distant locations need not be of an economic nature, i.e. based on consideration of compared profitability, but it is still tempting to consider the problem in terms of entrepreneurial policy. If it is taken for granted that the costs and inconveniences of land and water transportation in themselves constituted no insuperable obstacle, one should consider the positive aspects of decentralized production.

a. *the search for available or cheaper manpower*
The availability of adequate labor forces in the provinces might have encouraged some businessmen to relocate part of their production facilities at a time when Italy might have suffered from chronic manpower shortages. This is exactly what companies in industrialized nations are doing today in order to lower their labor expenses. We have seen in the general introduction to this chapter that at La Graufesenque potters and kiln operators were assisted by non-skilled workers (Ateleia's slaves) who performed menial, though essential, tasks. However, this was certainly not the primary reason for the development of provincial branches, as the manpower needed for such an operation was not great.

b. *increase in flexibility*
The advantage of having branch workshops in various areas allowed local managers to respond to the fluctuations of the market in a much faster and more efficient way than a distant producer would have been able to do. Provincial production became massive in the second century A.D., and the phenomenon of decentralization of the production, if it really occurred, might have corresponded to a stage in the economic history of Rome when Italian producers were

---

15 (1991) 1-43 demonstrate, through the analysis by X-Ray Fluorescence of some 121 lamps found in the legionary camp of Vindonissa (first century A.D.), that 90 % of the lamps were imported from Modena, Lyons, and Trier, while the rest was imported from minor workshops, none of which was located in Vindonissa. It is remarkable that the lamps found in Raetia (Regensburg), signed with names from Northern Italy, and dated to the second and third centuries A.D. were in part the products of local workshops, while all imports came exclusively from Modena.

in the process of losing their external markets and had therefore to be more sensitive to qualitative and quantitative changes in demand in the provinces. Rostovzeff's view on the decline of the Italian economy as a consequence of the loss of external markets in the second century A.D., criticized by Harris and defended by Bailey and Procaccini, need not be questioned on the basis of the organization of the lamp industry.[368]

5. *Organization of the production*

The marks found on factory lamps are not any more explicit than those found on terra sigillata pottery. Some common names, such as Communis, Crescens, Felicio, Felix, Fronto, Ianuarius, Inventus, Optatus, Saturninus, Titius, Vibius, are found on both artifacts, but we do not know whether they refer to the same persons.[369] There is no way to tell if they were agents or independent entrepreneurs (including slaves with *peculium*), because the marks on lamps, consisting often of a single *cognomen* (= Group III), do not provide as much information—ambiguous as it is—as those on terra sigillata pottery (cf. above). We do not know either whether the names refer to potters, branch managers or factory owners, as the genitive ATIMETI could be understood as (*opus*) ATIMETI, or (*ex officina*) ATIMETI, or (*ex figlinis*) ATIMETI.[370]

a. *marks, symbols, and letters*
Three interesting facts are worth mentioning in the context of a study of the system of production. First, the presence of symbols or single letters next to the signature of the lampmaker deserves some attention. E. Buchi regards them as evidence that large producers were trying to avoid the inconvenience of centralized production by entrusting part of it to small potters.[371] The symbols would serve as a sign of identification, i.e. as guarantee of the integrity of the product. They might also reflect internal practices within the same workshop, although this would not account for the fact that the same

---

[368] M. Rostovtzeff, *SEHRE*[2] (1957) 173-74; W.V. Harris, *JRS* 70 (1980) 133; D.M. Bailey (1987) 63; and P. Procaccini (1981) 513.

[369] Some Ateius's lamps are also attested, cf. *CIL* XV 6316 and perhaps 6313.

[370] E. Buchi, *Lucerne del Museo di Aquileia. I. Lucerne Romane con marchio di fabbrica* (Aquileia 1975) XXXVI-XLI.

[371] E. Buchi (1975) XXXVI.

symbol appears on the products of several independent firms. For instance, a dot surrounded by a circle above the mark is shared by the firms of Agilis, Atimetus, Bebianus, Cerialis, Communis, Favor, Fidelis, Fortis, Fronto, Iegidius, Litogenes, Lucius, Nerius, and Octavius. Temporary collaboration between workshops might account for this fact,[372] but one should remark that these symbols are extremely common (dot, palm, star) and are not specific to lamps, as any numismatist could attest.[373]

On the other hand the lamps of Fortis bear thirteen different symbols and eight different letters (F, I, N, A, L, P, S, and E): Buchi suggests that these letters represent individual *officinatores*, which is quite possible, but it is not the only possible explanation.[374] Each letter could be connected with an individual worker within the same workshop, perhaps reflecting the owner/manager's policy aimed at favoring internal competition. Another possibility is that every letter refers to a period of production of the same unit and has nothing to do with the personnel.[375]

b. *lid and tank: mould links*

In contrast with vessels, lamps were made out of two moulds, one for the top part and one for the bottom one. The top part, i.e. the lid, is often singularized by some decorative elements and the bot-

---

[372] W.V. Harris, *JRS* 70 (1980) 138 compares it to a similar phenomenon attested in the pottery industry in Lezoux, referring to H. Vertet – A. and J. Lasfargues, "Remarques sur les filiales des ateliers de la vallée du Pô à Lyon et dans la vallée de l'Allier," in *I problemi della ceramica romana di Ravenna, della Valle padana e dell'alto Adriatico, atti del Convegno internazionale, Ravenna . . . 1969* (Bologna 1972) 273-82, esp. 275 and 277.

[373] E.L. Will, *JFA* 6 (1979) 344, n. 14 thinks that the symbols found on Sestius amphora stamps "trace their ancestry back to coin-types and to the symbols on Greek amphora stamps."

[374] For instance, FORTIS / A; FORTIS / N, etc. E. Buchi (1975) 65-93, cited by W.V. Harris, *JRS* 70 (1980) 140, n. 97.

[375] G. Schneider – E. Wirz, *Doc. et Trav. IGAL* 15 (1991) 9 demonstrate that some lamps from Vindonissa made in the Trier area (= their Group D) and stamped FORTIS, FORTIS/I, or FORTIS/F have the same chemical composition. They conclude that they were made in the same workshop at different times, or by several workshops using the same clay. In the context of symbols found on amphora stamps, E.L. Will, *JFA* 6 (1979) 344 says: "Whether the Sestius devices [= symbols] refer to a particular potter or pottery or estate or inspector or year, among other possible interpretations, their variety is best exemplified at Cosa." The fact that many symbols are represented in one shipwreck (Grand Congloué, cf. Will 343) might speak against this second hypothesis (different times).

tom part, i.e. the tank, bears the signature. The combination of a lid and a tank makes a single product, a lamp, that can be identified in the same way as a coin is identified by two dies. The comparison between lamps and coins is not idle, because ideally, if we had large enough series of lamps with the same design, we should be able to establish mould links in order to trace signs of cooperation between potters, transfers of personnel or moulds from one workshop to another, or internal changes. Due to the ratio of preserved lamps to the total output and due to the state of cataloguing for those lamps which have been recovered, instances of mould links are rare, but they exist. For example, the same upper mould was used in the case of two lamps bearing different marks on their lower part (L CAE-SAE or FLORENT).[376] The nature of the relationship between these two people is not clear, but it is possible that they were successive managers of the same workshop. This hypothesis seems to me more convincing than that calling for an association of, or collaboration between, independent potters, but it is not verifiable. As we know nothing of the relationship between producers of moulds and lampmakers, provided that they were two distinct groups of people, isolated cases of mould links are of limited value at this point in the study of the organization of the production.

c. *generations of moulds*

W.V. Harris rests his case for the existence of branch workshops in the provinces partly on the fact that if lamps made in the provinces were unauthorized copies of Italian lamps they would exhibit differences in size—the extent of which is unclear to me—as secondary moulds were made out of an existing (imported) lamp. On the basis of median length figures, Harris asserts that lamps bearing the marks of Italian makers found and assumedly made in Pannonia are not significantly smaller than their Italian models, but the very evidence he presents could be used to prove the opposite.[377] Underlining the "limited value" of the size criterion, Harris compares the median length of selected factory lamps and points out that, for instance, FORTIS lamps from Ulpia Traiana/Sarmizegetusa in Dacia have a median length of 8.1 cm, while FORTIS lamps from

---

[376] C. Bémont–J. Bonnet, "Lampes et fabricants de lampes," *RCRF* 23/24 (1984) 135-54, esp. 148 and Pl. XIV, p. 153.

[377] W.V. Harris, *JRS* 70 (1980) 133-34, n. 56 and Table II.

Pannonia have a median length of 8.5 cm to be compared to those found in Aquileia, which are 9.6–9.7 cm long. Provided that these measurements are reliable and significant, they *do* illustrate a steady decline in size corresponding to the distance from the original place of manufacture in Northern Italy. Dacian lamps would thus have been made out of moulds derived from secondary Pannonian moulds based on an Italian model.

Moulds were often made out of an archetype, and the decoration or marks could be printed on the archetype or added on individual moulds.[378] One archetype could produce several generations of moulds, with the consequence that each generation would be smaller and less precise than its model.[379] Each mould was used to produce a certain number of lamps, and the degree of wear of the mould determined the precision of the decoration on the lamps. What confuses the issue of the origin of lamps is that second- or third-generation moulds are not less likely to have been used by those potters employed in the original workshop than by unauthorized imitators in the provinces. The measurements provided by Buchi for the lamps from Aquileia illustrate the possible range of size variations among lamps produced by a single firm and found within a delimited area.[380]

To return to the case of Pannonian lamps, it is interesting to note the large number of moulds which have been recovered in this province. Harris knows of fifty lower moulds for factory lamps—twelve of them bearing the mark FORTIS—"in addition to many moulds for the upper halves and for other types of lamps."[381] If it is true that these moulds "almost certainly originated in Northern Italy"—and I do not know on what ground this statement is based—

---

[378] C. Pavolini, in W.V. Harris (ed.), *The Inscribed Economy* (1993) 65-71 remarks that stamps were not always carved in the matrix.

[379] A. Provoost, "Les lampes antiques en terre cuite. Introduction et essai de typologie générale avec des détails concernant les lampes trouvées en Italie," *AC* 45 (1976) 5-39 and 550-86, esp. 14-18, with the presentation (p. 15) of an hypothetical genealogical tree based on a study by D.M. Bailey, in *OAth.* 10 (1965) 15-17 (non vidi).

[380] The questionable assumption that *surmoulage* as a technic was practiced only by unauthorized imitators undermines the argument against branch workshops presented by E.W. Haley, *MBAH* 9 (1990) 1-12, esp. 9.

[381] W.V. Harris, *JRS* 70 (1980) 135, with reference to D. Iványi, *Die pannonischen Lampen. Eine typologisch-chronologische Übersicht* (Budapest 1935) 26-27; 310-19; and Pl. LXXIV ("viel reicher an Modeln als an Modellen").

they point toward a significant trade in moulds. As Pannonian consumers were keen on purchasing the lamps made, or at least signed, by Fortis and his Italian colleagues, it made sense for the producers to respond to signs of lasting market opportunities by exporting a certain number of moulds rather than × times more lamps. The Pannonian moulds unfortunately are silent about the identity of the potters who used them, agents or independent buyers, to supply the market with lamps bearing an Italian trademark. One can argue that if Italian lampmakers had opened branch factories in Pannonia they would not have gone through the trouble of exporting the moulds from Italy, except perhaps at the initial stage. Sooner or later, they would have equipped these subsidiary workshops with all the specialists required to carry on the Italian tradition of lampmaking at the lowest cost. The same hypothesis is verified in the case of Ateius's workshop producing terra sigillata in Lyons (cf. above).

d. *social obscurity of the producers*

In spite of the mass of preserved artifacts, little is known about individual firms. As FORTIS lamps are best represented, it is worthwhile summarizing the scanty information preserved about their manufacturer(s). It has been argued that the main center of production was located near Mutina (modern Modena), either in a place today called Savignano sul Panaro, where a mould for tile was found with the inscription AD FORN(*acem* or *-aces*) CAT(. . .?) L AEMILII FORTIS,[382] or in Magreta, where a mould for FORTIS lamps was found in a potters' workshop.[383] The production of FORTIS lamps seems to have started in the second half of the first century A.D., probably around the middle of Vespasian's reign, as the mark FORTIS is represented at Pompeii. In the late first century A.D., three main centers of production (near Modena, in Lyons, and near Trier) exported FORTIS lamps to the legionary camp of

---

[382] *CIL* XI 6689, no. 12. Cf. W.V. Harris, *JRS* 70 (1980) 131, n. 34, quoting A. Crespellani, *BdI* (1875) 192-95, who indicates that the same kiln produced FORTIS lamps and points out that a place nearby was called (in the sixteenth century) 'Campo Forte'. Cf. now M.C. Parra, "La fornace di Savignano sul Panaro," in *Misurare la terra: centurazione e coloni nel mondo romano. Il caso modenese* (Modena 1983) 103-08, reporting the inscription on a brick found in a workshop with some moulds for *Firmalampen*. Cf. also G. Schneider–E. Wirz, *Doc. et Trav. IGAL* 15 (1991) 13.

[383] M.C. Parra, "La fornace di Magreta," in *Misurare la terra: centurazione e coloni nel mondo romano. Il caso modenese* (Modena 1983) 89-102. Cf. also G. Schneider–E. Wirz, *Doc. et Trav. IGAL* 15 (1991) 13.

Vindonissa. During the second century, only the Italian workshop
retained its vocation for long-distance exports (Raetia), while branch
workshops in the Rhine region, in Raetia, and in the other Danube
provinces produced for a local or regional market.[384] The firm continued to produce lamps until the beginning of the third century,[385]
and the sheer length of the period of activity shows that the firm long
outlived its founder.[386] It is possible that some of Fortis's workshops were also engaged in the production of other clay artifacts,
such as amphorae.[387]

6. Conclusion

Lamps signed by Italian manufacturers were exported from the
main workshop as main, supplementary, or return cargoes; they
were also produced locally in subsidiary workshops or by transient
potters, or illegally imitated by local, unaffiliated producers. Not
one of the above solutions seems to have been so prevalent as to
eliminate the others, but Harris's model is strongly supported by the
practicality of branch workshops and the existence of a legal system
promoting and protecting this type of managerial arrangement.
Transfers of moulds facilitated the decentralization of the production, but makes it more difficult for modern historians to establish
the exact circumstances under which the production of lamps was
carried out in the provinces. One—not necessarily the most important one—of many purposes for decentralizing the production could

---

[384] G. Schneider – E. Wirz, Doc. et Trav. IGAL 15 (1991) 13, suggesting, on the
basis of the chemical analysis of the products found in Vindonissa (first century
A.D.) and Regensburg (mid-second to mid-third century), that Fortis had three
main workshops (Group A/B [Modena], C1 [Lyons], D [Trier]), another large one
in Cologne (Group K), and about seven minor, perhaps temporary ones (Group
F2 [Frankfurt-Nied], F3 [?], C3 [perhaps Lausanne/Vidy], X [perhaps near
Regensburg/Raetia], V [Raetia], W [Raetia or Noricum], and Z [perhaps Panno-
nia]).

[385] E. Buchi (1975) 66-67 discusses various theories about this phenomenon.
Cf. also P. Panazza, Le lucerne romane della Valcamonica (Brescia 1984) 95.

[386] This fact, combined with the quantity of lamps bearing the same mark, the
variety of their fabrics, and the wide range of their distribution induced D.M.
Bailey (1980) 275-76 (cited by G. Schneider – E. Wirz, Doc. et Trav. IGAL 15 [1991]
4) to consider them as imitation by local lampmakers rather than the product of
workshops controlled by the Fortis family. Contra, cf. above, p. 236, and n. 114.

[387] CIL IX 6079, no. 29 (Brundisium). Cf. E. Buchi (1975) 65-93, esp. 70; and
W.V. Harris, JRS 70 (1980) 142, nn. 120 and 121.

have been to respond to changing tastes and needs of customers located at some distance from the original center of production, at a time when provincial lamps were gaining in popularity in the provinces and tended to supersede Italian imports.

Symbols and individual letters found on lamps next to the signature of the manufacturer can be interpreted as evidence for the organization of the workshop, where the activity of the workers was stimulated through internal competition, or as a sign of cooperation between workshops belonging to different manufacturers. Thus, moulds or designers could be exchanged, which explains how the same lid is found in combination with tanks signed by two different producers.

Unauthorized imitations cannot be identified by their comparatively smaller size, because moulds could be duplicated, or made out of existing lamps, in the same way by both authorized workshop managers and imitators. Exported and copied moulds probably existed in great numbers and were used by either of these two groups. However, G. Schneider and E. Wirz convincingly demonstrate that the phenomenon of unauthorized copies must have been rather limited:

> From the series of 121 analysed lamps no more than 14 could have been made in minor centers and thus be unauthorized copies. Nearly 90 percent of the lamps from this legionary camp [Vindonissa], however, were manufactured at only three major lampmaking centers, all of them very distant from Vindonissa. This makes it very likely that the centers in Modena, Lyon and Trier (?) must have been production branches of the larger firms. It would be hard to believe that unauthorized copies were made nearly exclusively in three large centers far away from the place where they were sold and used.[388]

The case of Vindonissa shows that it takes more sophisticated methods to trace the origin of lamps to branch workshops than to demonstrate the common occurrence of exports or to postulate the practice of unauthorized reproductions.

Finally, there was no intermediate category, such as "non-institorial freedmen" employed or authorized by Italian firm owners "to establish subsidiary workshops...which probably achieved a certain measure of independence from the parent concern."[389] Work-

---

[388] G. Schneider–E. Wirz, *Doc. et Trav. IGAL* 15 (1991) 9 and 13, against Loeschcke's hypothesis (recorded p. 3) that all *Firmalampen* belonging to techniques (= Groups) B, C, and D were unauthorized copies of imported Italian lamps.

[389] E.W. Haley, *MBAH* 9 (1990) 11-12, rejecting Harris's theory of branch

shops were either subsidiary or independent, and their respective operators were managers appointed by the firm owner in the first case, and entrepreneurs running their own business in the second case. Passages from the former situation to the latter were possible, and undoubtedly occurred, but such changes were unlikely to bear on the physical appearance of the production. At best, the promotion from the rank of workshop manager to that of independent entrepreneur could affect the structure of the stamps and/or the range of the distribution of the artifacts. However, this remains an hypothesis.[390]

F. Conclusion

The study of workshop managers in the ceramic industry rests on the examination of signatures stamped or painted on clay artifacts. The identification of the place of origin and destination of these roughly datable artifacts can be used to reconstruct commercial movements to be explained in terms of managerial policy in response to changes in the economic conjuncture. The opening of new markets presented entrepreneurs with an array of economic and managerial choices for the purpose of expanding their activity both horizontally and vertically. Limitations in the technology of transport made the enlargement of existing enterprises in the central point of production less profitable than the opening of branches in areas of development. The availability of an experienced work force and the guarantee offered by the legal system made it profitable to entrust the management of subsidiary workshops or outlets to agents. These workshop managers were tied to their principals by economic, social, and/or legal bonds. Consumers could count on products of equal quality and lower price than imports. The rise of a stiff competition among individual producers and regions called for drastic adjustments in manufacturing and marketing policy. These were achieved through diversification of the production, relocation of workshops, and eventual emancipation or abandonment of subsidiary centers of production.

---

production of terracotta lamps in Roman Spain, where most lamps are thought to be the result of importation and temporary imitations. The production of hypothetical "non-institorial freedmen" would have remained "negligible."

[390] Cf. above, the section on terra sigillata.

The managerial system used in the clay industry seems to have been borrowed from agricultural concerns (*fundi*), and was adapted to both rural and urban contexts. The manufacture of containers for the export of staples produced on agricultural estates and the exploitation of clay districts located in the vicinity of farmsteads for the production of building material must have directly benefited from the existence of the *vilicus* system.

Units of production were centered around kilns, the operation of which was not necessarily carried out by potters involved in making moulds and artifacts. Because of conditions characteristic of the pottery industry, such as the need for abundant supply of fuel for firing, nucleated centers of production, such as those in Arezzo, Lyons, La Graufesenque, or Lezoux, turned out to be very prosperous, though not long-lasting. Cooperation between workshops, through exchanges of moulds, *poinçons*, and personnel, was not uncommon. Such phenomena are illustrated by the archaeological material and by scattered evidence for temporary partnerships.

The division of labor, at the level of the extraction and preparation of the clay, the making of tools, the shaping or casting of artifacts, the operation of the kiln, storage management, marketing and distribution, is similar to what can be seen in the context of farm management. By having several potters or group of potters working side-by-side within the same workshop, the firm owner or manager could foster a climate of internal competition aimed at increasing the qualitative and quantitative level of the production. Some firms are known to have employed numerous workers at various places at the same time.

The names appearing in the stamps provide some evidence concerning the social background of potters and their place in Roman (Italian and provincial) society and economy. The content of the stamps occasionally permits identifying some slaves or freedmen among the people operating workshops producing tablewares, amphorae, and building material (stamps on terracotta lamps are more elliptic). *Tria nomina* (*praenomen* + *nomen* + *cognomen*) often point toward free status (freedman or freeborn). Many stamps, however, exhibiting *tria nomina* in an abbreviated form (or genitive) and on two different lines (*praenomen* + *nomen* / *cognomen*) could refer to two different persons, employer and employee, or principal and manager. The legal status of the latter remains unclear, although Greek *cognomina*, quite common in the stamps, usually point toward slave

or freed status. The stamps are almost never specific about the nature of the legal relationship between the two persons represented in
them. In the brick industry, for instance, male and female *officinatores* belonged to all social strata from slave up to the equestrian
order, but neither the slave, almost certainly an *institor*, nor the
knight, probably a contractor, advertised in any specific terms the
nature of his position with regard to the owner of the clay district/
brickyards where he operated.

Occasionally, the position of a name in a stamp permits identifying its bearer as a principal. Such people usually belonged to the
upper classes (cf. for instance, C. Laecanius Bassus, who produced
amphorae, belonged to the senatorial order, and A. Decius Alpinus,
whose name is associated with the production of building material,
was perhaps a member of the municipal elite in Southern Gaul).
However, the evidence is deceiving, because a succession of great
entrepreneurs, whose wealth, political influence, and birth pertained to the upper class, were likely to produce on a larger scale and
therefore to leave more visible traces of their activity than a lower-
middle-class potter, whose career was limited to a short period of
time (five to twenty-five years) during which he conducted operations on a moderate scale. Modest potters, such as the lampmaker
C. Clodius, existed nonetheless, and perhaps formed a majority.
They too may have relied on *institores* for the manufacture or distribution of their products.

Finally, it seems that in many ways the various types of material are
complementary. The picture that various types of artifacts and stamps
provide about exports, branch workshops, and the social fabric of
people involved in the clay industry is apparently similar for all four
sectors examined in this chapter, each case study illuminating to various extents specific aspects of the organization of Roman manufacturing activities. More could perhaps be learned from the study
of the organization of other similar activities, such as the marble,[391]

---

[391] Bibliography and state of the question in H. Dodge, "Ancient Marble
Studies: Recent Research," *JRA* 4 (1991) 28-50, esp. 34-36, with reference to the
recent work of J.C. Fant. The main evidence is provided by some inscriptions from
Docimium (Phrygia), classified by types (I-III, from Domitian to the third century), the later one (starting around 130's–150's and developing until 236) containing various types of information (consular date, name of *officina*, name of the foreman of the *caesura*, and identification numbers of the *locus* and *bracchium*, cf. *CIL*
III 7029 = *ILS* 8722c). Cf. J.C. Fant, *Cavum antrum Phrygiae: The Organization and
Operations of the Roman Imperial Marble Quarries in Phrygia* (Oxford 1989) esp. 33-41

stone,[392] metal,[393] wood,[394] and glass industries.[395]

---

on the personnel employed in the *caesurae*, *bracchia*, and *officinae* of imperial marble quarries, and about the role of military centurions in the organization of units of production; *idem*, "Ideology, Gift, and Trade: A Distribution Model for the Roman Imperial Marbles," in W.V. Harris (ed.), *The Inscribed Economy* (1993) 145-70. Cf. also J.-P. Morel (1976) 304-08; D. Mustilli, *Botteghe di scultori, marmorarii, bronzieri e caelatores in Pompei* (Naples 1950). On travelling *officinae*, cf. P. Pensabene, in *Ricerche e studi (Museo Provinciale "Francesco Ribezzo," Brindisi)* 6 (1972) 9-39. H. Dodge (above, p. 39) points out that certain quarries had agencies overseas (for instance, at Leptis Magna), where specialized sculptors were sent to satisfy a highly discriminating market; cf. J.B. Ward-Perkins, *JRS* 41 (1951) 89-104; and *idem*, *PBSR* 48 (1980) 23-69.

[392] R. Bedon, *Les carrières et les carriers de la Gaule romaine* (Paris 1984), esp. 147-98; and 199-220; and C. Dubois, *Etudes sur l'administration et l'exploitation des carrières dans le monde romain* (Paris 1908).

[393] J.-P. Morel (1976) 287-93; P. Ørsted, *Roman Imperial Economy and Romanization. A Study in Roman Imperial Administration and the Public Lease System in the Danubian Provinces from the First to the Third Century A.D.* (Copenhagen 1985), esp. 171-250; J.D.C. Boulakia, "Lead in the Roman World," *AJA* 76 (1972) 139-44; O. Davies, *Roman Mines in Europe* (Oxford 1935); S. Dusanic, "Aspects of Roman Mining in Noricum, Pannonia, Dalmatia and Moesia Superior," *ANRW* II.6 (1977) 52-94; J.F. Healy, *Mining and Metallurgy in the Greek and Roman World* (London 1978); J. Kunow, *Der römische Import in der Germania libera bis zu den Markomannenkriegen. Studien zu Bronze- und Glasgefässen* (Neumünster 1983); *idem*, "Die capuanischen Bronzegefässhersteller Lucius Ansius Epaphroditus und Publius Cipius Polybius," *BJ* 185 (1985) 215-42.

[394] J.-P. Morel (1976) 301-04; and R. Meiggs, *Trees and Timber in the Ancient World* (Oxford 1982).

[395] J.-P. Morel, "La ceramica e il vetro," in F. Zevi (ed.), *Pompei 79* (Naples 1979) 255-61; D.B. Harden, "Ancient Glass, II: Roman," *AJ* 126 (1970) 44-77; and M. Sternini, "I vetri," in W.V. Harris (ed.), *The Inscribed Economy* (1993) 81-94.

CHAPTER FIVE

DIRECT MANAGEMENT AND PUBLIC ADMINISTRATION: FOUR CASE STUDIES

A. Introduction

Direct management through agents developed as a legal system during the last two centuries of the Republican period. The *vilicus* system, as it has been referred to earlier, was certainly devised in the agricultural context of the villa economy and extended to workshops and other kinds of facilities organized as managerial units. It was born out of

(a) the necessity for wealthy people to rely on agents to carry out economic activities that their life-style, political and economic engagement, and social prejudices prevented them from pursuing personally;

(b) the desire, on the part of the elite, to retain some degree of control over the economic activities of their dependents without curtailing the latter's aptitudes to engage in highly profitable pursuits where technical and managerial skills were put to work for the benefit of the former;

(c) the structure of Roman society, in which a significant part of the population—all persons *alieni iuris*, including slaves, dependents-in-power, and women-in-power—was originally denied the legal capacity of entering into binding contracts;

and (d) the practice of regarding real estate property as an adequate guarantee for contracts made by agents. The combination of these factors resulted in the fruitful cooperation of the haves and the have-nots in almost all areas of economic life. Social peace in the business community was the consequence of a well understood community of interest, which was recognized and fostered by the Roman praetor at an early stage.

The *vilicus* system rested on the appointment (*praepositio*) of an agent by the principal to the head of an economic unit identified with a piece of real property (*fundus, hortus, praedia, officina, statio, mansio, mutatio, stabulum, taberna, deversorium, horreum, pistrina, insula, domus, aedes, aedis, mensa*, etc.), on the horizontal division of labor within that unit (*familia*), and on an efficient hierarchic system of control with several levels of administration (*dominus*; *procurator*, *curator*; *actor*, *dispensator*; *vilicus*, *officinator*, *institor*; *praefectus*, *magister*, *monitor*, *optio*).

In the present chapter, I will investigate how this system of management, which developed in relation to private enterprises, proved successful enough to be adopted in various areas of the economy and administration of the Roman empire. One obvious avenue of research consists in looking up the prosopography of *vilici* and *actores* and describing the many economic activities in which they engaged. The problem linked with this approach is that it is often not possible to go any further than emphasizing the existence of the pattern of management without being able to reach any enlightening conclusions.

Another way of tracking down managers would be to focus on the evidence about *familiae*[1] and to assume that they formed the staff of one managerial unit under the responsibility of a *vilicus*, *officinator*, or their like. This approach, however, would fail to take into account all one-person managerial units.

In some areas, a great deal is known about the activities of *vilici* at the head of a *familia*. I have discussed elsewhere[2] the application of the *vilicus* system in the administration of the water supply, of which we have a very detailed account by Frontinus, *curator aquarum* under Nerva. This author describes at great length the history of the water supply of the City of Rome, the functions of the water commissioner (*curator*) and his deputy (usually, an imperial freedman with the rank of *procurator*), the technical details of the distribution of water to individual landowners through signed lead pipes, the role of the *aquarii* in regulating this process, and their interaction with private contractors (*redemptores*).[3] The staff responsible for the construction, or at least the maintenance, of the system was divided into

---

[1] Dessau, *ILS* indices p. 420; 699; and 950.

[2] Cf. my paper "Workshop Managers" in W.V. Harris (ed.), *The Inscribed Economy: Production and Distribution in the Roman Empire in the Light of instrumentum domesticum* (*JRA* Suppl. 6, Ann Arbor 1993) 171-81.

[3] Frontin., *Aq.* Book Two, especially 96-119. Cf. S.D. Martin, *The Roman Jurists and the Organization of Private Building in the Late Republic and Early Empire* (Brussels 1989) 61; and C. Bruun, *The Water Supply of Ancient Rome. A Study of Roman Imperial Administration* (Helsinki 1991), with a full bibliography and an extensive collection and discussion of the primary material.

two brigades (*familiae aquarum*) of unequal sizes including *vilici*, *castellarii*, *circitores*, *silicarii*, *tectores*, and other *opifices*, one being composed of 240 public slaves, originally bequeathed by Agrippa, the other of 460 imperial slaves. The picture is completed by the fact that Frontinus's account is corroborated by epigraphical evidence recording *vilici* attached to a specific aqueduct[4] and other slaves attached to an administrative unit called *statio*.[5] In Bononia, and possibly elsewhere, *vilici* were responsible for the production of lead pipes, as some stamped signatures suggest.[6]

A different approach would consist in investigating the main areas of Roman economic life in order to identify *institores* in various trades (garment, perfume, food, banking industry, etc.), but this would lead to a great deal of repetition and to the same inconclusive statements as in my quest for *institores* in the clay industry (cf. above, Chapter Four). Through the legal sources, we know that business managers were to be found in many activities, but there is little nonlegal evidence supporting this fact.

In this chapter, I will discuss four areas of public life as case studies, each of which will serve a different purpose. I will start with the investigation of the system of tax collection in order to demonstrate how the *vilicus* system was adopted by the companies of publicans and how it went through major administrative reforms—the possible shift to a system of collection carried out by individual tax farmers, and, above all, its takeover by the imperial administration—without being drastically altered in its concept. Second, I will turn to recreational facilities, and show how the public and imperial administrations superseded to some extent private enterprise, without renouncing the *vilicus* system as a type of management. Third, I will focus on the imperialization and militarization of the system by examining the road system and the introduction and development of the postal service and requisitioned transport. And finally I will address the question of the internal organization of a particular type of economic unit, the Roman mint, a symbol of state sovereignty, the efficiency of which reflected on the general economic, political, and social well-being of the whole empire. Throughout the

---

[4] *CIL* VI 8495-8496 and 33732-33733.

[5] *CIL* VI 8489 and 36781.

[6] *CIL* XI 725 and 731-36; and *AE* 1976, no. 214 (= *Not.Scav.* 1932, pp. 42-50, late first century A.D.?).

chapter, the complementarity of different types of evidence should yield some colorful, dynamic pictures of Roman systems of management.

B. Tax collection (VECTIGALIA)

The *vilicus* system is well attested in the context of the collection of certain kinds of taxes. Most of the evidence is provided by Greek and Latin inscriptions roughly datable to the Imperial period and originating from the provinces.[7] Italian material exists, but it is less abundant and often less specific. The main features of the Roman system of tax collection are described in literary and legal sources, but some aspects of its chronological development remain unclear.[8] Besides, regional differences are hard to trace: the evidence is abundant in some areas (Illyricum, Gaul, Africa, Egypt, Asia Minor) and almost nonexistent in others (Spain, Britain, Lower Germania). Before discussing the role of managers (*vilici* and *actores*) in tax collection, it is necessary to present a brief outline of the history of tax collection in the late Republic and early Empire.

1. *Historical outline*

During the Republican period and the early Empire, the collection of various taxes was farmed to private contractors, because the Roman state lacked the means, skill, and political willingness to deal with this kind of task directly. Until the Severan period, these private entrepreneurs were organized in companies of publicans (*socii* or *publicani*), who established an empire-wide infrastructure, composed of central and regional offices supervising collection centers

---

[7] J. Carlsen collects and discusses all the material in his forthcoming book, *Vilicus. A Study in Roman Estate Management*.

[8] This picture has been recently redrawn to a considerable extent by the studies of M.R. Cimma, *Ricerche sulle società di publicani* (Milan 1981); and P.A. Brunt, "Publicans in the Principate," in *Roman Imperial Themes* (Oxford 1990) 354-432. The recent publication of an important inscription from Ephesus (*Monumentum Ephesenum*, or *Lex portorii Asiae* = νόμος τέλους ᾿Ασίας εἰσαγωγῆς καὶ ἐξαγωγῆς κατά τε γῆν καὶ κατὰ θάλασσαν), dated to A.D. 62 but including provisions passed in 75 B.C. and at various times between these two dates, provided new information about the structure and organization of toll stations, cf. H. Engelmann – D. Knibbe, "Das Zollgesetz der Provinz Asia. Eine neue Inschrift aus Ephesos," *Epigraphica Anatolica* 14 (1989).

located in cities and harbors, and along provincial and imperial
borders. The contracts for the right to collect various kinds of taxes
were farmed out for five years at public auctions organized in Rome
by the censors. It has been argued that during the Principate, this
task was taken over by imperial procurators and by the prefect of the
treasury (*praefectus aerarii Saturni*).[9] Even though it is likely that the
same companies were able to renew their contracts, newcomers
could displace incumbents.[10] In case of a change of company after
a period of time, the successful bidders would probably take over the
local infrastructure—buildings and staff—established by their predecessor, so that continuity at the practical level would be ensured.
This was facilitated by the fact that, in Roman private law, the
transfer of ownership of a managerial unit could include its managerial and technical staff, livestock, and equipment (cf. Chapter
Two).

Because of their semi-public functions, the companies of publicans (*societates vectigalium*) were considered as a particular type of
partnership which was not dissolved by the coming or withdrawal/
death of one of the partners/shareholders (*socii*).[11] Their factual
permanence may explain why they seem to have been endowed at
an early stage with some kind of juristic personality (*corpus*).[12] In

---

[9] W. Eck, *Die staatlichen Organisation Italiens in der hohen Kaiserzeit* (Munich 1979)
115; and P.A. Brunt (1990) 357 and 377. On imperial procurators supervising the
collection of taxes, cf. Dessau, *ILS* IV, pp. 426-32; H.G. Pflaum, *Les carrières procuratoriennes équestres* (Paris 1960-61). The emperor himself could take care of it, following Caesar's example (cf. Alfenus Varus [7 *dig.*] *Dig.* 39.4.15). The *Lex portorii Asiae*
shows that under the reign of Nero these matters were in the hands of three
ἐπιμεληταὶ τῶν δημοσίων προσόδων (*curatores publicorum vectigalium*, referred to by
Tacitus, *Ann.* 15.18: "tres dein consulares, L. Pisonem, Ducenium Geminum,
Pompeium Paulinum vectigalibus publicis praeposuit") whose appointment seems
to have been exceptional; cf. *Epigr.Anatol.* 14 (1989) Introduction (= *Praescript,*
lines 1-7, with commentary pp. 35-37) and sect. 62 (144-147).
[10] P.A. Brunt (1990) 369, n. 55, with reference to Cic., *Att.* 1.17.9 for evidence
of "keen competition for the Asian tribute in 61 B.C." Cf. also Paulus (5 *sent.*) *Dig.*
39.4.9 *pr.* (= *Sent.* 5.1a.1), where the *calor licitantis* is reported to have inflated the
bid "ultra modum solitae conductionis."
[11] Pomponius (12 *ad Sab.*) *Dig.* 17.2.59 *pr.*; and Ulpianus (31 *ad ed.*) *Dig.*
17.2.63.8. Cf. J. Plescia, "The Development of the Juristic Personality in Roman
Law," *Studi Sanfilippo* I (Milan 1982) 487-524, esp. 500-01, and n. 29; and P.A.
Brunt (1990) 372-75.
[12] Gaius (3 *ad ed. prov.*) *Dig.* 3.4.1. On the legal position of the companies and
their staff (*familiae publicanorum*), cf. *Dig.* 39.4. Cf. also C. Nicolet, "Deux remarques sur l'organisation des sociétés de publicains à la fin de la République romaine," in H. van Effenterre (ed.), *Points de vue sur la fiscalité à Rome* (Paris 1979)

dealing with state authorities, the companies were represented by an agent (*manceps*, *redemptor*, or *conductor*) who negotiated the contract and had to provide sureties (*praedes*) and securities (*praedia*). Insofar as the *socii* stood as sureties, *manceps* and *socii* were jointly liable for the contract. The legal relationship between *manceps* and *socii* was determined by private contract.[13] Thus, the *manceps* was some kind of legal representative of the company, but there is no evidence that he did anything else but bid for the contract and negotiate its terms with state officials.

The internal administration of the companies was entrusted to annually elected *magistri* and remained centralized in Rome. In the provinces, local administrative centers were headed by officials called *promagistri*. These representatives had the capacity to make binding agreements (*pacta*)[14] and were in charge of supervising the collection of one or more kinds of taxes or of some other state revenues, tasks in which they were assisted by a numerous, hierarchically organized staff (*familia publicanorum*, cf. below). For our purpose, it is important to note that "the rights and duties of tax collectors were regulated by the praetor's edict at Rome and by the edicts of governors in the provinces."[15] Tax collectors could sue the taxpayers and take pledges from them. Conversely, the *socii*, or, presumably, their representatives (*magistri* and *promagistri*), could be sued by any person who had been wronged (*furtum*, *damnum*, or *iniuria*) by a member of the *familia publicanorum*. If successful, the plaintiff could obtain redress from any of the *socii*.[16] There is, however, no explicit evidence for the contractual liability of *socii* for the

---

69-95; E. Badian, *Publicans and Sinners* (Ithaca/London 1972) 69-70; and *idem*, *Gnomon* 56 (1984) 45-48, reviewing M.R. Cimma (1981) who suggests (95-98; and 242-43) that it was only in the first century A.D. that *societates* were given a limited juristic personality. Cf. also the qualified statement by P.A. Brunt (1990) 368-71.

[13] P.A. Brunt (1990) 360-63.

[14] Ulpianus (4 *ad ed.*) *Dig.* 2.14.14: "Item magistri societatium pactum et prodesse et obesse constat." Cf. P.A. Brunt (1990) 370.

[15] P.A. Brunt (1990) 358, with reference to *Dig.* 39.4 *passim*. Gaius wrote a commentary *Ad edictum praetoris urbani titulo de publicanis* (*Dig.* 39.4.5 and 19.1.19), which indicates that publicans were under the jurisdiction of the urban praetor.

[16] P.A. Brunt (1990) 358-59 and 364-66, with reference to the *Lex metalli Vipascensis* (*FIRA* I², no. 105, lines 16, 34-35, 40-41, 45, and 53) for the right to take pledges extended to the *conductor*, his *socius* and/or his *actor*; and to Ulpianus (55 *ad ed.*) *Dig.* 39.4.3.1, Paulus (52 *ad ed.*), citing Labeo and the emperor Hadrian, *Dig.* 39.4.4, and Modestinus (2 *de poenis*) *Dig.* 39.4.6, about the liability of the publicans for the wrongdoings of their staff.

transactions negotiated by authorized agents (*actores*, *vilici*, *praepositi*, etc.). If this silence of the sources had to be accounted for, it may be due to the fact that collecting taxes did not give rise to an intense contractual activity on the part of the managers of *stationes* (cf. below). Here again, the recently published *Lex portorii Asiae* provides valuable information: it records a consular decree from L. Caninius Gallus and Q. Fabricius (2 B.C.) which stipulates that "if someone makes a contract with a tax farmer or his agent in connection with customs affairs, the contract is legal."[17]

Until recently, it was believed that the system underwent some drastic change at the beginning of the second century A.D.: the farming of taxes would have been transferred from the companies of publicans to personally liable contractors (*conductores*). As *conductores* had already been resorted to on a smaller scale during the preceding period, the novelty would have consisted in the gradual abolition of the companies of publicans. From then on, the imperial treasury would have dealt only with people who allegedly offered better financial guarantees. P.A. Brunt has recently challenged this theory, showing that the evidence for individual contractors is scarce and inconclusive and pointing out that several legal texts of the late-second and third centuries continue to refer to the activity of publicans as a contemporary phenomenon.[18] Thus, in the middle of the second century, the jurist Gaius brings up the fact that the companies in charge of collecting taxes and other revenues from the exploitation of gold and silver mines and saltworks were granted corporate status as a privilege.[19] After him, Ulpianus decries the well-known

---

[17] *Epigr. Anatol.* 14 (1989) sect. 48 (= lines 113-114): [Λεύκιος Κανίνιος Γά]λλος, Κόιντος Φαβρίκιος ὕπατοι προσέθηκαν· ἐάν τις περὶ τῶν τελῶν τούτων πρὸς δημοσιώνην ἢ ἐ[πίτρο]πον συνθῆται, [ὃ ἂν ἐκ πίστεως ἀγαθῆς γένηται] νόμιμον ἔστω{ι} (vac.) and the commentary on this passage (pp. 118-19). *Pactiones* negotiated by tax farmers with communities rather than individuals are mentioned by Cicero (*Cons. Prov.* 5.10; *QFr.* 1.1.12; *Att.* 5.14; *Fam.* 13.65, etc.). Cf. A.N. Sherwin-White, *Roman Foreign Policy in the East (168 B.C. to A.D. 1)* (Norman, OK 1984) 232-33, n. 117.

[18] P.A. Brunt (1990) 354-432, esp. 370-71 and 386-414, convincingly arguing against the thesis defended by S.J. de Laet, *Portorium. Etude sur l'organisation douanière chez les Romains, surtout à l'époque du Haut-Empire* (Bruges 1949) and generally accepted since then.

[19] Gaius (3 *ad ed. prov.*) *Dig.* 3.4.1 *pr.*: "Paucis admodum in causis concessa sunt huiusmodi corpora: ut ecce vectigalium publicorum sociis permissum est corpus habere vel aurifodinarum vel argentifodinarum et salinarum."

audacity and arrogance of the "factions" of publicans,[20] who are still mentioned in the *Sententiae* of Pseudo-Paulus, dated to the late third century A.D.[21] Even though individual tax farmers (*conductores*) may not have displaced the companies of publicans during the second century A.D., as was commonly believed until recently, there is no reason why the former should be discarded altogether from the history of tax collection: both companies and individual tax farmers could have lived side-by-side. The "paucity of evidence" pointed out by Brunt provides nothing more than an argument from silence, and in any case rests on the assumption that those *conductores* whose staff is attested in second- and third-century inscriptions were indeed attached to the companies.

Be that as it may, it seems that some change did occur in the later part of the second century, as the imperial administration became increasingly involved in the process of tax collection. It is true that imperial procurators appear in this context at an early date (first century A.D.), but it seems that at first they were only in charge of farming out the tax to the publicans and of supervising their activities. According to Brunt, the initial involvement of imperial officials was made necessary by a change in the terms of the contracts, whereby tax farmers would pay a percentage of what they collected instead of a lump sum determined at the time of auction; this reform followed the introduction of new taxes by Augustus and resulted from the difficulty for potential bidders to make a reasonable estimate of their likely profits. Since the switch from lump sum to percentage system had made cheating easier on the part of the publicans, closer supervision was required. Thus, the imperial bureaucracy developed side-by-side with, and more or less on the pattern of, the companies of publicans. There is, however, inescapable evidence that

---

[20] Ulpianus (38 *ad ed.*) *Dig.* 39.4.12 *pr.*: "Quantae audaciae, quantae temeritatis sint publicanorum factiones, nemo est qui nesciat. Idcirco praetor ad compescendam eorum audaciam hoc edictum proposuit: 'Quod familia publicanorum furtum fecisse dicetur, item si damnum iniuria fecerit et id ad quos ea res pertinet non exhibetur, in dominum sine noxae deditione iudicium dabo.'" Since the praetor's edict cited here is much older than Ulpianus's time, one may surmise that the jurist refers to an historical fact deemed familiar to his readers rather than to the contemporary situation. Therefore, the passage is not so cogent as assumed by P.A. Brunt (1990) 370. The same remark applies to Gaius's passage (quoted in the preceding note: "permissum est" may refer to a more or less recent past).

[21] Paulus (5 *sent.*) *Dig.* 39.4.9.4 (= *Sent.* 5.1a.5): "Socii vectigalium si separatim partes administrent, alter ab altero minus idoneo in se portionem transferri iure desiderat."

by the time of Commodus imperial procurators assisted by imperial freedmen and slaves did more than supervising the publicans, at least in certain areas (Illyricum, and perhaps Gaul and Africa). This may have been a temporary expedient to make up for the dearth of tax farmers, as an alternative for compulsory service.[22]

Finally, army officers are occasionally attested as tax collectors. This was the case, for instance, in third-century Palestine, where the crop tax was paid in kind to a *kitron*, who has been identified as a centurion.[23] The involvement of the Roman army in the collection of taxes both in kind and in money was connected with the collectors' need for protection in the climate of insecurity that developed by the early third century A.D., especially in the countryside. Thus, a *vilicus* probably in charge of a toll station in the capacity of agent of either tax farmers or the emperor(s) appears together with a *beneficiarius* (specialized non-commissioned officer) in an inscription from Moguntiacum (Upper Germania).[24] Another factor was that the military had become one of the main recipients of the produce of taxation, and therefore had a stake in ensuring its proper collection, storage, and distribution.[25] Under these circumstances, tax collection often borders on extortion.

2. *Taxes and appropriation*

In the Republican period, after the abolition of the *tributum* (an annual contribution that citizens imposed on themselves to cover war expenditures) in 167 B.C., the main income of the Roman state came from the *vectigalia*. These included:

– all kinds of revenues from public and private properties (pasture tax = *scriptura*; tithe = *decuma*, collected only in the provinces);

---

[22] P.A. Brunt (1990) 381-86 and 414-20, stressing (416) that there is no evidence for the involvement of imperial officials as tax collectors before Commodus and after Alexander Severus.

[23] D. Sperber, "The Centurion as Tax-collector," *Latomus* 28 (1969) 186-89, citing a text in Tosefta, *Demai* 6.3, where the tax was paid by the tenant of land owned by a Samaritan. The text was edited ca. 230 and the situation it describes belongs most likely to the second or early third century.

[24] *CIL* XIII 11816 (= 6731 + 6768, "...be(neficiarius) co(n)s(ularis) / c(um) vil(ico) p(osuit)").

[25] On soldiers as tax collectors, cf. R. MacMullen, *Soldier and Civilian in the Later Roman Empire* (Cambridge, MA 1963) 58-62.

- revenues from state monopolies (tax on salt, minium, sylphium);

- customs dues (*portoria*, first mentioned in Capua and Puteoli in 199 B.C., abolished in Italy by a *Lex Caecilia* of 60 B.C., and reestablished soon after);[26]

- and the tax on manumission (*vicesima libertatis*, established in 357 B.C.).[27] The proceeds of these taxes went to the main public treasury called *aerarium Saturni*, or to some separate account inside of it.[28]

During the Principate, several new taxes were introduced by the imperial government in order to cope with increasing expenditures linked to the rising cost of bureaucracy and political bribery. In A.D. 6, Augustus introduced a five percent tax on inheritance (*vicesima hereditatium*), the proceeds of which went to the *aerarium militare*.[29] A year later, pressured by the need of money for wars and for the support of the newly created fire brigades (*vigiles*), the same emperor imposed a two percent tax on the sale of slaves, the proceeds of which went to the *fiscus*. By A.D. 43, the rate of this tax had been raised to four percent (*vicesima quinta venalium mancipiorum*).[30]

At times, the rulers (triumvirs or emperors) would establish new imposts limited to the city of Rome to satisfy their urgent needs for cash.[31] Suetonius reports that Caligula introduced new taxes on

---

[26] The law for abolition had been introduced by the praetor Q. Metellus Nepos, cf. Dio 37.51.3; Cic., *Att.* 2.16.1; and *QFr.* 1.1.33. *Portoria* were reintroduced at least partially by Caesar (Suet., *Iul.* 43.1: "peregrinarum mercium portorium instituit") and perhaps completely by the triumvirs in 42 (Dio 47.16.3, who, however, does not explicitly say it). On *portoria*, cf. S.J. de Laet (1949); and P.A. Brunt (1990) 425-32.

[27] W. Eck, *Die staatlichen Organisation Italiens in der hohen Kaiserzeit* (Munich 1979) 114-24; K.R. Bradley, "The *vicesima libertatis*. Its History and Significance," *Klio* 66 (1984) 175-82; and M. Albana, "La *vicesima libertatis* in età imperiale," *QC* 9 (1987) 41-76.

[28] C. Nicolet, *Tributum. Recherches sur la fiscalité directe sous la République romaine* (Bonn 1976) 13-15.

[29] S.J. de Laet, "Note sur l'organisation et la nature juridique de la *vicesima hereditatium*," *AC* 16 (1947) 29-36; H.G. Pflaum, "Une inscription bilingue de Kos et la perception de la *vicesima hereditatium*," *ZPE* 7 (1971) 64-68; and *idem*, "Subproc(urator) XX hereditatium regionis Hellespontiacae et Pergameiae," *ZPE* 18 (1975) 11-12; C. Nicolet (1976) 95-98; and W. Eck (1979) 125-45.

[30] Dio 55.31.4; *CIL* VI 915 (= *ILS* 203) is a dedication, dated 43, by the "[socii] publici XX libertatis and XXV venal(ium);" and Tac., *Ann.* 13.31 (A.D. 56). Cf. W.V. Harris, "Towards a Study of the Roman Slave Trade," *MAAR* 36 (1980) 117-40, esp. 121 and 135-36, n. 44.

[31] For the various taxes introduced by the triumvirs, cf. C. Nicolet (1976)

eatables (*pro edulibus*), on lawsuits and legal proceedings (*pro litibus ac iudiciis*), on porters' wages (*ex gerulorum quaestibus*), and on prostitutes (*ex capturis prostitutarum*).[32] Some of these taxes, which Suetonius calls outrageous, may not have survived Caligula's reign. The collection was carried out by private contractors at first, and subsequently by officers of the praetorian guard. We also hear of taxes on vegetables[33] and on lavatories (*vectigal urinae*) introduced by Vespasian.[34] In the second and third centuries A.D., the sources record a tax on the obstruction of sunlight (*solarium*),[35] and various charges imposed on landlords for the maintenance of the water- and sewer-systems (*pro aquae forma* and *cloacarium*).[36] These taxes were presumably collected by the staff subordinated to the commissioner of public works ("qui operibus publicis procurat," i.e. the *curator operum publicorum*) or directly by the staff in charge of the maintenance of each utility, since these taxes were meant to support them.[37] Finally, there was a tax specific to the city of Rome, but akin to the *portorium* in its concept: the *vectigal foricul(i)ari et ansarii promercalium* was a tax on goods for sale imported within the Pomerium, except when these goods were intended for the personal use of the carrier or his household.[38] This tax, the proceeds of which went to the *fis-*

89-90. These taxes were imposed mostly on the senatorial class. Cf. also J. Le Gall, "Les habitants de Rome et la fiscalité sous le Haut-Empire," in H. van Effenterre (ed.), *Points de vue sur la fiscalité à Rome* (Paris 1979) 113-26.

[32] Suet., *Calig.* 40. A prostitute tax was also collected in the most remote places of the empire, as some customs regulations show (*IGRR* I 1183, 16-17 = tariff of Coptus, A.D. 90 and *IGRR* III 1056, col. 2a, *ad finem* = tariff of Palmyra, A.D.137 reconstructed from the Aramaic version). Cf. T.A.J. McGinn, "The Taxation of Roman Prostitutes," *Helios* 16 (1989) 79-110, esp. 87-90, corrected by R.S. Bagnall, "A Trick a Day to Keep the Tax Man at Bay? The Prostitute Tax in Roman Egypt," *BASP* 28 (1991) 5-12, who convincingly demonstrates that the Egyptian evidence is limited to Upper Egypt between A.D. 111 and 188. The connection between the tax recorded by Suetonius and the Egyptian/Palmyrene tax cannot be taken for granted.

[33] Pliny, *HN* 19.56.

[34] Suet., *Vesp.* 23.5; Dio 65.14.5; and Juv. 3.37-38.

[35] *CIL* VI 1585 and Ulpianus (68 *ad ed.*) *Dig.* 43.8.2.17.

[36] Ulpianus (21 *ad Sab.*) *Dig.* 30.1.39.5.

[37] Frontin., *Aq.* 118.

[38] *CIL* VI 1016 a-c and *CIL* VI 31227 (= *ILS* 375, between 177 and 180): Marcus Aurelius and Commodus are said to have set up a few stones "propter controversias quae / inter mercatores and mancipes / ortae erant, uti finem / demonstrarent vectigali foriculiari et ansarii / promercalium secundum veterem legem semel dum/taxat exigundo." Cf. also *CIL* VI 8594 ("quidquid usuarium invehitur / ansarium non debet"), which is reminiscent of a provision of a *lex censoria* pertain-

cus, was collected by private contractors (*mancipes*), perhaps also called *foricarii*,[39] but one inscription found in the center of Rome records a *vilicus vectigalis* who could have been linked with this particular tax.[40]

Municipal governments also levied various kinds of taxes to pay for public works (building and maintenance of city walls, public buildings, streets, sewers, aqueducts, latrines, and street lighting) and services (religious services, baths and entertainment, food supply, embassies, etc.) which burdened most cities and towns of the empire.[41] The collection of municipal taxes was farmed out or entrusted to wealthy individuals as compulsory public services (*munera*, λειτουργίαι).[42]

This list is certainly not comprehensive, but it illustrates the diversity of the revenues on which the Roman empire lived.[43]

3. *Method of collection*

Most of the available—non-papyrological—evidence concerning the collection of taxes refers to the collection of customs dues (*portoria*) and of the taxes on inheritance (*vicesima hereditatium*) and on manumission (*vicesima libertatis*) during the Principate. Consequently, we have to extrapolate from this information in order to understand how the system may have worked for the collection of other

---

ing to the Sicilian *portorium* and recorded by the Republican jurist Alfenus Varus (7 *dig.*) *Dig.* 50.16.203. Cf. J. Le Gall (1979) who convincingly argues for a new interpretation of the word *foricul(i)arium*.

[39] Paulus (*sing. de usur.*) *Dig.* 22.1.17.5: "Fiscus ex suis contractibus usuras non dat, sed ipse accipit: ut solet a foricariis, qui tardius pecuniam inferunt, item ex vectigalibus."

[40] *CIL* VI 779 (= 30830) and commentary of *CIL* VI 31227 (reporting that the inscription was found at Santa Sabina). On the role of *vilici* in tax collection, cf. below.

[41] W. Liebenam, *Städteverwaltung im römischen Kaiserreiche* (Leipzig 1900) 2-68, esp. 21-30; and W. Langhammer, *Die rechtliche und soziale Stellung der magistratus municipales und der decuriones* (Wiesbaden 1973) 96-122, esp. 118-19.

[42] W. Liebenam (1900) 417-30, with reference (419, n. 1) to legal sources from the late first century A.D. onwards (*Dig.* 50.4-7).

[43] This diversity is best attested in Egypt, cf. S.L. Wallace, *Taxation in Egypt from Augustus to Diocletian* (Princeton 1938). It is necessary to emphasize that the most significant part of the revenues of Rome came from land tax (*tributum soli*) and poll tax (*tributum capitis*) levied in the provinces; cf. L. Neesen, *Untersuchungen zu den direkten Staatsabgaben der römischen Kaiserzeit* (Bonn 1980), reviewed and expanded by P.A. Brunt, "The Revenues of Rome," *JRS* 71 (1981) 161-72 (= *Roman Imperial Themes* [1990] 324-46).

taxes, and how it may have developed during the Republican period. The collection of taxes in kind obviously entailed problems substantially different from taxes in money, but will not be discussed in
this context.[44]

Customs dues were collected at toll stations (*stationes, portus,*
τελώνια, παραφυλακαί).[45] In the province of Asia, these facilities,
the size of which was strictly regulated, could be erected on public
land.[46] They seemed to have been organized on the pattern of a
rural household: a tax farmer (*conductor*, τελώνης, δημοσιώνης) or a
vilicus (οἰκονόμος, καθήμενος ἐπὶ τὸ τελώνιον, ἐπίτροπος)[47] was in
charge of running the operations with the assistance of a staff composed of accountants, clerks, and inspectors. In the province of Asia,
the name of the tax farmer (τελώνης, δημοσιώνης) or that of his

---

[44] Cf. now R. Duncan-Jones, *Structure and Scale in the Roman Economy* (Cambridge 1990) 187-98, who has, however, little to say about the practical aspect of
tax collection.

[45] *AE* 1989, no. 341f (Catina/Sicily); *AE* 1956, no. 262 (= *CIL* V 1864, Iulium
Carnicum/*Regio* X); *AE* 1934, no. 234 (Aquileia/*Regio* X, between 211 and 217);
CIL V 7211 (Avigliana/Alpes Cottiae); *CIL* V 7264 (Segusio/Alpes Cottiae); *CIL*
V 7852 and *AE* 1955, no. 205 (Pedo/Alpes Maritimae); *AE* 1945, no. 123 (Acau-
num/Alpes Graiae et Poeninae); *CIL* XIII 5244 (Turicum/Upper Germania); *AE*
1938, no. 154 (Poetovio/Pannonia); *AE* 1952, no. 192 (Aquae Bassianae/Panno-
nia, 206); *AE* 1981, no. 24 (Dardania/Moesia, 225); *CIL* VIII 12134 (= *ILS* 1654,
Bisica/Africa); NT, *Matth.* 9.9 and *Mark* 2.14 (Capernaum/Galilee); *Epigr.Anatol.*
14 (1989) sect. 10 (lines 26-28); 23 (lines 56-57); and 51 (lines 117-120) (τελώνιον);
and sect. 12-15 (lines 29-40); 17 (lines 42-45); and 39 (lines 88-96) (παραφυλακή).
For a legal definition, cf. Ulpianus (68 *ad ed.*) *Dig.* 50.16.59: "'Portus' appellatus
est conclusus locus, quo importantur merces et inde exportantur: eaque nihilo
minus statio est conclusa atque munita. Inde 'angiportum' dictum est.''

[46] *Epigr.Anatol.* 14 (1989) sect. 12 (lines 29-32): ὁ τὸ τέλος ἐξηγορακὼς ἐν αἷς ἂν
πόλεσι καὶ τόποις ἐν τῶι τῆς ἐκμισθώ[σεως νόμωι ... διατεταγμένον ἦι, ὅπως ὁ κ]ατὰ
θάλασσαν καὶ ὁ κατὰ γῆν εἰσάγων ἢ ἐξάγων τῶι τελώνηι προσφωνῆι καὶ ἀπογράφηται,
ἐὰν βούληται [ἐν ταύταις ταῖς πόλεσι πάσαις καὶ τόποις παραφυλακ]ῆς ἢ ἀπογραφῆς
ἢ οἰκήσεως χάριν ἀνὰ ἓν ἐποίκιον ἐχέτω, ἐφ' ὧι οὔτε ἐν ἱερῶι οὔτε ἐν [τόπωι ἀνετῶι,
ἀλλ' ἐν δημοσίωι τόπωι ἔσται· καὶ ἐκεῖ μὲν π]αραφυλακὰς ἐχέτωσαν, παρὰ ποταμῶι
δὲ Ῥυνδάκωι μίαν παραφυλακήν· and sect. 30 (lines 71-72): ἕκαστον ἐποίκιον,
μῆκος ποδῶν τεσσαράκοντα, πλάτος ποδῶν τεσσαράκοντα, ἐν δημοσίωι τόπωι
[ἔστω] μήτε ἐν ἱερῶι μήτε ἐν τεμένει μήτε [ἐν τόπῳ ἀνετῷ· κ]αὶ τῶι τελώνηι
οἰκοδομῆσαι ἐξέστω. (vac.) Cf. also sect. 13 (lines 32-36).

[47] *Epigr.Anatol.* 14 (1989) sect. 4 (lines 13-15); 6 (lines 16-20); 10 (lines 26-28),
a provision belonging to the earliest part of the law and dated to 75 B.C.); 16 (lines
40-42); 23 (lines 56-57, with commentary, p. 85); 48 (lines 113-114); and 51
(117-120). The phrase τελώνης/δημοσιώνης ἢ ἐπίτροπος, which is recurrent in this
document, has been rightly compared to the phrase used in the second-century-
A.D. *Lex metalli Vipascensis* (*CIL* II 5181 = *ILS* 6891 = *FIRA* I², no. 105, *passim*):
"conductor socius actorve eius." About the title ἐπίτροπος as the equivalent of the
Latin *procurator*, cf. above Chapters One and Three.

general agent (ἐπίτροπος) was to be posted in a visible place in the toll station and gave the manager the right to collect tolls or fines (τέλος ἤ μισθός = *portorium mercesve*). This rule, which is similar to the legal provision regarding the appointment (*praepositio*) of private business managers,[48] was recorded in the A.D.-62 version of the *Lex portorii Asiae*, but is known to have been introduced earlier, either by consular decree in A.D. 5 or as part of the original enactment in 75 B.C.[49]

Vilici could also be attached to one of the provincial administrative centers located at Lugdunum, Virunum, Aquincum, Poetovio, Carthage, Ephesus, etc.[50] It is often difficult to determine to which category each *vilicus* belonged. In Dalmatia, one Hermes Fortunat(ianus?) had an underground shrine (*spelaeum*) built and dedicated to Mithra at his own expense: he was the slave *vilicus* of C. Antonius Rufus, who had contracted for the collection of the *p(ublicum) p(ortorium)* while holding the position of *praefectus veh(iculorum)*.[51] Hermes's benefaction was made possible by the fact that he could obviously dispose of significant funds, probably in the form of

---

[48] For the practice of posting a written document (*lex praepositionis, proscriptio, iussum*, or σύστασις) in facilities run by business managers, cf. Chapter One.

[49] *Epigr.Anatol.* 14 (1989) sect. 51 (lines 117-120): π[ρὸς δημοσιώνην ἤ τὸν ἐπί]τροπον αὐτοῦ ἀπογραφέσθω, παρὰ τούτωι, ὃς ἂν φανερῶς ἐν τῶι τελων[ίωι] ἤ προγεγραμμένος, ἐν οἷς ἂν τόποις δημο[σιώνη ἐποίκιον χάριν τε]λωνίας ὑπάρχῃ. Cf. also sect. 10 (lines 26-28): ἐπὶ τοῦ τελώνου ἤ ἐπι[τρόπου, ὃς ἂν τέλους εἰσπράξεως χά-ριν ἐπὶ τοῦ τελωνίου ἐκ]είνου χωρὶς δόλου πονηροῦ προγεγραμμένος ᾖ· and sect. 23 (lines 56-57): ἐν οἷς ἂν τόποις κατὰ τοῦτον τὸν νόμον τελώνιον δημοσιώνου ὑπάρχῃ, ἐν τοῖς τόποις τούτοις τέλος ἤ μισθὸν [δημοσιώνης ἤ ἐπί]τροπος λαμβανέτω.

[50] S.J. de Laet, *Portorium* (Bruges 1949) 105-08; 247-54; and 370-414. P.A. Brunt (1990) 385 suggests that imperial slaves attached to procurators mostly controlled tax collectors and were not involved in collection themselves. Brunt, however, acknowledges (416) that the evidence for imperial *scrutatores* (for instance, *AE* 1974, no. 485, *statio Bilachiniensis*, between Larice and Santicum/Noricum, and perhaps *AE* 1933, no. 160, *statio Lamudensis*, near Kumanovo/Upper Moesia, 211), who examined taxable goods, speaks against this theory: "It might also be doubted if for mere supervision the procurator needed *vilici* and the like at each toll-station, yet imperial slaves are found in these posts with exactly the same designation as employees of the conductores. It may reasonably be concluded that between the reigns of Commodus and Alexander Severus they were employed as collectors; thereafter evidence fails us."

[51] *AE* 1894, no. 22 (= *ILS* 4225 = *CIL* III 13283, Senia/Dalmatia). Another *vilicus* (Mercator) subordinated to a *praefectus vehiculorum* is known from an inscription found at Szeged, on the other side of the Danube (Sarmatian territory); cf. A. Mócsy, *Pannonia and Upper Moesia. A History of the Middle Danube Provinces of the Roman Empire* (London/Boston 1974) 100-01.

a *peculium*.[52] This is confirmed by four inscriptions from Poetovio
(Pannonia) which show that the same (C.) Antonius Rufus had
other *vilici* who were assisted by some *vicarii*: Prudens is first attested
as the underslave of the *vilicus* Primus,[53] before becoming himself a
vilicus with his own underslave named Felix.[54] The fourth inscription from the same location was set up by Optimus, the underslave
of the *vilicus* Vitalis, who was working for a different contractor, (Q.)
Sabinius Veranus.[55] It is impossible to ascertain whether all these
vilici were active contemporaneously and whether their functions
where the same in all cases. The tax farmers C. Antonius Rufus and
Q. Sabinius Veranus are well attested in the Illyrian provinces
around the middle of the second century A.D. and may have been
partners or members of the same company of publicans.[56]

Vilici employed in administrative centers may have ranked higher
than their colleagues attached to *stationes*, and therefore would have
been more likely to advertise their position: at Poetovio, an imperial
slave was responsible for the tax on inheritance collected in both
Upper and Lower Pannoniae.[57] A *vilicus summarum sociorum quattuor
publicorum Africae* was presumably located at Carthage, where he

---

[52] Other *vilici* involved in tax collection made similar expenditures; cf. *CIL*
VIII 12134 (= *ILS* 1654, "sua impensa restituit et ampliavit"); *AE* 1952, no. 192
("templum (Dardaniae) ex voto a solo restituit"); *AE* 1945, no. 123 (where a *verna
a(gens) v(ices) v(ilici)* . . . "aedem vetustate [c]onlabsam restituit"); *AE* 1934, no. 234
(where an imperial *ser(vus) vil(icus) vect(igalis) Illyric(i) praep(ositus) q(uin)q(uagesimae)*
"stationes utrasq(ue) empori ex comm(odis) suis ampliavit et restituit").

[53] *AE* 1899, no. 77 (= *ILS* 4245, dedication to "natura dei"). Another underslave of Primus, named Festus, made a dedication to Mithra (*AE* 1899, no. 74 =
ILS 4242).

[54] *AE* 1899, no. 75 (= *ILS* 4244, dedication to Petra Genetrix, who gave birth
to Mithra).

[55] *AE* 1899, no. 76 (= *ILS* 4243, dedication to Mithra). Bellicus, the *vilicus* of
the *statio P(o)etobionen[sis]*, had a *vik(arius)* named Castricius who set up an inscription for his health (*AE* 1981, no. 24, Dardania/Moesia, 225).

[56] About C. Antonius Rufus, cf. *PIR* I, p. 104, no. 693 and *PIR* I², p. 169, no.
871; *CIL* III 5117 (in the capacity of imperial procurator) and 5122 (both inscriptions from Atrans/Noricum); *CIL* V 820 (Aquileia, abbreviated "CARCPP" =
"C. Antonius Rufus conductor publici portorii"); in A.D. 157, he seems to have
been associated with one Saturninus (perhaps T. Iulius Saturninus, cf. O.
Bounegru, *Dacoromania* 6 [1981-82] 121-32, non vidi), cf. *CIL* III 1568 (Meha-
dia/Dacia). On Q. Sabinius Veranus, cf. *CIL* III 4015 and 4017 (Poetovio/Upper
Pannonia); and *CIL* III 5146 (*balnea Romana* near Tueffer/Noricum), where he had
another *vilicus* named Fructus.

[57] *CIL* III 4065 (*vern(a) vil(icus) XX hered(itatium) utrarumq(ue) Pann(oniarum)*, late
second century).

might have been in charge of the financial department of the company for the whole province.[58] Such *vilici* were certainly no small fries: at Aquincum, a *vilicus*, whose association with the imperial fiscal administration is only conjectural, had his seat reserved in the amphitheater, next to a warden in charge of a military prison (*kar(cerarius) leg(ionis)*) and to an army veteran.[59] This kind of privilege was usually reserved to powerful interest groups or colleges.

In many cases, each kind of tax was farmed separately to a company or to an individual contractor. Thus, at Nicopolis/Lower Moesia, another Hermes was employed as *vilicus* by three well-known tax farmers belonging to the *gens* Iulia, Ianuarius, Capito, and Epaphroditus, who had contracted for the collection of the *p(ublicum) p(ortorium) Illyrici et ripae Thraciae*.[60] Toll stations of the *vectigal* (= *portorium*) *Illyricum* are attested north and east of Aquileia.[61] In the Gallic Alps, *vilici* were attached to *stationes* of the *XL (quadragesima) Galliarum*;[62] and in Asia Minor, they collected the *XXXX (quadragesima) portuum Asiae* at Miletus and Iasus.[63] Private and imperial slaves are also attested as *vilici* in the context of the collection of the *vicesima libertatis*[64] and of the *vicesima heredita-*

---

[58] *CIL* VIII 1128 (= *ILS* 1873). A *vil(icus) summar(um)* was working in the office of the *vicesima hereditatium* at Thermae Himeraeae/Sicily (*CIL* X 7347 = *ILS* 1559) and at Segusio/Alpes Cottiae (*CIL* V 7264), but other *vilici summarum* may have been in charge of public finances (*CIL* V 737 = *ILS* 4869 and, possibly, *AE* 1934, no. 240, both from Aquileia).

[59] *CIL* III 10493d (probably third century). Cf. J. Kolendo, "La répartition des places aux spectacles et la stratification sociale dans l'Empire romain," *Ktèma* 6 (1981) 301-15, esp. 313.

[60] *AE* 1902, no. 122 (= *CIL* III 751 = *ILS* 1855). Cf. also *CIL* III 6124 and 5121 (= *ILS* 1464 and 1857, Atrans/Noricum). For contractors, cf. *CIL* III 5121 and 7429 (= *ILS* 1857 and 1465).

[61] *CIL* V 820 and *AE* 1934, no. 234 (Aquileia); *CIL* V 1864 (= *AE* 1956, no. 262, Iulium Carnicum/Regio X); *CIL* V 8650 (= 64*, Glemona/Regio X); *CIL* V 5081 (= *ILS* 3160, Sublavio/Regio X); *AE* 1899, no. 74-77 (= *ILS* 4242-4245) and *AE* 1938, no. 154 (Poetovio/Pannonia); *AE* 1894, no. 22 (Vratnik/Dalmatia); *AE* 1952, no. 192 (Aquae Bassianae/Pannonia); and *CIL* III 8042 (Celeia/Noricum). Cf. G. Alföldy, *Noricum* (London/Boston 1974) 116-17; 164-65; and 254-56 (with additional references); and P.A. Brunt (1990) 425-27.

[62] *CIL* XII 717 (= *ILS* 1565, Arelate/Narbonensis); *CIL* XII 2348 (= *ILS* 4816, Fines Allobrogum/Gaul); *AE* 1897, no. 4 (= *ILS* 9035) and *AE* 1945, no. 123 (Acaunum); *CIL* V 7852 (= *ILS* 1854) and *AE* 1955, no. 205 (Pedo); and, possibly, *CIL* V 7264 (Segusio) and *CIL* V 7211 (Avigliana/Alpes Cottiae). Cf. now G. Mennella, "La *quadragesima Galliarum* nelle Alpes Maritimae," *MEFRA* 104 (1992) 209-32.

[63] *CIL* III 447 (= *ILS* 1862, bilingual); *BCH* 10 (1886) 267; and *AE* 1979, no. 610.

[64] *CIL* IX 4681 (= *ILS* 1865, Reate/Regio IV); *CIL* XI 5032 (Mevania/Regio

tium.[65] For the latter tax, we have a few inscriptions showing that
the *vilicus* sometimes held simultaneously the position of treasurer
(*vilicus et arcarius XX hereditatium*).[66] By the time of Tiberius, the collection of taxes could also be farmed out as a package deal to single
companies. Thus, in Africa, the *quattuor publica* comprised the *portorium*, the *vicesima hereditatium*, the *vicesima libertatis*, and the *vicesima
quinta venalium mancipiorum*.[67] Some inscriptions from Tripolitania
show that there was a distinction between maritime and inland tax
collection, a practice already attested at Termessus/Pisidia in the
Republican period.[68]

When the system of tax collection was taken over by the imperial
administration, the supervision of regional centers was entrusted to
the care of imperial *procuratores* and the terminology of functions, if
not the hierarchic structure, may have undergone some change.
Thus, an imperial freedman bearing the title of *praepositus vicesimae
libertatis* in the provinces of Bithynia, Pontus, and Paphlagonia made
a dedication at Ancyra to his *nutritor*, L. Didius Marinus, whose
successful career included the position of *procurator vectigalior(um)
[p]opul(i) R(omani) quae sunt citra Padum*.[69] It seems that the title of

---

VI); *AE* 1975, no. 202 (Telesia/*Regio* IV); *CIL* XIII 7215 (= *ILS* 1866, Monguntia-
cum/Upper Germania); *ILS* 1867 (= *CIL* III 7287, Athenae/Achaia, bilingual);
CIL II 1742 (Gades/Baetica); *CIL* XIII 1130 (Poitiers/Gallia Lugdunensis); Cf.
K.R. Bradley, *Klio* 66 (1984) 177, n. 17.

[65] *AE* 1959, no. 261 (Patavium/*Regio* X); *CIL* X 7347 (= *ILS* 1559, Thermae
Himeraeae/Sicily); *AE* 1950, no. 256 (Olisipo/Lusitania); *CIL* II 2214 (Cordu-
ba/Baetica); *AE* 1954, no. 194 (Nemausus/Narbonensis); and *CIL* III 1996 (= *ILS*
1557, Salonae/Dalmatia).

[66] *CIL* II 2214 (Corduba/Baetica); *CIL* III 1996 (= *ILS* 1557, Salonae/Dalma-
tia); and *AE* 1959, no. 261 (Patavium/*Regio* X).

[67] *AE* 1925, no. 73 (Cuicul/Numidia, *vilicus Cuiculi IIII publicu(rum*, sic)
Afric(ae); *AE* 1942-43, no. 63 (Sitifis/Africa Procons., *vilicus quattuor publicorum Africae*). Cf. P.A. Brunt (1990) 382.

[68] *AE* 1952, no. 62 (Leptis Magna/Tripolitania, "...Aug(usti) N(ostri) ver/na
vegtig(alis) (*sic*) / IIII p(ublicorum) A(fricae) vil(icus) / Lepcis Mag(nae) / terrestris /
...''); and *AE* 1954, no. 20 (= *AE* 1926, no. 164, Leptis Magna/Tripolitania,
"...Aug(usti) ser(vus).../...vil(icus) / marit[imus(?)] et XX (vicesimae) /
hered(itatium) Lepc(is) / Magn(ae)...''). Cf. also *Lex Antonia de Termessibus* (*ILS*
38 = *FIRA* I², no. 11, p. 135-37, col. II, ll. 31-34, 71 B.C.): "Quam legem portorieis terrestribus maritumeisque / Termenses maiores Phisidae capiundeis intra
suos / fineis deixserint, es lex ieis portorieis capiundeis / esto, ...''). Cf. also *Lex
portorii Asiae* (*Epigr.Anatol.* 14 [1989] sect. 13, lines 32-36, with commentary pp. 76-
77, and *passim*).

[69] *CIL* III 249 (= 6753 = *ILS* 1396, Ancyra/Galatia, dated ca. 200 on the basis
of *CIL* IX 338 = *ILS* 6121).

the dedicator of this inscription refers to a position ranking at the same level as those *vilici* who were attached to regional administrative centers, but some doubt remains because another imperial *procurator* attached to the same area was honored with the laudatory terms of *optimus et sanctissimus praepositus* at Carales (Sardinia).[70] By contrast, *praepositi stationis* may have occasionally replaced *vilici* in the early third century,[71] if not before.[72] It is remarkable that most, if not all, of the preserved instances of *praepositi* in the context of tax collection were freedmen, whereas most *vilici* were slaves.

Each *vilicus* was commanding a staff (*familia*)[73] including substitutes (*vicarii*), controllers (*contrascriptores*), search officers (*scrutatores*), toll collectors (*portitores*), and ordinary servants (*servi*).[74] A few inscriptions discovered, published, or revised in the last few years provide a fresh glimpse of a new category of servants attached to the toll stations: *circitores* may have constituted a flying squad, whose task was to control subsidiary roads and trails in mountainous areas. However, there is no evidence that there was ever more than one *circitor* attached to a single *statio*.[75] Besides, it is remarkable that at

---

[70] *CIL* X 7584 (= *ILS* 1359). Compare with *CIL* II 1085 (= *ILS* 1406, Ilipa/ Baetica) where Irenaeus, an imperial *disp(ensator) portus Ilipensis* dedicated an inscription to L. Cominius Vipsanius Salutaris (a member of the equestrian order with a great administrative career behind him) whom he calls "praepositus sanctissimus." This inscription may have nothing to do with tax collection; *contra*, cf. P.A. Brunt (1990) 407.

[71] *CIL* V 5090 (= *ILS* 1561, imperial freedman, Vallis Atesis, near Tridentum/*Regio* X); *CIL* V 7643 (imperial freedman, Ager Saluzzensis/*Regio* IX); *AE* 1919, no. 21 (imperial freedman, Genava/Narbonensis); *CIL* XIII 5244 (imperial freedman, Turicum/Upper Germania); *AE* 1934, no. 234 (Aquileia, 211/217); *CIL* III 10301 (Intercisa/Lower Pannonia, 222/235). Cf. S.J. de Laet (1949) 413, nn. 1-2; and 471-72, with reference to *Cod. Theod.* 13.5.17.

[72] *CIL* III 1568 (Mehadia/Dacia, A.D. 157) was dedicated by one M. Valerius Felix, who was an employee of the tax farmers Rufus and Saturninus (cf. above). He says in the most elliptic manner (lines 3-4) that he was a "t(abularius?) p(romotus?) ex pr(aeposito?) IV (?) stationis / Tsiernen(sis)."

[73] *Familia publicanorum* (Ulpianus [55 *ad ed.*] *Dig.* 39.4.1.5; and *idem* [38 *ad ed.*] *Dig.* 39.4.12.2); *familia vectigalis* (*CIL* VIII 22670 a = *ILS* 8918 = *AE* 1906, no. 34, Leptis Magna, A.D. 202); or *familia vicesimae libertatis* (*CIL* V 3351 = *ILS* 1870, Verona/*Regio* X). Cf. P.A. Brunt (1990) 364-65; 371-72; 385; 406; and 416.

[74] *ILS* 1851-1873 (*servi et liberti publicanorum*).

[75] *AE* 1984, no. 740 (= *AE* 1938, no. 91, Ratiaria/Upper Moesia); *AE* 1985, no. 714 (Aquae Iasae/Upper Pannonia); and *AE* 1989, no. 334 (Augusta Praetoria/*Regio* XI). Cf. G. Walser, "Circitor Publici Portorii," in M. Piérart–O. Curty (eds.), *Historia Testis. Mélanges d'épigraphie, d'histoire ancienne et de philologie offerts à T. Zawadski* (Fribourg 1989) 153-58, who suggests that the abbreviation "Pra" in the inscription from Aosta should be filled as [*Augustae*] *Pra[et(oriae)*] instead of

least two (perhaps three) out of four known *circitores* were free, and
that one of them, Flavius Hermadion, who is attested elsewhere
(Poetovio, and perhaps Rome), was rich enough to dedicate to the
Nymphs at Aquae Iasae a silver cup weighing no less than two
pounds.[76] With such status and wealth, *circitores* were unlikely to
have withstood cold and rainy weather in the woods, and should
perhaps be regarded as regional inspectors. This hypothesis is consistent with what is known about *circitores* in another sector of the imperial administration: in Rome, *circitores* attached to the water supply department ranked below station managers (*vilici*) and water
tower foremen (*castellarii*), but above skilled workers (*silicarii, tectores
aliique opifices*).[77]

Some rare instances of promotions are recorded: Eutyches, who
presumably served the same contractors as Hermes from Nicopo-
lis/Lower Moesia (cf. above) started as the substitute (*vicarius*) of the
vilicus Benignus at Atrans/Noricum and became *contrascriptor* at a
different *statio* at Boiodurum.[78] In the same way, the imperial slave
Felix ran the *statio Pontis Augusti* in the capacity of *vilicus* after being
promoted from the position of substitute (*vicarius*) at another *statio*
called Micia.[79] Finally, an imperial *vilicus portorii Illyrici* became *dispensator rationis extraordinariae provinciae Asiae*, and served in both qualities the same *procurator*.[80]

It is probable that the accounting and bookkeeping was handled
by specialists and treasurers (*tabularii, tabellarii, arkarii, librarii, commentarienses, dispensatores, actores*/πραγματευταί), who were not neces-

---

pra[ep(ositus)]. A similar view is presented about the inscription from Ratiaria (*AE*
1984, no. 740), where "PP" is to be read as *p(ublici) p(ortorii)*. Cf. J. Sasel,
Ratiariensia 2 (1984) 77-80 (non vidi).

[76] Flavius Hermadion: *AE* 1985, no. 714 (Aquae Iasae); *ILJug* 1145 (Poetovio);
and *CIL* VI 731 (= *ILS* 4239, Rome).

T. Iulius Optatus: *AE* 1938, no. 91 (= *AE* 1984, no. 740, Ratiaria).

Μᾱρκος Λούκιος κιρκίτωρ: *Ann. Univ. Sofia, Fac. d'hist. et philolog.* 42 (1945-
1946) 21, cited by G. Walser (1989) 158, n. 26 and J. Sasel, *Ratiariensia* 2 (1984)
79 (*Asklepieion*, Glava Panega/Bulgaria).

The fourth known *circitor* (*AE* 1989, no. 334, Augusta Praetoria) is almost certainly an imperial slave (named Bassus).

[77] G. Walser (1989) 155-56, nn. 16-17, citing Frontin., *Aq.* 116; *CIL* X 711
(Surrentum/*Regio* I) and *CIL* VI 8749 (Rome) (= *ILS* 1712-1713).

[78] *CIL* III 5121 (= *ILS* 1857, found at Atrans on the Sava River). Several *vilici*
are attested there: *CIL* III 5117 and 13522.

[79] *CIL* III 1351 (= 7853 = *ILS* 1860, Micia/Dacia).

[80] *CIL* III 8042 (Celeia/Noricum) and *CIL* III 6575 (= 7127 = *ILS* 1421,
Ephesus).

sarily subordinated to the *vilicus*. According to P.A. Brunt, *actores* were given "some power to act on behalf of the administration,"[81] but the evidence is scarce and inconclusive: in Rome, an imperial freedman was attached to the *IIII Galliarum* in the first century A.D.,[82] and an imperial slave was attached to the *vicesima hereditatium*.[83] At Aquileia, the *actor* Processus dedicated an inscription to an *adiutor* named Dionysius, possibly his own assistant.[84] At Lilybaeum/Sicily, a private (?) slave was attached to the administration of the *portorium*.[85] One Galenus (possibly a slave) who bore the title of *actor*/πραγματευτής dedicated a trilingual inscription (Latin/ Greek/Palmyrene dialect), found on the agora of Palmyra and dated to A.D. 174, to L. Antonius Callistratus who had contracted in the capacity of *manceps*/τεταρτώνης for the collection of what may have been a twenty-five percent tax on merchandise called *IIII* (*quarta*) *merc*(*ium adventiciarum* or -*aturae*).[86] At Halicarnassus/Asia, two πραγματευταί were employed by M. Aurelius Mindius Matidianus Pollio, *conductor* and imperial *procurator*, and had the toll station refurbished.[87] In nearby Ephesus, P. Curtius Faustus, whose free status is revealed by the use of *tria nomina*, introduces himself as the *actor* representing a company in charge of collecting the five percent tax on manumissions.[88] The places of find of most of the inscriptions recording *actores* involved in tax collection may suggest that they were attached to regional administrative centers. This impression, however, seems to be contradicted by a third-century inscription mistakenly ascribed to Virunum/Noricum and recording an imperial *v*[*il*(*icus*)] (or *v*[*erna*] *actor* [*st*]*at*(*ionis*), provided that the restoration is correct.[89] There is no doubt that a *vilicus* and an *actor*

---

[81] P.A. Brunt (1990) 385, as opposed to *vilici* and *praepositi*, who "are presumably persons placed at the head of a particular office or group of other employees."

[82] *CIL* VI 8591 (= *ILS* 1564).

[83] *CIL* VI 38003. Cf. also *P.Ross.Georg.* II 26 (A.D. 160) and W. Eck (1979) 138 and 141.

[84] *CIL* V, Suppl. 239.

[85] *CIL* X 7225 (= *ILS* 6769, *servus actor portus Lilybitani*).

[86] *AE* 1947, no. 180. Cf. M.R. Cimma (1981) 214-18. On τεταρτῶναι, cf. H. Seyrig, *Syria* 22 (1941) 263-66.

[87] *ILS* 8858 (= *AE* 1897, no. 17 = *OGIS* 525), where the principal was an ἀρχώνης μ λι[μ]ένων Ἀσίας, in addition to his position of imperial procurator, Bithyniarch (twice) and Asiarch in charge of the temples of Ephesus.

[88] *AE* 1930, no. 87: Πόπλιος Κούρτιος Φαῦστος ἄκτωρ κοινωνῶν εἰκοστῆς ἐλευθερίας ἑαυτῶι καὶ....

[89] *CIL* III 11549. Cf. G. Alföldy (1974) 256, who ascribes it to another location.

could coexist in the same *statio*, as was the case at Mehadia/Dacia.[90]

Who owned the slave members of the staff of the *stationes*? Most of them probably belonged to the companies of publicans (*socii*) or to the tax farmers (*conductores*). Ulpianus, however, reports that both publicans and tax farmers (whom he indiscriminately designates as *publicani*) also employed hired labor, either free or slave.[91] The *familia vectigalis* was subject to particular rules, but any slave belonging to a publican or tax farmer was not necessarily attached to the *familia*.[92]

It is not sure whether the structure of the staff which carried out the collection of taxes was modified at the times when the system changed from publicans to private contractors and to direct collection by the imperial administration. It seems that the hierarchic organization became increasingly complicated with the later phases, but this was quite natural. On the other hand, it is possible that the lesser availability of inscriptions for the earlier period would affect the picture.

4. A late-Republican crux

Vilici involved in tax collection are not attested during the Republican period, and the evidence for the position of toll station manager is scarce. A noticeable exception is provided by Cicero, who incidentally describes the organization of the system of tax collection in Sicily in a speech aimed at uncovering the shady activities of the governor of this province.[93] The affair involved two representatives of the company of publicans which had taken on contract the collection

---

About *actores* in tax collection, cf. S.J. de Laet (1949) 335-36; 374, n. 1; 381; 388; 394; and 414.

[90] *CIL* III 1565 (212/217, "...sub cura Iul(ii) Pa/terni proc(uratoris) / Syntrophus / vil(icus)") and 1573a ("...Eutyches act(or) / P. Aeli Antipatri ex voto posuit"). The case of the *praepositus* (*CIL* III 1568, Mehadia/Dacia, 157) is reserved since the position, if it existed, would be connected with the *statio Tsernensis* (cf. above).

[91] Ulpianus (55 *ad ed.*) *Dig.* 39.4.1.5: "Familiae nomen hic non tantum ad servos publicanorum referemus, verum et qui in numero familiarum sunt publicani: sive igitur liberi sint sive servi alieni, qui publicanis in eo vectigali ministrant, hoc edito continebuntur."

[92] Ulpianus (55 *ad ed.*) *Dig.* 39.4.1.5: "Proinde et si servus publicani rapuit, non tamen in ea familia constitutus, quae publico vectigali ministrat, hoc edictum cessabit."

[93] Cic., *2Verr.* 2.69.167–78.191.

of customs dues in Syracuse and of grazing dues in the whole province of Sicily in the late 70's B.C. One L. Canuleius, whose function was to run the office or toll station in the harbor of Syracuse ("qui in portu Syracusis operas dabat"), had sent reports to the *magistri* of the company in Rome concerning the criminal activities (theft and tax evasion) perpetrated by Verres.[94] Another official involved in the scam, L. Carpinatius, was the *promagister* of the *scriptura* of Sicily. After sending the same kind of negative reports concerning unspecified wrongdoings, Carpinatius had become Verres's accomplice and had worked successfully to overturn the latter's bad reputation among the *socii* of the company.

The nature of the relationship between L. Canuleius and L. Carpinatius has been interpreted differently by modern scholars. J. Carcopino, H. de la Ville de Mirmont, S.J. de Laet, and J.P.V.D. Balsdon all see in Canuleius a "chef du bureau des douanes de Syracuses" subordinated to L. Carpinatius.[95] E. Badian, however, regards it as probable that Canuleius was also a *promagister*, explaining that the expression "operas dare," which "implies, in the Roman aristocratic view of things, a rather lowly station in life," is not inconsistent with this interpretation.[96] Cicero's account is somewhat confusing, because he keeps jumping back and forth from one case to the other. However, he never suggests that Carpinatius was influential in permitting Verres to export "quantities of gold, silver, ivory, purple dye, garments from Malta, lots of carpets, numerous vessels from Delos and vases from Corinth, loads of wheat and honey" from Syracuse without paying any customs dues.[97] He may have known and approved of it, but had no hand in it. Conversely, Canuleius had nothing to do with the fraudulent financial trans-

---

[94] Cic., *2Verr.* 2.70.171: "Furta quoque istius permulta nominatim ad socios perscripserat, ea quae sine portorio Syracusis erant exportata."

[95] J. Carcopino, *La loi de Hiéron et les Romains* (Paris 1914) 97; H. de la Ville de Mirmont, *Cicéron. Discours* III (Budé edition, Paris 1923) 148, n. 1; and 155, n. 1; S.J. de Laet, *Portorium* (Brugge 1949) 69, n. 3; and 105, n. 4; and J.P.V.D. Balsdon, "Roman History, 65-50 B.C. Five Problems," *JRS* 52 (1962) 134-41, esp. 135-36.

[96] E. Badian, *Publicans and Sinners* (Ithaca 1972) 75-76; and 140, nn. 41-44, provides parallels (n. 42) for the expression "operas dare pro magistro" in Cicero's work (*Fam.* 13.65.1, to which one should add *Att.* 11.10.1). On L. Canuleius, cf. S.J. de Laet (1949) 105-06; and C. Nicolet, *L'ordre équestre à l'époque républicaine* II (Paris 1974) 825, no. 80.

[97] Cic., *2Verr.* 2.72.176 and 74.182-183.

actions that took place between Carpinatius and Verres, alias Verrucius. This seems to indicate that both employees were acting independently and could very well hold similar positions (one in connection with the collection of *portoria*, the other in connection with the collection of the *scriptura*), even though the title of *promagister* is never explicitly used in reference to Canuleius.[98]

Thus, Cicero's report provides no evidence that the collection of customs dues was comprised within the sphere of competence of the *promagister* in charge of the collection of the pasture tax (*scriptura*) for the whole area, or that the actual work of collection at each *statio* was being carried out by a deputy whose title remains unknown. Some uncertainty remains, however, concerning the nature of the functions of *promagistri*. Badian suggests that they were "in charge of the keeping of the accounts as well as of collecting the actual taxes."[99] The fact that they were paid employees—*operas dare* refers to *locatio operarum*—does not imply that they were involved in anything more than supervisory work. If we were able to establish how many *promagistri* were employed by the company of publicans which had secured the contract for the collection of the "scriptura et sex publica" in Sicily,[100] we would be in a better position to estimate to what extent they were personally involved in the operation. Concerning the number of *promagistri*, Badian rightly says that there is no way to tell. However, Cicero draws the attention of the judges to the fact that the loss incurred by the company, as reported by Canuleius (60,000 sestertii in two months), represented only part of the total sum that the publicans may have lost to Verres, because this figure does not take into account the exports that could have been made illegally from other Sicilian ports, such as Agrigentum, Lilybaeum, Panhormus, Thermae, Halaesa, Catina, and Messana. As Cicero does not tell who would bear this unestimated loss, it is possible to surmise that in each of these harbors, there was one of Canuleius's colleagues, representing the same or another company of publicans. If the same company had a contract for the collection of customs dues in the whole island, the *promagister* stationed in Syracuse probably had agents in the other ports. This hypothesis could be supported by one inscription found in Lilybaeum and originally set up

---

[98] E. Badian (1972) 140, n. 42.
[99] E. Badian (1972) 75.
[100] Cic., *2Verr.* 3.71.167.

by one Lo(n)gus, a slave who bore the title of *actor port(us* or *-orii)* *Lilybit*[*a*]*ni*.[101] This document, however, is certainly to be dated much later (second century A.D.) and does not tell anything about Republican conditions. It only suggests that slave agents could have been appointed to a *statio* for the purpose of collecting customs dues, and that Syracuse might not have always been the regional administrative center in Sicily, or at least, not the only one.

The system of collection taken on contract by companies of publicans remained in place during the Principate.[102] The epigraphical evidence for this period is more abundant and provides some interesting cases of *vilici* appointed by *socii*. At Capua (*Regio* I), we find one Epap(h)ra, *vilicus* of the *socii Sisaponenses*, who had been buried and commemorated by his concubine. This company of publicans is already mentioned by Cicero and was in charge of collecting revenue from the mines located at Sisapo in Baetica.[103] At Carthage, an inscription records the name of one Onomastus, *vilicus summarum* of the *socii quattuor publicorum Africae*.[104] Finally, in Gaul, a *soc(iorum) XL vil(icus) ad Tur(?)* dedicated an inscription to Mater Mithrae.[105]

The relationship between *promagistri* and *vilici* remains uncertain, because they are never mentioned together in ancient texts and inscriptions. One exception might be provided by a Latin inscription from Africa recording the joint dedication of a shrine (*aedicula*) to Venus by two *promagistri soc(iorum) IIII (quattuor) publicorum Africae* and its subsequent renovation by a *vilicus*.[106] Nothing indicates, however, that the *vilicus* was subordinated to the *promagistri*. Whether or not these Imperial inscriptions illustrate Republican conditions remains a matter of guess.

---

[101] *CIL* X 7225. The inscription commemorates Salvius Plotinus and Salvia Rufa.

[102] P.A. Brunt (1990) 354-432, esp. 356; 360; and 366 (cf. above). Cf., for instance, *AE* 1964, no. 239 (Albintimilium/*Regio* IX); and *AE* 1975, no. 202 (Telesia/*Regio* IV). *Promagistri* are still attested in Sicily and in Asia in the early second century A.D., cf. *CIL* III 14195 (= *ILS* 7193-7195, A.D. 103/4); *AE* 1924, no. 80 (Ephesus/Asia, Trajanic); *AE* 1930, no. 87 (Ephesus); and *Inscr. Corinth* 8.3.100. Cf. M. Albana, *QC* 9 (1987) 59-60; and 72-76.

[103] *CIL* X 3964 (= *ILS* 1875); Cic., *Phil.* 2.19.41; and Pliny, *HN* 33.118.

[104] *CIL* VIII 1128 (= *ILS* 1873, Carthage).

[105] *CIL* XII 2348 (= *ILS* 4816). The place could be Turicum/Upper Germania, where a *praepositus* in charge of a *statio* of the *XL Galliarum* is attested (*CIL* XIII 5244).

[106] *AE* 1923, no. 22 (= *ILAfr* 257, Thuburbo Maius/Africa Proconsularis).

Very little is known concerning the lower positions in the system of collection of the *vectigalia* in the Republican period. In the case described by Cicero, the *promagister* Carpinatius was assisted by a bookkeeper—the one who tampered with the accounts—who was a "servus societatis qui tabulas conficeret," namely a *tabularius*.[107] The rest of the staff was made of *portitores*[108] and of *custodes*. As we have seen above, the evidence for the early Empire is more abundant but hardly more explicit about the nature of the operations performed at toll stations and about the respective responsibilities of the members of their staff.

5. *Conclusion*

The application of the *vilicus* system to the organization of the collection of taxes, in particular of customs dues, is attested from the first to the third century A.D. and may go back to the late Republican period, for which the evidence is not explicit. In the provinces, it is possible that most known *vilici* were connected with tax collection, a fact which illustrates the lasting and widespread success of the *vilicus* system for direct management.

Fiscal *vilici* were presumably appointed by the representatives of the companies (*magistri* or *promagistri*), by tax farmers, or by imperial officials (*procuratores*). They seem to have been in charge of administrative units called *stationes*, and were assisted by a specialized staff. The transactions performed by these *vilici*, like the rights and duties of their principals (*socii, conductores, magistri, promagistri, procuratores*), were regulated by the edict of the urban praetor in Italy and by the edicts of the governors in the provinces. In that sense, the managers of toll stations were typical *institores*.

The same system of management was presumably in use in both provincial administrative centers and in the *stationes*. Even though it is difficult to trace any development in the way the system was run, I do not see any reasons why management should have been significantly affected by the transfer of the organization from the com-

---

[107] Cic., *2Verr.* 2.76.186-78.191, esp. 77.188. The *tabulae* were the books recording the loans granted by Verres through Carpinatius.

[108] Plaut., *Tri.* 810 and 1107. *Portitores* were entitled to break seals to examine the goods going through their customhouse. On lower positions in the *familia publicanorum* during the Republican period, cf. M.R. Cimma (1981) 84-87.

panies of publicans to individual tax farmers (*conductores*) and finally to the imperial administration. In any case, *vilici* are attested at all three stages of development.

C. Entertainment

The steady progress of urbanization in Roman Italy during the late Republican and early Imperial periods led to significant improvements in the life-style of a wide range of the population. What had been before the preserve of the wealthy became increasingly accessible to the majority of town dwellers, as most Italian cities—and the same is true of many places all over the empire—displayed as necessary features a forum surrounded by public buildings, streets and public places with porticoes, markets, aqueducts, sewage systems, and all kinds of recreational facilities for sports and cultural activities.[109] In many cases, the infrastructure had initially been created with private means for private use, but the search for economic or political profits induced some owners to switch to the commercial exploitation of such facilities. What started as a luxury and privilege soon became a necessity and a right, and both the municipal and the imperial administrations had to intervene in order to make these amenities accessible at the lowest cost—or free of charge—and on a regular basis.

This section will try to demonstrate how the management of public facilities, such as (a) baths; (b) libraries; and (c) places of mass entertainment (theater, amphitheater, and circus), was devised at first by private owners and/or entrepreneurs before it was taken over by the municipal and imperial administration, which entrusted these facilities to the care of *curatores* and *procuratores*. All three types of units share similar features in their organizational structure, which they seem to have borrowed from agricultural estates (*vilicus* system). It is obvious that the list of urban managerial units geared toward the satisfaction of the needs of private individuals and of the community as a whole, either on a commercial or civic basis, could have been much longer. Such a list would include temples (*aedes, templa*), residential buildings (*praetoria, domus, insulae*), civic buildings (*curiae, basilicae, saepta, villae publicae, aeraria*), prisons (*carceres*),

---

[109] M. Rostovtzeff, *The Social and Economic History of the Roman Empire*[2] (Oxford 1957) 142-43.

police and fire stations (*castra, stationes, excubitoria*), aqueducts (*aquae, lacus, castella, stationes, munera*), granaries (*horrea*) and cellars (*cellae*), markets (*fora, macella*), stores and workshops (*tabernae*), bakeries (*pistrina*), etc.[110] Several of these units are known to have been managed by a *vilicus* or his like (*aedituus, praepositus, optio*, etc.), but will not be the object of a specific study in this book.

1. *Baths*

By contrast with the Greeks, the Romans never developed the practice of keeping separate public sports grounds (*gymnasia*). The Roman way was to integrate it in the broader institution of baths (*balnea*).[111] Thus, we know that a ball court (*sphaeristerium*) was attached to a public bath in early Imperial Rome. Likewise, in Pliny's villa at Tifernum Tiberinum, a luxurious bath complex contained a ball court which was large enough to accommodate several teams playing different games at the same time. The same is true of his Laurentine villa. In a famous letter to Lucilius, Seneca describes the baths located below his apartment, and complains about the groans of out-of-breath weight lifters and the nuisance of ball players counting points. In larger complexes, such as the Baths of Caracalla or Diocletian, customers could find gymnasia and stadium, in addition to other kinds of amenities for their physical and intellectual pleasure.[112]

Private baths existed before the creation of public baths and were

---

[110] On the function and location of such facilities in Rome, cf. L. Homo, *Rome impériale et l'urbanisme dans l'antiquité* (Paris 1951); H. Jouffroy, *La construction publique en Italie et dans l'Afrique romaine* (Strasboug 1986); J.E. Stambaugh, *The Ancient Roman City* (Baltimore/London 1988); and E. Brödner, *Wohnen in der antike* (Darmstadt 1989).

[111] On baths management, cf. the essential articles by O. Robinson, "Baths: An Aspect of Roman Local Government Law," *Sodalitas. Studi in onore di A. Guarino* III (Naples 1984) 1065-82; and M. Wissemann, "Das Personal des antiken römischen Bades," *Glotta* 62 (1984) 80-89. I have not seen H. Meusel, *Die Verwaltung und Finanzierung der öffentlicher Bäder zur römischen Kaiserzeit* (Diss. Köln 1960). On baths, cf. E. Brödner, *Die römischen Thermen und das antike Badewesen: eine kulturhistorische Betrachtung* (Darmstadt 1983); J. Delaine, "Recent Research on Roman Baths," *JRA* 1 (1988) 11-32; H. Manderscheid, *Bibliographie zum römischen Badewesen unter besonderer Berücksichtigung der öffentlichen Thermen* (Munich 1988); I. Nielsen, *Thermae et Balnea. The Architecture and Cultural History of Roman Public Baths* (Aarhus 1991); and F. Yegül, *Baths and Bathing in Classical Antiquity* (forthcoming).

[112] Mart. 12.82 and 14.163; Pliny, *Ep.* 5.6.27; *idem, Ep.* 2.17.12; and Sen., *Ep.* 56.1-2. Cf. L. Homo (1951) 414-19.

parts of the architectural structure of wealthy houses. It is unclear when private establishments were first open to outsiders, but the earliest evidence goes back to the end of the third century B.C.: some Roman officials and businessmen are said to have been suffocated in the baths by a rebellious mob in Campania in 216 B.C.,[113] and it is quite possible that private baths started being exploited for commercial purposes even earlier. Cicero mentions the baths owned by M. Iunius Brutus, in addition to the *Balneae Seniae* and *Balneae Pallacinae*, and there are good reasons to think that it was a good business.[114] The opening of private baths to the public, under the supervision of the aediles,[115] made the practice accessible to lower classes, and it is not surprising that members of the elite found there a way to gain popularity by providing the population of Rome with lavish buildings and occasionally free access to them.[116] Agrippa was reportedly one of the very first benefactors to have planned the construction of public baths on the Campus Martius, which he provided with a well organized staff. The establishment became public at his death.[117]

No matter how numerous, spacious, convenient and popular the imperial baths were, they never totally superseded private and pub-

---

[113] Liv. 23.7.3. Dio 15.30 (Zonaras 9.2) has Hannibal in the role of the villain and places the event in the town of Nuceria. Cf. O. Robinson, *Sodalitas* III (1984) 1065.

[114] Cic., *Clu.* 51.141; *Cael.* 25.61-62; and *Rosc.Am.* 7.18; and Juv. 7.3-5, mocking the initiative of two unknown poets attracted by the business ("cum iam celebres notique poetae / balneolum Gabiis, Romae conducere furnos / temptarent"). Cf. O. Robinson, *Sodalitas* III (1984) 1066-67, who suggests that there was a difference in the Latin terminology between privately owned baths opened to the public (*balineae* or *balinea* [plur.]) and private baths for personal use (*balineum*); cf. Varro, *Ling.* 9.68; Ulpianus (18 *ad Sab.*) *Dig.* 7.1.13.8; and Papinianus (7 *resp.*) *Dig.* 32.91.4. The distinction was not always respected, cf. Labeo (4 *post. a Iavoleno epit.*) *Dig.* 19.2.58.2; and *FIRA* I², no. 105, lines 19-31 (*Lex metalli Vipascensis*, second century A.D.), where the *conductor balinei* (*socius actorve eius*) collects half an as from every male customer and an as from every female customer.

[115] That is what Agrippa did during his aedileship in 33 B.C., cf. Dio 59.43.1-4; Pliny, *HN* 36.121; and Sen., *Ep.* 86.10. Cf. W. Eder, *Servitus Publica* (Wiesbaden 1980) 97-98.

[116] The entrance fee in Rome seems to have been one *quadrans* for the men and one *semis* for the women (from the mid-first century B.C. to the end of the first century A.D.). Lead tokens, dating from the Flavian to the Antonine period, have been found; cf. R. Turcan, "Jetons romains en plomb. Problèmes de datation et d'utilisation," *Latomus* 47 (1988) 626-34.

[117] Dio 53.27. Cf. D.E. Strong, "The Administration of Public Building in Rome During the Late Republic and Early Empire," *BICS* 15 (1968) 97-109, esp. 103.

lic baths, and this is true especially outside of Rome.[118] Pliny mentions the existence of three public establishments in the settlement (*vicus*) located in the vicinity of his Laurentine estate. He himself would not have considered it unfitting for a man of his status to use them under certain circumstances.[119] To this effect, Pliny donated a sum of money—the exact amount is not preserved—to his native town of Comum for the construction of public baths, for their decoration, and for their maintenance.[120] Under normal circumstances, public money would have been injected into the business.

We have some evidence concerning baths management, which would have been entrusted either to private contractors (*conductores*, *mancipes*)[121] or to business managers. A combination of the two was also possible: at Vipasca (Lusitania), the contractors (*conductor sociusve*), who had leased the baths from an imperial procurator, could be represented by a business manager (*actor*).[122] There is not much evidence about the management of private establishments. There is a slight chance, however, that one of the five private dedications referring to an *institor* is to be connected with baths. The inscription was found in Roman baths located near Tüffer in the province of Noricum. A freeborn, Tattus, had dedicated a monument there for himself and his relatives, including one Tatto, who, at age 15, was

---

[118] The mid-fourth-century *Catalogue of the Fourteen Districts of the City* (*Curiosum Urbis Romae*) lists the number of baths for each region, and the high figure suggests that it includes private, public, and imperial baths, though the summary might reflect only the number of imperial (and public?) establishments. The evidence for other cities points toward the same phenomenon: at Pompeii around 79, there were three public establishments, one at least under construction (J. Stambaugh [1988] 267), and the same number at Ostia by the time of Hadrian (*ibid.* 272-274); at Timgad (Numidia), one counts no less than 12 public baths in the late second century (*ibid.* 285).

[119] Pliny, *Ep.* 2.17.

[120] *ILS* 2927 (= *CIL* V 5262). On the financial burden represented by the maintenance and operation of baths by municipal government, cf. W. Liebenam, *Städteverwaltung im römischen Kaiserreiche* (Leipzig 1900) 93-98. In the late third century, the *calefactio thermarum* was a liturgy, cf. Hermogenianus (1 *epit.*) *Dig.* 50.4.1.2 and Arcadius Charisius (*sing. de mun. civ.*) *Dig.* 50.4.18.5. The supply of oil for the baths was an aspect of the *cura annonae* (*cura balnearia*), cf. W. Langhammer, *Die rechtliche und soziale Stellung der magistratus municipales und der decuriones* (Wiesbaden 1973) 177, n. 914.

[121] Labeo (4 *post. a Iavoleno epit.*) *Dig.* 19.2.58.2; and Africanus (8 quaest.) *Dig.* 20.4.9 *pr.* The owner is responsible for repairs, cf. *FIRA* I², no. 105, lines 19-31 (*Lex metalli Vipascensis*, second century A.D.), while the daily maintenance is the task of the contractor.

[122] *FIRA* I², no. 105, line 24.

the agent of one Mocianus.[123] The connection is fragile, and the detail unclear, but the management of so costly a facility would hardly be carried out by someone who was rich enough to own or rent it. Wealthy Romans who could afford to keep their own baths, such as the Statilii Tauri, had slaves *balneatores* take care of them.[124] Technical problems were fixed by skilled workers called *fabri balneatores*.[125] At Pompeii, a freedman named Ianuarius was the keeper of an establishment owned by one M. (Licinius) Crassus Frugi, perhaps to be identified with the consul of A.D. 27. The facilities must have been quite luxurious, because the inscription advertises both sea and fresh water.[126]

Imperial baths were also operated by a servile staff called *familia thermensis*, the manager of which was called a *vilicus*.[127] He was probably the person who made arrangements to secure water and fuel supply, who hired staff workers to perform menial tasks (*custodes*), and who contracted for building maintenance. Imperial *vilici* were also in charge of public baths, because public slaves are not attested in this function in Italy. It must be stressed, however, that the emperor Trajan, in response to Pliny's question concerning the fate of convicts in Bithynia, asserts that "people of this kind are usually employed in baths, in sewage cleaning and in street and road construction".[128] These people were more likely to be employed as cleaners and attendants than as managers.

As noted above, private ownership did not entail private use.[129]

---

[123] *CIL* III 13523.

[124] *ILS* 7412 (= *CIL* VI 6243).

[125] *ILS* 7718a (= *CIL* VI 9395-9396). Cf. M. Wissemann, *Glotta* 62 (1984) 80-89, who divides the jobs connected with the operation of baths into six categories (central administration – technical jobs – cashier – cloakroom – body care – maintenance).

[126] *CIL* X 1603. On M. Licinius Crassus Frugi, cf. Pliny, *HN* 31.5.

[127] The term *familia thermensis*, however, is attested only in a private dedication from Patavium (*CIL* V 1886). For *vilici* attached to baths, cf. *CIL* VI 8676 (*Thermae Neronianae*); and 8679 (*Thermae Bybliothecae Graecae*); *AE* 1924, no. 105 (Rome, *Thermae Neronianae*); and *MAAR* 10 (1932) 73 (Rome, *Balineum Caenidianum*).

[128] Pliny, *Ep.* 10.32.2 "solent enim eiusmodi [homines] ad balineum ad purgationes cloacarum item munitiones viarum et vicorum dari." It is unclear whether Trajan had a Bithynian context in mind rather than an Italian one, but A.N. Sherwin-White, *The Letters of Pliny: A Historical and Social Commentary* (Oxford 1966) 606 points out that drainage and sewerage were more developed in the West than in the Greek East (with references to Strabo 14.1.37 [646] and Pliny, *Ep.* 10.98). Cf. F. Millar, "Condemnation to Hard Labour in the Roman Empire, from the Julio-Claudians to Constantine," *PBSR* 52 (1984) 124-47, esp. 134-35.

[129] W. Liebenam (1900) 19-20; and 94, n. 4.

Private baths could be rented by a municipal aedile on a yearly basis for free use by the population.[130] Such arrangements probably made the reliance on baths managers inescapable, and various schemes were possible: the manager could be (a) the owner of the baths (called *balneator* by Alfenus); (b) a private slave belonging either to the owner of the baths or to the magistrate who rented them; (c) a paid employee; or (d) a subcontractor.

The advantage of having a slave manager at the head of such an establishment consisted in sparing the owner the mark of infamy regularly attached to those operating such businesses. Ulpianus reports that in some provinces baths, like inns and taverns, were used as a cover for prostitution, and that the baths manager was regarded as a pimp (*leno*). The sign ''balinea'' promised more than it says, not unlike our ''salons de massage.''[131]

Supervising magistrates or commissioners (*curatores*) are rarely mentioned in the sources, because the *cura balinei* became a liturgy at an early stage. In the late second and early third centuries A.D., famous athletes were granted the honor of being overseers of imperial baths, a function which was probably merely honorific and did not carry much obligation on the part of its holder.[132]

2. Libraries

Libraries, both public and private, were rather common in the Hellenistic world. The major institutions at Alexandria, Pergamum,

---

[130] Alfenus Varus (3 *dig. a Paulo epit.*) *Dig.* 19.2.30.1: ''Aedilis in municipio balneas conduxerat, ut eo anno municipes gratis lavarentur: post tres menses incendio facto respondit posse agi cum balneatore ex conducto, ut pro portione temporis, quo lavationem non praestitisset, pecuniae contributio fieret.''

[131] Ulpianus (6 *ad ed.*) *Dig.* 3.2.4.2 (on the praetorian edict concerning *qui fecerit lenocinium*): ''lenocinium facit qui quaestuaria mancipia habuerit: sed et qui in liberis hunc quaestum exercet, in eadem causa est. Sive autem principaliter hoc negotium gerat sive alterius negotiationis accessione utatur, (ut puta si caupo fuit vel stabularius et mancipia talia habuit ministrantia et occassione (*sic*) ministerii quaestum facientia: sive balneator fuerit, velut in quibusdam provinciis fit, in balineis ad custodienda vestimenta conducta habens mancipia hoc genus observantia in officina, lenocenii tenebitur.''

[132] *W.Chr.* 156 (Naples, 194); *IGRR* IV 1519 (Sardis, 212/217): ἐπὶ βαλ[ανείων τ]οῦ Σεβαστοῦ. The latter did not necessarily hold the function in Asia, because he is known to have been honored in other dedications, one of them from Rome. Cf. W. Langhammer (1973) 98-99; and 126; and W. Liebenam (1900) 414-15, and n. 5, referring to *CIL* II 4610 (Baetulum/Tarraconensis) and *CIL* II 5354 (Burguillos/Baetica) as evidence for *curatores balnei*.

and Antioch are known to have been headed by famous scholars and became intellectual centers of primary importance. These libraries contained the private collections of the kings and were reserved to select users.

In the Roman world, private libraries existed before the time of Caesar: Aemilius Paullus, Sulla, and Lucullus reportedly brought back many books from their military campaigns in the Greek East, and kept them as part of the booty.[133] Some private collections could be fairly extensive: Cicero's friend Atticus was famous for keeping several copyists to take care of his personal library.[134] Private libraries belonged to the nobility and were often kept in rural or suburban villas.[135] The books which were frequently used were considered part of the farm equipment, the others which were only stored there were excluded from it.[136] There is little evidence concerning the staff of librarians who took care of these private collections,[137] but, in view of the terminology used in the context of the

---

[133] Plut., *Aem.* 28.11; *Luc.* 42.1-2; *Sull.* 26.1-4; Lucian, *Ind.* 4; and Isid., *Orig.* 6.5.1. On Roman libraries, cf. G. Cavallo (ed.), *Le biblioteche nel mondo antico e medievale* (Rome/Bari 1988), esp. the contributions by L. Canfora, "Le biblioteche ellenistiche" (5-28) and P. Fedeli, "Biblioteche private e pubbliche a Roma e nel mondo romano" (31-64). Cf. also V.M. Strocka, "Römische Bibliotheken," *Gymnasium* 88 (1981) 298-329; A.J. Marshall, "Library Resources and Creative Writing at Rome," *Phoenix* 30 (1976) 252-64; K. Preisendanz, *Kl. Pauly* I (1964) cols. 892-96, s.v. *Bibliothek(en)* and 896-97, s.v. *Bibliothekswesen*; C. Wendel, "Das griechisch-römische Altertum," in *Handbuch der Bibliothekswissenschaften* III.1 (1955) 51-145, especially 119; 126-28; and 139-45 ("Die Bibliotheksverwaltung im Altertum" with a study of the staff, 143-44); idem, "Bibliothek," *RLAC* (1954) 231-74 (= *Kleine Schriften zum antiken Buch- und Bibliothekswesen* [Cologne 1974] 165-99); and R. Cagnat, "Les bibliothèques municipales dans l'empire romain," *MMAI* 38,1 (1909) 1-26, esp. 25. I have not seen R. Fehrle, *Das Bibliothekwesen im alten Rom. Voraussetzungen, Bedingungen, Anfänge* (Wiesbaden 1986).

[134] Nep., *Att.* 13.3 and 14.3 ("plurimi librarii"). In the third century A.D., the poet Serenus Sammonicus reportedly owned ca. 62,000 rolls (SHA, *Gord.* 18.3).

[135] Plut., *Luc.* 42; and Cic., *Fin.* 3.2.7-8. The books were brought back in 66 B.C. from the Mithridatic War and arranged on the same pattern as the library of Alexandria in his villa at Tusculum. The *Villa dei Papiri* at Herculaneum was offered by L. Calpurnius Piso Caesoninus (cons. 58 B.C.) to the philosopher Philodemus of Gadara, whose library was partly found there (cf. below).

[136] Ulpianus (20 *ad Sab.*) *Dig.* 33.7.12.34: "Instructo autem fundo et bibliothecam et libros, qui illic erant, ut quotiens venisset, uteretur, contineri constat. Sed si quasi apotheca librorum utebatur, contra erit dicendum." Cf. also Paulus, *Sent.* 3.6.51: "Instructo fundo legato libri quoque et bibliothecae quae in eodem fundo sunt legato continentur."

[137] Cicero, whose libraries were located in Rome, Cumae, Antium, and Tusculum, speaks of *librarii*, *librarioli*, and *glutinatores* (*Att.* 4.4a.1 [56 B.C.]; 4.5.3 [56]; 4.8.2 [56]; and *QFr.* 3.5.6 [54]); cf. T. Dorandi, *ZPE* 50 (1983) 25-28. Cicero's

management of public and imperial libraries in Rome, one can surmise that the estate manager (*vilicus*) was involved.[138] In so far as
private libraries were circulating books among the friends of the
owner, someone had to make the decision which book could taken
out by whom. Atticus seems to have been particularly picky about
this rule, since even Cicero had to present the person in charge a
written permission from Atticus himself in order to borrow a book
in the latter's absence.[139]

As far as public libraries in Rome are concerned, there is no trace
of any before the first century B.C.[140] In the aftermath of his victory, on the way to which parts of the Great Library at Alexandria
had been burned down in 48 B.C.,[141] Caesar planned the construction of the largest library of Greek and Latin books. For this purpose
he appointed M. Varro, an established scholar at this time and the
author-to-be of a treatise *De Bibliothecis*, as a commissioner (*curator*)
to be in charge of procuring and classifying the books.[142] As a result
of Caesar's assassination, the project was never carried out, but
Caesar had set a precedent that was followed a few years later (ca.
39 B.C.) by C. Asinius Pollio, who, as Pliny the Elder reports, was
the first to use the proceeds of his campaigns to make public the talents of mankind.[143] Once again, Varro was asked to coordinate the
enterprise. Augustus followed on, founded a library (ca. 28 B.C.)
in the portico of the temple of Apollo on the Palatine, and appointed

---

slave Dionysius, who was in charge of his master's library, stole some books and
fled to Dalmatia (*Fam.* 13.77.3 [46] and 5.10a.1 [44]).

[138] In the same way, the *vilicus* of the *domus Tiberiana* (*ILS* 1629 = *CIL* VI 8655)
may have been both a house manager and a library manager, since it is known that
a major collection was located there (Gell., *NA* 13.20.1).

[139] Cic., *Att.* 4.14.1 (writing from Cumae or Pompeii to Atticus who was on a
trip to Epirus in 54 B.C.).

[140] J. Stambaugh, *The Ancient Roman City* (Baltimore/London 1988) 121; 139;
350, n. 39; and 351, n. 41 for a list of known public libraries in Rome; and P. Fedeli
(1988) 48-51, who discusses the evidence concerning the development of public
libraries in Rome and who mentions that fourth-century regionaries (*Curiosum* and
Notitia) provides the dubiously-high figure of 28 (29) public libraries in Constantine's time; cf. L. Homo (1951) 292-93.

[141] It seems established now that in spite of Plutarch's assertion (*Caes.* 49.6), the
destruction was limited to some book depository located in the harbor area. Cf.
A.K. Bowman, *Egypt after the Pharaohs* (London 1986) 225; and Mustafa El Abbadi,
The Life and Fate of the Ancient Libraries of Alexandria (Paris 1990) (non vidi).

[142] Suet., *Iul.* 44.4: "curam comparandarum ac digerendarum [bibliotheca-
rum]."

[143] Pliny, *HN* 7.115 and 35.10; Ov., *Tr.* 3.1.71-72. The library was located in
the temple of *Libertas*.

as (pro)curator ("cui ordinandas bibliothecas delegaverat") Cn. Pompeius Macer, another famous scholar, whom he forbade to publish or circulate Caesar's early works.[144]

It is not clear when the position of *procurator bibliothecarum Graecarum et Latinarum* (*a bibliothecis* – ἐπίτροπος βυβλιοθηκῶν ʿΡωμαικῶν τε καὶ ʿΕλληνικῶν) was created, but we know the names of several scientific and literary writers and of one jurist who had held the position from the reign of Nero to the reign of Antoninus Pius. All of them were of equestrian rank (*ducenarii* or *sexagenarii*) and were very close to the emperor.[145] I suspect that the position encompassed all public and imperial libraries of the city of Rome.

Lower levels of management are more elusive: according to Suetonius, C. Melissus was born free, then exposed and raised as a slave. After his manumission, he became close to Augustus who entrusted him with the supervision of both libraries of the *Porticus Octaviae*.[146] The wording of Suetonius's account is quite similar to that used in describing Macer's appointment (cf. above); therefore, it is not inconsistent with the position of procurator. An inscription dated to the reign of Claudius or Nero and presenting an imperial freedman, Ti. Claudius Scirtus, in the capacity of *procurator bybl(iothecae* or *-iothecarum?*),[147] suggests that Melissus was a freedman procurator. By contrast with Macer, Melissus's function comprised only the administration (*cura bybliothecarum ordinandarum*) of the libraries of the *Porticus Octaviae*. In the same way, C. Iulius Hyginus, a Spanish slave manumitted by Augustus, was the head of the Palatine Library.[148] So it seems that equestrian and freed procurators of

---

[144] Suet., *Iul.* 56.7; and *Aug.* 29.3.

[145] H.-G. Pflaum, *Les carrières procuratoriennes équestres* III (Paris 1960-1961) 1023 gives the names of known officials with various titles (*a bibliothecis – proc. bibliothecarum – proc. rationum summarum privatarum bibliothecarum*); cf. in particular Pflaum's entries B (Cn. Pompeius Macer); 46 (Dionysius Alexandrinus); 96 (C. Suetonius Tranquillus); 105 (L. Iulius Vestinus); 110 (Valerius Eudaimon); 141 (L. Volusius Maecianus). It is remarkable that L. Iulius Vestinus had been Great Priest of Alexandria and of all Egypt and director of the Museum (ἐπιστάτης), a position of considerable prestige that was assigned by the emperor himself since Augustus (Strabo 17.1.8 [794]; for the earlier period, cf. *OGIS* 104 and 172). In his subsequent career, he was appointed *procurator a studiis* and then *ab epistulis* (*IGRR* I 136, Rome, reign of Hadrian). I have not seen L.D. Bruce, "The *procurator bibliothecarum* at Rome," *Journal of Library History* 18 (1983) 143-62.

[146] Suet., *Gram.* 21: "quo delegante, curam ordinandarum bibliothecarum in Octaviae porticu suscepit."

[147] The inscription was found in Naples, cf. *ILS* 1587 (= *CIL* X 1739).

[148] Suet., *Gram.* 20: "praefuit Palatinae bibliothecae."

libraries lived side by side, which is not entirely surprising, as freedmen are found playing the role of deputies of equestrian officials in
other areas of imperial administration. The difference between them
consisted perhaps in the scale of their attributions, the equestrian
official supervising all the libraries of the capital while his freedman
counterpart was assigned a group or just a pair of libraries.

The management of individual libraries, or of a section of it, was
left to a *vilicus*. Thus, Saturninus was a *ser(vus) vil(icus) a bybl(iotheca)
Lat(ina)*,[149] and Hymnus Aurelianus was the *vilicus* of the *bybliotheca
Latina Porticus Octaviae*.[150] In this latter library—which had been
dedicated shortly after 23 B.C. by Octavia, Augustus's sister, to
honor and commemorate her son Marcellus[151]—the Greek and
Latin sections were administered separately. It is not known whether
this practice was always respected, but we happen to know that some
private libraries were organized in two distinct sections, reflecting
the wealth and the education of their owner. Thus, Trimalchio
sounds all the more presumptuous, when he refers to his twin
libraries (some editions have even three!), considering his limited
education.[152] In the Villa dei Papiri at Herculaneum, 1073 rolls
were found in five different locations. The Latin texts are few (less
than 60) and come mostly from a box (*capsa*) on the verge of being
transferred to a different location within or outside of the villa
(perhaps to be rescued from impending destruction in A.D. 79).
The scarcity of Latin rolls in a library constituted probably in the
first century B.C. suggests that a significant part of the collection
(the Latin section) has not yet been found.[153]

---

[149] *AE* 1959, no. 300 (Rome, Neronian date).

[150] *ILS* 1971 (= *CIL* VI 2347 = 4431). Hymnus belonged to a funerary association in which he was the head of a *decuria*; cf. L. Halkin, *Les esclaves publics chez les
Romains* (Paris 1897) 123, who discusses the inscription and provides parallels (*CIL*
VI 5199; 5208; 5361; and 5362). Even slaves and women could hold the position
of *decurio*.

[151] Plut. *Marc.* 30.

[152] Petron., *Sat.* 48.4. Cf. R.J. Starr, "Trimalchio's Libraries," *Hermes* 115
(1987) 252-53; and N. Horsfall, "'The Use of Literacy' and the Cena Trimalchionis," *G&R* 36 (1989) 74-89 and 194-209, esp. 80 and 82, with reference to Lucian's
pamphlet *Against the Uneducated Man Who Buys Many Books*.

[153] G. Cavallo, "I rotoli di Ercolano come prodotti scritti: quattro riflessioni,"
Scrittura e civiltà 8 (1984) 5-30; F. Longo Auricchio – M. Capasso, "I rotoli della Villa ercolanese: dislocazione e ritrovamento," *BCPE* 17 (1987) 37-47; and M. Capasso, *Manuale di papirologia ercolanese* (Lecce 1991) 65-83, who suggests that the room
where 840 rolls were found could have been a sort of depository for both Latin and
Greek texts. Others speak of a workshop, the actual library being still undiscovered.

To return to the *Bybliotheca* of the *Porticus Octaviae*, one can surmise that if Hymnus Aurelianus was in charge of the Latin section of the library, another *vilicus* was probably in charge of the Greek section. Hymnus may have been an imperial slave who once belonged to a certain Aurelius, but it is surprising that he did not advertise his status of member of the imperial household. His connection with Octavia's dedication entitled him to an epitaph on the *Columbarium* of the Marcelli. Additional evidence concerning the staff of the library of the *Porticus Octaviae* suggests that Hymnus, like his predecessor or successor Montanus Iulianus,[154] was a public slave. This is illustrated by a couple of inscriptions concerning two members of the staff, Soterichus Vestricianus and Philoxenus Iulianus.[155] To sum up, it seems that Augustus employed an independent freedman, C. Melissus, to supervise the administration of a privately-founded, but publicly-run library, the owner of which was a member of the imperial family; each section was run by a public *vilicus* at the head of a *familia publica*.[156] Obviously, the Romans were not so sensitive as we are regarding the distinction between private, public, and imperial sectors.

By contrast with the libraries of the *Porticus Octaviae*, the Greek and Latin libraries attached to the temple of Apollo in Rome were staffed with imperial slaves.[157] Imperial *vilici a bybliotheca* are attested both in Rome and at Ostia.[158] The trend seems to show a progressive takeover by the imperial household of positions originally filled by public slaves.[159]

Libraries were often part of a larger architectural complex, such as a villa, a temple precinct, or baths (cf. above). Conversely, they were sometimes sheltering other activities: an imperial slave named Onesimus is recorded as *vilicus therma[rum] bybliothec(ae) Gra[ecae]*.[160] In that case, it is possible that the whole complex was run by a common staff. Often, however, libraries were housed in separate, in-

---

154 *CIL* VI 4435.
155 *ILS* 1970 (= *CIL* VI 2349 = 5192) and *ILS* 1972 (= *CIL* VI 2348).
156 L. Homo (1951) 264.
157 *ILS* 1588-1589 (= *CIL* VI 5188-5189).
158 *CIL* VI 8744 (A.D. 126); and *ILS* 1590 (= *CIL* XIV 196).
159 W. Eder (1980) 164 and 168; L. Halkin (1897) 100ff. considers that the turning point in the gradual shift from public to imperial management was the destruction of the library of the *Porticus Octaviae* under Titus (in 80) and its reconstruction under Domitian.
160 *CIL* VI 8679.

dependent buildings: Vespasian reserved some space on his *Forum Pacis* for the purpose of a library and a museum.[161]

Public libraries were not confined to the city of Rome: ca. A.D. 97, Pliny the Younger donated one at the cost of 1,000,000 sestertii to his native town of Comum with an additional sum of money (100,000 sestertii) for its maintenance (*tutela*).[162] It is likely that the town of Comum used part of the money to support a *vilicus a bybliotheca* and a few public slaves or contracted with a skilled librarian to operate the facility. There is no evidence concerning this point.[163] We know of other public libraries at Tibur, Volsinii, Tortona, Centumcellae, and Mediolanum, to limit the list to Italy.[164] These institutions seem to have been run by the municipalities, even though they had been created by private donations. One cannot exclude, however, the existence of imperial libraries outside Rome: the library at Suessa was called *b[y]bl[i]otheca M[ati]diana* and was probably built by, or dedicated to, Hadrian's mother-in-law who had died in 119.[165] The building was obviously used for public events, such as the drawing of official documents. An inscription recording an imperial *vilicus* was found at Ostia, which suggests that a public/imperial library existed in this town.[166] Since Suessa and Ostia

---

[161] For the administration of museums, cf. J. Beaujeu, "A-t-il existé une direction des musées dans la Rome impériale?" *CRAI* (1982) 671-88, discussing *ILS* 7213 (= *CIL* VI 10324, *Lex collegi Aesculapi et Hygiae*, A.D. 153) commemorating Flavius Apollonius, an imperial procurator "qui fuit a pinacothecis" and his assistant (*adiutor*), an imperial freedman. According to Beaujeu, the function was probably created by Hadrian on the model of the *procurator a bybliothecis* and suppressed by Antoninus Pius (SHA, *Ant. Pius* 7.6-7) to be taken over by another department. There is no evidence for a *vilicus pinacothecae*, but since museums were often located in temples, baths (*thermae*, cf. above), libraries, porticoes, and parks (*horti* and *saepta*), many an *aedituus* and *vilicus thermarum, a bybliotheca, horti* or *saeptorum* (*ILS* 9029 = *CIL* VI 37175 = *AE* 1910, no. 114) acted as museum curator; cf. L. Homo (1951) 264-65; 410-11; 417; and 597-98.

[162] Pliny, *Ep.* 1.8; and *ILS* 2927 (= *CIL* V 5262).

[163] M. Rostovtzeff, *SEHRE*² (1957) 601, n. 10 mentions that "the little city of Teos organized its own library and spent money to have books copied, to pay librarians and to restore books (*SEG* II 584, first century B.C. or A.D.?). Unfortunately, this inscription is in a very bad condition, and cannot be dated with certainty."

[164] Cf. L. Richardson, "The Libraries of Pompeii," *Archaeology* 30 (1977) 394-402, esp. 400-02 in which the author identifies the so-called *Sacellum Larum Publicorum* as one of the earliest buildings providing archaeological evidence for a public library. For a list of known public libraries in Italy and the rest of the empire (Athens, Halicarnassus, Ephesus, Miletus, Prusa, Smyrna, Pergamum, Carthage, and Timgad), cf. P. Fedeli (1988) 51-52.

[165] *ILS* 6296 (= *CIL* X 4760, A.D. 193).

[166] *ILS* 1590 (= *CIL* XIV 196).

were located in the vicinity of Rome, the management of these two libraries could be actively supervised by the imperial procurator.

What were the tasks to be performed by library staff (*a bybliotheca*), private, public, or imperial? The main functions of the librarians were to buy books, to copy or improve some manuscripts,[167] to replace them in case of wear, to get an idea about their content in order to place them in an appropriate location, and finally to circulate them. In a famous letter addressed to his tutor Fronto, Marcus Aurelius describes what happened when the same book was wanted by more than one person: the second-in-line had to put pressure on the librarian (*bibliothecarius*) in order to get a hold of the coveted roll, and all the more so when the reader in possession of the book was the emperor.[168]

The management of public libraries in Rome was in the hand of the imperial bureaucracy and therefore subject to change with it. A dubious tradition recorded by the *Scriptores Historiae Augustae* attributes to the reign of Aurelian (270-275) the transfer of the procuratorship of public libraries to the Urban Prefect.[169] That such a change actually took place is demonstrated by the fact that by 372, the Urban Prefect in Constantinople was assisted by a staff of seven *antiquarii*, four for the Greek section, and three for the Latin one, which incidentally indicates that the division between Greek and Latin sections had been maintained. Their job consisted in copying and repairing manuscripts. Besides, the emperor called for the appointment of a larger number of people of lowly status (*condicionales*) to run the facilities.[170] There is no reason to think that the hierarchic structure attested at the level of the staff of the library during the early Empire had been discarded, but there is no proof either for its continuing existence.

---

[167] The making of magical handbooks provides a glimpse of the organizational structure of copyists' workshops; cf. F. Maltomini, "I papiri greci," *SCO* 29 (1979) 55-134, in part. 56, nn. 2-3, shows that his first papyrus is copied (partially) in five other papyri (2-6). The identification of several hands, as well as the multilingual features of the handbook (texts in Greek, Coptic, and Aramaic), which was made on the basis of "ricettari, fatture specifiche e amuleti," imply an important workshop. For archaeological evidence for a "laboratory" where handbooks were produced (and tested?), cf. R. Wünsch, *Antikes Zaubergerät aus Pergamon* (Berlin 1905) (non vidi).

[168] Fronto, *Ep.* 4.5: "Igitur Tiberianus bibliotecarius tibi subigitandus est." Cf. also Gell., *NA* 19.5.4.

[169] SHA, *Aur.* 1.7.

[170] Constitution of Valens addressed to the Urban Prefect Clearchus (*Cod. Theod.* 14.9.2).

3. *Performing arts and sports*

The monuments designed for mass entertainment included theaters
and concert halls, amphitheaters, circuses, naumachiae, and stadia.
According to fourth-century documents (*Curiosum Urbis Romae*,
Notitia de Regionibus, *Breviarium*, Polemius Silvius, Zacharias) combined with earlier evidence, it seems that the population of Rome
had at its disposal no less than four theaters, one concert hall, five
amphitheaters supported by five gladiatorial schools (*ludi*), four circuses, four naumachiae, and one Greek stadium.[171] Some of these
facilities being in operation for a short period of time, this list constitutes a maximun, but it illustrates the importance of public buildings with recreational purposes in Rome, a phenomenon which is
matched in many cities all over the empire, as the archaeological evidence shows. Some of these buildings existed already in the late
Republican period, and, like baths and libraries, were often born
out of the generosity of private individuals.

As will be obvious in this section, the entertainment industry was
in the hands of private entrepreneurs in the beginning, and was little
by little financed, supervised, and finally organized by the state,
municipal, and, above all, imperial administration.[172] Private enterprise might have suffered a lethal blow in A.D. 27 with the col-
lapse of the amphitheater at Fidenae, which, according to Tacitus,
left fifty thousand people dead.[173] The cause of the disaster was attributed to the cheap construction of the wooden structure set up by
a local freedman who was driven more by greed than by political
ambition. What Tacitus does not say is whether Atilius was a free
entrepreneur acting on his own initiative to take advantage of the
proximity of the Roman crowds or whether he had been commissioned by municipal magistrates. The wording of the decree of the
senate (''ne quis gladiatorium munus ederet, cui minor quadringen-
torum milium res, neve amphitheatrum imponeretur nisi solo firmi-
tatis spectatae'') taken in the aftermath of this tragedy suggests that

---

[171] L. Homo (1951) 293-98. W. Liebenam (1900) 113-21, esp. 114, shows that
in the middle of the fourth century A.D., 175 days of the year were occasions for
games (10 for festivals, 64 for the circus, and 101 for the theater), but these figures
represent undoubtedly a peak.

[172] *Res Gestae* 22-23 provides the list of performances paid for by Augustus. On
the financial aspect of entertainment, cf. M.A. Cavallaro, *Spese e spettacoli: Aspetti
economici-strutturali degli spettacoli nella Roma giulio-claudia* (Bonn 1984).

[173] Tac., *Ann.* 4.62-63.

Atilius was a mere speculator. From then on, entertainment businessmen were supposed to have equestrian census, which makes it quite likely that they were relying on business managers.

a) *theaters*
In spite of the fact that many plays from antiquity have been preserved, we know very little about their production. In one of Plautus's prologues, which may have been rewritten in a later period, one character says that the success of the play would benefit the company (*grex*), its owners or directors (*domini*), and those who hired them (*conductores*).[174] A theatrical company (*grex, caterva,* or *factio*[175]) was a group of artists (*histriones, mimi, pantomimi, archimimi, scaenici,* etc.) who were partners,[176] hired employees, or slaves. A company could not exist without a general manager or impresario, called *locator*, who was in charge of negotiating contracts with playwrights and possibly the owner of facilities on which the play would be staged. *Locatores* are known mostly through the inscriptions they sometimes set up to honor or commemorate one deserving or deceased member of the company.[177] Thus, the *locator* could be the owner of all or some of the company actors,[178] in which case he could be referred to as *dominus scaenicorum* or *dominus gregis*.[179] Nothing prevented him from being an actor himself and an active member of the company. The position of *locator* may also have been an elective office.[180] T. Uttiedius Venerianus died at age 75 after act-

---

[174] Plaut., *Asin.* 3. Cf. W. Beare, *The Roman Stage. A Short History of Latin Drama in the Time of the Republic* (London 1950) 156-62; E. Rawson, "Theatrical Life in Republican Rome and Italy," *PBSR* 53 (1985) 97-113; and H. Leppin, *Histrionen. Untersuchungen zur sozialen Stellung von Bühnenkünstlern im Westen des römischen Reiches zur Zeit der Republik und des Prinzipats* (Bonn 1992).

[175] *ILS* 5204 (= *CIL* XII 737, Arelate/Gallia Narbonensis), although the term could apply to supporters.

[176] *ILS* 5217 (= *CIL* VI 10109, "sociarum mimarum").

[177] *ILS* 5195 (= *CIL* V 5889, Mediolanum/*Regio* XI: "D. M. / curante Calopodi locatore / Theocriti Augg. lib / Pyladi / pantomimo / honorato / splendidissimis / civitatib. Italiae / ornamentis / decurionalib. ornat. / grex / Romanus / ob merita eius / titul. memoriae / posuit"); and *ILS* 5203 (= *CIL* XII 3347, Nemausus/Gallia Narbonensis: "D. [M.] / Afrodis [...] / symmele[...] / grex Ga[ll.] / Memphi et / Paridis, P. M. et / Sextis administran/tibus").

[178] Ulpianus (20 *ad Sab.*) *Dig.* 32.73.3: "Proinde si quis servos habuit proprios, sed quorum operas locabat vel pistorias vel histrionas vel alias similes, an servorum appellatione etiam hos legasse videatur?"

[179] *CIL* IV 3877 and 5399 (both from Pompeii). Cf. E.J. Jory, "*Dominus gregis?*" *CPh* 61 (1966) 102-05.

[180] *ILS* 5206 (= *CIL* XIV 2299, Albanum/Latium), where an imperial freed-

ing 37 years as a Latin mime and 18 years as the company's impresario.[181] Fairly young people are also attested in this position.[182] When the *dominus scaenicorum* and the *locator scaenicorum* were two different persons, one can surmise that the latter was a business manager whose contracts with third contracting parties (*conductores*, *mancipes*) made the former fully and jointly liable to an *actio institoria*. There is no direct evidence for such a scheme, but it is possible that Ambivius Turpio, who appears on stage as producer and actor-manager in Terence's *Hecyra* and who may have been a freedman,[183] worked in the capacity of agent on behalf of some unknown owner. Company owners sometimes belonged to the elite: at Vienna/Narbonensis, the company called "scaenici Asiaticiani" may have been owned[184] by a relative of the senator Valerius Asiaticus, a character well known for his intrigues in the reign of Caligula and Claudius and whose family was considered large and powerful by Tacitus.[185] It is quite likely that under these circumstances the *dominus* would rely on a business manager to run the show.

Theater people sometimes belonged to associations (*corpus scaenicorum*) administered by a *magister*/secretary (*scriba*): in addition to his

---

man had been elected *locator diurnus* (= *diuturnus?* i.e. long-term, regular agent?). Cf. H. Leppin (1992) 183-84, who states that the term *diurnus* resists any definitive explanation, but who suggests that it should be understood as a mark of higher status (special guest); the same author (184-86) interprets *electus* as *adlectus*.

[181] *ILS* 5208 (= *CIL* III 7343, Philippi/Macedonia): "...archimim(us) Latinus et oficialis (*sic*)...promisthota...." Cf. also *SEG* XXX 593 (Serrai/Macedonia, II/III), featuring two προμισθῶται; *SEG* XXXIII 466 (= *AE* 1910, no. 16, Larissa/Thessaly, I B.C., προμισθώτης); and *CIL* VI 10092 (*locator scaenicorum*); *contra*, H. Leppin (1992) 90, n. 20.

[182] The *locator scaenicorum* Q. Gavius Armonius died at age 24, cf. *ILS* 5207 (= *CIL* VI 5819 = 10093).

[183] Terence, *Hecyra* 28-57; and *Haut.* 30-34. Cf. E. Rawson, *PBSR* 53 (1985) 112; and M. Brozek, "Einiges über die Schauspieldirektoren und die Komödiendichter im alten Rom," *StudClas* 2 (1960) 145-50.

[184] Actors often mentioned the company to which they belonged; cf. *ILS* 5202 (= *CIL* V 2787, Verona/*Regio* X, "in greg(e) Veturian(a)"); and *ILS* 5204 (= *CIL* XII 737, Arelate/Narbonensis, "Dis / Manibus / Primigeni / scaenici ex / factione Eudoxi").

[185] *ILS* 5205 (= *CIL* XII 1929). For Valerius Asiaticus (*suff. cons.* in A.D. 35), cf. Tac., *Ann.* 11.1-3 (A.D. 47): "genitus Viennae multisque et validis propinquitatibus subnixus;" and *ILS* 212, col. II, lines 14-17 (= *FIRA* I², no. 43, pp. 283-84): "ut dirum nomen la/tronis taceam, et odi illud palaestricum prodigium, quod ante in do/mum consulatum intulit, quam colonia sua solidum civitatis Roma/nae beneficium consecuta est."

position of elected agent (*locator*, cf. above), the imperial freedman M. Aurelius Plebeius was *scriba et magister perpetuus corporis scaenicorum Latinorum*. In this capacity, he had reportedly managed the affairs of the association with incomparable good faith.[186]

Theatrical companies were usually not attached to a specific theater, but were hired on a contractual basis. It is not clear whether the *conductores* or *mancipes*[187] who hired them owned the facilities (theater or stage) where the performance took place, or had to rent them as well. There was no need for permanent structures, which in any case did not exist in Rome before the mid-first century B.C. (theater of Pompey, 55 B.C.).[188] By this time, it is possible that some staff members, such as the stage director (*choragus*), the crier (*praeco*), the ushers (*dissignatores*), and the security personnel (*conquisitores*), if not the artists themselves, were permanent employees of a specific establishment.

During the Principate, some actors were members of the imperial household,[189] which suggests that they belonged to imperial companies administered by a freedman *procurator scaenicorum*,[190] perhaps in connection with other imperial services, such as the department of performing arts (*summum choragium*) and the costume department (*a veste scaenica*, cf. below).

b) *amphitheaters*

Gladiatorial games usually took place in amphitheaters,[191] although other locations, such as theaters and public places, were also used. These events were organized by Roman and municipal magistrates,

---

[186] *ILS* 5206 (= *CIL* XIV 2299, Albanum/Latium), ("inconp[arabi]li fide rem publ[icam ger]enti corpor[is supra]scripti...."); *ILS* 5228 (= *CIL* III 3980, Siscia/Upper Pannonia), *magister mimariorum*; and *ILS* 5205 (= *CIL* XII 1929, Vienna/Gallia Narbonensis, "Scaenici asiaticiani et qui in eodem corpore sunt, ...").

[187] *ILS* 5206 (= *CIL* XIV 2299, Albanum/Latium), set up by the *manc[ipes] gregum do[minorum] Augg.*

[188] Tac., *Ann.* 14.20. J.A. Shelton, *As the Romans Did* (New York/Oxford 1988) 338, n. 185 rightly remarks that permanent theaters existed much earlier in Roman towns closer to Greek influence (for instance, in Pompeii by the early second century B.C.).

[189] *ILS* 5206 (= *CIL* XIV 2299, Albanum/Latium); *ILS* 5225 (= *CIL* VI 4886); *ILS* 5227 (= *CIL* VI 10129); etc.

[190] *ILS* 5268 (= *CIL* VI 10088). For imperial companies (*greges dominorum Augg.*), cf. above *ILS* 5206 (= *CIL* XIV 2299, Albanum/Latium).

[191] *ILS* 5051-5163 and 9340-9343. Cf. P. Sabbatini Tumolesi, *Epigrafia anfiteatrale dell' occidente romano* (Rome 1988) 127-29.

by appointed commissioners (*curatores munerum*),[192] and by the emperors represented by members of the imperial administration (freedmen *procuratores a muneribus*[193] or *procuratores munerum*[194]). The central administration was probably enormous. It coordinated the efforts of other services, such as those which supplied the cloths (*ratio vestiaria* or *ratio vestium scaenicae et gladiatoriae* [*et venatoriae*]) headed by an imperial freedman *a commentariis rationis v. s. et g. (et v.*);[195] those which supplied the animals for the *venationes*;[196] and those which supplied the weapons to individual schools.[197] We can only guess the structure of the bureaucracy assisting these officials.[198]

Amphitheaters were managed by *vilici* at the head of a slave household. Hyacinthus, a slave who dedicated an inscription to his concubine and their daughter, was the manager of the first stone amphitheater in Rome.[199] The amphitheater belonged to the Statilii

---

[192] *ILS* 5066 (= *CIL* IX 1705, Beneventum/*Regio* II), freedman (?) Augustalis; *ILS* 6201 (= *CIL* XIV 2114, Lanuvium/Latium), municipal aedile; *ILS* 6295 (= *CIL* X 6090, Caieta/Latium), military officier. On *curatores ludi* and *curatores muneris publici*, cf. W. Liebenam (1900) 371, n. 3 and 372, n. 3. During the Republican period and the early Principate, the *cura ludorum* was part of the duties of aediles. W. Langhammer (1973) 155-56 shows that by the time of Severus Alexander all functions of the aediles, including the *cura ludorum*, had been taken over by *curatores* as liturgies (*ibid.* 180-82); cf. Hermogenianus (1 *epit.*) *Dig.* 50.4.1.2; and Langhammer 247.

[193] *ILS* 1567 (= *CIL* XI 3612, Caere, under Domitian).

[194] *ILS* 1738 (= *CIL* VI 8498, Rome, under Commodus). This man converted to Christianity.

[195] *ILS* 1766 (= *CIL* VI 10089). The service was divided into three or more departments, each of which was presumably run by a freed *praepositus*, cf. *ILS* 1762 (= *CIL* VI 8555, *a veste venatoria*); *ILS* 5160 (= *CIL* VI 3756, *a veste gladiatoria*); and *ILS* 1764 (= *CIL* VI 8553, *praepositus vestis scaenicae*).

[196] *ILS* 1578 (= *CIL* VI 8583, *procurator Laurento ad elephantos*); *AE* 1955, no. 181 (Ostia, *praepositus camellorum*); *ILS* 5159 (= *CIL* VI 10209, *praepositus herbariarum*), who supplied grazing (= bait) animals; and *ILS* 5158 (= *CIL* VI 10208, *adiutor ad feras*). About trade in wild animals, cf. the mosaics at Piazza Armerina (Sicily); and F. Bertrandy, "Remarques sur le commerce des bêtes sauvages entre l'Afrique du Nord et l'Italie (IIe s. av. J.-C. – IVe s. ap. J.-C.)," *MEFRA* 99 (1987) 211-41.

[197] *ILS* 5153 (= *CIL* VI 10164, *praepositus armamentario ludi Magni*).

[198] For a *tabularius a muneribus*, cf. *CIL* VI 10162 et 33981 (same person). Every school (*ludus*, cf. below) employed secretaries (*CIL* VI 352 = 30746, *commentariensis*), accountants (*ILS* 5154 = *CIL* VI 10166, *dispensator*), physicians (*ILS* 5152 = *CIL* VI 10173, *medicus*), messengers (*ILS* 5127 = *CIL* VI 10165, *cursor*), and musicians (Sabbatini Tumolesi, p. 43, no. 36 and Juv. 3.34-37, *cornicen* or *cornicularius*).

[199] *ILS* 5155 (= *CIL* VI 10163). Cf. A. Manodori, *Anfiteatri, circhi e stadi di Roma* (Rome 1982) 46; and J.-C. Golvin, *L'amphithéâtre romain* (Paris 1988) 52-53, who points out that since the amphitheater was destroyed in the fire of 64, it must have been built only partly in stone.

Tauri, an ancient noble family from Lucania close to the rulers in the triumviral and Julio-Claudian periods. Their interests in the building industry in the first century A.D. are well attested. The facility was run by their slaves, among whom one finds, in addition to the above mentioned *vilicus*, one *custos et vicarius de amphitheatro* and one *ostiarius ab amphitheatro*.[200] It is interesting to note that the Statilii Tauri were involved in both the construction and the management of public and private facilities.[201]

Combat personnel was called *familia gladiatoria*, was quartered in a school (*ludus*), and was directed by a *lanista*.[202] In the case of the *Ludus Magnus* in Rome, the administration was in the hands of an equestrian procurator.[203] If the imperial administration had a *de facto* monopoly over the game business in the capital, private enterprise was thriving in other towns: at Venusia (*Regio* II), C. Salvius Capito employed his own slaves and the slaves of other *domini* (*servi alieni*) as well as free(d) men as gladiators. In addition to the recruits (*tirones*) who went probably through some kind of general training, all fighters had a specific function which was determined by the kind of weapon they bore, by the kind of technique they used in combat, or by their ethnic origin. Thus, they were called *retiarii* (who used a net and a trident), *sagittarii* (archers), *mirmillones* and *hoplomachi* (heavily armed), *velites* (lightly armed), *scissores* (who used a sharp weapon), *manicarii* (who used a hook), *paegniarii* (fencing specialists), *secutores* (who ran after their opponent), *provocatores* (who stimulated the fighters), *equites* and *essedarii* (mounted on a horse or on a cart), *Thraeces*, *Samnites*, and *Galli*.[204] Each group had a trainer (*doctor*, ἐπιστάτης), and there is evidence for some internal hierarchy (*primus palus*).[205] Recruitment was entrusted to equestrian *procuratores familiarum gladiatoriarum* who operated in the provinces.[206]

---

[200] *CIL* VI 6226-6228.

[201] S.D. Martin, *The Roman Jurists and the Organization of Private Building in the Late Republic and Early Empire* (Brussels 1989) 64-65.

[202] *ILS* 5151 (= *CIL* X 1733, Naples); FIRA I², no. 49, *passim* (= *ILS* 5163 = *CIL* II 6278, Italica/Baetica); and *ILS* 9340 (Sardes/Asia). According to the *Lex Iulia municipalis* (*Tabula Heracleensis*, 45 B.C.), the function carried a social stigma comparable to pimps and prostitutes; cf. *FIRA* I², no. 13, line 123 (p. 149).

[203] *ILS* 2773 (= *CIL* VI 1645); and *ILS* 9002.

[204] *ILS* 5083 and 5083a (= *CIL* IX 465-466). For the *familia gladiatoria Caesaris*, cf. *ILS* 5084 and 5084a (= *CIL* VI 631-632, Rome, Via Labicana, 177), which also includes *pagani* (civilians? as opposed to *milites*).

[205] *IGRR* I 207 (Rome), where the gladiator was promoted from *primus palus* to the rank of ἐπιστάτης; and *ILS* 5103 (= *CIL* VI 10175, Rome).

[206] *ILS* 1396 (= *CIL* III 249 = 6753, Ancyra), where L. Didius Marinus was

c) *circuses*

Horse and chariot racing, which took place in the circus, were organized as a competition among various teams backed by a fan club (*factiones*).[207] The competing charioteers (*agitatores, aurigae, bigarii, cursores*) belonged to one of four stables distinguished by a specific colour (*pannus*), i.e. the red (*russata factio*), the blue (*veneta f.*), the green (*prasina f.*), and the white (*alba f.*). In the early Principate, each stable was owned by a private businessman of equestrian status,[208] but by the fourth century, this function was taken over by the emperor. Within the same stable, there was an established hierarchy among runners: A. Antonius Albanus was a *cursor* who had a position of leader (*supra cursores*) among his colleagues of the green faction.[209] Even though manumitted and free charioteers are known to have switched from one team to another,[210] it seems that senior charioteers became more and more involved in the administration of the team to which they belonged, and by the end of the third century, the factions were usually run by a "player manager" or *factionarius*.[211] After the imperial takeover, the teams were attached to an hippodrome.

One early Imperial inscription provides evidence for a *vilicus* of the *familia quadrigaria* of Titus Ateius Capito, who was presumably

---

successively *procurator familiarum gladiatoriarum* in Gaul, Britain, Spain, Germania, and Raetia on one hand, and in Asia, Bithynia, Galatia, Cappadocia, Lycia, Pamphylia, Cilicia, Cyprus, Pontus, and Paphlagonia on the other. Cf. also *ILS* 1397 (= *CIL* X 1685, Naples) for a procurator operating from Alexandria throughout Egypt; *ILS* 1412 (= *CIL* V 8659, Concordia/*Regio* X) for Gallia Transpadana; *ILS* 9014 (Puteoli) for Aemilia Transpadana, both Pannoniae, and Dalmatia; and perhaps *AE* 1989, no. 339c (Tauromenium/Sicily).

[207] *ILS* 5277-5316. In *ILS* 5295 (= *CIL* VI 10069) and *ILS* 5305 (= *CIL* VI 10072), the faction is called *grex* (compare above, about theatrical companies). Cf. A. Cameron, *Circus Factions. Blues and Greens at Rome and Byzantium* (Oxford 1976), esp. 5-23; E. Rawson, "Chariot-racing in the Roman Republic," *PBSR* 36 (1981) 1-16; J. Humphrey, *Roman Circuses* (Berkeley, CA 1985), who has little to say about personnel; and V. Olivá, "Chariot Racing in the Ancient World," *Nikephoros* 2 (1989) 65-88, esp. 78-88.

[208] SHA, *Comm.* 16.9; Plin., *HN* 10.34; Suet., *Ner.* 22.3 and 5.2; and Dio 55.10.5 (recording that Augustus allowed senators to practice this kind of activity).

[209] *ILS* 5279 (= *CIL* VI 33944).

[210] *ILS* 5281 (= *CIL* VI 10063); *ILS* 5286 (= *CIL* VI 10049); *ILS* 5287 (= *CIL* VI 10048, starting his career in A.D. 122). Cf. A. Cameron (1976) 201-02.

[211] *ILS* 5296 (= *CIL* VI 10058) and *ILS* 5297 (= *CIL* VI 10060, A.D. 275), both of them possibly freedmen being referred to as *domini et agitatores*, the former as *pater et magister et socius*, the latter as *sui temporis primus et solus factionarius ob gloria(m)*.

in charge of maintaining the facilities where the charioteers of the blue faction kept their material and horses, and trained.[212] Each stable employed a large staff (*familia panni*) composed of the maintenance crew, guards, attendants assigned to specific locations within the circus, veterinarians, grooms, etc.[213] The servile staff was property of the team, and after manumission, would be identified as *liberti factionis*.[214] In the Byzantine period, the staff of the hippodrome was called a τάξις and was directed by an *actuarius* who was also responsible for the organization of the races. As A. Cameron puts it, "the administration of the games, the hiring and firing of staff and performers, the procuring, breeding, and training of animals and so forth, was in the hands of the hippodrome professionals."[215]

4. *Conclusion*

Vilici are attested as managers of various types of private, public, and imperial facilities. There were no noticeable differences between all three areas of administration. Private *vilici* were probably appointed by the entrepreneur who owned (*dominus*) or took out on contract (*redemptor, manceps, conductor*) the management of the facility. Public *vilici* were appointed by the representatives (magistrates or *curatores*) of the state or of the municipality. Imperial *vilici* were subordinated to imperial procurators and supervised the staff (*familia*) assigned to the facility. The scope of their appointment could vary from the administration of a department within an institution (Greek or Latin library) to the management of a whole unit. The servants on the staff, whose composition sometimes attest a high level of division of labor, could form a blend of private, public, and imperial slaves and freedmen, and free labor.

---

[212] *ILS* 5313 (= *CIL* VI 10046). A. Manodori (1982) 134 considers the *vilicus* as a slave entrusted with the care of the horses belonging to the faction. E. Rawson, *PBSR* 36 (1981) 8, n. 35 thinks that the inscription has been possibly misread and refers to a partnership between T. Ateius Capito and one P. Annius Chelidonius.

[213] The same inscription (*ILS* 5313) records *conditores, succonditores, tentores, medici, spartores* (or *sparsores*), *moratores, viatores*. Other functions are known: *hortores* (*ILS* 5307 = *CIL* VI 33949a), *cellarii* (*ILS* 5309 = *CIL* VI 33945).

[214] *ILS* 5311 (= *CIL* VI 10077).

[215] A. Cameron (1976) 16-17.

D. COMMUNICATIONS

In the late Republic and during the Principate, people traveled widely for economic, political, military, or simply personal reasons. Several centuries of conquest had pushed the limits of the empire further and further, and the ensuing *pax Romana* facilitated the exploitation of the newly acquired provinces. The necessity to transmit messages and to transport persons and goods required the establishment of a complex infrastructure, which fostered economic activity in places otherwise fairly remote from the main urban centers. This infrastructure consisted in an adequate road system combined with a network of relay stations providing wagons, draft or mount animals, drivers, food, fodder, and lodging. Although the Roman state and army had a primary interest in the existence and reliability of the system, private businessmen used it as well. The first step was the construction of the road system by the Roman army, starting at the very end of the fourth century B.C.[216]

1. *Roads*

The traditional view is that Roman roads were built for and by the army. This is certainly true as far as mid-Republican roads are concerned, but the role of civilian entrepreneurs should not be underestimated, especially during the next phase of road work. Their main tasks consisted in extending and maintaining the existing network. Siculus Flaccus, a land surveyor thought to have been active in the second half of the first century A.D., says that public roads were built under the supervision of commissioners (*curatores viarum*)[217] by private contractors (*mancipes* or *redemptores*).[218] During

---

[216] L. Casson, *Travel in the Ancient World* (Toronto 1974) 163-225.

[217] Siculus Flaccus, *De condic. agror.* (C. Thulin (ed.), *Corpus Agrimensorum Romanorum* I [Leipzig 1923] 110). In a later period, commissioners were performing a *munus personale*; cf. Hermogenianus (1 *epit.*) *Dig.* 50.4.1.2; and Arcadius Charisius (*sing. de mun. civ.*) *Dig.* 50.4.18.7 and 15. Cf. W. Langhammer (1973) 183-84; P. Culham Ertman, *Curatores viarum: A Study of the Superintendents of Highways in Ancient Rome* (Diss. Buffalo 1976), esp. 93-137, who reconstructs (102-04) the structure of the staff in charge of road maintenance (*familia viarum*) by comparison with the staff attached to the water supply (*familia aquarum*); W. Eck, *Die staatliche Organisation Italiens in der hohen Kaiserzeit* (Munich 1979) 25-87; and H.-C. Schneider, *Altstrassenforschung* (Darmstadt 1982) 61-64, who summarizes various opinions.

[218] Tacitus, *Ann.* 3.31 (A.D. 21); *CIL* VI 8468 (Cn. Cornelius Cn. f. Sab(atina) Musaeus as *manceps Viae Appiae*); and *CIL* VI 8469 (Diadumenus ma[nceps] *viarum*

the Republican period, state contracts were farmed out by the censors, and their execution was supervised by commissioners whose term of office was not limited to a one-year period.[219]

How those private contractors carried out their obligations is not known, but one can assume that they employed their own private slaves and/or hired workers. An incidental remark by the emperor Trajan points toward the use of convicts, i.e. public slaves (*servi poenae*) on construction sites, which might indicate that municipalities sometimes carried out the work directly, under the supervision of the magistrates or commissioners.[220] There is no evidence for the lower levels of the hierarchic structure, and it is not known whether commissioners or contractors were acting through agents (*vilici*, *actores*, *praepositi*, or *institores*) to buy the necessary material, and sometimes to hire supplementary workers or draft animals. The only hint we have supporting this hypothesis is the passage of Labeo, cited by Ulpianus, where he includes among *institores* those who have been appointed to take work contracts.[221]

Laurentinae et Ardentinae). *CIL* VI 3824 (= 31603 = *ILS* 5799 = *ILLRP* 465, Republican, under Sulla [?]) contains a contract made by the *curator viarum and quaestor urbanus* Titus Vibius Temuudinus with several *mancipes* for work to be done—including the construction of a bridge—on the Via Caecilia: a sum of money had been appropriated with the consent of the people. One of the *mancipes* was a freedman, another a freeborn; cf. W. Eck (1979) 59, who considers that the same contractors were in charge of building the roads and the infrastructure attached to them, such as bridges and relay stations. The system was not always very efficient. Dio reports (59.15.4) a conflict that opposed Caligula and the senator Cn. Domitius Corbulo to the commissioners and contractors (ἐργολαβήσαντες) because of the bad conditions of the roads under Tiberius.

[219] D.E. Strong, "The Administration of Public Building in Rome During the Late Republic and Early Empire," *BICS* 15 (1968) 97-109, esp. 98, referring to the arrangement made by the L. Metellus, who divided the *Via Salaria* into three sections and entrusted each of them to the responsibility of a *curator*.

[220] Pliny, *Ep.* 10.32.2. It is possible that convicts worked for private contractors or under the supervision of soldiers, cf. F. Millar, "Condemnation to Hard Labour in the Roman Empire," *PBSR* 52 (1984) 124-47, esp. 126.

[221] Ulpianus (28 *ad ed.*) *Dig.* 14.3.5.2: "Labeo quoque scripsit, si quis pecuniis faenerandis, agris colendis, mercaturis *redempturisque faciendis* praeposuerit, in solidum eum teneri." Labeo is otherwise known to have been influential in "framing the discussion of the parties' liabilities" in work and labor contracts, cf. S.D. Martin, *The Roman Jurists and the Organization of Private Building in the Late Republic and Early Empire* (Brussels 1989) 21, n. 7 (with further references). A possible instance of an *institor* in the building industry is provided by Cicero, *2Verr.* 1.49.129ff, where P. Iunius, "homo de plebe Romano" and connected with D. Brutus, is in charge of maintaining the temple of Castor and Pollux; cf. Martin 132-33. The passage by Ulpianus has been interpreted differently by A. di Porto, "Impresa agricola ed attività collegate nell'economia della villa. Alcune tendenze organizzative,"

The bill was footed by the state or municipal treasuries and sometimes by local landowners, though the *Res Gestae* and scores of milestones found all over the empire show that the imperial *fiscus* was deeply involved. Users did not have to pay any toll, and the collection of customs dues at provincial borders was never intended to cover the cost of maintenance, at least directly.

2. *Inns*

People traveling over long distances had to stop on the way to get food and rest. Along the road, there were urban centers, villages, or isolated facilities of varying standing where services were provided. In the Republican period, these facilities were always privately run. Travelers would try to get hospitality from local people, as a favor from friends or as a service from total strangers, in farmsteads or inns (*tabernae deversoriae, cauponae, deversoria, stabula, hospitalia, centenaria(e?)*).[222]

In Plautus's *Pseudolus*, Harpax, an agent who came from out of town to do some business, is staying at a *taberna* located just outside the city-gate and kept by an old woman. There he can find food and lodging.[223] The tradition of providing full board is attested around the middle of the second century B.C. in Cisalpine Gaul by Polybius, who reports that travelers were rarely charged more than half an as per day.[224] Varro, following the Sasernas' approach to extended exploitation of a farmstead, suggests that when a farm is

---

Sodalitas. Scritti in onore di A. Guarino VII (Naples 1984) 3235-77, esp. 3248ff. Di Porto considers that Labeo refers to three different aspects of the activity of farm managers (namely moneylending, farming, and marketing the products), an interpretation which would be supported by a passage by Paulus (29 *ad ed.*) *Dig.* 14.3.16 (cf. Chapters One and Three).

222 The only evidence for the latter is *AE* 1984, no. 723 (Savaria/Upper Pannonia). On inns and innkeepers, the basic work remains T. Kleberg, *Hôtels, restaurants, et cabarets dans l'Antiquité romaine* (Uppsala 1957) 74-97, esp. 79 and 88-89. Cf. also A. Mau, *PW* 7 (1910) cols. 1806-08, sv. *caupona*; G. Hermansen, "The Roman Inns and the Law. The Inns of Ostia," in J.A.S. Evans (ed.), *Polis and Imperium. Studies in Honour of E.T. Salmon* (Toronto 1974) 167-81; L. Casson (1974) 197-218, esp. 208; J.E. Parker, "Inns at Pompeii," *Cronache Pompeiane* 4 (1978) 5-53; R. Chevallier, *Voyages et déplacements dans l'empire romain* (Paris 1988) 66-78; and now J.-M. André–F.-M. Baslez, *Voyager dans l'Antiquité* (Paris 1993).

223 Plaut., *Pseud.* 658-664.

224 Polyb. 2.15.6: ὡς μὲν οὖν ἐπὶ τὸ πολὺ παρίενται τοὺς καταλύτας οἱ πανδοκεῖς, ὡς ἱκανὰ πάντ' ἔχειν τὰ πρὸς τὴν χρείαν, ἡμιασσαρίου (τοῦτο δ' ἔστι τέταρτον μέρος ὀβολοῦ), σπανίως δὲ τοῦθ' ὑπερβαίνουσιν.

located along a road in a suitable place a tavern should be built to make an additional profit.[225] His advice was undoubtedly followed: because of a regrettable incident involving police brutality, we know that the cultivators (*vilicus* and *inquilini*) employed on some estates belonging to the future emperor Claudius operated establishments serving hot food.[226] Large estates could even breed draft and pack animals and saddle horses in order to provide travelers with needed replacement allowing them to continue their journey.[227]

Wealthy landowners living in Rome and bound to visit once in a while their distant estates would keep facilities along the road (*deversoria*) and send notice of their forthcoming passage to their keepers. Their friends would certainly be invited to use the facilities, should they come by.[228] The emperor who set out for a trip would find a luxurious mansion (*praetorium*) tended by an imperial slave or freedman and his staff, ready to welcome him.[229] At the other end of the social spectrum, travelers would stop wherever they could find a roof. In Apuleius's *Metamorphoses*, the main characters decide to put up for the night at a place formerly managed by a *vilicus*.[230]

Innkeepers (*caupones, stabularii*, etc.) belonged to the lower classes. Some owned their establishment, others acted as *institores*.[231] The practice of appointing a business manager to run an inn is attested by Ulpianus, who states that "we will consider as innkeepers or

---

[225] Varro, *Rust.* 1.2.23: "Neque ideo non in quo agro idoneae possunt esse non exercendae, atque ex iis capiendi fructus: ut etiam, si ager secundum viam et opportunus viatoribus locus, aedificandae tabernae devorsoriae, quae tamen, quamvis sint fructuosae, nihilo magis sunt agri culturae partes."

[226] Suet., *Claud.* 38.2.

[227] Cato, *Agr.* 10.1-5 and 11.1-5, listing, as part of the equipment of an olive-yard and of a vineyard, teamsters and muleteers; oxen, pack asses, and draft donkeys; yokes, harnesses, and pack saddles. All this was meant for use on the farmstead, but could be sold or rented out if necessary. Cf. also Varro, *Rust.* 2.6.5, showing that in Apulia pack animals bred on the estate were used to transport the production (grain, oil, wine, etc.) from the farmstead to the sea. Cf. D.V. Sippel, "Some Observations on the Means and Cost of the Transport of Bulk Commodities in the Late Republic and Early Empire," *AncW* 16 (1987) 35-45, esp. 37, nn. 11-12; and 39.

[228] Cicero owned several of these places, one for instance at Sinuessa (*Fam.* 12.20, 46 B.C.; and *Att.* 14.8.1, 44 B.C.). On some occasions he stopped at his friend M. Aemilius Philemon's near the Pomptine Marshes (*Fam.* 7.18.3, 53 B.C.).

[229] A *vilicus de praetorio* is attested at Ostia, cf. *CIL* XIV 199 (= *ILS* 1582).

[230] Apul., *Met.* 8.22. The *vilicus* was a slave who was put to death by his master, because his sexual disloyalty had driven his concubine to commit suicide.

[231] This could be the case in *CIL* V 5931 (= *ILS* 7474, Mediolanum/*Regio* XI), and in *CIL* XI 866 (Mutina/*Regio* VIII).

stablekeepers those who operate an inn or a stable, or *their man-agers*, but not those who perform menial tasks, such as house and kitchen servants."[232] Among the few *institores* recorded in the in-scriptions, one was probably an innkeeper: Vitalis, son and slave of C. La(e?)vius Faustus and still an adolescent of 16, was the manager of the *Taberna Apriana* which was probably located along a road in the vicinity of Philippi/Macedonia. In his epitaph, he asks the travelers he cheated in his lifetime on behalf of his principal to for-give him and to respect his parents. The young manager must have been pretty vicious, since his father/principal—who probably set up the inscription—obviously felt that he had reasons to fear retaliation or boycott on the part of previous customers.[233]

In Roman law, innkeepers were liable for the safekeeping of their guests' belongings.[234] This provision, introduced in the praetor's edict, translates the harsh reality of life. Inns were not safe, and guests had to guard against other guests, outsiders, and the host himself. Cicero, Valerius Maximus, Petronius, Juvenal, Apuleius, and Augustine have some frightening stories to tell about crimes committed against unfortunate travelers.[235] Scores of known inn-keepers were women, who were often regarded as prostitutes, pro-curesses, or witches.[236] As we have seen, nothing prevented women from being business managers.[237]

---

[232] Ulpianus (14 *ad ed.*) *Dig.* 4.9.1.5: "Caupones autem et stabularios aeque eos accipiemus, qui cauponam vel stabulum exercent, institoresve eorum. ceterum si qui opera mediastini fungitur, non continetur, ut puta atriarii et focarii et his similes." The phrase "institoresve eorum" could be a gloss, but certainly reflects a plausible situation during the Principate.

[233] *CIL* III 14206, no. 21 (= *ILS* 7479 = *AE* 1898, no. 148): "Vitalis C. Lavi Fausti / ser(vus), idem f(ilius), verna domo / natus, hic situs est. Vixit / annos XVI, institor tabernas / Aprianas a populo acceptus / idem ab dibus ereptus. Rogo vos, viatores, si quid minus / dedi me(n)sura, ut patri meo adicere(m) / ignoscatis; rogo per superos / et inferos, ut patrem et matre(m) / commendatos (h)abeatis. / Et vale."

[234] *Dig.* 4.9. J.A. Crook, *Law and Life of Rome (90 B.C. –A.D. 212)* (Ithaca, NY 1967) 226-28.

[235] Cic., *Inv. Rhet.* 2.4.14; Val. Max. 1.7.10; Petron., *passim*; Juv. 8.171ff.; Apul., *Met.* 1.8; August. *De Civ. D.* 18.18. Cf. R. Chevallier (1988) 72-74.

[236] Ulpianus (1 *ad leg. Iul. et Pap.*) *Dig.* 23.2.43 *pr.*: "Palam quaestum facere dicemus non tantum eam, quae in lupanario se prostituit, verum etiam si qua (ut adsolet) in taberna cauponia vel qua alia pudori suo non parcit;" and 8-9: "Lenam accipiemus et eam, quae alterius nomine hoc vitae genus exercet. Si qua cauponam exercens in ea corpora quaesturaria habeat... dicendum hanc quoque lenae appel-latione contineri." Cf. N. Moine, "Augustin et Apulée sur la magie des femmes d'auberge," *Latomus* 34 (1975) 350-61, esp. 353 with a list of women *cauponae* in inscriptions (for instance, *CIL* VI 9824 and *CIL* IX 2689).

[237] Ulpianus (28 *ad ed.*) *Dig.* 14.3.7.1.

Inns, like other types of economic units (*fundus*, *officina*, *taberna*, etc.), comprised the building (or the parts of it) used for this particular purpose, fully equipped with the necessary furniture (*supellectile*), such as beds (*lecti*), chamber pots (*matellae*), lamps (*candelabra*), etc; and the staff, including the manager (referred to as *caupo*(*na*), *stabularius*, *hospes*, *hospita*(*lis*), *vilicus*, *institor*, *insularius*, or *procurator*) and the other regular employees (*atriarii*, *ianitores*, *ministri*, *pueri*, *vinariae*, *ministrae*, *ancillae*).[238] Ulpianus reports that (female) innkeepers who used their establishment as a brothel tried to register the prostitutes as staff members and consequently as parts of the *instrumentum cauponium*.[239]

The private system of temporary housing described above was supplemented during the Principate by the creation of public facilities. Since these were available only to certain categories of people, the competition of the public system never caused any disruption in the private sector.

3. *Postal service (cursus publicus, vehiculatio)*

To transmit news and personal messages, in an oral or written form, everybody had to rely on messengers, because audio-visual methods of communications (such as smoke, fire, or drum signals) were never highly developed.[240] The role of messengers could be performed by

---

[238] Pomponius (6 *ad Sab.*), quoting Servius, *Dig.* 33.7.15 *pr.*: "Si ita testamento scriptum sit: 'quae tabernarum exercendarum instruendarum pistrini cauponae causa facta parataque sunt, do lego', his verbis Servius respondit et caballos, qui in pistrinis essent, et pistores, et in cauponio institores et focariam, mercesque, quae in his tabernis essent, legatas videri." Cf. also Paulus (4 *ad Sab.*), citing Neratius, *Dig.* 33.7.13 *pr.*: "Tabernae cauponiae instrumento legato etiam institores contineri Neratius existimat: sed videndum ne inter instrumentum tabernae cauponiae et instrumentum cauponae sit discrimen, ut tabernae non nisi loci instrumenta sint, ut dolia vasa ancones calices trullae, congiaria sextaria et similia: cauponae autem, cum negotiationis nomen sit, etiam institores."

[239] Ulpianus (1 *ad legem Iuliam et Papiam*) *Dig.* 23.2.43.9: "Si qua cauponam exercens in ea corpora quaestuaria habeat (ut multae adsolent sub praetextu instrumenti cauponii prostitutas mulieres habere), dicendum hanc quoque lenae appellatione contineri." Cf. above.

[240] "Pyrotelegraphy" was invented by the Persians (Hdt. 9.3) and probably used in Classical Greece and in Ptolemaic Egypt, as some papyri mention some πυρσουροί (*P. Gur.* 22 and *SB* VI 9302, both III B.C.). In a Roman context, a system of signs was used by the emperor Tiberius in order to be informed of the development of Seianus's conspiracy (Suet., *Tib.* 65.2). Cf. E. Van't Dack, "Postes et télécommunications ptolémaïques," *CE* 37 (1962) 338-41.

merchants, travelers, servants, friends, or relatives, on a more or less occasional basis. In the third century A.D., the government used professional civil servants recruited in various groups, from the slaves to the apparitorial classes (*tabellarii, cursores, equites, Numidae, commentarienses, geruli, iuvenes*), or soldiers and secret service agents (*speculatores, beneficiarii, frumentarii, agentes in rebus*).[241]

a. *creation of the system*

Before Augustus, there was no regular postal service in Roman Italy, which is not to say that communications were not very intense. Officials, like everybody else, had to rely on their own resources to carry messages from places to places. Upper-class people, in particular the magistrates of the Roman Republic, are known to have used in some occasions the infrastructure set up by companies of publicans. Otherwise, messengers had to rely on their own connections or on privately-run relay stations (*praetoria, tabernae, deversoria*, or *stabula*) along the main military roads of the empire, between population centers.

Suetonius reports that the postal service was created by Augustus.[242] The new system was perhaps inspired by the Persian system still in use in a few regions in the eastern part of the empire— Augustus or his adoptive father could have observed its efficiency in Egypt, where it had achieved a high level of sophistication under the Ptolemies. Relay stations were presumably managed by an ὡρο-γράφος who was in charge of keeping the registers in which were recorded the names of incoming and outgoing messengers, the time of their arrival and departure, and the number of letters they were carrying. The staff was made up of a camel driver (καμηλίτης), a policeman (ἔφοδος) and a host of message carriers (βυβλιαφόροι): one document lists some fourty four employees who were all paid by the royal treasury. The high number of people involved in the trans-

---

[241] R. Chevallier, *Roman Roads* (Berkeley/L.A. 1976, first publ. in French in 1972) 181-84.

[242] Suet., *Aug.* 49.3. On the organization of the postal service, cf. H.-G. Pflaum, "Essai sur le cursus publicus sous le Haut-Empire romain," *MMAI* 14.1 (1940) 189-390; E. Kornemann, *PW* 22 (1953) cols. 995-1014, s.v. *Postwesen*; S. Mitchell, "Requisitioned Transport in the Roman Empire: A New Inscription from Pisidia," *JRS* 66 (1976) 106-31; R. Chevallier (1976) 178-201; W. Eck, *Die staatliche Organisation Italiens in der hohen Kaiserzeit* (Munich 1979) 88-110; W. Eder, *Servitus publica* (Wiesbaden 1980) 90; H.-Chr. Schneider, *Altstrassenforschung* (Darmstadt 1982); and J. Stambaugh, *The Ancient Roman City* (Baltimore/London 1988) 253-54.

mission of messages can be accounted for by the particular geographical structure of Egypt, where lines of communication followed the Nile Valley in the majority of cases.[243]

There is no way of knowing when relay stations were first established or how they were run at the beginning. My guess is that we are dealing with a slowly developing process at the start of which public and imperial messengers requisitioned logistical support from private individuals and communities on the way on a random basis. However, things steadily changed: in Italy, for instance, the system of relay stations seems to have been fairly extensive by the end of the Julio-Claudian period. Plutarch reports that in A.D. 68 the public slaves (δημόσιοι οἰκέται) dispatched by the consuls could find fresh horses, food, and lodging upon presentation of a diploma at relay stations set up by the magistrates of Italian municipalities.[244]

In the provinces, the development is similar, and some valuable evidence even appears at an earlier date: under the reign of Tiberius, the inhabitants of the Pisidian town of Sagalassus were requested to provide transportation within a radius of 35 to 55 km from their town. The service (*ministerium*, λειτουργία) comprised, in the words of Sextus Sotidius Strabo Libuscidianus, the imperial legate of praetorian rank who issued the edict, providing transportation at a fixed rate per *schoenus* and free lodging ''lest all other services be exacted without payment from unwilling people.''[245] The service was available to senators, knights, centurions, imperial freedmen and slaves, as long as they were on official duty, but people doing private business, whatever their rank and occupation, were not eligible. The provision about free lodging is consistent with the laws on

---

[243] H.-G. Pflaum, *MMAI* 14.1 (1940) 206-09, quoting *P.Hib.* 110 (255 B.C.); and *P.Oxy.* IV 710 (111 B.C.) (= *W.Chr.* 435 and 436). Cf. now S.R. Llewelyn, *ZPE* 99 (1993) 41-56.

[244] Plut., *Galba* 8 (ἐν ταῖς τῶν ὀχημάτων ἀμοιβαῖς = *mutationes* or *mansiones*).

[245] *AE* 1976, no. 653. Cf. S. Mitchell, *JRS* 66 (1976) 106-31, who publishes for the first time a bilingual edict dated to the early reign of Tiberius which recalls earlier regulations edicted by Augustus and confirmed by Tiberius about who was entitled to use the postal service (*vehiculatio*), at what price, and within which limits. The section most relevant for our purpose starts at line 23: '' . . . Mansionem omnibus qui erunt ex comitatu nostro et militantibus ex omnibus provinciis et principis optimi libertis et servis et iumentis eorum gratuitam praestari oportet, ita ut reliqua ab invitis gratuita non e(x)sigant'' (= σταθμὸν πᾶσιν τοῖς τε μεθ' ἡμῶν καὶ τοῖς στρατευομένοις ἐν πάσαις ἐπαρχείαις καὶ τοῖς τοῦ Σεβαστοῦ ἀπελευθέροις καὶ δούλοις καὶ τοῖς κτήνεσιν αὐτῶν ἄμισθον παρασχεθῆναι δεῖ, τἄλλα δὲ [. . .]).

hospitium introduced in the Republican period, but contains one sign of improvement compared to the previous situation: *gratuita mansio* did not imply the loss of a regular and substantial source of profits for local people and authorities, since civil servants and soldiers billeted in provincial cities had never been expected to pay for their stay; under these circumstances, hospitable communities were probably happy to get away with limited plundering and abuse as a result of the passage of official retinues. The point of providing a *mansio* free of charge was to keep traveling officials away from the population and to serve as an incentive for them to pay for transport services. There is no basis for S. Mitchell's contention that the term *mansio* (σταθμός) in the Pisidian inscription cannot have the technical meaning of relay station because the extensive system of *mansiones* would not yet have been developed at such an early date.[246] It can be argued, however, that this inscription provides evidence for the creation of the system in the eastern provinces. Thus, other emperors adopted a similar policy by presiding over the creation of relay stations along the main military roads in various parts of the empire: in 61, Nero ordered T. Iulius Ustus (probably for Iustus), procurator of the province of Thracia, to supervise the building of shops and residences.[247] The *Taberna Apriana* run by the *institor* Vitalis near Philippi in Macedonia may have been opened around this time to fill the same purpose.[248] In 137, Hadrian created a new road across the Egyptian desert from the Red Sea harbor of Berenike to the city of Antinoe in the Nile Valley. An inscription found there records that he established along the road "an abundant water supply, relay and police stations."[249]

The rulers were quite aware of the financial burden that these services represented for Italian and provincial communities, and several of them, Claudius, Nerva, Hadrian, Antoninus Pius, and Septimius Severus tried to relieve them from this duty—or at least promised to do so.[250] The expenses generated by such services were

---

[246] S. Mitchell, *JRS* 66 (1976) 127.

[247] *ILS* 231 (= *CIL* III 6123 = *AE* 1912, no. 193, found near Serdica/Thracia): "...[ta]bernas et praeto[ria pe]r vias militare[s fie]ri iussit pe[r T. Iuli]um Ustum proc[urator pro]vinciae Thrac[iae]." A milestone bearing the name of the same procurator was found in the same region, cf. *AE* 1916, p. 17.

[248] *ILS* 7479 (= *CIL* III 14206, no. 21 (cf. above).

[249] *IGRR* I 1142: ...ὑδρεύμασιν ἀφθόνοις καὶ σταθμοῖς καὶ φρουρίοις διειλημμένην ἔτεμεν.

[250] *ILS* 214 (= *CIL* III 7251 Tegea, A.D. 49), on which cf. M. Rostovtzeff,

gradually taken over by the imperial *fiscus* and the administration of the *mansiones* farmed out to private contractors (*mancipes*). These reforms were abandoned during the disruptions that took place in the third century, and the burden fell back onto provincial communities. Therefore, it is not surprising to see the emperor Julian involved in the same effort and taking similar measures in 362/363.[251]

b. *upper level of administration (a vehiculis, praefecti vehiculorum)*
The postal service was administered from the time of its creation by a *praefectus vehiculorum*.[252] By the reign of Trajan, we have evidence for imperial freedmen (*a vehiculis*),[253] who could represent a recent

---

SEHRE[2] (1957) 79 and 569-70, n.2; *BMC* [Imp.] III 21, nos. 119-120; and *RIC* II 229f, coins bearing the legend "vehiculatione Italiae remissa"; SHA, *Hadr.* 7.5: "Statim (*rather than ms.* statum) cursum fiscalem instituit, ne magistratus hoc onere gravarentur;" SHA, *Ant. Pius* 12.3: "vehicularium cursum summa diligentia sublevavit;" SHA, *Sev.* 14: "Post haec, cum se vellet commendare hominibus, vehicularium munus a privatis ad fiscum traduxit." As the same measure is known to have been enacted by the emperor Julian (cf. below), one can wonder whether the reforms attributed to Hadrian, Antoninus Pius, and Septimius Severus, at least in this particular aspect, could not be the result of an anachronistic transposition on the part of the authors of the *Historia Augusta*. Cf. also W. Eck (1979) 94-99, esp. 97, n. 50.

251 *ILS* 755 (= *CIL* V 8987, Concordia/*Regio* X): "...remota provincialibus cura, cursum fiscalem breviatis mutationum spatiis fieri jussit."

252 W. Eck (1979) 90-94 convincingly argues that the position of *praefectus vehiculorum* probably already existed in the first century A.D. and was introduced by Augustus himself. Eck's case rests on the historical development of the title *praefectus* (instead of *procurator*), on some fragmentary inscriptions from Buthrotum/Epirus (*AE* 1950, no. 170, under Claudius) and from the Colonia Claudia Apriensium/Thracia (*AE* 1973, no. 485, revised by W. Eck, *Chiron* 5 [1975] 365-92, Vespasianic), and on the redating of *ILS* 1434 (= *CIL* X 6976, Messana/Sicily) to the reign of Nero on the basis of the identification of L. Baebius Iuncinus with a member of the *consilium* of the prefect of Egypt in 63 (*P.Fouad* 21). This evidence sets the passage by Statius referring to Plotius Grypus (a member of the senatorial order) in a new prospective (cf. Statius, *Silv.* 4.9.17-19: "Te Germanicus arbitrum sequenti(s?) / Annonae dedit omnium late / Praefecit stationibus viarum."). F. Bérard, "La carrière de Plotius Grypus et le ravitaillement de l'armée impériale en campagne," *MEFRA* 96 (1984) 259-324, esp. 277ff.; and 282-306, considers that Plotius was in charge of the army supply in 92 on the basis of an exceptional appointment, which included the supervision of all imperial roads and relay stations on the way from Rome to the Danube during Domitian's Sarmatian campaign. Cf. also *AE* 1955, no. 225 (Cyrrhus/Syria, before 108, *PP bis praef. vehic.*).

253 *CIL* VI 8542 (M. Ulpius Crescens, *ab vehiculis*, and his son M. Ulpius Saturninus, *a commentari(i)s vehiculorum*) and *CIL* VI 8543 (T. Flavius Saturninus, *tabularius a vehiculis*). At Ephesus, we find an imperial freedman who started his career as *adiutor procuratoris ab ornamentis*, then became *acceptor vehiculorum*, before being entrusted with procuratorial positions in various provinces (*I.v.Ephesos* III [= *IK* XIII] 855 and 855a). The latter two could even be pre-Trajanic. Cf. W. Eck (1979) 109-10.

addition to the system perhaps connected with a reform of the *cursus publicus* recorded by Aurelius Victor.[254] In the second century, equestrian prefects were of centenarian or ducenarian rank.[255] It seems that there were two kinds of prefects, a single individual at the head of the central administration, and several officials assigned to a set of roads in a specific area. This is illustrated by an inscription dedicated to the emperor Caracalla in 214 by the *mancipes et iunctores iumentarii viarum Appiae Traianae item Anniae cum ramulis* who were reportedly subordinated to three *praefecti vehiculorum*.[256] H.-G. Pflaum thought that prefects of both categories were operating from the city of Rome.[257] If this hypothesis is correct, one can wonder how they managed to carry out the task for which they were appointed, namely the supervision of the *mancipes*, who ran the service at the local level on a contractual basis (five-year leases), and, presumably, *praepositi* (cf. below). The job of the *praefecti vehiculorum* required a minimum amount of traveling, even though one cannot rule out that they relied heavily on their subordinates.[258]

c. *management of relay stations (mancipes, praepositi)*
The evidence for the management of the *mansiones* and *mutationes* is late and fragmentary. Our main source is the Theodosian Code which includes several imperial constitutions issued in the second half of the fourth century.[259] This is admittedly beyond the time limit chosen for this study, but there is something to be gained from

---

[254] Aur. Vict., *Caes.* 13.5: "Simul noscendi ocius, quae ubique e re publica gerebantur, admota media publici cursus. Quod equidem munus satis utile in pestem orbis Romani vertit posteriorum avaritia insolentiaque." Cf. W. Eck (1979) 96-97.

[255] *ILS* 1358 (= *CIL* X 7580, Carales/Sardinia). In the third century, they were sometimes of sexagenarian rank (*ILS* 1433 = *CIL* VI 1624 = *CIL* XIV 170, Ostia, 247 or 248).

[256] *ILS* 452 (= *CIL* VI 31338a). Cf. W. Eck (1979) 100-03.

[257] H.-G. Pflaum, *MMAI* 14.1 (1940) 288, because of the place of discovery (in Rome) of three inscriptions referring to regional *praefecti* (*CIL* VI 31338a; 31369; and 31370). Cf. W. Eck (1979) 101.

[258] For the staff assisting the *praefecti vehiculorum*, cf. W. Eck (1979) 108-10, listing an *advocatus fisci at vehicula per Flaminiam* and *per Transpadum et partem Norici* (*ILS* 9018 = *CIL* VIII 26582, Thugga/Africa Proconsularis, under Gallienus), and the imperial freedmen mentioned above (*tabularius a vehiculis* in *CIL* VI 8543, Vespasianic; an *a vehiculis*, and his son *a commentariis vehiculorum* in *CIL* VI 8542, Trajanic; and the *acceptor ve[hic]ulorum* from Ephesus in *I.v.Ephesos* III [= *IK* XIII] 855 and 855a).

[259] *Cod. Theod.* 8.5.

examining the later evidence in order to understand how the system may have worked in an earlier period.

The terminology used to refer to the facilities and to their managers is admittedly loose. In an imperial constitution regulating the use of the postal service, the emperors Valens, Gratian, and Valentinian were unable to come up with a set of terms designating without ambiguity all types of managers of relay stations.[260] *Mancipes* and *praepositi* are both attested otherwise and require some discussion.

Mancipes, who are not attested before the third century A.D., but who could have been active long before, probably negotiated their contract with the *praefecti vehiculorum*. They were each assigned to a relay station for a period of time, often limited to five years.[261] They were recruited among those provincials who qualified for service in the governor's staff, as personal accountants (?), or, if necessary, among local councillors (*decuriones*).[262] Their job (*munus*) consisted in personally engaging in the supervision of their staff at work, limiting the number of post-horses allowed to leave the station, inspecting the post warrants (*diplomata*), and requisitioning wagons and fodder for the animals.[263] They were not allowed to absent themselves from their relay station for more than a certain number of days each month,[264] but the mere existence of this rule may suggest that the *mancipes* had a tendency to make only occasional appearances, while delegating the day-to-day operation to subordinates.

The *praepositi* are even harder to grasp, because the evidence is more elusive. A constitution of the emperor Constantine addressed to the Praetorian Prefect Felix and dated to 335 recalls a complaint made by the *decuriones* of Africa concerning the fact that people of high standing—who, they say, had been *flamines*, civil priests, or magistrates—were forced to become *praepositi* of the public post stations, "a duty which, in each municipal council, men of a lower

---

[260] *Cod. Theod.* 8.5.35 (378): "...[ei] qui praepositi vocantur aut mancipes, publico denique cursui nomine aliquo praesunt."

[261] *Cod. Theod.* 8.5.23.1 (365); and 8.5.36 (381). For the classical period, cf. W. Eck (1979) 107-08.

[262] *Cod. Theod.* 8.5.23 *pr.* (365); 26 (365); 34 (377); and 51 (392).

[263] *Cod. Theod.* 8.5.35 (378); and 8.5.23.3 (365).

[264] *Cod. Theod.* 8.5.36 (381).

grade and rank customarily perform.''[265] The fact that we are dealing with a text dating from one or two generations earlier than the
evidence relative to the *mancipes* might be significant.

Like *mancipes*, *praepositi* are said to perform a compulsory service
(*munus*): this might be a peculiarity of the fourth century, and it is
quite likely than in an earlier period *mancipes* and *praepositi* were paid
or were offered some other kind of incentive to do their job. It is not
clear when the position became a liturgy, but the change probably
did not occur before the Severan reform. In the fourth century, *praepositi* belonged to the class of city councillors (*decuriones*), but they
seem to have always ranked below *mancipes* on the social ladder. O.
Seeck rightly points out that if there was a difference of functions between *mancipes* and *praepositi*, the evidence does not permit establishing whether it was connected to the type of facilities respectively entrusted to them, because both managers are attested at the head of
both *mansiones* and *mutationes*.[266] One can surmise that the difference between *mancipes* and *praepositi* was more significant in an earlier period (first or second century A.D.), when the management of
private and public economic or administrative units was either
farmed out to tenants or contractors or entrusted to the care of business managers. By the fourth century, both positions had become
compulsory, but remaining signs of social distinctions may imply
different types of liability. Thus, *praepositi* may have been agents of
the emperor (appointed by the official in charge of supervising the
road system) or of the local municipal government. There is no evidence that *praepositi* could be appointed by *mancipes*, but one cannot
exclude that the model attested in agriculture and tax collection,
whereby a lessee (*conductor*) would appoint an agent (*vilicus*), was also
applied in the context of relay stations.

The staff assisting either a *manceps* or a *praepositus* was called a
familia.[267] It was composed of muleteers (*muliones*), cartwrights (*car-
pentarii*), and veterinarians (*mulomedici*) who received a subsistence
allowance and clothing, but no salary, because they were public
slaves.[268] Other sources mention grooms (*hippocomi* and *iunctores*

[265] *Cod. Theod.* 12.1.21.
[266] O. Seeck, *PW* 4.2 (1900) s.v. *cursus publicus*, cols. 1846-63, esp. 1857.
[267] *Cod. Theod.* 8.5.21 (364).
[268] *Cod. Theod.* 8.5.31 (370); and 8.5.58 (398).

iumentarii).[269] They were skilled workers likely to be induced into working for wealthy landowners in times of manpower shortage. Some emperors took steps to curb this practice by imposing a fine on the solicitors and by returning the slaves to their relay station "with their wives, children, and all their *peculium*."[270] This rescript illustrates the relative independence of the members of the staff and how their importance was recognized—in this case, at least—by the grant of family life and property rights.

d. *various types of facilities (stationes, mansiones, mutationes)*
Relay stations were not all the same: some were probably very modest, and comprised nothing more than a stable, a workshop, and living quarters for the staff. These were called *mutationes*. Others would be much more sophisticated, and were meant to accommodate travelers for the night. Those were called *mansiones*. The use of these facilities was restricted to the bearers of a diploma. Thus, an imperial *tabellarius* could claim in his verse epitaph that he, a pedestrian, had carried his diploma through the whole region.[271]

It would make sense that along a certain road all stations were approximately of the same size, with a similar number of horses and carts to be determined by the density of the traffic and reduced to a minimum in order to keep the cost of exploitation as low as possible. As supply was limited, regulation was needed to determine the number of animals or wagons that could be requisitioned by any one official, and such regulations are preserved from the age of Tiberius to the fourth century.[272] *Mutationes* were presumably more numer-

---

[269] *Cod. Theod.* 8.5.37 (382). Procopius, *Hist. Arc.* 30.4, speaks of ἱπποκόμοι at each station in proportion to the number of horses (κατὰ λόγον τοῦ τῶν ἵππων μέτρου). Cf. also *ILS* 452 (= *CIL* VI 31338a, 214); *CIL* VI 31369-31370; and *AE* 1985, no. 462 (= *AE* 1975, no. 429, Porta Iovia near Villafranca, on the Via Postumia/*Regio* X, *mancipes iumentarii* at *stationes*). *Collegia iumentariorum* are also found at Mediolanum/*Regio* XI (*ILS* 7295 = *CIL* V 5872, Porta Vercellina et Iovia), Forum Sempronii/*Regio* VI (*ILS* 7294 = *CIL* XI 6136, Porta Gallica) and Rome (*ILS* 7296 = *CIL* VI 9485). Cf. W. Eck (1979) 107-08, esp. n. 90 with more evidence from Brixia/*Regio* X (*CIL* V 4211 and 4294), and Vicus Martis Tudertium/*Regio* VI or VII (*CIL* XI 4749); and *idem*, "*Superiumentarii et muliones* im privaten Personal des Statthalters," *ZPE* 90 (1992) 207-10, with evidence from Carnuntum/Upper Pannonia and Apulum/Dacia.
[270] *Cod. Theod.* 8.5.58 (398).
[271] *ILS* 1710 (= *CIL* VIII 1027, Carthage): "...dip[l]oma circavi totam regione(m) pedestrem...."
[272] Cf. the Pisidian inscription cited above (*AE* 1976, no. 653) and the provisions contained in the *Theodosian Code*, e.g., 8.5.35 (378).

ous than *mansiones*, because any traveler would need from five to eight *mutationes* each day, but only one *mansio* where he would spend the night. The distribution of *mutationes* and *mansiones* was affected by the geographical environment, since, in mountainous areas, some places were unsuitable for overnight stays. The distribution of *mansiones* and *mutationes* on various roads are recorded for different periods in third- or fourth-century *Itineraries* (*Itinerarium Antoninianum*, *I. Burdicalese*, *I. Hierosylamitum*, and the Peutinger Table).[273] One should point out, however, that *mansiones*, which presumably were more important than *mutationes*, are more likely to have left some traces, such as a place-name, a mention in one of the ancient Itineraries or in the literary sources, some archaeological remains, or an inscription. A recent survey of Northern Italy records a total of seventy-seven *mansiones* in *Regiones* VIII-XI, versus thirty-two *mutationes* and twenty *stationes*.[274]

e. takeover by the military

In the course of time, two phenomena affected the management of the relay stations of the *cursus publicus*. First, the lack of security in the countryside induced the emperors to post soldiers along the military roads to police them. Thus, Hadrian combined σταθμοί and φρούρια along the new Via Hadriana in Egypt.[275] The practice became widespread in the second and third centuries. These detachments were attached to a *statio*, hence their name of *stationarii*.[276] The second phenomenon, which is in fact an extension of the first one, consists in the creation of the *annona militaris* under Septimius Severus and the increasing importance of taxes collected in kind, the consequence of which was reflected by the need to create a new network of collection and distribution centers. As the soldiers became more and more involved in the organization of the corn supply, the

---

[273] R. Chevallier (1976) 185-89.

[274] R. Chevallier, *La romanisation de la Celtique du Pô* (Paris/Rome 1983) 527-52 (with a detailed analysis of the basis on which he assigns these facilities to each of the three categories), with, respectively, 9 *mansiones*, 4 *mutationes*, and 5 *stationes* in *Regio* VIII; 13, 0, 6 in *Regio* IX; 33, 9, 4 in *Regio* X; and 22, 19, 5 in *Regio* XI. Other regional surveys are available; cf., for instance, S. Crogiez, "Les stations du *cursus publicus* en Calabre: un état de la recherche," *MEFRA* 102 (1990) 389-431.

[275] *IGRR* I 1142 (cf. above).

[276] On the encroachment of the military on civilian life, cf. R. MacMullen, *Soldier and Civilian in the Later Roman Empire* (Cambridge, MA 1963) esp. 55-59, with the relevant evidence cited in n. 20.

stationes intended as collection centers soon coincided with the relay and police stations.[277]

A few inscriptions, mainly from the eastern part of the empire, illustrate this development. At Gebze in Bithynia, along the road connecting Nicomedia with Thracian Chalcedon, two soldiers of the sixth equestrian cohort were in charge of the *stationes* (note the plural) and kept registers and accounts, while muleteers took care of the transport service. As the inscription, which is dated to the third century, is dedicated to a commissioner of Caesar's draft animals, it was at first thought to refer to the administration of an imperial breeding stud. But since the place is known to have harbored a relay station for centuries afterward, it is possible that there was already one at the time of the inscription.[278]

The second example belongs to Thracia and can be dated to the year 202.[279] The emperors created a new market-place (ἐμπόριον) at Pizos by transferring part of the population of neighboring villages to the new settlement and offering them various privileges. The reason behind this measure is obscure, but the beginning of the decree issued by the procuratorial governor of the province refers to the contentment of the emperors concerning the provisioning of the relay stations (τῇ προόψει τῶν σταθμῶν ἠσθέ[ν]τες): the foundation of a market, comparable to the establishment of local fairs in the early Middle Ages, was perhaps thought to contribute to maintaining the relay station by fostering local economic prosperity. The settlers—the inscription records 174 names of people coming from nine villages—were offered an exemption from contribution to the corn supply, and from compulsory public services, especially as guards, policemen, and managers of the public postal service, which

---

[277] SHA, *Alex. Sev.* 47: "milites expeditionis tempore sic disposuit ut in mansionibus annonas acciperint." Cf. D. van Berchem, "L'annone militaire dans l'empire au IIIe siècle," *MSAF* 10 (1937) 118-202, esp. 187; *idem*, "L'annone militaire est-elle un mythe?" *Armées et fiscalité dans le monde antique* (Paris 1977) 331-36. On *praepositi annonae* attested at Gorsium (Lower Pannonia, A.D. 213), an important crossroad where a *statio* might have been located, cf. J. Fitz, *Alba Regia* 12 (1971) 254.

[278] *AE* 1923, no. 44 (= *IGRR* III 2). L. Robert, *Hellenica* X (Paris 1955) 46-62 provides a new reading: οἱ ἐπὶ τῶν στατιώνων τῶν ἀκτῶν καὶ νουμέρων καὶ οἱ [μ]ουλίωνε[ς] οἱ ἐπεστῶτες συνωρία. The person to whom the inscription is dedicated was an ἐπιμελητὴς κτήνων Καίσαρος.

[279] *IGRR* I 766 (= *IGBulg* III,2 1690). Cf. G. Seure, *BCH* 22 (1898) 480-91 and 522-557; and M.I. Rostovtzeff, *The Social and Economic History of the Roman Empire*² (Oxford 1957) 426-27; and 724-25, n. 51.

that the gathering of manpower for the management of the relay station was not the principal motivation behind the imperial enactment.[280] The new ἐμπόριον was to be ruled partly by civilian officials chosen among the leaders of the villages (nine τόπαρχοι
βουλευταί) and partly by the military (ἐπιστάθμοι στρατιῶται), who
would take over the management of the guest-residences (πραιτώ-
ρια) and of the baths (βαλανεῖα) from the current commissioners
(ἐπιμεληταί), suggesting that the construction of these buildings
antedates the foundation of the ἐμπόριον.

The inscription from Pizos provides the best illustration of a phenomenon which must have been very common, though not universal, at this period, at least in the eastern part of the empire, whereby
private and imperial administration was superseded by the military.[281] It is not surprising to find soldiers and civilians involved in
joint ventures: in Moguntiacum/Upper Germania, a *beneficiarius con-
sularis* set up an inscription with a *vilicus* whose function is not specified, but who was probably attached to a relay station or to a center
for the collection of taxes.[282] A fourth-century imperial constitution
acknowledges the continuing coexistence of both systems of management by inflicting separate penalties upon managers of the public post found guilty of not respecting the regulation relative to the
number of post-horses that could be dispatched every day from any
relay station: soldiers would be demoted from their rank and civilians sent to temporary exile.[283]

The militarization of the postal service was increased by the involvement of secret service agents as inspectors and imperial couri-
ers.[284] An inscription from Thermae Selinuntinae (Sicily) dated to
the 340's records the construction of a *statio* by a *p(rae)p(ositus) cursus
publici* acting on behalf of two governors (*consulares*) of the province
of Sicily. The *praepositus* was an *agens in rebus* of the highest (ducena-

---

[280] Lines 39-42 (= *IGBulg* III,2 1690, e 59-62): μεγάλας δωρεάς, τουτέστιν
πολειτικοῦ σεί[τ]ου [ἀν]εισφορίαν καὶ σ[υντελ]είας βουργαρίων καὶ φρουρῶν καὶ
ἀνγαρειῶν ἄνεσιν.
[281] M. Rostovtzeff, *SEHRE*[2] (1957) 448-49. The archaeological evidence suggests that the situation was quite similar in the western part of the Empire, cf. H.
Bender, *Archäologische Untersuchungen zur Ausgrabung Augst-Kurzenbettli. Ein Beitrag zur
Erforschung der römischen Rasthäuser* (Frauenfeld 1975) 125-35.
[282] *CIL* XIII 11816. Cf. R. MacMullen (1963) 58-59, and above.
[283] *Cod. Theod.* 8.5.35 (378).
[284] A.H.M. Jones, *The Later Roman Empire* (Norman, OK 1964) 578; and 830-
34.

rian) rank.[285] In the early fifth century, the *praepositi* who belonged
to the category of confidential agents (*curiosi*) were liable to the ancient discipline applying to imperial servants.[286]

The takeover by the military did not bring drastic changes to the
management of the postal service, as far as the daily routine was
concerned. Problems remained the same. Coming from the top of
the hierarchic structure, orders were directed indifferently to soldiers and civilians. What mattered was the efficiency of the system.
Those most likely to notice the difference were the people who would
stop or start being called upon as managers, whether it meant relief
from heavy financial burden or denied access to a desirable position
of power. The difference would be all the more noticeable depending
on how the system was subsidized.

4. *Conclusion*

The establishment of a sophisticated network of roads, inns, relay
stations, and vehicles is the result of the joint effort of private entrepreneurs, public officials, imperial servants, and the army. The
maintenance and running of the facilities were carried out by representatives of these four categories, although a shift toward compulsory public service and takeover by the military is noticeable by the
second and third centuries A.D. A complete standardization of the
administration was never achieved nor sought, but fourth-century
sources show that the various types of relay stations (*stationes*, *mansiones*, and *mutationes*) were usually run by *mancipes* or *praepositi*, a combination which seems to represent the dichotomy tenancy-agency
analyzed in the context of the management of agricultural estates
(cf. Chapter Three). The strong interest of the military in the organization of the food supply (*annona militaris*), combined with a
general tendency toward militarization of the imperial administration in the third century and later, accounts for the presence of soldiers at the head of some of these facilities.

---

[285] *ILS* 5905 (= *CIL* X 7200): "Pro beatitudine / temporum dd. (dominorum)
nn. (nostrorum) / Constanti et / Constantis AAuugg. (Augustorum) / stationem
a solo fece/runt Vitrasius Orfitus et Fl. / Dulcitius vv. (viri) cc. (clarissimi) consulares / p(rovinciae) S(iciliae), instante Fl. Valeriano / ducenario, agente in reb(us)
et p(rae)p(osito) cursus / publici."
[286] *Cod. Theod.* 6.29.9 (412).

E. Coinage

1. *Historical outline*

The Romans started issuing their own silver coinage in the last decade of the fourth century B.C. at the earliest. During the third century, the Roman coinage was made of struck gold (staters) and silver
(didrachms), and cast bronze (asses) denominations, very similar to
the Greek monetary system existing in Southern Italy and Sicily at
the same period. In 211 B.C., a new system was introduced. It was
based on a sextantal standard and its central element was the silver
denarius of ten asses. Around 140 B.C., the denarius was retariffed
at sixteen asses, and the sestertius of four asses became the official
unit of reckoning.[287] During the next three and a half centuries,
Roman coinage went through various vicissitudes, none of which is
likely to have drastically affected the basic monetary concepts adopted in the early period. This summary outline should suffice to show
that by the beginning of our period (ca. 200 B.C.) the Roman mint
was already a respectable institution, firmly rooted in Roman public
life. The minting of coins was a state monopoly based on statutes
enacted by a popular assembly.[288] The physical process of striking,
carried out under the authority of magistrates and the overall control
of the senate, was entrusted to an economic or administrative unit,
the mint, the management and internal organization of which constitute the focus of this section.

2. *General administration of the mint*

Before dealing with the mint proper and its staff, it is necessary to
concentrate on the authorities commissioning its operation. In contrast with the technical aspect of minting, our sources are likely to
provide some evidence about some drastic changes at the command
level entailed by the evolution and transformation of Roman political institutions during the Republic and the Principate.

---

[287] T.V. Buttrey, "On the Retariffing of the Roman Denarius," *ANSMusN* 7
(1957) 57-65; and M.H. Crawford, *Coinage and Money under the Roman Republic* (Ber-
keley/L.A. 1985) 28-29; 55-56; and 144-45.

[288] M.H. Crawford, *Roman Republican Coinage* II (Cambridge 1974) 610-18 (=
RRC); and H.B. Mattingly, "The Management of the Roman Republican Mint,"
AIIN 29 (1982) 9-46, esp. 18-22.

a. *moneyers*

The predominant figures in the administration of coinage production during the Republican period were the moneyers, *tresviri monetales* (or *quattuorviri* now and then from 44 to 4 B.C.). These officials were probably magistrates of lower rank elected or appointed annually.[289] They belonged to the college of lower magistrates (*vigintisexviri*, reduced to twenty under Augustus) which had been created in 289 B.C according to Pomponius,[290] or, more plausibly, around the time of the introduction of the denarius (211 B.C.). The full title was *IIIviri aere argento auro flando feriundo*, college of three men in charge of casting and/or striking bronze, silver, and gold. During the Republican and triumviral periods, the names of moneyers—single or in a group—appear on the reverse of coins, which illustrates their involvement in the minting process, at least at a supervisory level. Such a signature served undoubtedly a political purpose; by recording the identity of the official(s) in charge of the minting process, it represented an additional guarantee against tampering with the weight and purity of the coins. The moneyers were responsible for selecting the types of the dies. Because of its political implication, this powerful instrument of propaganda was later taken over by the emperor and his aides, or, on occasion, by a more or less submissive senate.

Although the moneyers' names no longer appear on imperial coinage, the office is attested in numerous inscriptions until the beginning of the third century A.D. and ranks close to the bottom of the senatorial career.[291] It is thought that during the Principate moneyers were appointed by the emperor, but it is not clear which functions they had. Minting policy was implemented by the imperial household, and the position of moneyer may have been a sine-

---

[289] A.M. Burnett, "The Authority to Coin in the Late Republic and Early Empire," *NC* 137 (1977) 37-63, esp. 37-44, convincingly argues that the moneyers were appointed by the consuls—they were often relatives of the consuls in charge—and that they should be regarded as the consuls' agents, acting within the limits of the consuls' *imperium*. Cf. also H.B. Mattingly, *AIIN* 29 (1982) 9-16.

[290] Pomponius (*sing. enchiridii*) *Dig.* 1.2.2.30: "Constituti sunt eodem tempore et quattuorviri qui curam viarum agerent, et triumviri monetales aeris argenti auri flatores, et triumviri capitales qui carceris custodiam haberent, ut cum animadverti oporteret interventu eorum fieret."

[291] *ILS* IV, *indices* p. 412. Cf. J.R. Jones, "Mint Magistrates in the Early Roman Empire," *BICS* 17 (1970) 70-78, with a complete prosopography. Jones points out that the abbreviation *IIIviri* is rendered as *tresviri* in the Republican period and as *triumviri* during the Empire.

cure or a test of loyalty: a successful (i.e. problem-free) tenure of office was a first step towards the consulship.[292]

During the Republican and Augustan periods, the *tresviri monetales* were not the only magistrates entitled to sign coins. The prerogative was sometimes claimed by other Roman magistrates (such as the praetors, quaestors, or aediles), by municipal magistrates (*duoviri*), or by proconsular governors and military commanders in the field.[293] In some cases, these magistrates, especially those with *imperium*, were substituting for the authority behind the moneyers and were in charge of *ad hoc* mints. Thus, some coins struck in Spain bear the legend PERMISSV AVGVSTI; others, produced at Gergis, display the legend PERM L VOLVSI PROCOS; finally, the *IIviri coloniae deducendae*, who founded the colony of Narbo in Southern Gaul, signed an issue struck by five moneyers.[294]

b. *Julius Caesar's praepositi*

The moneyers were eclipsed during the Principate by the appearance and rise of other officials picked among the members of the imperial household (slaves and freedmen) or belonging to the growing equestrian bureaucracy. The trend started at the end of the Republican period, when Julius Caesar engaged in an act of blatant arrogance—described as no less than *dominatio*, *licentia*, and *arrogantia*—by appointing his own slaves at the head of the mint and of the fiscal administration.[295] The nature of the functions of these slaves *praepositi* is unclear, but it would be surprising if they were mere technicians or mint workers. It would certainly be more sensible to picture them supervising the workshop(s) or even in charge of the whole organization of the minting process.[296]

---

[292] J.M. Jones, *A Dictionary of Ancient Roman Coins* (London 1990) 187-90, s.v. mint magistrates. A.M. Burnett, *NC* 137 (1977) 54 suggests that the imperial moneyers were attached to one side of a dual minting system in which the bronze coinage would have been under the control of the senate and carried out by the moneyers, while the precious metal coinage would have been under the control of the emperor and his aides.

[293] M.H. Crawford, *RRC* II (1974) 598-604, who points out that some of these issues might have been illegal.

[294] M. Crawford, *RRC* I (1974) 282; and A.M. Burnett, *NC* 137 (1977) 58-59.

[295] Suet., *Iul.* 76.3: "Praeterea monetae publicisque vectigalibus peculiares servos praeposuit."

[296] C.H.V. Sutherland, "*Monetae. . .peculiares servos praeposuit*: Julius Caesar and the Mint of Rome," *NC* 145 (1985) 243-45 dates the event referred to in this passage to the mid-40's B.C. and rightly considers that "their (= the appointed

Suetonius, who reports the story, was obviously shocked by the intrusion of slaves in an area which was until then regarded as the preserve of the senatorial aristocracy. Caesar may have signaled his readiness to work with whoever appeared loyal to him, regardless of the social background of the appointee. Besides, the rupture with the past was not so drastic as it sounded, since the practice of personal appointment by the highest magistrate(s) of the state was long established (cf. above). In their capacity of private agents of the dictator, the *servi peculiares praepositi* represented the first instance of the gradual replacement of Republican magistracies by personal appointees of the ruler. And in fact, this trend is emphasized by Suetonius, who reports other rumors pertaining to the same phenomenon: Caesar had allegedly planned to move his capital to Alexandria or Troy, to entrust the management (*procuratio*) of the city of Rome to his friends, and to live off the diverted resources of the empire while pressuring Italy with his levies.[297] By appointing dependents and friends as *praepositi* and *procuratores*, Caesar acted as the quintessential tyrant treating the Roman state as his private property. The move conveyed an unambiguous political message to his opponents by showing that the empire could survive without the cooperation of a distrusted political class. In this particular instance, agency proved to be an efficient alternative to Republican institutions.

c. *equestrian procurators*

By the time of Trajan, a new official is attested in inscriptions: the *procurator monetae*, of equestrian rank.[298] He was probably a general

---

slaves') task can only have been to implement policy for the mint; and questions of policy would necessarily include the quantity and quality of coinage to be struck, its apportionment between the coinage-metals, and the types it bore;" and *idem*, *Roman History and Coinage, 44 B.C. –A.D. 69* (Oxford 1987) 1-3.

[297] Suet., *Iul.* 79.3: "Quin etiam varia fama percrebruit migraturum Alexandream vel Ilium, translatis simul opibus imperii exhaustaque Italia dilectibus et procuratione urbis amicis permissa."

[298] M. Peachin, "The *procurator monetae*," *NC* 146 (1986) 94-106 lists thirteen entries from the early second to the mid-third century, and five more in the next century (until 371-2). This list rightly does not include (101, n. 37) C. Iulius Quadratus Bassus, who was engaged in a senatorial career and attested as ἐπιμελη[τὴς μονήτη]ς (or [...χαλκο]ῦ) χρυσοῦ ἀργύρου χαράγματος under Domitian (*AE* 1933, no. 268, Pergamum). This man should be regarded as a *IIIvir a.a.a.f.f.* rather than as a (*pro*)*curator* of the reorganized imperial mint. Cf. C.H.V. Sutherland, "The Personality of the Mints under the Julio-Claudian Emperors," *AJP* 68 (1947) 47-63, esp. 51, n. 11; and A.N. Sherwin-White, *The Letters of Pliny: A Historical and Social Commentary* (Oxford 1966) 274-75, discussing Pliny, *Ep.* 4.9.1.

administrator, but there is no evidence that he had a say in the selection of coin types or in decisions pertaining to the quantity and quality—in terms of coin denomination and metal purity—of the coinage to be produced annually to meet the needs of the imperial government.[299] All modern scholars agree that the first occurrence of a *procurator monetae* in the sources provides nothing more than a *terminus ante quem* and that the office could have been created before the reign of Trajan. The lack of evidence can be attributed to chance, to the fact that second-century inscriptions are more numerous than earlier ones, and also to the possibility that the position might have been held first by imperial freedmen.[300]

The truth is that, from Augustus to Trajan, we know next to nothing about the administration of the imperial mint. The textual evidence is limited to an allusion by Statius to the freedman Claudius Etruscus, who reportedly held the position of *a rationibus* from 55 to 82.[301] The duties of the *a rationibus* included the *cura domus Augustianae*, the *cura statuarum*, and the *cura monetae*, all three tasks implying the apportionment of precious metals. The *procurator monetae* cannot have displaced the *a rationibus* (or *rationalis*), since the latter position is still attested in the late third century: during the reign of Aurelian, the so-called revolt of the moneyers was instigated by the *rationalis* Felicissimus, who was probably a freedman (in spite of Aurelian's alleged statement in the letter).[302]

---

[299] M. Peachin, *NC* 146 (1986) 104-05 argues that such decisions were made by the (*procurator* or *magister*) *a rationibus* or by his successor, the *rationalis summae rei* and, in the fourth century, the *comes sacrarum largitionum*.

[300] G. Boulvert, *Esclaves et affranchis impériaux sous le Haut-empire romain. Rôle politique et administratif* (Naples 1970) 65-67 is sceptical about the employement of imperial slaves in the Roman mint under Augustus and supports Hirschfeld's view that the *triumviri monetales* were still in charge of all denominations during the Principate. According to Boulvert, the technical task was perhaps farmed out to private contractors (*ILS* 1470 = *CIL* VI 8455, but the inscription is to be dated certainly two centuries later, cf. below). The same author suggests (264) that in the second century A.D. the equestrian procurator was assisted by a freedman procurator, which is quite sensible, but it is worth stressing that there is not any more evidence for such a position in the second century than in the first.

[301] Statius, *Silv.* 3.3.103-105: "quod domini celsis niteat laquearibus aurum / quae divum in vultus igni formanda liquescat / massa, quid Ausoniae scriptum crepet igne Monetae." M. Peachin, *NC* 146 (1986) 104, n. 58 stresses that this text provides the only evidence about the connection between the *a rationibus* and the mint.

[302] SHA, *Aur.* 38.2-3: "auctore Felicissimo, ultimo servorum, cui procurationem fisci mandaveram;" Eutrop., *Breviarium* 9.14; Aur. Vict., *Caes.* 35.6; and *idem*,

The lack of evidence concerning mint administrators in Rome in the early first century, apart from the *triumviri monetales*, is also due to the fact that there was no mint in Rome issuing gold and silver coinage from the 20's B.C. to the 50's A.D.[303] During this period, the mint producing gold and silver coinage had been transferred to Lugdunum, and there is some evidence that imperial slaves were attached to the mint there.[304]

d. *conclusion*

During the Republic and the Principate, the administration of the Roman mint, and possibly of other mints as well, was entrusted to agents. Mint managers were at first junior magistrates, later members of the imperial household, and finally equestrian officials. Decisions concerning types, quantity, quality (purity), and denominations were usually made, or at least inspired, by the holder of the *cura monetae*, i.e. the magistrate (*consul* or *proconsul*) who appointed the mint manager, the senate, the emperor, or his finance minister (*a rationibus*). Departure from this principle could have dreadful consequences: meddling with coin types was a crime of high treason (*maiestas*), and tampering with the purity or weight was a crime akin to counterfeiting.[305]

Epit. 35.4. On the whole episode, cf. E. Bernareggi, *"Familia monetalis,"* NAC 3 (1974) 177-91, esp. 182-91.

[303] A.M. Burnett, *NC* 137 (1977) 61-62, and especially n. 143 (where he argues against the traditionally accepted date under Caligula for the return of the precious-metal mint to Rome). This move is linked to the decision of Augustus to renounce the consulship, and his concern to retain control of the gold and silver coinage through his *imperium proconsulare* (*ibid.* 57-60). Some temporary issues in precious metal are attested in Rome from 19 to 12 B.C., cf. C.H.V. Sutherland, *AJP* 68 (1947) 55; and J.D. Mac Isaac, *The Location of the Republican Mint of Rome and the Topography of the Arx of the Capitoline* (Diss. J. Hopkins Univ. 1987).

[304] Strabo, 4.3.2 (192), mentions such a mint at Lugdunum: καὶ γὰρ ἐμπορίῳ χρῶται, καὶ τὸ νόμισμα χαράττουσιν ἐνταῦθα τό τε ἀργυροῦν καὶ χρυσοῦν οἱ τῶν Ῥωμαίων ἡγεμόνες. It is not clear, however, whether he meant an imperial or proconsular mint, which in the case of Augustus did not matter since he had been granted an *imperium proconsulare* over the Gallic and Spanish provinces in 27 B.C. The existence of a servile staff is proved by *ILS* 1639 (= *CIL* XIII 1820, under Tiberius): "Nobilis Tib. / Caesaris Aug. / ser(vus) aeq(uator) monet(ae) / hic adquiescit / Iulia Adepta coniunx / et Perpetua filia d.s.d." Cf. A.M. Burnett, *NC* 137 (1977) 56 and 59. The mint at Lugdunum was protected by a unit of the urban cohort *ad monetam* attested in an inscription dated to the reign of Claudius (*ILS* 2130 = *CIL* XIII 1499).

[305] E. Bernareggi, *NAC* 3 (1974) 188-89 on the significance of the moneyers' revolt in 270-271.

While mint managers were expected to implement the political and economic policy defined by higher authorities, they still had important managerial decisions to make with regard to staff organization, technical aspects of production, bookkeeping, and subcontracting. The administrative structure of mints was in many ways similar to the hierarchic structure identified in the context of the *vilicus* system in agriculture, tax collection, etc., with a multilevel chain of command. It is not the place here to discuss the relationship between the general administrators of the mint and those holding the authority to strike coinage,[306] but some attention should be paid to the lower level, i.e. the internal organization of the mint.

3. *Internal organization of the mint*

The technical and administrative staff of the Roman mint is known through some eighteen Latin inscriptions of Imperial dates, but since most of the positions mentioned in these documents are not attested otherwise, we have to rely on a linguistic analysis of the terminology used in these documents in order to determine what these positions represented.[307]

a. *officinatores*

The staff was composed in part of *officinatores* or mint workers with no specification. One of the Trajanic inscriptions found on the Caelian Hill, where the Roman imperial mint was presumably located, lists sixteen *officinatores* of libertine status, and nine other employees of servile status in a dedication to Fortuna.[308] These *officinatores* were attached to the imperial mint producing gold and silver coinage,[309] and the exact nature of their functions is not clear. The

---

[306] C.H.V. Sutherland, *AJP* 68 (1947) 47-63; and A.M. Burnett, *NC* 137 (1977) 37-63.

[307] R.A.G. Carson, "System and Product in the Roman Mint," in R.A.G. Carson–C.H.V. Sutherland (eds.), *Essays in Roman Coinage Presented to H. Mattingly* (Oxford 1956) 227-39; M.R. Alföldi, "Epigraphische Beiträge zur römischen Münztechnik bis auf Konstantin den Grossen." *SNR* 39 (1958-59) 35-48; J. Lafaurie, "*Familia monetaria,*" *BSFN* 27 (1972) 267-71; and E. Bernareggi, *NAC* 3 (1974) 177-91.

[308] *ILS* 1634 (= *CIL* VI 43, 28 Jan. 115).

[309] "officinatores monetae / aurariae argentariae / Caesaris n(ostri)." A.M. Burnett, *NC* 137 (1977) 53 uses this inscription as evidence for a separate mint for gold and silver coinage. G. Boulvert (1970) rightly assumes that these *officinatores* were members of the imperial household.

term *officinator* might be a generic term including everybody working in a workshop (*officina*), from foremen and skilled workers down to mere handworkers (*mediastini*), but a comparison with the evidence pertaining to other industries (for instance, brick- and tilemaking) and other relevant documents concerning mint personnel indicates that it was not the case.[310] *Officinatores* may have performed a managerial function, for instance as supervisors of individual *officinae*.[311]

The same inscription indicates that the *officinatores* were possibly subordinated to an *optio et exactor auri argenti aeris* named Felix, and to a mere *optio* named Labanus, both of libertine status. The wording of the text of the inscription suggests that both were included among the *officinatores*. The rank of *optio* has a military flavor,[312] but, since the term is already used to designate a civilian function ("assistant") by Plautus (*Asin.* 101), it is not clear which sector borrowed it from the other (civilian from military, or *vice versa*). It is probable that Felix ranked higher than Labanus. The former combined the rank of *optio* with the position of *exactor*,[313] which suggests that he was the official in charge of collecting precious metals in bullion form from a different department (*fiscus* or *aerarium?*) and of handing them over to mint workers to strike coins. One could wonder why a foreman attached to the mint producing gold and silver coinage should have been entrusted with the collection of bronze, but A.M. Burnett rightly points out that the purity of the silver coinage called for an input of ca. 20 percent of bronze.[314] In addition, the hierarchic superiority of Felix over Labanus is emphasized by the fact that the same Felix appears in two other dedications, once alone and once with another group of mint workers.[315]

---

[310] Cf. my paper "Workshop Managers," in W.V. Harris (ed.), *The Inscribed Economy* (1993) 173, nn. 12-15; and below.

[311] R.A.G. Carson (1956) 234, against M.R. Alföldi, *SNR* 39 (1958-1959) 42, n. 33. J. Lafaurie, *BSFN* 27 (1972) 269 considers that *officinatores* belonged to the clerical staff and may have included some specialists, such as accountants and engravers.

[312] C.H.V. Sutherland, *AJP* 68 (1947) 48-49; M. Peachin, *NC* 146 (1986) 105, n. 65.

[313] Cf. also *AE* 1927, no. 87 (Greek inscription from Perinthos, Thracia, III/IV?).

[314] A.M. Burnett, *NC* 137 (1977) 54 considers that this inscription, which he wrongly dates to the reign of Hadrian on the basis of a misprint in *ILS* I, p. 344 (read, n. 2 to nos. 1634-1635, 115 instead of 119), "does not, however, prove a single system of administration for all three coin metals."

[315] *CIL* VI 42 and 44 (to Apollo and Hercules, respectively).

b. *technical staff*

The second inscription[316] was dedicated by Felix on the same day (28 Jan. 115) in cooperation with the *signatores, suppostores,* and *malliatores.* This second group of mint workers was composed of thirty freedmen and thirty slaves, plus three other people of uncertain status. It is remarkable that, even though all names in both lists[317] are very common, there are very few overlaps (Primigenius among the freedmen, and Zosimus and Helius among the slaves), which unambiguously indicates that the two groups are distinct from one another. The conclusion to be drawn from this fact is that the term *officinatores,* found in *CIL* VI 43, did not include the skilled workers listed in *CIL* VI 44, whose functions will be analyzed below.

The arrangement of the list, in four columns (I-IV) underneath category labels, might reflect the composition of the second group. In Column I (*signatores*) are listed seventeen workers, namely twelve freedmen and five slaves. In Column II (*suppostores*) are listed eleven workers, namely seven freedmen and four slaves. In Column III (*malliatores*) are listed eighteen workers, namely eleven freedmen and seven slaves.[318] Column IV is usually understood as an extension of Column III and therefore lists additional *malliatores,* fourteen slaves and three other persons of uncertain status who might form a separate category.[319] One of these three workers (Asclepius) was certainly a slave of Felix. G. Boulvert thinks that they were freeborn (*ingenui*), but their names (Sallustius Hermes / Mevius Cerdo / Asclepius Felicis) suggest that the first two were freedmen who did not belong to the imperial household (Hermes and Cerdo are *cognomina* with a definite servile flavor, and Sallustius and Mevius are *gentilicia* well attested in the second century A.D.). They had been set apart probably because of their status of outsiders (*mercennarii?*), and Boulvert correctly suggests that they were hired, probably by the

---

[316] *ILS* 1635 = (*CIL* VI 44).

[317] *ILS* 1634 and 1635 (= *CIL* VI 43 and 44).

[318] It seems that Column III could be either considered independently from Columns II and IV, or linked with Column IV. The second solution has been more popular on the basis of the succession of freedmen and slaves. Cf. M.R. Alföldi, *SNR* 39 (1958-1959) 36-38; and J. Lafaurie, *BSFN* 27 (1972) 269. As the photograph shows, it is unlikely that Columns II and III should be grouped together, because each of the first three columns is carefully aligned just below the respective titles designating the categories of workers, cf. J.S. and A.E. Gordon, *Album of Dated Latin Inscriptions* II (Berkeley/L.A. 1964) 38-40, Pl. 77b.

[319] G. Boulvert (1970) 265 and 266, n. 22.

manager, to perform particularly exhausting jobs. Thus, we end up with seventeen *signatores*, eleven *suppostores*, and thirty-two (thirty-five) *malliatores*, with a rough ratio of 2:1:3. Another solution would be to read the four columns separately, with respectively seventeen *signatores*, eleven *suppostores*, eighteen *malliatores*, and fourteen (or seventeen) additional workers (*mediastini?*), whose status (slaves or hired workers) implies the performance of menial jobs. The ratio then becomes approximately 3:2:3:3. Since one cannot exclude the possibility that a typical workday at the mint was divided into shifts of uneven lengths between categories of workers, it is unclear whether these figures and ratios are significant, and whether they carry some information about the organization of the work.

A short description of the respective functions provides a better understanding of the organizational structure of workshops. The task of *malliatores* seems to be self-evident. They were the workers wielding the hammer (*malleus*) and striking ready-made cast flans with a reverse die. If all *malliatores* from Column III were working simultaneously, there would have been eighteen anvils side by side in the mint. If one counts the workers in Column IV among the *malliatores*, the number of anvils goes up to thirty-two (or thirty-five). It is possible, however, that given the exhausting nature of the work the workers operated through rotation, with two or three *malliatores* per anvil.[320] The number of anvils would then be somewhere between eleven and seventeen, which corresponds to the respective numbers of *suppostores* and *signatores* in the inscription.

Suppostores were probably in charge of laying, and holding by means of tongs, the hot flans on the anvil where the obverse die was fixed and probably to take the new coins off the anvil after they had been struck.[321] It has been suggested, on the basis of telling "misstrikes," that several coins could be struck simultaneously.[322] The

---

[320] T.F. Carney, "The Working of the Roman Mint," *New Zealand Numismatic Journal* 10.5 (Dec. 1961) 154-58, esp. 156-57 states that the actual process of striking implies an upper die struck by two *malliatores*, an operation which would account for the high relief of coins especially in the mid-first century A.D.

[321] I do not follow G. Boulvert (1970) 265 who thinks that *suppostores* were in charge of melting the metal and preparing the flans, which I believe to be the function of the *flaturarii* (cf. below). Lafaurie, *BSFN* 27 (1972) 270 suggests that the *suppostores* were in charge of weighing the coins.

[322] M. Crawford, *RRC* II (1974) 582. An interesting case, dating to the early period of Roman coinage (286-268 B.C.), is provided by a group of coins (*as*) still attached together by melted metal, cf. F. Panvini Rosati, *La moneta di Roma re-*

necessity to adjust a line of reverse dies above flans lying upon obverse dies would have required the cooperation of two *suppostores* for
each strike, but there is no evidence supporting such a ratio (2:1 of
suppostores to *malliatores*), unless one speculates that the workers in
Column IV were assigned as assistants to official *suppostores*. Thus,
the personnel listed in Columns II and IV would make up to fourteen pairs of *suppostores*.

The role of the *signatores* is more problematic. The *Oxford Latin
Dictionary* suggests that they were responsible for stamping bars of
assayed metals. They might also have had something to do with
the addition of control marks, letters, numerals, or symbols on the
dies.[323] M. Crawford points out that the marks on the Republican
coinage of L. Sulla and L. Manlius Torquatus were scratched on the
dies "as a sort of last-minute extra" or that they were placed elsewhere than on the dies.[324] Thus, the *signatores* would have been instrumental in providing each issue with proper identification related
to the mint authority and to administrative subdivisions. The addition of a "signature," in the form of (abbreviated) names and various types of marks, constituted an intermediary stage between the
process of die engraving by *scalptores* and the actual striking of the
coins.[325]

The *scalptores*, or die engravers, formed their own unit, which was
headed by a *praepositus* assisted by a deputy (*adiutor*).[326] During the

---

pubblicana. Storia e civiltà di un popolo. Bologna 17 aprile – 22 maggio 1966 (Catalogo)
(Bologna 1966) 35, Pl. IV, no. 15, cited by L. Tondo, "Una officina monetaria
romana a Gubbio?" *SE* 53 (1985) [1987] 141-42.

[323] For the purpose of marks, letters, numerals, and symbols, which are also
found in connection with amphora production (cf. Chapter Four), see O. Picard,
"L'administration de l'atelier monétaire de Thasos au IVe siècle," *RN* 29 (1987)
7-14, who suggests, in connection with Greek coinage, that the symbols may reflect
a production by phases and were probably meant to facilitate the administrative
control over the production.

[324] M.H. Crawford, "Control-marks and the Organization of the Roman
Republican Mint," *PBSR* 34 (1966) 18-23, esp. 22.

[325] I do not follow Boulvert's suggestion ([1970] 266) that *signatores* were doing
the same job as *scalptores*. A similar view is shared by H. Zehnacker, *Moneta.
Recherches sur l'organisation et l'art des émissions monétaires de la République romaine
(289-31 av. J.-C.)* (Rome 1973) 55, n. 5.

[326] *ILS* 1638 (= *CIL* VI 8464, Rome, probably under the reign of Hadrian or
Antoninus Pius). The imperial freedman, P. Aelius Felix, also called Novellius,
atiutor (sic) *praepos(iti) scalptorum sacrae monetae* is certainly a different person from the
optio et exactor mentioned above (whose complete name, as a freedman of Trajan,
would have been M. Ulpius Felix. The abbreviation can also be filled as *adiutor*

Republican period, at least, it seems that homogeneity of style was not required, and that the die engravers attached to the mint were divided into two main schools and might have supplied different workshops (*officinae*, cf. below).

The preparation of the flan was entrusted to *flaturarii*,[327] and it seems that this task was sometimes farmed out to contractors: an inscription, dated to A.D. 115, lists five imperial freedmen as *conduc[tores] flaturae argen[tar](iae) monetae Cae[saris]*.[328] The melting process was not necessarily always strictly divided by metal, since around the same period, one M. Ulpius Symphorus, a freedman of the emperor Trajan, advertised himself as *flaturarius auri et argenti moneta[e]*.[329] Nothing indicates that M. Ulpius Symphorus was acting as a contractor rather than as the emperor's agent. As for other public services, the performance of specific tasks could be either under direct management or farmed out to contractors, and both systems of management may have been applied successively to any specific operation.

The case of the *flaturarii* demonstrates that imperial servants were not barred from bidding for public contracts. This is confirmed by the case of Hermes, an imperial freedman attested as *[man]ceps (a)erariae mo[ne]tae*, which means that he had contracted—perhaps on behalf of a company or partnership—for the management of some (or all) operations pertaining to the production of bronze coinage.[330] When it was the case, it is not clear who had the competence to let the contract out. Likely candidates are the imperial *procurator monetae* for gold and silver coinage, and the *triumviri monetales* for bronze coinage. In a later period (third century), the equestrian P. Calvius Sp. f. Iustus had contracted for the management of five workshops (*officinae*) producing bronze coinage and for the casting of silver.[331]

(*alicuius*, e.g., *procuratoris*) *p(rae)p(ositus) scalptorum*, in which case the foreman of the die engravers would have been the deputy of the mint administrator.

[327] Some *flaturarii* attested in inscriptions might not be connected with the mint, but with some metal industry, cf. *CIL* VI 9418-9420 and *CIL* X 3967 (cf. below).

[328] *CIL* VI 791.

[329] *CIL* VI 8456.

[330] *CIL* XIV 3642 (Tibur).

[331] *ILS* 1470 (= *CIL* VI 8455): "mancips (*sic*) officinarum aerariarum quinquae (*sic*) item flaturae argentariae." For the date, cf. A.M. Burnett, *NC* 137 (1977) 53, n. 96, based on the existence of five *officinae* in Rome, which, according to him, did not occur before the third century A.D. Even though the Roman state was not issuing a silver coinage any more by then, billion coinage (*antoninianus*)

The technical staff of the imperial mint also included one or several *aequatores*, who were probably responsible for checking the homogeneity of the coins, in terms of their physical appearance.[332] It cannot be excluded that *aequatores* were also—or rather—in charge of testing the weight, purity, and shape of the flans before coinage. It has been suggested that the term might refer to a totally different function, i.e. the balancing of accounts,[333] which should have been treated then in the next section (clerical staff). In conclusion, one should mention that the various technical operations described above are represented on a wall painting from Pompeii (House of the Vettii), which shows, from right to left, Cupids melting, casting, and weighing flans before striking under the supervision of Iuno Moneta.[334]

c. *clerical staff*

After the coins had been physically produced, they had to be tested, stored, and distributed. These functions were entrusted to *nummularii*, who were supervised by a *superpositus*[335] and seem to have been distinct from, and possibly ranked above, *officinatores*.[336] Thus, in a twofold inscription dated to the reign of Trajan, M. Ulpius Secundus was an *off(icinator) mon(etae)* when he buried his wife Claudia Festa and a *nummularius offic(inarum* or *-inae?) monetae* at the time of his death.[337] Each denomination was treated separately, as two of

---

requested the input of both bronze and silver. For the number of *officinae* at various periods, cf. below.

[332] *ILS* 1639 (= *CIL* XIII 1820, Lugdunum, under Tiberius).

[333] J.M. Jones (1990) 7, s.v. *aequator*.

[334] E. Bernareggi, *NAC* 3 (1974) 177-79 (Photograph in M. Rostovtzeff, *The Social and Economic History of the Roman Empire*[2] [Oxford 1957] 96, Pl. XV, 3, who regards them as goldsmiths [*aurifices*]).

[335] *ILS* 1637 (= *CIL* VI 8461). The deceased, C. Iulius Thallus, who was at 33 a "superpositus auri monetae numulariorum," had probably acquired some technical and managerial skills while he was the manager (*actor?*) of the lead workshops of the Regio Trastiberina and the Trigarium ("qui egit officinas plumbarias Trastiberina (regione) et Trigari").

[336] *ILS* 1636 (= *CIL* VI 298) is a dedication by the "officinatores et nummularii officinarum argentariarum familiae monetari[ae]."

[337] *CIL* VI 8463a and b. Cf. G. Boulvert (1970) 266, n. 21, following F. Vittinghof (*PW* 17 [1937] col. 2044, s.v. *officinatores monetae*), fills the abbreviation "offic( )" with "offic(inator)." According to Boulvert, the two functions were held successively (in progressive or regressive order), and it is unlikely that *nummularii* should be counted among *officinatores*.

the inscriptions cited above seem to suggest.[338] J. Andreau is certainly right to consider the *nummularii* as employees ("essayeurs-changeurs") dealing with coins rather than with flans, as the word *nummus* ("coin" from the Greek νόμος, "statutory unit of currency") would suggest. The role of distributor can be inferred from what is known about private *nummularii* in other areas of business life. I am skeptical about the existence of another category of controller, the *probator*, at least during the Principate. The existence of such a function has been conjectured by J. Lafaurie on the basis of a text by Africanus who cites the Augustan jurist Mela.[339] The passage, however, clearly indicates that the *probatio* was performed by the *nummularius* with whom the money was deposited. Admittedly, the title of *probator* is attested on a stamped gold bullion from Naples,[340] but both the onomastic and the terminology point toward a fourth-century date, or even later.

Finally, strict accounting was necessary in order to keep track of the quantity of metal (in flans or bullions) delivered to the mint and of coins leaving it. This task was entrusted to *dispensatores (rationis monetae)* who were always slaves. They handled the cash once it was ready for use and probably did the bookkeeping.[341]

All mint workers and employees belonged to the *familia monetalis* (or *monetaria*).[342] Even though most known mint workers belong to the imperial household, it seems that provincial mints could employ public slaves.[343] As noted above, they were organized by units of

---

[338] J. Andreau, *La vie financière dans le monde romain. Les métiers de manieurs d'argent (IVe siècle av. J.-C.-IIIe siècle ap. J.C.)* (Rome 1987) 207-09. The metal specification does not always appear in the title, cf. *CIL* XIII 11311 (Trier), where Anulinus Polibius introduces himself as *nummularius s(acrae) m(onetae) Au[g](usti) n(ostri)*.

[339] Africanus (8 *quaest.*) *Dig.* 46.3.39: "Si, soluturus pecuniam tibi, iussu tuo signatam eam apud nummularium, quoad probaretur, deposuerim, tui periculi eam fore Mela libro decimo scribit." Cf. J. Lafaurie, *BSFN* 27 (1972) 268.

[340] Published in 1941 by L. Breglia and cited by Lafaurie (270): FLAVIVS FLAVIANVS PROBATOR SIGNAVIT AD DIGMA / LVCIANVS OBRYZVM PRIMVS SIGNAVIT. Cf. also *AE* 1976, no. 590a-d (379–383).

[341] *ILS* 1633 (= *CIL* VI 239) and *CIL* VI 8454. Both are imperial slaves. Cf. G. Boulvert (1970) 429-33.

[342] *ILS* 1633 (= *CIL* VI 239) and *ILS* 1636 (= *CIL* VI 298).

[343] Ulpianus (7 *de off. procons.*) *Dig.* 48.13.8 *pr.*: "Qui, cum in moneta publici operarentur, ..." Ulpianus discusses the *crimen peculatus* (regarded as different from forgery): were found guilty of it those who steal coins from the imperial mint, and those mint workers who "freelanced." On stealing coins as a method of resistance on the part of slaves, cf. K.R. Bradley, "*Servus Onerosus*: Roman Law and the Troublesome Slave," *Slavery & Abolition* 11 (1990) 135-57, esp. 142 and 155, n. 32.

specialists (*signatores, malliatores, suppostores, flaturarii, scalptores, aequatores, nummularii*, etc.) and were subordinated to a procurator assisted by *praepositi, superpositi, optiones, adiutores*, and *officinatores*. Some fourth-century evidence suggests that the chain of command was not drastically modified as a result of third-century upheavals in the monetary system and of the major reforms introduced by Diocletian and his colleagues: a dedication was set up in honor of the emperor Constantine by Valerius Rusticus, *rat(ionalis) s(ummae) r(ei)* with rank of *vir perfectissimus*, through the agency ("curante") of one Valerius Pelagius, *v(ir) e(gregius) s(acrae) m(onetae) u(rbis)*. The latter was obviously a procurator of the mint, and he reportedly acted jointly with the managers of individual units or workshops ("una cum p(rae)p(ositis) et officinatoribus").[344]

d. *competing officinae*

While the inscriptions demonstrate that the personnel of the mint was divided into units of specialists, the coins themselves provide evidence for another kind of internal division, i.e. into units of production. This pattern was not explicitly recorded on the coins before the middle of the third century A.D., but it seems to have been in use already during the Republican period, at least intermittently. The mint was organized by metal denomination and by workshops (*officinae*), the number and size of which might have increased just before the middle of the third century as a result of the debasement of silver coinage, which had to be compensated by larger issues of billon coinage. The history of this aspect of mint organization has been studied by several scholars. P.V. Hill traces five *officinae* from 98 until 107, seven in 107-108, five again from 109 until 128, six from 129 until 189, five again from 189 until 196, and six afterwards.[345] Most recently, R.A.G. Carson records the existence of six *officinae* striking coinage for Nero, Galba, Vitellius, Nerva,

---

[344] *CIL* VI 1145. *Praepositi* were sometimes confused with *procuratores*. Cf. M. Peachin, "*Praepositus* or *procurator*?" *Historia* 36 (1987) 248-49, discussing a possible mistake by Ammianus Marcellinus (22.11.9) about the title of Dracontius, the head of the mint at Alexandria in 363.

[345] P.V. Hill, *The Undated Coins of Rome (A.D. 98-148)* (London 1970) 2-5, pointing out that some of these *officinae* were entrusted to the care of some members of the imperial family. In view of the number of *officinae* identified during the reign of Trajan (sixteen freedmen and nine slaves in *CIL* VI 43), it is clear that each *officina* employed more than one *officinator*. One can think of joint managers, of different shifts, or of a division by metal or denomination.

Antoninus, Pertinax, Severus Alexander, Maximinus, Gordian I and II, and Balbinus and Pupienus. These six *officinae* would have been reduced to five under Pertinax, Didius Iulianus, and for the whole period between 193 and 196. Carson concludes that

> it is evident at a number of points in the imperial coinage that the mint of Rome operated as an organization of a specific number of *officinae* each producing coinage with a given reverse. The evidence for this theory, and specifically for an organization in six *officinae* comes in the reign of Philip when for the first time the antoniniani carry each the number of the six producing *officinae* marked by Roman numbers I to VI or Greek numerals A-S.[346]

As noted above, an equestrian entrepreneur had contracted for the management of five *officinae aerariae*.[347] Similarly, in the early fourth century, the short-lived mint at Ostia had on its staff a *praepositus mediastinorum de moneta oficina* (sic) *prima*,[348] from which one can infer the existence of several *officinae* (*secunda*, *tertia*, etc.). The Trajanic inscriptions expounded above show that minting was conducted as a very large—by ancient standards—industrial enterprise, carried out at times by dozens of employees organized along highly sophisticated lines, quite similar to the pattern developed in private concerns. The size of the enterprise, and the highly sensitive nature of its economic function, called for division into managerial units to facilitate control over the production, both in qualitative and quantitative terms.

Since the later evidence provides more detailed information about the organization of *officinae*, it is necessary to summarize first what is known in this period before turning to the earlier material. In the late Roman and early Byzantine periods, the minting of coins was the responsibility of the *comes sacrarum largitionum*, the successor of the *a rationibus* and *rationalis summae rei*.[349] His *officium* comprised the structure and personnel of both mint and treasury and was com-

---

[346] R.A.G. Carson, *Coins of the Roman Empire* (London/New York 1990) 14, 21, 23, 35, 46, 59-61, 73 (quotation), and 76-77. On the validity of this statement, cf. W.E. Metcalf's review of Carson's book (forthcoming in *ANSMusN*). Dr. Metcalf kindly brought this information to my attention.

[347] *ILS* 1470 (= *CIL* VI 8455).

[348] *ILS* 1640 (= *CIL* XIV 1878).

[349] M.F. Hendy, "The Administration of Mints and Treasuries, 4th to 7th Centuries, with an Appendix on the Production of Silver Plate," in *The Economy, Fiscal Administration and Coinage of Byzantium* (London 1989) 1-18.

posed of 446 members, divided into eighteen departments (*scrinia*). The staff was divided into two sectors (managerial and technical). Every individual staff member was assigned a rank or grade (out of seven). Equestrian officials, who held managerial functions, ranked as *perfectissimi, ducenarii, centenarii*, or *epistulares* and made up approximately one fourth (ca. 134 people) of the whole staff. Freedmen and slaves, who performed clerical or manual tasks, belonged to three lower categories (*Formae I-III*) and made up the remaining three fourths (ca. 312 people). The ratio between managerial and technical staff varied from one *scrinium* to another.[350]

In the fourth century, for instance, the gold mint was divided into ten workshops (*officinae*) operated by *aurifices solidorum*. On the basis of the charter of the personnel of the Palatine *officium* of the *comes sacrarum largitionum*[351] that shows thirty *aurifices solidorum* in *Forma II*, M.F. Hendy points out that each of the ten workshops was a unit of three workers, two *suppostores* holding the anvil die, and one *signator* handling the hammer die. The combination of two *suppostores* and one *malliator* is illustrated by a coin from the Vienna collection (Bundessammlung, Wien), the reverse of which shows two workers sitting on the floor and holding something upon a kind of stool, while a third worker, standing, wields a hammer.[352] The staff in charge of melting, shaping, weighing and correcting the flan did not belong to the actual *officinae*. The group of *aurifices solidorum* in the charter included one *ducenarius*, seven *centenarii*, six *epistulares*, and nine employees from *forma I*, who performed these and other administrative tasks. Furthermore, Hendy points out that the *officina* number (marks A-I on the reverse of coins) was

> engraved *after* the remainder of the reverse die had been cut, and (that) the occasional alteration of the number suggests that perhaps at the end of the day or of the work-session control of the dies reverted to an outside authority, whence they were redistributed—normally but not invariably—to the same *officinae* on the recommencement of work.[353]

Each metal was coined in separate workshops, possibly with differ-

---

[350] *Cod. Iust.* 12.23.7 (384); *Notitia Dignitatum* (ca. 400); Cassiodorus, *Variae* 12.6.7 (490-526). Cf. A.H.M. Jones, *LRE* I (1964) 583-86.

[351] A.H.M. Jones, *LRE* I (1964) 583, based on *Cod. Iust.* 12.23.7 (A.D. 384).

[352] J. Lafaurie, *BSFN* 27 (1972) 270 provides a photograph of this coin.

[353] M.F. Hendy (1989) 4. This remark, made in reference with the gold coinage, is not necessarily valid for other denominations.

ent administrative structures or internal organizations. For instance, it can be shown that the dies were kept outside the *officinae* for the gold coinage, but inside for the copper coinage. Since security requirements were not the same for each denomination, such discrepancies are not surprising.

In the fourth century, as before that time, a mint was administered by a procurator and divided into *officinae*. The terminology designating ranks and specialties might have changed over time, but it seems to me unlikely that the overall organization of the production of coinage underwent major changes, except for the increase in number and size of workshops in the third century.

Why did mint administrators maintain an internal division, based on a certain number of units of production, rather than simply increase or decrease the personnel involved in one single unit? According to D.W. Mac Dowall,

> the purpose of any officina system was clearly to divide the work at the mint between a number of responsible divisions of manageable proportions, and to exercise a degree of administrative control over the coins produced by different divisions. The purpose of any such organisation would be lost if mint inspectors were not able to distinguish easily the product of differing officinae to apportion blame for any lapse from standards.[354]

The *officina* system is certainly the product of some sophisticated managerial policy. Admittedly, quality control could be achieved none the less if the minting of coins was concentrated in one single unit of production, for instance by giving each of the mint workers involved in the actual process of striking a personal die symbol. It seems, however, that the dies were returned to a central depository and reissued at random to workers on the next workday. Thus, patterns of die links lead P. Bastien to assume the existence in the late third century A.D. of a central room where dies were stored every night before being redistributed randomly to any *officina* the next morning. Because obverse-die links are more frequent than reverse-die links (one obverse die being connected with several reverse dies), Bastien suggests that reverse dies, bearing the mark of the *officinatores*, were returned to the same *officina* or stayed in the workshop

---

[354] D.W. Mac Dowall, "The Organisation of the Julio-Claudian Mint at Rome," in R.A.G. Carson–C.M. Kraay (eds.), *Scripta nummaria romana. Essays Presented to H. Sutherland* (London 1978) 32-46, esp. 33.

overnight while obverse dies, bearing the portrait of the emperor, were stored properly for protection.[355]

How early is this division into separate units of production attested? In his study of the coinage of Galba, C.M. Kraay observes that three, possibly five (A-E), units were active simultaneously. These *officinae* would have been self-contained units placed under the control of one of the moneyers. One *officina*, however, seems to have developed as a separate mint at an early stage, and could have been located elsewhere (in Gaul or in Spain). The same author remarks that "the continuous activity of *officinae* from reign to reign should not be expected. The organization must have involved a very small technical staff, including both administrative and metallurgical experts, which could be rapidly expanded by signing on casual labor." Accordingly, Kraay speculates that this pattern of subdivision of the mint could have been initiated in A.D. 64 and need not have been permanent.[356]

The process has been best observed by T.V. Buttrey in his study of the denarius coinage of P. Crepusius, one of the *tresviri monetales* in 82 B.C.[357] Crepusius issued massive quantities of coins, first individually, and then jointly with his colleagues, L. Marcius Censorinus and C. Mamilius Limetanus. The obverse bears a unidentified laureate head (representing perhaps Apollo or Jupiter Feretrius) alone or with one of twenty-four symbols and/or one of twenty-one letters (A-X), which makes up a total of 479 different obverse dies. The reverse bears a horseman brandishing a spear with one Roman numeral from 1 to 519, which corresponds to the number of reverse dies.

Symbols, letters, and numerals provide the basis for establishing the order of Crepusius's coinage. Buttrey points out that the symbol groups were not struck one after the other, but that up to group 18 (symbol of a hooked staff) they were struck in pairs.[358] This suggests that two anvils or two sets of anvils were in operation simultaneously. Thus, it seems that the workplace was divided into two sections, i.e. either two *officinae* or two divisions of the same *officina*.

---

[355] P. Bastien, "Liaisons de coins de revers et officines des ateliers monétaires romains," *Cercle d'études numismatiques* 5.4 (Oct.-Dec. 1968) 73-78.

[356] C.M. Kraay, *The Aes Coinage of Galba* (New York 1956) 25-32 and 58-59.

[357] T.V. Buttrey, "The Denarii of P. Crepusius and Roman Republican Mint Organization," *ANSMusN* 21 (1976) 67-108.

[358] T.V. Buttrey, *ANSMusN* 21 (1976) 89.

Obverse dies never passed from one section to the other, whereas reverse dies were used indiscriminately in either section.[359]

This internal division is also reflected at the level of the style of the engraving. Two engravers (or two schools of engravers) were at work at the same time, one exhibiting a fine style and producing symbols with an agricultural or pastoral flavor, the other turning out dies of a less refined style with symbols representing divine attributes.[360] Finally, from group 18 to 24, Crepusius's coinage was struck at one (set of) anvil(s) only, while the other was used for the production of the joint issue of the moneyers of 82 B.C.[361]

The system was too idiosyncratic to convey any messages to the bearers of the coins, i.e. economic agents in general. The conclusion that it was meant for internal use is almost inescapable,[362] and the disparity of the marks from one issue to another suggests that they represented a decision by (one of) the moneyers. As to the meaning of the marks, Buttrey remarks that "since Crepusius's obverse letters or symbol-letter combinations are each unique to the die, as are the reverse numbers, the marks provide an easy identification of the individual die for bookkeeping, and a cumulative check on die production."[363] However, control of the quality and quantity of the output of the mint could be done without resorting to a two-anvil system. Why then did the moneyers resort to this type of organizational structure? Perhaps in order to facilitate the evaluation of the productivity of the workers. By having two (or more) autonomous units working side-by-side and doing the same thing, the managers could compare their respective outputs, reward the better unit, and put pressure on the worse one to improve its productivity. Internal competition was fostered by the division of the workforce into independent units of comparable size and composition.[364]

---

[359] M.H. Crawford, *PBSR* 34 (1966) 22 suggests, on the basis of the evidence provided by the Agrinion hoard, that the two-workshop system attested between 135 and 125 B.C. worked alternatively on a yearly basis. Other instances of dual systems point toward a division of *officinae* between moneyers.

[360] T.V. Buttrey, *ANSMusN* 21 (1976) 90-93.

[361] T.V. Buttrey, *ANSMusN* 21 (1976) 102.

[362] M.H. Crawford, *PBSR* 34 (1966) 22 comes to the same conclusion on the ground that the marks scratched on the issue of L. Sulla and L. Manlius Torquatus were not intended to survive on the coin.

[363] T.V. Buttrey, *ANSMusN* 21 (1976) 104.

[364] This interpretation has been suggested to me by Dr. W.E. Metcalf at a Seminar of the American Numismatic Society (Spring 1986). However, Buttrey (107) points out that the two-anvil system "is good evidence for a kind of organiza-

If one accepts the suggestion that the Roman mint, both during the Republic and the Empire, was divided into two or more *officinae* performing identical tasks, it is necessary to examine whether each of these *officinae* formed a managerial unit. If the administrative structure of the Roman mint were copied from the model provided by the management of agricultural estates—and the intensive division of labor and the four-level administrative structure offer some striking similarities—then we would expect to find an intermediate managerial level between the mint administrator (*triumviri monetales* or *procurator*) and the mint workers, which would be filled by a *vilicus* or any other official acting as unit manager.

The obvious candidate for this position is the *optio et exactor* attested in the Trajanic inscriptions examined in the previous section. This official is attested in dedications set up by at least two distinct groups of mint workers and it has been suggested that, as an imperial freedman, he was more likely to be an agent of the emperor than of the imperial procurator.[365]

As minting was carried out—at least until the end of the Republican period—in or near the temple of Iuno Moneta,[366] one may wonder whether the temple staff had anything to do with the management of the minting facilities. But the only known *aedituus de moneta* should be dated later than the removal of the mint from the temple of Iuno Moneta and therefore cannot be regarded as relevant in the context of mint organization. This inscription might at best provide the latest evidence for the existence of the temple of Iuno Moneta.[367]

---

tion control in the Republican mint, but not necessarily of deliberate subdivisions into officinae, each with its operational individuality if not autonomy.'' This is true, and the interpretation presented here remains speculative.

[365] M.R. Alföldi, *SNR* 39 (1958-59) 46 rightly points out that ''this official [= the *optio et exactor*] is an imperial freedman, whose agency secures complete imperial control of the mint.'' This type of *exactor* has nothing to do with the fourth-century official (*vir clarissimus*) attested as ''exactor auri et argenti provinciarum III'' (= Sicily, Sardinia, and Corsica) in an inscription from Atella (*Regio* I), cf. *ILS* 1216 (= *CIL* X 3732).

[366] J.D. Mac Isaac, *The Location of the Republican Mint of Rome and the Topography of the Arx of the Capitoline* (Diss. J. Hopkins Univ. 1987) esp. 111-16 and 124 argues that the Republican mint was located not on the Arx, but at its base, before its transfer to the Caelian in 47/46 B.C.

[367] *ILS* 3533 (= *CIL* VI 675, late first century A.D.), a joint dedication to Silvanus by Ti. Claudius Herma *aedituus de moneta*, by T. Flavius Evaristus and Ti. Claudius Sostratus, both *aeditui port*(*icus*) *Crep*(*ereiae?*), and by Sex. Caelius Encolpius.

As a working hypothesis, one should examine whether the *vilicus* system might be recognized in mint organization. The basis for such an investigation is to be found in Suetonius's remark that Julius Caesar treated the organization of both mint and tax collection in the same way.[368] As the *vilicus* system is well attested for the latter during the Principate, there may be some reason to think that the same system was applied to the former. Among recorded Italian *vilici*, there is one potential candidate for such a position. One Blastus, *vilicus ab III m*(?), was the servant of one Livineius Regulus, to be possibly identified with the *quattuorvir monetalis* of 42 B.C. or one of his sons.[369] The inscription was found in Rome and the abbreviation *ab III m*(?) has never been satisfactorily interpreted.

Another reason why the presence of *vilici* in a mint should not be surprising is that it seems that an *officina monetalis* was very much like an *officina plumbaria*, where lead material (pipes, etc.) was produced.[370] There is even one case where a member of the managerial or technical staff was transferred from one sector to the other: C. Iulius Thallus, who was in charge of some (imperial?) lead workshops located beyond the Tiber, became the foreman (*superpositus*) of the *nummularii* attached to the gold mint in Rome.[371] The evidence pertaining to the metal industry can supplement that concerning the mint: *vilici* are attested as managers of lead workshops. At Capua, a joint dedication was made by one Eutychus, *vili[cus] a plumbo* and one Euagogus, *a flam(ine?)*, who might have been one of the metal casters (*flaturarius*). A *vilicus plumbariorum* is also attested at Verona, and several *vilici* signed lead pipes from Bononia.[372]

If no *vilicus* can be securely identified in connection with the mint,

---

[368] Suet., *Iul.* 76.3. Cf. above.

[369] *CIL* VI 33400.

[370] C. Bruun, *The Water Supply of Ancient Rome. A Study of Roman Imperial Administration* (Helsinki 1991); and my paper "Workshop Managers," in W.V. Harris (ed.), *The Inscribed Economy* (1993) 177.

[371] *ILS* 1637 (= *CIL* VI 8461): "D(is) M(anibus) / fecit Mindia Helpis C. Iulio Thallo / marito suo bene merenti, qui egit / officinas plumbarias Transtiberina (regione) / et Trigari(o), superposito auri monetae / numulariorum, qui vixit ann(is) XXXIII m(ensibus) VI / ...."

[372] *CIL* X 3967 (Capua/*Regio* I); and *AE* 1946, no. 136 (Verona/*Regio* X); *CIL* XI 725 and 731-736; and *AE* 1976, no. 214 (Bononia/*Regio* VIII). These *vilici* were either public or imperial slaves or the agents of public contractors (*conductores, mancipes, redemptores*). A connection between the metal industry and the mint was suggested by J.D. Mac Isaac (1987) 111-16 in his attempt at localizing the mint at the base of the Arx, where metal workshops are known to have been located.

one should perhaps look through the inscriptions for another title that might designate the person in charge of a managerial unit. The first position that comes to mind is that of *officinator*. We have seen that it is difficult to figure out what their function was in the minting process. Perhaps we should think of a managerial role for them. This hypothesis would be consistent with what *officinatores* seem to be in other contexts, for instance in the brick and tile industry. Thus, Donatus, the imperial slave *officinator* who dedicated an inscription to the God Silvanus on the Caelian Hill, in the vicinity of the imperial mint, would be on a similar standing as the numerous *vilici* who dedicated their inscription to the same deity.[373]

The scarcity of evidence, however, leaves a great deal of uncertainty as to the title and function of managers of *officinae monetales*. The continuous existence of such managers seems to be supported by the above-mentioned fourth-century inscription which lists, next to the *rationalis summae rei*, a *proc(urator) s(acrae) m(onetae) u(rbis) una cum p(rae)p(ositis) et officinatoribus*.[374] The fourth-century *praepositi* could include all kinds of managers and foremen, but they are best understood in the light of Suetonius's remark about Caesar setting, in his capacity of self-appointed *curator monetae*, his own slaves as managers of the departments of the mint.

4. *Conclusion*

During the Republican period, mints were operated by a staff—which is never described in written sources—under the supervision of lower magistrates. Julius Caesar was the first to take over the organization of the mint, to the head of which he appointed his own slaves. It seems likely that the reform introduced at this time consisted in bringing in the *vilicus* system, although the title is never explicitly attested in the context of mint management. The subsequent division of power under Augustus between the emperor and the traditional institutions of the Roman state left the members of the *familia Caesaris* in charge of the gold and silver coinage. Second- and third-century inscriptions offer a glimpse of the social and technical

---

[373] *AE* 1909, no. 99, to be compared with *CIL* VI 586; 615; 619; 623; 662; 664; 666; 679; 696; 31010; etc. Cf. P.F. Dorcey, *The Cult of Silvanus* (Leiden 1992) 116–20.

[374] *CIL* VI 1145.

composition of the *familia monetalis* and reveal a sophisticated division of labor. Later material seems to confirm the result of die studies of some issues of Republican coinage pointing toward the division of the mint into several *officinae* for the purpose of establishing internal competition resulting in higher productivity. This last point is admittedly speculative.

F. Conclusion

Through these five studies I have tried to demonstrate how the *vilicus* system seems to have been applied indifferently in private, public, and imperial administration. In some cases, public servants are found supplementing private or imperial slaves and freedmen. The execution of administrative tasks was supervised by the magistrates of the Roman state or of Italian and provincial municipalities— these tasks often required a closer supervision by longer-term *curatores*—and ultimately by imperial officials (*procuratores* and *praefecti*) or army officers. The actual work was carried out by a more or less permanent, hierarchically organized staff composed of specialists and often owned by private contractors (*socii, conductores, mancipes, redemptores*), the state or a municipality (*servi publici*), or the emperor (*familia Caesaris*). Among these skilled workers, a few individuals were bound to be endowed with some financial and contractual power to allow them to carry out the day-to-day business without requiring the personal involvement of higher officials. Delegation had long been recognized to be the key to efficiency.

It is quite likely that the passage from one system to the other did not necessarily affect the actual management of these services at their lower level. The stability which resulted from such a structure of management partly accounts for the limited references in the literary sources to these administrative reforms.

Finally, it is clear that the managers of public or imperial facilities were usually appointed by representatives of the state/city or of the emperor. These representatives could have been Roman magistrates in the case of the administration of the Republican mint; during the Principate, however, state or city commissioners (senatorial or municipal *curatores*) and imperial officials (equestrian or freed *procuratores*) were undoubtedly responsible for such appointments. Consequently, one can wonder who would have been liable for the contracts negotiated by public or imperial *actores, vilici, officinatores,* and their likes. The question may sound idle, since it would be ludicrous to think that a customer of imperial baths who felt cheated by the slave manager would have dared sue the bath commissioner, not to mention the emperor. However, there were cases in which the contractual power of a public or imperial servant would have benefitted from the acknowledgement of the additional liability of his superior. Let us envisage the same public/imperial bath manager buying firewood to heat the installations. If he could not rely on his own organization to provide it, he had to approach a private supplier, thus competing with other potential buyers. What would have been the incentive of the supplier to deal with the public/imperial servant who could go back on his word with impunity, while the other buyers, principals or agents, could at least be sued in case of nonobservance of any of the provisions of the contract?

In this respect, a set of passages by the classical jurists Ulpianus et Paulus—which have usually been considered interpolated—should be looked at from a different prospective. Ulpianus says that if the appointment of a business manager has been made by a *procurator*, a *tutor*, or a *curator*, the principal remains liable to an *actio institoria*;[375] further on, he adds that an appointment made by an unauthorized administrator, once ratified, would be considered valid.[376] In connection with the first provision, Paulus states that the *procurator*—*tutor* and *curator* are left out—would be jointly liable to an *actio institoria*.[377] It is likely that the phrasing of these passages is post-classical,[378] which is not to say that the idea behind them should be discarded. Insofar as the emperor was theoretically a private individual looking after the interests of the Roman state on a voluntary basis and in a spirit of munificence and selfless dedication, the legal position of his representatives was not different from that of the agents of any other citizen: third contracting parties dealing

[375] Ulpianus (28 *ad ed.*) *Dig.* 14.3.5.18: "Sed et si procurator meus, tutor, curator, institorem praeposuerit, dicendum erit veluti a me praeposito dandam institoriam actionem."

[376] Ulpianus (28 *ad ed.*) *Dig.* 14.3.7 *pr.*: "Sed et si quis meam rem gerens praeposuerit et ratum habuero, idem erit dicendum."

[377] Paulus (30 *ad ed.*) *Dig.* 14.3.6: "Sed et in ipsum procuratorem, [si omnium rerum procurator est,] dari debebit institoria."

[378] P. Angelini, *Il procurator* (Milan 1971) 252, n. 297: "la parola *curator*, senza specificazioni, non può appartenere ad un classico." Cf. also S. Solazzi, "Procurator senza mandato," *RIL* 56 (1923) 735-47 (= *Scritti* II [Naples 1957] 569-78, esp. 569-70); and O. Behrends, "Die Prokuratur des klassischen römischen Zivilrechts," *ZRG* 88 (1971) 215-99, esp. 295-96.

with them had a legal remedy either against the agent (*actio directa*) or against the principal (*actio institoria/exercitoria/quod iussu/de in rem verso/de peculio/tributoria*).

Cases involving the agents of the state or of a municipality are admittedly more complicated. Although this is not the place to discuss the problems arising from the lack of corporate law in ancient Rome or the subtleties of the development of the juristic personality in Roman law, it is necessary to state a few points.[379] While the Roman state should be considered a necessary sovereign corporation governed by public law, towns were necessary corporations governed by private law. This point is explicitly stated by Gaius.[380] Internal matters were managed by the assembly of citizens, the council, and the magistrates (= organs), while external matters were dealt with by agents (*syndicus/actor*) representing the *municipium*.[381] By the late Republican period, towns were entitled to sue and liable to be sued, which implied the right to own, acquire, and tranfer property.[382] The liability of municipal *duumviri* and of the town itself, incurred in connection with the management of public affairs, was extended

---

[379] I follow J. Plescia, "The Development of the Juristic Personality in Roman Law," *Studi Sanfilippo* I (Milan 1982) 487-524.

[380] Gaius (3 *ad ed. prov.*) *Dig.* 50.16.16: "Eum qui vectigal populi Romani conductum habet, 'publicanum' appellamus. Nam 'publica' appellatio in compluribus causis ad populum Romanum respicit: civitates enim privatorum loco habentur."

[381] Gaius (3 *ad ed. prov.*) *Dig.* 3.4.1.1: "Quibus autem permissum est corpus habere collegii societatis sive cuiusque alterius eorum nomine, proprium est ad exemplum rei publicae habere res communes, arcam communem et actorem sive syndicum, per quem tamquam in re publica, quod communiter agi fierique oporteat, agatur fiat." Ulpianus (8 *ad ed.*) *Dig.* 3.4.2: "Si municipes vel aliqua universitas ad agendum det actorem, non erit dicendum quasi a pluribus datum sic haberi: hic enim pro re publica vel universitate intervenit, non pro singulis." Cf. also Paulus (9 *ad ed.*) *Dig.* 3.4.6; Ulpianus (5 *ad ed.*) *Dig.* 2.4.10.4; Ulpianus (48 *ad ed.*) *Dig.* 42.1.4.2; Maecianus (12 *fideicom.*) *Dig.* 36.4.12; and Iulianus (40 *dig.*) *Dig.* 36.1.28 *pr.* Cf. J. Plescia, *Studi Sanfilippo* I (1982) 505, n. 49.

[382] Ulpianus (10 *ad ed.*) *Dig.* 3.4.7 *pr.*: "Sicut municipum nomine actionem praetor dedit, ita et adversus eos iustissime edicendum putavit. Sed et legato, qui in negotium publicum sumptum fecit, puto dandam actionem in municipes." J. Plescia, *Studi Sanfilippo* I (1982) 506 considers that the praetor's edict referred to in this passage is to be dated to the period 80-50 B.C. Cf. also Marcianus (3 *inst.*) *Dig.* 1.8.6.1, about common property of towns (*theatra, stadia et similia, servi communes*). The right to manumit public slaves was enjoyed by the city council (*ordo*), but in the provinces the approval of the governor was necessary, cf. *Cod. Iust.* 7.8.1 (*Imp. Gordianus A. Epigono*). It goes back to the Republican period (Varro, *Ling.* 8.41), and was extended to all types of corporations (*collegia*) by Marcus Aurelius, cf. Ulpianus (5 *ad Sab.*) *Dig.* 40.3.1. Cf. W. Liebenam, *Städteverwaltung im römischen Kaiserreiche* (Leipzig 1900) 66-67.

beyond the year in office of the magistrates.[383] Finally, it is interesting to note that Macer and the emperors Alexander Severus and Diocletianus/Maximianus compare the state or a municipality (*res publica*) to a ward (*pupillus/-a*).[384] This evidence demonstrates that the administration of municipal property was governed by private law. Consequently, municipal commissioners (*curatores*) and public *actores/vilici* were in a similar legal position as private guardians and agents, respectively.[385] The principle of the liability of *curatores* could be regarded as an incentive for them to apply special care in the management of public funds.[386] Accessorily, it was perhaps more practical to bring a lawsuit against an individual, no matter how powerful, than against a community.

---

[383] Paulus (1 *ad ed. praet.*) *Dig.* 44.7.35.1: "In duumviros et rem publicam etiam post annum actio datur ex contractu magistratuum municipalium."

[384] Macer (2 *de appellationibus*) *Dig.* 49.1.9; *Cod. Iust.* 11.30.3 (*Imp. Alexander A. Saturnino*): "Rem publicam ut pupillam extra ordinem iuvari moris est." *Cod. Iust.* 2.53.4 (*Impp. Diocletianus et Maximianus AA. Prisciano*): "Res publica minorum iure uti solet ideoque auxilium restitutionis implorare potest." Cf. J. Plescia, *Studi Sanfilippo* I (1982) 505, n. 50.

[385] Cf. F. Jacques, *Le privilège de liberté* (Paris 1984) 267.

[386] J.C. Fant, *The curatores rei publicae in Italy, from their Inception to the Death of Commodus* (Diss. Univ. of Michigan 1976) 102-06.

CONCLUSION

The practice of doing business through agents predates the second century B.C. and was certainly not a Roman invention. There are numerous examples in Classical Greece illustrating this fact. Plutarch, for instance, reports how Pericles administered his family estate in a most unconventional way. Doing away with the normal practice of aiming at self-sufficiency, the fifth-century Athenian statesman employed an agent named Evangelos to sell in bulk the production of his estate, to buy all necessary commodities on the market, and to keep track of all receipts and expenditures. Since Pericles was against storing staples, Evangelos was probably instructed to sell the products immediately after the harvest, even though, at this time of the year, prices were low as large supplies of all kinds of agricultural products were dumped on the market. While Pericles's relatives may have expressed some dismay over the losses incurred as a result of the poor timing of the sale, they do not seem to have questioned his reliance on a business agent.[1] The case of Evangelos was hardly exceptional. In Demosthenes's speech *Against Phormio*, the slave Lampis was appointed as shipmaster by his master Dio,[2] and the list of similar examples could be greatly extended. Even though our knowledge of agency in Greek laws, including Athenian law, is rather sketchy,[3] it is clear that the Romans should be credited with the introduction of drastic innovations in their legal system which both reflect the importance of agency in the Roman economy in the mid- and late-Republican period, and account for the growing role of business managers in the next centuries.

Because of their social and legal status, slaves, foreigners, and family dependents (*alieni iuris*) were deprived of property rights and unable to make binding contracts with customers and contractors.

---

[1] Plut., *Per.* 16.3-6.

[2] J. Rougé, *Recherches sur l'organisation du commerce maritime en Méditerranée sous l'Empire romain* (Paris 1966) 333, n. 4, with reference to U.E. Paoli, "Il prestito marittimo nel diritto attico," in *Studi di diritto attico* I (Florence 1930) 106-09.

[3] M.I. Finley, *The Ancient Economy*[2] (London 1985) 221, n. 2, citing L. Gernet, *Droit et société dans la Grèce ancienne* (Paris 1964, first published in 1955) 151-72; and E.L. Kazakevitch, "Slave Agents in Athens," *VDI* (1961) no. 3, 3-21 (in Russian).

Although this situation did not bar them altogether from engaging in economic activities, it constituted a major obstacle for their involvement in complex business transactions requiring reciprocal commitment from both parties. In order to facilitate such business transactions, the Roman Republican praetor devised a twofold system, whereby the contracts made by people with no legal personality acting as business agents and managers would involve both their own liability—to no immediate effect—and that of the people who had commissioned them. The liability of the latter group was defined by the scope of the commission (specific task [*iussum*] or permanent appointment [*praepositio*]), and by the extent of the principal's enrichment (*de in rem verso*). In addition, a different kind of arrangement, based on the grant of a personal, legally fictitious endowment (*peculium*), provided both principal and third contracting party with a limited protection: while the former would at most lose his/her dependent's *peculium*, the latter could obtain redress up to the total value of the *peculium* without having to prove the principal's initial agreement to his dependent's business activities. All these legal remedies had their limits, but represented a major improvement by comparison with the previous situation, in which third contracting parties were left with no effective legal remedy against either agent or principal.

Slaves, foreigners, and dependent people had not waited for the law to change to get involved in business transactions. Thus, one or two generations before the creation of the *actiones adiecticiae qualitatis* (in the late second century B.C.), Cato the Elder reportedly gave his slaves loans which enabled them to buy other slaves, to train them, and then to resell them with a profit.[4] M.I. Finley rightly states that "in practice . . . a substantial part of the urban commercial, financial and industrial activity in Rome, in Italy, and wherever else in the empire Romans were active, was being carried on in this way by slaves and freedmen from the third century B.C. on."[5] During the second century B.C. the social and economic conditions changed in such a way as to make the adjustment of the law of agency desirable, not to say inevitable. I suggested that such an evolution was triggered by the rise of absentee landownership in connection with the development of the villa economy, and that the growth of sea-

---

[4] Plut., *Cato Maior* 21.7-8.
[5] M.I. Finley (1985) 64.

borne trade is to be seen more as a consequence than as a cause of the economic development usually associated with the introduction of the praetorian remedies. Long ago, M. Rostovtzeff had already recognized that the origin of agency lies in the sudden availability of new land (as a result of the conquest) and manpower (enslaved prisoners of war) in the late third and second century B.C. Borrowing the capitalistic system of management from the Greeks of the Hellenistic period, the Roman nobility invested its newly acquired wealth in landowning, moneylending, and industry.[6]

The ancient economy was mainly based on agricultural production. Private land was divided into economic or managerial units (*fundi*), the exploitation of which was carried out by the landowner, entrusted to a farm manager (*vilicus*), or rented to a tenant (*conductor* or *colonus*). Farm managers were mostly slaves, and were in charge of operations implying fairly developed technical, organizational, and managerial skills. The villa economy soon became diversified and sophisticated enough to require from them that they enter into legal contracts with outsiders, in order to buy tools and equipment, sell surpluses or even part of the production, buy or hire additional hands and specialized workers, sell or rent out idle and unnecessary ones, etc. While some farm managers undoubtedly took part in fieldwork, others were too busy with managerial tasks to do so, and chose to rely on a staff organized along paramilitary lines, featuring squads, squad-leaders, and specialists. The farmstead, with its equipment, livestock, technical and managerial staff, provided third contracting parties with a sense of security in their dealing with business managers. This was the essence of the *vilicus* system, as described by Roman agricultural writers of the classical period (Cato, Varro, and Columella).

The development of non-agricultural activities as part of the villa economy called for an extension of the functions of the *vilicus*. The management of workshops producing building material, containers for the storage and marketing of agricultural products, and various types of artifacts for household consumption and/or export, implied a new division of labor within the villa, and the establishment of new levels of supervision: between the landowner/principal and the farm managers, various types of administrative agents were in charge of

---

[6] M. Rostovtzeff, *The Social and Economic History of the Roman Empire*[2] (Oxford 1957) 17-19.

keeping accounts, handling cash, and assisting farm managers. Insofar as ancient Greek novels reflect the social reality of the time of their composition, the *Love Story of Chaereas and Callirhoe* by Chariton of Aphrodisias (dated between 100 B.C. and A.D. 200, most likely around the middle of the first century A.D.) features a "general" manager, Leonas, employed by a rich Greek landowner from Miletus, Dionysios, buying a female slave from a pirate/slave dealer and entrusting her to the care of a farm manager named Phocas.[7] In this context, it is remarkable that Leonas must turn to a professional lawyer in town in order to draw a written contract (καταγραφή) to validate his purchase.[8] Large estates located in Asia Minor or Syria managed by a farm manager (οἰκονόμος) employing slave labor commanded by squad leaders (ἐπιστάται) under the supervision of an overseer (ἐργοστόλος) were a common feature of second-/third-century-A.D. Greek novels.[9] In Achilles Tatius's *Leucippe and Clitophon*, the manager (διοικητὴς τῶν χωρίων) is again pictured as buying a female slave for his master.[10] This may be a literary topos,

---

[7] Chariton, *Chaereas and Callirhoe* 1.12.8-2.1.9. Leonas introduces himself as a διοικητὴς τῶν ὅλων (1.12.8), while Phocas is presented as an οἰκονόμος (2.1.1). For the hypothetical date of composition of the novel—which is different from the dramatic date (fourth century B.C.)—cf. B.P. Reardon, *The Form of Greek Romance* (Princeton 1991) 17, n. 3.

[8] Chariton, *Chaereas and Callirhoe* 2.1.4 and 6: βάδιζε εἰς τὴν ἀγοράν· Ἄδραστος δὲ ὁ ἐμπειρότατος τῶν νόμων διοικήσει τὰς καταγραφάς. On this sale, cf. F. Zimmermann, "Kallirhoes Verkauf durch Theron. Eine juristisch-philologische Betrachtung zu Chariton," in *Aus der byzantinischen Arbeit der DDR* I (Berlin 1957) 72-81 (non vidi); and E. Karabélias, "Le Roman de Chariton d'Aphrodisias et le droit. Renversement de situation et exploitation des ambiguités juridiques," in G. Nenci–G. Thür (eds.), *Symposion* 1988 (Cologne 1990) 368-96, esp. 382-89.

[9] Chariton, *Chaereas and Callirhoe* 3.7.3 and 4.2.1-15, about the organization on the estate owned by Mithridates, satrap of Caria. The work in the field is directed by an ἐργοστόλος (4.2.2), the slaves are organized in squads of sixteen men and watched by an ἐπιστάτης (4.2.5-6), and the estate is managed by an οἰκονόμος (4.2.6 and 8). In Xenophon of Ephesus's *Ephesiaca* (1.14-2.12), the commander of the Phoenician pirates, Apsyrtos, is a merchant who owned an estate near Tyre which was probably entrusted to a bailiff. In Longus's *The Pastorals of Daphnis and Chloe*, the estate of the town-dweller Dionysophanes is located some 35 km away from Mytilene (Lesbos), and is managed by the slave Lamon (3.31.3). Cf. S. Saïd, "La société rurale dans le roman grec ou la campagne vu de la ville," in E. Frézouls (ed.), *Sociétés urbaines, sociétés rurales dans l'Asie Mineure et la Syrie hellénistiques et romaines. Actes du colloque de Strasbourg (novembre 1985)* (Strasbourg 1987) 149-71, esp. 156-62.

[10] Achilles Tatius, *Leucippe and Clitophon* 5.17.9-10; 6.3.3-4; and 7.7.3. The author describes an estate owned by a rich woman from Ephesus, Melite, and managed by a διοικητής named Sosthenes, who bought Leucippe from a slave dealer and put her to work in the field (5.17.3-6 and 5.18.4). The interest of Sosthenes's case is that, because of his cruelty toward Leucippe, his appointment was cancelled

but it underlines a specific activity performed by various kinds of business managers, namely making contracts. The position of διοικητής in the novels corresponds either to that of *procurator*/ἐπίτροπος or to that of *actor*/πραγματευτής. The latter position is first mentioned in Columella's treatise and shows up in inscriptions from Italy around the middle of the first century A.D.; it seems to reflect a more sophisticated stage in estate management, whereby the manager was no longer strictly attached to the managerial unit he was in charge of. This legal development was recorded by classical jurists, according to whom it was no longer instrumental for the manager to be appointed to the head of a specific business (*taberna*, etc. as *locus praepositionis*) for the *actio institoria* to be given against the principal to third contracting parties.

Most of the ancient evidence suggests that, in the early history of the *actio institoria*, only dependent people (slaves and persons-in-power) could be appointed as business managers. Although it seems that by the time of Cicero, *vilici* could be freedmen, free(d) business managers remain rare during the whole period. So are persons-in-power in the same position, even though their legal situation was similar to that of slaves. It is true that, now and then, one hears of some *filius familias* involved in some business deal of his father's.[11] But the overwhelming majority of business managers were slaves, male or female, adults or teenagers, and the reason why it was so is not easy to explain. The position of business managers must have retained a strong servile flavor, and even lower-class people (freeborn and freedmen) may have been careful to avoid any ambiguity about their status and then reluctant to take such a position. Conversely, it was perhaps the result of a deliberate choice on the part of the principals to select their trusted representatives among the members of their slave household. Besides, it is possible that third contracting parties, like Harpax in Plautus's *Pseudolus* (608 ff.), were reluctant to deal with non-slave agents for fear of being unable to prove the connection between agent and principal, and thus to lose the benefit of an *actio institoria* in case of litigation. Finally, one cannot exclude that the evidence is biased. Slaves seem to be much

---

by Melite (5.17.10: Ἡ δὲ τὸν μὲν τῆς διοικήσεως, ἧς εἶχεν, ἀπέπαυσεν . . . and 6.3.3: Ὁ γὰρ Σωσθένης ὁ τὴν Λευκίππην ἐωνημένος, ὃν ἡ Μελίτη τῆς τῶν ἀγρῶν ἐκέλευσεν ἀποστῆναι διοικήσεως . . .).

[11] This is the case, for instance, of Lucius, in Pseudo-Lucian's *The Ass* (1). As a result of the advanced age of men at marriage, nearly 60% of all youths would

easier to detect as business agents or managers than free(d) people, because it is assumed that, as slaves, they were working on behalf of their master. However, this is not necessarily true. As M.I. Finley puts it "unlike slave bailiffs and managers, those who had a *peculium* were working independently, not only for their owners but also for themselves. And if the business were on any scale above the minimal, their *peculium* was likely to include other slaves along with cash, shops, equipment and stock-in-trade."[12] In the mass of stamped signatures preserved on clay artifacts, it is always difficult to determine whether a person signed in the capacity of entrepreneur, business manager, contractor, or mere employee.

The difference between business managers and other employees with responsibilities, such as foremen, overseers, treasurers, comptrollers, coaches, etc. lies in the ability of the first mentioned to make valid contracts. In each managerial unit, the person(s) in charge of making decisions about short-term and long-term policy had to be able to determine how the facility was to be furnished and organized, how much and what kind of labor, tools, equipment, raw material was to be put to work in order to achieve the goals of the enterprise. The combination of various factors of production is the key to profitability of any economic venture, and ancient managers, who were often stuck with a fixed number of slave workers, needed to be able to rent them out in times of underemployment within the enterprise, and to supplement them with outside labor in peak periods (harvest season, etc.). The lack of communication between manager and principal forced the former to take initiative when one factor of production needed to be replaced or adjusted. Besides, it is likely that managers were often more competent than absentee principals to make difficult choices regarding purchases of equipment, hiring of skilled workers, and marketing of the production.

It is difficult to say whether or not business managers formed a homogeneous social class. They are likely to have been diversely successful, and this alone should serve as a reminder of the discrepancy among them in terms of economic power. Urban positions were probably more coveted than rural ones; some functions, such as tax collection, bath- and innkeeping, were branded with infamy;

---

have lost their *paterfamilias* by the time they reached the age of 20; cf. R.P. Saller, *CP* 82 (1987) 21-34, esp. 33 (Table II).

[12] M.I. Finley (1985) 64.

others, such library management, were held in higher repute. Public and imperial servants enjoyed a special status. Those managers who commanded a numerous and diversified staff must have been wooed not only by their subordinates, but also by the rest of the local community, especially by those hopeful hirelings gravitating around the enterprise. Others, who were in charge of small enterprises, must have been ignored like any other worker. In spite of the classical jurists' contention that men and women, boys and girls, were treated equally in the position of business manager, it is likely that the more desirable the position the more likely that it was filled by an adult male. We do have some evidence about child and female labor, but it is hopelessly short on the subject of managerial jobs.[13] One can wonder whether the provisions of the *Senatusconsultum Velleianum* (A.D. 46?), barring women from incurring liability for the benefit of others (*intercessio*), and of the *Senatusconsultum Macedonianum* (under Vespasian), barring persons-in-power from taking out loans, may have adversely affected the ability of women and youngsters to work as business managers.[14] In any case, slaves and lower-class people were unlikely to be concerned with these kinds of legal subtleties. The only trade where female managers might have been common was as inn-/brothelkeeper, hardly something to be excited about

---

[13] K.R. Bradley, "Child Labour in the Roman World," *Historical Reflections/ Réflexions historiques* 12 (1985) 311-30; T. Wiedemann, *Adults and Children in the Roman Empire* (London 1989) 153-56; J. Le Gall, "Métiers de femmes au *Corpus Inscriptionum Latinarum*" *REL* 47 (1969) 123-30; S.B. Pomeroy, *Goddesses, Whores, Wives, and Slaves. Women in Classical Antiquity* (New York 1975) 190-204; S. Treggiari, "Jobs for Women," *AJAH* 1 (1976) 76-104; S. Treggiari, "Lower Class Women in the Roman Economy," *Florilegium* 1 (1979) 65-86; N. Kampen, *Image and Status: Roman Working Women in Ostia* (Berlin 1981); and S.R. Joshel, *Work, Identity, and Legal Status at Rome. A Study of the Occupational Inscriptions* (Norman, OK/London 1992). I have not seen M. Eichenauer, *Untersuchungen zur Arbeitswelt der Frau in der römischen Antike* (Frankfurt 1988).

[14] On the *SC Velleianum*, cf. *Dig.* 16.1 and *Cod. Iust.* 4.29; on the *SC Macedonianum*, cf. *Dig.* 14.6 and *Cod. Iust.* 4.28. The literature on either enactment is enormous, and can be traced through J.A. Crook, "Feminine Inadequacy and the *Senatusconsultum Velleianum*," in B. Rawson (ed.), *The Family in Ancient Rome* (London/Sydney 1986) 83-92; M. Kaser, *Das römische Privatrecht* I^2 (Munich 1971) 532, nn. 26-33; and 667, nn. 2-13; and R. Zimmermann, *The Law of Obligations. Roman Foundations of the Civilian Tradition* (Cape Town 1990) 145-52, esp. 148-49 and nn. 215-221, who points out that the provision of the *SC Velleianum* applied to situations where women stood surety, incurred joint obligations, gave security for another by the way of pledge, released a debtor by way of *novatio*, took out a loan on somebody else's behalf, even in connection with contracts of sale, hire, and mandate.

from a feminist point-of-view. Again, the evidence might be biased against women and children.

The nature of the social and personal relationship between agent and principal is also elusive. The success of the *vilicus* system in agriculture as well as in other sectors of the Roman economy speaks in favor of a genuine understanding between the two groups. Business managers who served as cover for the nobility involved in despised economic activities were to be trustworthy employees, whose discretion and honesty were instrumental in maintaining the respectability of their principals. The point of relying on a business manager would have been missed if, as a result of the latter's shady activities, the owner of a brothel found himself repeatedly involved in litigation against cheated customers. In any case, there was ample ground for defining a community of interest which, translated into a general policy, would have benefitted both employer and employee, no matter how large the social gap between the two. In this respect, slaves are not likely to have been more amenable than freeborn managers, because of their unavoidable propensity to passive resistance in case of compulsion or harsh treatment. For people in managerial positions, the carrot has always been more efficient than the stick. Like students, employees fare better when they know that they are expected to succeed:

> FELICITER SIT
> GENIO LOCI
> SERVVLE VTERE
> FELIX TABERN
> AM AUREFI
> CINAM

Let us wish good fortune to the Genius of this place. Young slave, good luck with the management of this goldsmith's shop.[15]

---

[15] *CIL* VII 265 (= *ILS* 3651 = *RIB* I 712, Norton, Yorkshire, *tabula ansata* used as a building stone, probably as a sign on the wall of the shop set up by the manager's principal/master).

BIBLIOGRAPHY

M. Albana, "La *vicesima libertatis* in età imperiale," *QC* 9 (1987) 41-76.

B. Albanese, "*Iudicium contrarium* e *ignominia* nel mandato," *Iura* 21 (1970) 1-51.

M.R. Alföldi, "Epigraphische Beiträge zur römischen Münztechnik bis auf Konstantin den Grossen." *SNR* 39 (1958-59) 35-48.

G. Alföldy, "Die Freilassung von Sklaven und die Struktur der Sklaverei in der römischen Kaiserzeit," *RSA* 2 (1972) 97-129.

G. Alföldy, *Noricum* (London/Boston 1974).

L. Amirante, "Sulla schiavitù nella Roma antica," *Labeo* 27 (1981) 26-33.

L. Amirante, "Lavoro di giuristi sul peculio. Le definizioni da Q. Mucio a Ulpiano," *Studi Sanfilippo* III (Milan 1983) 3-15.

J.-M. André – F.-M. Baslez, *Voyager dans l'Antiquité* (Paris 1993).

J. Andreau, *Les affaires de Monsieur Jucundus* (Rome 1974).

J. Andreau, "Originalité de l'historiographie finleyenne et remarques sur les classes sociales," *Opus* 1 (1982) 181-85.

J. Andreau, "Les financiers romains entre la ville et la campagne," in P. Leveau (ed.), *L'origine des richesses dépensées dans la ville antique* (Aix-en-Provence 1985) 177-96.

J. Andreau, *La vie financière dans le monde romain. Les métiers de manieurs d'argent (IVe siècle av. J.-C.-IIIe siècle ap. J.C.)* (Rome 1987).

P. Angelini, "Osservazioni in tema di creazione dell'*actio ad exemplum institoriae*," *BIDR* 71 (1968) 230-48.

P. Angelini, *Il procurator* (Milan 1971).

H. Ankum, "*Mancipatio* by Slaves in Classical Roman Law?" *Acta Juridica* (1976) 1-18.

P. Apathy, "*Procurator* und *solutio*," *ZRG* 96 (1979) 65-88.

P. Arthur, "Roman Amphorae and the *Ager Falernus* under the Empire," *PBSR* 50 (1982) 22-33.

A.E. Astin, *Cato the Censor* (Oxford 1978).

D. Atkinson, "A Hoard of Samian Ware from Pompeii," *JRS* 4 (1914) 27-64.

J.-J. Aubert, "Workshop Managers," in W.V. Harris (ed.), *The Inscribed Economy* (1993) 171-81.

E. Badian, *Publicans and Sinners* (Ithaca/London 1972).

E. Badian, "Marius' Villas: The Testimony of the Slave and the Knave," *JRS* 63 (1973) 121-32.

R.S. Bagnall, "A Trick a Day to Keep the Tax Man at Bay? The Prostitute Tax in Roman Egypt," *BASP* 28 (1991) 5-12.

D.M. Bailey, *A Catalogue of the Lamps in the British Museum* I-III (London 1975-1988).

D.M. Bailey, "The Roman Terracotta Lamp Industry. Another View About Exports," in T. Oziol and R. Rebuffat (eds.), *Les lampes de terre cuite en Méditerranée* (Lyons 1987) 59-63.

D.M. Bailey, "Lamps Metal, Lamps Clay: A Decade of Publications," *JRA* 4 (1991) 51-62.

J.P.V.D. Balsdon, "Roman History, 65-50 B.C. Five Problems," *JRS* 52 (1962) 134-41.

G. Barker, "The Archaeology of the Italian Shepherd," *PCPhS* 215 (n.s. 35) (1989) 1-19.

P. Bastien, "Liaisons de coins de revers et officines des ateliers monétaires romains," *Cercle d'études numismatiques* 5.4 (Oct.-Dec. 1968) 73-78.

R. Beare, "Were Bailiffs Ever Free Born?" *CQ* 28 (1978) 398-401.

W. Beare, *The Roman Stage. A Short History of Latin Drama in the Time of the Republic* (London 1950).

J. Beaujeu, "A-t-il existé une direction des musées dans la Rome impériale?" *CRAI* (1982) 671-88.

O. Behrends, "Die Prokuratur des klassischen römischen Zivilrechts," *ZRG* 88 (1971) 215-99.

C. Bémont–J. Bonnet, "Lampes et fabricants de lampes," *RCRF* 23/24 (1984) 135-54.

N. Benke, "Zu Papinians *actio ad exemplum institoriae actionis*," *ZRG* 105 (1988) 592-633.

H.S. Bennett, "The Reeve and the Manor in the Fourteenth Century," *EHR* 41 (1926) 358-65.

H.-P. Benöhr, *Der Besitzerwerb durch Gewaltabhängige im klassischen römischen Recht* (Berlin 1972).

F. Bérard, "La carrière de Plotius Grypus et le ravitaillement de l'armée impériale en campagne," *MEFRA* 96 (1984) 259-324.

D. van Berchem, "L'annone militaire dans l'empire au IIIᵉ siècle," *MSAF* 10 (1937) 118-202.

D. van Berchem, "L'annone militaire est-elle un mythe?" *Armées et fiscalité dans le monde antique* (Paris 1977) 331-36.

E. Bernareggi, "*Familia monetalis*," *NAC* 3 (1974) 177-91.

F. Bertrandy, "Remarques sur le commerce des bêtes sauvages entre l'Afrique du Nord et l'Italie (IIᵉ s. av. J.-C.–IVᵉ s. ap. J.-C.)," *MEFRA* 99 (1987) 211-41.

I. Bieżuńska-Małowist, "Les esclaves payant l'ἀποφορά dans l'Egypte gréco-romaine," *JJP* 15 (1965) 65-72.

P. Bistaudeau, "A la recherche des villas d'Ausone," *Caesarodunum* 15bis (1980) 477-87.

H. Bloch, *I bolli laterizi e la storia edilizia romana* (Rome 1947) (= *BCAR* 64 [1936] 141-225; 65 [1937] 83-187; and 66 [1938] 61-221).

H. Bloch, "*Consules suffecti* on Roman Brick Stamps," *CP* 39 (1944) 254-55.

H. Bloch, "The Roman Brick-stamps not Published in Volume XV, 1 of *CIL*," *HSPh* 56/57 (1947) 1-128 (= *S*).

H. Bloch, "Supplement to Volume XV,1 of *CIL* Including Complete Indices to the Roman Brick Stamps," *HSPh* 58/59 (1948) 1-104.

J.P. Bodel, *Roman Brick Stamps in the Kelsey Museum* (Ann Arbor 1983).

J.P. Bodel, *Freedmen in the Satyricon of Petronius* (Diss. Univ. of Michigan 1984).

J.E. Bogaers, "Foreign Affairs," in B. Hartley–J. Wacher (eds.), *Rome and her Northern Provinces* (Gloucester 1983) 13-32.

J.E. Bogaers–P. Stuart, "Augusta Raurica und die Dea Nehalennia," *JAK* 1 (1980) 49-58.

P. Bonnassie, "Survie et extinction du régime esclavagiste dans l'Occident du haut moyen âge (IVᵉ–XIᵉ s.)," *Cahiers de civilisation médiévale* 28 (1985) 307-43.

G. Boulvert, *Esclaves et affranchis impériaux sous le Haut-Empire romain. Rôle politique et administratif* (Naples 1970).

G. Boulvert, *Domestique et fonctionnaire sous le Haut-Empire romain. La condition de l'affranchi et de l'esclave des princes* (Paris 1974).

L. Bove, *Documenti processuali delle Tabulae Pompeianae di Murecine* (Naples 1979).

K.R. Bradley, "The *vicesima libertatis*. Its History and Significance," *Klio* 66 (1984) 175-82.

K.R. Bradley, "Child Labour in the Roman World," *Historical Reflections/Réflexions historiques* 12 (1985) 311-30.

K.R. Bradley, "*Servus Onerosus*: Roman Law and the Troublesome Slave," *Slavery & Abolition* 11 (1990) 135-57.

G. Brodribb, "Markings on Tile and Brick," in A. McWhirr (ed.), *Roman Brick and Tile* (Oxford 1979) 211-21.

M. Brozek, "Einiges über die Schauspieldirektoren und die Komödiendichter im alten Rom," *StudClas* 2 (1960) 145-50.

L.D. Bruce, "The *procurator bibliothecarum* at Rome," *Journal of Library History* 18 (1983) 143-62.

P.A. Brunt, "Two Great Roman Landowners," *Latomus* 34 (1975) 619-35.

P.A. Brunt, "Free Labour and Public Works at Rome," *JRS* 70 (1980) 81-100.

P.A. Brunt, "The Revenues of Rome," *JRS* 71 (1981) 161-72 (= *Roman Imperial Themes* [1990] 324-46).

P.A. Brunt, "Publicans in the Principate," in *Roman Imperial Themes* (Oxford 1990) 354-432.

C. Bruun, *The Water Supply of Ancient Rome. A Study of Roman Imperial Administration* (Helsinki 1991).

E. Buchi, *Lucerne del Museo di Aquileia. I. Lucerne romane con marchio di fabbrica* (Aquileia 1975).

R.J. Buck, *Agriculture and Agricultural Practices in Roman Law* (Wiesbaden 1983).

W.W. Buckland, *The Roman Law of Slavery. The Condition of the Slave in Private Law from Augustus to Justinian* (New York 1908).

W.H. Buckler, "Labour Disputes in the Province of Asia," in W.H. Buckler–W.M. Calder (eds.), *Anatolian Studies Presented to Sir William M. Ramsay* (Manchester 1923) 27-50.

G. von Bülow, "Militärische und zivile Keramikproduktion in den römischen Provinzen am Rhein und an der oberen Donau," *Klio* 57 (1975) 233-40.

M. Buora, "Sul commercio dei laterizi tra Aquileia e la Dalmazia," *AAAd* 26 (1985) 209-26.

A. Burdese, *Autorizzazione ad alienare in diritto romano* (Turin 1950).

A. Burdese, "*Actio ad exemplum institoriae* e categorie sociali," *BIDR* 74 (1971) 61-82 (= *Studi G. Donatuti* I [Milan 1973] 191-210).

A. Burdese, "Controversie giurisprudenziali in tema di capacità degli schiavi," *Studi Biscardi* I (Milan 1982) 147-80.

A. Burdese, "Considerazioni in tema di peculio c.d. profettizio," *Studi Sanfilippo* I (Milan 1982) 71-111.

P. Bürgin, "Figuli im römischen Recht," *RCRF* 23/24 (1984) 123-27.

A.M. Burnett, "The Authority to Coin in the Late Republic and Early Empire," *NC* 137 (1977) 37-63.

I. Buti, *Studi sulla capacità patrimoniale dei servi* (Naples 1976).

T.V. Buttrey, "On the Retariffing of the Roman Denarius," *ANSMusN* 7 (1957) 57-65.

T.V. Buttrey, "The Denarii of P. Crepusius and Roman Republican Mint Organization," *ANSMusN* 21 (1976) 67-108.

R. Cagnat, "Les bibliothèques municipales dans l'empire romain," *MMAI* 38,1 (1909) 1-26.

M.H. Callender, *Roman Amphorae with Index of Stamps* (London 1965).

A. Cameron, *Circus Factions. Blues and Greens at Rome and Byzantium* (Oxford 1976).

L. Canfora, "Le biblioteche ellenistiche" in G. Cavallo (ed.), *Le biblioteche nel mondo antico e medievale* (Rome/Bari 1988) 5-28.

M. Capasso, *Manuale di papirologia ercolanese* (Lecce 1991).

A. Carandini, "Produzione agricola e produzione ceramica nell'Africa di età imperiale. Appunti sull'economia della Zeugitana e della Bezacena," *Studi Miscellanei* 15 (1970) 95-122.

A. Carandini, "Il vigneto e la villa del fondo di Settefinestre nel Cosano: un caso di produzione agricola per il mercato transmarino," *MAAR* 36 (1980) 1-10.

A. Carandini, *Schiavi in Italia. Gli strumenti pensanti dei Romani fra tarda Repubblica e medio Impero* (Roma 1988).

A. Carandini, "L'economia italica fra tarda repubblica e medio impero considerata dal punto di vista di una merce: il vino," in *Amphores romaines et histoire économique* (Rome 1989) 505-21.

A. Carandini *et al.* (eds.), *Settefinestre: Una villa schiavistica nell'Etruria romana* (Modena 1985).

J. Carlsen, "Considerations on Cosa and Ager Cosanus," *ARID* 13 (1984) 49-58.

J. Carlsen, "Estate Management in Roman North Africa. Transformation or Continuity?" in A. Mastino (ed.), *L'Africa romana* VIII (Sassari 1991) 625-37.

J. Carlsen, "*Magister pecoris*. The Nomenclature and Qualifications of the Chief Herdsman in Roman Pasturage," *ARID* 20 (1991) 57-64.

J. Carlsen, "*Dispensatores* in Roman North Africa," in A. Mastino (ed.), *L'Africa romana* IX (Sassari 1992) 97-104.

J. Carlsen, "The *vilica* and Roman Estate Management," in H. Sancisi-Weerdenburg *et al.* (eds.), *De agricultura. In memoriam P.W. de Neeve* (Amsterdam 1993) 197-205.

J. Carlsen, *Vilicus. A Study in Roman Estate Management* (forthcoming).

T.F. Carney, "The Working of the Roman Mint," *New Zealand Numismatic Journal* 10.5 (Dec. 1961) 154-58.

M.-B. Carre, "Les amphores de la Cisalpine et de l'Adriatique au début de l'empire," *MEFRA* 97 (1985) 207-45.

R.A.G. Carson, "System and Product in the Roman Mint," in R.A.G. Carson – C.H.V. Sutherland (eds.), *Essays in Roman Coinage Presented to H. Mattingly* (Oxford 1956) 227-39.

R.A.G. Carson, *Coins of the Roman Empire* (London/New York 1990).

J. Carter, "Rural Architecture and Ceramic Industry at Metaponto, Italy, 350-50 B.C.," in A. McWhirr (ed.), *Roman Brick and Tile* (Oxford 1979) 45-64.

L. Casson, *Travel in the Ancient World* (Toronto 1974).

M.A. Cavallaro, *Spese e spettacoli: Aspetti economici-strutturali degli spettacoli nella Roma giulio-claudia* (Bonn 1984).

G. Cavallo, "I rotoli di Ercolano come prodotti scritti: quattro riflessioni," *Scrittura e civiltà* 8 (1984) 5-30.

G. Cavallo (ed.), *Le biblioteche nel mondo antico e medievale* (Rome/Bari 1988).

D. Cavazzoni, "Un complesso produttivo fittile di età romana a Santo Marino (Poggio Berni [provincia di Forlì]). Relazione topografica preliminare," *Stud-Romagn* 34 (1983) 67-85.

G. Cerulli Irelli, "Officina di lucerne fittili a Pompei," in *L'instrumentum domesticum di Ercolaneo e Pompei nella prima età imperiale* (Rome 1977) 53-72.

R. Chevallier, *Roman Roads* (Berkeley/L.A. 1976, first publ. in French in 1972).

R. Chevallier, *La romanisation de la Celtique du Pô* (Paris/Rome 1983).

R. Chevallier, *Voyages et déplacements dans l'empire romain* (Paris 1988).

R. Chevallier, *Les potiers antiques (monde romain)* (Tours 1990).

T.J. Chiusi, "Landwirtschaftliche Tätigkeit und *actio institoria*," *ZRG* 108 (1991) 155-86.

M.R. Cimma, *Ricerche sulle società di publicani* (Milan 1981).

A. Claus, *Gewillkürte Stellvertretung im römischen Privatrecht* (Berlin 1973).

H. Cockle, "Pottery Manufacture in Roman Egypt: A New Papyrus," *JRS* 71 (1981) 87-97.

D. Colls *et al.*, "L'épave Port-Vendres II et le commerce de la Bétique à l'époque de Claude" *Archaeonautica* 1 (1977) 93-103.

H. Comfort, "Late Ateius Signatures," *RCRF* 4 (1962) 5-25.

G. Cornil, "Explication historique de la règle *alteri stipulari nemo potest*," *Studi Riccobono* IV (Palermo 1936) 241-58.

M. Corsi-Sciallano – B. Liou, "Les épaves de Tarraconaise à chargement d'amphores Dr. 2-4," *Archaeonautica* 5 (1985).

E. Costa, *Le azioni exercitoria e institoria* (Parma 1891).

L. Cracco Ruggini, "Vicende rurali dell'Italia antica," *RSI* 76 (1964) 261-86.

D.J. Crawford, "Imperial Estates," in M.I. Finley (ed.), *Studies in Roman Property* (Cambridge 1976) 35-70.

M.H. Crawford, "Control-marks and the Organization of the Roman Republican Mint," *PBSR* 34 (1966) 18-23.

M.H. Crawford, *Roman Republican Coinage* (Cambridge 1974) (= *RRC*).

M.H. Crawford, "Economia imperiale e commerci estero," in *Tecnologia, economia e società nel mondo romano* (Como 1980) 207-17.

M.H. Crawford, *Coinage and Money under the Roman Republic* (Berkeley/L.A. 1985).

S. Crogiez, "Les stations du *cursus publicus* en Calabre: un état de la recherche," *MEFRA* 102 (1990) 389-431.

J.A. Crook, *Law and Life of Rome, 90 B.C. –A.D. 212* (Ithaca, NY 1967).

J.A. Crook, "*Patria potestas*," *CQ* 17 (1967) 113-22.

P. Culham Ertman, *Curatores viarum: A Study of the Superintendents of Highways in Ancient Rome* (Diss. Buffalo 1976).

N. Cuomo di Caprio, "Proposta di classificazione delle fornaci per ceramica e laterizi nell'area italiana dalla preistoria a tutta l'epoca romana," *Sibrium* 11 (1971-1972) 371-461.

R.I. Curtis, "A Personalized Floor Mosaic from Pompeii," *AJA* 88 (1984) 557-66.

R.I. Curtis, "Product Identification and Advertising on Roman Commercial Amphorae," *AncSoc* 15-17 (1984-86) 209-28.

R.I. Curtis, "A. Umbricius Scaurus of Pompeii," in *Studia Pompeiana e Classica in Honor of W.F. Jashemski* (New York 1988) 19-50.

R.I. Curtis, *Garum and Salsamenta. Production and Commerce in Materia Medica* (Leiden 1991).

J.H. D'Arms, *The Romans on the Bay of Naples* (Cambridge, MA 1970).

J.H. D'Arms, *Commerce and Social Standing in Ancient Rome* (Cambridge, MA 1981) (= *CSSAR*).

D. Daube, "Actions between *pater familias* and *filius familias* with *peculium castrense*," *Studi E. Albertario* I (Milan 1950) 433-74.

D. Daube, *Roman Law: Linguistic, Social and Philosophical Aspects* (Edinburgh 1969).

J. Delaine, "Recent Research on Roman Baths," *JRA* 1 (1988) 11-32.

C. Delplace, "Les potiers dans la société et l'économie de l'Italie et de la Gaule au Ier siècle av. et au Ier siècle ap. J.-C.," *Ktèma* 3 (1978) 55-76.

A. Deman, "Réflexions sur la navigation fluviale dans l'Antiquité," in T. Hackens – P. Marchetti (eds.), *Histoire économique de l'Antiquité* (Louvain 1987) 79-106.

J. Deneauve, *Les lampes de Carthages* (Paris 1969).

S. Dixon, "Polybius on Women and Property," *AJP* 106 (1985) 147-70.

C. Domergue, "Un envoi de lampes du potier Gaius Clodius," *MCV* 2 (1966) 5-40.

P.F. Dorcey, *The Cult of Silvanus. A Study in Roman Folk Religion* (Leiden 1992).

P.J. Drury, "The Production of Brick and Tile in Medieval England," in D.W. Crossley (ed.), *Medieval Industry* (London 1981) 126-42.

J.-C. Dumont, "Le gentilice: nom de citoyen ou d'esclave?" *Ktèma* 6 (1981) 105-14.

J.-C. Dumont, *Servus. Rome et l'esclavage sous la République* (Rome 1987).

R.P. Duncan-Jones, "Some Configurations of Landholding in the Roman Empire," in M.I. Finley (ed.), *Studies in Roman Property* (Cambridge 1976) 7-33.

R.P. Duncan-Jones, *The Economy of the Roman Empire: Quantitative Studies*² (Cambridge 1982).

R.P. Duncan-Jones, *Structure and Scale in the Roman Economy* (Cambridge 1990).

P.M. Duval – R. Marichal, "Un 'compte d'enfournement' inédit de La Graufesenque," *Mélanges d'archéologie et d'histoire offerts à A. Piganiol* III (Paris 1966) 1341-52.

S.L. Dyson, "Some Reflections on the Archaeology of Southern Etruria," *JFA* 8 (1981) 79-83.

W. Eck, *Die staatlichen Organisation Italiens in der hohen Kaiserzeit* (Munich 1979).

W. Eck, "*Superiumentarii et muliones* im privaten Personal des Statthalters," *ZPE* 90 (1992) 207-10.

W. Eder, *Servitus Publica* (Wiesbaden 1980).

H. Engelmann – D. Knibbe, "Das Zollgesetz der Provinz Asia. Eine neue Inschrift aus Ephesos," *Epigraphica Anatolica* 14 (1989).

R. Etienne, "Ausone, propriétaire terrien et le problème du *latifundium* au IVᵉ siècle ap. J.-C.," in M. Christol *et al.* (eds.), *Institutions, société et vie politique au IVe siècle ap. J.-C.* (Rome 1992) 305-11.

E. Ettlinger, "Vorbemerkungen zu einer Diskussion des Ateius-Problems," *RCRF* 4 (1962) 27-44.

E. Ettlinger, "How was Arretine Ware Sold?" *RCRF* 25/26 (1987) 5-19.

E. Ettlinger *et al.*, *Conspectus formarum terrae sigillatae italico modo confectae* (Bonn 1990) (= *Conspectus*).

G. Fabre, *Libertus* (Rome 1981).

P. Fabricius, *Der gewaltfreie Institor im klassischen römischen Recht* (Würzburg 1926).

J.C. Fant, *The curatores rei publicae in Italy, from their Inception to the Death of Commodus* (Diss. Univ. of Michigan 1976).

J.C. Fant, "Ideology, Gift, and Trade: A Distribution Model for the Roman Imperial Marbles," in W.V. Harris (ed.), *The Inscribed Economy* (1993) 145-70.

P. Fedeli, "Biblioteche private e pubbliche a Roma e nel mondo romano" in G. Cavallo (ed.), *Le biblioteche nel mondo antico e medievale* (Rome/Bari 1988) 31-64.

E. Fentress – D. Kennit – I. Valenti, "A Sicilian Villa and its Landscape (Contrada Mirabile, Mazara del Vallo 1988)," *Opus* 5 (1986) [1990] 75-95.

M.I. Finley, "Private Farm Tenancy in Italy before Diocletian," in M.I. Finley (ed.), *Studies in Roman Property* (Cambridge 1976) 103-21.

M.I. Finley, *The Ancient Economy*² (London 1985).

D. Flach, *Römische Agrargeschichte* (Munich 1990).

G.B. Ford, jr., "The Letters of Pliny the Younger as Evidence of Agrarian Conditions in the Principate of Trajan," *Helikon* 5 (1965) 381-89.

L. Foxhall, "The Dependent Tenant: Land Leasing and Labour in Italy and Greece," *JRS* 80 (1990) 97-114.

T. Frank, "Notes on Roman Commerce," *JRS* 27 (1937) 72-79.

J.M. Frayn, *Subsistence Farming in Roman Italy* (London 1979).

A. Freschi, "Il relitto A delle Tre Senghe (Isole Tremiti). – Relazione preliminare 1981-1982," in *Archaeologia subacquea* (*BA* Suppl. 4, Rome 1982 [1983]) 89-100.

E. Frézouls, "La vie rurale au Bas-Empire d'après l'oeuvre de Palladius," *Ktèma* 5 (1980) 193-210.

B.W. Frier, "Law, Technology, and Social Change. The Equipping of Italian Farm Tenancies," *ZRG* 96 (1979) 204-28.

M. Fruyt, "La plurivalence des noms d'agents latins en -tor: lexique et sémantique," *Latomus* 49 (1990) 59-70.

P. Garnsey, "Independent Freedmen and the Economy of Roman Italy under the Principate," *Klio* 63 (1981) 359-71.

V. Gassner, "Zur Terminologie der Kaufläden im Lateinischen," *MBAH* 3 (1984) 108-15.

J.L. Gay, "L'*in rem versum* à l'époque classique," *Varia. Etudes de droit romain* II (Paris 1956) 155-280.

F. Ghionda, "Sul *magister navis*," *Riv. dir. navigaz.* 1 (1935) 327-55.

M. Giacchero, *Edictum Diocletiani et collegarum de pretiis rerum venalium* (Genova 1974).

A. Giardina (ed.), *Società romana e impero tardoantico* (Rome/Bari 1986) (= *SRIT*).

A. Giardina – A. Schiavone (eds.), *Società romana e produzione schiavistica* (Bari 1981) (= *SRPS*).

G. Giliberti, *Servus quasi colonus: forme non tradizionali di organizzazione del lavoro nella società romana* (Naples 1981).

G. Giliberti, *Legatum kalendarii* (Naples 1984).

J.-C. Golvin, *L'amphithéâtre romain* (Paris 1988).

A.E. Gordon, "On the First Appearance of the *cognomen* in Latin Inscriptions of Freedmen," *Univ. of Calif. Publ. in Class. Philol.* (1935) 151-58.

W.M. Gordon, "Agency and Roman Law," *Studi Sanfilippo* III (Milan 1983) 341-49.

C. Goudineau, *Bolsena IV. La céramique arétine lisse. Fouilles de l'Ecole Française de Rome à Bolsena (Poggio Moschini) 1962-1967* (Paris 1968).

C. Goudineau, "Céramique arétine à reliefs de Bolsena," *MEFR* 80 (1968) 167-200.

C. Goudineau, "Un nouveau vase de L. Sarius Surus," *MEFRA* 80 (1968) 527-45.

M. Grazia Celuzza – E. Regoli, "Gli insediamenti nella Valle d'Oro e il fondo di Settefinestre," in A. Carandini *et al.* (1985) 48-59.

K. Greene, *The Archaeology of the Roman Economy* (Berkeley/L.A. 1986).

E.W. Haley, "The Lamp Manufacturer Gaius Iunius Draco," *MBAH* 9 (1990) 1-12.

L. Halkin, *Les esclaves publics chez les Romains* (Paris 1897).

G. Hamza, "Einige Fragen der Zulässigkeit der direkten Stellvertretung in den Papyri," *AUB* (*iur.*) 19 (1977) 57-67.

G. Hamza, "Fragen der gewillkürten Stellvertretung im römischen Recht," *AUB* (*iur.*) 25 (1983) 89-107.

G. Hamza, "Zur Frage der Stellvertretung im Willen anhand der *P.Amh.* 90 und *P.Oxy.* 501," *AUB* (*iur.*) 30 (1988/89) 55-65.

H. Harrauer – P.J. Sijpesteijn, "Ein neues Dokument zu Roms Indienhandel. P.Vindob. G40822," *AAWW* 122 (1985) 124-55.

W.V. Harris, "Roman Terracotta Lamps: The Organization of an Industry," *JRS* 70 (1980) 126-45.

W.V. Harris, "Toward a Study of the Roman Slave Trade," *MAAR* 36 (1980) 117-40.

W.V. Harris, *Ancient Literacy* (Cambridge, MA 1989).

W.V. Harris, "Trade and the River Po: A Problem in the Economic History of the Roman Empire," in J.-Fr. Bergier (ed.), *Montagnes, fleuves, forêts dans l'histoire* (St. Katharinen 1989) 123-33.

W.V. Harris, "Roman Warfare in the Economic and Social Context of the Fourth Century B.C.," in W. Eder (ed.), *Staat und Staatlichkeit in der frühen römischen Republik* (Stuttgart 1990) 494-510.

W.V. Harris (ed.), *The Inscribed Economy: Production and Distribution in the Roman Empire in the Light of instrumentum domesticum* (*JRA* Suppl. 6, Ann Arbor 1993).

M. Hassall, "Britain and the Rhine Provinces: Epigraphic Evidence for Roman

Trade," in J. du Plat Taylor–H. Cleere (eds.), *Roman Shipping and Trade: Britain and the Rhine Provinces* (London 1978) 41-48.

W.E. Heitland, *Agricola. A Study of Agriculture and Rustic Life in the Graeco-Roman World from the Point of View of Labour* (Cambridge 1921).

T. Helen, *Organization of Roman Brick Production in the First and Second Centuries A.D.* (Helsinki 1975).

M.F. Hendy, "The Administration of Mints and Treasuries, 4th to 7th Centuries, with an Appendix on the Production of Silver Plate," in *The Economy, Fiscal Administration and Coinage of Byzantium* (London 1989) 1-18.

J. Hengstl, "Einige juristische Bemerkungen zu drei Töpferei-Mieturkunden," *Studi Biscardi* IV (Milan 1983) 663-73.

G. Hermansen, "The Roman Inns and the Law. The Inns of Ostia," in J.A.S. Evans (ed.), *Polis and Imperium. Studies in Honour of E.T. Salmon* (Toronto 1974) 167-81.

A. Hesnard–P.A. Gianfrotta, "Les bouchons d'amphores en pouzzolane," *Amphores romaines et histoire économique* (Rome 1989) 393-441.

P.V. Hill, *The Undated Coins of Rome (A.D. 98-148)* (London 1970).

D. Hobson, "Women as Property Owners in Roman Egypt," *TAPhA* 113 (1983) 311-21.

B. Hofmann, "Marques de potiers, de producteurs de moules et de fabriquants de poinçons," *RCRFCommunicationes* 2.11 (1970) 61-62.

B. Hofmann, "Les relations entre potiers, fabricants de moules et artistes producteurs de poinçons," *RCRF* 13 (1971) 5-20.

L. Homo, *Rome impériale et l'urbanisme dans l'antiquité* (Paris 1951).

N. Horsfall, " 'The Use of Literacy' and the Cena Trimalchionis," *G&R* 36 (1989) 74-89 and 194-209.

J. Humphrey, *Roman Circuses* (Berkeley, CA 1985).

P. Huvelin, *Etudes d'histoire du droit commercial romain* (Paris 1929).

D. Iványi, *Die pannonischen Lampen. Eine typologisch-chronologische Übersicht* (Budapest 1935).

J.-P. Jacob–H. Leredde, "Un aspect de l'organisation des centres de production céramique: le mythe du 'cartel' ", *RCRF* 21/22 (1982) 89-94.

F. Jacques, *Le privilège de liberté. Politique impériale et autonomie minicipale dans les cités de l'Occident romain (161-244)* (Rome 1984).

T.O. Jefferson–G.B. Dannell–D. Williams, "The Production and Distribution of *terra sigillata* in the area of Pisa, Italy," in A.C and A.S. Anderson (eds.), *Roman Pottery Research in Britain and North-West Europe* (Oxford 1981) 161-71.

P. Johnson, *A History of the Jews* (New York 1988).

A.H.M. Jones, *The Later Roman Empire, 284-602. A Social, Economic, and Administrative Survey* (Norman, OK 1964) (= *LRE*).

J.M. Jones, *A Dictionary of Ancient Roman Coins* (London 1990).

J.R. Jones, "Mint Magistrates in the Early Roman Empire," *BICS* 17 (1970) 70-78.

E.J. Jory, "*Dominus gregis?*" *CPh* 61 (1966) 102-05.

S.R. Joshel, *Work, Identity, and Legal Status at Rome. A Study of the Occupational Inscriptions* (Norman, OK/London 1992).

H. Jouffroy, *La construction publique en Italie et dans l'Afrique romaine* (Strasboug 1986).

M. Just, "Ansätze zur Anscheinsvollmacht im römischen Recht. D. 14, 3, 19, 3; 14, 5, 8: ein Beispiel spätklassischer Rechtspraxis," in W. Barfuss (ed.), *Festschrift für K.H. Neumayer zum 65. Geburtstag* (Baden-Baden 1985) 355-87.

W. Kaltenstadler, *Arbeitsorganisation und Führungssystem bei den römischen Agrarschriftstellern (Cato, Varro, Columella)* (Stuttgart 1978).

W. Kaltenstadler, "Arbeits- und Führungskräfte im *Opus Agriculturae* von Palladius," *Klio* 66 (1984) 223-29.

W. Kaltenstadler, "Betriebsorganisation und betriebswirtschaftliche Fragen in *Opus Agriculturae* von Palladius," in H. Kalcyk – B. Gullath – A. Graeber (eds.), *Studien zur alten Geschichte S. Lauffer zum 70. Geb.* (*Historia* 2, Rome 1986) 501-57.

N. Kampen, *Image and Status: Roman Working Women in Ostia* (Berlin 1981).

E. Karabélias, "Le Roman de Chariton d'Aphrodisias et le droit. Renversement de situation et exploitation des ambiguités juridiques," in G. Nenci – G. Thür (eds.), *Symposion* 1988 (Cologne 1990) 368-96.

M. Kaser, *Das römische Zivilprozessrecht* (Munich 1966) (= *RZ*).

M. Kaser, *Das römische Privatrecht*² (Munich 1971-1975) (= *RP*).

M. Kaser, "Zum Wesen der römischen Stellvertretung," *Romanitas* 9 (1970) 333-55.

M. Kaser, "Stellvertretung und 'notwendige Entgeltlichkeit'," *ZRG* 91 (1974) 146-204.

D.P. Kehoe, "Lease Regulations for Imperial Estates in North Africa," *ZPE* 56 (1984) 193-219; and *ZPE* 59 (1985) 151-72.

D.P. Kehoe, *The Economics of Agriculture on Roman Imperial Estates in North Africa* (*Hypomnemata* 89, Göttingen 1988).

D. Kehoe, "Allocation of Risk and Investment on the Estates of Pliny the Younger," *Chiron* 18 (1988) 15-42.

D.P. Kehoe, "Approaches to Economic Problems in the Letters of Pliny the Younger. The Question of Risk in Agriculture," *ANRW* II.33.1 (1989) 555-90.

D.P. Kehoe, *Management and Investment on Estates in Roman Egypt during the Early Empire* (Bonn 1992).

H.-J. Kellner, "Warum signierte PRO(vincialis)?" *RCRFCommunicationes* 2 (1969) 47-49.

J.M. Kelly, "The Growth-Pattern of the Praetor's Edict," *IJ* 1 (1966) 341-55.

A. Kirschenbaum, *Slaves, Sons, and Freedmen in Roman Commerce* (Jerusalem/Washington 1987).

H.T. Klami, "*Mandatum* and Labour," *ZRG* 106 (1989) 575-86.

T. Kleberg, *Hôtels, restaurants et cabarets dans l'Antiquité romaine* (Uppsala 1957).

R. Knütel, "Die Haftung für Hilfspersonen im römischen Recht," *ZRG* 100 (1983) 340-443.

F. Kolb, "Zur Statussymbolik im antiken Rom," *Chiron* 7 (1977) 239-59.

J. Kolendo, "La répartition des places aux spectacles et la stratification sociale dans l'Empire romain," *Ktèma* 6 (1981) 301-15.

C.M. Kraay, *The Aes Coinage of Galba* (New York 1956).

W. Kunkel, *An Introduction to Roman Legal and Constitutional History*² (Oxford 1973, based on the sixth German edition).

H. Kupiszewski, "Des remarques sur les *statuliberi* en droit romain classique," in I. Bieżuńska-Małowist – J. Kolendo (eds.), *Actes du colloque sur l'esclavage, Nieborow 2-6 XII 1975* (Warsaw 1979) 227-38.

V.I. Kuziščin, *La grande proprietà agraria nell' Italia romana* (Rome 1984) (first published in Russian in 1976).

A. Labisch, *Frumentum commeatusque. Die Nahrungsmittelversorgung der Heere Caesars* (Meisenheim am Glan 1975).

S.J. de Laet, "Note sur l'organisation et la nature juridique de la *vicesima hereditatium*," *AC* 16 (1947) 29-36.

S.J. de Laet, *Portorium. Etude sur l'organisation douanière chez les Romains, surtout à l'époque du Haut-Empire* (Bruges 1949).

J. Lafaurie, "*Familia monetaria*," *BSFN* 27 (1972) 267-71.

P. Landvogt, *Epigraphische Untersuchungen über den οἰκονόμος* (Strasbourg 1908).

W. Langhammer, *Die rechtliche und soziale Stellung der magistratus municipales und der decuriones* (Wiesbaden 1973).

A. La Regina, "Rivista di epigrafia italica," *SE* 44 (1976) 284-88.

J. and A. Lasfargues – H. Vertet, "L'atelier de potiers augustéen de la Muette à Lyon," *Notes d'épigraphie et d'archéologie lyonnaises* (Lyons 1976) 61-80.

E. Lattanzi – M. Letizia Lazzarini – F. Mosino, "La tegola di Pellaro (Reggio Calabria)," *PP* 44 (1989) 286-310.

S. Lauffer, *Diokletians Preisedikt* (Berlin 1971).

M.-P. Lavizzari Pedrazzini, "Artigianato colto e di tradizione ellenistica nella transpadana di età augustea. La ceramica 'tipo Aco'," *RCRF* 25/26 (1987) 255-80.

J. Le Gall, "Métiers de femmes au *Corpus Inscriptionum Latinarum*" *REL* 47 (1969) 123-30.

J. Le Gall, "Les habitants de Rome et la fiscalité sous le Haut-Empire," in H. van Effenterre (ed.), *Points de vue sur la fiscalité à Rome* (Paris 1979) 113-26.

M. Lemosse, "La procédure contre l'esclave débiteur, une nouvelle révélation romanistique," *RD* 62 (1984) 225-29.

O. Lenel, *Palingenesia iuris civilis* (Leipzig 1889).

O. Lenel, *Das Edictum Perpetuum*[3] (Leipzig 1927).

C. Lepelley, "Liberté, colonat et esclavage d'après la Lettre 24*: la juridiction épiscopale *'de liberali causa'*," in *Les Lettres de Saint Augustin découvertes par J. Divjak* (Paris 1983) 329-42.

H. Leppin, *Histrionen. Untersuchungen zur sozialen Stellung von Bühnenkünstlern im Westen des römischen Reiches zur Zeit der Republik und des Prinzipats* (Bonn 1992).

P. Le Roux, "L'huile de Bétique et le prince sur un itinéraire annonaire," *REA* 88 (1986) 247-71.

P. Leuregans, "L'origine administrative du terme *locatio* dans la *locatio-conductio* romaine," *Eos* 65 (1977) 303-22.

P. Leveau (ed.), *L'origine des richesses dépensées dans la ville antique* (Aix-en-Provence 1985).

M.A. Levi, *"Liberi in manu,"* *Labeo* 22 (1976) 73-80.

B. Levick, "The Senatus Consultum from Larinum," *JRS* 73 (1983) 97-115.

W. Liebenam, *Städteverwaltung im römischen Kaiserreiche* (Leipzig 1900).

L. de Ligt, *Fairs and Markets in the Roman Empire. Economic and Social Aspects of Periodic Trade in a Pre-industrial Society* (Amsterdam 1993).

B. Liou, "Les amphores à huile de l'épave Saint-Gervais 3 à Fos-sur-mer: premières observations sur les inscriptions peintes," in J.M. Blázquez Martínez (ed.) *Producción y comercio del aceite en la antigüedad* (Madrid 1980) 161-75.

B. Liou – J.-M. Gassend, "L'épave Saint-Gervais 3 à Fos-sur-mer (milieu du IIe siècle ap. J.-C.). Inscriptions peintes sur amphores de Bétique. Vestiges de la coque," *Archaeonautica* 10 (1990) 157-264.

B. Liou – A. Tchernia, "L'interprétation des inscriptions sur les amphores Dr. 20," in *Epigrafia della produzione e della distribuzione. VIIe rencontre de l'Ecole Française de Rome, 5-6 juin 1992* (Preatti, pp. 73-82).

W. Litewski, "La responsabilité du mandataire," *Index* 13 (1983-84) 106-39.

E. Lo Cascio, *"Oberarii (obaerati). La nozione della dipendenza in Varrone,"* *Index* 11 (1982) 265-84.

S. Loeschcke, *Lampen aus Vindonissa. Ein Beitrag zur Geschichte von Vindonissa und des antiken Beleuchtungswesens* (Zurich 1919).

F. Longo Auricchio – M. Capasso, "I rotoli della Villa ercolanese: dislocazione e ritrovamento," *BCPE* 17 (1987) 37-47.

G. Longo, *"Actio exercitoria, actio institoria, actio quasi institoria,"* *Studi G. Scherillo* II (Milan 1972) 581-626.

M.-F. Loyzance, "A propos de Marcus Cassius Sempronianus Olisiponensis, *diffusor olearius*," *REA* 88 (1986) 273-84.

G. MacCormack, "*Nexi, judicati*, and *addicti* in Livy," *ZRG* 84 (1967) 350-55.

G. MacCormack, "The Lex Poetelia Papiria," *Labeo* 19 (1973) 306-17.

G. MacCormack, "The Liability of the Mandatary," *Labeo* 18 (1972) 156-72.

G. MacCormack, "The Early History of the *actio de in rem verso* (Alfenus to Labeo)," *Studi Biscardi* II (Milan 1982) 319-39.

G. MacCormack, "The Later History of the *actio de in rem verso* (Proculus to Ulpian)," *SDHI* 48 (1982) 318-67.

D.W. Mac Dowall, "The Organisation of the Julio-Claudian Mint at Rome," in R.A.G. Carson–C.M. Kraay (eds.), *Scripta nummaria romana. Essays Presented to H. Sutherland* (London 1978) 32-46.

J.D. Mac Isaac, *The Location of the Republican Mint of Rome and the Topography of the Arx of the Capitoline* (Diss. J. Hopkins Univ. 1987).

R. MacMullen, *Soldier and Civilian in the Later Roman Empire* (Cambridge, MA 1963).

R. MacMullen, *Roman Social Relations* (New Haven/London 1974) (= *RSR*).

R. MacMullen, "Late Roman Slavery," *Historia* 36 (1987) 359-82.

R. MacMullen, *Corruption and the Decline of Rome* (New Haven/London 1988).

G. Maetzke, "Notizie sulla esplorazione dello scarico della fornace di CN. ATEIVS in Arezzo," *RCRF* 2 (1959) 25-27.

F. Maltomini, "I papiri greci," *SCO* 29 (1979) 55-134.

D. Manacorda, "The *Ager Cosanus* and the Production of the Amphorae of Sestius: New Evidence and a Reassessment," *JRS* 68 (1978) 122-31.

D. Manacorda, "L'*Ager Cosanus* tra tarda Repubblica e Impero: forme di produzione e assetto della proprietà," *MAAR* 36 (1980) 173-84.

D. Manacorda, "Produzione agricola, produzione ceramica e proprietari nell' *Ager Cosanus* nel I° a.C.," *SRPS* II (1981) 3-54.

D. Manacorda, "Schiavo 'manager' e anfore romane: a proposito dei rapporti tra archeologia e storia del diritto," *Opus* 4 (1985) 141-51.

D. Manacorda, "Le anfore dell'Italia repubblicana: aspetti economici e sociali," in *Amphores romaines et histoire économique* (Rome 1989) 443-67.

D. Manacorda, "Produzione agricola, produzione ceramica e proprietà nella Calabria romana tardo-repubblicana: L'epigrafia delle anfore," in *Epigrafia della produzione e della distribuzione. VIIᵉ rencontre de l'Ecole Française de Rome, 5-6 juin 1992* (Preatti, pp. 15-24).

D. Manacorda, "Appunti sulla bollatura in età romana," in W.V. Harris (ed.), *The Inscribed Economy* (1993) 37-54.

D. Manacorda–C. Panella, "Anfore," in W.V. Harris (ed.), *The Inscribed Economy* (1993) 55-64.

A. Manodori, *Anfiteatri, circhi e stadi di Roma* (Rome 1982).

R. Marichal, "Quelques graffites inédits de la Graufesenque (Aveyron)," *CRAI* (1971) 188-212.

R. Marichal, "Nouveaux graffites de la Graufesenque," *REA* 76 (1974) 85-110 and 266-99.

R. Marichal, "Nouvelles fouilles et nouveaux graffites de la Graufesenque," *CRAI* (1981) 244-72.

R. Marichal, *Les graffites de La Graufesenque* (*Gallia* Suppl. 47, Paris 1988).

F. Marino, "Appunti sulla falsificazione del marchio nel diritto romano," *ZRG* 105 (1988) 771-75.

E. Maróti, "The *vilicus* and the Villa-system in Ancient Italy," *Oikumene* 1 (1976) 109-24.

E. Maróti, "Die Rolle der freien Arbeitskraft in der Villa-Wirtschaft im Zeitalter der Republik," *AArchHung* 32 (1989) 95-110.

A.J. Marshall, "Library Resources and Creative Writing at Rome," *Phoenix* 30 (1976) 252-64.

R. Martin, "Pline le Jeune et les problèmes économiques de son temps," *REA* 69 (1967) 62-97.

R. Martin, "*Familia rustica*: les esclaves chez les agronomes latins," *Actes du colloque 1972 sur l'esclavage* (*Annales littéraires de l'Université de Besançon* 163, Paris 1974) 267-97.

S.D. Martin, *The Roman Jurists and the Organization of Private Building in the Late Republic and Early Empire* (Brussels 1989).

T. Martin, "L'atelier de Valery (Tarn): ses rapports avec ceux de Montans," *Figlina* 1 (1976) 1-12.

T. Martin, "Fouilles de Montans. Notes préliminaires sur les résultats de la campagne 1975," *Figlina* 2 (1977) 51-78.

F. de Martino, "Studi sull'*actio exercitoria*," *Riv. dir navigaz.* 7 (1941) 7-31 (repr. in F. de Martino [1982] 148-70).

F. de Martino, "Ancora sull'*actio exercitoria*," *Labeo* 4 (1958) 274-300 (repr. in *Mnemeion Solazzi* [Naples 1963] 25-51 and in F. de Martino [1982] 171-99).

F. de Martino, *NNDI* 6 (1960) 1088-92, s.v. *exercitor*.

F. de Martino, *Diritto privato e società romana* (Rome 1982).

R. Matijasic, "Cronografia dei bolli laterizi della figlina Pansiana nelle regioni adriatiche," *MEFRA* 95 (1983) 961-95.

D.J. Mattingly, "Oil for Export? A Comparison of Libyan, Spanish and Tunisian Olive Oil Production in the Roman Empire," *JRA* 1 (1988) 33-56.

H.B. Mattingly, "The Management of the Roman Republican Mint," *AIIN* 29 (1982) 9-46.

T. Mayer-Maly, "Probleme der *negotiorum gestio*," *ZRG* 86 (1969) 416-35.

F. Mayet, "Les *figlinae* dans les marques d'amphores Dressel 20 de Bétique," *REA* 88 (1986) 285-305.

L. Mazzeo Saracino, "Terra sigillata nord-italica" in *Enciclopedia dell'arte antica. Atlante dell forme ceramiche* II (1985) 175-280.

A.M. McCann, "The Portus Cosanus: A Center of Trade in the Late Republic," *RCRF* 25/26 (1987) 21-70.

A.M. McCann et al., *The Roman Port and Fishery of Cosa: A Center of Ancient Trade* (Princeton 1987).

T.A.J. McGinn, "The Taxation of Roman Prostitutes," *Helios* 16 (1989) 79-110.

S. McGrail, "The Shipment of Traded Goods and of Ballast in Antiquity," *Oxford Journal of Archaeology* 8 (1989) 353-58.

N. McKendrick, "The Typology and Organisation of Enterprise," in S. Cavaciocchi (ed.), *L'impresa. Industria, commercio, banca (secc. XIII-XVIII)* (Florence 1991) 77-94.

A. McWhirr (ed.), *Roman Brick and Tile: Studies in Manufacture, Distribution and Use in the Western Empire* (Oxford 1979).

R. Meiggs, *Roman Ostia*² (Oxford 1973).

R. Meiggs, *Trees and Timber in the Ancient Mediterranean World* (Oxford 1982).

G. Mennella, "La *quadragesima Galliarum* nelle Alpes Maritimae," *MEFRA* 104 (1992) 209-32.

P. Meylan, "Révocation et renonciation du mandat en droit romain classique," *Studi G. Grosso* I (Turin 1968) 463-82.

J.H. Michel, "Quelques observations sur l'évolution du procurateur en droit romain," *Etudes J. Macqueron* (Aix-en-Provence 1970) 515-27.

G. Micolier, *Pécule et capacité patrimoniale. Etude sur le pécule, dit profectice, depuis l'édit 'de peculio' jusqu'à la fin de l'époque classique* (Lyons 1932).

P.S. Middleton, "Army Supply in Roman Gaul. An Hypothesis for Roman

Britain,'' in B.C. Burnham – H.B. Johnson (eds.), *Invasion and Response: The Case of Roman Britain* (Oxford 1979) 81-97.

H. Mielsch, *Die römische Villa. Architektur und Lebensform* (Munich 1987).

F. Millar, "Condemnation to Hard Labour in the Roman Empire, from the Julio-Claudians to Constantine," *PBSR* 52 (1984) 124-47.

S. Mitchell, "Requisitioned Transport in the Roman Empire: A New Inscription from Pisidia," *JRS* 66 (1976) 106-31.

A. Mócsy, *Pannonia and Upper Moesia. A History of the Middle Danube Provinces of the Roman Empire* (London/Boston 1974).

N. Moine, "Augustin et Apulée sur la magie des femmes d'auberge," *Latomus* 34 (1975) 350-61.

I. Molnár, "Object of *locatio conductio*," *BIDR* 85 (1982) 127-42.

I. Molnár, "Subjekte der *locatio-conductio*," *Studi Sanfilippo* II (Milan 1982) 413-30.

I. Molnár, "Verantwortung und Gefahrtragung bei der *locatio-conductio* zur Zeit des Prinzipats," *ANRW* II.14 (1982) 583-680.

R. Monier, *Manuel élémentaire de droit romain* I[6] and II[4] (Paris 1947-1948).

P. Moreau, *Clodia religio. Un procès politique en 61 av. J.-C.* (Paris 1982).

J.-P. Morel, "Aspects de l'artisanat dans la Grande Grèce romaine," in *La Magna Grecia nell'età romana. Atti del XV convegno . . . (Taranto, 5-10 ott. 1975)* (Naples 1976) 263-324.

J.-P. Morel, "La produzione della ceramica campana. Aspetti economici e sociali," *SRPS* II (1981) 81-97.

J.-P. Morel, "Les producteurs de biens artisanaux en Italie à la fin de la République," in *Les bourgeoisies municipales italiennes aux IIe et Ier siècles av. J.-C.* (Paris/Naples 1983) 21-39.

J.-P. Morel, "La manufacture, moyen d'enrichissement dans l'Italie romaine," in Ph. Leveau (ed.), *L'origine des richesses dépensées dans la ville antique* (Aix-en-Provence 1985) 87-111.

J. Muñiz Coello, "*Officium dispensatoris*," *Gerion* 7 (1989) 107-19.

L. Neesen, *Untersuchungen zu den direkten Staatsabgaben der römischen Kaiserzeit* (Bonn 1980).

P.W. de Neeve, *Colonus. Private Farm-tenancy in Roman Italy during the Republic and the Early Empire* (Amsterdam 1984).

P.W. de Neeve, "*Fundus* as Economic Unit," *RHD* 52 (1984) 3-19.

P.W. de Neeve, "A Roman Landowner and his Estates: Pliny the Younger," *Athenaeum* 78 (1990) 363-402.

B. Nicholas, *An Introduction to Roman Law* (Oxford 1962).

C. Nicolet, *Tributum. Recherches sur la fiscalité directe sous la République romaine* (Bonn 1976).

C. Nicolet, "Deux remarques sur l'organisation des sociétés de publicains à la fin de la République romaine," in H. van Effenterre (ed.), *Points de vue sur la fiscalité à Rome* (Paris 1979) 69-95.

H. Niederländer, *Die Bereicherungshaftung im klassischen Recht* (Böhlau 1953).

I. Nielsen, *Thermae et Balnea. The Architecture and Cultural History of Roman Public Baths* (Aarhus 1991).

C. Noke, "Accounting for Bailiffship in Thirteenth[-]Century England," *Accounting and Business Research* 42 (1981) 137-51.

D. Nörr, "Zur sozialen und rechtlichen Bewertung der freien Arbeit in Rom," *ZRG* 82 (1965) 67-105.

G. Olcese, "Archeologia e archeometria dei laterizi bollati urbani: primi risulti e prospettive di ricerca," in W.V. Harris (ed.), *The Inscribed Economy* (1993) 121-28.

V. Olivá, "Chariot Racing in the Ancient World," *Nikephoros* 2 (1989) 65-88.

D. Oschinsky, *Walter of Henley and Other Treatises on Estate Management and Accounting* (Oxford 1971).

A. Oxé, "Zur älteren Nomenklatur der römischen Sklaven," *RhM* 59 (1904) 108-140.

A. Oxé, "Die Töpferrechnungen von der Graufesenque," *BJ* 130 (1925) 38-99.

A. Oxé–H. Comfort, *Corpus Vasorum Arretinorum* (Bonn 1968) (= *CVArr*).

P. Panazza, *Le lucerne romane della Valcamonica* (Brescia 1984).

S. Panciera, "*Olearii*," *MAAR* 36 (1980) 235-50.

J.E. Parker, "Inns at Pompeii," *Cronache Pompeiane* 4 (1978) 5-53.

M.C. Parra, "La fornace di Magreta," in *Misurare la terra: centurazione e coloni nel mondo romano. Il caso modenese* (Modena 1983) 89-102.

M.C. Parra, "La fornace di Savignano sul Panaro," in *Misurare la terra: centurazione e coloni nel mondo romano. Il caso modenese* (Modena 1983) 103-08.

J. Paterson, "'Salvation from the Sea': Amphorae and Trade in the Roman World," *JRS* 72 (1982) 146-57.

J. Paterson, "Roman Tankers," *LCM* 13 (1988) 62.

J.R. Patterson, "Crisis: What Crisis? Rural Change and Urban Development in Imperial Apennine Italy," *PBSR* 42 (1987) 115-46.

C. Pavolini, "Le lucerne nell'Italia romana," *SRPS* II (1981) 139-84.

C. Pavolini, "Le lucerne romane fra il III sec. A.C. e il III sec. D.C.," in P. Lévêque–J.-P. Morel (eds.), *Céramiques hellénistiques et romaines* II (Paris 1987) 139-65.

C. Pavolini, "I bolli sulle lucerne fittili delle officine centro-italiche," in W.V. Harris (ed.), *The Inscribed Economy* (1993) 65-71.

M. Peachin, "The *procurator monetae*," *NC* 146 (1986) 94-106.

M. Peachin, "*Praepositus* or *procurator?*" *Historia* 36 (1987) 248-49.

D.P.S Peacock, *Pottery in the Roman World: An Ethnoarchaeological Approach* (London/New York 1982).

D.P.S Peacock–D.F. Williams, *Amphorae and the Roman Economy* (London/New York 1986).

J.T. Peña, "Two Studies of the Provenience of Roman Pottery Through Neutron Activation Analysis," in W.V. Harris (ed.), *The Inscribed Economy* (1993) 107-20.

L. Peppe, *Studi sull'esecuzione personale* I (Milan 1981).

J. Percival, "Seigneurial Aspects of Late Roman Estate Management," *EHR* 84 (1969) 449-73.

J. Percival, "*P.Ital.* 3 and Roman Estate Management," *Hommages à M. Renard* II (Brussels 1969) 607-15.

H.-G. Pflaum, "Essai sur le *cursus publicus* sous le Haut-Empire romain," *MMAI* 14.1 (1940) 189-390.

H.G. Pflaum, *Les carrières procuratoriennes équestres* (Paris 1960-61).

H.G. Pflaum, "Une inscription bilingue de Kos et la perception de la *vicesima hereditatium*," *ZPE* 7 (1971) 64-68.

H.G. Pflaum, "*Subproc(urator) XX hereditatium regionis Hellespontiacae et Pergameiae*," *ZPE* 18 (1975) 11-12.

M. Picon *et al.*, "Recherches sur les céramiques d'Ateius trouvées en Gaule," *RCRF* 14/15 (1972/1973) 128-35.

M. Picon–J. Lasfargues, "Transfert de moules entre les ateliers d'Arezzo et ceux de Lyon," *RAE* 25 (1974) 61-69.

M. Picon–J. Garmier, "Un atelier d'Ateius à Lyon," *RAE* 25 (1974) 71-76.

J. Plescia, "The Development of the Juristic Personality in Roman Law," *Studi Sanfilippo* I (Milan 1982) 487-524.

J. Plescia, "The Development of Agency in Roman Law," *Labeo* 30 (1984) 171-90.

T.F.T. Plucknett, *The Medieval Bailiff* (*The Creighton Lecture in History*, London 1954).

M. Polak, "Some Observations on the Production of Terra Sigillata at La Graufesenque," *AKB* 19 (1989) 145-54.

S. Pollard, "Industrial Management and the Beginnings of Industrialization in Europe," in S. Cavaciocchi (ed.), *L'impresa. Industria, commercio, banca (secc. XIII-XVIII)* (Florence 1991) 95-118.

S.B. Pomeroy, *Goddesses, Whores, Wives, and Slaves. Women in Classical Antiquity* (New York 1975).

A. di Porto, "Impresa agricola ed attività collegate nell'economia della villa. Alcune tendenze organizzative," *Sodalitas. Scritti in onore di A. Guarino* VII (Naples 1984) 3235-77.

A. di Porto, *Impresa collettiva e schiavo 'manager' in Roma antica (II sec. a.C. –II sec. d.C.)* (Milan 1984) [1985].

G. Prachner, *Die Sklaven und Freigelassenen im arretinischen Sigillatagewerbe* (Wiesbaden 1980).

P. Procaccini, "Ancora a proposito dell''industria' delle lucerne nell'impero romano. Note in margine ad un recente studio di storia economica," in L. Gasperini (ed.), *Scritti in memoria di F. Grosso* (Rome 1981) 507-21.

A. Provoost, "Les lampes antiques en terre cuite. Introduction et essai de typologie générale avec des détails concernant les lampes trouvées en Italie," *AC* 45 (1976) 5-39 and 550-86.

G. Pucci, "La produzione della ceramica aretina. Note sull''industria' nella prima età imperiale," *DArch* 7 (1973) 255-93.

G. Pucci, "La ceramica italica (terra sigillata)," *SRPS* II (1981) 99-121.

G. Pucci, "Pottery and Trade in the Roman Period," in P. Garnsey *et al.* (eds.), *Trade in the Ancient Economy* (Berkeley/L.A. 1983) 105-17.

G. Pucci, "Schiavitù romana nelle campagne. Il sistema della villa nell'Italia centrale," in A. Carandini *et al.* (eds.), *Settefinestre. Una villa schiavistica nell'Etruria romana* I (Modena 1985) 15-21.

G. Pucci, "Terra sigillata italica" in *Enciclopedia dell'arte antica. Atlante delle forme ceramiche* II (1985) 359-406.

G. Pucci, "A Sigillata Kiln in Valdichiana (Central Etruria)," *RCRF* 27/28 (1990) 15-23.

G. Pucci, "I bolli sulle terra sigillata fra epigrafia e storia economica," in W.V. Harris (ed.), *The Inscribed Economy* (1993) 73-79.

G. Pugliese, "In tema di *actio exercitoria*," *Labeo* 3 (1957) 308-43 (= *Studi F. Messineo* IV [Milan 1959] 287-326).

N. Purcell, "The *apparitores*: A Study in Social Mobility," *PBSR* 51 (1983) 125-73.

N. Purcell, "Wine and Wealth in Ancient Italy," *JRS* 75 (1985) 1-19.

G. Raepsaet, "Aspects de l'organisation du commerce de la céramique sigillée dans le Nord de la Gaule au IIᵉ [et IIIᵉ] siècle[s] de notre ère, I: Les données matérielles," *MBAH* 6 (1987) 1-27.

G. Raepsaet – M.-Th. Raepsaet-Charlier, "Aspects de l'organisation du commerce de la céramique sigillée dans le Nord de la Gaule au IIᵉ [et IIIᵉ] siècle[s] de notre ère, II: Négociants et transporteurs. La géographie des activités commerciales," *MBAH* 7 (1988) 45-69.

G. Ramilli, "Un *saltuarius* in una epigrafe dell'agro Bresciano," *Suppl. ai Comment. dell'Ateneo di Brescia* (1975) 77-88.

J. Ramin – P. Veyne, "Droit romain et société: les hommes qui passent pour esclaves et l'esclavage volontaire," *Historia* 30 (1981) 472-97.

D.W. Rathbone, "The Development of Agriculture in the *Ager Cosanus* during the

Roman Republic: Problems of Evidence and Interpretation," *JRS* 71 (1981) 10-23.

D.W. Rathbone, "The Slave Mode of Production in Italy," *JRS* 73 (1983) 160-68.

E. Rawson, "The Ciceronian Aristocracy and its Properties," in M.I. Finley (ed.), *Studies in Roman Property* (Cambridge 1976) 85-102.

E. Rawson, "Chariot-racing in the Roman Republic," *PBSR* 36 (1981) 1-16.

E. Rawson, "Theatrical Life in Republican Rome and Italy," *PBSR* 53 (1985) 97-113.

M. Reinhold, "Usurpation of Status and Status Symbols in the Roman Empire," *Historia* 20 (1971) 275-302.

P. Remark, *De amphorarum inscriptionibus Latinis quaestiones selectae* (Diss. Bonn 1912).

L. Richardson, "The Libraries of Pompeii," *Archaeology* 30 (1977) 394-402.

V. Righini, "Officine artigianali e nuclei industriali nella villa romana," in *La Villa Romana, Giornata di Studi, Russi, 10 maggio 1970* (Faenza 1971) 29-36.

L. Robert, *Etudes anatoliennes* (Paris 1937).

L. Robert, *Hellenica* X (Paris 1955).

F.M. de Robertis, "I lavoratori liberi nelle *familiae* aziendali romane," *SDHI* 24 (1958) 269-78.

F.M. de Robertis, "*Locatio operarum* e status del lavoratore," *SDHI* 27 (1961) 19-45.

F.M. de Robertis, *Lavoro e lavoratori nel mondo romano* (Bari 1963).

O. Robinson, "Baths: An Aspect of Roman Local Government Law," *Sodalitas. Studi in onore di A. Guarino* III (Naples 1984) 1065-82.

E. Rodriguez-Almeida, "Bolli anforari del Monte Testaccio, introducción," *BCAR* 84 (1974-1975) 119-248.

E. Rodriguez-Almeida, "Monte Testaccio: I *mercatores* dell'olio della Betica," *MEFRA* 91 (1979) 873-975.

E. Rodriguez-Almeida, "El Monte Testaccio, hoy: Nuevos testimonios epigráficos," J.M. Blázquez Martínez (ed.) *Producción y comercio del aceite en la antigüedad* (Madrid 1980) 57-100.

E. Rodriguez-Almeida, "Vicissitudini nella gestione del commercio dell'olio betico da Vespasiano a Severo Alessandro," *MAAR* 36 (1980) 277-90.

E. Rodriguez-Almeida, "Altri *mercatores* dell'olio betico," *DArch* 1 (3rd series) (1983) 79-86.

P. Rosafio, "*Inquilini*," *Opus* 3 (1984) 121-31.

P. Rosafio, *Studies in the Roman Colonate* (Diss. Cambridge 1991).

M. Rostovtzeff, *The Social and Economic History of the Roman Empire*² (Oxford 1957).

J. Rougé, *Recherches sur l'organisation du commerce maritime en Méditerranée sous l'Empire romain* (Paris 1966) (= *ROCMMER*).

J. Rougé, "La justice à bord du navire," *Studi E. Volterra* III (Milan 1971) 173-81.

J. Rougé, "Prêt et société maritime dans le monde romain," *MAAR* 36 (1980) 291-303.

J. Rougé, "Droit romain et sources de richesses non foncières," in Ph. Leveau (ed.), *L'origine des richesses dépensées dans la ville antique* (Aix-en-Provence 1985) 161-75.

P. Sabbatini Tumolesi, *Epigrafia anfiteatrale dell' occidente romano* (Rome 1988).

S. Saïd, "La société rurale dans le roman grec ou la campagne vu de la ville," in E. Frézouls (ed.), *Sociétés urbaines, sociétés rurales dans l'Asie Mineure et la Syrie hellénistiques et romaines. Actes du colloque de Strasbourg (novembre 1985)* (Strasbourg 1987) 149-71.

G. Salmeri, "Un *magister ovium* di Domizia Longina in Sicilia," *ASNP* 14 (1984) 13-23.

J.W. Salomonson, "*Litterae Africanae*. Ein Tonfragment mit kursiver lateinischer Inschrift in der archäologischen Sammlung der Utrechter Universität," in

J. den Boeft–A.H.M. Kessels (eds.), *Actus. Studies in honor of H.L.W. Nelson* (Utrecht 1982) 343-93.

R. Samson, "Rural Slavery, Inscriptions, Archaeology and Marx," *Historia* 38 (1989) 99-110.

G. and M. Sautel, "Note sur l'action *quod iussu* et ses destinées post-classiques," *Mélanges H. Lévy-Bruhl* (Paris 1959) 257-67.

W.K. Scarborough, *The Overseer. Plantation Management in the Old South*[2] (Athens, GA 1984).

W. Scheidel, "Zur Lohnarbeit bei Columella," *Tyche* 4 (1989) 139-46.

W. Scheidel, "Feldarbeit von Frauen in der antiken Landwirtschaft," *Gymnasium* 97 (1990) 405-31.

W. Scheidel, "Free-born and Manumitted Bailiffs in the Graeco-Roman World," *CQ* 40 (1990) 591-93.

W. Scheidel, "Sklaven und Freigelassene als Pächter und ihre ökonomische Funktion in der römischen Landwirtschaft (Colonus-Studien III)," in H. Sancisi-Weerdenburg *et al.* (eds.), *De agricultura. In memoriam P.W. de Neeve* (Amsterdam 1993) 182-96.

E. Schindler-Kaudelka, "Zur Bedeutung der Signaturen auf norditalischer Reliefkeramik," in E. Weber–G. Dobesch (eds.), *Römische Geschichte, Altertumskunde und Epigraphik. Festschrift für A. Betz zur Vollendung seines 80. Lebensjahres* (Vienna 1985) 557-64.

O. Schlippschuh, *Die Händler im römischen Kaiserreich in Gallien, Germanien und den Donau Provinzen, Rätien, Noricum und Pannonien* (Amsterdam 1974, repr. with additions in 1987).

G. Schneider–E. Wirz, "Chemical Answers to Archaeological Questions–Roman Terracotta Lamps as Documents of Economic History," *Doc. et Trav. IGAL* 15 (1991) 1-43.

G. Schneider, "X-ray Fluorescence and the Production and Distribution of Terra Sigillata and Firmalampen," in W.V. Harris (ed.), *The Inscribed Economy* (1993) 129-37.

H.-C. Schneider, *Altstrassenforschung* (Darmstadt 1982).

F. Schulz, *Principles of Roman Law* (Oxford 1936).

F. Schulz, *History of Roman Legal Science* (Oxford 1946).

F. Schulz, *Classical Roman Law* (Oxford 1951).

H.H. Seiler, *Der Tatbestand der negotiorum gestio im römischen Recht* (Cologne/Böhlau 1968).

H.H. Seiler, "Zur Haftung des auftraglosen Geschäftsführers im römischen Recht," in D. Medicus–H.H. Seiler (eds.), *Studien zum römischen Recht M. Kaser zum 65. Geb. gewidmet* (Berlin 1973) 195-208.

H.H. Seiler, "Bereicherung und *negotiorum gestio*," in H.P. Benöhr *et al.* (eds.), *Iuris Professio* (Vienna/Cologne/Graz 1986) 245-57.

M.E. Sergeenko, "*Villicus*," in I. Biezuńska-Małowist (ed.), *Schiavitù e produzione nella Roma repubblicana* (Rome 1986) 191-207 (= *VDI* 4 [1956] 46-54).

F. Serrao, *Enciclopedia del diritto* 21 (Milan 1971) 827-34, s.v. *institor*.

P. Setälä, *Private domini in Roman Brick Stamps of the Empire* (Helsinki 1977).

B.D. Shaw, "Rural Markets in North Africa and the Political Economy of the Roman Empire," *AntAfr.* 17 (1981) 37-83.

A.N. Sherwin-White, *The Letters of Pliny: A Historical and Social Commentary* (Oxford 1966).

A.N. Sherwin-White, *Roman Foreign Policy in the East (168 B.C. to A.D. 1)* (Norman, OK 1984).

G. Siebert, "Signatures d'artistes, d'artisans et de fabricants dans l'antiquité classique," *Ktèma* 3 (1978) 111-31.

D.V. Sippel, "Some Observations on the Means and Cost of the Transport of Bulk Commodities in the Late Republic and Early Empire," *AncW* 16 (1987) 35-45.

V.A. Sirago, *L'Italia agraria sotto Traiano* (Louvain 1958).

B. Sirks, *Food for Rome. The Legal Structure of the Transportation and Processing of Supplies for the Imperial Distributions in Rome and Constantinople* (Amsterdam 1991).

T.P. Smith, *The Medieval Brickmaking Industry in England, 1400-1450* (London 1985).

S. Solazzi, "Procurator senza mandato," *RIL* 56 (1923) 735-47 (= *Scritti* II [Naples 1957] 569-78).

S. Solazzi, "L'età dell'*actio exercitoria*," *Riv. dir. navigaz.* 7 (1941) 185-212 (= *Scritti di diritto romano* IV [Naples 1963] 243-64).

S. Solazzi, "*Procurator* ed *institor* in *D*.14.3.5.10," *SDHI* 9 (1943) 104-13 (= *Scritti di diritto romano* VI [1972] 548-56).

G. Soricelli, "Un'officina di N. Naevius Hilarus a Cuma," *ArchClass* 34 (1982) 190-95.

D. Sperber, "The Centurion as Tax-collector," *Latomus* 28 (1969) 186-89.

P.P. Spranger, *Historische Untersuchungen zu den Sklavenfiguren des Plautus und Terenz*[2] (Wiesbaden/Stuttgart 1984).

E.M. Štaerman – M.K. Trofimova, *La schiavitú nell'Italia imperiale* (Rome 1975).

J.E. Stambaugh, *The Ancient Roman City* (Baltimore/London 1988).

R.J. Starr, "Trimalchio's Libraries," *Hermes* 115 (1987) 252-53.

P. Stein, "The Place of Servius Sulpicius Rufus in the Development of Roman Legal Science," in O. Behrends *et al.* (eds.), *Festschrift F. Wieacker zum 70. Geb.* (Göttingen 1978) 175-84.

M. Steinby, "La cronologia delle *figlinae* doliari urbane dalla fine dell'età repubblicana fino all'inizio del III secolo," *BCAR* 84 (1974-1975) 7-132.

M. Steinby, *PW* Suppl. 15 (1978) cols. 1489-1531, s.v. *Ziegelstempel von Rom und Umgebung*.

M. Steinby, "Appendice a *CIL* XV,1," *BCAR* 86 (1978/79) 55-88.

M. Steinby, "La diffusione dell' opus doliare urbano," *SRPS* II (1981) 237-45.

M. Steinby, "I senatori e l'industria laterizia urbana," *Tituli* 4 (1982) 227-37.

M. Steinby, "L'industria laterizia di Roma nel tardo-impero," in A. Giardina (ed.), *Società romana e impero tardo-antico* II (Roma/Bari 1986) 99-164.

M. Steinby, *Indici complementari ai bolli doliari urbani (CIL XV,1)* (Rome 1987).

A. Steinwenter, *PW* 10 (1919) cols. 1306-08, s.v. *iussum*.

A. Steinwenter, *Fundus cum instrumento* (Vienna/Leipzig 1942).

M. Sternini, "I vetri," in W.V. Harris (ed.), *The Inscribed Economy* (1993) 81-94.

J. Stopford, "The Organization of the Medieval Tile Industry," *Oxford Journal of Archaeology* 11 (1992) 341-63.

M.J. Strazzulla, "Le produzioni [terrecotte architettoniche] dal IV al I A.C.," *SRPS* II (1981) 187-207.

K. Strobel, "Einige Bemerkungen zu den historisch-archäologischen Grundlagen einer Neuformulierung der Sigillatenchronologie für Germanien und Rätien und zu wirtschaftsgeschichtlichen Aspekten der römischen Keramikindustrie," *MBAH* 6 (1987) 75-115.

V.M. Strocka, "Römische Bibliotheken," *Gymnasium* 88 (1981) 298-329.

D.E. Strong, "The Administration of Public Building in Rome during the Late Republic and Early Empire," *BICS* 15 (1968) 97-109, esp. 103.

J. Suolahti, M. Steinby, *et al.*, *Lateres Signati Ostienses* (Rome 1978) (= *LSO*).

C.H.V. Sutherland, "The Personality of the Mints under the Julio-Claudian Emperors," (1947) 47-63.

C.H.V. Sutherland, "*Monetae. . .peculiares servos praeposuit*: Julius Caesar and the Mint of Rome," *NC* 145 (1985) 243-45.

C.H.V. Sutherland, *Roman History and Coinage, 44 B.C. -A.D. 69* (Oxford 1987).
A. Swiderek, "Les Καίσαρος οἰκονόμοι de l'Egypte romaine," *CE* 45 (1970) 157-60.
R.J. Talbert, *The Senate of Imperial Rome* (Princeton 1984).
P. Taponeco Marchini, "La fabbrica pisana di Ateio," *Antichità Pisane* 1 (1974) 3-9.
F. Tassaux, "Laecanii. Recherches sur une famille sénatoriale d'Istrie," *MEFRA* 94 (1982) 227-69.
A. Tchernia, "D. Caecilius Hospitalis et M. Iulius Hermesianus," in J.M. Blázquez Martínez (ed.) *Producción y comercio del aceite en la antigüedad* (Madrid 1980) 155-60.
A. Tchernia, *Le vin de l'Italie romaine* (Rome 1986).
Y. Thomas, "Droits domestiques et droits politiques à Rome. Remarques sur le pécule et les *honores* des fils de famille," *MEFRA* 94 (1982) 527-80.
J.-O. Tjäder, *Die nichtliterarischen lateinischen Papyri Italiens aus der Zeit 445-700* I (Lund 1955).
R. Tomber, "Evidence for Long-distance Commerce: Imported Bricks and Tiles at Carthage," *RCRF* 25/26 (1987) 161-74.
S. Tortorella, "Le lastre Campana," *SRPS* II (1981) 219-35.
S. Treggiari, *Roman Freedmen during the Late Republic* (Oxford 1969) (= *RFLR*).
S. Treggiari, "Jobs for Women," *AJAH* 1 (1976) 76-104.
S. Treggiari, "Lower Class Women in the Roman Economy," *Florilegium* 1 (1979) 65-86.
S. Treggiari, "Sentiment and Property: Some Roman Attitudes," in A. Parel – T. Flanagan (eds.), *Theories of Property. Aristotle to the Present* (Calgary 1979) 53-85.
S. Treggiari, "Urban Labour in Rome: *mercennarii* and *tabernarii*," in P. Garnsey (ed.), *Non-slave Labour in the Greco-Roman World* (Cambridge 1980) 48-64.
R. Turcan, "Jetons romains en plomb. Problèmes de datation et d'utilisation," *Latomus* 47 (1988) 626-34.
G. Uggeri, "Un insediamento romano a carattere industriale (relazione preliminare degli scavi sull'argine d'Agosta, 1971-1973)," *Musei Ferraresi* 3 (1973) 174-86.
G. Uggeri, *La romanizzazione dell'antico delta padano* (Ferrara 1975).
G. Uggeri, "La navigazione interna della Cisalpina in età romana," *AAAd* 29 (1987) 305-54.
G. Uggeri, "Aspetti archeologici della navigazione nella Cisalpina," *AAAd* 36 (1990) 175-96.
W. von Uxkull-Gyllenband, *PW* 19.1 (1937) cols. 13-16, s.v. *peculium*.
E. Valiño, "Las *actiones adiecticiae qualitatis* y sus relaciones basicas en derecho romano," *AHDE* 37 (1967) 339-436; and *AHDE* 38 (1968) 377-480.
E. Van't Dack, "Postes et télécommunications ptolémaïques," *CE* 37 (1962) 338-41.
M. and P. Vauthey, "Les courants artistiques et économiques de l'industrie céramique dans l'Antiquité d'Arezzo aux confins de l'Empire à travers la Gaule romaine," *RACF* 12 (1973) 115-26.
M. Vegas, "Aco-Becher," *RCRF* 11/12 (1969-1970) 107-24.
D. Vera, "Strutture agrarie e strutture patrimoniali nella tarda antichità: l'aristocrazia romana fra agricoltura e commercio," *Opus* 2 (1983) 489-533.
D. Vera, "Simmaco e le sue proprietà: struttura e funzionamento di un patrimonio aristocratico del quarto secolo d.C.," in F. Paschoud (ed.), *Colloque genevois sur Symmaque* (Paris 1986) 231-76.
M. Verguet, "La marque de Clarianus sur briques, tuiles et tuyaux d'hypocauste. Epoque des Antonins," *RAE* 25 (1974) 239-44.
H. Vertet – A. and J. Lasfargues, "Remarques sur les filiales des ateliers de la

vallée du Pô à Lyon et dans la vallée de l'Allier,'' in *I problemi della ceramica romana di Ravenna, della Valle padana e dell'alto Adriatico, atti del Convegno internazionale, Ravenna . . . 1969* (Bologna 1972) 273-82.

P. Veyne, ''Mythe et réalité de l'autarcie à Rome,'' *REA* 81 (1979) 261-80.

P. Veyne, ''Le dossier des esclaves-colons romains,'' *RH* 265 (1981) 3-25.

K. Visky, ''L'affranchi comme *institor*,'' *BIDR* 83 (1980) 207-20.

A. Wacke, ''Die adjektizischen Klagen im Überblick. I. Von der Reeder- und der Betriebsleiterklage zur direkten Stellvertretung,'' forthcoming in *ZRG* 111 (1994).

H. Wagner, ''Zur wirtschaftlichen und rechtlichen Bedeutung der Tabernen,'' *Studi A. Biscardi* III (Milan 1982) 391-422.

W. Waldstein, *Operae libertorum. Untersuchungen zur Dienstpflicht freigelassener Sklaven* (Wiesbaden/Stuttgart 1986).

G. Walser, ''*Circitor publici portorii*,'' in M. Piérart–O. Curty (eds.), *Historia Testis. Mélanges d'épigraphie, d'histoire ancienne et de philologie offerts à T. Zawadski* (Fribourg 1989) 153-58.

A. Watson, *Contract of Mandate in Roman Law* (Oxford 1961).

A. Watson, *The Law of Obligations in the Later Roman Republic* (Oxford 1965).

A. Watson, *Law Making in the Later Roman Republic* (Oxford 1974) (= *JRS* 60 [1970] 105-19, slightly revised).

P.R.C. Weaver, *Familia Caesaris* (Cambridge 1972).

P.R.C. Weaver, ''Children of Freedmen (and Freedwomen),'' in B. Rawson (ed.), *Marriage, Divorce, and Children in Ancient Rome* (Oxford 1991) 166-90.

C.M. Wells, ''L'implantation des ateliers de céramique sigillée en Gaule. Problématique de la recherche,'' *Figlina* 2 (1977) 1-11.

C.M. Wells, ''Manufacture, Distribution and Date: Some Methodological Considerations on the Dating of Augustan Terra Sigillata,'' *RCRF* 17/18 (1977) 132-40.

C. Wendel, ''Das griechisch-römische Altertum,'' in *Handbuch der Bibliothekswissenschaften* III.1 (1955) 51-145.

J. van der Werff, ''Sekundäre Graffiti auf römischen Amphoren,'' *AKB* 19 (1989) 361-76.

K.D. White, ''The Productivity of Labour in Roman Agriculture,'' *Antiquity* 39 (1965) 102-07.

K.D. White, *Roman Farming* (London 1970).

C.R. Whittaker, ''Labour Supply in the Later Roman Empire,'' *Opus* 1 (1982) 171-79.

C.R. Whittaker, ''Trade and the Aristocracy in the Roman Empire,'' *Opus* 4 (1985) 49-75.

C.R. Whittaker, ''Circe's Pigs: From Slavery to Serfdom in the Later Roman World,'' in M.I. Finley (ed.), *Classical Slavery* (London 1987) 88-122.

C. Wickham, ''Marx, Sherlock Holms, and Late Roman Commerce,'' *JRS* 78 (1988) 183-93.

F. Wieacker, *Römische Rechtsgeschichte* (Munich 1988).

F. Wiedemann *et al.*, ''A Lyons Branch of the Pottery-making Firm of Ateius of Arezzo,'' *Archaeometry* 17 (1975) 45-59.

T. Wiedemann, *Adults and Children in the Roman Empire* (London 1989).

K. Wiesmüller, *PW* Suppl. 12 (1970) cols. 365-72, s.v. *exercitor*.

E.L. Will, ''The Sestius Amphoras: A Reappraisal,'' *JFA* 6 (1979) 339-50.

E.L. Will, ''Ähnlichkeiten zwischen Stempeln auf Amphoren und auf arretinischen Gefässen,'' *RCRF* 23/24 (1984) 9-11.

T.P. Wiseman, ''Tile-stamps and Roman Nomenclature,'' in A. McWhirr (ed.), *Roman Brick and Tile* (Oxford 1979) 221-30.

M. Wissemann, "Das Personal des antiken römischen Bades," *Glotta* 62 (1984) 80-89.

D.A. Wren, *The Evolution of Management Thought*[3] (New York 1987).

S.E. Wunner, *Contractus. Sein Wortgebrauch und Willensgehalt im klassischen römischen Recht* (Cologne/Graz 1964).

R. Yaron, "Sale of Wine," in D. Daube (ed.), *Studies in the Roman Law of Sale dedicated to the memory of F. de Zulueta* (Oxford 1959) 71-77.

S. Zabehlicky-Scheffenegger, "Die Geschäfte des Herrn Lucius G. – ein Arbeitsbericht," *RCRF* 21/22 (1982) 105-15.

S. Zabehlicky-Scheffenegger, "Frühe padanische Filialen einiger arretinischer Töpfereien," *RCRF* 29/30 (1991) 95-104.

C. Zaccaria, "Per una prosopografia dei personaggi menzionati sui bolli delle anfore romane dell'Italia nordorientale," *Amphores romaines et histoire économique* (Rome 1989) 469-88.

H. Zehnacker, *Moneta. Recherches sur l'organisation et l'art des émissions monétaires de la République romaine (289-31 av. J.-C.)* (Rome 1973).

F. Zevi, "Appunti sulle anfore romane," *ArchClass* 18 (1966) 208-47.

R. Zimmermann, *The Law of Obligations. Roman Foundations of the Civilian Tradition* (Cape Town 1990).

APPENDIX

PROSOPOGRAPHY: BUSINESS MANAGERS IN LATIN INSCRIPTIONS

The following list of inscriptions is divided into three groups: the first group includes all *institores* (A) recorded in Italy and throughout the Empire, i.e. one instance in Noricum and another one in Macedonia; the second group includes all *vilici* (B), *vilicae* (B'), and *subvilici* (B'') recorded in Italy and Sicily; the third group includes all *actores* (C), *actrices* (C', one instance), and former *actores* (C'', *ex actore*)[1] recorded in Italy and Sicily.

First column: Each entry is given a reference number (A1-A5; B1-B201, B'202-B'206, B''207-B''210; C1-C151, C'152, C''153-C''156).

Second column: References to standard collections are arranged in the following order: *Corpus inscriptionum latinarum* (*CIL* I², V, V Suppl., VI, IX, X, XI, XIV, XV); *l'année épigraphique* (*AE*, chronological order); *Notizie degli scavi di antichità* (*Not.Scav.*); *Ephemeris epigraphica* (*Eph.Ep.*); other publications. Corresponding references to H. Dessau's *Inscriptiones latinae selectae* (*ILS*), to A. Degrassi's *Inscriptiones latinae liberae rei publicae* (*ILLRP*), and to the *Inscriptiones Italiae* (*Inscr.It.*) are provided when available. Within the first group, Italian *institores* (*CIL* VI, IX, and XI) are listed before provincial *institores* (*CIL* III). The place of origin is recorded by its Latin name (when known) followed by the Augustan region to which it belonged (I-XIV, Rome, Vetus Latium, Alpes Cottiae, Alpes Maritimae, Sicily).

Third column: Name of business manager, which sometimes permits us to determine his/her legal status (free(d) or slave; private, public, imperial servant; cf. sixth column).

Fourth column: Name of principal and other information concerning his/her social or economic position. Famous characters in this column are instrumental in dating inscriptions.

---

[1] It is sometimes difficult to distinguish a former *actor* (*ex actore*) from a comptroller (*exactor*). Cf. E. de Ruggiero, *Diz. Epigr.* 2 (1912) 2176-78, s.v. *exactor*; and G. Boulvert, *Esclaves et affranchis impériaux sous le Haut-Empire romain. Rôle politique et administratif* (Naples 1970) 38, n. 153; 184, n. 653; and 222, n. 113.

Fifth column: Occupation of business manager, determined on the basis of the text of the inscription or, sometimes, on the basis of its archaeological context (baths, quarries, fistula stamps, tile stamps, etc.). Lack of specification may suggest that a *vilicus* was attached to an agricultural estate, and that an *actor* was supervising the production of several estates, but other occupations are not ruled out.

Sixth column: Legal status (S. = *servus* [= slave]; V. = *verna* [homebred slave or freedman]; *vicarius/vicaria* [slave belonging to the *peculium* of another slave]; L. = *libertus/libertinus/liber* [freedman-freedwoman/freeborn]; P. = public servant; I. = imperial servant) and marital status (M = married) followed by the legal status of the spouse. Even though it is likely that most business managers were slaves, a mere servile *cognomen* is no proof of servile status, as it can apply to freedmen or even freeborn as well.

Seventh column: Age of business manager. I did not try to speculate the age on the basis of the length of tenure or of marriage, since the time of their inception is never specified.

Eighth column: Date of inscription. Dates based on stylistic or palaeographic evidence are left out.[2] Most of the dates rest on consular dating or on the mention of otherwise known characters (especially when principals belong to the senatorial order).

---

[2] Very few inscriptions recording *institores*, *vilici*, or *actores* can be checked on the basis of published photographs. While in Rome, I planned to visit a few archaeological sites to see the relevant stones, but I was unable to secure permission to do so.

A. *Institores* (Italy and provinces)

No.	Reference/Origin	Name of business manager	Name of principal	Occupation	Status	Age	Date
A1	*CIL* VI 10007 (= *ILS* 7608), Rome	Faustus	(One of the) Po[pilii?]	unguentarius	?	?	I?
A2	*CIL* IX 3027 (= *ILS* 7546), Teate Mar- rucinorum (IV)	Dionysius	Cn. Mamilius Primus *or* Q. Avidius Bassus	sutor/caligarius	?	?	?
A3	*CIL* XI 1621 (= *ILS* 7607), Florentia (VII)	Adiectus	Sex. Avidius Eutychus	seplasiarius	S./?	?	?
A4	*CIL* III 13523, Tüffer/Noricum	Tatton	Mocianus?	balneator?	?	15	?
A5	*CIL* III 14206, no. 21 (= *ILS* 7479 = *AE* 1898, no. 148), Karrakavak/Macedonia	Vitalis	C. La(e?)vius Faustus	tabernarius	S.V./?	16	?

B. *Vilici (Italy and Sicily)*

No.	Reference/Origin	Name of business manager	Name of principal	Occupation	Status	Age	Date
–	*CIL* I² 1825 = *CIL* IX 4053						
B1	*CIL* V 706, Ager Tergestinus (X)	Aquilinus	AVGVSTI	?	?/M (I.L.)	?	II/III
B2	*CIL* V 737 (= *ILS* 4869), Beligna/Aquileia (X)	Felix	colonia Aquileiensium	v. summarum	P.S.?/?	?	?
B3	*CIL* V 810, Aquileia (X)	Velox	Ti. Claudius Macro, conductor fer(rariarum) Nor(icarum)	metallarius/ferrarius?	S./?	?	II
B4	*CIL* V 820, Aquileia (X)	Eleuther	C. A(?) R(?), c(onductor) p(ortorii) p(ublici)	v. vectigalis?	?	?	?
B5	*CIL* V 878, Aquileia (X)	Syntrophus	T. Statilius Taurus Sissena P[o]ntif(ex), cos. 16	?	?	?	I
B6	*CIL* V 1864 (= *AE* 1956, no. 262), Iulium Carnicum (X)	Respectus	T. Iulius Perseus, c(onductor) p(ublici) p(ortorii) vec(ti)gal(is) Illyr(ici)	v. vectigalis (v. stat(ionis) [Gl]em(oniensis))	S./?	?	?
B7	*CIL* V 2803, Patavium (X)	?	municipium Patavinorum	v. aerarii	P.?/?	?	?
B8	*CIL* V 4503, Brixia (X)	Quartio	colonia Brixianorum	v. (et) a[rc]ar(ius) or v. a[er]ar(ii)	P.S./M (L.)	?	?
B9	*CIL* V 4507, Brixia (X)	Cosmus	colonia Brixianorum	?	P.S./?	?	?
B10	*CIL* V 5081 (= *ILS* 3160), Eisack Valley (X)	Mercurialis	AVGVSTVS N(oster)	v. vectigalis (statio portorii)	I.S./?	?	?
B11	*CIL* V 5500, Lacus Verbanus (XI)	Asellio	M. Aurelius Lucilianus	?	?	?	?
B12	*CIL* V 5558, Lacus Verbanus (XI)	Eutyches	the Fulvii		S./?	?	?
B13	*CIL* V 5668, Ager Mediolanensis (XI)	Bucolus	M. C(?) (= ? municipium Comensium)	?	P.S.?/?	?	?

Continued.

No.	Reference/Origin	Name of business manager	Name of principal	Occupation	Status	Age	Date
B14	CIL V 5858, Mediolanum (XI)	Epitynchanus	M. M(?) (= ? municipium Mediolanensium)	v. ark(arius)	P.S.?/?	?	?
B15	CIL V 6673, Vercellae (XI)	Zosimus	M. V(?) (= ? municipium Vercellensium)	?	P.S.?/?	?	?
B16	CIL V 7211, Avigliana (Alpes Cottiae)	?	CAESAR	v. vectigalis (v. stationis Matronis)	I.S./?	?	?
B17	CIL V 7264, Segusio (Alpes Cottiae)	Neritus	Satrius? (or socii XL Galliarum?)	v. vectigalis (v. summarum)	?	?	?
B18	CIL V 7449, Vardagate (IX)	Eyaefu?	the Firmani	?	S.?/?	?	?
B19	CIL V 7739, La Spezia (IX)	Tellius Censorinus	?	?	L.?	?	?
B20	CIL V 7852 (= ILS 1854), Pedo (Alpes Maritimae)	Flaminalis	M. Tarquinius Memor, conductor XL Galliarum	v. vectigalis (v. stationis Pedonensis)	S./M (?)	?	?
B21	CIL V 8650 = 64*, Glemona (X)	Onesimus	?	v. vectigalis (Illyrici)	S.?/M (?)	?	?
B22	CIL V Suppl. 166, Aquileia (X)	Acutius	(colonia Aquileiensium?)	?	P.S./?	?	?
B23	CIL VI 56 (= ILS 5453), Rome	Astrapton	CAESAR	?	I.S./?	?	?
B24	CIL VI 203, Rome	Artemidorus	?	?	?	?	?
B25	CIL VI 276, Rome/praedia Peduceana	Daphnus	TITVS	agricola	I.S./?	?	69-81
B26	CIL VI 278, Rome	Dorus	?	agricola?	?	?	?
B27	CIL VI 532 (= ILS 3738 = IG XIV 1012), Rome	Hermes	AVGVSTVS	agricola?	I.L./?	?	?
B28	CIL VI 586, Rome	Ampliatus	Hilarus, Augg. libertus	?	S./?	?	II/III

Continued.

No.	Reference/Origin	Name of business manager	Name of principal	Occupation	Status	Age	Date
B29	CIL VI 615, Rome	Higinus	P. Quintius Zosimus or Cn. Turpilius Cn. f. Geminius	?	S./?	?	?
B30	CIL VI 619, Rome	Speratus	HADRIANVS	?	I.S./?	?	117-138
B31	CIL VI 619, Rome (later restoration)	Dubitatus	CARACALLA	?	I.S.?/?	?	198-217
B32	CIL VI 623 (= ILS 3521), Rome/horti Aciliorum	Tychicus	Glabrio n(oster)	agricola/topiarius (v. hortorum)	S./?	?	?
B33	CIL VI 662 (= CIL VI 30807), Rome	Astus	?	?	?	?	?
B34	CIL VI 664, Rome	[?]lus	?	?	?	?	?
B35	CIL VI 666, Rome	Callistus	C. Caelius Helius	?	?	?	?
B36	CIL VI 679, Rome	Heuretus	?	?	?	?	?
B37	CIL VI 679, Rome	Callimorphus	?	?	?	?	?
B38	CIL VI 696 (= ILS 3564 = AE 1977, no. 146), Rome	Euphranides	Valerius?	?	?	?	?
B39	CIL VI 696, etc.	Pergamus	Valerius?	?	?	?	?
B40	CIL VI 718 (= CIL VI 30818 = ILS 4199), Rome	Alcimus	Ti. (Iulius Aquilinus Castricius Saturninus) Claudius Livianus (cf. AE 1924, no. 15)	?	?	?	II
B41	CIL VI 745, Rome/praedia Maeciana	Victor	?	agricola	S./?	?	154 or 177
B42	CIL VI 758, Rome	Abascantus	Decyda	?	?	?	?

Continued.

No.	Reference/Origin	Name of business manager	Name of principal	Occupation	Status	Age	Date
B43	CIL VI 774 + 842 (= ILS 3725 + 3726), Rome	Fuscus	AVGG. NOSTRI	?	I.V./?	?	II/III
B44	CIL VI 779, Rome	Primus	?	v. vectigalis	?	?	?
–	CIL VI 842 = 774						
B45	CIL VI 2347 = 4431 (= ILS 1971), Rome/Via Appia (Columbarium Marcellae)	Hymnus Aurelianus	(one of the Marcelli or the emperor)	bibliothecarius (b. Latina Porticus Octaviae)	?	?	I
B46	CIL VI 3929, Rome/Via Appia (Columbarium Liviae)	Philomusus	(M. Livius) Tertius	?	L.?/?	?	I
B47	CIL VI 4226 (= ILS 1620), Rome/Via Appia (Columbarium Liviae)	Calamus Pamphilianus	Ti. Claudius Caesar Augustus Germanicus (CLAVDIVS or NERO)	horrearius (horrea Lolliana)	?	?	I
–	CIL VI 4431 = 2347						
B48	CIL VI 4435, Rome/Via Appia (Columbarium Marcellae)	Montanus Iulianus	?	bibliothecarius (b. Octaviae Latina)	?	?	I
B49	CIL VI 4450, Rome/Via Appia (Columbarium Marcellae)	Helenus	Regillus	?	?	?	I
B50	CIL VI 7528, Rome/Via Appia	F(lavius?) Isidorus	AVG. (one of the Flavians?)	?	I.L.?/?	?	69-?
B51	CIL VI 7660, Rome/Via Appia	?	(one of the Gabii?)	?	?	?	?
B52	CIL VI 8495 (= ILS 1612), Rome/horti Casaliorum (Porta Capena)	Sabbio	?	aquarius (aqua Claudia)	I.S./M (L.)	?	?
B53	CIL VI 8495, etc.	Sporus	?	aquarius (aqua Claudia)	I.S./M (I.L.)	?	?
B54	CIL VI 8496 + 33729, Rome/Via Labicana	Amicus	?	aquarius (aqua Marcia)	?	?	?
B55	CIL VI 8650, Rome/Via Appia	M. Aurelius	AVG.	atriensis? (v. domus Aug.)	I.L./M (I.L)	?	II?

Continued.

No.	Reference/Origin	Name of business manager	Name of principal	Occupation	Status	Age	Date
B56	CIL VI 8655 (= ILS 1629), Rome	Iucundus	TIBERIVS?	atriensis? v. domus Tib.)	?/M (L.)	?	I
B57	CIL VI 8669 (= ILS 1617), Rome/horti Maiani	Felix	CAESAR	agricola/topiarius (v. hortorum Maianorum)	I.S./M (I.L.)	?	I?
B58	CIL VI 8672, Rome/horti Sallustiani	?	[A]VG.	agricola/topiarius? ([vilicu]s hortorum [Sall]ustianor(um))	I.L./?	?	I?
B59	CIL VI 8676, Rome/thermae Neronianae	Flavius [. . . .?]	AVG.	balneator (v. thermar(um) N[eronianarum?]	I.L.?/M (L.)	?	69.?
B60	CIL VI 8679 (= ? MAAR 10 [1932] 73), Rome/thermae bibliothecae Graecae	Onesimus	CAESAR N(oster)	balneator/bibliothecarius (v. therma[rum] bybliothecae Gra[ecae])	I.?/?	?	?
B61	CIL VI 8684 (= ILS 7375), Rome or Puteoli (I)	Auximus	?	agricola? (v. a Tritones, perhaps the name of a villa)	?	?	?
B62	CIL VI 8744, Rome/Via Labicana	[Eutyc]hes	CAES(ar) N(oster)	bibliothecarius	I.S./?	?	126
B63	CIL VI 8759, Rome	Atticus	[Epa]phroditus Aug. L. [a cu]biculo	?	?/M (I.L.?)	?	?
B64	CIL 9005 (= ILS 1795), Rome	Coetus Herodianus	AVGVSTVS	agricola/topiarius (v. in hortis Sallustianis)	I.?/?	?	43
B65	CIL VI 9089 = 33761 (= ILS 9244), Rome/Porta Flaminia	P. Aelius Barbarus	AVGVSTI (probably M. AVRELIVS and L. VERVS)	agricola?	I.L./?	?	II/III

Continued.

No.	Reference/Origin	Name of business manager	Name of principal	Occupation	Status	Age	Date
B66	CIL VI 9090, Rome	Pylades Cosmianus	Imp. Caes. Nerva TRAIANVS Optimus Aug. Germanicus Dacicus	?	I.S./?	?	II
B67	CIL VI 9102, Rome/Via Prenestina	Alexander	?	?	?	?	?
B68	CIL VI 9102, etc.	Oboedus	?	?	?	?	?
B69	CIL VI 9472 (= ILS 7373), Rome	Cladus	Messala	agricola/topiarius (v. supra hortos)	?	?	I?
B70	CIL VI 9483, Rome	[?]ius	?	insularius? ([a M]ercurio sobrio)	?	?	?
B71	CIL VI 9983, Rome or perhaps from Pesaurum (VI)	Archelaus	?	?	?	?	?
B72	CIL VI 9984, Rome/Porta Capena	Eros Cutta Clodianus	?	?	P.L.?/?	?	?
B73 –	CIL VI 9985, Rome/Aventinus CIL VI 9986 = CIL XI 4422	Gaa?	?	?	?	?	?
B74	CIL VI 9987 = 33819, Rome	Martialis	T. Sextius (Magius?) Lateranus ? (cos. 94)?	?	?/M (?)	?	I/II?
B75	CIL VI 9988, Rome/Quirinal	Modestus	?	?	?/M (I.L.?)	35 + ?	69-?
B76	CIL VI 9989 (= ILS 7370), Rome	Sabinianus	Memmia Iuliane (sic)	?	S./?	?	?
B77	CIL VI 9990, Rome	Iul[ianus?]	?	agricola/topiarius? (horti Antoniani?)	?	?	?
B78	CIL VI 9990a, Rome	[?]ius	?	agricola/topiarius?	?	?	?
B79	CIL VI 10046 (= ILS 5313), Rome	Docimus	T. Ateius Capito	quadrigarius (v. familiae quadrigariae)	?	?	I

Continued.

No.	Reference/Origin	Name of business manager	Name of principal	Occupation	Status	Age	Date
B80	CIL VI 10163 (= ILS 5155), Rome/Via Latina (Columbarium of the Statilii Tauri)	Hyacinthus	(Statilii Tauri)	ab amphitheatro	?/M (I.L.)	?	I?
B81	CIL VI 10251 (= ILS 7336), Rome	Cosmus	?	?	S.?/?	?	?
B82	CIL VI 13328, Rome/Via Latina	Numida Medaurianus (from colonia Theveste)	AVG(ustus) N(oster)	?	I.S./?	?	?
–	CIL VI 30807 = 662						
–	CIL VI 30818 = 718						
B83	CIL VI 30855 (= ILS 1621 = Eph.Ep. IV 723a), Rome	Zmaragdus	CAESAR AVG(ustus)	horrearius (v. horreorum Galbianorum)	I.S.?/M? (?)	?	I?
B84	CIL VI 30934 (= ILS 4343), Rome/Via Portuensis	Leonas	?	aedituus? (of the temple of Jupiter Beheleparus)	?	?	?
B85	CIL VI 30983 (= ILS 3840), Rome/Monte Testaccio (praedia Galbana)	Felix	AVGVSTVS	agricola	I.S.V./?	?	?
B86	CIL VI 30983, etc.	Aspergus Regianus	AVGVSTVS	agricola	I.S. or L./?	?	?
B87	CIL VI 30983, etc.	Vindex	AVGVSTVS	agricola	I.S.V./?	?	?
B88	CIL VI 31010, Rome/Grottaferrata	Onesimus (perhaps the same character as in CIL VI 36823)	?	?	?	?	?
B89	CIL VI 32461 (= Eph.Ep. IV 872), Rome or Puteoli (I)	[?]ibus	?	agricola?/aeditus? (his wife was a sacerdos of the Bona Dea)	?/M (?)	?	?

Continued.

No.	Reference/Origin	Name of business manager	Name of principal	Occupation	Status	Age	Date
B90	CIL VI 33400, Rome (Columbarium Livineorum)	Blastus	(L.?) Livineus Regulus (IIIvir/IVvir monetalis ca. 42 B.C.)	officinator monetalis?	?	?	I B.C.
–	CIL VI 33729 = 8496						
B91	CIL VI 33732, Rome/Villa Casalia/Caelius Mons	[Di]adumenus	?	aquarius	?/M? (I.L.)	?	?
B92	CIL VI 33733 (= ILS 1611), Rome/Viae Salaria and Pinciana	Euporus	CAESAR	aquarius	I.S./M (?)	?	?
–	CIL VI 33761 = 9089						
–	CIL VI 33819 = 9987						
B93	CIL VI 36786 (= AE 1912, no. 36), Rome/Monte Testaccio	Cocceius	A. Atinius Phosphorus?	horrearius	?	?	?
B94	CIL VI 36786, etc.	Cosmus	A. Atinius Phosphorus?	horrearius	?	?	?
B95	CIL VI 36786, etc.	Pyramus	A. Atinius Phosphorus?	horrearius	?	?	?
B96	CIL VI 36786, etc.	Eutyches	Moschus?	horrearius	?	?	?
B97	CIL VI 36786, etc.	Vinicius	?	horrearius	?	?	?
B98	CIL VI 36786, etc.	Dius	?	horrearius	?	?	?
B99	CIL VI 36823, Rome/Via Labicana	Onesimus (perhaps the same character as in CIL VI 31010)	?	?	S./?	?	?
B100	CIL VI 37175 (= ILS 9029 = AE 1910, no. 114), Rome/Via Flaminia	Callimachus	(Populus Romanus?)	agricola/atriensis? (v. saeptorum ope(rarum) pub(icarum) agr(ariarum?))	P.S.?/?	?	?

Continued.

No.	Reference/Origin	Name of business manager	Name of principal	Occupation	Status	Age	Date
B101	CIL VI 37827, Rome/Via Ostiensis	Phronimus	?	?	?/M (L.)	30	?
B102	CIL VI 37828, Rome	Priscus	CAESAR	?	I.S.?/M (?)	32	?
B103	CIL VI 37829, Rome/Viae Salaria and Pinciana	?	C. Lucretius?	?	S.?/M (?)	?	?
B104	CIL IX 59, Brundisium (II)	Maximus	(colonia Brundisinorum?)	?	P.S.?/M (L.)	50	?
B105	CIL IX 163, Brundisium (II)	Phoebus	C. Evellianus Procles?	?	S./?	18	?
B106	CIL IX 472, Venusia (II)	Pyramus	(colonia Venusiensium?)	?	P.S./?	?	?
B107	CIL IX 820, Luceria (II)	Antipater	?	?	?/M (S.?)	?	?
B108	CIL IX 1456 (= ILS 3806), Ligures Baebiani (II)	Tricunda	Ti. Claudius Nero	?	S./?	?	11
B109	CIL IX 2484, Saepinum (IV)	Constans	Neratii	?	?/M (?)	?	?
B110	CIL IX 2485, Saepinum (IV)	Primigenius	Neratius Proculus	?	S./M (S.)	?	?
B111	CIL IX 2829, near Uscosium (IV)	Stepeanus	?	?	?	?	?
B112	CIL IX 3028 (= ILS 7367), Teate Marrucinorum (IV)	Hippocrates	Plautius	agricola (v. familiae rusticae)	?	?	?
B113	CIL IX 3056, Interpromium (IV)	Firmus	(L.?) Varius Ambibulus (cos. anno incerto)	?	?/M (?)	?	?
B114	CIL IX 3103, Sulmo (IV)	Phota	Cervia Psyche	?	?	?	?
B115	CIL IX 3446, Peltuinum (IV)	Daphinus (sic)	Vibulena Quartilla and Aponia Tertulla	?	S./M? (S.)	?	?
B116	CIL IX 3517, Furfo (IV)	[A]p[r]ulleus?	Pa[m]phi[l]ius (?)	?	?	?	?

Continued.

No.	Reference/Origin	Name of business manager	Name of principal	Occupation	Status	Age	Date
B117	CIL IX 3571, Pagus Fificulanus (IV)	Festus (possibly the same character as the actor in CIL IX 3579)	(Ti.) Catius (Caesius) Fronto (suff. cos. 96)	?	?	?	I/II
B118	CIL IX 3617, Aveia (IV)	Glaucus	Nepos	?	?/M (S.)	?	?
B119	CIL IX 3651, Cerfennia (IV)	Felix	?	agricola? (v. et familia de fundo Favill[e]niano)	?/M (L.)	?	?
B120	CIL IX 3701, Marruvium (IV)	Paternus	(one of the Camerii?)	?	?/M (?)	50	?
B121	CIL IX 3908, Alba Fucens (IV)	[Er]os?	?	?	?	?	?
B122	CIL IX 4053 = I² 1825 (= ILLRP 197), Carseoli (IV) or Tibur	Philargyrus	Corrius	?	?	?	I
B123	CIL IX 4664, Aquae Cutiliae (IV)	Cinura	?	?	?	?	?
B124	CIL IX 4681 (= ILS 1865), Reate (IV)	Hyginus	?	v. vectigalis (vicesima libertatis)	?/M (?)	?	?
B125	CIL IX 4877, Trebula Mutuesca (IV)	Probus	Flavius Sa[binus]?	?	?	?	?
B126	CIL IX 5460, Falerio (V)	Apollo	?	?	?	?	?
B127	CIL X 1561, Puteoli (I)	Diognetus	CAESARES	?	?	?	II/III
B128	CIL X 1746 (= ILS 6337), Puteoli (I)	Demetrius	Herodes Aphrodisii f. Ascalonita (from Ascalon in Coele Syria)?	agricola?	?	?	?
B129	CIL X 1749, Puteoli (I)	Hermias	AVGVSTVS	?	I.S./M (?)	?	?
B130	CIL X 1750 (= ILS 7368), Baiae (I)	Mystes	CAESAR	?	I.S.?/M (I.L.)	?	?

Continued.

No.	Reference/Origin	Name of business manager	Name of principal	Occupation	Status	Age	Date
B131	CIL X 1751, Puteoli/Baiae (I)	Martialis	CAESAR	?	I.S.?/M (L.?)	?	?
B132	CIL X 3964 (= ILS 1875), Capua (I)	Epap(h)ra	socii Sisapo[n]enses	v. vectigalis (metalli)	S.?/M (S.?)	?	?
B133	CIL X 3967, Capua (I)	Eutychus	?	plumbarius/monetalis?	?	?	?
B134	CIL X 4917 (= Anthol.Lat. 2.2 = Carm.Epigr. 468, no. 1015), Venafrum (I)	Narcissus	T. Titucius Florianius and Teia L.f. Galla	?	S./?	25	?
B135	CIL X 5081 (= ILS 7372), Atina (I)	C. Obinius C.l. Epicadus	C. Obinius?	agricola?	L./M (L.), perhaps not before retirement	?	?
B136	CIL X 6637 (= CIL VI 8639), Antium (I)	[?]ctus	?	?	?	?	48
B137	CIL X 6637, etc.	Albanus	?	?	?	?	67
B138	CIL X 7041 (= ILS 7371), Catina (Sicily)	Gallicanus	?	agricola (v. Afinianis (praediis))	?	45	?
B139	CIL X 7347 (= ILS 1559), Thermae Himeraeae (Sicily)	Secundus	? (procurator XX hereditatium?)	v. vectigalis (v. summarum XX hereditatium)	?	?	?
B140	CIL X 8217 (= ILS 3523), near Capua (I)	Ursulus	Diana Tifatina?	aedituus?/agricola? (v. aedis or agrorum Dianae)	?	?	?
B141	CIL XI 725, Bononia (VIII) (fistula stamp)	Cinnamus	L. Rufius (+) Sex. Pontius, quaestores	plumbarius/aquarius?	P.S.?/?	?	?
B142	CIL XI 731, Bononia (VIII) (fistula stamp)	Acutus	?	plumbarius/aquarius?	?	?	?

Continued.

No.	Reference/Origin	Name of business manager	Name of principal	Occupation	Status	Age	Date
B143	*CIL* XI 732, Bononia (VIII) (fistula stamp)	Campanus	?	plumbarius/aquarius?	?	?	?
B144	*CIL* XI 733, Bononia (VIII) (fistula stamp)	Dignus	?	plumbarius/aquarius?	?	?	?
B145	*CIL* XI 734, Bononia (VIII) (fistula stamp)	Lausus	?	plumbarius/aquarius?	?	?	?
B146	*CIL* XI 735, Bononia (VIII) (fistula stamp)	Peculiaris	?	plumbarius/aquarius?	?	?	?
B147	*CIL* XI 736, Bononia (VIII) (fistula stamp)	L. Publicus Asclepius	colonia Bononiensium	plumbarius/aquarius?	P.L./?	?	?
B148	*CIL* XI 1231 (= *ILS* 6673), Placentia (VIII)	Onesimus	colonia Placentinorum	macellarius	P.S./M (L.)	?	?
B149	*CIL* XI 1320, Luna (VII)	Aithales	Florus	officinator?	S./?	?	98-?
B150	*CIL* XI 1327, Luna (VII)	Felix	?	?	?	?	?
B151	*CIL* XI 1356 (= *ILS* 7228), Luna (VII)	Hilario	?	marmorarius (found in the marble quarries at Carrara)	?	?	22
B152	*CIL* XI 1751, Volaterrae (VII) = *CIL* XI 2916 = *CIL* XIV 2420	Urbicus	colonia Volaterranorum	?	P.S.?/?	43	?
B153	*CIL* XI 3549, Centumcellae (VII)	Pamphilus	Doryphorus, dispensator Augusti	?	?/M? (S.?)	?	?
B154	*CIL* XI 4422 = VI 9986, Ameria (VI)	Glaphyrus	Roscia	?	S./M? (S.)	?	?
B155	*CIL* XI 5032, Mevania (VI)	Apulus	?	v. vectigalis (v. vicesimae libertatis)	?	?	?
B156	*CIL* XI 6073, Urvinum Mataurense (VI)	Verecundus	Urbinates	v. ab alim(entis)	P.S./?	?	?

Continued.

No.	Reference/Origin	Name of business manager	Name of principal	Occupation	Status	Age	Date
B157	CIL XI 6947, Luna (VII)	Hermes	Baebius Nymphodotus	?	?	?	?
B158	CIL XIV 196 (= ILS 1590), Ostia (I = Vetus Latium)	Alcimus	CAESAR	bibliothecarius (v. a bybliotheca Marcia)	I.?/?	?	?
B159	CIL XIV 198, Ostia (I = Vetus Latium)	Ianuarius	CAESAR	?	I.S.V./M (L.)	?	69-?
B160	CIL XIV 199 (= ILS 1582), Ostia (I = Vetus Latium)	T. Flavius Olympicus	?	atriensis? (v. de praetorio)	I.?L./M (L.)	40	69-?
B161	CIL XIV 255 II 30 (= ILS 6153, in part), Ostia (I = Vetus Latium)	Dativus	(colonia Ostiensium?)	? (v. familiae publicae)	P.S./?	?	?
B162	CIL XIV 2420, Bovillae (I = Vetus Latium) (= CIL XI 2916, Visentium [VII])	Chryseros Drusianus	Ti. CAESAR?	?	I.S.?/M (L.)	?	I?
B163	CIL XIV 2726, Tusculum (I = Vetus Latium)	Moschus	?	?	?/M? (S.)	?	?
B164	CIL XIV 2751, Tusculum (I = Vetus Latium)	[?]ches	[Mess]alina?	?	?	?	?
B165	CIL XIV 4471, Ostia (I = Vetus Latium)	?	HADRIANVS	?	I.?	?	II
B166	CIL XIV 4570 (= AE 1922, no. 93), Ostia (I = Vetus Latium)	Maximianus	SEPTIMIVS SEVERVS + CARACALLA (through Callistus, imperial procurator)	agricola (v. praediorum Rusticelianorum)	I. S.?V./?	?	205

Continued.

No.	Reference/Origin	Name of business manager	Name of principal	Occupation	Status	Age	Date
B167	AE 1906, no. 100 (= *Inscr.It.* X.1 592a-b), Pola/Histria (X)	Anconius	?	agricola?	?	?	?
–	AE 1910, no. 114 = *CIL* VI 37175						
–	AE 1912, no. 36 = *CIL* VI 36786						
–	AE 1922, no. 93 = *CIL* XIV 4570						
B168	AE 1923, no. 69, Rome/Via Portuensis	Butaessoror?	?	?	?/M (L.)	?	?
B169	AE 1924, no. 15, Rome?	Hierus	Ti. Iulius Aquilinus Castricius Saturninus Claudius Livianus (Praefectus Praetorio under Hadrian, cf. *CIL* VI 718)	?	?	?	II
B170	AE 1924, no. 15, etc.	Asylus	Ti. Iulius etc. Livianus	?	?	?	II
B171	AE 1924, no. 105, Rome/Via Salaria	Martialis	?	balneator? (thermae Neronianae)	?	?	?
B172	AE 1929, no. 155, Sorrentum (I)	Athictus	AVGVSTVS	?	I.S.?	31	?
B173	AE 1934, no. 234, Aquileia (X)	Eutyches	CARACALLA	v. vectigalis (Illyric(i) praep(ositus) q(uin)q(uagesimae)	I.S./?	?	211-217
B174	AE 1937, no. 61, Rome/Via del Porto di Ripagrande (Trastevere)	Chryses	L. Clodius Iustus Egnatus Priscus	cellarius (v. cellae Civicianae)	?	?	111

Continued.

No.	Reference/Origin	Name of business manager	Name of principal	Occupation	Status	Age	Date
					?	?	?
B175	AE 1939, no. 150, Ostia (I = Vetus Latium)	Olympicus	Plato (dietarcha Caesaris)?	?	?	?	?
B176	AE 1946, no. 136, Verona (X)	Phoebus Veronens(is)	(colonia Veronensium?)	plumbarius (v. plombariorum)	P.S.?/?	?	?
—	AE 1956, no. 262 = CIL V 1864						
B177	AE 1959, no. 261, Patavium (X)	Aristius	(one of the emperors)	v. vectigalis (arkarius et v. XX hereditatium)	I.S./?	?	?
B178	AE 1959, no. 300, Rome/Vatican	Saturninus	NERO CAESAR?	bibliothecarius (a bibliotheca Latina)	I.S.?/M (I.S.)	?	54-68
B179	AE 1961, no. 175, Trebiano (IX)	[Cl]arus or [Hi]larus	Petinia Posilla	?	?	?	?
B180	AE 1966, no. 106, Padula (II)	Secundio	Helvia Procula	?	?/M (L.)	?	?
B181	AE 1968, no. 110a, Latina/Borgo Grappa (I)	Zosimus	?	?	?/M (I.L.)	?	?
B182	AE 1975, no. 202, Telesia (IV)	Bargathes	socii (vicesimae libertatis)	v. vectigalis (v. vicensimae)	S./M? (L.)	?	?
B183	AE 1975, no. 313, region of the Marsi (IV)	Diphilus	Sex. Agilenius?	?	?	?	?
B184	AE 1977, no. 87, Rome/Via Appia	Philocrates	?	?	?/M? (L.)	?	?
—	AE 1977, no. 146 = CIL VI 696						
B185	AE 1978, no. 80, Fundi/Latina (I)	Diodorus	Vipsanius	?	?/M? (L.)	?	?
B186	AE 1980, no. 229, Capua (I)	[B]rittius [Ale]xander	M. Brittius (= ? M. Bruttius Praesens)	?	L./M? (L.)	?	?

Continued.

No.	Reference/Origin	Name of business manager	Name of principal	Occupation	Status	Age	Date
B187	AE 1980, no. 230, Capua (I)	M. En(nius) Elp(idius)	?	faenerator? (v. anato(cismi))	L./?	?	?
B188	AE 1980, no. 476, Luna (VII)	Athenio	CAESAR N(oster)		?	?	?
B189	AE 1985, no. 314, Petelia (III)	Euctus	Petelini		?	23	?
B190	AE 1987, no. 188, Rome	F[lavius?] Phoebion	AVGVSTI		I.L.V./?	?	II/III
B191	AE 1989, no. 195, Brundisium (II)	?	?		?	120, or 70	?
B192	AE 1989, no. 209 (= Not.Scav. 1894, p. 407), Nursia (IV)	Communis	C. Orfidius Benignus [local senator and general in Otho's army, killed in 69]		?	?	ca. 69
B193	AE 1989, no. 212, Val-nerina/Visso (IV)	Onesimus	CA[esar] N(oster)		?	?	I/II
B194	AE 1989, no. 341f, Catina (Sicily)	Ma[?]	?	v. vectigalis (v. st[a(tionis) port(us)])	?	?	?
—	Not.Scav. 1894, p. 407 = AE 1989, no. 209						
B195	Not.Scav. 1897, p. 405, no. 8, Rudia (II)	Bialus	Cn. Senius		?	?	?
B196	Not.Scav. 1923, p. 369, Rome/Via Salaria (Columbarium)	Serenus	CAESAR		I.S./M? (I.L.)	?	?
B197	Not.Scav. 1932, p. 46, Bononia (VIII) (fistula stamp)	Super		plumbarius/aquarius?	?	?	?
B198	Not.Scav. 1932, p. 46, Bononia (VIII) (fistula stamp)	Aphrodisius	?	plumbarius/aquarius?	?	?	?
—	Eph.Ep. IV 723a = CIL VI 30855						

Continued.

No.	Reference/Origin	Name of business manager	Name of principal	Occupation	Status	Age	Date
—	*Eph.Ep.* IV 872 = *CIL* VI 32461						
B199	*Eph.Ep.* VII 1247, Lacus Albanus (I = Vetus Latium)	Abascantus	CAESAR N(oster)	?	I.S./M (?)	?	?
B200	*MAAR* 10 (1932) 73, Rome	Onesimus	CAESAR N(oster)	balneator (v. balinei Caenidiani)	?	?	?
B201	R. Meiggs, *Roman Ostia*² (Oxford 1973) 343, Ostia (I = Vetus Latium)	Agathon	CAESAR	saltuarius	I.S./?	?	?

B'. Vilicae (Italy)

No.	Reference/Origin	Name of business manager	Name of principal	Occupation	Status	Age	Date
B'202	*CIL* I² 504 = XV 6905 (= *ILLRP* 1193), Rome (graffito on a terracotta lamp)	Statia	?	officinatrix?	?	?	I B.C.
B'203	*CIL* V 7348, Staffarda (Alpes Cottiae)	?	?	?	?	?	?
B'204	*CIL* X 5081 (= *ILS* 7372), Atina (I)	Trebia C.l. Aphrodisia	C. Obinius?	agricola?	L./M (L.), perhaps not before retirement	?	?
B'205	*CIL* XI 356, Ariminum (VIII)	Zoila	?	?	S./?	?	?
B'206	*CIL* XI 871 (= *ILS* 7369), Mutina (VIII)	Nicen?	Damas, statul{l}i(ber?) *or one* Stat{u}<i>lli(us?)	?	S. vicaria/?	?	?
—	*CIL* XV 6905 = *CIL* I² 504						

B". Subvilici (Italy)

No.	Reference/Origin	Name of business manager	Name of principal	Occupation	Status	Age	Date
B"207	*CIL* VI 9991 (= *ILS* 7374), Rome	Lupercus	?	agricola/topiarius (horti Antoniani)	I.(?)S./?	?	?

Continued.

No.	Reference/Origin	Name of business manager	Name of principal	Occupation	Status	Age	Date
B″208	CIL X 6638 (= *Inscr.It.* XIII.1 31), Antium (I)	Primus	?	?	?	?	42
B″209	CIL X 6638, etc.	Nemphius Delianus	?	?	?	?	51
B″210	*Eph.Ep.* VII 1248, Lacus Albanus (I = Vetus Latium)	Aciva	CAESAR N(oster)	?	I.S./M (I.L.)	?	?

C. Actores (Italy and Sicily)

No.	Reference/Origin	Name of business manager	Name of principal	Occupation	Status	Age	Date
C1	CIL V 90, Pola (X)	Fortunatus	Iulius Fronto (cf. Tac., Hist. 1.20 and 2.26; Dig. 48.19.5)	?	?/M (?)	?	I
C2	CIL V 1035, Aquileia (X)	Hyginus	?	?	?	?	?
C3	CIL V 1049, Aquileia (X)	?	?	?	?	?	?
C4	CIL V 1939, Concordia (X) (= CIL XI 6545) (= ILS 8165), Sassina/Meldula (VI)	Alexander	?	?	?/M (?)	?	?
C5	CIL V 5005 (= ILS 3761), Tridentum/praedia Tublinat(ia) (X)	Druinus	M. No[nius] Arrius Mucianus, clarissimus vir (cos. 201)	agricola (a. praediorum Tublinat(ium))	?	?	II/III
C6	CIL V 5048, Ausugum (X)	Anthus	?, clarissimus vir, cos.?	?	?	?	?
C7	CIL V 5318, Comum (XI)	Trophimus	M.C. (= private individual or municipium Comensium)	?	P.S.?/?	?	?
C8	CIL V 7473, Industria (IX)	[G]a[l]lus?	Desticius Iuba, clarissimus vir	?	S./?	?	?
C9	CIL V 8116, Verona (X) (signaculum)	Onesimus	L.N.V.	?	?	?	?
C10	CIL V 8237, Aquileia (X)	Domitius Zosimus	Domitius Terentianus	a. in rationibus	L./?	?	244
C11	CIL V Suppl. 239, Aquileia (X)	Processus	?	?	?	?	?
C12	CIL VI 41, Rome	Crescens	Domitia Lucilla	?	?	?	II
C13	CIL VI 272, Rome	Aristides	Mummia Laenila C.f.	?	S./?	?	?
C14	CIL VI 306, Rome	Crescentianus	?	?	?	?	?
C15	CIL VI 306, Rome	Florus	?	?	?	?	?
C16	CIL VI 306, Rome	Tychius	?	?	?	?	?

Continued.

No.	Reference/Origin	Name of business manager	Name of principal	Occupation	Status	Age	Date
C17	CIL VI 365 + 366 (= ILS 4321 + 4321a), Rome	Paezon	Aquillia Bassilla	?	?/M (?)	?	?
–	CIL VI 366 = 365						
–	CIL VI 585 = CIL XI 3732						
C18	CIL VI 669, Rome	?	AVGVSTVS	?	I.S./?	?	?
C19	CIL VI 671 = 30808 = 36751 (= ILS 3543), Rome	Eutyches	ANTONINVS PIVS FELIX AVGVSTVS (= CARACALLA)	agricola/topiarius? (horti Aroniani)	I.S./?	?	III
C20	CIL VI 688, Rome	Securus	Aurelius Verianus	?	?	?	?
C21	CIL VI 721 = 30820 (= ILS 1615), Rome/praedia Romaniana	Atimetus	AVGVSTI N(ostri)	agricola	I.S./?	?	II/III
C22	CIL VI 1464, Rome	At[t]alicus	L. Mummius Felix Cornelianus (praetor kandidatus, XVvir sacris faciundis, tribunus plebis, quaestor kandidatus, sevir equitum Romanorum turmae secundae, Xvir stlitibus iudicandis)	?	S./?	?	?
C23	CIL VI 3709 = 30997, Rome	Onesimus	?	?	?	?	?
C24	CIL VI 3714 = 31007, Rome	Crescentianus	Orfitus	?	?	?	?
C25	CIL VI 3728 = 31046, Rome	? (but more than one)	Praefectus Urbi? (in charge of the forum suarium)	a. de foro suario?	?	?	?
C26	CIL VI 6995, Rome/Via Latina (Columbarium)	Prosodus	Ti. Claudius Paris	?	?/M (?)	30	?
C27	CIL VI 7284a, Rome/Monumentum Volusiorum	Verec[un]dus	the Volusii Saturnini	?	?/M (L.)	?	I

Continued.

No.	Reference/Origin	Name of business manager	Name of principal	Occupation	Status	Age	Date
C28	CIL VI 7367, Rome/Monumentum Volusiorum	Primus Rhodismianus	Q.N.? (rather, one of the Volusii)	?	?/M (?)	?	I
C29	CIL VI 8591 (= ILS 1564), Rome	Iucundus	AVGVSTVS	a. vectigalis (XL Galliarum)	I.L./M (I.L.)	?	?
C30	CIL VI 8688, Rome	C. Iulius Bassus Aemilianus	CAESAR	a. patrimonii (ad Castorem et ad loricatam ad auctoritatem)	I.L./?	?	?
C31	CIL VI 8696, Rome	Antiochus	Plotina Augusta (Trajan's wife)	?	I.S.?/?	?	105-122
C32	CIL VI 8697, Rome	Calocaerus	AVGVSTVS?	?	I.S.?/?	?	?
C33	CIL VI 8850 (= ILS 1545), Rome	Nitor	Domitia Augusta (Domitianus's wife, died in 126)	a. a frumento	I.S.?/M (I.L.)	35	?-126
C34	CIL VI 9108, Rome	Apsyrtus	?	? (his father was an horrearius)	?	?	?
C35	CIL VI 9109, Rome	Atimetus	C. Iulius Proculus	?	?	?	?
C36	CIL VI 9110, Rome	Atticus	P. Marus	?	?/M (L.)	?	?
C37	CIL VI 9111, Rome	Carpus	?	?	?	25	?
C38	CIL VI 9112, Rome/near Monte Testaccio	Efficax	Iulii Iustus et Secundus	?	S./?	?	?
C39	CIL VI 9113, Rome/outside Porta Collinensis	Eunus	Caecilius Silvanus	?	?/M (?)	?	?
C40	CIL VI 9114 (= ILS 7377), Rome	Felix	M. Salvius Otho (emperor in 69, or his ancestor?)	?	S./M (S.)	60	?-69
C41	CIL VI 9115, Rome	Fructuosus	the Paebii (?)	?	?/M (?)	?	?

Continued.

No.	Reference/Origin	Name of business manager	Name of principal	Occupation	Status	Age	Date
C42	CIL VI 9116, Rome	Hector	Suellius Onesimus? (= the recipient of the dedication)	?	?	?	?
C43	CIL VI 9117, Rome	Heliades	T. Flavius Chryseros? (= the recipient of the dedication)	?	?	?	?
C44	CIL VI 9118, Rome	Hermes	Cocceia Bassa	?	?/M (L.)	?	?
C45	CIL VI 9120, Rome	Lunesis	Aurelius Apollonius	?	S./M (L.)	?	?
C46	CIL VI 9121, Rome	P(h)osphorus	?	?	?/M (?)	?	?
C47	CIL VI 9122, Rome	Sollemnis	L. Veianius Achilleus	?	S./M (?)	?	?
C48	CIL VI 9123, Rome	Successus	C. Marcius Nicephorus	?	?	?	?
C49	CIL VI 9124, Rome or Verona (X)	Thallus	C. Seius Phaedrus	? (a. domo Veronae)	S./?	25	?
C50	CIL VI 9125, Rome	Theagenes	Valeria Polla	? (the principal is known to have owned a tilery, cf. CIL XV 235)	?/M (?)	?	II
C51	CIL VI 9126, Rome	Theseus	Silvius Stephanus?	?	?	?	?
C52	CIL VI 9127, Rome	Tyrannus	(Valeria) Polla nostra	?	?	?	II
C53	CIL VI 9128 = 37771, Rome	Victor	?	?	?	?	?
C54	CIL VI 9129, Rome	Pyl[?] or Clemens	?	?	?	?	?
C55	CIL VI 9130 (= ILS 7402), Rome/Forum Sempronii	Flavianus	?	notarius et a.	S./M (L.?)	?	?
C56	CIL VI 10229 (= ILS 8379a), Rome (Testamentum L. Dasumii Tusci)	Encolpius	L. Dasumius Tuscus (Dig. 40.5.36 pr.)	?	?	?	108

Continued.

No.	Reference/Origin	Name of business manager	Name of principal	Occupation	Status	Age	Date
C57	CIL VI 29712 (= ILS 6187), Rome	Pergamus	Q. Petilius Felix (pr(aetor) et q(uin)q(uennalis) L(aurentium) L(avinatium))	?	?/M? (L.)	?	?
—	CIL VI 30808 = 671						
—	CIL VI 30820 = 721						
—	CIL VI 30997 = 3709						
—	CIL VI 31007 = 3714						
—	CIL VI 31046 = 3728						
C58	CIL VI 31652, Rome	Faustinus	Tib.(?) Claudia Camilla Alfidia Celonide (?) C.f. + Claudia Papia Netonia (?) Insteia Praenestina + L. Insteius L.f. Hor. (?) Flaccianus Pr(aetor) K(andidatus), trib(unus) pl[l](ebis) k(andidatus), quaest(or) urb(is), sevir turmarum, Xvir stlitib(us) iudicand(is), sodalis Hadrianal[is]	a. ark(arius) ex Africa	S./?	?	II
C59	CIL VI 31716, Rome	Martialis	C. Iulius Camilius Galerius Asper	?	?	?	III
C60	CIL VI 31807 (= Eph. Ep. IV 834), Rome	Diogenes	r(es publica) Calenorum (from Cales, in Umbria or Campania)	?	P.S./?	?	?
C61	CIL VI 33823, Rome	Gattaba?	the Aurelii?	?	?	?	?
C62	CIL VI 33824, Rome	Callipus	L. Caecilius Iovinius	?	?/M (?)	?	?

Continued.

No.	Reference/Origin	Name of business manager	Name of principal	Occupation	Status	Age	Date
C63	CIL VI 33825, Rome	Niceros	Cleander	?	?	?	?
C64	CIL VI 33826, Rome	?	?	?	?	?	?
C65	CIL VI 33827, Rome	[?]stomia?	?	?	S./?	?	?
C66	CIL VI 33828, Rome	Eros	M. Publicus Rufus (p(rimus) p(ilaris)?)	p(rae)p(ositus)?	?/M (?)	?	?
—	CIL VI 36751 = 671						
C67	CIL VI 37750, Rome	Ephesius	CAESAR	?	?	?	?
—	CIL VI 37771 = 9128						
C68	CIL VI 38003, Rome	Antiochus Galbianus	CAESAR	a. vic(esimae libertatis or hereditatium? cf. P.Ross.Georg. II 26, A.D. 160)	I.S./M (?)	?	?
C69	CIL IX 322, Cannae (II)	Rhodanus	Sal(via?) Rec(epta?)	?	S./?	?	?
C70	CIL IX 425 (= ILS 3197), Venusia (II)	[S]agaris	one of the Bruttii Praesentes	(the same actor is attested as οἰκονόμος = vilicus in a Greek inscription from the same place, cf. IGRR I 464)	?	?	II
C71	CIL IX 473 = 476, Venusia (II)	?	one the Bruttii Praesentes	?	?	?	?
C72	CIL IX 1717, Beneventum (II)	Epigonus	?	?	?	?	?
C73	CIL IX 2113, Ager Beneventanus (II)	Trophimus	?	?	?	?	?
C74	CIL IX 2123 (= ILS 3718), Vitulanum (II)	Polytimus	Umbrius Liberalis	?	?	?	?
C75	CIL IX 2798, Aufidena (IV)	?	Ulpia[nus or -na?]	?	?	?	?

Continued.

No.	Reference/Origin	Name of business manager	Name of principal	Occupation	Status	Age	Date
C76	CIL IX 2827 (= ILS 5982), Buca (IV)	M. Paquius Aulanius	municipium Histoniensium	?	L./?	?	late I
C77	CIL IX 3052, Interpromium (IV)	Strategicus	Statilius Barbarus, clarissimus vir (cos. 157?, legatus Thraciae 196/197, cf. CIL VI 1522 = ILS 1144; PIR III, pp. 258-59, no. 591)	?	?/M (?)	?	late II
C78	CIL IX 3076 (= ILS 3555), Sulmo (IV)	Felicissimus	?	?	?	?	?
C79	CIL IX 3579, Pagus Fificulanus (IV)	Festus (possibly the same character as the vilicus in CIL IX 3571)	Ti. (Catius) Caesius Fronto (cos. 96)	?	?/M (L.)	?	late I
C80	CIL IX 3652, Cerfennia (IV)	Successus	C. Iul[l]ius Iul?]ianus	?	S./M (?)	?	?
C81	CIL IX 4129 (= ILS 7300b), Aequiculi (IV)	Helius	L. Iulius Fronto	?	S.?/M (S.)	?	?
C82	CIL IX 4326, Ager Amiterninus (IV)	C(?)	?	?	S./M (S.)	?	?
C83	CIL IX 4513 (= ILS 3378), Ager Amiterninus (IV)	Niceforus	P. Betulenus Aper	?	?	?	?
C84	CIL IX 5377, Firmum Picenum (V)	Philumenus	?	?	?/M (?)	?	?
C85	CIL IX 5829, Auximum (V)	Restutus	?	a. ali(mentorum?)	?/M (L.)	?	?
C86	CIL IX 6083, no. 43, Movrea/Antinum (IV) (signaculum)	Marcus	one of the Cotrii	?	?	?	?

Continued.

No.	Reference/Origin	Name of business manager	Name of principal	Occupation	Status	Age	Date
C87	CIL IX 6083, no. 48, Larinum (II) (signaculum)	Epaphrobus	Aemilia C.f. Caricla	?	?	?	?
C88	CIL IX 6083, no. 49, Aeclanum (II) (signaculum)	[E]rg(asimus?)	D. Tit(ius) Lib(eralis)?	?	L.?/?	?	?
C89	CIL IX 6083, no. 111, Septempeda (V) (signaculum)	Picentinus	Bassil(ius) N(oster)	?	S./?	?	?
C90	CIL IX 6083, no. 124, colonia Tegoliti or Gioliti? (V) (signaculum)	Romanus	Calpurnius N(oster)	?	?	?	?
C91	CIL IX 6083, no. 130, Aeclanum (II) (signaculum)	Salutaris	Mariana Valeriana C.f.	?	S./?	?	?
C92	CIL IX 6083, no. 163, Palata (IV) (signaculum)	Vest(?)	AVGVSTI N(ostri) (AVGG NN)	?	?	?	II/III
C93	CIL X 238, Grumentum (III)	Fuscinus?	L. Bruttius Crispinus, clarissimus vir?	?	S./?	?	?
C94	CIL X 284, Tegianum (III)	Herculanius	?	?	?	?	?
C95	CIL X 285, Tegianum (III)	Idaeus	Bruttia Crispina	?	?	?	177
C96	CIL X 419 + 420, Volceii (III) (III)	Dionysius	C. Bruttius?	?	?/M (?)	?	?
–	CIL X 420 = 419						
C97	CIL X 421, Volceii (III) (possibly the same character as AE 1969/1970, no. 173, A.D. 208)	Quintianus	?	?	?/M (?)	?	?
C98	CIL X 1909, Puteoli (I)	Hierocles	Caecilia Materna, clarissima femina	?	?/M (?)	?	?
C99	CIL X 1910, Puteoli (I)	Epaphroditus	Cn. Haius Proculus	?	S./?	?	?

Continued.

No.	Reference/Origin	Name of business manager	Name of principal	Occupation	Status	Age	Date
C100	*CIL* X 1911, Puteoli (I)	?	?	?	?/M (?)	?	?
C101	*CIL* X 1912, Puteoli (I)	Mallus	[?]iiaia	?	?	?	?
C102	*CIL* X 1913, Puteoli (I)	Onesimus	?	ferrarius/metallarius? (a. ferr.)	?/M (?)	?	?
C103	*CIL* X 4600, Caiatia (I)	Achilleus	?	?	?/M (L.)	?	?
C104	*CIL* X 4904, Venafrum (I)	Marcus	res p(ublica) Venafr(orum)	?	P.S.?/M (L.)	?	?
C105	*CIL* X 6592 (= *ILS* 7451), Velitrae (I)	Iulianus	?	agricola (a. et agricola optimus)	?/M (?)	40	?
C106	*CIL* X 7225 (= *ILS* 6769), Lilybaeum (Sicily)	Lo(n)gus	Salvius Plotinus and Salvia Rufa	a. vectigalis (a. port(us) or -(orii) Lilybitani)	S./?	?	?
C107	*CIL* X 8045, no. 12, Astutum (Sicily) (tegula)	Eulalus	L. Minicius Natalis (of African origin, under Trajan, *CIL* VIII 2478)	officinator (?)	?	?	I/II
C108	*CIL* X 8056, no. 154, Soluntum (Sicily) (vasculum)	?	C. Gau(?)	sum(m)a(rum) a.	?	?	?
C109	*CIL* X 8059, no. 29, Neapolis (I) (signaculum)	Alphius	(L. Valerius Messala) Thrasea Priscus (cos. 196, and later curator aquarum)	?	?	?	II/III
C110	*CIL* XI 140, Ravenna (VIII)	Philomellus	L. Romanus Iuvenalis	?	S./?	?	?
C111	*CIL* XI 576, Forum Popili (VIII)	Verecundus	?	?	?	?	?
C112	*CIL* XI 1952, Perusia (VII)	Nomicus	the Postumii	?	?/M (?)	?	?
C113	*CIL* XI 2657, colonia Saturnia (VII)	Carpus	?	?	?/M (?)	?	?
C114	*CIL* XI 2686 (= *ILS* 4036), Volsinii (VII)	Primitivus (perhaps the same character as *CIL* XI 2714)	Dea Nortia?	aedituus? (cf. *CIL* VIII 15894)	S./?	?	?

Continued.

No.	Reference/Origin	Name of business manager	Name of principal	Occupation	Status	Age	Date
C115	CIL XI 2714, Volsinii (VII)	Primitivus (perhaps the same character as CIL XI 2686)	res publica Volsiniensium	?	P.S./M (S)	?	?
C116	CIL XI 2997, Ager Viterbiensis (VII)	Antigonus	[R]ufius Festus (possibly procos. Africae 366) + Rufius Marcellinus, clarissimi viri	?	S./?	?	IV?
C117	CIL XI 3299, Forum Clodi (VII)	Polyaenus	?	?	?/M (?)	?	?
C118	CIL XI 3732 (= CIL VI 585), Lorium (VII)	Alexander	Faustina Augusta	?	?	?	II
C119	CIL XI 4427, Ameria (VI)	Primitivus	IMP. COMMODVS AVG. N(oster)	?	I.S.?/M (?)	?	180-193
C120	CIL XI 4661, Tuder (VI)	Augustianus	L. Romanus?	?	S./?	?	?
C121	CIL XI 4752, Vicus Martis Tudertium (VI)	Myrtilis	?	?	S./M? (S.)	?	?
C122	CIL XI 6076, Urvinum Mataurense (VI)	Felix	Postumia Varia, clarissima femina (perhaps related to T. Flavius Postumius Varus, praef. urbi in 271, CIL VI 1416-1417 and CIL VII 95)	a. qui gessit annis XIIII	S./M (S.)	40	III?
—	CIL XI 6545 = CIL V 1939						
C123	CIL XI 7391, Balneum Regis (VII)	Achilleus	?	?	?	?	?
C124	CIL XIV 203, Ostia (I = Vetus Latium)	Terentinus	?	?	?	22	?

Continued.

No.	Reference/Origin	Name of business manager	Name of principal	Occupation	Status	Age	Date
C125	CIL XIV 352b (= ILS 6149), Ostia (I = Vetus Latium)	?	Flavius Mosc(h)ylus, vir clarissimus	?	?	?	251
C126	CIL XIV 372 (= ILS 6158), Ostia (I = Vetus Latium)	Alexa[nder?]	L. Lepidus Eutychus (sevir Aug. idem quinq. in colonia Ostiensi et in municipio Tusculanorum et quinq. perpetuus corpor. fabrum navalium Ostiensium)	?	?	?	?
C127	CIL XIV 469 (= ILS 7376), Ostia (I = Vetus Latium)	Cerdon	M. Caesonius Spectatus	?	?	?	?
C128	CIL XIV 2251 (= ILS 3503), Ager Albanus (I = Vetus Latium)	Callistus	?	?	?	?	?
C129	CIL XIV 2301 (= CIL VI 9119), Ager Albanus (I = Vetus Latium)	Iunius	Fulvia Lucina	?	?	?	?
C130	CIL XIV 2569, between Tusculum and Mons Albanus (I = Vetus Latium)	Festianus	?	?	?	?	?
C131	CIL XIV 2792, Gabii (I = Vetus Latium)	Vetus Verus	L. Caecili[us ?]	?	?	?	?
C132	CIL XIV 4659, Ostia (I = Vetus Latium)	[He]rm[es]?	?	?	?/M (?)	?	?

Continued.

No.	Reference/Origin	Name of business manager	Name of principal	Occupation	Status	Age	Date
C133	CIL XV 1049, Rome (tegula) (= CIL X 8046, no. 5, Sardinia)	Earinus	Lucilla Veri (the mother of MARCVS AVRELIVS or, less likely, the wife of LVCIVS VERVS)	officinator (tile factory)	?	?	II
C134	CIL XV 8024, Rome (signaculum)	Lesbus	AVGGG NNN (SEPTIMIVS SEVERVS, CARACALLA, GETA?)	?		?	209-211
C135	AE 1912, no. 256, Fundi (I = Vetus Latium)	Asclepiades	?	?	?	?	337
C136	AE 1919, no. 56, Amiternum (IV)	Festus	Laber(ius?) Crispin(us?)	?	?	?	?
C137	AE 1934, no. 235, Aquileia (X)	Olympus	[L]aelius Speratus (CAESAR)?	?	?	?	?
C138	AE 1964, no. 87, Rome/Via Latina (catacomb)	Augustalis	d(omus) d(ivinae or -omitianae) a.	?/M (L.)	?	?	
C139	AE 1964, no. 94, Rome/Via Latina (catacomb)	Libicus	Paulina Asiatica? (CIL VI 28224 and PIR I², p. 72, no. 424)	?	?/M (?)	?	II
C140	AE 1968, no. 109, Latina/Satricum (I = Vetus Latium)	[P]actys	L. Caesonius L.f. Quirina Quintus Rufinianus Manlius Bassus, Salius Palatinus, pontifex maior, praetor, quaestor, curator albei Tiberis et Berebentanorum, consul (in 259 and again in 271), triumvir pr[...]ones tracto Piceno, curator Laviniensium, legatus Carthaginensium, vir clarissimus	?	L./?	?	III

Continued.

No.	Reference/Origin	Name of business manager	Name of principal	Occupation	Status	Age	Date
C141	AE 1969/1970, no. 173, Polla near Buccino/Volceii (III) (possibly the same character as CIL X 421)	Quintianus	Fulionianus? (= ? L. Fabius F.f. Gal. Cilo Septiminus Catinius Acilianus Lepidus Fulcinianus, suff. cos. 193 cos. 204 (CIL VI 1408-1410 and IGRR I 138, cf. PIR II, p. 45, no. 20)	?	?	?	208
C142	AE 1973, no. 132, Castrimoenium (I = Vetus Latium)	Crescens	M. Alfius Severus	lapidicinarius (vicinity of the quarries of Peperino at Marino)	?	?	ca. 160
C143	AE 1975, no. 387, Volci (VII)	Populonius	?	?	?/M (?)	?	III?
C144	AE 1976, no. 117, Nomentum (I = Vetus Latium)	?	[C. Brutti]us (C.l.) Parmenion?	?	?	30	?
C145	AE 1982, no. 292, Amiternum (IV)	?	C. Bruttius Pr[ae]sens	?	?	?	II
C146	AE 1984, no. 56, Rome (tegula)	Soterichus	T. Statilius Maximus (successor of M. Rutilius Lupus as owner of the figlinae Brutianae, after 123)	officinator? (tile factory)	?	?	123-?
C147	AE 1985, no. 189, Ostia (I = Vetus Latium)	Dionysius	Ummidia Quadratilla	?	?/M (?)	?	late I
C148	AE 1987, no. 140, Rome/Vatican	Hipponicus	Faustina Augusta (wife of MARCVS AVRELIVS)	?	S./M (I.L.)	?	II
C149	AE 1987, no. 238a, Artena/Signia (I)	Vernaculus	?	?	?/M (?)	42	?
C150	AE 1987, no. 284, Canusium (II)	Primus	Iunius Rusticus	?	?	?	?

APPENDIX

Continued.

No.	Reference/Origin	Name of business manager	Name of principal	Occupation	Status	Age	Date
–	Eph.Ep. IV 834 = CIL VI 31807						
C151	RemdLinc 24 (1969) 231, Volceii (III)	Callipus	?	?	?	?	?
	C'. Actrices (Italy)						
C'152	CIL XI 1730, Florentia (VII)	Prastinia Maximina	c(onsularis?)	actrix c(onsularis?) domus L.?/M (?)	?	?	?
	C". Exactores –ex actore? (Italy and Sicily)						
C"153	CIL VI 8673, Rome	T. Flavius Onesimus	AVGVSTVS (one of the Flavians)	agricola/topiarius? (horti Serviliani)	I.L./M (L.)	?	I?
C"154	CIL VI 8683 (= ILS 1616), Rome	Fortunatus	CAESAR N(oster)	agricola (exactor praediorum Lucilianorum)	I.S./M?	?	?
C"155	CIL VI 8697a, Rome	Phoebus	Octavia	?	?/M (L.)	?	?
C"156	CIL IX 4186, Amiternum (IV)	[?]s	?	disp. ex actor lar[?]	?	?	?

INDEX

A. Ancient Written Sources

In spite of the large amount of material used in this book and in view of its diffuseness, the listing is almost comprehensive, but does not include all the material in the appendix.

I. *Literary sources*

De Oratore
1.58.249:   154, 185
2.55.224:   77

Orationes Philippicae
2.19.41:   345
2.38.97:   28

Pro Plancio
26.64:   212

De Provinciis Consularibus
5.10:   328

Pro Sextio Roscio Amerino
7.18:   153, 349
7.20:   153
15.42-18.52:   153-54
17.48:   153
18.50:   153
38.111-39.115:   154

Pro Sestio
3.6:   166

Pro Marco Tullio
7.17:   184

Actio Secunda In Verrem (*2Verr.*)
1.49.129ff.:   369-70
2.69.167-78.191:   342-46
3.71.167:   344
5.7.16-17:   177-78
5.18.45:   114

COLUMELLA

De Re Rustica
1 *passim*:   182
1.1.19:   126
1.3.8-13:   127, 131
1.5.7:   177
1.6.7:   185
1.6.21:   209
1.6.23:   185
1.7.1:   118, 159
1.7.2-4:   131, 158
1.7.7:   190
1.8.5:   191
1.8.6:   170-71
1.9.7:   180
2.12.7:   127
2.12.8-9:   167

3.13.11-13:   171
3.21.10:   171
7.3.16:   177-78
11 *passim*:   182
11.1.3:   169
11.1.5 (= Xen., *Oec.* 12.3-4):   141-42
11.1.7:   151, 160
11.1.14:   118
11.1.17:   180
11.1.23:   170-71
11.1.24:   172
12 *passim*:   140, 177
12.3.6:   191
12.3.9:   142

CORPUS GLOSSARIORUM LATINORUM

6, p. 588:   33

DIO CASSIUS

Roman History
15.30 (= Zonaras 9.2):   349
37.51.3:   331
47.16.3:   331
53.27:   349
55.10.5:   366
55.31.4:   331
59.15.4:   368-69
59.43.1-4:   349
60.6.7:   25
60.12.3:   253
65.10.3:   25
65.14.5:   332

Fragmenta
11.43.20 (= Zon. 8.12):   122-23

DIO COCCEIANUS = DIO CHRYSOSTOMUS

Orationes
15.23:   194

DIODORUS SICULUS

Bibliotheca
5.13:   276
36.5.1:   33, 141-42

EPICHARMUS (= G. Kaibel, *Comicorum Graecorum Fragmenta*)

Frg. 212:   33

II. *Legal sources*

FONTES IURIS ROMANI ANTEIUSTINIANI
(= *FIRA*)
cf. also epigraphical and papyrological
sources

I², no. 65: 6, 16, 80, 81, 87

Fragmenta de iure fisci (= *FIRA* II²,
pp. 627-30)
6: 198
21: 198

Fragmenta quae dicuntur Vaticana (= *Frag.
Vat.* = *FIRA* II², pp. 461-540)
51: 3

GAIUS

Institutiones (= *FIRA* II², pp. 4-192)
1.18-19: 156, 185
1.52: 44
1.116-123: 43
1.122: 196
2.7: 162
2.31: 162
2.73: 97
2.86-96 (= *Dig.* 41.1.10): 42-44
2.200: 291
3.103: 41
3.104: 44
3.136 (= *Dig.* 47.7.2.2): 40
3.142-147: 112, 232
3.155-162: 105
3.163-167: 42, 44
3.199: 131
4.35: 46, 77
4.70: 50, 78
4.71: 6, 9, 14, 16, 52-53, 58-59, 78,
  87, 89, 91
4.72: 68
4.72a-74a: 64-66, 68, 82
4.75-76: 75

IUSTINIANUS

Codex
1.9.18 (= *Nov. Theod.*3.2.5-6): 27
2.12(13).16: 43, 186-87, 189
2.18: 110
2.36.1: 198
2.53.4: 412
3.26.9: 186, 187

4.25: 52-53, 58-59, 78-79, 109
4.26: 50, 52, 64, 66, 80
4.27: 42
4.28: 419
4.29: 419
4.35: 105
4.65: 112
6.3: 102
7.8.1: 411
7.32.1: 43
8.38.3 *pr.*: 41
10.42.9: 120
10.64.1: 120
11.30.3: 412
11.37: 188
11.53.1.1: 118
11.72: 186, 187
12.23.7: 402
12.57.12.3: 27, 28

Digesta
1.1.7.1: 76
1.2.2.30: 287
1.2.2.39: 77
1.2.2.44: 77
1.5.5.1: 194
1.8.6.1: 411
2.4.10.4: 187, 411
2.10.2: 61
2.13.4 *pr.*: 87
2.13.9 *pr.*: 107
2.14.2 *pr.*: 40
2.14.14: 327
3.2.4.2: 352
3.3: 106
3.3.1 *pr.*: 106
3.3.1.1: 106, 108
3.3.1.2: 107
3.3.35 *pr.*: 107
3.3.39.1: 107
3.3.42.2: 107
3.3.49: 105
3.3.58: 108
3.3.59: 108
3.3.63: 108
3.3.68: 107
3.3.74: 108
3.4: 40
3.4.1: 326-27
3.4.1 *pr.*: 328
3.4.1.1: 187, 411

Sententiae (cont.)
5.1a.1 (= *Dig.* 39.4.9 *pr.*): 326
5.1a.5 (= *Dig.* 39.4.9.4): 329
5.1a.8 (= *Dig.* 39.4.9.7): 308
5.2.2: 42

Frg. Leid. (ed. G.G. Archi *et al.* [1956])
p. 5, §3: 274

THEODOSIUS

Codex
2.30-32: 141
2.30.2: 186
2.31.1 (= *Cod. Iust.* 4.26.13): 52, 80,
  186
2.32: 66, 186
4.12.5: 143, 185
6.29.9: 385
7.13.8: 27
8.5: 378-85
8.5.21: 380
8.5.23: 379
8.5.26: 379
8.5.31: 380
8.5.34-37: 379, 381, 384
8.5.51: 379

8.5.58: 380, 381
9.29.2: 143
11.7.6: 141
12.1.21: 380
12.1.179: 185
12.1.6: 141
13.1.10: 168
13.5.17: 339
14.9.2: 359
16.5.36.1: 141, 173
16.5.65.3: 185
16.8.16: 27
16.8.24: 27

Mai. Nov.
7: 185

Nov. Val.
13.8: 145

XII TABLES (= *FIRA* I², pp. 21-75)

12.2.a: 75

ULPIANUS

Regulae
1.12 (= *FIRA* II², p. 263): 156

III. *Epigraphical sources*

A. SPECIAL CORPORA

AE
1894, no. 22 (= *CIL* III 13283 = *ILS*
  4225): 335, 337
1894, no. 32: 174
1895, no. 45: 174
1897, no. 4 (= *ILS* 9035): 174, 337
1899, nos. 74-77 (= *ILS* 4242-4245):
  174, 336, 337
1904, no. 180: 174
1906, no. 11: 186-87
1906, no. 30: 186-87
1908, no. 233: 174
1909, no. 99: 408
1911, no. 31: 256
1912, no. 256: **C135**; 186
1913, no. 210: 147
1916, p. 17: 376
1919, no. 21: 339
1923, no. 22 (= *ILAfr* 257): 174, 345
1924, no. 80: 345
1924, no. 105: **B171**; 174, 351

1925, no. 73: 174, 338
1926, no. 164 (= 1954, no. 20): 174,
  338
1927, no. 7: 173
1927, no. 50: 141
1927, no. 87: 393
1929, no. 155: **B172**; 157
1930, no. 53: 273-74
1930, no. 67: 34
1930, no. 87: 187, 341, 345
1931, no. 27: 213-14
1933, no. 160: 335
1933, no. 268: 389
1934, no. 234: **B173**; 174, 334, 336,
  337, 339
1934, no. 240: 337
1937, no. 61: **B174**; 174
1937, no. 141: 187, 193
1938, no. 53: 188
1938, no. 154: 174, 334, 337
1938, no. 168: 176
1939, no. 19 (= *IDR* II 107): 242
1942-1943, no. 61: 193

CVArr (cont.)
160-161: 287
162: 296
166: 287, 292
168, no. 34: 291
168-169: 287
174: 280
175: 296
176-177: 287
180-181: 287
182-186: 296
241: 292
274: 292
302: 292
315-316: 292
374-375: 292
387: 292
397: 207
448: 292
468: 207
473: 292
487: 292
525: 292
543: 292
548: 292
589: 292
647 (= 1625 = 2428): 291
730: 292
786: 293
818: 292
1007-1009: 209-10
1015: 292
1023: 293
1080-1110: 281
1545: 293
1565: 293
1641: 291
1647: 291, 293
1665-1666: 279, 291
1702: 292
1792-1819: 249-50
1850-1851: 293
1915: 292
1968-1975: 292
1985: 292
1988: 292
2024: 291
2040-2044: 291
2046: 209-10
2128: 291
2132: 302
2310-2311 (= 1838): 209-10
2343-2347: 294

2384-2459: 250
2392-2393: 209-10
2406 + 2409-2413: 290, 291
2418-2459: 290
2440: 207
2441: 290
2450-2451: 290

Eph.Ep. VII 1248: **B**″210; 252

FIRA
I², no. 8: 108, 184
I², no. 11: 338
I², no. 13: 365
I², no. 43: 362
I², no. 49: 365
I², no. 100: 118, 137-38
I², no. 103: 118
I², no. 105: 187, 327, 334, 349, 350
III², no. 88: 211
III², no. 92: 3, 98, 148

IGRR
I 136: 355
I 190: 34
I 207: 365
I 349: 34
I 359: 34
I 464 (= *CIG* 5875): 33, 34, 193, 195
I 766 (= *IGBulg* III,2 1690): 383, 384
I 1142: 376, 382
I 1183: 332
III 2 (= *AE* 1923, no. 44): 383
III 25 (cf. *CIL* III 333): 34, 196
III 1056: 332
III 1434: 160
IV 152: 160
IV 186 (= *SIG* 1229): 188, 274
IV 710 (= *CIL* III 7047): 292
IV 1519: 352

ILJug 1145: 340

ILLRP
430: 209
465: 368-69
738, 740-741, 743: 261
1151-1170: 227
1176: 264
1241: 264

ILS
642, Praef. 12 (I 23-26 Lauffer): 26-27, 31

JRS
4 (1914) 27-64: 214
21 (1931) 247: 214

JSGU 44 (1954) 111-12: 131

Ludowici, *Rheinzabern Töpfern* I-II (1901-1905): 209

MAAR 10 (1932) 73: **B200**; 174, 351

MAL 17 (1974) 101, no. 9: 237-38

Marichal, *Les graffites de la Graufesenque* (1988)
226-28 (25B = 169): 210
243, no. 211 (= *CRAI* [1981] 266 and 272): 211
260-62 (= *Germania* 7 [1923] 64-68): 209

Meiggs, *Roman Ostia*^{2} (1973) 343: **B201**; 174, 176, 177-78

Peacock, *Pottery in the Roman World* (1982) 143: 242

du Plat Taylor–Cleere (eds.), *Roman Shipping and Trade: Britain and the Rhine Provinces* (1978) 43, table I, no. 14: 188, 212, 274

PP 44 (1989) 286-310: 226-27

RCRF 23/24 (1984) 148 + Pl. XIV, p. 153: 313

Res Gestae Divi Augusti 22-23: 360

Rossignani, *Scavi di Luni* II (1977) 314, CM 5520, tav. 173, 9: 249-50

Sabbatini Tumolesi, *Epigrafia anfiteatrale dell'occidente romano* (1988) 43, no. 36: 364

Studi etruschi 44 (1976) 284-88: 224-26

StudRomagn 34 (1983) 67-85: 206

Thylander, *Inscriptions du port d'Ostie* (1952) A 74: 230

Whitcomb–Johnson (eds.), *Quseir al-Qadim 1978* (1979) 243-44: 270-71

IV. Papyrological sources

BGU I 300: 11

FIRA I^2, no. 99 (= *BGU* V 1210): 25-26

P.Cair.Zen. I 59 133: 254

P.Fay. passim: 34

P.Fouad. 21: 377

P.Giss. 40: 26

P.Gur. 22: 373

P.Hib. 110 (= *W.Chr.* 435): 375

P.Ital. 3: 118, 140, 145, 148

P.Mert.
I 18: 11
II 76: 254

P.Oxy.
I 94: 11
II 261: 11
III 501: 11
IV 710 (= *W.Chr.* 436): 375
XVII 2103 (= *FIRA* II^2, pp. 202-04): 52-53, 58-59, 68
XXXI 2616: 255
XLVIII 3384-3429: 35
L 3595-3597: 253-55
LI 3641: 35, 171
LVIII *passim*: 35

P.Ross.Georg. II 26: 187, 341

P.Sarap. passim: 35

P.Select. 18: 35

PSI IX 1035: 11

PSI dem. IX 1002: 254

V. Numismatic sources

B. General

(subjects, places, names)

internal organization of the mint 392-408

coloni 113, 134, 136-37, 143-46, 168, 188, 205, 209, 231

Cominius Vipsanius Salutaris, L. 339

comites sacrarum largitionum 401

Comitialis 282

commentarienses 340, 374, 378

commercium 101, 156

Commodus (emperor) 332

communication, audio-visual methods 373

compensation, monetary 71, 73, 96, 111

competition 214-16, 243, 248, 286, 300, 326, 405, 410

complementarity of agency and tenancy 162-68

compulsory services, see *munera, leiturgiae*

Comum 350, 358

concert hall 360

condemnatio 46, 53, 71, 77

condicionales 359

condictio 41, 82

conductores, see also *locatio, mancipes, redemptores* 15, 20, 113

  agriculture 129, 137-38, 143

  baths 350

  brick/tile industry 231

  tax collection 327-29, 342

  theaters 361-63

conquisitores 363

Constantinople 359

contacts

  between main workshops and branches 278

  between producers and consumers 201-02, 240, 276-77

container/content, weight ratio 261

contracts

  agricultural 131, 170-73

  between absent parties 40

  between manager and principal 104-14

  between slave and master 101-02, 113, 255

  breach of 47, 105

  negotiated by dependents 45

  negotiated by managers 5, 8, 154-55, 169-72, 179, 210-11, 361-62

  privity of 41

public 8, 31, 112, 241-42, 360, 379, 409-12

work/labor 20, 154, 171, 232-33, 369

Contrada Mirabile (Mazara del Vallo) 200

contrascribae/contrascriptores 294, 339-40

conveyance 43

cooks 182

Coptus 332

Corinth 343

Cornelii 295

Cornelius Scipio Aemilianus, P. 19

corpus, see personality, juristic

Cosa, and *Ager Cosanus* 162-67, 249-50, 272, 312

Cossutii 37

cost-efficiency 158

craftsmen, see also *opifices*, potters 19, 99, 181, 201-03

crates 214, 241, 307

Crepusius, P. 404-05

crisis, economic 31, 165, 248

cullei 260

culpa (standard of liability) 107, 110, 114

Cumae 184, 281, 353-54

cuppae, cuppulae 260

curae, curatores 52, 231, 241-42, 323, 409-12

  annonae 350

  aquarum 323

  balneariae/balnei 350, 352

  bibliothecarum 354-55

  domus Augustianae 390

  ludorum/munerum 364

  monetae 390-91, 408

  operum publicorum 332

  statuarum 390

  publicorum vectigalium 326

  viarum 367-68

cursus publicus 373-85

  creation 374-77

  upper level of administration 377-78

  management of relay stations 378-81

  facilities (*stationes, mansiones, mutationes*) 381-82

  takeover by military 382-85

Curiatius Cosanus, C. 236

Curtius Faustus, P. 341

Columbia Studies in the Classical Tradition publishes monographs by members of the Columbia University faculty and by former Columbia students. Its subjects are the following: Greek and Latin literature, ancient philosophy, Greek and Roman history, classical archaeology, and the classical tradition in its medieval, Renaissance and modern manifestations.

1. MONFASANI, J. *Georg of Trebizond.* A Biography and a Study of his Rhetoric and Logic. 1976. ISBN 90 04 04370 5
2. COULTER, J. *The Literary Microcosm.* Theories of Interpretation of the Later Neoplatonists. 1976. ISBN 90 04 04489 2
3. RIGINOS, A.S. *Platonica.* The Anecdotes concerning the Life and Writings of Plato. ISBN 90 04 04565 1
4. BAGNALL, R.S. *The Administration of the Ptolemaic Possessions outside Egypt.* 1976. ISBN 90 04 04490 6
5. KEULS, E. *Plato and Greek Painting.* 1978. ISBN 90 04 05395 6
6. SCHEIN, S.L. *The Iambic Trimeter in Aeschylus and Sophocles.* A Study in Metrical Form. 1979. ISBN 90 04 05949 0
7. O'SULLIVAN, T.D. *The* De Excidio *of Gildas: Its Authenticity and Date.* 1978. ISBN 90 04 05793 5
8. COHEN, S.J.D. *Josephus in Galilee and Rome.* His Vita and Development as a Historian. 1979. ISBN 90 04 05922 9
9. TARÁN, S.L. *The Art of Variation in the Hellenistic Epigram.* 1979. ISBN 90 04 05957 1
10. CAMERON, A.V. & J. HERRIN (eds.). *Constantinople in the Early Eighth Century: the Parastaseis Syntomoi Chronikai.* Introduction, Translation and Commentary. In conjunction with Al. Cameron, R. Cormack and Ch. Roueché. 1984. ISBN 90 04 07010 9
11. BRUNO, V.J. *Hellenistic Painting Techniques.* The Evidence of the Delos Fragments. 1985. ISBN 90 04 07159 8
12. WOOD, S. *Roman Portrait Sculpture 217-260 A.D.* The Transformation of an Artistic Tradition. 1986. ISBN 90 04 07282 9
13. BAGNALL, R.S. & W.V. HARRIS (eds.). *Studies in Roman Law in Memory of A. Arthur Schiller.* 1986. ISBN 90 04 07568 2
14. SACKS, R. *The Traditional Phrase in Homer.* Two Studies in Form, Meaning and Interpretation. 1987. ISBN 90 04 07862 2
15. BROWN, R.D. (ed.). *Lucretius on Love and Sex.* A Commentary on *De Rerum Natura* IV, 1030-1287 with Prolegomena, Text and Translation. 1987. ISBN 90 04 08512 2
16. KNOX, D. *Ironia.* Medieval and Renaissance Ideas about Irony. 1990. ISBN 90 04 08965 9
17. HANKINS, J. *Plato in the Italian Renaissance.* Reprint 1994. ISBN 90 04 10095 4
18. SCHWARTZ, S. *Josephus and Judaean Politics.* 1990. ISBN 90 04 09230 7
19. BARTMAN, E. *Ancient Sculptural Copies in Miniature.* 1992. ISBN 90 04 09532 2
20. DORCEY, P.F. *The Cult of Silvanus.* A Study in Roman Folk Religion. 1992. ISBN 90 04 09601 9
21. AUBERT, J.-J. *Business Managers in Ancient Rome.* A Social and Economic Study of Institores, 200 B.C.-A.D. 250. 1994. ISBN 90 04 10038 5